Poland's Place in Europe

Poland's Place in Europe

General Sikorski and the Origin of
The Oder-Neisse Line, 1939-1943

Sarah Meiklejohn Terry

Princeton University Press
Princeton, New Jersey

Copyright © 1983 by Princeton University Press

Published by Princeton University Press, 41 William Street,
Princeton, New Jersey

In the United Kingdom: Princeton University Press, Guildford, Surrey

All Rights Reserved

Library of Congress Cataloging in Publication Data will be
found on the last printed page of this book

This book has been composed in Linotron Sabon

Clothbound editions of Princeton University Press books
are printed on acid-free paper, and binding materials are
chosen for strength and durability

Printed in the United States of America by Princeton
University Press, Princeton, New Jersey

To my Parents

Contents

Maps

Preface

FOR FEW NATIONS is history so palpable a part of daily life as it is for Poland. Yet for few has access to their recent past been so circumscribed by official taboos. The extent of that deprivation—of the veil of censorship (and self-censorship) that has been drawn across even the formative events of state history—was brought home to me in a very personal way several years ago. As an exchange scholar in Warsaw in the fall of 1976, I was invited to present a preliminary version of this study at the Institute of History of the Polish Academy of Sciences. For a while, it looked as if the session might never get off the ground when, to a man, members of the Institute's World War II Study Group "regretted" that they had "prior commitments." Sikorski was still a "hot potato," others explained, and as recognized specialists on the period Study Group members were reluctant to risk public comment on a thesis as "provocative" as mine. In the end the session was held and, as the audience included at least half a dozen people with first-hand knowledge of the events in question, the formal presentations (mine and prepared comments by a Polish historian) were followed by a full three hours of lively, even heated, debate. Among the more animated participants was one Władysław Pałucki of the Institute's Geography Department, and until that day known to me only by the pseudonym, Antoni Błoński, under which he had published a book on Poland's western boundary in London during the war. (The book, *Wracamy nad Odrę [Return to the Oder]*, which argued for a boundary approximating the present Oder-Neisse line, is discussed in Chapter V.) At the close of the meeting, one of Pałucki's colleagues, who had remained silent throughout the discussion thanked me profusely. He too, he told me, had spent the war years in Britain, had read the "Błoński" book and, like many others, had been struck at the time by the logic of its message. Since returning to Poland, he and Pałucki had worked side by side at the Institute for nearly three decades. "But," he exclaimed with genuine emotion, "only today have I learned that Pałucki was the real author of that book! You have opened windows we have kept shuttered for thirty years."

By the time I returned to Poland in the summer of 1981, the atmosphere had changed radically. A year of crisis and unaccustomed candor had brought to the surface an insatiable thirst for truths past as well as present. Yesterday's taboos were this year's coffeehouse topics. Katyń, a word previously uttered in hushed tones only among family and close friends, was now displayed on lapel pins, the "t" unmistakably transformed into a Catholic cross. A friend's teenage son, himself the grandson of a Katyń victim, stunned his teachers by asking to address his classmates on the subject. By the end of the school year, most of the school's teachers had asked to see his sources (all published outside of Poland). Interest in General Sikorski, too, experienced something of a revival. Since the late 1960s the anniversary of his death had been marked only by a Catholic mass, and before that by no public observance at all. But in 1981, the 100th anniversary of his birth spawned a spate of articles in the still controlled press, a symposium sponsored by the Institute of Military History, and an official (although so far unsuccessful) campaign for the return of the general's remains from England for reburial in the cathedral of Kraków's Wawel Castle, traditional burial place of Polish kings.

These and similar developments marked only the beginning of a process, now cut short by the imposition of martial law, that the Poles referred to as filling in the "blank spaces" in their history. These "blank spaces" are many, especially for the period under scrutiny here. Nor are they limited to the official version of Polish history disseminated within Poland itself. Gaps and misconceptions concerning Poland's role in the early years of World War II abound in émigré and Western literature as well. It is my hope that the present book will make a contribution, however modest, to the process of filling in these "blank spaces."

MANY PEOPLE have assisted me in the completion of this book. I owe a special debt of gratitude to those who have shared with me their personal recollections: to Count Edward Raczyński, Poland's Ambassador to Great Britain from 1934 to 1945 and Acting Foreign Minister of the Polish Government-in-Exile in the critical years 1941 to 1943; to Władysław Pałucki, of the Institute of History of the Polish Academy of Sciences; and to Józef Winiewicz, a former official in the exile government and, at the time of his retirement in 1972, a Deputy Foreign Minister of Poland. Special thanks go also to Andrzej Korboński, of the University of California at Los Angeles, and Sanford Thatcher, of Princeton University Press, for their advice and encouragement through several drafts; and to Marilyn Campbell, also of the Press, who guided the manuscript through to publication. Others who have read and offered valuable comments and criticisms at various stages of the writing and revising process are Adam Ulam and Wiktor Weintraub, both of Harvard University, Anna Cienciala of the University of Kansas, Kamil Dziewanowski and Melvin Croan, both of the University of Wisconsin, and Roman Szporluk of the University of Michigan. I have not always taken the suggestions offered, but their comments prompted me to rethink or clarify issues and to produce what I hope is a better book.

In addition, a number of organizations and institutions have facilitated my research. Grants from the National Endowment for the Humanities, the International Research and Exchanges Board, the American Council of Learned Societies, and the Tufts University Committee on Faculty Awards made possible the essential research trips to the National Archives in Washington, the Hoover Institution at Stanford University, the Franklin D. Roosevelt Library in Hyde Park, the Public Record Office and Polish Institute in London, and to Warsaw. I am indebted to the staffs of all of these institutions for their cheerful cooperation and efficiency. But it is with special gratitude that I recall the unstinting and meticulous assistance given me by the late Regina Oppman of the Sikorski archives at the Polish Institute, and by her assistant and successor as archivist, Wacław Milewski. I also wish to thank the Controller of Her Majesty's Stationery Office for permission to quote Crown-copyright records in the Public Record Office.

Over the years the Russian Research Center at Harvard has provided a congenial and supportive environment in which to work. I am especially grateful to the Center's Administrative Assistant, Mary Towle, and to Rose DiBenedetto who, together with Jini Kelly of the Tufts Political Science Department, expertly typed much of the final manuscript; and to Melissa Stockdale for her assistance in proofreading and tracking down elusive references. Finally, I want to thank my husband, Robert Terry, not only for enduring my preoccupations, but for sharing many of the burdens of research and writing. His critical eye and aversion to "verbal weeds" have helped make this a more readable book, although of course final responsibility for content and style is mine alone.

Belmont, Massachusetts
January 1982

Map 1

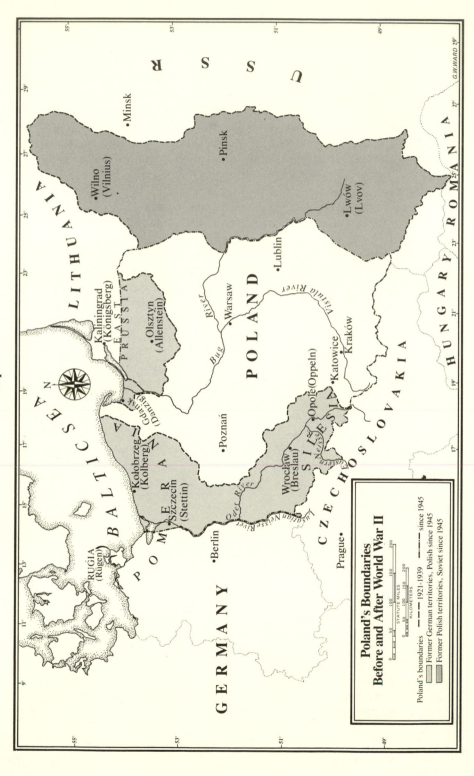

**Poland's Boundaries
Before and After World War II**

Poland's boundaries –––––– 1921–1939   –––––– since 1945

Former German territories, Polish since 1945

Former Polish territories, Soviet since 1945

STATUTE MILES
0   50   100   150   200

KILOMETERS
0   50   100   150   200

USSR

LITHUANIA

POLAND

GERMANY

CZECHOSLOVAKIA

HUNGARY

ROMANIA

BALTIC SEA

EAST PRUSSIA

POMERANIA

SILESIA

•Minsk

•Pinsk

•Wilno
(Vilnius)

•Lwów
(Lvov)

•Lublin

•Warsaw

•Kraków

Kaliningrad
(Königsberg)•

•Olsztyn
(Allenstein)

Gdańsk
(Danzig)•

•Kołobrzeg
(Kolberg)

•Szczecin
(Stettin)

•Poznań

•Berlin

Wrocław•
(Breslau)

Opole•(Oppeln)

•Katowice

Prague•

RUGIA
(Rügen)

Bug River

Vistula River

Oder River

Lusatian Neisse River

Map 1

N

G.W.WARD

Note on Geographical Terms

IN ANY STUDY of this kind, geographical place names pose special problems. Every city or river or mountain range that I refer to has at least two and, in some cases, as many as four working names, any or all of which may have been used by quoted sources. In view of the fact that there is no magic solution to this quagmire, a few words of explanation are in order.

First, with respect to the region as a whole: The area between Germany and Russia, traditionally known as Central or East Central Europe, is most often referred to today as Eastern Europe. Possibly this is a result of the Cold War division of Europe between East and West, which has left little room for intermediate status either from the ideological or territorial standpoint. Or perhaps it is because, now that the Soviet Union has become a Great Power, we tend to view her as flanking Europe but not of it. In either event, I have chosen here to revert to the term Central Europe for several reasons: because I am dealing with a period in which the traditional terminology still predominated, because this was the designation that Sikorski himself seemed to prefer, and because it reinforces the distinction between the general's conception of Poland's appropriate international posture and her traditional eastward orientation. While I have occasionally used "East Central Europe," "Eastern Europe" appears only in direct quotes. Likewise, in discussing Sikorski's plans for the postwar regional organization of Central Europe, and in particular of Poland and Czechoslovakia, I have favored the term "federation" over "confederation," again because I am concerned primarily with Sikorski's program and he preferred the tighter federal form of union. I am aware, of course, that the provisional agreement reached was for a looser confederation structure, and that the general's own statements were not entirely consistent on this point.

Specific place names fall roughly into three categories: those for which there is an English equivalent distinct from either the German or Polish, those for which there is no separate English equivalent, and a mixed category. The first category poses no problem and applies particularly to the names of the provinces which were transferred from Germany to Poland—e.g., Silesia (Schlesien in German, Śląsk in Polish), East Prussia (Ostpreussen, Prusy Wschodnie), and Pomerania (Pommern, Pomorze). The second category includes the names of cities and towns in the affected

xvi • Geographical Terms

territories. Known by their German names before 1945, they have gradually come to be referred to in English by their postwar Polish names; e.g., Stettin has become Szczecin, Breslau—Wrocław, Danzig—Gdańsk, and so forth. Since these cities remained German during the period under examination, and since they were referred to by their German names during the Great Power deliberations, I have also used those forms except when quoting sources that use the Polish names. Where the possibility for confusion exists, the alternative name is given in brackets. By the same token, when referring to cities in the prewar Polish eastern provinces, I have used the Polish spellings: Lwów rather than Lvov, Wilno rather than Vilna or Vilnius.

The names of the rivers which form the postwar boundary between Poland and Germany fall somewhere in between the first two categories. By and large, the basic German names Oder and Neisse have remained the accepted English forms, although one occasionally encounters the Polish Odra and Nysa (initially Nisa or Nissa). The confusion arises over the several adjectives which differentiate between the two tributaries of the Oder bearing the name Neisse, since the common English designations "eastern" and "western" do not generally appear in either the German or Polish forms. The so-called Western Neisse (i.e., the river along which the southern half of the postwar boundary runs) is in German the Lausitzer or Görlitzer Neisse, in Polish the Nysa Łużycka; while the Eastern Neisse (the subject of discussion among the Great Powers as an alternative boundary line) is called the Glatzer Neisse in German, the Nysa Kłodzka or Nysa Śląska in Polish. When referring to the former, I have used both the terms Western and Lusatian Neisse, although I prefer the latter; where for the sake of brevity simply Neisse is used (as in Oder-Neisse line), it is invariably a reference to this river. Where the Eastern Neisse is meant, the full name is used, and always the common English form. The reader may wish to refer to Maps 1, 5, and 6 to identify these and other geographical features.

Part One

The Historical Setting

I · *Introduction*

THE SO-CALLED "Polish Question" in World War II is one of those issues which have been so overworked in the literature of recent European history that the author rash enough to reopen any aspect of it has an obligation to reveal at the outset what new and dramatic evidence has been unearthed to make the exercise worth the reader's time. In this case, it is the question of the origin of the Polish-German boundary on the Oder and Lusatian Neisse rivers[1] that I propose to reopen and, in particular, the contribution made to the concept of such a boundary by the first prime minister of the Polish Government-in-Exile, General Władysław Sikorski. My justification for doing so is summed up in a brief memorandum, dated December 4, 1942, and submitted by Sikorski the following day, together with three longer supporting memoranda, to President Roosevelt (or, more accurately, to Under Secretary of State Sumner Welles for transmittal to Roosevelt). Because the contents of this memorandum are virtually unknown, and because it and the accompanying papers have been the subject of considerable controversy, it seems appropriate to quote it here in full:

MEMORANDUM CONCERNING THE WESTERN BOUNDARIES

I. Our approach to the problem of [Poland's] western boundaries is dictated by the necessity of:

—a lasting guarantee of the territories most basic to the economic development and defensive potential of the Polish-Czech federation, that is, the mouth of the Vistula and the industrial center in Silesia;

—the liquidation of the permanent threat such as East Prussia and Silesia constitute [when] held in the hands of the Germans as their base of attack;

---

[1] The basic facts of Poland's geographic shift at the end of the war are sufficiently familiar that they need only be summarized here: As a consequence of the Great Power agreements at Yalta and Potsdam, in February and July-August 1945 respectively, Poland lost to the Soviet Union all territories east of a boundary closely approximating the Curzon line, amounting to some 180,830 square kilometers or just over 46 percent of her prewar total. In the west and north she gained 102,836 square kilometers, including the former Free City of Danzig, the southern half of East Prussia, and all other prewar German territories east of the Oder and Lusatian (or Western) Neisse rivers. Poland's overall area was thereby reduced by one-fifth, from approximately 390,000 to 312,000 square kilometers, with the "Recovered Territories" as they were then called (or the "Western and Northern Territories" as they are generally referred to now) comprising just under one-third of the postwar total.

—*control over the mouth of the Oder, which possesses paramount importance for the federation as the artery directly linking our common center of Silesian industry with the sea*;

—the opening to us permanently of a route through the Baltic and the guaranteeing of communication with allies (naval bases on Bornholm, Rügen and Fehmarn);

—the creation of conditions for our effective and rapid intervention against Germany should it attempt to remilitarize. In this regard, *Western Pomerania based on the lower Oder and, secondly, the northwestern part of the Sudetes with an outlet toward Leipzig* are of paramount importance for the federation.

II. The problem of occupation consists in guaranteeing the freedom to execute in Germany the conditions of surrender imposed on her and, on the other hand, in creating for us the possibility of rapid economic, political and military reconstruction of our country.

In this connection the range of our (federated Poland's) interests includes:

a) *the zone up to the Oder and Lusatian Neisse with bridgeheads on the left bank* (as on the line of the Rhine);

b) key points on the western Baltic as well as [points] connecting it with the North Sea (Bornholm, Rügen, Fehmarn, the Kiel Canal) as a joint zone of Polish, British and American interests.

III. A Central-European Federation is a fundamental condition of the economic existence and, therefore, also of the security of the states along the Belgrade-Warsaw axis.

A federation based on strong foundations will be a guarantee likewise of the security of the United States, both in relation to Germany and also to any other forces which might again bring Europe to a state of chaos and, consequently, of war.

According to our conception, the basic elements of the federation include: Poland (with Lithuania), Czechoslovakia, Yugoslavia, Greece, (and Hungary).[2]

---

[2] This memorandum was first published by me in an article drawn from an earlier version of this study; see Sarah Meiklejohn Terry, "The Oder-Neisse Line Revisited: Sikorski's Program for Poland's Postwar Western Boundary, 1939-42," pp. 39-68. Several versions of the memorandum appear in different archival collections. This translation was made from the Polish original filed in the archive of the Polish Institute and Sikorski Museum, London (originally the General Sikorski Historical Institute, hereafter GSHI): A.XII.23/42, folio 1, no. 9 [emphasis added]. An English version, differing in only minor editorial details from the one presented here, is filed in the Archives of the Hoover Institution on War, Revolution and Peace, Stanford University (hereafter HIWRP): Ciechanowski Deposit, Box 93[84], folio: "General W. Sikorski's visit in Washington, Dec. 1942-Jan.1943." This and the accompanying memoranda are discussed in detail in Chapter V, the American reaction in Chapter X.

Although not all aspects of the above memorandum are self-explanatory, its immediate impact is to call into question what one might describe as the conventional wisdom concerning the origin and geopolitical significance of the Oder-Neisse line. This conventional wisdom is based on a stark black-and-white distinction between the policies of the "Moscow" and "London" Poles which holds, on the one hand:

—that the Polish-German boundary as established at the end of World War II was essentially a communist contrivance, fostered with Stalin's support by the wartime Union of Polish Patriots in Moscow and later by the Lublin Committee;

—that, despite the symbolic importance of a return to her historical boundaries in the west, from a practical standpoint the primary function of the Oder-Neisse line was to compensate Poland economically and territorially for the land she had lost in the east; and

—that, with respect to Poland's political orientation, a major consequence of this boundary was to bind her irrevocably to Russia, since Germany would never accept the loss of some 20 percent of her prewar territory.

By contrast, with respect to the London Poles this view holds:

—that the primary concerns of the Polish Government-in-Exile were retention of Poland's prewar eastern provinces (*kresy*, or "borderlands," as they were called) and the construction of a Central European federation as a barrier to the westward expansion of Soviet influence;

—that, being unwilling to countenance either territorial concessions in the east or the political dependence that would, inevitably in this view, follow from the absorption of so much German land in the west, the London Poles rejected the Oder line (with either Eastern or Western Neisse variant); and

—that, instead, the exile government sought only modest rectifications of Poland's borders with Germany, specifically removal of the East Prussian enclave and a straightening of the prewar frontier in eastern Pomerania and Upper Silesia.

Implicit in this view, though not always articulated, are the additional assumptions that the Great Powers, acting more or less in concert, in fact offered the exile government substantial territorial gains in the west in exchange for Poland's prewar east as a firm and consistent quid pro quo; and that Britain and the United States backed away from supporting the final Oder-Neisse line only because it went too far (to the Western rather than Eastern Neisse) and because, by the time of the Potsdam Conference, it was clear that Poland would be a communist state.

One cannot deny, of course, that there is some truth to this conventional wisdom. It is unquestionably true, for instance, that the Communists emerged from the war as the only organized political force that fully, indeed enthusiastically, supported all aspects of Poland's territorial shift. It is equally true that, in the final stage of the war, the Government-in-Exile wittingly rejected an Oder-Neisse frontier in the west just as it had, consistently throughout the war years, rejected the Curzon line in the east; that the exchange of eastern *kresy* for "Recovered Territories" has generally been regarded by the outside world, if not by the Poles themselves, as a matter of simple compensation; and that, for twenty-five years after the end of the war, the perpetuation of the Polish-German border quarrel, aggravated by the failure of the non-communist world to recognize the Oder-Neisse, did in fact serve to reinforce Warsaw's dependence on Moscow.

What is wrong with such statements and the assumptions that underlie them is not that they are untruths, but that they are half-truths whose continual repetition, almost in chorus, by virtually all parties at interest (a point to which I shall return momentarily) has been an all-too-effective deterrent to more critical scrutiny. They are half-truths in the sense that they are ahistorical, reflecting only the end product of events that unfolded over a period of six convulsive years. Moreover, they do so from a Cold War perspective, presenting the Oder-Neisse both as a product of and as a weapon in the competition between East and West. The result is a stereotyped view which gives little quarter to the complexities and ironies of Polish wartime politics and consequently distorts the policies not only of both the London and Moscow Poles, but of the Great Powers as well. It is a view that obscures the fact that the divisions within the London exile community were fully as deep and bitter as those between the London and Moscow camps and were occasioned by the same issue, i.e., the age-old question of "Poland's place in Europe." It is a view, moreover, that cannot fully appreciate the irony of the Communists' appropriation of an "Endek" dream.[3]

In opposition to this first set of assumptions I propose a second set, perhaps better referred to for the moment as hypotheses, and reflecting among other things the substance of the memorandum quoted above:

—first, that the concept of a Poland extended westward to the Oder and Neisse, as a practical policy rather than just an historical conception, first gained currency not among Polish Communists in Moscow, but within exile circles in London and in the non-communist Underground;

---

[3] The term "Endek" (or "Endecja"), derived from the initials N.D., refers to the right-wing National Democratic movement; see Chapter II below.

—that General Sikorski, as prime minister of the Polish Government-in-Exile from its inception in September 1939 until his death in July 1943, was the first Polish spokesman formally to propose such a boundary;

—that he did so within the framework of an overall reorientation of Poland's international posture based on a reconciliation with the Soviet Union—*including* a compromise settlement of the Polish-Soviet boundary dispute—as well as on a federation with Czechoslovakia and potentially with other Central European nations;

—that Sikorski did not conceive of territorial gains in the north and west *primarily* as compensation for possible losses in the east, but rather as justified in their own right by Poland's economic and strategic needs and by the needs of the federation;

—further, that he did not foresee absorption of so much German territory as inevitably rendering Poland dependent on Moscow, but as one prerequisite for the creation of a new balance of power in Central Europe—one in which Poland and the other small nations between Germany and Russia would cease to be the perennial flashpoints of Europe and become instead masters in their own houses and a positive factor in European prosperity and stability;

—that Sikorski was unsuccessful in implementing his policy in large measure because he failed to win over to his conceptions either a majority of his own countrymen or Poland's major allies—that, far from being assured a comprehensive settlement, he was subjected to a double standard whereby he was repeatedly urged to accept far-reaching concessions in the east with little prospect of more than minimal gains in the west;

—and, finally, that only after the collapse of Sikorski's policy— the collapse not only of his territorial program but, equally important, of the federation—did the Communists take up the Oder-Neisse idea, but only gradually and within a more limited context.

Perhaps the most startling realization of all is that the main period of Sikorski's pursuit fell in the two-and-one-half years between mid-1940 and the end of 1942, before Teheran (not to mention Yalta and/or Potsdam), before the Katyń discovery and the break in relations with Moscow, before the Polish Communists began to formulate their own boundary program, much of it while the latter were still in political limbo and while the Soviets were denying the very existence of Poland—in other words, before most of the landmark events that we now think of as having shaped the Polish settlement after the war.

IF the above scenario even remotely approaches the truth, then we are faced with a very intriguing question: why has the first set of assumptions concerning the origin of the Oder-Neisse line, what I have called the conventional wisdom, been so widely accepted for so long, while the second set has remained obscured or at best only dimly and incompletely perceived? The reasons are deceptively simple and fall roughly into two categories.

Several are related to the timing and character of the Sikorski period itself. For instance, in the torrent of memoirs, documents, and monographs about the "Polish Question" in World War II, the early years have generally been slighted in favor of the period more or less from the middle of 1943 on—and not without some logic. Not only was the later period with its Great Power conferences more dramatic; it was then that the decisions which in fact determined Poland's postwar territorial and political status were made. By contrast the Sikorski years are a study in frustration and failure. Second, for reasons related both to longstanding divisions in Polish politics and to the essentially disruptive nature of Sikorski's conceptions, the exile community was a hotbed of dissension and intrigue. In particular, his approach to relations with the Soviet Union was a source of intense and bitter dispute. Moreover, from the standpoint of confidentiality, the exile government's bureaucracies had all the virtues of Swiss cheese. Thus it is hardly surprising that the general, himself a controversial figure and by nature something of a loner, chose to keep discussion of his policy within a narrow circle of personal advisors. As a result, although the basic outlines of his strategy were common knowledge throughout the exile community—indeed, they were the subject of heated debate—details of his specific programs were not; and this was especially true of the more sensitive aspects of his policy. Finally, of course, Sikorski did not live to explain and defend his own policy but was killed together with several of his closest aides in a plane crash off Gibraltar on July 4, 1943.

A very different but equally important reason for the persistence of misconceptions about the development of the Oder-Neisse idea relates to the changing political environment in which this line became the boundary between Poland and Germany: first, to the post-Sikorski shift in the policy of the Government-in-Exile away from the general's vision of westward expansion toward a more rigid stand on Poland's prewar eastern boundary; and, second, to the growing rift in the Grand Alliance that made the Oder-Neisse boundary appear less an integral part of a common peace settlement than an opening move in the Cold War maneuvering that followed. In this new atmosphere it redounded to the interests of all parties concerned—of the Poles, both émigré and communist, of the Western powers as well as the Soviets, and also of the Germans—to paint a picture of stark contrasts between the policies of the communist and non-communist camps. What we have as a result is a deceptively uniform impression of Polish exile policy in which the major tenets and rigidities of the post-Sikorski period have been extrapolated backwards and applied to the general himself, who is then portrayed as having been above all a defender of Poland's territorial integrity within her pre-September 1939 boundaries, and as unwilling to seek more than modest gains in the north and west (if indeed the subject of such gains is mentioned at all) in order not to jeopardize Poland's position in the east.

Obviously sources representing such divergent points of view have not all appraised the Sikorski period in the same way. Each group has had its own axe to grind—past actions and policies to justify, as well as current and future interests to protect. Each has emphasized those points and events that best sustain its case, while playing down, distorting or simply ignoring those that might call it into question. Yet, stripped of these differences of interpretation, the overwhelming impression left by those books that have most shaped our understanding of the Polish Question in World War II is that the idea of shifting Poland westward to the Oder and Lusatian Neisse dates from the conversation between Stalin and Churchill at Teheran in late 1943, at which the latter made his now famous matchstick demonstration—"like soldiers taking two steps 'left close.' "[4]

SMALL WONDER that the conventional wisdom concerning the Oder-Neisse boundary has so rarely been challenged, or that it has been carried over into secondary sources of all political colorations. Small wonder, too, that as the boundary has gained acceptance and finally, in 1970, formal recognition by the German Federal Republic, interest in the question of its origin has flagged. Indeed, in view of the fact that with recognition the long controversy over the legitimacy of the Oder-Neisse boundary is now closed—in view also of the fact that Sikorski's efforts were an unmitigated failure, and that the actual establishment of the boundary occurred under circumstances incompatible with the basic premises of his policy—it is reasonable to ask what purpose a study of this sort serves. Is it merely an exercise in historical curiosity? Or does it in some way contribute to a broader understanding of Poland's lot in the last thirty-odd years? There is, of course, a certain satisfaction to be derived from helping to right the historical balance—from fitting into place some of the last missing pieces of a puzzle long unfinished and obscured by more recent history. This is particularly true when those new pieces substantially alter our perspective

---

[4] Winston S. Churchill, *Closing the Ring*, p. 362. For a discussion of source materials, see my Bibliographical Essay.

on the whole picture, in this case our image of the Polish Government-in-Exile. Even if this were the only reason for reassessing General Sikorski's premiership, it would be worth undertaking.

I would suggest however that, far from being of purely historical interest, the topic is relevant to the study of postwar Polish politics as well—and ultimately to an understanding of why, nearly forty years after the end of the war, Poland is again on center stage as the potential flashpoint of Europe. For, where a comparison of postwar communist policy with that of the exile government in the final war years provides a picture of stark contrasts, a similar comparison with the Sikorski period reveals several areas of continuity that have gone unnoticed at least in part because of our persistent misunderstanding of the origin of the Oder-Neisse line and of its intended political and economic significance. I am speaking here not merely of the similarities in territorial design already alluded to. More interesting are the similarities in overall conception of Poland's "place in Europe" and in the relationship of boundary changes to this central issue. For instance, if one examines closely the strategy pursued by the Polish Workers' Party in the first postwar years, one finds:

—that, even within the framework of an alliance with the Soviet Union, the Communists, with Stalin's destruction of their prewar party still fresh in their minds, also had reason to seek a reduction of Poland's vulnerability to Russian domination;

—that both saw the acquisition of the Oder-Neisse territories as promoting this end because of the added economic potential they would give Poland, because their loss would permanently weaken Germany, and because they would provide the geographic basis for a closer economic relationship with Czechoslovakia;

—that, while they could not espouse the political federation sought by Sikorski, the Communists did favor extensive economic cooperation between Poland and Czechoslovakia, based on what they too saw as a special community of interests among the smaller nations of Central Europe;

—and, finally, that both hoped for a continuation of Grand Alliance cooperation into the postwar period not only in order that Poland's new boundaries be recognized and guaranteed by both sides but, equally important, that Germany not become the focal point of East-West rivalry in Europe—a development that the Communists no less than Sikorski feared would open the way for renewed Russo-German collaboration at Poland's expense.

True, the Communists were scarcely more successful in implementing this basic strategy in the late 1940s than Sikorski had been earlier in the decade.

Of these several goals the only one they managed to achieve was retention of the Oder-Neisse boundary, but in circumstances that increased rather than lessened their dependence on Moscow. Yet these same themes have reemerged in one or another form whenever the international climate has turned propitious.

It would be very easy to overstate the parallels between Sikorski and the Communists, and I do not intend to carry the analogy any further. Even within the areas of similarity, there were important differences of emphasis and detail, due not only to ideological differences but also to the requirements of their respective political circumstances. (Among the more obvious: the latter had perforce to accept a greater degree of reliance on Soviet backing than any non-communist government could have tolerated; on the other hand, where federation was an integral and central part of Sikorski's program from the outset, the Communists appear to have taken up the idea of Polish-Czech economic cooperation belatedly, less out of principle than of necessity to offset wartime devastation compounded by blatant Soviet economic exploitation.) Nor do I mean to suggest that there was any direct link between the policies of the exile government under Sikorski and those of the postwar regime—although, as we shall see, the general's diplomatic efforts on behalf of Poland's westward expansion did contribute indirectly to the eventual establishment of an Oder-Neisse boundary by introducing and supporting the legitimacy of that idea in London and Washington.

Rather, the significance of the parallels lies in the fact that both policies represented broadly analogous attempts by Poles of widely disparate political persuasions to respond realistically to the fundamental dilemma posed by Poland's geography in the context of World War II and the postwar period—a dilemma to which the Communists were no more immune by virtue of their adherence to the Soviet faith than were their non-communist compatriots. That is, how to seek defense against one hostile and powerful neighbor (Germany) without falling into a position of unqualified reliance on a second (Russia), which itself had twice conspired with the first to erase Poland from the map of Europe—but without, at the same time, falling back into the progressive isolation that had brought her such disastrous consequences in 1939.

THIS is a story with many facets, not all of which can be explored with the same degree of detail. On the other hand, it is important to an understanding of the question of Poland's western boundary in this early wartime period that it not be isolated from the larger political context. For this is also the story of the last four years in the life of one of Poland's most controversial and least understood modern leaders, and of his attempt to find an enduring solution to that country's geopolitical dilemma. As such, it involves his efforts to found a Central European federation and to bring about a reconciliation in Polish-Soviet relations, based initially on the formation of a Polish Army to fight on the Soviet front—both aspects of his policy that have never been adequately clarified. Because of the central role that General Sikorski played in Poland's fortunes in these years, the ensuing chapters have been organized around first the development and then the disintegration of his policy, with particular attention to his plans for a Polish Army in the Soviet Union and for Central European cooperation, as well as to his territorial program.

II · The Burden of History

FEW NATIONS can rival Poland in the variety of configurations that she has assumed throughout history, ranging from her status as the largest European state at the height of the Polish-Lithuanian Commonwealth in the fifteenth century to her disappearances from the political map following the three partitions of 1772 to 1795, and once again in 1939. For all this, one of the more astonishing aspects of her checkered existence is the fact that her present boundaries approximate those within which she began her recorded history more than a thousand years ago—a fact that might seem to make her geographic meanderings in the intervening centuries somewhat irrelevant. Yet the changing dimensions of Poland's place in Europe have never been a matter simply of geography, or even of shifting alliances and enmities. Far more important has been the lasting burden on the psyche of the Polish nation, on their sense of national identity.

Speaking very broadly, Poland's history up to the time of the partitions can be divided into two sharply contrasting periods, the Piast and the Jagiellonian, each named after the dynasty that dominated it and each roughly four centuries in duration.[1] The Kingdom of the Piasts, first unified in the latter half of the tenth century in response to pressure from the German margraves, began its history with a western boundary that ran somewhat to the west of the lower course of the Oder and then southward to the Bohemian border along an irregular line between the Lusatian Neisse and the Kwisa and Bober rivers slightly to the east. (The southern sector of the boundary was probably not clearly defined, as this region was then sparsely inhabited and heavily forested; see Map 2.) Except for a brief period during the reign of her second king, Bolesław Chrobry (the Brave), when the Lusatian lands to the west and Bohemia and Moravia to the south came under the Polish crown, Poland's boundary with the Holy Roman Empire remained relatively stable for some two hundred years. It was in the latter part of the twelfth and early thirteenth centuries, under the influence both of internal dynastic divisions and of the Tatar invasion from the east, that Poland began to lose her grip on the west and along the

---

[1] For detailed treatment, see Oscar Halecki, *Borderlands of Western Civilization: A History of East Central Europe*, pp. 39-257; or Zygmunt Wojciechowski, "Poland and Germany: Ten Centuries of Struggle," in *Poland's Place in Europe*, ed. Z. Wojciechowski, pp. 85-316. For a briefer survey, see Samuel L. Sharp, *Poland: White Eagle on a Red Field*, pp. 17-41.

Map 2

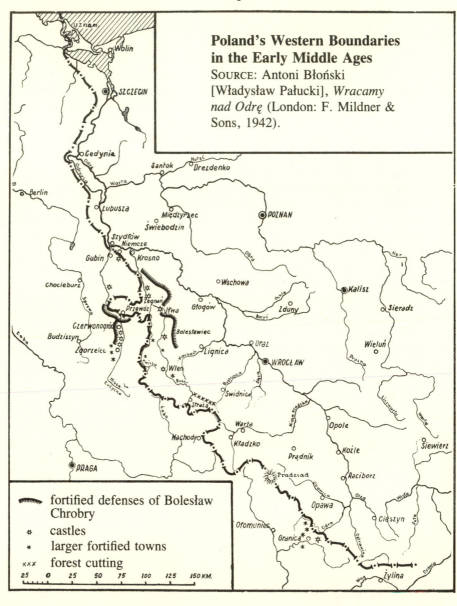

Poland's Western Boundaries in the Early Middle Ages

SOURCE: Antoni Błoński [Władysław Pałucki], *Wracamy nad Odrę* (London: F. Mildner & Sons, 1942).

Baltic, forfeiting first western Pomerania with the lower course of the Oder to the Mark of Brandenburg and somewhat later experiencing the first incursions of the Teutonic Knights in the northeast. The kingdom was reunified early in the fourteenth century, but only at the cost of further losses. The Order, called in to help reestablish the crown's control over Danzig, took over what remained of Polish Pomerania, thereby cutting her off completely from the sea. By mid-century Kazimierz the Great, the last of the Piast kings, had to recognize Bohemian suzerainty over Silesia, which already for several hundred years had been ruled as a separate duchy under another branch of the family. (Although gradually Germanized, Silesia did not come under Prussian rule until its conquest by Frederick the Great in the 1740s.) From this point—that is, the end of the Piast dynasty—until the first partition in 1772, the only change of moment in Poland's western boundary was the recovery of her access to the sea through Danzig and eastern Pomerania (then called Royal Prussia) in the fifteenth century.

In contrast to the gradual attrition of Poland's holdings in the west, her expansion to the east occurred almost by a single stroke, through the dynastic union with the Grand Duchy of Lithuania in 1386.[2] It was only in the reign of the last Piast, Kazimierz, that Poland's eastern boundary was extended beyond her ethnic limits to include the Ruthenian territories of Halich (later known as Eastern Galicia) and the western part of Volhynia. Now, with the assumption of the Polish crown by Grand Duke Jagiełło, Poland found herself attached to a loosely organized empire three times her own size, whose boundaries at their point of greatest expansion embraced much of the eastern Baltic coast and the entire Dnieper River basin— stretching, that is, across almost all of what we know today as Estonia, Latvia, Belorussia, and the Ukraine as well as a slice of Russia proper. The eastern limits of the Commonwealth fluctuated over the centuries, at times reaching almost to Moscow (see Map 3). Although by the time of the partitions it had lost its foothold on the Black Sea as well as most of its territories east of the Dnieper, the dual monarchy still comprised an empire at least twice the size of ethnic Poland and Lithuania combined.

Ironically the union, which was originally sought to enable both states to counter the challenge posed by the Teutonic Order, had the long-term effect of diverting Poland's attention away from the German danger and toward the east. It also marked the beginning of her transformation from a cohesive, ethnically homogeneous state into the dominant force in a vast multinational federation. For, despite the disparity in size between the two

[2] In addition to the sources cited in the preceding note, see M. K. Dziewanowski, *Joseph Piłsudski: A European Federalist, 1918-1922*, chap. 1.

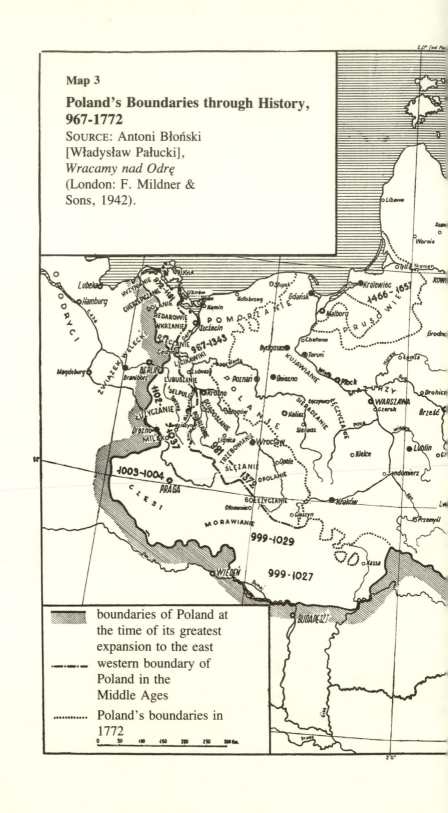

Map 3

Poland's Boundaries through History, 967-1772

SOURCE: Antoni Błoński [Władysław Pałucki], *Wracamy nad Odrę* (London: F. Mildner & Sons, 1942).

boundaries of Poland at the time of its greatest expansion to the east

western boundary of Poland in the Middle Ages

Poland's boundaries in 1772

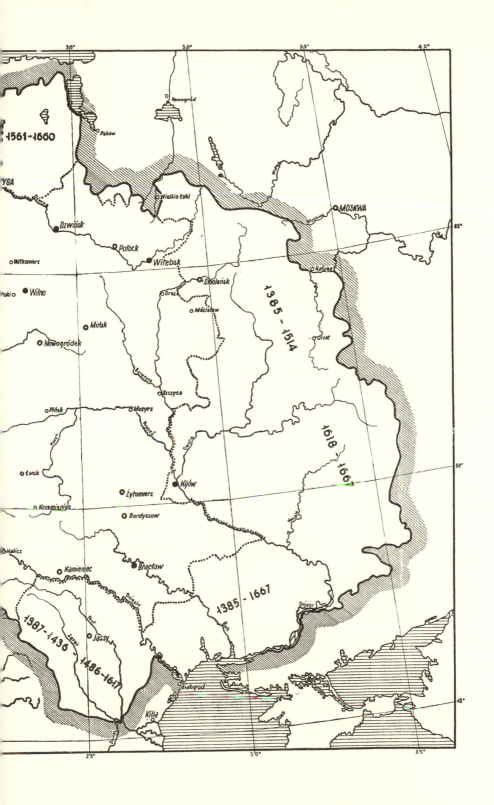

1561-1660

YGA

Psków

Dźwińsk

Nowogród

Wielkie Łuki

Witkomierz

Połock

Wilno

Witebsk

Smoleńsk

Orsza

Mścisław

Kaługa

MOSKWA

1385 - 1514

Mińsk

Nowogródek

Orzet

Pińsk

Mozyrz

Rzyca

Łuck

Krzemieniec

Żytomierz

Kijów

Berdyczow

1618 - 166

Halicz

Kamieniec

Bracław

1385 - 1667

1387 - 1436

Jassy

1486 - 1617

Dniepr

Kilia

Białogród

partners, Poland represented the more advanced civilization to which the Lithuanian and Ukrainian upper classes naturally gravitated. (In this way even Vilnius, or Wilno, the ancient capital of ethnic Lithuania, became in the end a predominantly Polish city.) This process was greatly accelerated midway in the life of the Jagiellonian state when, under the Union of Lublin of 1569, what had been merely a dynastic union took on the forms (if not always the substance) of a more unified federal political structure in which large areas of the Ukraine came under direct Polish administration. The Polish gentry now settled these areas in large numbers, more often than not becoming the dominant element economically, as well as politically and culturally.[3]

Although the Piast and Jagiellonian conceptions never clashed directly in prepartition Poland, the contrasts between these periods of her history posed two fundamental questions for later generations of Poles seeking the resurrection of their nation: First, what was Poland? Was her basic identity geographic or ethnic? Historico-political or cultural? And, second, how best could the continued existence of the Polish nation and culture be ensured? It is these two questions, rather than the issues that traditionally determine one's place on the political spectrum, that have been the source of the most rending division in Polish politics over the last two hundred years.

To define that division as one between those who have favored a return to the original Piast state and those who have looked to a revival of the Jagiellonian empire would obviously be an oversimplification. The Piast model as a geographic concept did not gain much of a following until shortly before and during the Second World War. Moreover, in view of the ethnic changes wrought in western Poland over the centuries, neither model offered an appropriate vessel for the wine of modern nationalism. Rather, Polish politics is more commonly described in terms of geopolitical orientations: in terms of the opposition between "realism" and "idealism," or between "positivism" and "romanticism."[4] Yet neither are the dynastic designations wholly alien to the philosophical differences of the opposing sides.

For the realists, Poland was first and foremost an ethnic and cultural

[3] On the eve of the Bolshevik Revolution, there were an estimated 1 to 1.8 million Poles in the western Ukraine (i.e., west of the Dnieper) and they were still a dominant element in the agricultural economy; ibid., p. 223. The nature of this federation or Commonwealth, especially the degree of unity achieved, has been a subject of debate among historians; see, e.g., Oswald P. Backus III et al., "The Problem of Unity in the Polish-Lithuanian State: A Discussion," pp. 411-55.

[4] See especially Andrzej Micewski, *Z geografii politycznej II Rzeczypospolitej: Szkice,* especially pp. 335-99; and Adam Bromke, *Poland's Politics: Idealism vs. Realism.*

entity, whose preservation could not be risked for mere political or territorial gain. Not that they would always disclaim political aspirations, but they subordinated politics to the need to conserve and strengthen the nation's human capital. Second, if the realists did not subscribe to the Piast conception in the strict geographical sense, they did regard the western provinces where Poland began her history and where the Poles remained the dominant ethnic element as those most important to the nation's existence.[5] More than this, they believed that excessive expansion to the east had weakened Poland internally, thereby contributing to her downfall. Third, and as a consequence of their ethnic and geographic orientation, the realists saw Germany—or, more accurately, Prussia whose growth had occurred at the expense of Poland's heartlands—as their mortal enemy. For them the only rational course open to the Poles was to seek an accommodation with the one partitioning power with whom they shared a common interest vis-à-vis Germany: Russia.

Where the realists tailored their goals to what they perceived to be Poland's limited political prospects, the idealists took their cue from the Romantic poet, Adam Mickiewicz: "Measure your powers by your purpose, not your purposes by your powers." For them Poland was an historical entity, one which they identified with the "Golden Age" of the Jagiellonian Commonwealth. Their most important goal was the recovery of political independence and, in the first decades after partition, they were willing to settle for nothing less than a restoration of the 1772 frontiers. Entwined with this political conception was the notion of Poland as the last outpost of Western civilization, to whom history had assigned the dual role as bearer of that civilization to the east and as the defender of western Europe from the inundations of assorted infidels. (Hence the tendency to embellish Poland's role in saving Europe from the Mongols in 1241 and Vienna from the Turks in 1683.) Of the three partitioning powers the idealists saw Russia, the occupier of the vast majority of what were in their view Polish territories, as their archenemy. Unlike the realists, they did not favor reliance on a second partitioner (although they were not averse to flirting with Prussia); rather, they looked to the West, and especially to France, for the assistance that they believed Poland richly deserved for her sacrifices.[6]

The realist school, which put in its first abortive appearance in the interlude between the first and second partitions, came into its own only in the aftermath of the disastrous insurrection of 1863 which was followed

---

[5] "Western" here is meant in the context of the Poland of 1772, and not as a reference to her post-World War II Western or "Recovered" Territories.

[6] Sharp, *Poland: White Eagle*, pp. 20-21, 38-39, and 44-60; Bromke, *Poland's Politics*, pp. 7-10.

by an intensification of oppressive policies in both the Russian and Prussian partitions. Perceiving that revolutionary tactics and the preoccupation of the romantics with independence could only lead to the total destruction of the nation, the realists, or "positivists" as they called themselves in this period, urged the Poles to eschew political activity and to turn their energies to internal "organic reform"—to renounce "radical utopias which profess to change society overnight" in favor of "slow and gradual progress." By the turn of the century, however, the very success of the positivist program, as well as frustration with continued political oppression, had led to a revival of political activism which found its expression in the modified realism of the National Democratic movement under Roman Dmowski. Although a nationalist par excellence who looked forward to the eventual reestablishment of an independent Poland, Dmowski was also a realist in his appreciation of the limits imposed by Poland's geography, in his emphasis on her western provinces and on the need to seek a rapprochement with Russia. "Either with the Germans or the Russians," he wrote in 1901, "no third possibility exists." With the outbreak of World War I he urged the Poles to support the Russian war effort, his hope being that a Russian victory over the Central Powers would result in the unification of all Polish lands under tsarist rule, such unification leading first to autonomy and ultimately to independence.[7]

Apparent Russian indifference to his efforts to promote rapprochement, followed in 1917 by the Bolshevik Revolution, caused Dmowski to reassess his previous policy. Where he had foreseen a close association with a tsarist Russia, his fundamental conservatism would not brook the same degree of cooperation with a Soviet Russia. Moreover, the pending defeat of both Russia and Germany greatly enhanced the prospects for a truly independent Poland. Transferring his activities from St. Petersburg to the West, Dmowski organized a Polish National Committee to represent Poland's interests in the capitals of the West and eventually at the Peace Conference. There was more to the move than a mere change of physical location; it also marked a shift away from the "realist" position. Not only did he espouse immediate independence but, in moving away from a policy of reliance on Russia, he moved closer to the idealist position on Poland's eastern boundaries. In the west, Dmowski limited his proposals to those territories to which the Poles had a legitimate ethnic claim: the boundary of 1772 together with all of Upper Silesia (including the Oppeln district) and the ethnically Polish districts of East Prussia; the rest of East Prussia would either be an autonomous province of Poland or a separate state, but

---

[7] Bromke, *Poland's Politics*, pp. 5 and 10-16; Dziewanowski, *Piłsudski*, pp. 38-39 and 48-49; and Titus Komarnicki, *Rebirth of the Polish Republic: A Study of the Diplomatic History of Europe, 1914-1920*, pp. 40-41 and 48-49.

in either event removed from German control.[8] In the east, however, Dmowski presented claims considerably broader than Poland would have been entitled to on purely ethnic grounds. In a memorandum submitted to President Wilson in October 1918, he conceded that "there is no good solution" to the Polish-Russian boundary problem but proposed that the most acceptable one could be reached by "dividing the territory of the eastern Polish provinces [i.e., as of 1772] into two parts: the western part, where the Polish element is more numerous and the Polish influence decisively predominant, should belong to the Polish state; and the eastern part should remain in Russia's possession." Moreover, Dmowski foresaw that these areas of mixed or even predominantly non-Polish population would be incorporated into Poland not on a federated basis or with rights of local autonomy, but as integral parts of a centralized nation state. As one historian of the period has commented: "At the bottom of this suggestion was the idea that the peoples of the ethnically mixed intermediate zone between Poland proper and Russia proper were not yet mature enough for independent existence, and that the Poles would be able to assimilate the western fringes of the area in due time."[9]

After leading the Poles into two disastrous uprisings in 1830 and 1863, the reprisals for which only aggravated their already difficult situation, idealism fell into disfavor for much of the remainder of the nineteenth century. When it reemerged, it too took a somewhat modified form under the guidance of Józef Piłsudski, a leader of the Polish Socialist Party (the nationalist wing of Polish socialism) and Dmowski's chief political rival. In line with the idealist tradition, Piłsudski rejected the view that the former Polish-Lithuanian federation had been a mistake that had contributed to Poland's downfall. On the contrary, he believed it had saved both nations from dismemberment or destruction at the hands of the Teutonic Order and Muscovy in the fourteenth century, allowing them to survive in relative freedom and prosperity until the end of the eighteenth. Given their precarious geography, only a revival of the union could ensure their future survival. For him, therefore, while Russia was the main enemy (against

[8] For Dmowski's program on the western boundary, see: Komarnicki, *Rebirth of the Polish Republic*, p. 326; Marian Seyda, *Pół wieku walki o granicę polsko-niemiecką*, p. 7; and Henryk Zieliński, "Poglądy polskich ugrupowań politycznych na sprawę Ziem Zachodnich i granicy polsko-niemieckiej (1914-1919)," in *Problem polsko-niemiecki w Traktacie Wersalskim*, ed. J. Pajewski, pp. 206-207.

[9] Dziewanowski, *Piłsudski*, p. 95. See also Komarnicki, *Rebirth of the Polish Republic*, pp. 480-90; Micewski, *Z geografii politycznej*, pp. 102-103; and Kay Lundgreen-Nielsen, *The Polish Problem at the Paris Peace Conference: A Study of the Policies of the Great Powers and the Poles, 1918-1919*, pp. 33-34. Dmowski's proposed line would have allowed the Russians to retain almost all of their acquisitions from the 1772 and 1793 partitions.

whom he even sought military support from the Japanese in 1904), Germany was not a potential ally except in a tactical sense.

On the other hand, Piłsudski departed from the idealist conception in his realization that the tide of nationalism sweeping through the several peoples of the old Commonwealth would not allow for the return of a structure in which Polish influence predominated over the others. Rather, he wanted to see a largely ethnic Poland in free association with independent states in Lithuania, Belorussia, and the Ukraine. His ideas on Poland's eastern boundary provide an interesting contrast to Dmowksi's and, indeed, were unacceptable to the National Democrats and many others as well. In the north, he believed that Wilno, despite its Polish majority, should go to Lithuania—although, should the latter not join a federation, he would insist that Wilno and other ethnically Polish districts remain with Poland. In relation to the Ukraine, Piłsudski proposed a division of Eastern Galicia such that only the western part with Lwów and the neighboring oil fields would remain with Poland, a gesture that he hoped would win over the reluctant Ukrainians to a common struggle against Russia.[10]

For Piłsudski as for Dmowski, the simultaneous collapse of all three partitioning powers was a major turning point. At the beginning of the war, he had been willing to accept an "Austrian solution"—that is, the unification of Russian-held Congress Poland with Austrian-held Galicia under the Dual Monarchy, the least oppressive of the partitioners. At the time, such a solution had seemed to be the best that Poland could hope for; moreover, cooperation with Austria had allowed Piłsudski to form his Polish legions. Now, with Russia in revolution and the Central Powers on the verge of defeat, he seized the opportunity to pursue his dream. But in his preoccupation with federation, Piłsudski led the Poles into a war with Russia that very nearly resulted in the destruction of their newly resurrected state and that cost them dearly in their relations with the West and in their boundary struggle with Germany.[11]

[10] For a book-length study of Piłsudski's federation plan, see Dziewanowski, *Piłsudski*, especially chaps. 2, 3, 5, 7, and 13. See also Bromke, *Poland's Politics*, pp. 25-30; Komarnicki, *Rebirth of the Polish Republic*, pp. 450-56; Micewski, *Z geografii politycznej*, pp. 102-103; and Lundgreen-Nielsen, *The Polish Problem*, pp. 50-52. It is worth noting that Piłsudski's minimum boundary demands in the east, while more modest than Dmowski's, would still have left a fair number of Lithuanians, Belorussians, and Ukrainians within Poland proper.

[11] This is not to suggest that Piłsudski or the Poles bear primary responsibility for the 1919-20 war, which grew out of the Bolsheviks' desire to reincorporate as much of the tsarist empire's non-Russian western borderlands as possible, Poland included—or, if faced with the impossibility of reabsorbing Poland proper, to limit her to a small and vulnerable rump state, possibly for later sacrifice to a revolutionized Germany. Thus, Piłsudski's military initiatives (beginning with the seizure of Wilno in April 1919), if not entirely defensive in nature, can fairly be described as a preventive war. On the other hand, Piłsudski seriously

In the end, Poland got the worst of both worlds. Piłsudski, despite his apparent sensitivity to the issue, seriously underestimated the force of national feelings on both sides—that is, the anti-Polish sentiment especially among the Lithuanians and Ukrainians, and the chauvinistic nationalism of his own countrymen. The 1919-20 war with the Soviets, ended by the Treaty of Riga on March 18, 1921, was settled more in accordance with Dmowski's ideas than Piłsudski's. Although Poland received substantial areas of predominantly non-Polish population, including all of Eastern Galicia and Polish Wilno with its non-Polish environs, they were too small to form the basis of a federal structure yet too large to be successfully absorbed into a centralized nation-state. At the same time, their incorporation into Poland virtually ensured the hostility of her neighbors to the east and north. (Lithuania refused to establish diplomatic relations with Warsaw until 1938.)[12]

Moreover, in part as a result of their preoccupation with the east, the Poles failed to secure their most vital interests vis-à-vis Germany in the west: in Upper Silesia, which was divided to Poland's disadvantage following a plebiscite on March 20, 1921, two days after the signing of the Riga Treaty; in southern East Prussia, which was returned in its entirety to Germany following a plebiscite in July 1920 that coincided with the Soviet march on Warsaw; and in Danzig (Gdańsk), ostensibly to become a Free City but in fact dominated by German political and economic interests. Thus Poland emerged from the First World War with boundaries that satisfied neither ethnic nor strategic and economic criteria. Instead of the promised free access to the sea, she received only a narrow corridor, which served merely to aggravate relations with a hostile Germany in possession of salients into her economic centers from three directions.[13]

---

overestimated Poland's relative power—he once described Russia, Red and White, as "cadavers." This misjudgment led him, in the joint Polish-Ukrainian assault on Kiev in April-May 1920, into a grave overextension of Polish strength for goals that lacked full support or understanding at home and alienated the Western powers on whom Poland would ultimately depend. For detailed studies of this period, see Piotr S. Wandycz, *Soviet-Polish Relations, 1917-1921*; and Norman Davies, *White Eagle, Red Star: The Polish-Soviet War, 1919-20*.

[12] Komarnicki, *Rebirth of the Polish Republic*, Pt. II, chaps. 4-8; and Dziewanowski, *Piłsudski*, chaps. 15-17.

[13] One cannot say for sure how much Poland's ambitions and military activities in the east prejudiced her interests in the west and north. What can be said with some certainty is that the allied Polish Commission at Versailles initially recommended the unconditional incorporation into Poland of all of Upper Silesia and Danzig and the demilitarization of what would remain of German East Prussia following the plebiscite in the Allenstein (Olsztyn) district; and that the British delegation—led by Lloyd George, by all accounts a firm disbeliever in Poland's capacity for self-rule—exploited growing Western unease over Polish military advances into non-Polish areas in the east in his efforts to revise the Commission's recommendations in Germany's favor. See Lundgreen-Nielsen, *The Polish Problem*, espe-

The mood of the nation in the interwar period was also an unfortunate blend. As is so often the case in political as well as religious movements, the subtleties of a Dmowski's or a Piłsudski's thoughts were lost on the masses of their followers. On the one hand, although Dmowski never entirely abandoned his realist outlook—consistently rejecting the idea that an independent Poland could survive between a hostile Germany and Russia, and believing that an eventual accommodation with the latter was necessary to offset the greater threat from the former—the mass of his National Democratic followers (or Endeks as they were called after their initials) were as ardently anti-Bolshevist and as wedded to a "two-enemy" policy as the Piłsudskiites. On the other hand, while Piłsudski himself never gave up his federalist ideals or his tolerance for other nationalities, it was Dmowski's incorporationist, chauvinistic nationalism that dominated the mood of Piłsudski's followers in the Sanacja.[14] While their leaders appear to have grasped the unreality of the "great power" mystique (*mocarstwość*) they preached, too many Poles tended to forget that the resurrection of their state was the result not merely of their own political genius and military strength, but of an accident of history which had temporarily weakened both Germany and Russia while leaving unchanged their underlying geographic dilemma.[15]

WITH their boundaries in the east, west, and north as barriers to normal relations with neighbors on those sides, the one remaining direction in which the Poles might have looked to bolster their security and economic stability was to the south. The most immediate possibility would have been some form of union with Czechoslovakia, and beyond her with the

cially pp. 197-205, 294, 357-62, and 413. Some interesting background papers on the Polish-German boundary settlement, drawn up by the Research Department of the British Foreign Office [F.O.R.D.] during 1942 and 1943, appear in the Foreign Office archives; see files FO 371/34595 and 34596, PRO. See also Robert Machray, *The Problem of Upper Silesia*, chaps. 4-5; Komarnicki, *Rebirth of the Polish Republic*, Pt. II, chap. 2; and Piotr S. Wandycz, *France and Her Eastern Allies, 1919-1925: French-Czechoslovak-Polish Relations from the Paris Peace Conference to Locarno*, chap. 1.

[14] "Sanacja" was the name given by Piłsudski to the movement that ruled Poland after his May 1926 coup. Literally "sanitation" or "purification," the term symbolized Piłsudski's intention to lead the nation into moral and political reform. See, for instance, Antony Polonsky, *Politics in Independent Poland 1921-1939: The Crisis of Constitutional Government*, pp. 147-85; and Edward D. Wynot, Jr., *Polish Politics in Transition: The Camp of National Unity and the Struggle for Power, 1935-1939*, especially chap. 2.

[15] The national mood of interwar Poland is perhaps best evoked by Czesław Miłosz in his part autobiography, part social history, *Native Realm: A Search for Self-Definition*. See also Micewski, *Z geografii politycznej*, pp. 262-72; and Bromke, *Poland's Politics*, pp. 17-18 and 31-43. For an extreme expression of the "great power" myth, see Juliusz Łukasiewicz, *Polska jest mocarstwem*. See p. 183 below.

other small nations of Central Europe, themselves largely products of the disintegration of the Austro-Hungarian Empire and the Versailles settlement. To judge by the number of proposals and supportive statements that began to find expression in various quarters even before the war had ended, the prospects that some combination or combinations of states would emerge must, initially at least, have seemed promising. As early as November of 1916, a British Foreign Office memorandum recommended linking Bohemia with Poland.[16] In October 1918, on the eve of the Armistice, the Czech leader Thomas Masaryk proposed that "the German plan of *Mitteleuropa* [should be replaced] by a positive plan of organization of the host of smaller nations located between the Germans and the Russians." Dmowski, at that time president of the Polish National Committee in Paris, agreed but suggested an even closer union between Poles and Czechs.[17] Eduard Beneš, who would later speak of his plan as a "United States of Central Europe," argued for a gradual approach: "The Czechs," he wrote on the eve of the Peace Conference, "now look for natural allies; an alliance in the East with the Poles and in the South with the Yugoslavs. These alliances will be close and can even lead to an economic union (which means a federation) and a united Poland and Bohemia will have a common port on the Baltic Sea. . . ."[18] Others, too, including the Hungarian federalist advocate Oscar Jászi, saw a Danubian federation as the only rational means of solving the complex nationality problems of the successor states and of easing the economic dislocations that would inevitably follow the breakup of Austria-Hungary.[19] In the end, however, none of these proposals came to pass. Indeed, in retrospect they were doomed to failure from the start, not only by the spirit of exuberant and intolerant nationalism that dominated Central European politics in the twenty years between the wars, but equally by the Western democracies' abdication of their responsibilities in the region.

On the level of Polish-Czech relations, there were at least three serious obstacles to federation, or even to the establishment of close political and economic ties. The first was the fact that, within weeks of the war's end, relations between the two nations were poisoned by the dispute over Teschen Silesia and thereafter never broke out of a pattern of petty nationalistic

[16] Komarnicki, *Rebirth of the Polish Republic*, p. 165n.

[17] Dziewanowski (*Piłsudski*, pp. 79-80 and notes) indicates that Piłsudski also made an approach to Masaryk; see also Komarnicki, *Rebirth of the Polish Republic*, p. 356.

[18] Komarnicki, *Rebirth of the Polish Republic*, pp. 367-68.

[19] For a general discussion of federal plans for Central Europe after World War I, see Stephen Borsody, *The Tragedy of Central Europe: The Nazi and Soviet Conquest of Central Europe*, pp. 17-60.

rivalries.[20] Second, the final course of Poland's western and Baltic boundaries was itself a negative factor; for, both the German Silesian wedge separating the Polish and Czech industrial districts and Poland's failure to gain outright control of the port city of Danzig substantially diminished the potential benefits of economic cooperation.[21] Third and most damaging to the prospects for closer relations were the profound differences between the Polish and Czech attitudes toward the Soviet Union. The Czechs, having no common frontier and therefore no outstanding territorial disputes with the Soviets, looked on them as potential Slav allies against Germany.[22] Hence they wanted no part of a federation scheme that could in any way be interpreted as a *cordon sanitaire*. In the same vein, they admonished the Poles to limit their territorial claims to their ethnic boundaries in order to facilitate good relations with the Soviet Union.[23] Whatever the soundness of this advice, it was understandable in light of the Teschen affair, and in light of the substantial German and Hungarian minorities in Czechoslovakia, that the Poles would view the Czech stance as more than a little hypocritical.

The pattern of relations at the broader regional level was no more auspicious and, in one sense at least, paralleled the Polish-Czechoslovak experience; that is, the boundaries laid down after the war served more often as barriers than as bridges to cooperation. Even had the principle been fairly applied, it is doubtful that national self-determination would have proven a reliable guide to delineating frontiers in a region of such mixed populations as Central Europe. As it was, the territorial settlement effected in the Danube Valley was less an expression of self-determination than a vindictive peace imposed by the victors (Czechoslovakia, Rumania,

---

[20] Their mutual embitterment affected both political and economic relations in ways damaging to the long-term interests of each side. For instance, the Poles spurned Czech efforts to bring them into the Little Entente, while both sides attempted to exclude the other's exports. See ibid., pp. 34-35; and Ferdynand Zweig, *Poland Between Two Wars: A Critical Study of Social and Economic Change*, p. 15. For detailed accounts of the Teschen affair, see Komarnicki, *Rebirth of the Polish Republic*, pp. 35-72; and Wandycz, *France and Her Eastern Allies*, chap. 3.

[21] Komarnicki has suggested that the Czechs abandoned the federation idea in part because the final Versailles decisions deprived Poland of her natural outlet to the sea, and notes that Beneš's concept of a Slav *Mitteleuropa* at one point included the "possible prolongation [of Poland]: Lithuania, Latvia, Estonia, etc." *Rebirth of the Polish Republic*, pp. 367-68.

[22] Borsody (*The Tragedy of Central Europe*, pp. 40-41) has noted that Beneš was one of the first to argue for recognition of the Soviet Union and for enlisting her in an anti-German coalition as the best way of forestalling German-Soviet collaboration.

[23] Piotr S. Wandycz, *Czechoslovak-Polish Confederation and the Great Powers, 1940-43*, p. 2. For an interesting comparison of Polish and Czech policies in the interwar period, see Wandycz's "Pierwsza Republika a Druga Rzeczpospolita: Szkic," pp. 3-20, and Edward Raczyński's rejoinder in *Zeszyty Historyczne*, no. 30 (1974), pp. 234-35.

and Yugoslavia) on the vanquished (Hungary and Bulgaria). As one student of Danubian politics has summed up the prospects for federation (in a comment, by the way, that applies to Poland as much as to her neighbors to the south):

> . . . it is doubtful whether any one of the Danubian countries was really ready for a higher form of co-operation, . . . Their post-war record shows a consistent shying away from the idea of national equality, which was prerequisite to true reconciliation. Jealous and suspicious, infected by the spirit of intolerance, the Danubian states lacked the good will and moderation needed for a federation. . . .
>
> . . . victors or vanquished, reactionaries or democrats, revisionists or anti-revisionists, all the regimes in the Danube Valley had one thing in common: they were strongly nationalistic. Nationalism coupled with democracy was certainly a lesser evil than nationalism coupled with reaction. Nevertheless, a peaceful evolution in the Danube Valley depended as much on the abandonment of the nationalist dogma that viewed the state as a vehicle of power directed against another nation, as on the universal extension of democracy. Only thus, if at all, could the national states of the post-Habsburg era have evolved towards a federal union of the Danubian peoples.[24]

Lest the Central Europeans be held solely responsible for their disunity and weakness, it should be remembered that these nations had scant chance for survival, much less genuine prosperity or stability, without the concern and support of the Great Powers who had overseen their creation. Instead the West, with the partial exception of France, chose to treat them as unwanted stepchildren, with a disdain perhaps best captured by E. H. Carr's advice to the Council of Allied Ambassadors in 1920 "not to take the new nations of Europe too seriously" as their affairs "belong principally to the sphere of farce."[25] On those few occasions when the Central Europeans managed to put aside their differences long enough to present a common economic front, the West responded with indifference and apparent incomprehension of the consequences German domination of the region would have for all Europe.[26]

[24] Borsody, *The Tragedy of Central Europe*, pp. 37 and 52.

[25] Quoted in Davies, *White Eagle, Red Star*, p. 105.

[26] For instance, in 1930 all six countries, presenting themselves as an Agrarian Bloc, tried without success to gain preferential treatment for their exports. The following year, the so-called Tardieu Plan proposed an economic union of Central Europe backed by a large reconstruction loan from France; however, the French dropped the plan under German and Italian pressure. In 1932 the Stresa Conference approved preferential treatment and subsidies for Central European grain exports, but these were never put into effect. A. Jordan, *Oder-Neisse Line: A Study of the Political, Economic and European Significance of Poland's*

During the summer and early fall of 1938, when the danger posed by Nazi Germany was too obvious to be ignored any longer, the Czechs made several gestures in the direction of repairing relations with Poland, including a hint of a possible compromise settlement in Teschen.[27] But it was too little, too late. Moreover, by now the Polish government was in hands wholly unsympathetic to Czechoslovakia's plight, believing her an unnatural hybrid whose disappearance would actually be in Poland's interest because it would weaken Soviet influence in Europe.[28] Poland's complicity in the first stage of Czechoslovakia's dismemberment, by coordinating her seizure of Teschen with the Munich crisis of September 1938, was a fitting if tragic end to two decades of unenlightened relations.

DESPITE the preoccupation of official policy and national mood with an eastern orientation, there was also in interwar Poland a western orientation—a distinctly secondary trend which, by virtue of its small but cohesive organizational structure, might properly be called a "Western School." Although many of its members were associated with one or another branch of the National Democrats, it was not a political movement as such, and the evidence indicates that up until the very eve of World War II its influence on Endek policy was negligible. Rather, the Western School was primarily an academic current with some social action and journalistic offshoots, concentrated almost entirely in the provinces carved from the former Prussian partition: Pomerania, Poznania, and Silesia. Its most im-

---

Western Frontier, pp. 76-77. The diaries of Sir Alexander Cadogan, permanent under secretary in the British Foreign Office from 1938 to 1950, offer insight into the equanimity with which the British viewed the expansion of German influence in East Central Europe in the interwar period. Writing in 1937 (and paraphrased in part by the editor), Cadogan argued "from the premiss that Germany had suffered undoubted injustice from the Versailles Treaty and the manner of its application." Moreover, he did not see that Britain "could or should prevent Germany from exercising economic domination over Central and Eastern Europe. He presumed that 'German hegemony' in Central Europe would not mean 'conquest in the ordinary sense of the word. In Czechoslovakia, Hungary, Yugoslavia, Roumania and Greece there are nearly 60,000,000 non-German inhabitants. It cannot surely be suggested that Germany could conquer and rule so many diverse elements. And if she could, I should have thought her hands would be full enough without any adventures against us.' " *The Diaries of Sir Alexander Cadogan, O.M., 1938-1945*, ed. David Dilks, pp. 14-15. For a major new study of British and French complicity in the economic origins of World War II, see David E. Kaiser, *Economic Diplomacy and the Origins of the Second World War: Germany, Britain, France, and Eastern Europe, 1930-1939*.

[27] Wandycz, *Czechoslovak-Polish Confederation*, pp. 24-26; Jordan, *Oder-Neisse Line*, p. 92.

[28] Polonsky, *Politics in Independent Poland*, pp. 475-76; Wandycz, *Czechoslovak-Polish Confederation*, pp. 18-19. For a detailed study of this period, one that seeks to explain though not necessarily to defend Polish behavior, see Anna M. Cienciala, *Poland and the Western Powers, 1938-1939: A Study in the Interdependence of Eastern and Western Europe*.

portant component organizations were: the West-Slavonic Institute, estab-lished under the aegis of the University of Poznań in 1921; the Baltic Institute, founded in Toruń in 1926; the Silesian Institute, founded in 1933 in Katowice; and the Association for the Defense of the Western Border-lands (often referred to by the initials Z.O.K.Z. after its Polish name Związek Obrony Kresów Zachodnich), also founded in 1921 with head-quarters in Poznań and the only one of the four organizations with a social action and public education, rather than academic, orientation.[29]

Although the scholars of the Western School started from some of the same premises as the realists—that is, that Poland's future, like her distant past, lay in her western provinces where the Poles constituted the dominant ethnic element and, therefore, that Germany (more accurately Prussia) was her most dangerous enemy—their focus was quite different. Being pri-marily historians, archeologists, Slavicists, and geographers, they took a broader and longer view of what constituted Poland's "west," a view unencumbered for the most part by political boundaries or even by con-temporary ethnic and linguistic divisions. Building on the work of earlier geographers, who by the turn of the century were already beginning to describe the line of the Oder and Lusatian Neisse as the "natural" limit of Poland's part of the North European plain,[30] they turned their attention to documenting the Slavic heritage of the Oder basin and the long struggle there between Polish and German cultures. The range of their interests can

[29] The term "Western School" apparently does not date from the interwar period. I first encountered it in an article that appeared shortly after World War II (Kiryl Sosnowski, "Polska wraca na Dolny Śląsk," pp. 278-81). Although Sosnowski used the term with reference only to Poznań-based activities, the designation properly applied to all of these organizations not only because their interests were analogous, but likewise because their memberships overlapped and they often cooperated with one another. For a brief description of the work of the West Slavonic Institute and the Z.O.K.Z., see: Zygmunt Dulczewski and Andrzej Kwilecki, *Społeczeństwo wielkopolskie w osadnictwie Ziem Zachodnich*, pp. 16-17 and 150. A more recent monograph on the Z.O.K.Z. is Marian Mroczko, *Związek Obrony Kresów Zachodnich, 1921-1934: Powstanie i działalność*. For the Baltic Institute: Józef Borowik, "Nauka polska a Pomorze Szczecińskie," pp. 178-82. For the Silesian Institute: Kazimierz Popiołek, "Instytut Śląski," p. 125; and Marek Stanisław Korowicz, *W Polsce pod sowieckim jarzmem*, p. 77.

Not all the activities of the Western School were concentrated in the western provinces. Considerable interest was shown, for instance, by the Lwów journal *Ruch Słowiański*, edited by Professor T. Lehr Spławiński, noted Slavicist and later a founding member of the postwar Western Institute in Poznań. There was also a special Silesian section of the Polish Academy of Sciences in Cracow, which operated in cooperation with the Silesian Institute.

[30] The arguments advanced for this line then were the same as those during World War II—that is, the complementarity of the Oder and Vistula river basins and the fact that the Oder and Neisse form an almost straight line across the narrowest part of the North European plain. For a survey of these early views, as well as similar studies dating from the interwar period, see Maria Kiełczewska, *O podstawy geograficzne Polski*, especially pp. 13-33.

readily be seen from a random selection of titles: "The Territorial Development of Prussia in Relation to Poland's Homelands"; "Poland on the Vistula and Oder in the Xth Century"; "The Historical Relationship of the Poles to the Sea"; "Silesia and Pomerania as Symbols of Our Independence"; "The Separation of Silesia from Poland in the XIVth Century"; "At the Front of the National Struggle in Opole"; "The Polish Problem in Silesia in the Light of Recent German Literature"; "The Folk Songs of Pomerania"; "Coal and the Sea"; and "The Conquest of Prussia and its Colonization by the Teutonic Order."[31] Despite the obvious implications, none of the institutes openly advocated revision of the frontiers with Germany; nor did they address directly the related questions of the eastern boundary or Polish policy toward Russia. In all probability, they resisted the former course as impolitic and, at least after 1934, likely to invite retaliation in some form by the government. Once this restraint was removed by the outbreak of World War II, however, the surviving members of these groups played a key role in the Underground movement for an Oder-Neisse boundary.[32]

In contrast to the scholarly wing of the Western School, the focus of the Z.O.K.Z. was distinctly contemporary and more avowedly anti-German. An outgrowth of earlier plebiscite committees in Silesia and East Prussia, the Association took upon itself the dual tasks of defending the cultural interests of Poles remaining on the German side of the frontier and of eliminating German influence from the economic and cultural life of Poland. The first goal it pursued through a number of educational, cultural, and recreational programs aimed especially at Polish youth in Germany; the second, through its publications which concentrated on pop-

---

[31] These titles all represent books or chapters from books published by the Baltic and Silesian Institutes; in addition, each published a journal: *Jantar*, published quarterly by the Baltic Institute between 1937 and 1939; *Slavia Occidentalis*, published annually by the West-Slavonic Institute from 1921; and *Zaranie Śląskie*, first published under other auspices in 1907 and then jointly with the Silesian Institute after 1933. The last named also published a series of "Communiqués" and a second series of reports on economic problems in Silesia. Of the three, only the Baltic Institute seems to have published for foreign consumption. Between 1933 and 1936, a series of pamphlets appeared in English under the general rubric "The Baltic Pocket Library"; starting in 1935 it published, also in English, the journal *Baltic Countries* (A Survey of the Peoples and States on the Baltic with special regard to their History, Geography and Economics).

[32] See Dulczewski and Kwilecki, *Społeczeństwo wielkopolskie*, pp. 17-19; Borowik, "Nauka polska," pp. 182-83; also Leopold Gluck, *Od ziem postulowanych do ziem odzyskanych*. The most interesting aspect of the Western School's existence is unfortunately beyond the scope of this study, but deserves at least passing mention. That is the very central role that the successor institutions played during the first three to four postwar years, before they succumbed to Stalinization, in providing expertise and policy guidelines for the takeover and absorption of the Recovered Territories.

ularizing Poland's western heritage and constantly reminding the Poles of the ever-present German danger. Although it also took no official position on further boundary corrections, there could be little doubt that the Association's members remained wholly unreconciled to the loss of southern East Prussia and the Oppeln district. At the end of 1933 its aggressive anti-Germanism ran afoul of the pending Polish-German Non-Aggression Declaration of January 1934. Apparently at the behest of the Germans, the Polish government forced it to change its name from Association for the Defense of the Western Borderlands to the more innocuous Polish Western Association (Polski Związek Zachodni), and to temper its anti-German tone.[33]

Not directly related to the activities of the Western School was the appearance of four pamphlets, all dating from the 1920s and all advocating in some degree revision of Poland's frontiers with Germany. Of these, three limited their proposals to part or all of the original Polish demands at Versailles (with particular emphasis on East Prussia), and are not of further interest here.[34] The fourth, published under the pseudonym "Consulibus" and entitled *The Experiences and Errors of Our Foreign Policy in Light of the Tasks of the Moment*, merits passing comment because it anticipated in several respects the programs developed early in the war by the exile wing of the Western School, which in turn influenced Sikorski's policy. Moreover, the fact that the author most likely had Socialist ties indicated that interest in this matter extended beyond right-wing Nationalist circles.[35] Of particular interest are Consulibus's views on Silesia. Chastising both Poles and Czechs for their "political immaturity," he contended that had the two nations presented a common front at the Peace Conference, instead of bickering "over a few square miles in Teschen," "the Silesian question would have been settled in quite a different manner, to the benefit of all Europe and of Czechoslovakia and Poland." Instead they have paid

[33] Mroczko, *Związek Obrony Kresów Zachodnich*, pp. 242-43; and Marian Wojciechowski, *Stosunki polsko-niemieckie, 1933-1938*, p. 119, n. 9. See also the report of a speech by the postwar secretary general of the P.Z.Z., Czesław Pilichowski, in *Głos Ludu*, November 11, 1946. The main prewar publication of the Z.O.K.Z. was *Strażnica Zachodnia [Western Watchtower]*, published from 1922-1933 and, under the new organization, from 1937-1939.

[34] Stanisław Bukowiecki, *Polityka Polski niepodległej: Szkic programu* (Warsaw, 1922); Stanisław Grabski, *Uwagi o bieżącej historycznej chwili Polski* (Lwów[?], 1923); and Stanisław Srokowski, *Z krainy Czarnego Krzyża: Uwagi o Prusiech Wschodnich* (Poznań, 1925). All three are summarized in Ernst R. B. Hansen, *Poland's Westward Trend*.

[35] Consulibus [pseudonym], *Doświadczenia i błędy naszej polityki zagranicznej wobec zadań chwili*; see also Hansen, *Poland's Westward Trend*, pp. 76-92 (although his translations are not always accurate). In all probability, Consulibus's real name was Włodzimierz Wakar (1885-1933), a statistician and economist at Warsaw's Higher School of Trade and one of the founders of the interwar Socio-Economic Institute, also in Warsaw. The Institute was a radical, predominantly Socialist institution, from which Endek influences were excluded.

the "disastrous price" of seeing their most vital economic districts divided and virtually surrounded by Germany. Therefore, a "fundamental demand" of both countries should have been the "shortening to the greatest extent possible" of their frontier with the Reich. Consulibus then proposed the following line, one, it should be noted, that would have left about half of Lower as well as all of Upper Silesia on the Polish-Czech side: "The German boundary should have run from the Kłodzko [Glatz] valley [west of] Wrocław [Breslau] and thence toward Poznań province, while the Polish-Czech border [should have] run somewhat to the west of the Oder from Wrocław to Bogumin." Apart from Silesia, the writer also wanted to see all of East Prussia removed from German control and divided between Poland and Lithuania.[36]

Just how much influence these various efforts had on Polish opinion is impossible to say. There is little evidence to suggest they had any. On the other hand, the Sanacja regimes of the 1930s certainly did not encourage the public expression of opinions of this stripe. It was only in 1939, in the last months before the war, that the political mood seemed to change. In that year three books in a more popular vein appeared: two depicting the rising tide of Polish-German tensions ("The Mobilization of German forces in Poland" and "The Frontier Struggle Continues"),[37] the third an immensely popular journalistic travelogue through the Polish districts of Germany ("The Land Gathers Dust").[38] Also in the spring of 1939, the chairman of the National Party, Kazimierz Kowalski, stated in a speech that in the event of another war Poland must seek to gain a foothold in the Lusatian Marshes and on the lower Oder. That summer another leading Endek spokesman, Jędrzej Giertych, wrote in a series of articles entitled "Polish Districts Under German Domination" that;

> after the coming war, should it end with the defeat of Germany, Poland should annex Gdańsk, East Prussia, Upper and Central Silesia including Wrocław, and Central Pomerania including Kołobrzeg [Kolberg]; [Poland] should also create a chain of small buffer states under

[36] Consulibus, *Doświadczenia i błędy*, especially pp. 21-26. The author was equally radical in his proposals for the eastern boundary (a fact that tends to confirm his Socialist rather than Endek ties): Wilno should be given to Lithuania, while the predominantly Ukrainian territories east of the Bug and Stryj rivers should be given local autonomy on grounds that "the most effective defense of the western borderlands is neutralization of the hostility to this time of five million of our citizens in the east." Ibid., pp. 43-49 and 128-34.

[37] J. Winiewicz, *Mobilizacja sił niemieckich w Polsce* (Poznań, 1939); and E. Męclewski, *Walka graniczna trwa* (Poznań, 1939). Winiewicz was to play a role in the development of Sikorski's program as an official in the exile government's Ministry for Peace Conference Preparations.

[38] Józef Kisielewski, *Ziemia gromadzi prochy*. See also Sosnowski, "Polska wraca na Dolny Śląsk," pp. 280-81; and Borowik, "Nauka polska," p. 180.

her protectorship and occupation in the territory along the lower Oder and even beyond the Lusatian Neisse (i.e. in Lusatia).[39]

As it turned out, Giertych's series was never completed. On September 1, 1939, Germany invaded Poland from three directions. On September 17th, the Soviet Union moved in to occupy her eastern half, ostensibly to protect the fraternal Belorussian and Ukrainian populations, but in reality in accord with the still-secret protocol to the Nazi-Soviet Non-Agression Pact of August 23rd. By September 29th, with Poland defeated and her government in flight, the two occupying powers had divided the spoils a second time. As Soviet Foreign Commissar Molotov exulted to the Supreme Soviet a month later, "one swift blow to Poland, first by the German Army and then by the Red Army, and nothing was left of this ugly offspring of the Versailles treaty . . . "[40]

Yet, in once again effacing her from the map, her two powerful neighbors had reopened the debate—not least among the Poles themselves—over the question of Poland's place in Europe. What follows is only part of the story of how this question was resolved to return her six years later to the geographic position from which she had started her history one thousand years before. Nor is it the decisive part, since I do not cover the diplomatic maneuverings of the final years of World War II that led directly to the establishment of Poland's western boundary on the Oder and Neisse. But it is an interesting part of the story, one long obscured and distorted, and important to a full understanding of the burden that history and geography place even today on the Polish nation.

[39] Both Kowalski's speech and Giertych's thesis are reported in Jędrzej Giertych, *Pół wieku polskiej polityki: Uwagi o polityce Dmowskiego i polityce polskiej lat 1919-1939 i 1939-1947*, pp. 180-81, n. 77. M. Kamil Dziewanowski, formerly Professor of History at Boston University and presently at the University of Wisconsin-Milwaukee, recalls that similar ideas were expressed by members of the Union of Poles in Germany [Związek Polaków w Niemczech] in Berlin, where he was a Polish correspondent in the late 1930s. Dziewanowski also recalls a cartoon which appeared in the *Volkische Beobachter* sometime around the middle of August 1939, the caption to which can be appreciated only in German. The picture showed a German soldier facing a Polish soldier across a barbed-wire frontier. In an obvious reference to gathering war clouds and to the approaching war-or-peace decision, the German says: "Die Entscheidung Kommt näher—entweder . . . oder . . ." To which the Pole replies: "Wir haben schon an der Oder entschieden."

[40] For documents relating to these events, see: *Documents on Polish-Soviet Relations, 1939-1945*, ed. the General Sikorski Historical Institute 1:38-54 and 65 [cited hereafter as *Documents*].

Part Two

Program and Promise

III · *The Unlikely Iconoclast*

THE TOUCHSTONE of General Sikorski's policy was his conviction that Poland's international posture must be a realistic reflection of her geography. As one wartime adviser wrote of him later: "Sikorski felt that sentiments should not obscure the realities of politics and history. Emotions pass, but geography remains. And geography has placed Poland between Germany and Russia."[1] This was a conviction that was at once unexceptionable, yet one that marked a significant departure from the underlying assumption of twenty years of Polish foreign policy: to wit, that Poland could successfully and more or less singlehandedly maintain a balance between her two hostile and more powerful neighbors. In light of Sikorski's forced retirement both from the central political stage and from active military service for the better part of the interwar period, it was probably inevitable that personal estrangement from Piłsudski and his successors—in particular, Colonel Józef Beck, Poland's foreign minister from 1932 to 1939—would be translated into bitter, even exaggerated criticism of their policies. Yet the overtones of personal rancor should not be allowed to overshadow the validity of the general's belief that his predecessors' miscalculation of Poland's relative power had contributed to the country's fatal isolation.[2]

Sikorski's intention to change the course of Polish policy was summed up in the statement that "Poland has entered upon the path of political realism with determination." To the Polish prime minister "political realism" meant discarding once and for all the notion that Poland could afford "simultaneous struggles on two fronts." It meant, too, that Poles must recognize the qualitative distinction between the mortal threat posed by "the Germany of today . . . , [with whom] there can be no agreement, no compromise," and her "differences" with Russia—"most difficult and disputable differences" to be sure, but ones that "are the outgrowth of history, and of the situation of Poland and Russia" and that "should be decided in conformity with the interests of both states and on behalf of

---

[1] This remark by Józef Retinger, an important but enigmatic figure in Sikorski's wartime entourage, is recorded in *Joseph Retinger: Memoirs of an Eminence Grise*, ed. John Pomian, p. 109; see also Stanisław Strumph-Wojtkiewicz, *Siła złego*, pp. 179-80. For additional comments on Retinger's role, see Chapter VIII, note 115, below.

[2] Wandycz, *Soviet-Polish Relations*, pp. 143, 182, and 284-85; and Wynot, *Polish Politics in Transition*, pp. 21-22.

the common aims of mankind. . . . '' Hence, point one of Sikorski's policy: reconciliation and alliance between Poland and the Soviet Union, based on ''mutual good faith and mutual respect for each other's national independence and sovereignty''—and, crucial to his conception, the mutually recognized self-interest of each side. Speaking to the National Council of the Government-in-Exile in London in February 1942, he said:

> . . . An honest understanding with the Soviets should ensure a lasting security for Poland. Otherwise—as the course of history has proved—we would be doomed to simultaneous struggles on two fronts, and the prospect would be dark indeed. This understanding will be no less beneficial to the other side. A strong Poland will be capable of withholding the everlasting German *Drang nach Osten*. It will afford our neighbor an opportunity of accomplishing great tasks and furthering the development of the enormous areas and untold wealth of the U.S.S.R. Unquestionably the possibilities of Russia in this regard are boundless. I am therefore confident that the differences that still divide us will disappear. . . .

By way of demonstrating Poland's good faith, the prime minister stressed that ''the final solution [of Polish-Soviet differences] . . . is not a task for present days. Our first and foremost obligation is to crush our common foe.'' As her most important contribution to this effort, Poland would organize an army on Russian territory to fight side by side with the Soviet Army. In return Sikorski expressed the hope for a like demonstration of Soviet good faith: ''We must trust that the Soviet peoples will not forget that in the hour of their gravest trials we stood up beside them and that they realize what significance a strong and friendly Poland confronting Germany has for them.''[3] In less circumspect language, the ''differences

---

[3] These several quotations are from Prime Minister Sikorski's statement over Soviet radio following signing of the Polish-Sovet Declaration of December 4, 1941, and his speech to the National Council of the Polish Government-in-Exile, February 24, 1942; in *War and Peace Aims of the United Nations*. Vol. I: *September 1, 1939-December 31, 1942*, ed. Louise W. Holborn, pp. 466-67 and 470-71.

The theme that Poland must discard its ''two-enemy'' posture was a recurrent one throughout the Sikorski period. In a broadcast to Poland on July 31, 1941, he said: ''The Nation will reject all idea of any kind of co-operation with Germany. But, led by an infallible instinct, it realizes that in its geographical situation it needs an understanding with one of its great neighbors, in order to resist the other effectively.'' *Documents*, 1:145. Again, in a report to the Council of Ministers on January 12, 1942, he declared: ''One of the most dreaded solutions for us would be a negotiated peace with Germany. For Poland it would be a calamity as great as a lost war. . . . Only Germany's total collapse can bring about the desired results.'' Ibid., p. 266. Leon Mitkiewicz, an aide to Sikorski, confided to his diary in mid-1940 that the general ''considers it impermissible, under any pretext, to bind the future of the Polish Nation with Germany.'' *Z gen. Sikorskim na obczyźnie (fragmenty wspomnień)*, p. 74.

that still divide us'' was a reference to conflicting Polish and Soviet claims to Poland's prewar eastern provinces. He clearly hoped at first that the sobering experience of joint battle against Germany would overcome Soviet suspicions and convince them that they had more to gain by returning these territories—which, after all, were minuscule in the Soviet scale but which comprised nearly half of Poland—in exchange for a loyal and strong ally. But, as Soviet intransigence became increasingly evident, he would prove willing to compromise even on this most sensitive issue.

Yet Sikorski's policy was not simply a revival of Dmowski's "realism." However sincere his professed desire for friendly relations with Moscow, and however firm his conviction that such relations were a sine qua non of Poland's future security, he was acutely aware of the danger that his country might be pulled from the German fire merely to be tossed back into the Russian skillet. "I stress most emphatically," he wrote in September 1941 to General Anders, then commander of the newly formed Polish Army in the Soviet Union:

> that Poland upholds now and will uphold in the future the full independence of her political line, and that in no case will she agree to become a tool of the policy of any Power. She desires to preserve her independence in the political field, and to secure the place which is due her in post-war Europe . . . We wish to cooperate closely and loyally with the USSR, during this war and after it. However, we do not wish to go further than that. *Realizing that the New Poland will be basically different from that of yesterday, we shall nevertheless oppose the transplanting of communist ideas on our soil.* Neither do we agree to disappear in the Pan-Slav melting-pot.[4]

Nor, as the bitter experience of the interwar period had demonstrated, could Poland escape the imperatives of her geography through alliances with the West. Friendship and promises of support from that quarter, however welcome and necessary, had proved an inadequate substitute for political and economic strength at home. Only by securing a stronger territorial base and by combining with the other small nations of Central Europe could the Poles hope to bring to bear sufficient economic resources and political bargaining power to withstand the German pressure from the west and, at the same time, avoid absorption by the Russian east. Hence the second and third aspects of Sikorski's foreign policy program: the establishment of a Polish-Czechoslovak federation, involving the coordination of a wide range of foreign and domestic policies and forming the nucleus for a broader Central Europe union; and substantial territorial

[4] *Documents*, 1:162-63 [emphasis added].

acquisitions in the north and west at Germany's expense, in order both to improve Poland's (and the federation's) strategic and economic position while weakening Germany's war potential—and, in the final analysis, to compensate Poland for the lands she would lose in the east.

The two distinguishing marks of Sikorski's program were its innovativeness and its iconoclasm. By innovativeness I do not mean to suggest that the individual components of his program were in any way original to the Polish leader. On the contrary, as we shall see, he borrowed liberally from others especially in the development of his boundary and federation proposals. Intellectually, then, his role was not so much that of an innovator as a synthesizer who adapted ideas already current to his own appraisal of the conditions and limits imposed on Poland's future security and independence by her geographical situation. But this should not blind us to the innovative, even revolutionary, character of his synthesis, which promised nothing less than a wholesale reorientation of Poland's internal structure and external relationships, with ramifications extending to the balance of power in the entire Central European region.

Sikorski's iconoclasm lay in the fact that his program broke either implicitly or explicitly with some of the most cherished myths of Polish policy in the interwar years: that Poland was a great power who could alone maintain her integrity between two hostile and larger neighbors; that not Germany but Russia, especially a Bolshevik Russia, posed the greatest danger to the Poles;[5] and that Poland had no vital interest in the existence of Czechoslovakia, much less in making sacrifices for a common interest. Less specific but equally important was a sense of righteousness especially common in the Polish exile community, a feeling that because Poland had suffered so much her allies had a duty, without compromise, to undo the wrongs done to her. Since none of these myths automatically died with the demise of the Second Republic, Sikorski's challenge was to arouse intense opposition which would in turn seriously limit his maneuverability and chances for success.

Still a third characteristic of the general's policy was its apparent plasticity. I say apparent because I see this quality as related less to the substance of his ideas than to the constraints inherent in the position of a secondary power in exile—in particular, the aggravation of internal divisions due to isolation from one's native constituency, and the lack of

---

[5] According to a 1937 report by the Czechoslovak ambassador in Warsaw to his government in Prague, Sikorski tried indirectly to dissuade the French from extending a loan to the Polish government without a firm guarantee that the latter would reorient its military capabilities away from an exclusively anti-Russian orientation. Quoted in Józef Kowalczyk, *Za kulisami wydarzeń politycznych z lat 1936-1938 (w świetle raportów posła Czechosłowacji w Warszawie i innych archiwaliów)*, pp. 18-19.

leverage over great powers whose interests may differ from those of the exile government but on whom the latter is nonetheless dependent. In these circumstances, with the obstacles to his goals as numerous as the variables of the political and military situation, the Polish leader had little choice but to seek to shape a more rational foundation for Polish policy through a combination of public circumspection and private probing.

The coincidence of these three characteristics poses a thorny analytical problem for the unwary historian: the dual overt-covert nature of Sikorski's behavior together with the unorthodox and controversial nature of his ideas tend to blur one's image of his policy, often leaving the impression that it was disjointed and inconsistent—or, at best, that his postwar program developed by fits and starts. This impression is neither wholly accurate nor wholly inaccurate. It is misleading in that the fragmentary nature of available documentation of the Sikorski government's inner workings and deliberations[6] places the observer in a position analogous to someone who, walking along one side of a fence, can catch only occasional glimpses through cracks and knotholes of the action taking place on the other side: the pieces of the action observed may appear to be disconnected scenes fitting no coherent pattern, whereas they may in fact represent successive steps on a continuum.

In another sense, however, the characterization of "fits and starts" is reasonably accurate. Certainly it is appropriate if one follows the development of Sikorski's strategy—as to a large extent we must—through his attempts to present that strategy to Poland's major allies, rather than through the evolution of his own thinking, of which we have little direct evidence. Here the pattern was determined by events and circumstances more or less beyond the control of the exile government: sudden changes in the course of the war, for instance, or allied policies to which the Poles had to accommodate themselves, or the interminable discord that marked Polish exile politics. Unquestionably some of these events had a catalyzing effect on the development of Sikorski's political program. Thus, as one aide recounts, it was "particularly in the period between the fall of France in [June] 1940 and the German attack on Soviet Russia in [June] 1941"—a year that, following Germany's sweep through Western Europe, witnessed the inconclusive Battle of Britain, growing Nazi-Soviet tensions in the east, unmistakable signs that London was seeking a rapprochement with

---

[6] The lack of this type of source material applies throughout the Sikorski period, but is especially critical for the years 1942-43. General Marian Kukiel, former professor of history and a defense minister in the exile government, laments: "Internal affairs and the work of the government during 1942 and 1943 are an area almost untouched by research; reportorial material is scanty." Marian Kukiel, *Generał Sikorski: Żołnierz i mąż stanu Polski walczącej*, p. 245, n. 30.

Moscow, and the final establishment of a Czechoslovak exile government—
that "General Sikorski's political conceptions concerning Poland's postwar
policy and defining her position in the future structure of Europe and the
world finally crystallized."[7] On the other hand, it is just as certain that
other circumstances severely impeded his ability to articulate those conceptions, forcing him to mute, defer, or even abandon in public positions
that he knew were vital to Poland's interests, while espousing others—for
the sake of "Allied unity" for instance—that he believed inimical to his
goals. As we shall see, this was particularly true of the Anglo-American
policy of deferring decisions on territorial issues to the end of the war.

In still a third sense, the appearance of disorganization and inconsistency
in Polish policy was a function of the essentially disruptive nature of
Sikorski's conceptions, a fact that caused the Poles' image to suffer by
comparison, say, with the Czechs'. It is infinitely easier, in both domestic
and foreign relations, to pursue a policy of *status quo ante* than it is to
propose changes that, quite literally, would revolutionize a country's internal social and economic structure as well as its external relations. The
latter course is far more likely to challenge vested interests, to menace the
sacred cows of the Old Order, so to speak. It is more likely, therefore, to
evoke resistance from elements whose cooperation, or at least benevolent
neutrality, is essential. Often the positions Sikorski was forced to assume
to pacify his domestic critics were incompatible with the programs for
which he was seeking support among Poland's allies. Thus, depending on
how one looks at the available sources, his policy may seem integrated or
disjointed, his behavior consistent or erratic, his goals realistic or quixotic.

In order to bring some semblance of order out of the chaos we must
try, without losing sight of the total context in which he operated, to
separate out those elements of Sikorski's behavior that were central to his
long-range strategy from those that were more tactical or defensive in
nature. Thus, for the sake of clarity and at the risk of some repetition, the
remaining chapters in Part II will examine Sikorski's strategy more or less
in isolation from the problems that plagued it, except insofar as they helped
to shape its development. Part III analyzes the obstacles that brought about
the collapse of that strategy and will, finally, assess the consequences of
its collapse not only for the Polish Government-in-Exile, but for postwar
Poland as well.

FROM a personal as well as a political standpoint, the general was at first
blush an unlikely candidate for the role of iconoclast—in particular on
questions related to Polish-Soviet relations and the eastern boundary. Much
attached to his native Eastern Galicia, he had spent his days as an engi-

---

[7] Mitkiewicz, *Z gen. Sikorskim*, preface.

neering student in Lwów to which he later returned as a district military commander. In addition, he shared the traditional background of the Polish officer corps, and had played a major role both in the organization of Piłsudski's legions during World War I and in the defense of Warsaw during the Polish-Soviet war of 1919-20. Although he later broke with the marshal over the issues of civilian control of the military and the direction of Polish foreign policy, he apparently made (or permitted others to make) several attempts at a reconciliation before Piłsudski's death in 1935. Moreover, Sikorski's political predispositions could scarcely be described as radical: in foreign policy he favored a return to Poland's traditional alliance with France, while domestically he was by most accounts a liberal democrat who favored a political structure more or less on the French parliamentary model. The Polish leader with whom he was most closely associated in the interwar years was former Prime Minister Ignacy Paderewski and, to the extent that he allowed himself to become involved in the political intrigues of this period (as he did against the post-Piłsudski "Colonels' regime"), it was for the purpose of restoring Poland to constitutional rule based on a coalition of the moderate center.[8]

Nonetheless, even a cursory review of Sikorski's role first in the pre-1919 independence movement, and later in interwar Polish politics, reveals important insights into the personal qualities and policy concerns that had made him a controversial figure at home well before he assumed the premiership of the exile government, and that were to mark his tenure in that office. A man of considerable self-confidence and ambition—many would add uncommon vanity—he nevertheless retained an open and agile mind. Even in his earliest forays into public life, Sikorski displayed a certain aloofness from organized political parties, an unwillingness to be confined by labels and rigid ideologies. Nor did he shrink from bold or unpopular initiatives, whether in the area of military strategy or politics. For instance, it was Sikorski who, during his first brief stint as prime minister between December 1922 and May 1923, ordered an acceleration of preparatory work for construction of the port at Gdynia—a move that reflected a forehanded concern for Poland's security vis-à-vis Germany.[9] It was during this same period that he incurred the lasting enmity of the Endecja by proposing to increase taxes on higher incomes.[10] A decade

[8] For accounts of Sikorski's pre-World War II activities, see: Kukiel, *Generał Sikorski*, chap. 1-4; Micewski, *Z geografii politycznej*, pp. 291-306; Karol Popiel, *Generał Sikorski w mojej pamięci*, pp. 9-83; Olgierd Terlecki, *Generał ostatniej legendy: Rzecz o gen. Władysławie Sikorskim*, pp. 7-83; and Roman Wapiński, *Władysław Sikorski*, pp. 11-219.

[9] Terlecki, *Generał ostatniej legendy*, p. 52; and Kukiel, *Generał Sikorski*, p. 59.

[10] Terlecki, *Generał ostatniej legendy*, p. 52. The insinuation made by one of his biographers (Wapiński, *Władysław Sikorski*, pp. 204-219) that Sikorski's views in the late 1930s were in many respects analogous to those of the Endecja—incredibly with no discussion of the irreparable split within the Nationalist movement in that period—is extremely misleading.

later his book *The Future War*, in which he accurately foresaw many of the strategic and technological innovations of the approaching Second World War, showed him again to be a man ahead of his times, capable of shedding the straitjacket of outworn ideas.[11] Moreover, as a result of his numerous trips abroad, primarily to France where he was well connected in the top echelons of the military establishment, he had acquired a more sober perspective on Poland's international standing than was in vogue among his compatriots.

While these were qualities that were to facilitate Sikorski's dealings with the Allies, they were also ones that set him apart from the majority of Poles, and especially those associated with the Piłsudski and post-Piłsudski regimes. About the only point on which friend and foe could agree was that he was a man of extraordinary energy and industriousness, as well as organizational talent. Beyond that, however, the qualities deemed positive by his admirers tended to be viewed with skepticism or outright distrust by his detractors. Where the former saw detached objectivity and flexibility, the latter saw opportunism and indecisiveness; uncanny foresight to some was to others unwarranted and naive optimism. In fact, Sikorski's outstanding quality of leadership was neither prescience nor unalloyed optimism, but the fact that his vision was focused on the future rather than rooted in the past—that he perceived opportunities and contingencies others could not or did not want to see, and that he was determined to seize every opening to pursue his goals.[12] In light of the rending divisions that plagued

While it is true that several prominent Endek politicians were associated with him both in the 1930s and in exile, they were from the avowedly democratic wing, by then distinctly out of favor, and had either broken openly with the movement or had withdrawn from active participation. A more accurate representation of Sikorski's political orientation at this time was that he sought collaboration with moderates in a number of parties, and that the bulk of the Endecja viewed him as "practically an extreme radical" whose policies were too "pro-French and pro-Jewish" for their tastes. See Terlecki, *Generał ostatniej legendy*, pp. 76-77. For a more accurate view of the state of affairs within the Endecja in this period, see Jerzy Janusz Terej, *Rzeczywistość i polityka: Ze studiów nad dziejami najnowszymi Narodowej Demokracji*, chap. 1; and Micewski, *Z geografii politycznej*, pp. 261-77.

[11] Władysław Sikorski, *Przyszła wojna: Jej możliwości i charakter oraz związane z nim zagadnienia obrony kraju.* See further comment below.

[12] E.g., he has been accused both of opportunism in pursuit of personal power (Wapiński, *Władysław Sikorski* pp. 188-89 and 204-213) and of excessive optimism (Terlecki, *Generał ostatniej legendy*, pp. 73-79) in the period of intense political maneuvering toward the end of Piłsudski's rule and following his death. However, Sikorski and his associates were not the only ones to attempt to take advantage of the temporary disorientation and weakness within the Sanacja. Indeed, it is not unreasonable to suppose that it was similar moves on the part of the extreme right-wing Nationalists that helped spur him to action. Although this attempt at coalescing the moderate opposition—in the form of the so-called "Front Morges"—bore little fruit at the time, the groundwork laid then (1936/37) would pay off a few years later when many of those associated with the earlier effort became Sikorski's closest and

Polish politics toward the end of the interwar period, to say nothing of the conspiratorial climate fostered by an exile existence, it was virtually inevitable that Sikorski's motives as well as his policies would be called into question.

Typical of the lack of appreciation accorded Sikorski's views was the reception given his book, *The Future War*, when it appeared in 1934. Drawing in part on his own experiences in the 1919-20 Polish-Soviet war, in which he is said to have led the first motorized infantry assault, he predicted that both armored vehicles and air power, rather than being tied to the infantry or cavalry, would acquire increasingly independent functions—indeed, that high-speed tanks would be the main offensive weapon of the next war. In addition, he stressed the element of strategic surprise, the importance of flexibility and technological change, and the prospect for "total war." Although well received abroad—the book was translated into French and English under the less appropriate titles of *La guerre moderne* (Paris, 1935) and *Modern Warfare* (London, 1942), and was apparently prescribed reading within the Soviet General Staff—Sikorski's military views were ignored by the Polish military establishment.[13] By and large his supple intellect would also go unappreciated when, as prime minister of the Government-in-Exile, he turned it to Poland's political problems.

most loyal collaborators in exile. Concerning the Front Morges, named after the Swiss town in which Paderewski lived, see Polonsky, *Politics in Independent Poland*, p. 418, and Micewski, *Z geografii politycznej*, pp. 257-59; and Wynot, *Polish Politics in Transition*, pp. 31-32 and 46-47. For a recent Polish monograph, see Henryk Przybylski, *Front Morges w okresie II Rzeczypospolitej*.

[13] For summaries see: Davies, *White Eagle, Red Star*, pp. 268-70; Terlecki, *Generał ostatniej legendy*, pp. 64-71; and Wapiński, *Władysław Sikorski*, pp. 192-95. Kukiel (*Generał Sikorski*, p. 75) suggests that it was Stalin who ordered its use by the Soviet General Staff; more likely it was Marshal Tukhachevsky who, as Davies points out, also participated in the 1919-20 Polish-Soviet war and after whose purge in 1937 the Red Army reassumed a "static, defensive posture."

IV · *Sikorski's Russian Gambit*

WHILE Sikorski's conciliatory stance toward Russia was a radical departure from the policy of Poland's prewar governments, it in no way marked a change in the general's personal position; indeed his approach to Polish-Soviet relations was characteristic of the distance that separated him from the Sanacja. Throughout the interwar period he saw Germany as constituting the greater danger to Poland and, at least in the latter half of the 1930s, advocated the formation of an anti-German coalition including the Soviet Union; he held his own country at least partially responsible for the failure of such a coalition to materialize. Writing in 1935, for example, he deplored Poland's signing of a nonaggression declaration with Germany the previous year:

> It has broken the ring of isolation with which Germany was sur-rounded from the moment of victory of the National Socialist revo-lution. From this moment, Poland follows in the footsteps of German diplomacy. Together with Germany, we stand opposed in Europe to the principles of collective . . . security. . . . In so doing, we forget the fact that what is beneficial for Germany in a given instance is for Poland disastrous in the full sense of that word. Preparing herself for revenge, Germany strives consistently to divide her opponents . . . and disrupt alliances. . . .[1]

On the need to draw the Soviet Union into an anti-German coalition he wrote in 1936:

> The military alliance of Italy and the Third Reich must accelerate the coalescing of Europe against Germany. The coalition should as quickly as possible embrace Soviet Russia. Without reliance on Rus-sia, the peace bloc will not prevail. The very fact of coming to an agreement with Russia will enormously enhance the chances of saving the peace. . . . Should an agreement with Russia not be reached—the danger of war will increase beyond measure.[2]

---

[1] From Sikorski's prewar diaries; quoted in Strumph-Wojtkiewicz, *Siła złego*, pp. 14-15. Other excerpts from his diaries appear in "General Sikorski's 1936-9 Diary (extracts)," pp. 26-42; although it was stated here that the "full text" of the *Diaries* was "due to be published by the Ossolineum Press," they had yet to appear by 1982.

[2] Strumph-Wojtkiewicz, *Siła złego*, pp. 15-16. The author also includes a quote from

In retrospect there can be little doubt that Sikorski was unduly optimistic about the prospects of an anti-German or anti-Axis coalition, particularly one that included the Soviet Union or that would have assigned priority to protecting the small states lying between Russia and Germany. As the Munich Agreement would show two years later, the West was only too willing to appease Hitler's appetite in the east out of a false hope that that would dissuade him from turning his sights westward. On the other hand, the demands advanced by the Soviet side in the course of the summer 1939 negotiations with Britain and France were a clear indication that Poland and the Baltic States could not expect better treatment from that quarter.[3]

But the question at issue here is not so much the accuracy of Sikorski's critique of Polish policy in the 1930s, nor even the realism of his vision of future relations with the USSR—a matter for later judgment—but the sincerity and consistency of his desire to rearrange Poland's geopolitical orientation and thus of his approach to Polish-Soviet relations. Here the evidence is clear. Indeed, the fact that in the end Stalin joined with Hitler to erase Poland once again from the map in no way altered his view, including his assessment of Poland's share in the blame. Repeating that view to his intelligence chief in the exile government, Leon Mitkiewicz, in 1940, he stressed "that the only correct policy for Poland is reliance on a close alliance with Czechoslovakia, supported by Soviet Russia, as

---

another Polish general to the effect that, while Sikorski was not eager to see the Red Army march through Poland, he did countenance Polish-Soviet military cooperation in the form of bases for the Soviet air force on Polish soil; ibid., p. 18. Stanisław Kot, a long-time associate of Sikorski and the first ambassador from the Government-in-Exile to Moscow, has suggested that these views dated back to the early 1920s: ". . . Already in 1923, as Chairman of the Council of Ministers, in his famous speech in Poznań, [Sikorski] foresaw Germany's permanent hostility toward the reconstruction of the Polish state and carved out his future political line. Despite the fact that he had organized recruitment for the Legions against Tsarist Russia and that he was a victorious leader against Bolshevik Russia, he bore no grudge against Russia; and from the time of Hitler's seizure of power, he constantly probed the possibilities of finding an ally in Russia. Following the Hitler-Bolshevik pact and the seizure of the eastern territories by the Soviets, he took note of any information concerning friction between the two and foresaw the moment when Soviet Russia might find herself in the Allied camp. . . ." Stanisław Kot, *Listy z Rosji do Gen. Sikorskiego*, pp. 11-12.

[3] For a surprisingly frank statement of the view that Western Europe could take some solace from Hitler's eastward expansionism, see the excerpt from *The Cadogan Diaries*, ed. Dilks, in Chapter II, note 26, above. Concerning Soviet demands during the 1939 negotiations, see Adam B. Ulam, *Expansion and Coexistence: The History of Soviet Foreign Policy, 1917-1967*, pp. 274-75; and Edward J. Rozek, *Allied Wartime Diplomacy: A Pattern in Poland*, pp. 24-25. In his memoirs of the period, Churchill strongly implies that Poland was responsible for the breakdown of Anglo-French negotiations with the Soviet Union; Winston S. Churchill, *The Gathering Storm*, pp. 390-91. For a more balanced account, suggesting that both sides hung back in the hope of reaching a settlement with Germany, see Cienciala, *Poland and the Western Powers*, pp. 245-47.

well as on active friendship and alliances with the Western Democracies.''[4] Nor was the general's view of Germany as Poland's primary adversary limited to a Nazi Germany; rather, he accepted the premise espoused by German rulers since Frederick the Great, namely that Prussia and Poland are incompatible geographical and political concepts. "Prussia," he declared in his broadcast to the Polish nation of June 23, 1941, "must be overthrown and destroyed in order that there be a place for Poland in the family of free nations.''[5]

FALSE START—JUNE 1940

Indicative of the depth of Sikorski's conviction that Poland's future security would depend on a Polish-Soviet rapprochement is the fact that he began laying the groundwork for such an accommodation in 1940. In late May of that year he asked Sir Stafford Cripps, then en route to Moscow as a special emissary of the British Government, to probe the possibilities for a normalization of Polish-Soviet relations should the Nazi-Soviet pact come unstuck.[6] With the fall of France a few weeks later, he intensified his

[4] Mitkiewicz, *Z gen. Sikorskim*, p. 65 [entry for June 30, 1940].

[5] In the translation of this speech in *Documents*, 1:110-12, this passage is rendered: "The Germans must be overthrown, they must be disabled and destroyed . . .'' However, the original Polish phrasing—"Prusy muszą być obalone i zniszczone . . .''—makes it clear that Sikorski meant "Prussia," not "Germans" or even "Prussians," thus implying not merely the defeat of Germany but the actual elimination of Prussia as a geographic and political entity. The Polish phrasing appears in the *Biuletyn Zachodnio-Słowiański* (Edinburgh), no. 4-5 (August 1941):4. That Sikorski was concerned with the German danger and Poland's western boundaries prior to Hitler's rise to power is indicated by a passage in his book *Polska i Francja* (1931), in which he stated that Poland's western territories were a matter of "first rank importance to the state" and that "these territories demand a more active and effective defense than [has been the case] in the past." Wapiński, *Władysław Sikorski*, p. 186.

[6] Stanislaw Kot, *Rozmowy z Kremlem*, pp. 6-7; also Kot, *Listy z Rosji*, p. 12; and Rozek, *Allied Wartime Diplomacy*, pp. 51-52. Kukiel (*Generał Sikorski*, pp. 110-11) does not mention a Sikorski-Cripps meeting, but does say that a memorandum was prepared for Ambassador Cripps concerning Soviet treatment of the population in Poland's eastern provinces. Whether the memo touched on other aspects of Polish-Soviet relations cannot be stated with certainty, as no copy was found in General Sikorski's papers; that it did, however, is implied by Terlecki (*Generał ostatniej legendy*, pp. 119-20).

As for Sir Stafford's special mission to Moscow, the British War Cabinet had decided on May 18th to dispatch him, on a short and well-defined tether, to ascertain the prospects for improving Anglo-Soviet economic cooperation and for reducing Nazi-Soviet economic cooperation. When the Soviets declined to accept a special emissary, London was faced with a choice between recalling Cripps and admitting the failure of their overture, or appointing him as ambassador with far broader responsibilities than the War Cabinet had intended to give him. Given both his lack of diplomatic experience and his strongly pro-Soviet leanings, the choice was a most unfortunate one from the Polish point of view. For a none-too-flattering account of Cripps's first year in Moscow, see H. Hanak, "Sir Stafford Cripps as British Ambassador in Moscow, May 1940 to June 1941," pp. 48-70.

efforts to establish contact with Moscow for the purpose of discussing both future relations and, more immediately, the possible formation of a Polish army from reserves in the eastern provinces as well as prisoners-of-war being held in the Soviet Union. To appreciate the boldness of these moves, we must remember that they occurred fully a year before Hitler's June 1941 attack put an end to Nazi-Soviet collaboration, and thus at a time when Moscow was still publicly celebrating the demise of an independent Polish state.[7] Moreover, reports filtering out of the Soviet-occupied territories told of mass repression and deportations.[8] Such circumstances would seem inauspicious at best for arranging future relations, much less for raising a national army on the territory of a state with which one is de facto still at war.

Yet Sikorski's reasoning was by no means farfetched. On the contrary, he had compelling reasons of both a positive and negative nature for seeking an accommodation at this time. Among the positive incentives was his desire to explore every course that might lead to an amelioration of conditions in Soviet-occupied Poland and to the release of the literally hundreds of thousands of Polish deportees and prisoners-of-war in Russia proper. This concern was a recurring theme in Sikorski's policy and one of the few goals he would eventually attain, if only partially. More critical to the timing of his effort, however, was his belief that the Soviets' attitude toward Poland might in fact be less intractable than indicated by their public stance, that the latter possibly reflected less an irrevocable denial of Poland's right to exist than a desire not to provoke their Nazi allies, and that the climate of Nazi-Soviet relations had now soured to the point where Stalin might be willing to establish some form of contact or cooperation with the Poles. Already some six months earlier, in early November 1939, word had reached the Government-in-Exile through private channels concerning Moscow's conditions for the creation of an "ethnographical Poland," in a context suggesting that the Soviets saw a mutually

---

[7] Following Foreign Commissar Molotov's speech of October 31, 1939, in which he declared that "nothing was left of this ugly offspring of the Versailles treaty," the Russians avoided all mention of "Poland." Soviet-occupied areas were called the "Western Ukraine" or "Western Belorussia," depending on which Soviet Republic they had been incorporated into, while Nazi-occupied areas were referred to as "Germany." Where use of the word "Poland" proved unavoidable, it was preceded by "*byvshaya*," or "former." Rozek, *Allied Wartime Diplomacy*, pp. 46-47. British Ambassador Cripps, reporting back to General Sikorski in June 1941 on his efforts to raise the Polish issue with the Soviets, also remarked on their avoidance of any mention of "Poland"; *Documents,* 1:106.

[8] Between September 1939 and June 1941, the Soviets deported into central Russia and Siberia some 1.7 million people from the occupied eastern provinces. Of these, an estimated 230,000 were Polish soldiers and officers taken prisoner in September 1939. For a general account of Soviet treatment of the population of eastern Poland in this period, see Rozek, *Allied Wartime Diplomacy*, pp. 36-51.

acceptable solution to the Polish problem as removing a serious obstacle to their "gradual inclusion in the anti-German coalition."[9] In addition, they were apparently eager to make use of Poland's trained military manpower and were trying (without success) to form purely Polish units within the Red Army.[10] Moscow's reported conditions—most importantly, the demand that Poland recognize in advance the incorporation of her eastern provinces into the Soviet Union and acquiesce to the status of a political satellite—were clearly unacceptable.[11] Yet it was not unreasonable for Sikorski to hope that now, in June 1940, in the wake of yet another demonstration of Germany's formidable power and faced with the Soviet Union's growing isolation, Stalin might be amenable to genuine negotiations.[12]

Equally compelling were the negative forces pushing Sikorski toward accommodation. Renewed British efforts to improve relations with Moscow, together with the German sweep through France and the Low Countries, had brought conflicting pressures to bear on the Poles. On the one hand, they were keenly aware that a rapprochement between their principal

[9] The Soviets were reportedly ready to support the reestablishment of an ethnographic Poland, "with the possible rectification in her favor of the boundary with the Soviets," in exchange for formal Polish recognition of the incorporation into the Soviet Union of the Western Ukraine and Western Belorussia. In addition, they would "support the cause of Poland as an independent state, without attempting to incorporate her into the Union of Soviet [Socialist] Republics, naturally under the condition of a friendly Polish policy in relation to the Soviets." These conditions were conveyed to the exile government in a letter from a Polish colonel, Jan Kowalewski, then in Bucharest; quoted in Kukiel, *Generał Sikorski*, pp. 99-100. Later Kukiel mentions that similar conditions were suggested to at least one Polish political figure in Lwów at the end of October 1939; ibid., p. 130. In late June 1940, just as the incident in question was coming to a close, yet another feeler concerning the possibility of establishing contact with Moscow was transmitted by a Polish attaché in Bucharest; PRM 22/1, GSHI.

[10] Władysław Pobóg-Malinowski, *Najnowsza historia polityczna Polski, 1864-1945*, Vol. 3: *Okres 1939-1945*, pp. 156-57.

[11] The Polish government's rejection of the notion of an "ethnographical Poland" was not occasioned solely by its claim to the Soviet-occupied eastern territories, but more particularly by its desire to see Poland's future boundaries determined in accordance with her economic and strategic needs, and by a desire not to concede its bargaining position in advance of a comprehensive settlement. These issues are discussed in detail below.

[12] A staff memorandum circulating within the exile government (then still in France) during the first part of June 1940, concluded that at the time of a German victory in the West, the Soviets would have to reckon with the fact that they were next in line; Kukiel, *Generał Sikorski*, p. 110. Rozek (*Allied Wartime Diplomacy*, p. 48) notes that a "striking reversal" of the Soviets' anti-Polish attitude occurred around the middle of 1940, due to "cooling relations between the Nazis and the Soviets." See also Mitkiewicz (*Z gen. Sikorskim*, pp. 364-65) for a contemporary Polish appraisal of Nazi-Soviet relations in the Balkans, and Ulam (*Expansion and Coexistence*, pp. 295-98) for an analysis of Soviet anxieties at this juncture.

ally and one of the partitioning powers could jeopardize Poland's most vital interests, especially should it take place without her participation.[13] At issue were not only Poland's existence as an independent state and her claims to her prewar eastern boundaries, though these were the most obvious concerns. Also at stake was the Poles' natural desire to have a voice in such decisions as the postwar treatment of Germany and the future structure of Central Europe. As it turned out, their concerns were neither misplaced nor premature. In its abortive attempt to achieve a rapprochement with Moscow, the British Government would shortly offer "to recognize, on a temporary basis pending a general settlement . . . at the end of the war, Soviet *de facto* control of the areas which have been occupied by the Red Army since the beginning of the war." Although Lord Halifax, then in his last days as British foreign secretary, would claim that "the question of sovereignty would of course remain unaffected by such recognition," it is hardly surprising that the Poles protested this move as prejudicial to their interests.[14] Moreover, at least within the prime minister's entourage, they were cognizant of the unfavorable disposition of much of British opinion toward their cause.[15]

In another sense, however, an Anglo-Soviet rapprochement was vital to Poland. Without it and without a belief on the part of the British in the

[13] Another staff memo, this one dated May 15, 1940, discussed among other matters "the desire of the Allies for an understanding with the Soviets [and] . . . foresaw accurately the consequences of such an understanding for the cause of our eastern territories"; Kukiel, *General Sikorski*, p. 110. Several weeks later, Mitkiewicz noted in his diary: "In view of these diplomatic maneuvers of the British Government, we must hurry if we are not to be left out in the cold, and begin thinking seriously about initiating our own direct talks with Soviet Russia. It seems to me that it is rather risky to put our quarrels with Soviet Russia in anyone else's hands. We will have more to lose than gain by this, since we will not be able to decide for ourselves concerning our vital interests." *Z gen. Sikorskim*, pp. 68-69.

[14] See Halifax's letter of November 27, 1940, to Polish Foreign Minister August Zaleski, in PRM 20/36, GSHI; reprinted with Zaleski's reply in *Documents*, 1:98-101; also *The Great Powers and the Polish Question, 1941-1945: A Documentary Study in Cold War Origins*, ed. Antony Polonsky, pp. 78-79. This was scarcely the first occasion for Polish concern over Allied, and especially British, willingness to concede Poland's eastern half to the Soviets. The British had never been keen on the Riga line, had deliberately limited their guarantee to Poland's boundaries with Germany and, as early as October 1939, had hinted broadly at their willingness to accept the Molotov-Ribbentrop partition line as a return to the Curzon line recommended during the 1919-20 Polish-Soviet war. For more detailed discussion of British and American policy on the eastern boundary, see Chapters VIII and X below.

[15] Indicative of the tenor of influential British opinion at this time was a collection of essays on the postwar settlement, written mostly by members of Parliament, which appeared in the summer of 1940: *After the War: A Symposium of Peace Aims*, ed. William Teeling. Of the fourteen contributors, only two or three could have been considered pro-Polish—the remainder being indifferent, uninformed, or simply hostile; for a review of the book from the Polish point of view, see PRM 20/13, GSHI. See also Chapter VIII below.

Soviet Union's eventual entry into the war on the side of the Allies, the Poles could well fear that a besieged and isolated Britain would opt for what, in Sikorski's view, would be the worst of all possible outcomes—a negotiated peace with Germany. The most detailed exposition of this fear was a memorandum to Sikorski from his newly appointed chief of military intelligence, Leon Mitkiewicz, dated July 1, 1940. Reviewing events of the preceding weeks, Mitkiewicz foresaw two alternatives for the course of the war in the near future: (1) a German offensive against Great Britain, with temporary concessions to Russia in the East, or (2) conclusion of the war in the West through a conciliatory attitude toward the British Empire, with the immediate initiation of military operations in the East to recoup Germany's position there, especially in the Balkans. Examining further the prospects for a negotiated peace in the West, for which he perceived support among financial and conservative circles in both Britain and the United States, Mitkiewicz saw the possibility that such a peace might include promises on Germany's part to resurrect Poland, the Baltic countries and even Czechoslovakia. But, he warned, such an outcome would hold grave danger for Poland:

> The conclusion of the war now by Great Britain would leave us under compulsion either to submit to the Germans or to wait in the role of émigrés for further changes, carried out without us. This applies to the Government and Armed Forces abroad. The people at home will have no choice. They will remain under the Germans.

Therefore Mitkiewicz concluded, "we must make every effort:

> 1. to convince the Government of Great Britain that a Russo-German conflict is inevitable and that, in view of this, the greatest sacrifice connected with holding out even in the most difficult defensive war will pay off completely;
> 2. to establish indirectly, or even directly, contacts with Moscow for the purpose of posing the question of Poland there, in view of the evident change in Soviet policy towards Germany.[16]

Faced with these several and sometimes contradictory pressures, Sikorski developed a strategy which he would follow over the next three years:

[16] Mitkiewicz, *Z gen. Sikorskim*, pp. 363-65. Fears of a negotiated settlement between Germany and Great Britain were not entirely unfounded. Even Churchill admitted that those "who do not understand the temper of the British race" could easily have expected such a peace in the circumstances of June 1940; Winston S. Churchill, *Their Finest Hour*, pp. 226-27. In November of that year, British Ambassador Cripps remarked to some American diplomats that "if increased collaboration with the Nazis followed the Molotov visit [to Berlin], the possibility could not be excluded that 'influential circles' in Great Britain might begin to press for a separate peace with Germany on an anti-Soviet basis. . . ." Charles E. Bohlen, *Witness to History, 1929-1969*, p. 103.

"Nothing about us without us."[17] That is, he chose a course which he hoped would afford Poland the greatest possible initiative and influence in matters affecting her national interests. At this particular juncture, May-June 1940, that meant initiating an attempt to restore Polish-Soviet contacts in order, first, not to be isolated within the Allied camp should an Anglo-Soviet rapprochement come about and, second, to maximize Poland's influence on the future resolution of Polish-Soviet differences.

For the time being, Sikorski's efforts came to naught. As British Ambassador Cripps would report back a year later, he had been unable even to raise the Polish issue with the Soviets—although the fact that he also made scant progress toward an Anglo-Soviet reconciliation took some urgency out of the Polish probe.[18] In the process, however, the attempt did produce a preliminary "exchange" of Soviet and Polish conditions for renewing contacts, in the form of two drafts of a memorandum from the Polish Government-in-Exile to the British Foreign Office expressing the former's posture vis-à-vis the Soviet Union. According to the first version, which is generally viewed as reflecting a position acceptable to the Soviets, Poland would declare her readiness to follow a policy "not in any way . . . directed against the interests of Soviet Russia"; while demanding "the restitution of Poland's status quo," she "would nevertheless be ready to agree to some territorial changes concerning the ethnographically White-Russian and Ukrainian regions along the Polish-Russian border." In addition, the Polish Government would take "a benevolent attitude" toward the march of Soviet troops through Poland and would "collaborate with the Soviet authorities" in raising a Polish army to fight the Germans; in return, Poland would "expect . . . a change in the Soviet attitude toward Polish nationals in the part of Poland which is under Soviet occupation."[19]

This was the version that awaited Sikorski in London on the morning of June 19th, the day he flew from a rapidly collapsing France for his first meeting with Winston Churchill. Finding the Soviet conditions "vague and excessive"—indeed they represented little improvement over those

---

[17] "*Nic o nas bez nas*"; Kukiel, *Generał Sikorski*, p. 130. Later, in January 1942, when Cripps informed Sikorski that Stalin wished to see Poland expand "at the expense of Germany only" but would most likely demand the Curzon line in the east, Sikorski interrupted saying: "In a word to push Poland from the East to the West, . . . but that cannot be done without Polish consent"; *Documents*, 1:271.

[18] *Documents*, 1:106-107. Concerning Cripps's difficulties in Moscow, see Hanak, "Sir Stafford Cripps," pp. 59-67.

[19] For several accounts of this incident, see: Edward Raczyński, *W sojuszniczym Londynie: Dziennik Ambasadora Edwarda Raczyńskiego 1939-1945*, pp. 70-73; Kukiel, *Generał Sikorski*, pp. 110-11 and 129-31; Mitkiewicz, *Z gen. Sikorskim*, pp. 50-51, 65, 68-69, and 74-75; Pobóg-Malinowski, *Najnowsza historia*, 3:150-58; and Terlecki, *Generał ostatniej legendy*, pp. 117 and 119-20. For the full text of this first version, see Raczyński, *W sojuszniczym Londynie*, pp. 71 (Polish) and 419 (English).

conveyed to the Poles in late 1939[20]—the general directed Ambassador Raczyński to revise the memo that same morning. This second, Polish, version was fundamentally different from the first: "The Polish Government, regarding the defeat of Germany as its principal war aim," would not hinder Anglo-Soviet talks; on the other hand, it would "spare no effort to improve the tragic situation of the Polish population under Soviet occupation." Should this condition be met, Poland would be ready "with the consent of Soviet authorities" (implying retention of control by the Poles) to form a Polish army for use against Germany; this army would be formed from reserves in the occupied areas as well as from Soviet-held prisoners-of-war (unmentioned in the first draft), and would number about 300,000 men. The Polish draft also proposed attaching an unofficial Polish observer to the British embassy in Moscow. On the boundary issue, it stated that nothing in the memorandum should be construed as abrogating any "rights of the Polish State violated by Soviet aggression," but it did not specifically invoke the Treaty of Riga.

It was this Raczyński version that was handed to British Foreign Secretary, Lord Halifax, on the afternoon of the 19th.[21] Within a few days, however, the memorandum was withdrawn at the insistence of Polish President Raczkiewicz and Foreign Minister Zaleski, who then used the incident as a pretext for trying to oust Sikorski from the premiership. In light of the fact that the rest of his government knew nothing of Sikorski's participation in this "exchange" of views until after the Polish draft had been handed to the Foreign Office, he must of course bear some respon-

[20] Mitkiewicz's account of his conversation with Stefan Litauer (see following note) makes it clear that, behind the vague wording, the Soviets were still demanding a strictly ethnographical Poland under Soviet political control. *Z gen. Sikorskim*, pp. 50-51.

[21] For the full text of the second version, see Raczyński, *W sojuszniczym Londynie*, pp. 72-73 (Polish) and 420 (French). The fact that the first version was drafted by the pro-Soviet London correspondent of the Polish Telegraph Agency, Stefan Litauer, together with the local Tass representative, has led some observers to suggest that the entire incident was instigated by Moscow. In light of evidence now available from the Foreign Office archives, however, it is far more likely that the initiative came from the British side. Having dispatched Cripps to Moscow for the transparent purpose of weaning the Soviet Union away from Germany, by mid-June the British found themselves in the unhappy position either of withdrawing him, in effect an admission of failure, or of offering Stalin "greater inducements" to curtail Soviet-German cooperation. Among the "greater inducements" suggested was one that "the British government, with the consent of the Polish, should discuss with [the Soviet government] a new Soviet-Polish frontier which would leave to the Soviet Union the Ukrainian and White Russian populations formerly in Poland." It was further decided that Cripps be provided with a personal message from Churchill to Stalin along these lines. (Hanak, "Sir Stafford Cripps," p. 60.) It would appear that it was these pending developments that prompted Sikorski's sudden flight to London, arranged by the ubiquitous Mr. Retinger (see Chapter VIII, note 115, below), and that his purpose was both to push forward with his earlier initiative via Cripps (see note 6 above) and to insure that it was his views that prevailed.

sibility for the ensuing brouhaha.[22] The ostensible reason for this irregular (most likely illegal) procedure was the impossibility of consulting with his colleagues due to the chaotic situation in France, from where the Government-in-Exile was evacuating. The more probable explanation is that Sikorski—his hand forced by the British initiative toward Moscow, and knowing full well that Zaleski and Raczkiewicz (plus a number of others) would oppose his actions (and especially his failure to invoke the Riga boundary)—preferred not to consult them. This *modus operandi* would become familiar, especially after Soviet entry into the war deepened the divisions among the Poles.

At the time and later, critics charged that Sikorski's actions were not only blatantly illegal but had done irreparable damage to the Polish cause—damage that could not be undone by mere withdrawal of the memorandum. "In foreign policy," wrote one, "there are no events that can be considered 'null and void.' Submission of a memorandum and its withdrawal after six days is not the same as not having submitted it. In this episode Polish policy appeared to the British government as impulsive, rash, susceptible to diverse influences, not to be taken seriously."[23] On the other hand, more sympathetic observers point to the incident as "prov[ing] the goodwill of the Poles and show[ing] that Sikorski's instinct was sound and farsighted"[24]—or as "undoubtedly help[ing] the British form an opinion of Sikorski as a partner in future eastern initiatives . . . and, particularly valued in British political life, as a flexible politician."[25] On balance, despite the indisputable fact that his initiative was premature—despite also the initial British inclination to pour cold water on the whole idea of a Polish-Soviet rapprochement as "not practical"[26]—the second, more sym-

---

[22] For accounts of this government crisis, which lasted into the latter part of July, see: Raczyński, *W sojuszniczym Londynie*, pp. 73-79; Kukiel, *Generał Sikorski*, pp. 131-36; Mitkiewicz, *Z gen. Sikorskim*, pp. 78-81; Pobóg-Malinowski, *Najnowsza historia*, 3:158-62; and Terlecki, *Generał ostatniej legendy*, pp. 120-25. The attempt to remove Sikorski from the prime minister's post, in favor of Zaleski, was by no means occasioned solely by this memo affair; more to the point, the opposition was taking advantage of the collapse of France (where Sikorski had strong political backing) and the move to England (where Zaleski was better known and well regarded). For early British appraisals of the two men, see Chapter VIII, note 111, below.

[23] Adam Pragier, *Czas przeszły dokonany*, p. 613; Pragier, a prominent Socialist politician in exile, became one of the more vocal critics of Sikorski's policies.

[24] From Retinger's memoirs; *Joseph Retinger*, ed. Pomian, p. 110.

[25] Terlecki, *Generał ostatniej legendy*, p. 120.

[26] Despite the remark widely attributed to Halifax on returning the memo to Zaleski—to the effect that, in view of the unorthodox manner of its delivery, he had half expected its withdrawal and therefore had not made use of it (or possibly even read it)—a copy was in fact circulated within the Foreign Office and retained in the files. From the appended minutes it is clear that the general lack of enthusiasm was occasioned not by a view of Sikorski's

pathetic appraisal would appear to be closer to the truth, although Sikorski would not reap the benefits of his gamble for another year.

THE POLISH-SOVIET AGREEMENT OF JULY 1941

Sikorski's failure at this time—mid-1940—either to win over his own government to a policy of renewing contacts with Moscow, or to bring about a modification in Moscow's attitude toward Poland, did nothing to alter his basic conviction. Throughout the year preceding Hitler's attack on Russia, the Polish leader remained convinced both of the inevitability of a Nazi-Soviet conflict and of the need for a Polish-Soviet alliance as the foundation of future Polish policy.[27] On June 18, 1941, he met again with British Ambassador Cripps; with the imminence of war between Germany and Russia now obvious to virtually everyone except Stalin,[28]

policy as rash or inconsistent but, in addition to doubts concerning Soviet receptivity, by a view of the Polish exile community at large as so inalterably anti-Russian as to make such a rapprochement unworkable. C7880/7177/55, FO 371/24482, PRO. The same entry contains a report of Halifax's meeting with Sikorski, also on June 19th. Sikorski's views, as reported here by the foreign secretary, are consistent with those expressed in the memorandum as submitted. Indeed, they go somewhat further, first, in criticizing the prewar government's "policy of provocation" toward the Soviet Union and, second, in setting as conditions for renewed contacts with Moscow only " that the question of the eastern frontier of Poland [be] freely discussed and [that] the persecution of Poles in Soviet-occupied Poland cease." In the end, all reference to Polish-Soviet relations was deleted from Churchill's letter to Stalin, dated June 25th, although a draft of the 24th had included a paragraph along the lines of the memorandum. See Hanak, "Sir Stafford Cripps," p. 61n.

[27] In his diary entry for June 30, 1940, following one of his first long talks with Sikorski, Mitkiewicz recorded: "According to Gen. Sikorski conflict between Germany and Russia is inevitable. . . . Personally, the General is in favor of seeking an understanding right now with Soviet Russia and of beginning direct talks immediately; he considers this all the more necessary, being completely informed about the steps already taken by the British Government toward cooperation with Russia." A few days later, he noted: ". . . Gen. Sikorski is aware of the fact that staking everything, our existence as a Nation and State, solely on the one British card constitutes a serious danger; for, even in the event of victory by Great Britain in the war with Germany, we ourselves will still have to take care of settling postwar relations with Soviet Russia. Mainly from these considerations, . . . he is for an understanding with Soviet Russia already now, during this war." Z gen. Sikorskim, pp. 65 and 74-75; see also entries for March 23 and April 15, 1941, ibid., pp. 110 and 136. In addition, an exposition of the basic principles of Polish foreign policy, drafted sometime in the fall of 1940, and Sikorski's instructions to Jan Ciechanowski as the exile government's newly appointed ambassador to the United States, dated January 15, 1941, both anticipate eventual Soviet participation in the war on the side of the Allies. PRM 35/16 and PRM 40a/2, GSHI.

[28] Pobóg-Malinowski (*Najnowsza historia*, 3:170-71), reporting that the Polish government made light of the German buildup and viewed it as merely "an attempt to intimidate Russia," has tried to demonstrate that Sikorski shared the belief that war between Germany and Russia was not imminent and that he changed his view only as a result of this June 18th meeting, at which Sikorski reportedly gave Cripps a detailed account of the German buildup in Poland,

they discussed at some length the desirability of assisting the Russians, including the formation of a Polish army within the Soviet Union. Sikorski was agreeable provided Moscow changed its attitude toward Poland; Cripps, admitting that he had so far been unable to raise the Polish issue in Moscow, thought "the situation could change radically" now.[29]

The start of the German offensive four days later gave Sikorski the opportunity he had been waiting for. In a June 23rd broadcast "to the Polish Nation" but intended also for Soviet ears—a broadcast in which his statements again did not reflect prevailing opinion within the government[30]—he hailed the collapse of the "policy of German-Bolshevik cooperation begun at Rapallo," calling it "a sequel very favorable to Poland" which "changes and reverses the former situation." Foreseeing that the German armies would bog down in Russia's vastness, he reaffirmed Poland's "irreconcilable" enmity toward Germany and offered her aid to Russia. In return, he asked that the hundreds of thousands of Polish deportees and prisoners-of-war in the Soviet Union be released to join the struggle against Hitler, and expressed his assumption "that in these circumstances Russia will cancel the Pact of 1939 [which] should logically bring us back to the position" of the Treaty of Riga.[31]

---

concluding: "All this information showed that the Germans were well prepared to start an offensive against Russia very shortly. Hitler was convinced that he would be able to finish that war very quickly, and then attack Britain also before winter." *Documents*, 1:104. But in a comprehensive memorandum on the state of preparedness along the Russo-German front, which he presented to Churchill on May 23rd, Sikorski had already stated that German preparations were at most two weeks away from full readiness; at this point, he was somewhat skeptical of the immediacy of a German attack on grounds (all too accurate as it happened) of timing and the marginal benefits in terms of foodstuffs and raw materials to be gained by the Germans in the short run. PRM 39a/22, GSHI; partial text in *Documents*, 1:102-103. Thus it is not true that Sikorski did not foresee the possibility of a Russo-German war. What is true is that the Polish exile community in general—including apparently many of Sikorski's closest advisors—did not anticipate such a war and that, in all probability, Sikorski received much advice to this effect. One exception, Ambassador Raczyński, noted the prevalence of the opposing view: "Personally, despite the official opinion of our authoritative circles—which, when it comes to the Russian problem, are ruled by emotional reactions and therefore are always in error—I was convinced that an armed German-Soviet conflict would break out at any moment. . . . [Foreign Minister] August Zaleski was always and invariably of another opinion. For him, German-Soviet quarrels were always mock, aimed at 'more effective blackmail' of Great Britain and her friends. Mr. Zaleski has been feeding us this doctrine for a year." *W sojuszniczym Londynie*, p. 118 (this passage is omitted from the English edition).

[29] *Documents*, 1:103-108; and Pobóg-Malinowski, *Najnowsza historia*, 3:171.

[30] Pobóg-Malinowski (*Najnowsza historia*, 3:172-73) writes that President Raczkiewicz and Ministers Zaleski and Sosnkowski wanted to block the opening of negotiations. On June 22nd, the Council of Ministers passed a resolution to the effect that cooperation with Russia was not possible "under present conditions." See also pp. 184-89 below.

[31] *Documents*, 1:108-112.

In the negotiations that followed and that eventually led to the signing of the Polish-Soviet Agreement of July 30, 1941, the initial positions of the two sides were essentially the same as those exchanged the year before:[32] For its part, the Soviet government was prepared to give Poland, along with Czechoslovakia and Yugoslavia, facilities to form a "national committee" in the USSR; a Polish military force would be formed by this committee to fight with the Russian armies against Germany, and all Polish prisoners-of-war (whose number Moscow placed at less than one-tenth the Polish estimate) would be handed over to the Polish "national committee." For the future, "Soviet policy was to favour the establishment of an independent . . . ethnographical Poland." Sikorski pressed for modification on all points. First, he refused outright the formation of a Polish "national committee" which he saw as a revival of Pan-Slavism, this time of a "red" variety. Instead, he insisted that Moscow recognize the legal continuity of the Polish state and government by establishing diplomatic relations with the Government-in-Exile. Second, while agreeing that a Polish army in the Soviet Union would be operationally subordinate to the Soviet military command, he insisted that it be an autonomous and sovereign force with a commander appointed by and subordinate to Polish headquarters in London. Third, he demanded the release of all Polish citizens being held by the Russians, whether as prisoners-of-war or as political offenders; he demanded also that Moscow permit the creation under the Polish embassy of a relief organization to serve the million or more refugees and prisoners. Fourth and finally, Sikorski rejected emphatically and repeatedly the idea of an "ethnographical" Poland; on the contrary, he insisted that the Soviet government renounce its treaties of August and September 1939 with Germany, adding that he would interpret such renunciation as "automatically" returning Polish-Soviet relations to their legal status from before September 1, 1939. He could agree that the question of postwar boundaries "need not be discussed in detail at present," so long as the Soviet government did not "declare that the frontiers of 1939 would *not* be restored."[33]

The agreement as finally signed gave Sikorski his minimum conditions,

[32] The basic documents relating to these negotiations and the text of the final Agreement are reprinted in ibid., pp. 114-45. The most complete record is to be found in the British Foreign Office files, FO 371/26755 and 26756, PRO. Probably the most balanced overall narrative account of the negotiations, especially of Sikorski's motives and of the opposition to the agreement, is in Kukiel, *General Sikorski*, pp. 164-80. See also Rozek, *Allied Wartime Diplomacy*, pp. 52-65.

[33] "Record of conversation between General Sikorski and Ambassador Maisky," July 5, 1941, in *Documents*, 1:117-18 [emphasis in the original]; also C7492/3226/55, FO 371/26755, PRO. Sikorski's handling of this question is especially interesting and does not support the contention that he agreed to a formula that avoided mention of the Riga Treaty only under pressure from the British; see pp. 124-26 below.

though not all in precisely the form he hoped. The boundary issue ended in a standoff: while the Soviets declared "that the Soviet-German treaties of 1939 relative to territorial changes in Poland have lost their validity," they steadfastly refused to countenance Sikorski's interpretation of that renunciation. On the other hand, he succeeded in eliminating all reference to "ethnographical" frontiers. On the prisoner issue—on which Moscow proved fully as intractable as on boundaries—he had to settle for a grant of "amnesty," thus implying that the prisoners had been guilty of something; the question of a Polish relief organization was put off to a later agreement.[34] On the other two points however, concerning diplomatic relations and the Polish Army, the provisions of the agreement were essentially in accord with Sikorski's demands. In addition, he got from the British a public (though dubious) declaration to the effect that "His Majesty's Government do not recognize any territorial changes which have been effected in Poland since August 1939."[35]

Both the British Foreign Office and the U.S. Department of State viewed the agreement as a victory for the Poles, though admittedly a partial and tentative one, for which their prime minister deserved the lion's share of the credit. Foreign Secretary Eden later wrote of the signing: "General Sikorski's statesmanship deserved any credit that might be due for this. Our part was only patient diplomacy tinged with anxiety for what the future must hold for the Poles as the weaker partner." In a similar vein, Ambassador Ciechanowski cabled from Washington that the agreement was viewed in the United States as a "diplomatic success for the Polish government."[36]

On the other hand, virtually all contemporary Polish assessments, as

[34] The Soviet government proclaimed amnesty for all Poles living on Soviet territory on August 12, 1941; see Kukiel, *Generał Sikorski*, p. 177, and *Documents*, 1:145-46. Retinger later suggested that use of the word "amnesty" instead of "release" in the English text of the Agreement was a "grave mistake"; *Joseph Retinger*, ed. Pomian, p. 119. However, it is almost certain that "amnesty" was used at the insistence of the Soviets as the price of their agreeing to release the Poles at all; see Ambassador Cripps's two cables of July 26th from Moscow, in C8377/3226/55, FO 371/26756, PRO. Very early in the negotiations Sir Alexander Cadogan, permanent under secretary in the Foreign Office, identified the prisoner issue as the most troublesome: "Only real difficulty [is] question of release of Polish *political* prisoners in Russia . . ." *The Cadogan Diaries*, ed. Dilks, p. 391 [entry for July 5, 1941; emphasis in the original].

[35] This declaration was as ambiguous as the Polish-Soviet Agreement itself; moreover, whatever beneficial effect it might have had was largely negated by Foreign Secretary Eden's statement in Commons the next day that it did not "involve any guarantee of frontiers by His Majesty's Government." *Documents*, 1:142-44.

[36] Anthony Eden, *The Reckoning: The Memoirs of Anthony Eden, Earl of Avon*, p. 316; and Kukiel, *Generał Sikorski*, pp. 174-77. Eden's praise of Sikorski in this instance is fully reflected in the internal Foreign Office minutes; see, e.g., C8306/3226/55, FO 371/26756, PRO.

well as many later ones—whether critical or otherwise—have ascribed Sikorski's behavior in this sequence of events to one or several of the following motives and circumstances: outright vanity and personal ambition, especially an overriding ambition to command a large army; undue haste both in starting negotiations and in concluding the agreement; naiveté concerning Soviet motives and designs; Anglo-American pressure to come to an agreement with Moscow regardless of the costs to Polish national interests; and, a variant of this last, Sikorski's subservience to Britain's pro-Soviet machinations despite Washington's willingness to support Poland's just demands (i.e., the pre-September 1939 eastern boundary).[37] Many of the criticisms leveled at Sikorski reflected the deep divisions that existed within the exile community not only over how best to protect Poland's vital interests, but even over what those interests were. In particular, the charges of ambition and haste often masked feelings, widespread at the time, that there was no need to deal with the Soviet government because it would quickly collapse under the Nazi onslaught and that, in any event, Poland had done her bit and now it was up to others to carry the military burden. We shall discuss these divisions in some detail later. What is of interest at the moment is, first, the extent to which the several motives and pressures imputed to him did in fact influence Sikorski's decision to negotiate and sign an agreement with the Soviets and, second, what he expected or hoped Poland would gain from it.

There is unquestionably some truth to the claim that the Poles were under considerable Allied pressure, and primarily from the British, to reach some kind of *modus vivendi* with Moscow (although not to the myth that the Americans were inclined to rescue them from unpleasant concessions). As Churchill himself would later write:

> In this summer of 1941, less than two weeks after the appearance of Russia on our side in the struggle against Germany, we could not force our new and sorely threatened ally to abandon, even on paper, regions on her frontiers which she had regarded for generations as

[37] Pobóg-Malinowski's treatment of Sikorski is the most scathing, not only in regard to the signing of the July 1941 agreement but throughout his tenure. Having already attributed his behavior in the June 1940 memo incident to "personal ambition" and "visions of a 300,000-man army," Malinowski repeats these charges here; he also faults Sikorski for his "short-sightedness" and "wishful thinking," for his "total ignorance" of Russia, and for having knuckled under to British pressure to sign quickly despite orders from President Raczkiewicz to wait for an American "guarantee" of Poland's eastern boundary. *Najnowsza historia*, 3:151-53 and 174-88. Wacław Jędrzejewicz (*Polonia amerykańska w polityce polskiej*, pp. 50-51) claims that Washington warned the Poles against quick conclusion of an agreement. Other critical accounts, though devoid of personal attacks on Sikorski, include: Pragier, *Czas przeszły dokonany*, pp. 632-52; and Michał Sokolnicki, *Dziennik Ankarski, 1939-1943*, pp. 240-57.

vital to her security. There was no way out. The issue of the territorial future of Poland must be postponed until easier times. We had the invidious responsibility of recommending General Sikorski to rely on Soviet good faith in the future settlement of Russian-Polish relations, and not to insist at this moment on any written guarantees for the future.[38]

Yet, accepting that such pressure existed, the question remains whether it measurably altered the substance of Sikorski's policy. Here the evidence is mixed, but on balance suggests that the constraints on him were more than offset by the opportunity to set in motion the strategy he had been developing for more than a year.

The most serious constraints, largely ignored by the general's detractors, flowed more from circumstances beyond his control than from specific demands made of the Polish government: most importantly, from Churchill's unconditional offer of aid to Stalin and from the knowledge that, for Britain, Poland's friendship "could not outweigh the enormous power of the Soviet Union . . . , without which a victorious conclusion to the war was unimaginable . . ."[39] He had to act, as he had tried to do a year earlier, in order that Poland not find herself isolated within the Allied camp by an Anglo-Soviet rapprochement which now, in the wake of the German offensive, had become a reality. It must also be acknowledged that the mediating role played by the Foreign Office was indispensable in breaking down Moscow's aversion to *any* agreement with the Poles. The full diplomatic record bears ample witness to the tedious and difficult course of the month-long negotiations, and to the considerable patience and sensitivity to Polish concerns on the part of the British officials most intimately involved.[40] As General Kukiel later wrote: "there was urging, but there was also honest assistance."[41]

[38] Winston S. Churchill, *The Grand Alliance*, p. 391.

[39] See e.g. Kukiel, *Generał Sikorski*, pp. 164-67. During a luncheon meeting on July 3rd with Labour Secretary Ernest Bevin and Assistant Under Secretary at the Foreign Office William Strang, Sikorski (according to the Polish report of the discussion) "did not hide" the fact that he had found Churchill's June 22nd speech "not satisfactory, either from the Polish point of view or from its overall contents, or rather lack of them"—a transparent reference to the lack of conditions attached to Churchill's promise of aid to Russia. PRM 39b/8, GSHI. This comment is not reported in the British account of the meeting (C7458/3226/55, FO 371/26755, PRO).

[40] FO 371/26755 and 26756, PRO, *passim*. Concerning Moscow's reluctance to entertain the idea of any agreement with the exile government, including threats as late as July 18th to break off the negotiations and set up its own Polish "national committee" in the Soviet Union, see especially: C7016, C7423, C8028, and C8377/3226/55 in the FO files indicated above. Moscow's attitude toward the Government-in-Exile is discussed in Chapter VIII below.

[41] Kukiel, *Generał Sikorski*, p. 174. The need for British assistance in bringing the Soviets

By contrast, the more specific and direct pressures most often alluded to by Sikorski's critics (and some of his supporters as well)—in particular, Churchill's insistence on revisions to Sikorski's June 23rd broadcast to Poland, and alleged British pressure to sign the agreement before the arrival of an American "guarantee" of Poland's prewar eastern boundary[42]— appear to have had a negligible impact on his policy. On the first point, it is a matter of documentary record that the Polish leader toned down some references to the Soviet Union following a last-minute meeting with Eden, although he successfully resisted pressure to delete a passage on Polish POWs and internees.[43] In light of the fact that the original text had

to the negotiating table could be dismissed only by those who did not want an agreement. Thus, despite its obvious immodesty, there is likely a good deal of truth in the following statement made by Sikorski in December 1941, as he passed through Turkey en route home from Moscow, and recorded by the Polish ambassador in Ankara: "I state that, despite circulating rumors, it was not the English who maneuvered me into Polish-Soviet negotiations, but I [who] maneuvered Eden into them, so that Great Britain would participate alongside us. There was no British pressure on us in this matter, but my pressure on England." Sokolnicki, *Dziennik Ankarski*, p. 292. The following month, in a secret report to his Council of Ministers in London, Sikorski again discounted Allied pressure; *Documents*, 1:264.

[42] For the most important critical accounts, see note 37 above. It is interesting that even many of Sikorski's defenders repeat the charges of British pressure here. For instance, Rozek (*Allied Wartime Diplomacy*, pp. 61-63), while much gentler in his treatment of the prime minister than Malinowski, places the blame on the British at the expense of portraying the true dimensions of intragovernmental dissension. He would have us believe Sikorski actually sympathized with Ministers Zaleski, Sosnkowski, and Seyda, who resigned from the government in protest; he also asserts that Sikorski signed under heavy British pressure and despite the offer of an American "guarantee." Jan Ciechanowski (*Defeat in Victory*, pp. 37-38) suggests that Sikorski shared Churchill's "romantic attitude" toward Russia. Stanisław Mikołajczyk (*The Pattern of Soviet Domination*, pp. 17-18), although he accepted the agreement as the best the Poles could get, placed greatest blame on British pressure to maintain "Allied unity." Raczyński (*W sojuszniczym Londynie*, pp. 120-25), although he later changed his mind, initially opposed an agreement and wrote that it came about as a result of pressure from both the British and the Americans. Even Mitkiewicz (*Z gen. Sikorskim*, pp. 150-53 and 167-68), despite his own stated belief that a "radical change" in Polish policy toward the Soviet Union was essential, blamed British pressure as well as Sikorski's haste for the decision to postpone the boundary issue. For a British view of prevailing Polish attitudes toward the agreement with Moscow, see Ambassador Cecil Dormer's report to Eden of July 22nd, in C8306/3226/55, FO 371/26756, PRO.

[43] British displeasure with the original text is evident from the notation in Cadogan's diary for the 23rd, about "an impossible broadcast Sikorski wants to let off at 10.30. Tried to put it into shape, and left A. [Eden] to grapple with S. [Sikorski]." *The Cadogan Diaries*, ed. Dilks, p. 390. The Foreign Office record of their 9 p.m. meeting at the Ritz Hotel indicates that Eden, on Churchill's instructions, proposed "some rather drastic amendments . . . to avoid a gratuitous attack on Russia," and that Sikorski "accepted all the amendments" (apparently with little or no argument) except the proposal to delete the prisoner issue (which Eden thought would be more easily settled by private negotiation). C7007/151/55, FO 371/26718, PRO. Similarly, Stanisław Stroński writes that Sikorski accepted those changes affecting phrasing and tone, but not those that "encroached on essential content." "O układzie polsko-rosyjskim z 30.7.1941," p. 101.

to pass muster with a Council of Ministers which only the day before had opposed cooperation with Moscow "under present circumstances" and which insisted on an unconditional invocation of the Riga boundary—both positions that Sikorski had abandoned fully a year earlier—such pressure may not have been entirely unwelcome. Indeed, it is possible, even probable, that he actually exaggerated the extent of British pressure throughout the negotiations in order to persuade reluctant members of his government to accept an agreement he thought essential.[44] On the second point, the expectation of an American "guarantee" of the Riga boundary was wholly unfounded and was largely the product of Washington's inscrutable ambiguity on territorial questions, which in turn fostered wishful thinking on the part of some Polish officials, in particular the Polish ambassador in Washington. After determining for himself that no such guarantee would be forthcoming, Sikorski signed the agreement in defiance of President Raczkiewicz's order to wait.[45]

In the final analysis, it is probably a mistake to conclude that in signing the Polish-Soviet Agreement of July 30, 1941, Sikorski was swayed wholly or even mainly by external factors. A second and equally credible explanation of the Prime Minister's motives—one consistent not only with his actions in the critical months of June and July 1941, but also with those of the preceding and subsequent years—is simply that he believed a Polish-Soviet rapprochement to be essential to Poland's future existence. However painful and costly such an accommodation with Russia might be for his country, the only alternatives were total extinction as an independent state or a junior partnership with Germany, which at best (assuming a German victory in which Sikorski did not believe) would offer Poland the forms of nationhood but never its substance. No, Poland's only hope lay in an Allied victory over Germany and, as a logical consequence, in a permanent and powerful Russian presence on her eastern flank. Writing more than a decade later, Stanisław Kot, Sikorski's first ambassador to Moscow and one of his closest confidants in this period, spoke of the continuity of his thinking:

> No Englishman inspired Sikorski with the idea that, in the event of war between Germany and Russia, it would be necessary to stand on the side of Russia. This was his deep conviction, thought out long

---

[44] Concerning the attitude of the Polish government, see note 30 above. It is entirely possible that Sikorski submitted the text to the British in advance in the expectation that they would press for changes and as a way of shifting the onus to them. Pobóg-Malinowski (*Najnowsza historia*, 3:182, n. 52) accuses him of overstating to the Council of Ministers his efforts to press the Polish viewpoint on the British during the negotiations.

[45] See, e.g., Eden's cable to Halifax, by then British ambassador in Washington, of July 29, 1941; C8498/3226/55, FO 371/26756, PRO. For further discussion, see pp. 281-82 below.

beforehand. . . . Passivity seemed to him nonsense; he did not believe that we had anything to gain by observing from a neutral standpoint the course of the Russo-German war. He knew that the Allies would exert every effort to help Russia. He feared that if the Poles stood in the way of these efforts, even morally by expressing a wish for the defeat of the Soviets and for the conquest of Russia by Hitler, then the Polish cause would surely not gain in importance but, on the contrary, would vanish from the concerns of the Allies and from the international arena. . . . Poland would become passive material for crushing by the steamroller of war.[46]

In Kot's view, Sikorski was neither naive nor hasty in concluding the agreement with the Soviets, nor was he motivated by a personal ambition to command a large army. On the contrary, the former ambassador testified to the importance the prime minister attached to the timing of the agreement and to the central role a Polish army in the Soviet Union was to play in his strategy of reconciliation:

Sikorski was anxious to seize the opportunity when Russia found herself in a difficult situation to conclude a pact with her. He understood that, when her position improved, she would not be inclined to accept conditions that suited us. He did not believe in a German victory. He placed a higher value on the forces . . . of the Soviets than was accepted in the camp of the Piłsudskiites, who had learned little in this regard. He did not place trust in the reliability of the Bolsheviks' word, but he took account of their realism. He knew how to demonstrate to Russia those Polish qualities with which even she would have to reckon; and the rapid establishment of a Polish army, valiant and patriotic, in connection with the Soviet Army he regarded as a guarantee of real cooperation. . . .[47]

But by his own admission, it was the plight of the Poles in the Soviet Union that gave Sikorski his most compelling motive to reach an early agreement. "Some Poles did not understand," he wrote on August 3rd to General Anders, himself just released from Moscow's Lubianka prison,

[46] Kot, *Listy z Rosji*, p. 11. See also Sikorski's July 31st broadcast to Poland, in *Documents*, 1:144-45.

[47] Kot, *Listy z Rosji*, p. 13. Noting the "great malice" of some of Sikorski's critics, Kukiel (*Generał Sikorski*, p. 174) writes: "What after all was the alternative? Had he not seized the initiative in his own hands, a 'National Committee,' possibly with a composition more representative than the later 'Committee of National Liberation,' would have arisen in Moscow already in July and would have begun to create a Polish 'peoples' army subordinate to Soviet Russia . . ."

"that, at a moment when at issue is the liberation of hundreds of thousands of [their] fellow countrymen, this above all must decide the argument."[48]

One need only scan the protocols of his negotiating sessions with Soviet Ambassador Maisky to realize that Sikorski was fully aware of the issues left unresolved by the agreement. The evidence suggests that he looked on it not as a solution but as an opening, which provided not the Polish-Soviet understanding he sought but only the minimum basis on which such an understanding could be built. Again Professor Kot is instructive:

> When they [his opponents] said to him that, without guarantees—and who would or could give them?—the Soviets will not keep their word, he answered that no verbal guarantees or formulas will be respected if we do not come down to facts, which lay the real foundations for cooperation. He regarded the joint crossing of Polish divisions with the Red Army into Poland as a stronger guarantee of respect for Polish sovereignty than all the pacts that could be concluded.[49]

Sikorski also knew that to take advantage of this opening would require not only the good will of both Russians and Poles, but a healthy measure of foresight and cooperation from their now mutual allies as well. What he could not know in advance was that, in the final analysis, all would be found wanting and that what he hoped was merely a beginning actually marked the high point of his achievement. He would spend the next two years—the last two of his life—battling to retain the advantages he had gained here.

[48] Kukiel, *Generał Sikorski*, pp. 174-75. Kukiel added here that Sikorski had said to him shortly thereafter: "You know, when I had to sign this agreement and I was struggling with myself over whether to wait still longer, I heard as if a whisper from a thousand lips—hurry, save us." See also Kot, *Rozmowy z Kremlem*, pp. 7-8; and Mikołajczyk, *Pattern of Soviet Domination*, p. 18.

[49] Kot, *Listy z Rosji*, p. 13.

V · *Toward a New Central Europe*

As WE have already seen in Chapter II, the contentious nationalisms that dominated the mood in the Central European successor states following the First World War gave little quarter to suggestions for an effective regional organization. By the 1930s, however, their patent incapacity separately to solve their problems had revived interest in plans for cooperation, especially in the economic sphere. On a smaller scale, the idea of Polish-Czechoslovak cooperation followed a similar pattern. Although early ruminations over a federation fell victim to the poisonous state of political relations engendered by the Teschen dispute, proposals for looser forms of association were revived sporadically throughout the interwar period.

The Polish-German boundary, as the immediate occasion for the outbreak of World War II, posed even more urgent problems. From the very beginning it had been a source of dissatisfaction and tension on both sides. Poland's dissatisfaction stemmed from the fact that the Versailles settlement had failed to meet her minimum demands in Silesia, Danzig, and East Prussia. As a result her most vital centers—her modest industrial district and access to the sea—were gravely exposed while more than a million Poles were left, mostly in compact communities, on the German side of the frontier. Although the idea of returning to Poland's original boundaries in the north and west remained a dream nurtured only by a small group of scholars and political activists, there was a growing recognition as the war approached of the need for borders that would be fairer from an ethnic point of view and that would provide greater economic and military security.

It should come as no surprise then that these ideas—both the proposals for some sort of Central European organization and the demand for a rectification of Poland's frontiers with Germany—resurfaced more or less independently in several quarters in the early stages of the war.[1] However,

---

[1] For a survey of Polish views of a future Polish-German boundary during the early war years, see Marian Orzechowski, *Odra-Nysa Łużycka-Bałtyk w polskiej myśli politycznej okresu drugiej wojny światowej*, pp. 13-152. Early British interest in both a Central European federation and a westward shift of Poland's boundary with Germany is reported in Włodzimierz T. Kowalski, *ZSRR a granica na Odrze i Nysie, 1941-1945*, pp. 21 and 25. See also Raczyński, *W sojuszniczym Londynie*, p. 57; Eden, *The Reckoning*, pp. 85-86; and Teeling, ed., *After the War*, especially the contributions by Alan Graham, M. P. and Sir Hugh Molson, M.P. An unusual German proposal for the reorganization of Central Europe is Edgar Stern-Rubarth's *Exit Prussia: A Plan for Europe*.

the forms in which they resurfaced varied widely. Often they were vaguely conceived, and the two ideas were not necessarily related to each other. Many, especially proposals for boundary revisions, were more on the order of political slogans than thought-out practical programs. Nor did they all draw the same conclusions from the realities of Poland's geographic situation. On the contrary, while some at least implied a reorientation of Poland's international posture, others represented a reaffirmation of prewar "great power" aspirations and a "two-enemy" stance. For instance, at least one radical Nationalist group coupled a claim to a western boundary approximating the Oder-Neisse with demands for a vast expansion of Poland's eastern holdings[2]—a notion that assumed the defeat and breakup of the Soviet Union and was hardly compatible with a policy of Polish-Soviet reconciliation.

THE "WESTERN SCHOOL" IN EXILE

As an influence on the development of Sikorski's policy, two of these programs seem to have been important. The first and more comprehensive of these was the one set forth by the *Biuletyn Zachodnio-Słowiański* (or *West-Slavonic Bulletin*), a short-lived scholarly publication out of Edinburgh, which appeared sporadically between September 1940 and June 1942,[3] and which seems to have been a kind of exile offshoot of Poland's interwar "Western School."[4] The *Bulletin*'s program is of interest not only because it represented the earliest and most coherent argument both for a

[2] Orzechowski, *Odra-Nysa-Bałtyk*, pp. 76-79; also Terej, *Rzeczywistość i polityka*, pp. 157-58, n. 110; and Kot, *Listy z Rosji*, p. 72.

[3] In all nine issues were published: nos. 1 and 2 were circulated first in mimeographed form in September and November 1940, and then were reissued early the next year in journal format; nos. 7 and 8 (also called nos. 1 and 2, 1942) were issued under the name *Ruch Zachodnio-Słowiański*; no. 9 was also called "no. 1 English Series" and contained translations of articles that had appeared in earlier issues. The *Bulletin* probably fell victim to the political wars that raged within the Government-in-Exile, which could exert control through paper-rationing. According to Stanisław Strumph-Wojtkiewicz (*Gwiazda Władysława Sikorskiego*, p. 184), the Ministry of Information "hindered the appearance of the *Bulletin* over a long period" because it feared that demands for a western boundary on the Oder and Neisse would jeopardize Poland's claims to her prewar eastern territories. At one point, the *Bulletin* itself stated that it was experiencing difficulties "beyond the control of the editors" (no. 4/5, August 1941, p. 32); and certainly the designation of the final issue as "no. 1 English Series" indicated the intention of the editors to continue publication.

[4] Describing themselves as "long-time activists in the movement for reconciliation among the Slavs," the *Bulletin*'s founders proclaimed as their goal to "instill deeply in the consciousness of all Poles, Czechs, Slovaks, Lusatians and other Western Slavs this idea [of the unification of the Western Slavs] . . ." "Od redakcji," *Biuletyn Zachodnio-Słowiański*, no. 1 (September 1940):1.

Central European federation and for Poland's territorial expansion to the west,[5] but more particularly because it integrated these two ideas in much the same way as Sikorski was later to do. Moreover, since documentation of Sikorski's program remains incomplete, the *Bulletin*'s programmatic statements and supporting analyses offer welcome insights into the rationale behind his proposals.

The basic premise of the *Bulletin*'s outlook was that Germany constituted the main danger to the Western Slavs, indeed the only threat to their very existence, and, as a corollary, that they could counter this threat only by overcoming their own weakness and disunity:

> . . . The Western Slavs, settled on the Vistula, Oder, Elbe and Danube, live at the greatest political crossroads of the world. At this point in Europe, there is not and cannot be room for small or weakly consolidated states. We Western Slavs will either exist as a uniform and cohesive power, or we will not exist at all.
>
> No other arguments are needed to justify our basic thesis that a lasting solution to the dangers always threatening from the direction of Germany . . . requires *not merely an alliance but a permanent political union of Poles, Czechs and Slovaks.*
>
> Just as Czechoslovakia and Yugoslavia, the first two political manifestations of the tendency toward voluntary unification of Slavic nations, arose as a result of the 1914 war, so as a result of the 1939 war a West Slavonic State must arise as the voluntary and permanent union of all Western Slavs.[6]

In contrast to the vague schemes bandied about in the interwar years, this union would be no loose organization of otherwise sovereign states, as was indicated by the proposed list of common functions: a common foreign policy and military command, a customs union and common currency, a joint economic plan for basic industries, a joint transportation system, a joint foreign trade policy, uniform scientific and educational systems, and a joint supreme court and legal code; unified state offices and bodies would include a single head of state, a federal parliament, and a federal government. In short: "The Poles and Czechs and Slovaks must all renounce absolute sovereignty, and not only for the material good of their common

---

[5] The basic programmatic statement of the "West-Slavonic" group appeared in two parts in the second and third issues of the *Biuletyn Zachodnio-Słowiański*: "Federacja Zachodnio-Słowiańska" (no. 2, November 1940, pp. 3-11) and "Związek polityczny narodów Europy Środkowej" (no. 3, February 1941, pp. 3-15). Both articles were signed with the initials Z.S. and were, in all probability, written by Zbigniew Stachowski, coeditor of the *Bulletin*. The "Western School" also continued to flourish in the Polish Underground; by and large, however, its work could not be published until after the war.

[6] "Federacja Zachodnio-Słowiańska," in ibid., no. 2, p. 3 [emphasis added].

state, but likewise in the name of satisfying their higher national ambitions."[7]

The editors of the *Bulletin* were fully aware that their proposal would require a fundamental change in the psyche of the Polish nation. In the lead editorial of their first issue, they lamented the narrow nationalism of their fellow countrymen[8] and warned that the Poles, together with the Czechs and Slovaks, would be able to achieve their "common ambitions" only insofar as they could "manage here and now to restrain their particularist ambitions."[9] By "common ambitions" the *Bulletin* had in mind above all a westward shift of Poland's boundary with Germany, a shift that the group saw as interdependent with the formation of a federation. On the one hand, extensive territorial gains could only be attained within the framework of a close federal union; on the other, such gains were an essential condition of the federation's economic success and strategic viability. "The appearance of our nations in the form of a single state organism," asserted the *Bulletin*:

> will immeasurably facilitate . . . the gaining of that western boundary to which we must raise legitimate claim. Acting separately, even if we were to act in complete solidarity . . . , we would surely not gain the whole area demanded—the glaring need for the annexation of which to Poland and Czechoslovakia emerges only when these two countries present themselves to the outside as a single state. . . .
>
> The form of a federal state is likewise the form affording the greatest possibilities for a rapid reconstruction of normal economic life, as well as the further intensive development of our war-devastated and exhausted countries. Such a structure can most easily promote the harmonizing of economic processes among the federated countries, with the optimal exploitation of the natural possibilities of each.[10]

A "cardinal error" of the Versailles settlement following World War I had been "the creation on the eastern frontiers of the Reich of two completely independent . . . states: Poland and Czechoslovakia, divided by a

---

[7] Ibid., p. 5. Stachowski reserves the word "state" (*państwo*) for the federation, referring to the component units as "nations" (*narody*) or "countries" (*kraje*).

[8] "We are fighting not only for Poland, but for all Western Slavdom, for a better world order. Our higher supranational consciousness is still immature. Egoism and pettiness are still too deeply ingrained in us. The struggle for the greatness of our tribe is at the same time a struggle for the transformation of our inner psyche. The struggle with ourselves is the most difficult struggle and, to put it bluntly, often hopeless." "Od redakcji," ibid., no. 1, p. 2.

[9] "Federacja Zachodnio-Słowiańska," ibid., no. 2, p. 5.

[10] Ibid., p. 4. This last paragraph is especially striking not only in view of Sikorski's later program, but in comparison with the program for Polish-Czechoslovak economic cooperation developed and partially implemented between 1947 and 1949 by the Communists. The economic argument has been most forcefully presented in Jordan, *Oder-Neisse Line*.

German wedge.'' Strategically, this had rendered "both of them incapable of adequately opposing alone the power of a Germany only temporarily prostrated.'' Economically, the "Silesian wedge" divided into three separate sectors the Silesian-Moravian industrial basin (one of four such coal basins in Europe), while a Pomeranian wedge between Poland's northwestern frontier and the Baltic left the natural outlet for this basin, the Oder river with its port at Stettin (Szczecin), in the hands of a hostile Germany. By including all of Silesia and Pomerania in their federation, the Poles and Czechs could rid themselves of the strategic horror of German salients protruding into their most vital industrial regions. Moreover, inclusion of Silesia and Pomerania would restore the basic economic complementarity of the Silesian and Moravian halves of the basin, placing within the borders of the federation not only its natural outlet to the north, but also all of the critical junction in the south through which—by a network of canals linking the Oder, Danube, and Vistula rivers—continuous water routes could be opened to the south and east.[11]

With these criteria in mind, the *Bulletin* defined the frontiers "to which we must raise legitimate claims" as follows: "the Baltic coast from the mouth of the Nieman to the island of Rugia [Rügen], the entire Oder basin as well as the basin of the upper Spree." In other words, East Prussia with Danzig, all of Pomerania, Upper and Lower Silesia, east and southeast Brandenburg "including both banks of the Oder along its middle course," as well as Upper and Lower Lusatia.[12] According to the map in the *Bul-*

[11] "Współpraca w przemyśle hutniczym i metalowo-przetwórczym: Z zagadnień polsko-czechosłowackiej wspólnoty gospodarczej," *Biuletyn Zachodnio-Słowiański*, no. 1, pp. 12-14; and T[adeusz] S[ulimirski], "Geopolityka ziem polskich," ibid., no. 4/5, pp. 5-12. Sulimirski points out (p. 9) that between 1919 and 1939 Poland possessed approximately the same western frontier as she had in 1772 just prior to the partitions, and that this frontier had left her in an indefensible position in both periods. The idea of a canal system linking up the major rivers of the region dates back to the late eighteenth century. During the war, the Germans began work on an elaborate system, based in part on earlier Polish plans and including a canal linking the Oder and Danube rivers. See Machray, *The Problem of Upper Silesia*, pp. 57-61.

[12] Lusatia is that part of Saxony lying along the upper Spree just to the west of the Lusatian Neisse and inhabited by remnants of a Slavic tribe closely related to the Czechs. See, e.g., Tadeusz Halewski, "Łużyce," *Ruch Zachodnio-Słowiański*, no. 8 (May 1942), pp. 3-6 and 8; also Tadeusz Sulimirski, *Poland and Germany, Past and Future*, pp. 17-21. Sulimirski proposed that the Lusatian lands, being too small to support an independent state, be incorporated into Bohemia with which they had long been associated. In general, the *Bulletin* group was more inclined toward the ethnic argument than Sikorski was to be. Editor Stachowski ("Federacja Zachodnio-Słowiańska," *Biuletyn Zachodnio-Słowiański*, no. 2, p. 7) gave as the "most important" argument justifying the proposed boundary "the fact that the vast majority of the population of these territories . . . are native Slavs, the closest kinsmen of the Poles and Czechs, or simply belong to Polish tribes"—germanized to be sure, but only by force and incompletely. See also Tadeusz Sulimirski, "Rdzenne ziemie słowiańskie," *Biuletyn Zachodnio-Słowiański*, no. 1, pp. 5-8.

letin's November 1940 issue (see Map 4), a boundary line embracing these territories would have run approximately thirty to fifty kilometers to the *west* of the Oder-Neisse boundary as eventually established, curving even further westward as it approached the Baltic. In addition to meeting the security and economic needs of the proposed federation, such a boundary would in the *Bulletin*'s view, contribute to general European stability by helping to "so weaken Germany that she will never again be capable of seeking revenge." In this way, "the repossession by a Federation of Western Slavs of the ancient Slavic lands in the west is a question of historical justice that also coincides with the interests of Europe as a whole."[13]

Implicit in both these views was a basic distrust of the idealistic and abstract guarantees characteristic of the post-World War I settlement and the League of Nations. In order to avoid a repetition of the situation in which the small nations of Europe were at the mercy of the willingness of the Great Powers to check aggression, supranational associations of the future should be regional in nature and be based on a community of interests, needs, and historical experience. Seeing such a community among the small nations lying between the Baltic, Black, and Adriatic Seas, the *Bulletin* favored, in addition to the West-Slavonic Federation of Poland and Czechoslovakia, the formation of a broader Central European Union. Its three main components would be the West-Slavonic Federation, a similar Association of Southern Slavs (Yugoslavia and Bulgaria), with a grouping of the two non-Slav states of Rumania and Hungary in between; other potential beneficiaries were Greece and Albania in the south and Lithuania in the north. The structure of this union would be much looser than that of the proposed Polish-Czechoslovak federation: there would be no central legislative or executive bodies, no common head of state; rather, the central agencies would be more on the order of coordinating committees for matters of foreign policy, defense, and economic cooperation with the union.[14]

The arguments presented by the *Bulletin* in support of such a Central European Union were more or less analogous to those for the more closely knit federation. The natural resource bases of the several components were complementary and provided most of the prerequisites for balanced economic growth. The main industrial center of the union would be the Sile-

---

[13] "Federacja Zachodnio-Słowiańska," *Biuletyn Zachodnio-Słowiański*, no. 2, pp. 6-8. The proposed boundary is described here as "proceed[ing] from the point where the Elbe passes between the Sudeten and Kruszcowe [Erzgebirge] ranges, and from there goes straight north toward the Baltic, approximately along the 14th meridian, only with a slight bend to the east to exclude the densely populated Berlin district; then further with a rather sharp curve back toward the northwest in order to embrace the whole of historic Pomerania, whose western extreme together with Rugia [Rügen] the Prussians conquered only in 1815."

[14] "Związek polityczny narodów Europy Środkowej," ibid., no. 3, pp. 3-11.

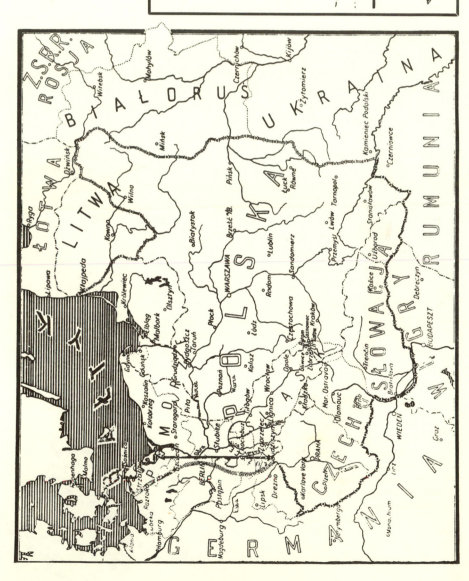

Map 4

"The Territory of the Western Slavs," according to the West-Slavonic Bulletin, November 1940

SOURCE: *Biuletyn Zachodnio-Słowiański* (Edinburgh), No. 2 (November 1940).

┄┄┄ boundaries prior to 1938

‧‧‧‧‧ provincial boundaries

▬▬▬ shortest line between Sudetes and Baltic, approx. 330 km.

〰〰〰 limits of predominantly Slavic ethnic elements

sian-Moravian basin within the West-Slavonic Federation; but Rumania would provide much-needed oil, while Yugoslavia would contribute important nonferrous metals (aluminum, copper, and chromium). And if, apart from Silesia and Moravia, the region was still predominantly agricultural, the union framework would afford better utilization of land than would be possible "with small organisms fenced off by customs barriers." Strategically, it would constitute a "land power" of between 110 and 120 million people, larger than Germany and second only to Russia on the European continent. The *Bulletin* also anticipated the creation of a comparable West European Union which, it was hoped, would supplant Germany as the primary trading partner of the Central European nations—a shift in trading patterns that would be greatly facilitated by the latter's control over the Baltic ports of Stettin and Danzig. Because any punitive measures that might be taken against Germany after the war would presumably be of a temporary nature, a Central European Union would have to be tied to the West by "a close and permanent alliance." However, such an alliance would no longer be a dependent relationship, but one of equals for mutual benefit.[15]

On the thorny subject of future relations with Russia the *Bulletin* group said little (in part, no doubt, because its basic programmatic statements were published during the period of Nazi-Soviet collaboration). Nonetheless, one can hazard several conclusions. The first is that they did not desire Russia's direct participation in the political, economic, or military organization of Central Europe. This is absolutely clear from the substance of their proposals, which emphasize the community of interests among the *small* nations of that region, resulting in large measure from their location between "the two great land powers" of Russia and Germany.[16] Indeed, the unwritten—or only partially expressed—hypothesis underlying the whole *Bulletin* program was that one result of the historical weakness of Central Europe had been that Germany and Russia had traditionally ordered their mutual relations at the expense of the small nations between them. The

---

[15] Ibid., pp. 10-14; see also Marian Książkiewicz, "Surowce mineralne Europy Środkowej," ibid., no. 6 (January 1942), pp. 14-21. The need for a permanent alliance was explained by the expectation that "the sparks of future wars will remain for several generations more in the form of states defeated in the present war; . . . Germany and Italy will remain . . . continually threatening because of their central position and continually strong because of the size of their populations." Moreover, although France would continue as a great civilization, she could no longer offset Germany's superior numbers and might; while Britain, in addition to being involved in distant parts of the world, had never represented sufficient land forces to break an aggressive continental power. "In the event of a new war with their ancient enemies," the Central European nations could "count only on themselves." "Związek polityczny narodów Europy Środkowej," pp. 12-14.

[16] "Związek polityczny narodów Europy Środkowej," p. 6.

second conclusion, the apparent contradiction notwithstanding, is that neither the proposed Polish-Czechoslovak federation nor the Central European Union was anti-Soviet in intent. On the contrary, such developments were seen as entirely compatible with Russia's interests and even as serving her security needs by providing a reliable and friendly buffer against "would-be aggressors" along her western and southwestern flanks, and thereby affording her "peaceful conditions in which to organize her economic life."[17]

The occasional references to the Polish-Soviet boundary issue were likewise restrained and conciliatory. "We strongly believe," read the November 1940 issue, that "the problem of our eastern territories, so painful for us in the present situation, can nonetheless be resolved . . . in a rational manner, consistent with our and also our eastern neighbors' vital interests." The "Eastern Slavs" must come to understand that it is in the "highest interest" of both sides to "be done with the fighting," and that "reliance on each other's protection . . . will afford us all maximum benefits." The author concluded that the issue would become "amenable to practical solution . . . when they, too, feel on their skin the effects of Germany's unrestrained lust for mastery over the world."[18] Early in 1941, the *Bulletin* defended the Riga line as "a kind of compromise" among historical alternatives and suggested that, in the absence of clear-cut ethnographical boundaries, "cultural influences" provided the "most rational criterion for dividing Central from Eastern Europe." But a later version of the same article added that a "final settlement will largely depend upon the further development of relations between neighbouring nations."[19]

A final consideration was the matter of timing. In the view of the *Bulletin* group, the new organization of Central Europe should come into effect immediately after the war. This was considered particularly critical for the success of the West-Slavonic Federation, where the devastation wrought by the war was "effectively smashing barriers and removing hindrances that until now have stood in the way of the unification of Poland and Czechoslovakia"—and where, therefore, it would be "utter nonsense" to resurrect separate political and economic structures. Equally important was the fear that any delay in forming the federation would jeopardize the attainment of its most vital economic and territorial demands. Recalling that, following World War I, foreign investment in defeated Germany had

[17] Kosta Todorov, "Free Bulgarians and Balkan Union," *West-Slavonic Bulletin*, no. 1 English Series (June 1942):6; see also "Do drugiego Grunwaldu," *Biuletyn Zachodnio-Słowiański*, no. 4/5, p. 4.

[18] "Federacja Zachodnio-Słowiańska," ibid., no. 2, p. 8.

[19] "Związek polityczny narodów Europy Środkowej," ibid., no. 3, p. 6; the final sentence appeared in the English summary published in the *Bulletin*'s no. 1 English Series, p. 4.

been far greater than in all the Central European states taken together, the *Bulletin* stressed the importance of appearing before the world as a single entity in order to obtain the foreign loans and investment capital essential for reconstruction. On the matter of boundaries, it warned that "these matters will perforce be decided immediately after the war" and what "occurs in the first postwar months, or perhaps even weeks, will undoubtedly endure for many long years." It was imperative, then, to take "maximum advantage" of the war period to organize the federation and to prepare the world to "accept our proposals after the war."[20]

PRESENTING a view similar to, though less comprehensive than that of the *West-Slavonic Bulletin* was Władysław Pałucki's book *Wracamy nad Odrę (Return to the Oder)*, written under the pseudonym Antoni Błoński.[21] This small but elegantly published volume appeared only in 1942, but is of interest because there is ample reason to believe, first, that Prime Minister Sikorski was aware of its contents at least by the end of 1940 (by which time the book was in fact written)[22] and, second, that it may have exerted a direct influence on his thinking. The author's focus was primarily on the ethnic and historical bases of Poland's claims to the Oder basin. Yet, like the *Bulletin*, his territorial proposals also stressed strategic and geopolitical considerations. "Historical experience shows all too clearly," he wrote:

> that the greatness and security of Poland will depend above all on what boundaries we have in the north and west. The war of 1914-18 did, to be sure, restore us to independence, but our independence . . . was neither complete nor secure. . . . [A]t the time of the conclusion of the Versailles Peace, the western world, despite previous experi-

[20] "Federacja Zachodnio-Słowiańska," ibid., no. 2, pp. 8-11.

[21] Antoni Błoński, *Wracamy nad Odrę: Historyczne, geograficzne i etnograficzne podstawy zachodnich granic Polski*. Pałucki used the pseudonym (derived from Błonie, his home village) primarily to protect his family in Poland but also because, as a soldier on active duty, he was not supposed to engage in politics. Pałucki was also connected with the *West-Slavonic Bulletin*, for which he wrote occasionally under the name Władysław Prawdzic. After the war and shortly before returning to Poland, where he worked for nearly thirty years in the geography department of the Institute of History of the Academy of Sciences, he published a second book on the subject of Poland's western boundary, this time under his real name: Władysław Pałucki [Antoni Błoński], *Ziemie Odzyskane: Szkice historyczne*.

[22] Confirming that the book was in fact completed by the end of 1940 (the Foreword is dated February 15, 1941), Pałucki told me in 1976 that publication had been held up for more than a year, primarily by the Polish Ministry of Information but indirectly also by the British. (He confirmed that publication of the *West-Slavonic Bulletin* had been similarly hampered and finally stopped.) His own book was eventually published at personal expense and through the generosity of friends, who included friends and political associates of Sikorski; see note 29 below.

ences, did not understand that Poland must either be large, with permanent and natural boundaries and broad access to the sea, or she will not be at all; and without her there will be neither peace nor equilibrium in Europe.[23]

Not surprisingly, he specifically rejected the use of plebiscites as an acceptable means for reaching territorial settlements. Even in Wilson's day, the "fine idea of national self-determination" had been "equitable only in a theoretical sense." "Today," after the genocidal policies of the Nazis, "no rational man would dare" suggest a return to plebiscites.[24] Rather, Poland must seek the shortest possible frontier with her ancient enemy to the west, a frontier that would "satisfy in every respect [her] strategic requirements." In the north, that meant the unconditional inclusion of East Prussia and Danzig in the future Polish state, thereby eliminating an "unprecedented historical-geographic monstrosity." In the west, his proposals were only slightly more modest than the *Bulletin*'s: Poland should return to the "Chrobry Line" (after King Bolesław Chrobry, 992-1025) which Pałucki called her "natural boundary with Germany." This line ran from the Czech frontier in the Sudeten mountains along the Kwisa and Bober rivers (tributaries of the Oder running parallel to and twenty-five to forty kilometers east of the Lusatian Neisse), thence along the Oder to the Baltic, leaving the port and bay of Stettin and the isle of Rügen on the Polish side.[25] To the west of this line along its southern sector, he proposed that Lusatia be restored as an "autonomous country" under a joint Polish-Czech military protectorate. On the subject of Polish-Czech relations in general, Pałucki said little; it is clear, however, that he thought some form of postwar West-Slav association essential and viewed the lack of such an understanding in 1918 as responsible for the Poles' and Czechs' failure to regain then the whole of Silesia together with Lusatia and eastern Brandenburg.[26]

Before returning to the development of Sikorski's program, one aspect of the proposals set forth by the *West-Slavonic Bulletin* and *Return to the Oder* deserves reiteration: in neither case was the idea of a Polish-German boundary shifted westward to the vicinity of the Oder and Lusatian Neisse seen as related to the question of Poland's eastern boundary with the Soviet Union. In justifying their proposals in the west, neither cited the need to compensate Poland for lands she might lose in the east;[27] nor did they

[23] Błoński, *Wracamy nad Odrę*, p. 25.

[24] Ibid., p. 114.

[25] Ibid. pp. 26, 56-58, and 113-14. The Chrobry line is shown on Map 2 in Chapter II.

[26] Ibid., pp. 113-15.

[27] In Błoński's (Pałucki's) view, written prior to June 1941, the Polish-Soviet border established by the 1921 Treaty of Riga was "not subject to discussion." Ibid., p. 8.

expect a consequence of Poland's westward expansion to be increased dependence on Russia. On the contrary, dependence on Russia for security against Germany was the antithesis of their programs. Both saw an Oder-Neisse boundary, or slight variants thereof, as fully justified by a combination of Poland's ethnic and historical rights and her economic and strategic needs; and they saw as its most promising consequence the chance for genuine economic and political independence from both of her great neighbors.

Although it is possible to show only tentative and circumstantial links between Pałucki or the *West-Slavonic Bulletin* and the Sikorski government, it is almost certain that one or the other, or both of these programs exerted a strong intellectual influence on the development of the prime minister's ideas concerning essential territorial gains for Poland as well as the postwar organization of Central Europe. The probable links between Sikorski and Pałucki are especially intriguing as they date from the early spring of 1940 when, shortly after his arrival in France from internment in Hungary, the latter set down his views in a seven-to-eight page memorandum intended for the former.[28] Although he never knew for sure that the memo had been brought to the prime minister's attention, during the ensuing months while he was writing his book he reports receiving support and encouragement from Generals Józef Haller and Marian Kukiel.[29] As both were long-time

[28] Pałucki told me in 1976 that he had given copies of the memo to Professor Stanisław Stroński, one of Sikorski's closest collaborators before and during the war, and to Colonel Antoni Bogusławski; the latter, in addition to his military position a well-known writer, had accompanied Sikorski during part of his flight from Poland in September 1939 and was apparently also an acquaintance of Adam Kulakowski, Sikorski's personal secretary. Pałucki first made his views known publicly in a series of lectures in Paris, also in the spring of 1940.

[29] In the Foreword to his book, Pałucki thanked Haller, at this time a minister without portfolio in the exile government, for his "friendly interest and support" (*Wracamy nad Odrę*, p. 8). During our conversations in 1976, he added that Haller had helped him acquire materials essential to his research and that Kukiel had also encouraged him although, as a deputy minister of defense, he could do so only privately. Still another mutual contact was Henryk Bagiński, who had maintained contact with Sikorski from their days at the Lwów Politechnik and who had written several books on the question of Poland's western boundary and access to the sea already in the interwar period; Pałucki met Bagiński while doing research at the British museum, and the latter later helped finance publication of his book. Finally, and on a more personal note, Sikorski's own daughter Zofia Leśniowska, bought up some 200 copies of the book for distribution among army posts, thereby helping in a very substantial way to recover publication costs.

Another source (Strumph-Wojtkiewicz, *Siła złego*, p. 184) has also reported that the Pałucki book caught Sikorski's interest and that, while he was not particularly struck by the historical and ethnographic arguments, he "immediately appreciated the economic and strategic significance of the concept of basing Poland on the Baltic and Oder." According to Strumph-Wojtkiewicz, this occurred in 1942 (when the book was actually published); however, other

military colleagues and political intimates of Sikorski,[30] it is improbable that they would not have brought views of such potential import to the attention of their old friend. While it is not possible to establish such a close connection between the exile government and the *Bulletin*, here too there were at least two channels through which Sikorski could have become familiar with its existence and contents.[31]

Needless to say, none of this is meant to suggest that either the "West-Slavonic" group or Pałucki was the source of Sikorski's basic strategy of alliance with the Soviet Union and Czechoslovakia against Germany. Such a strategy was, as we have already seen, firmly established in his own mind well before the war. It will become clear as well that close cooperation with the Czechs together with some boundary rectifications were part of his program for Poland's reconstruction from the earliest days of the war. Nonetheless, these policies appear to have taken on definitive shape only sometime in the late fall and winter of 1940-41, fully a year or more after they were first indicated in October 1939. It is here in the detailed shaping of his program that Sikorski appears to have seen in the Pałucki and *Bulletin* proposals the ideal complement to his own strategy. On the one hand, they were compatible with the shift he was seeking to bring about in Poland's policy toward the Soviet Union. At the same time, they promised to strengthen Poland's economic and strategic leverage, thereby reducing the risk of her being reabsorbed into the Russian orbit as she sought security from Germany. As we shall see from the evidence available, the similarities relate to the most crucial aspects of his policy: his coupling of territorial

evidence—including the development of Sikorski's own program, discussed below—suggests that, if the book influenced his thinking at all, he must have been aware of its contents at the earlier date, most likely through Generals Haller and Kukiel.

[30] Both Haller and Kukiel had been associated with Sikorski from their pre-World War I days in Lwów, Haller also in the "Front Morges" in the late 1930s.

[31] The first was the same Colonel Bogusławski mentioned in note 28 above; his article on the Southern Slavs ("Słowianie południowi") appeared in the third issue of the *Bulletin* in February 1941 (pp. 16-23). The second possible channel, though only after mid-1941, was Józef Winiewicz, prewar editor of the *Dziennik Poznański* and an anti-German publicist. Following his arrival in London in May 1941, he joined the staff of the exile government's Bureau of Political, Economic and Legal Studies (Biuro Studiów Politycznych, Ekonomicznych i Prawnych), later renamed the Ministry for Peace Conference Preparations (Ministerstwo Prac Kongresowych). Thereafter he did supply the *Bulletin* with some materials, but did not work closely with it and did not know the identity of the editors. (Perhaps the most serious obstacle to reconstructing the activities and connections of the *Bulletin* group is the fact that many of its contributors, including the coeditors, wrote under pseudonyms; only in one or two cases have I been able to establish their real identities.) Winiewicz was also a personal acquaintance of Count Edward Raczyński, Poland's ambassador in London and, after August 1941, acting foreign minister of the Government-in-Exile; Raczyński, *W sojuszniczym Londynie*, p. 116.

demands with a Polish-Czech federation; his definition of a Polish-German boundary to satisfy the economic and security requirements of the federation; his concept of the federation's internal structure and its relationship to the rest of Central Europe; his emphasis on the permanence of the German threat and on the need, regardless of whatever punitive measures might be taken against her after the war, to prepare for the eventual resurgence of Germany's aggressiveness; his insistence, therefore, on the independence—political, economic, and military—of the Central Europe of the future; and finally, his sense of urgency about the timing of decisions in these matters.

Where differences emerged—and there were differences of both detail and emphasis—they appear to have resulted largely from the fact that General Sikorski, unlike Pałucki or the scholars and journalists of the *Bulletin*, was constrained by political realities of both the intra-Polish and inter-Allied varieties: by the need to resolve Poland's relations with Moscow, a need that was apparent well before Hitler forced the Soviets into the war and that became thereafter increasingly urgent and pervasive in its effect; by the cleavages within the Polish community itself, which tended to delay unpleasant decisions vis-à-vis Moscow and thereby to paralyze all other aspects of Polish policy; and by the reluctance of the British and the Americans to discuss problems of a postwar settlement, especially territorial problems, during wartime. Each of these realities exerted different and often conflicting pressures on Sikorski; and all affected in some measure not only the substance of his programs for regional organization and territorial expansion in the west, but likewise the speed and manner in which he pursued them. In light of the obstacles that he faced, what is surprising is not that there is so little evidence of these programs (and especially his territorial program), nor that the evidence is sometimes conflicting. What is striking under the circumstances is that there is so much evidence, that these programs appear to have been developed so early in the war, and that Sikorski pursued them so doggedly.

THE QUEST FOR "REAL GUARANTEES"

On these questions of Poland's future boundaries and the postwar reorganization of Central Europe, the first phase of the Government-in-Exile is notable less for the detailed proposals it produced than for the framework it established for later policies. That framework was what Sikorski called "real guarantees," a concept that he opposed to the abstract and general guarantees of the Versailles peace. "Had it not been for the mistaken assumption at the Paris conference," read an early government circular:

that the League of Nations Charter would be not only a supplement, *but would remove the need to take into account strategic boundaries and other real guarantees*, the peace of the world would not have been broken so often in the course of twenty-five years, and the development of the League would not have been weakened and hampered. . . . For this reason also, in considering the rebuilding of the League, we shall defend the thesis: *not an international organization instead of real guarantees—but real guarantees to make possible the existence and development of international organizations.*[32]

This theme was to be hammered home again and again, perhaps most forcefully in Sikorski's January 12, 1942, report to the Council of Ministers: "Our security," he declared, "must not be thrown into the melting-pot of general security. Let us have no illusions on this point. The frontiers of future States will be of paramount importance for a long time."[33]

From the outset, the measures suggested by the Poles as "real guarantees" of their security fell into three categories: first, those that would "weaken Germany and render impossible imperialist escapades in the future"; second, and complementarily, those that would assure Poland "the foundations of security based on defensible strategic boundaries"; and third, those that would promote mutually beneficial cooperation among the smaller nations of Central Europe. None of these goals was spelled out in any detail at this stage. On the need to weaken German military potential, early documents (October to December 1939) spoke generally of "a reduction of the territory of Germany in the west and in the east, possibly her division into autonomous units." The only territory specifically mentioned, however, was East Prussia which "must be demilitarized and completely divested of its character as a German military base on the Baltic." Likewise, East Prussia (with Danzig) was the only area specified as essential to Poland's strategic needs, although it was made clear that this was only the most urgent "among other conditions." One of the "other conditions" the Poles had in mind was the incorporation in the southwest of the Oppeln district, or Opole Silesia—i.e., that part of Upper Silesia retained by Germany after World War I. (We should remember that these tentatively voiced claims, far from being novel or surprising, represented nothing more than a revival of Poland's territorial desiderata at the time of Versailles and were, moreover, based on strong ethnic as well as strategic arguments.) Polish conceptions of the future organization of Central Europe also appear to have been embryonic at this stage. While recognizing that the independence of Poland was inseparable from that of Czechoslovakia—

---

[32] Archiwum Ministerstwa Spraw Zagranicznych [AMSZ], pos. Bruksela 1940, "Raporty-Akta 1939-1940"; quoted in Kowalski, *Walka dyplomatyczna*, p. 152 [emphasis added].

[33] *Documents*, 1:265; see also Kukiel, *General Sikorski*, p. 92.

"the fate of Poland was foreclosed from the moment Hitler entered Prague"—
they spoke merely of "very close military cooperation" between the two
countries. At other times they referred to the need for a regional "assem-
blage . . . to create between the Baltic, Black and Adriatic Seas close and
harmonious cooperation of states, to resist the German pressure to the east
and to separate Germany from Russia."[34]

More important perhaps than the occasional particulars that can be gleaned
from these earliest documents was the Sikorski government's view that it
was time "already now [i.e., November 1939] to coordinate war aims and
the structure of Europe with our allies . . . [and] gradually to mold the
opinion of these same circles in the direction of agreeing on the foundations
of a future peace which would assure Poland . . . the foundations of
security."[35] Like the concept of "real guarantees," this sense of urgency
over the need to begin planning for the postwar world was to remain a
constant element of Sikorski's outlook.

Yet over the next year more or less (well into the fall of 1940), the
Poles appear to have made scant progress toward crystallizing their own
program, let alone arriving at a coordinated policy with their allies. The
reasons—or, more precisely, obstacles—were several. Most important in
all probability was the course of the war itself and the political consequences
thereof: the fall of France, the need to reestablish the Government-in-Exile
in London, and to rebuild for the second time in less than a year a Polish
army in the West, as well as the attempt already mentioned to oust Sikorski
from the premiership, reflecting *inter alia* sharp divisions over Poland's
foreign policy orientation. All these matters demanded the immediate attention of Sikorski's government and necessarily relegated longer-range
problems, such as postwar planning, to a back burner. A second reason
was the obvious reluctance of the British to discuss concrete postwar issues
on an official level. Though reportedly sympathetic to the Poles' desire to
rid themselves of the East Prussian enclave, Chamberlain and Halifax told
Polish Foreign Minister Zaleski in October 1939 that "the immediate aim
[of the Allies] . . . —the defeat of Germany—should also be the most
immediate goal of the Poles. . . . The resurrection of the Polish state
[would] depend on the outcome of the war." Hence it was "too early"
to take up boundary proposals.[36]

[34] From various documents in the AMSZ, 1939-1940; as quoted in Kowalski, *Walka
dyplomatyczna*, pp. 148-57; essentially the same material appears also in Kowalski, *ZSRR
a granica*, pp. 19-25.

[35] "Biuletyn Informacyjny MSZ nr 1," November 28, 1939; quoted in Kowalski, *Walka
dyplomatyczna*, p. 149.

[36] AMSZ, dok. S. Litauera; quoted in ibid., p. 153. British sympathy toward Polish claims
to East Prussia may well have been no more than diplomatic courtesy. Ambassador Raczyński

Perhaps for this reason, Sikorski soft-pedaled the question of Poland's postwar reconstruction during his own visit to London the following month, focusing his efforts instead on the more immediate problems of rebuilding a Polish fighting force in the West, establishing the foundation for military cooperation with the British, and in general gaining Poland's acceptance as a full-fledged ally. To the extent that he broached postwar issues at all during his official meetings, he did so obliquely and only in order to establish the principle that Poland should participate in the decisions that were to determine her future. (Hence his request for Polish representation on the Inter-Allied Military Committee was based on the presumption that the Committee would be discussing war aims, and "that the experience of 1919 demonstrates the errors committed as a result of the fact that the question of security in the military sense was not agreed upon prior to the peace conference.")[37]

Undaunted by the cool, even negative, reaction to their official overtures, the Poles pushed ahead with the establishment of an institutional structure for defining and promoting their postwar aspirations. In this they were encouraged, and to a certain extent impelled, by a distinctly more receptive attitude toward such discussions in unofficial or semiofficial British circles. Already in September 1939, the Royal Institute of International Affairs had been moved from London to Balliol College at Oxford where, under the directorship of Arnold Toynbee, it was being reconstituted as a kind of quasi-governmental planning and research arm of the Foreign Office.[38]

---

reported that, when he broached the same issue the following month, Halifax heard him out in silence, having already asked if Hitler's demands with respect to Danzig and the Corridor "hadn't after all been acceptable"; PRM 3/8j, GSHI. The British records of Zaleski's visit make no reference to postwar or territorial questions; see C16373 and C16424/16049/55, FO 371/23159, PRO.

[37] Report of General Sikorski's meeting with Lord Halifax, November 14, 1939; PRM 3/8a, GSHI. The British record of Sikorski's visit, together with appended Foreign Office minutes, also bear witness to the Poles' anxiety over being left out of decisions affecting their vital interests; see esp. C18557 and C18579/27/55, FO 371/23131, PRO.

Although territorial questions were not raised in the official talks, Sikorski did manage to pass along through indirect channels his appreciation of the fact "that the reconstruction of Poland in her pre-war frontiers is very problematic" and that, while it is not yet possible "to have any hard and fast ideas about Poland's future, . . . [should it prove] impossible to recover from Russia what has been lost, he aims at finding compensation elsewhere which would at the same time increase Poland's security." East Prussia is the only area mentioned, and only in the sense of its demilitarization under international control. See the report from Rex Leeper of the Foreign Office's Political Intelligence Department to Assistant Under Secretary Strang, November 25, 1939; C19288/27/55, FO 371/23131. PRO; extracted in *The Great Powers and the Polish Question*, ed. Polonsky, pp. 75-76. See also p. 122 below.

[38] This became the Foreign Research and Press Service (F.R.P.S.) which, sometime in the spring of 1943, was formally integrated into the Foreign Office as its Research Department (F.O.R.D.) and later that year moved back to London. For more details of its work, see pp. 158 and 166 below.

Map 5

The following month two high-level Polish visitors to Oxford concluded that the organization of a comparable Polish research center was "a matter of the greatest urgency," in order not only "to take advantage of the desire expressed on the English side for systematic cooperation" but, more importantly, to influence the development of British thinking, as yet still vague and unformulated, but already showing signs of moving in directions detrimental to Polish interests.[39] The product of these concerns was the Polish Research Centre, organized in the very early months of 1940 and tied through its governing council both to the Polish Embassy in London and the exile Ministry of Foreign Affairs in France, as well as to the Royal Institute itself. Although in no sense a policy-making body, the Centre's mandate covered a wide range of research and public information functions—for example, collecting and distributing information and documentation on Poland, maintaining a library, organizing lecture series, and issuing reports to the media.[40]

At approximately the same time, a second organization was being set up within the framework of the exile government at Angers. This was the so-called Bureau of Political, Economic and Legal Studies (Biuro Studiów Politycznych, Economicznych i Prawnych), later upgraded and renamed as the Ministry for Peace Conference Preparations (Ministerstwo Prac Kongresowych) and to become the agency most responsible for postwar planning. While few if any records from the earliest days of the Bureau's existence have survived, it seems to have turned its attention rather promptly to the need for a more definitive proposal for the future Polish-German frontier. According to one of the principals in this effort, a draft scheduled to be presented to the British and French at a secret tripartite meeting in France on May 10, 1940, foresaw major gains for Poland in the southern and northern sectors—including the Oppeln district and Eastern Pomerania

[39] The two visitors were Władysław Kulski, counselor to the Polish Embassy in London, on October 4th, and the distinguished Polish historian, Oscar Halecki, on the 17th and 18th; for their reports see Polish Government Collection, Box 507, folio: "Polskie Biuro Badań Politycznych," HIWRP. While both noted they had been cordially received and encouraged to set up a comparable Polish organization, both also reported predispositions among some of the principal researchers that were in direct opposition to the trend of Polish thinking. For instance, although William Rose, a long-time friend of Poland, was to head up the Polish section, others (such as the Russophile historian Bernard Pares) were not so well disposed. Both Kulski and Halecki remarked with some dismay on the widespread tendency to regard the Polish-Soviet boundary question as more or less settled, while the latter also noted "a certain fear of imposing on the Germans conditions that were either injurious or excessively irritating."

[40] Correspondence over the period from November 1939 to April 1940, concerning the formation of the Centre, as well as the report of its first meeting on April 11th, is to be found in ibid. For a limited amount of additional material on the Centre's subsequent activities, including a report for the period from March 31, 1940 through December 31, 1941, see a second folio ("Biuro Badań Politycznych"), also in Box 507.

up to a line running south from Kolberg (Kołobrzeg)—plus more modest corrections in the central sector around Poznań. As it happened, the meeting was interrupted, before the Poles had a chance to present their proposal, by news of the German invasion of France. With this the question of Poland's western boundary seems to have vanished from exile counsels for another six months.[41]

By contrast the idea of a regional federation in Central Europe fared rather better, not only among the scholarly planners at Oxford where the concept was being discussed with some enthusiasm, but within the Foreign Office itself. Indeed, at least in the early months of the war, it may have been the British who took the initiative in pressing the idea on the Poles.[42] But here, too, progress was slow—delayed first by internal disorganization and dissension between Czechs and Slovaks, and to a lesser extent by residual distrust between Poles and Czechs. It was only in mid-summer 1940 that an officially recognized Czechoslovak exile government was established. And the joint Polish-Czechoslovak Declaration that followed on November 11, 1940, signified less an agreement of substance on the future relationship of the two governments than a public affirmation of their intention to reach such an agreement.[43]

THE SIKORSKI MEMORANDA

Ironically it was just at this point—that is, November 1940—that we find the first comprehensive statement of Sikorski's conception of a postwar settlement corresponding to Poland's interests and security, here in the form of a memorandum addressed to British Labour Party leader and minister of labour in the War Cabinet, Ernest Bevin. This was followed over the next two years by three additional such statements, each consisting

[41] According to information provided by the late Witold Sworakowski of the Hoover Institution, Stanford University, December 1975. Mitkiewicz (*Z gen. Sikorskim*, p. 15) offers tantalizing but isolated evidence that the Poles were discussing even more far-reaching gains in the west at this early date. In his entry for February 20, 1940, he writes: ". . . in Section III of the General Staff, they (Klimecki, Marecki, Noël) are already seriously pondering the problem of Poland's future boundaries and the solution of the question of East Prussia and Lower Silesia. Our western boundary has according to them several variants: the most extensive reaches to Szczecin [Stettin] and Frankfurt on the Oder as well as Wrocław [Breslau], while maintaining our eastern boundary." He does not refer to the western boundary issue again for more than a year.

[42] Kowalski, *Walka dyplomatyczna*, pp. 153-54, and *ZSRR a granica*, pp. 21-22; also Kukiel, *Generał Sikorski*, p. 99. For an early British view of regional federations that might include Poland, see "The Problem of the Reconstruction of Poland," written in January 1940 by Frank Savery, counselor to the British Embassy to the Polish Government-in-Exile; C1762/116/55, FO 371/24470, PRO. See Chapter X, n. 72, below.

[43] Wandycz, *Czechoslovak-Polish Confederation*, pp. 34-39 and 45; for the text of the joint Declaration, see ibid., pp. 128-29, or *War and Peace Aims*, ed. Holborn, 1:452-53.

of a memorandum or set of memoranda prepared in connection with one of the general's three trips to the United States. For the first and second of these trips—in April 1941 and March 1942—the documentation is incomplete and secondary accounts contradictory. However, for the third and most important visit, in December 1942, we have available the full texts of the several memoranda submitted as well as a variety of supporting primary and secondary materials.

While these four statements differed, often markedly, in detail, tone and emphasis—each reflecting the exigencies of the respective moments—nonetheless all were set in the conceptual framework of "real guarantees" which Sikorski had established in the closing months of 1939. All stressed the need for a compact regional organization to enable the small nations of Central and East-Central Europe to resist German expansionism, in whatever form it might occur in the future; all projected either implicitly or explicitly a substantial shift westwards of Poland's boundary with Germany; all signaled, though in differing degrees, Poland's desire for a long-term reconciliation with the Soviet Union; and, finally, all posited the right of the Central European nations to participate in the decisions that would determine their fate.

November 1940. The Bevin memorandum is of interest not only for what it says (including the first mention in an official Polish document of the Oder River line), but also for its timing and the somewhat irregular manner in which it was presented. Coming as it did immediately after the signing of the preliminary Polish-Czechoslovak agreement of November 11th, one might at first glance assume that the memo reflected growing optimism on Sikorski's part that the climate of British opinion might now be more receptive to his concepts. Certainly the federation idea afforded a more acceptable context within which to express his territorial aspirations in the north and west; for it would allow him to relate these aspirations not merely to Poland's economic and strategic interests, but to those of the Central European region as a whole and especially of Czechoslovakia.

Other developments in the final months of 1940, however, were less auspicious. Growing Nazi-Soviet friction in the East, in and of itself a welcome sign, had had the the unpleasant effect of encouraging the British to intensify their efforts to achieve a rapprochement with Moscow by conceding some of the latter's demands in advance—in this case, de facto recognition of Soviet control over territories seized in 1939-40.[44] In addition, by October at the latest Sikorski had evidence from several quarters

---

[44] See the report of Zaleski's meeting with Halifax, November 18, 1940 (C12458/7177/55, FO 371/24482, PRO) and the follow-up letter from Halifax of November 27th (PRM 20/36, GSHI, reprinted in *Great Powers and the Polish Question*, ed. Polonsky, pp. 78-79); also Chapter IV, note 14, above.

that the tide of British opinion, never all that favorable to Poland, was turning increasingly against him. Particularly alarming was a report early that month of a "striking change" in the attitude of the postwar planning group at Oxford. According to the secretary general of the Polish Research Centre, the "prevailing opinion" there now was that:

> the definition of war aims is definitely not indicated for the present, because this can only play into the hands of the German propaganda machine. Moreover, I was particularly struck by the change of attitude at the institute with respect to the problem of the future reconstruction of Europe: by the disappearance of interest in the questions of European federation . . . about which there was so much talk during the first months of the war last year.

While the issue of "security" was being given highest priority, he added, the tendency was now to separate that issue from territorial, ethnic, or economic questions.[45]

Under the circumstances, then, the November memorandum should probably be viewed in somewhat the same light as the abortive attempt to reopen contacts with the Soviets five months earlier. That is, it was a calculated initiative taken not merely in reaction to a rapidly changing situation, but in an attempt to anticipate and shape future events—or, as the Poles had stated back in November 1939, another attempt "already now to coordinate war aims . . . with our allies" and "gradually to mold the opinion of these same circles in the direction of . . . a future peace which would assure Poland . . . the foundations of security."

That Sikorski should have chosen Bevin as the channel through which to communicate his views was hardly accidental. By this time the Poles had come to regard Halifax, now in his last weeks as foreign secretary, at best as uncomprehending of Polish concerns, and at worst as simply hostile.[46] In the search for a more sympathetic ear, the Labour minister was an obvious choice. Not only was Bevin a firm advocate of regional federations and of greater British involvement with the continent; he was also an acquaintance of Józef Retinger, Sikorski's close (if controversial) friend and adviser. Unquestionably it was Retinger, long associated with British Labour circles, who provided the contact.[47] Moreover, presenting

[45] Letter from Jan Baliński-Jundziłł to Raczyński, October 1, 1940; Polish Government Collection, Box 507, folio: "Polskie Biuro Badań Politycznych," HIWRP.

[46] Anthony Eden replaced Lord Halifax as secretary of state for foreign affairs in December 1940; however, the Poles could take only partial solace from the change as Halifax then became Britain's ambassador to Washington.

[47] Both by virtue of political inclination and marital ties, Retinger had long been well connected in British Labour circles, and apparently had first met Bevin in the 1920s; *Joseph Retinger*, ed. Pomian, p. 69. Prior to submitting his memorandum, Sikorski met with Bevin

his views to someone without formal foreign policy responsibilities no doubt allowed Sikorski to treat the memorandum more as a personal statement, and thus to be more candid and explicit on sensitive issues than he could have been in an official statement of policy passed through normal diplomatic channels. As we shall see, it would be another two years before he would again present his views to the Allies as boldly and explicitly as he did here.

The memorandum itself[48] began with a reiteration and elaboration of central themes of earlier Polish statements. Analyzing first the nature of the German problem, it stressed the geopolitical bases of German expansionism of which Hitlerism "constitutes merely a synthesis of previous German efforts" to establish hegemony over Europe. Only by avoiding the half-measures of the Versailles settlement will Europe be "capable of preventing the unleashing of a third war by Germany." Principal among the errors of Versailles had been the failure to "weaken the objective bases of German power" and the establishment of an international order in which economic considerations were subordinated to abstract political principles that "took little account of reality."

On the subject of the political restructuring of Europe, Sikorski suggested that a logical consequence of the weakening of France and changes in military technology would be greater involvement for Britain on the continent as a counterweight to Germany. But he attached greater significance to self-reliant regional organizations. Unions or federations should be created "only where there exists a community of interest, that is regional unions . . . especially desirable in the case of smaller states which, by entering into regional federations, could become viable partners for the great powers." Such a community of interests exists, he continued, among the nations of Central and Eastern Europe, and not only because of their

---

on November 1st at the former's residence; Retinger appears to have been the only other person present; see PRM 20/26, GSHI. For a further comment on Retinger, see Chapter VIII, note 115, below.

[48] "Memoriał Rządu Polskiego dla Min. Bevina," PRM 20/31, GSHI; for the English version, see C14/14/62, FO 371/26419, PRO. Excerpts included here are translated from the Polish original. This version, preserved among Sikorski's papers cited above, was circulated to a limited group of exile leaders, but only after the memo had been submitted both to Bevin and the Foreign Office. The covering letter merely states that "the Prime Minister has the honor of sending you the enclosed memorandum which has been submitted to Minister Bevin. This memorandum was drafted following a series of conversations with Minister Bevin and other British statesmen." Included on the circulation list are President Raczkiewicz, Foreign Minister Zaleski, and Marian Seyda, the minister in charge of the postwar planning office (Biuro Studiów). Whether or how much they knew about the memorandum in advance is pure conjecture. The copy to Bevin was apparently submitted on November 19th, and a second delivered the following day by Ambassador Raczyński to Cadogan in the Foreign Office; however, it was circulated within the exile government beginning only on the 22nd.

desire to maintain their independence from both Germany and Russia. "These states have many economic and cultural affinities, on the whole rather similar social problems, and could together become a significant factor in the European balance." As to the composition of such a federation, Sikorski admitted that "in today's conditions, it is difficult to prejudge which nations might enter into such a federation; in any event," he continued:

> the nucleus of such a union must be the two states bordering Germany in the east, that is: Poland and Czechoslovakia. Under favorable conditions, the federation could also include Hungary, Rumania, Lithuania and Yugoslavia. . . . Together a bloc of this type would represent not only a large number of people (about 80 million, which would not be small even in comparison with Germany and Russia), but in addition would constitute a union of states . . . with substantial possibilities for economic development. . . . In its striving for a reorganization of postwar Europe, the Polish Government would strive above all to bring about the establishment of a federation of states in Central and Eastern Europe, beginning with Czechoslovakia.

It would not be enough, however, to create a new balance of power in Europe. Measures must also be taken "to so weaken Germany that it would be incapable of unleashing" another war. And here Sikorski listed four such means: a) long-term occupation "for the purpose of instilling in the Germans recognition of the reality of [their] defeat . . . and of making impossible a repetition of the legend . . . of the invincible Germans"; b) "territorial changes in favor of Germany's neighbors to weaken Germany strategically and economically"; c) reparations; and d) certain temporary measures, such as "restoring the autonomy of the German states," to "hinder Germany's military resurrection." The memorandum also outlined essential strategic measures, in particular in the Baltic and North Sea area, to ensure a capacity for immediate reaction to any future German aggression.

It is only at this point, and "only within the framework of the preceding analysis," that the memorandum presented Poland's claims vis-à-vis Germany, stating that "the future Polish State [should] comprise a logical whole, viable, capable of defending its own interests and of playing a positive role in maintaining the European balance." Foremost among Poland's claims was, of course, "a definitive resolution of the centuries-long struggle . . . over Poland's free access to the sea":

> . . . Twice—in the 18th century and presently—Germany has attempted to settle this quarrel by annexing the province of Pomerania

to Germany. From the Polish point of view, the only solution that would prevent the perennial renewal of this quarrel would be the incorporation of East Prussia and Danzig into Poland, which among other things would put an end to constant German claims to the territory between the Reich proper and East Prussia . . . [and] would deprive Germany of the main German outpost in the east, whose only importance for the Reich is that it constitutes a springboard for expansion in the east of Europe. . . . In addition, Poland would not be, as in 1939, threatened by Germany on two fronts, west and north, with the northern front (East Prussia) dominating Poland's central provinces and lying scarcely more than 100 km. from the capital. . . .

Perhaps to suggest that the acquisition of East Prussia should not be viewed as compensation for concessions elsewhere, the memo noted that the province was "an exclusively agricultural area with very poor soils, and [had] always constituted a deficit area economically" for Germany, and that a "significant percentage" of the population was already Polish "by origin or language."

Turning to the question of Poland's western boundary with Germany, the memo pointed to "the strategic necessity of a shortening" of that line and to the desirability "in particular of moving the German boundary away from the Polish ports of Gdynia and Gdańsk [Danzig] as well as from the mouth of Poland's one great river, the Vistula." Although Sikorski did not further specify what boundary the Polish government might favor in the northwest, the next sentence is highly suggestive:

A change of this kind would be justified by the existence on the border regions of Germany of a population either Polish by language or of Polish origin—as well as by the fact that the German territory *to the east of the river Oder*, in particular Prussian Pomerania, is sparsely populated [emphasis added].

Finally, with respect to Silesia in the southwest, the memo declared that this was a "question of equal interest to both Poland and Czechoslovakia, which should jointly present their desiderata in this region," but that in general "the creation of a Union of Poland and Czechoslovakia would demand a shortening" of their respective boundaries with Prussian Silesia. Then, in a formulation that left the way open for claims beyond the Oppeln district, it continued:

In any event, from the Polish point of view, it is essential to call attention to the fact that so-called Prussian Silesia is inhabited to a very significant degree by a population of Polish origin or language.

In addition, the detachment from Germany of this region—a region that comprises one of the most important economic arsenals of German military potential—would be an effective blow to future German aspirations toward hegemony in Europe.

In conclusion, Sikorski acknowledged the enormous difficulties such a radical program would face. His plan, he said, "must be regarded as provisional" in nature; for

> in the present phase of the war, it is not yet possible to perceive clearly whether public opinion would be prepared for undertaking a far-reaching program of European federation immediately after the war. . . . Insofar as one can judge today, public opinion will only gradually be capable of accepting such a broad conception. . . .

Nonetheless, in a passage suggesting that he was anxious to counter the reluctance of Britain's postwar planners to define Allied war aims, the general declared, "it lies in the interest of the Allies that such a plan be carefully prepared and put forth now." Far from providing grist for German propaganda mills as the British feared, an Allied conception of the postwar world was essential to offset the influence of Hitler's New Order, already being "promoted throughout the world."

One final aspect of this memorandum deserving of our attention is what it reveals of Sikorski's attitude toward the Soviet Union. From the standpoint of what is actually said in the memo, that attitude can best be described as ambivalent. While he stated categorically that "Germany would constitute the greatest danger" to his proposed federation, he was clearly opposed also to direct Soviet involvement in the affairs of East-Central Europe. At one point, Russia is described as "a state with primarily Asiatic interests." More to the point, however, was the "uncertainty and traditional changeability of Russian policy" vis-à-vis Germany and the "probability [that] Russia will not be inclined to cooperate in an anti-German balance of power." In this respect the federation, with its more limited but also more constant interests, would be a more reliable element of European equilibrium. "Centuries-long experience," he concluded, "demonstrates that the Russian factor is politically uncertain, and that it is difficult to build on it any kind of political system. . . ."

That Sikorski should at this point have shown such reserve toward Moscow (which after all had yet to retrieve Poland from the dustbin of history) is hardly surprising. Not only were the Soviets still formally allied with Hitler; in the wake of the Russo-Finnish war, Soviet economic and military strength was widely discounted in the West. What is surprising is what was *not* stated in the memorandum: in all of its sixteen pages, there was not one word about Poland's eastern boundary, not one syllable in defense of the Riga Treaty—and that at a time when the British, in their quest for a rapprochement with Moscow, were wavering on these territorial issues.[49] In a number of respects, then, this was a quite remarkable document, devoid of the national egotism and great power pretensions of prewar Polish policy—one which foreshadowed in all important particulars the more detailed program Sikorski was to present two years later, and in which he challenged the Allies to think in terms of new solutions for Europe's problems.[50]

April 1941. Compared with the crisp detail of this memorandum for Bevin, the formulations (or what we know of them) of the one prepared for General Sikorski's first trip to the United States, in April 1941, are disappointingly vague and brief. Adding to the confusion is the fact that existing acccounts of this trip differ on a number of important points,[51] raising the possibility that more than one version of a memorandum was prepared and even that, in the end, none was submitted to the Americans. Yet this seems not to have implied a retreat on Sikorski's part. On the

[49] See note 44 above. In view of the fracas caused by his failure to invoke the Riga Treaty back in June, it is possible that his harsher references to the Soviets here were a trade-off for omission of the boundary question.

[50] The minutes attached to the copy in the Foreign Office file cited in note 48 above indicate that the memorandum met with a fair degree of interest and mixed reviews at the department level. However, it appears to have evoked little more than a patronizing yawn from more senior Foreign Office officials. In a cover note to Cadogan dated January 16, 1941, Assistant Under Secretary Strang wrote: "You have never, I think, seen this tiresome paper. The only thing we can think of doing with it is to circulate it to the War Aims Committee . . ." C741/14/62/, FO 371/26419, PRO. It was in fact printed and circulated, but there is no evidence that it had any impact on British thinking. A further indication of the Foreign Office's inclination to throw cold water on such discussions at this point was the response several months later to Bevin's query about the propriety of his meetings with Sikorski. The initial reaction was "that there is no need to raise any objections to these conversations," although Bevin should make a record of anything "interesting or important." However, on being reminded that the subject of these conversations was "the reorganization of the world [sic] after the war, and [that] some time ago the Poles sent Mr. Bevin a paper on this subject with a copy to Sir A. Cadogan," it was determined that "this sort of thing should not be encouraged." C5693/151/55, FO 371/26718, PRO. In the event, the Bevin-Sikorski meetings did continue, at least on an intermittent basis. For instance, they met on July 3, 1941, just two days before the opening of negotiations between the exile government and Moscow, and again on January 28, 1942, shortly after Sikorski's return from Moscow. (See p. 126 and Chapter X, note 35, below.) But on each occasion the Labour Minister was now accompanied (chaperoned?) by a second British official.

[51] See Ciechanowski, *Defeat in Victory*, pp. 18-22; Kowalski, *Walka dyplomatyczna*, pp. 183-89; Kukiel, *General Sikorski*, pp. 147-53; Mitkiewicz, *Z gen. Sikorskim*, pp. 105-48; Popiel, *Generał Sikorski w mojej pamięci*, pp. 124-34; Terlecki, *Generał ostatniej legendy*, pp. 134-37; and Józef Lipski, Edward Raczyński, and Stanisław Stroński, *Trzy podróże gen. Sikorskiego do Ameryki*, pp. 3-8.

contrary, an analysis of all of the pertinent materials strongly suggests that the discrepancies between his stated positions in November 1940 and April 1941 can be explained by the specific and limited purposes of this trip, and by his reading of the mood and sensitivities of the Americans.

The most extensive account is that of Sikorski's intelligence chief, Leon Mitkiewicz. Moreover, since the latter took part in what he has called the "final revisions" of the memorandum, his is probably the most reliable reflection of Sikorski's thinking at the time. According to his diary entry for March 23rd, the focal point of the prime minister's presentation to President Roosevelt was to be the future political organization of Central Europe:

> Gen. Sikorski's memorandum represents, in general political principles, a plan for the postwar organization of East-Central Europe. In this memorandum [he] develops his idea about the absolute necessity of creating a federation of the nations inhabiting the territory of East-Central Europe between the Baltic and Adriatic as the only fair and just solution capable of assuring peace and security in this part of Europe and, at the same time, of building a durable dam against German aggression to the East and South. General Sikorski argues that the German *Drang nach Osten* cannot be contained by the dispersed forces of weak states, [such as] the eastern and southern neighbors of the German Reich. The General further maintains in this memorandum that an East-Central European Federation, based on the three strongest nations of this region of Europe—Czechoslovakia, Yugoslavia and Poland—would be a sufficiently strong bloc to resist German attempts at territorial and ethnic expansion.[52]

Mitkiewicz did not list all the states Sikorski thought should be included in this bloc, nor did he distinguish between this wider bloc and a Polish-Czechoslovak federation. But according to Jan Ciechanowski, the Polish ambassador to the United States who also acted as interpreter during the Roosevelt-Sikorski conversation on April 8th, the prime minister spoke in terms of "an initial confederation of Poland and Czechoslovakia to which Poland desired to see added the three Baltic States, and, in time, possibly Hungary, Rumania, Greece, and Yugoslavia."[53]

The most important discrepancy among the several accounts of the visit

---

[52] Mitkiewicz, *Z gen. Sikorskim*, pp. 109-110. There is considerable confusion among the sources between the terms "federation" and "confederation," and between "Central" and "East-Central" Europe. In the narrative I have used "federation" and "Central Europe" because these are the terms used in the December 1942 documents for which we do have official texts. In so doing, however, I recognize that Sikorski himself was sometimes inconsistent and vague at this earlier stage.

[53] Ciechanowski, *Defeat in Victory*, p. 19.

arises over the substance of Sikorski's territorial views at this juncture. Only two sources admit that this critical question was even raised: Mitkiewicz and a present-day Polish historian who has written extensively on the "Polish Question" during World War II, W. T. Kowalski. The latter, quoting from a version of the Polish memorandum found in Foreign Ministry archives, has asserted that it "drew attention to the necessity of revising the western boundary of Poland in order to assure favorable conditions for realizing the concept of a Polish-Czechoslovak confederation." He continues:

> Analyzing the problem of Poland's western boundary as established after the First World War, the memorandum pointed to "its absurdity especially in the north and in Upper Silesia." It stressed in this regard that the Versailles Treaty allowed Germany "to exploit Upper Silesia as a military base separating Poland from the Czechoslovak Republic [and] rendering the boundaries of these two states virtually indefensible." Together with the unjust resolution of the problem of East Prussia, the frontiers [laid down by] the Versailles Treaty placed Poland in a hopeless strategic position vis-à-vis Germany.

Kowalski concludes that the implications of this passage—i.e., "the unconditional incorporation into Poland of East Prussia and Opole Silesia"— were "completely unequivocal," but adds that Sikorski did not make these demands explicit because he was not sufficiently familiar with the policy of the then neutral United States.[54]

Where Kowalski would have us believe that there had been during the preceding year absolutely no progress in Sikorski's thinking on territorial issues[55]—indeed, this formula represents a marked retreat from both the proposal prepared for the aborted May 1940 meeting and the Bevin memorandum in November—Mitkiewicz's diary offers an entirely different picture, one more consistent with these earlier positions. "With reference to matters directly touching the Polish state," he wrote, "the General's memorandum contains a justification for the right of the Polish Nation to boundaries in the west embracing all of East Prussia, German Pomerania

[54] Kowalski, *Walka dyplomatyczna*, pp. 185-86; this account appears almost verbatim in his other book, *ZSRR a granica*, pp. 26-27. The passages of this draft cited by Kowalski correspond substantially to several copies of a draft, one corrected in Sikorski's handwriting, among the general's papers; PRM 40b/1, GSHI. The last, especially the passage referring to the boundary with Germany, appears to be more in the form of guidelines for a draft than the actual text; also it does not include the portion beginning "to exploit Upper Silesia . . ." Unfortunately, the copies in the Sikorski Institute are not dated; also, since Western scholars do not have access to Polish state archives dating from September 1, 1939, I have not been able to compare the two texts.

[55] See especially Kowalski, *ZSRR a granica*, p. 50.

and the whole of Silesia, Upper and Lower . . . ."[56] The implications of this passage are equally obvious—that is, a Polish-German boundary running approximately along the Oder and Lusatian Neisse rivers. How to reconcile the apparently enormous discrepancy between two such "unequivocal" accounts? We should remember, first, that Kowalski and Mitkiewicz may have been writing from different drafts of the memorandum; if so, it is probable that Mitkiewicz's was the later one and the one that better reflected Sikorski's own thinking at this time.[57]

Even assuming they were working from the same version however, the conflict may be more apparent than real. Kowalski's suggestion that Sikorski's territorial aspirations were limited here to East Prussia and Opole Silesia is in all probability his own interpretation. (The rough draft of this passage in the copy found among the general's papers uses the vaguer and potentially more expansive formulation: "the incorporation of Prussia and takeover jointly with the Czechs of the Silesian Basin and arsenal.") Likewise, Mitkiewicz has said only that the memorandum provided the "justification" for a boundary embracing the areas listed, not that it explicitly expressed claims to these areas; nor is it clear whether his description represented Sikorski's conclusions or merely his own conclusions based on that "justification." In any event, even using the arguments cited by Kowalski, a close look at a map tends rather to support Mitkiewicz's interpretation, at least along the southern sector of the boundary. For the Silesian wedge, "separating Poland from the Czechoslovak Republic [and] rendering the boundaries of these two states virtually indefensible," was approximately 150 miles long; the incorporation into Poland of the Oppeln district alone would have eliminated less than a third of that wedge and done little to improve the strategic situation of either Poland or Czechoslovakia.

The probable explanation for these contradictory accounts is that Sikorski deliberately left the definition of his territorial program vague in this memorandum. Moreover, it is virtually certain that he did not present his territorial views in *any* form during this first, April 1941, trip to Wash-

[56] Mitkiewicz, *Z gen. Sikorskim*, p. 110. According to Mitkiewicz, the memorandum also included a defense of Poland's prewar eastern boundary, with emphasis on Wilno and Lwów; for discussion, see Chapter VI below.

[57] The pattern in preparing the memoranda for Sikorski's trips appears to have been for a first draft to be drawn up in the appropriate department or ministry; this draft would then be revised by Sikorski together with his closest aides; see Raczyński, *W sojuszniczym Londynie*, pp. 154-55, Kukiel, *Generał Sikorski*, p. 211, and Lipski, Raczyński, and Stroński, *Trzy podróże*, p. 17. Since security within the exile government, and especially within the Foreign Ministry, was less than ideal (e.g. Kot, *Listy z Rosji*, p. 235), it is quite possible that copies of the final drafts were not filed with the ministries. See pp. 190-98 below for additional comments concerning the effect of the opposition on the prime minister's *modus operandi*.

ington.[58] His most pressing reasons for wishing to see President Roosevelt at this time were to secure Lend-Lease aid and permission to recruit Polish-Americans for the Polish Army in Great Britain. While the Polish leader was fully cognizant of the "decisive influence" that the United States would exercise "on the final outcome of this war," he had instructed Ambassador Ciechanowski only a few months before that it was still "too early" to present Washington with detailed proposals. For the present, he continued, "the Polish Government attaches the greatest importance to the creation of a favorable atmosphere both among American officials, as well as within the population at large, for a full appreciation of our actions and goals"—above all by convincing the Americans that Poland was a staunch ally, willing and able to bear her share of the burdens of war, and that the events of September 1939 had "brought about a profound transformation in Poland's domestic and foreign policy," placing her "sincerely and wholeheartedly on the side of democracy."[59] Having been warned in advance that the United States was touchy about its still neutral status (and even advised for this reason not to make the trip), the prime minister clearly feared that he would jeopardize these more immediate military and political goals by pressing territorial issues prematurely.[60]

What is important to our argument at the moment, however, is not whether he actually presented his views to Roosevelt, but the state of development of his own thinking. To this extent we can reasonably con-

[58] Neither the Polish nor the American records of his official talks during this trip make even the slightest reference to territorial questions. Sumner Welles's letter to Roosevelt of April 7, 1941, briefing the president for his meeting with Sikorski the following day, is characteristic. Following mention of Sikorski's interest in recruitment for the Polish Army and Lend-Lease aid, Welles wrote: "He will wish to discuss with you post-war problems in Europe, but only in very general terms. . . . His general thesis is that no peaceful and prosperous Europe can be built up without a political and economic federation between Poland, Czechoslovakia and Hungary—and perhaps Rumania." But Welles gave no indication that Sikorski wished to discuss territorial questions. U.S. Department of State, *Foreign Relations of the United States: Diplomatic Papers* [hereafter *FRUS*], *1941*, 1:232-34. For the Polish record of the general's meetings with Welles and Roosevelt, as well as Ambassador Ciechanowski's report of the visit, see Ciechanowski Deposit, Box 66[84], folio: "Sprawozdanie z pobytu Pana Premiera i Naczelnego Wodza w Stanach Zjednoczonych (6-10/IV/1941)," HIWRP; also PRM 40c, GSHI.

[59] Sikorski's letter of instruction to Ciechanowski, newly appointed ambassador to the United States, January 15, 1941; PRM 40a/2, GSHI. This letter contains one of the most scathing references by Sikorski to the prewar government, in which he states that his government has not openly condemned the foreign policy of the last prewar years only for reasons of national interest. His concern to demonstrate Poland's determination to make the maximum military effort and her commitment to a democratic future runs through all the materials relating to this visit, including the draft memorandum cited in note 54 above.

[60] Mitkiewicz, *Z gen. Sikorskim*, pp. 110-11; and Lipski, Raczyński, Stroński, *Trzy podróże*, pp. 5-7.

clude that, while he may yet have been far from explicitly endorsing an Oder-Neisse line, he was by early 1941 well on the way to laying the foundations for precisely such a boundary proposal.

A second discrepancy concerning this first visit arises over the question of Sikorski's conception of a future federation and of Poland's relative position therein—that is, whether he foresaw for his nation a special role merely as a result of her being a catalyst and by virtue of her undeniably critical geographic location, or because of the presumed superior qualifications of the Poles for leadership. This may seem a subtle distinction. Yet it becomes relevant when one is attempting to draw the line between political concepts reminiscent of the old Polish-Lithuanian Commonwealth, in which the Poles were assumed to have some civilizing mission vis-à-vis less advanced peoples (e.g., Piłsudski's post-World War I plan for a federation with the Ukraine and Lithuania), and, on the other hand, proposals for a genuinely democratic federation in which all members would participate on an equal basis. The first are commonly associated rightly or wrongly with an affirmation of Poland's "great power" status and, in particular, with her eastward expansion and an anti-Russian orientation.[61] Since Sikorski was later accused by the Communists (Polish as well as Soviet) of imperialist pretensions and of spearheading a drive to revive the *cordon sanitaire* around the Soviet Union's western flank—and since such inclinations were prevalent in some exile and Underground quarters—it is important to determine what role he envisioned for Poland in the postwar organization of Central Europe, as well as how he defined its future relationship to the Soviet Union.

While, as we have seen, the Bevin memorandum of the previous November was totally lacking in intimations of a special role for Poland, accounts of this first U.S. trip are inconclusive (although none suggests that Sikorski was ever, at this or any other time, associated with notions of renewed eastward expansion).[62] For example, the draft memorandum

[61] As Wandycz has described Piłsudski's "federalist designs—for want of a better word"— he "wanted to undo the partitions and restore Poland, though in a new form, to her former might. Warsaw was to become the rallying point of smaller states in the East, with Russia driven back to the borders of Peter the Great's reign." *Soviet-Polish Relations*, p. 284. While entirely different from Piłsudski's vision, Foreign Minister Beck's concept of a "Third Europe," briefly discussed in the late 1930s as a solution to the power vacuum in East-Central Europe, was also based on quite different assumptions and goals from Sikorski's. For a detailed discussion of Beck's views, see Cienciala, *Poland and the Western Powers*, pp. 55-56 and 149-76.

[62] In an isolated and curious entry from February 1940, Mitkiewicz (*Z gen. Sikorskim*, p. 15) wrote: "As for our East, the views of our strategists from section III [of the General Staff] are very hazy. Possibly a federation composed of: Lithuania, Belorussia, the Ukraine, Poland, Czechoslovakia—and perhaps Hungary." He did not associate Sikorski with this

cited by Kowalski contains the following passage, which might easily leave the reader with the impression that the prime minister saw Poland in the role of *primus inter pares*:

> "In the international arena, the role of crystallizing agent in East-Central Europe will fall to Poland as the only one apparently capable of fulfilling [that role] in this part of the world. . . . Poland is, therefore, the key to equilibrium in East-Central Europe. She is the guarantee of the independence of the states situated between Russia and Germany and should be treated as such in the future, if the United States were not to have to intervene militarily every twenty-five years to salvage the peace and defend Europe."[63]

The draft makes no further reference to the relationship between a future Central European organization and the Soviet Union, but merely states that "the present [Polish] Government . . . recognizes sincerely and loyally the principle of peaceful cooperation with Russia." On the other hand, in defending Poland's right to her prewar eastern territories, it repeats the reference made in the Bevin memorandum to Russia's predominantly "Asiatic" character.[64] Kukiel, too, extracting from various speeches and press conferences during the trip, has quoted Sikorski as declaring among other things that there would be "several federated blocs" in the new Europe, with Poland as "one of the cornerstones of this structure"; and again that "Poland will be the core of the federation in the East, in accordance with her more than 500-year tradition."[65]

In contrast, Mitkiewicz's account of the preparations for the trip gives no indication that Sikorski implied for Poland any special leadership role apart from the undeniable fact that she, along with the Czechs and Yugoslavs, was one of the "three strongest nations of this region."[66] Likewise, Ciechanowski, whose account is concerned primarily with Sikorski's meetings with President Roosevelt and other officials, has suggested only that the prime minister "came as the spokesman of the smaller European Powers" and that he was "the first European . . . boldly to present in Washington the case of postwar Europe . . . the first to initiate the idea of European federation as the best way of creating political and economic

---

"hazy" notion, and he never mentioned it again. Even Kowalski, who views Sikorski's federation concept as "an anti-communist *cordon sanitaire*" (*Walka dyplomatyczna*, p. 289), does not suggest that he favored any eastward expansion.

[63] Kowalski, *Walka dyplomatyczna*, pp. 185-86, and *ZSRR a granica*, p. 26; this passage appears verbatim in the rough draft found among Sikorski's papers (note 54 above).

[64] These passages are not mentioned by Kowalski, but do appear in the rough draft.

[65] Kukiel, *Generał Sikorski*, p. 150.

[66] Mitkiewicz, *Z gen. Sikorskim*, p. 110.

security.''[67] Even more intriguing is Mitkiewicz's handling of the proposed federation's relationship with the Great Powers—including with the Soviet Union.

> General Sikorski . . . [writes] that, for the durability of the Federation's existence and for the securing of peace in Europe, it is indispensable that the new East-Central European Federation be tied by solid political, military and economic alliances with the Western Powers: [with] England, France and the United States, *as well as in the same degree with the Soviet Union.*[68]

Like the omission of the eastern boundary question in the Bevin memorandum, this last point is of interest as yet one more hint of Sikorski's flexibility toward Moscow well before "Operation Barbarossa."[69]

As with the contradictory interpretations of his territorial program, the most likely explanation for the confusion over Sikorski's approach to federation was the conflicting pressures under which he was operating. We should keep in mind that many of his statements on Poland's and the federation's future, both during this trip and later, were public remarks made largely to Polish audiences (from which he was hoping to recruit thousands of soldiers and among which he had constantly to be on guard against the opposition).[70] Moreover, as Kukiel has emphasized, Sikorski was anxious on this first trip to dispel the legacy of years of German propaganda to the effect that "Poland is a *Saisonstaat* for which there will be no place in the future Europe, and the Poles a romantic and capricious people capable only of causing humanity trouble."[71] In such circumstances, it was perhaps natural, if in retrospect unfortunate, for the exile leader to invoke his nation's grander past.

March 1942. The discrepancies among the several accounts of Sikorski's second American trip, in March of 1942, are if anything even greater than those concerning the first, at least insofar as the western boundary is concerned. Once again, virtually all sources fail to mention the existence of any memorandum, much less one specifying a future boundary with

---

[67] Ciechanowski, *Defeat in Victory*, pp. 18-19.

[68] Mitkiewicz, *Z gen. Sikorskim*, p. 110 [emphasis added].

[69] Although most of the materials relating to this visit make no reference to the subject, future Polish-Soviet relations were clearly on the general's mind. Both his instructions to Ambassador Ciechanowski of the previous January (PRM 40a/2, GSHI) and his request for a summary of topics for his meetings with Welles and Roosevelt (PRM 40b/2, GSHI) indicate a willingness to work out a compromise settlement with Moscow.

[70] Concerning the activities of the well-organized anti-Sikorski opposition among Poles in the United States, see Popiel, *Generał Sikorski w mojej pamięci*, pp. 127-30.

[71] Kukiel, *Generał Sikorski*, p. 150.

Germany; and once again, it is almost certain that no such memorandum was submitted to the Americans. Instead, accounts of the conversations that Sikorski and Foreign Minister Raczyński (who preceded the general to Washington by six weeks) had with Roosevelt, Under Secretary of State Sumner Welles, and other State Department officials, are almost entirely devoted to the question of *Soviet* territorial demands in the east and to the Poles' plea for an evenhanded observance of the Atlantic Charter.[72] Yet, it is equally certain that a memorandum was prepared—and even, as before, that there was more than one draft.

One version, which has perhaps done more than any other single document to obscure Sikorski's position on the western boundary, surfaced five years later on the pages of the London *Observer*. Writing at the time of the April 1947 Moscow Conference of Foreign Ministers, at which the possibility of revising the Oder-Neisse boundary in Germany's favor was being discussed, the *Observer*'s diplomatic correspondent suggested that the proposals then made by U.S. Secretary of State George Marshall bore a ''striking'' resemblance to those presented to Roosevelt by General Sikorski during the latter's March 1942 visit to Washington. And he summarized those proposals as follows:

1. East Prussia to be divided between Lithuania and Poland, giving the northeastern part with Insterburg [since 1945 Cherniakovsk] to Lithuania, the bulk of the province, with Koenigsberg [Kaliningrad], to Poland.

2. Frontier rectifications in Poland's favour in the northeastern part of Pomerania and West Prussia, moving the Polish frontier roughly to the area of Stolpmunde [Słupsk].

3. The upper Silesian coal basin and industrial area around Gleiwitz and Oppeln (roughly the plebiscite area of 1921) either to be divided between Poland and Czechoslovakia, or (preferably) to be united with Polish Upper Silesia and Teschen as a Polish-Czechoslovak economic condominium, possibly under some form of international industrial supervision.

[72] Ciechanowski, *Defeat in Victory*, pp. 93-103; Lipski, Raczyński, Stroński, *Trzy podróże*, pp. 9-15; Kukiel, *Genrał Sikorski*, pp. 194-97; Raczyński, *W sojuszniczym Londynie*, pp. 134-38; *Documents*, 1:310-12; *FRUS, 1942*, 3:111-16 and 123-33; and Mitkiewicz, *Z gen. Sikorskim*, pp. 216-41. Of these, only the last mentions the western boundary or a memorandum. The detailed reports of Raczynski's and Sikorski's numerous talks with American officials during this visit fully reflect this emphasis; see Ciechanowski Deposit, Box 67[84], folios: ''Amb. E. Raczyński w Washingtonie (II-III/1942),'' and ''Gen. W. Sikorski w USA (III-IV/1942),'' HIWRP; and Polish Government Collection, Box 424, folio: ''Stosunki Polsko-Amerykańskie: podróż Ministra Spraw Zagr. i Premiera, 1941-1942r,'' HIWRP.

"These demands," commented the writer, "represented the considered policy of the Polish Government . . . [which] deliberately abstained from more far-reaching claims in the considered interest of Poland herself."[73]

How the *Observer* came into possession of this version is not made clear. However, the fact that this rather than the later December memorandum surfaced at this particular time raises the suspicion that it was a politically motivated leak. After Sikorski's death, and especially after it became clear that the British and Americans did not favor pushing Poland as far west as the Oder-Neisse, the London Poles took great pains to deny that they had ever presented such extensive demands, and therefore, had an interest in leaking this version as the final and "considered" position of the Sikorski government. Moreover, while this may well have been *a* draft of the March memorandum, it is worth pointing out that point 2 would have accorded the Poles less than half of the additional territory in eastern Pomerania that they had been prepared to ask for as much as two years earlier, in May of 1940.[74]

Once again it is Mitkiewicz's diary that provides a quite different picture. In contrast to the emphasis in other accounts on the decidedly defensive purpose of this second trip, Mitkiewicz's account of the preparatory discussions indicates that Sikorski's mind was equally absorbed with the further "definition of Poland's . . . war aims and the postwar organization of Europe." In particular, his views on the proposed Central European federation, as an alternative to a general international organization on the post-World War I model, appear to have matured in the course of the preceding year—and in a direction strongly reminiscent of the programs set forth by the *West-Slavonic Bulletin* and Pałucki's *Return to the Oder*. Mitkiewicz has summarized Sikorski's views as the latter presented them to him orally in late February 1942:

"The postwar organization of the world should not, following the conclusion of this war, stop with the repetition of the idealistic theories of . . . President Wilson concerning the existence of a *Treuga Dei*

[73] *Observer* (London, April 13, 1947); quoted in *The Genesis of the Oder-Neisse Line in the Diplomatic Negotiations during World War II: Sources and Documents*, comp. and ed. Gotthold Rhode and Wolfgang Wagner, pp. 16-17. The editors were apparently unaware that a memo had been prepared for the March trip and suggested that the *Observer* correspondent had erred and that this proposal had been presented during Sikorski's third visit in December 1942, thus further confusing the issue. I have been able to find no trace of this memorandum in either the Polish or American archives.

[74] One possibility is that this was a draft prepared by the Biuro Studiów, headed by Dr. Marian Seyda who, while he concurred with Sikorski's overall strategy vis-à-vis Germany, believed that Poland could not afford such extensive claims as the Oder or Oder-Neisse line. Seyda's views are discussed below, pp. 269-70.

among all peoples, or with the creation of a new League of Nations stripped of the power to impose respect for established laws. . . . After this war, it is essential to prepare for and create such an international organization that peace will be genuine and will not be broken for a long time. . . . Cooperation among the three great powers of the world following the conclusion of this war . . . represents the only possibility of safeguarding the peace. Likewise, all the lesser and small nations should be included in this cooperation. To assure their participation in international affairs and to keep the great powers from using [the smaller nations'] forces for their own purposes, it is necessary that the lesser and small nations be joined in regional groupings. These groupings should be created on the basis of common economic interests and similarities, or of a cultural community. The most desirable solution for the region of East-Central Europe would be a federation, whose core would be Czechoslovakia, Poland and possibly Yugoslavia. The joining of the economic wealth and forces of Czechoslovakia and Poland, based on broad access to the Baltic Sea and possibly to the Adriatic, and their central position in Europe would result in a well-conceived Federation which would become an important element of economic and political stability for all of postwar Europe.''

Once again it was German expansionism that had to be contained:

''In the first instance it is necessary that Germany, as the state and nation which twice in the course of a quarter century has caused a world war, be permanently deprived of the bases of existence as a great power; . . . The pacification of Germany can ensure a long peace in Europe.''

Concerning relations with the Soviet Union, on the other hand, Sikorski's memorandum, far from suggesting a *cordon sanitaire*, recommended that:

''The present situation, when as a result of the German attack Soviet Russia has perforce become an ally of the Western Democracies, should be exploited above all to draw . . . [her] out of isolation. Only the genuine and fullest possible participation of the peoples of the Soviet Union in the international life organized after this war can guarantee that Soviet Russia will not in the future be an adversary of the western powers . . .''[75]

A second conversation several days later, as recorded in Mitkiewicz's diary entry for March 5th, provides some of the most interesting insights

[75] Mitkiewicz, *Z gen. Sikorskim*, pp. 216-17 [entry for February 24, 1942]; the quotation marks are in the original.

we have into the nature of the relationship Sikorski foresaw with the Soviet Union, and into his understanding of the revolutionary consequences of Poland's new political and territorial orientation for both domestic and foreign policies. "Above all," wrote Mitkiewicz, "General Sikorski regards as a cardinal condition for an understanding with Russia her approval of the [East-Central European] Federation." Assuming such approval:

> This Confederation—for this is how the General designated it—would conclude a military-political alliance with the Soviet Union against Germany, *and would be obligated to carry out appropriate changes in its internal life and in foreign policy, while continuing to remain in the democratic system.*

By now, according to this account, Sikorski had come to the realization that one such "appropriate" change had to be substantial concessions along the Polish-Soviet boundary in the east (a point that will be explored in the next chapter). "But," Mitkiewicz continued, "another aspect of this solution is extremely important—namely [that]:

> the alliance with Soviet Russia and the union with Czechoslovakia, as well as the change in the western boundary at the expense of former German lands, *would turn Poland together with the whole Federation with its front expressly toward the West, against Germany, and would delineate new directions for internal and external policy.*

Primary among Poland's tasks—and opportunities—would be her economic restructuring:

> For Poland, the absorption of the annexed western regions and the reconstruction of wartime destruction, together with the remodeling of our system, would be tasks for an estimated two to three generations at least. First among Poland's economic tasks should be the balancing of the uneconomic state of agriculture with the industrialization of the country in the new favorable conditions. General Sikorski told us that he strongly believes that this program will succeed, despite all difficulties.[76]

The implications of these passages for Poland's future western boundary were very broad indeed, going far beyond the specific but limited territorial demands mentioned in the *Observer* version of the March memorandum. (In fact, the only thing these two versions seem to have in common is the link between a boundary settlement and the proposed Polish-Czech federation.) First, the reference to turning Poland's "front expressly toward the West" is meaningful only if it is understood to imply the elimination

[76] Ibid., pp. 221-22 [emphasis added].

of the "Silesian wedge" between Poland and Czechoslovakia *and* the incorporation into Poland of the entire course of the Oder as the natural and shortest outlet to the west for the Silesian-Moravian industrial basin. In other words, the Oppeln district, Lower Silesia at least up to Breslau, and all of Pomerania westward to the lower Oder with its port at Stettin. Likewise, the reference to "balancing the uneconomic state of agriculture with the industrialization of the country in the new favorable conditions" leads to more or less the same conclusion. The incorporation merely of East Prussia (a poor and predominantly agricultural region) and the Oppeln district, for example, would have been insufficient to bring about this kind of transformation—with or without the small slice of eastern Pomerania foreseen in the *Observer* version.

These tentative conclusions are supported by a statement Sikorski himself made several months before his Washington trip, in which he expressed the hope that the "balance of forces in the ultimate stage of the war . . . will be to our advantage, and that the Polish State will expand its western frontiers." "It is history that pushes us in this direction," he continued,

> providing us with a unique occasion for putting right old wrongs and mistakes and enabling us to reinforce our strategic position in the West, to stem the perennial German drive to the East and to force it back. We shall have to do our utmost in this period in order to lay a firm foundation for a strong Poland, . . . by regaining old Slav territories, with wide access to the sea, and secure from the military point of view.[77]

Yet, despite the bold and sweeping references in this speech as well as in the preparatory discussions, Mitkiewicz's account indicates that the final version of the memorandum for this second visit with Roosevelt made only oblique references to Poland's territorial aspirations in the north and west,

---

[77] From Sikorski's report of the Council of Ministers, January 12, 1942; in *Documents*, 1:264. Several weeks later, in a context suggesting that Sikorski was making a discreet attempt to sound out British views on Poland's future western boundary, he told Churchill that Stalin had "declared to [him] that Poland must arise larger and stronger than before, that East Prussia must belong to Poland, that the Polish Western boundaries must be based on the river Oder. Stalin's tendency to push Poland to the West was obvious." Ibid., p. 274. This is the source of the notion that it was Stalin who gave Sikorski the idea of a boundary on the Oder; see, e.g., Heinz Günther Sasse, "The Prelude to the Expulsions and Oder-Neisse Line from 1939-1945," in *Eastern Germany: A Handbook*, Vol. II: *History*, ed. Göttinger Arbeitskreis, p. 379. We shall take up later the somewhat different and more troublesome question of whether Stalin actually offered Sikorski such a boundary (see pp. 245-60 below). For the moment, it is enough to note that the Oder concept was sufficiently prevalent in London and Underground circles that Sikorski did not have to go to Moscow to hear about it.

to the effect that "it is necessary that Germany . . . be permanently deprived of the bases of existence as a great power" and that "the joining of Czechoslovakia and Poland [be] based on broad access to the Baltic Sea."[78]

The source of the apparent contradiction, however, lies not so much in inconsistencies of policy as in the conflicting pressures to which the Sikorski government was increasingly subject in this period. Where the general's mood at the time of his first trip to Washington had been one of cautious optimism and initiative, his outlook a year later was distinctly more defensive. The intervening year had witnessed a number of changes in the situation of the exile government—some seemingly auspicious for the future of his program, others threatening to undermine that program before these favorable developments could bear fruit. Most important were the changes brought about by the German attack on Russia. The Polish-Soviet Agreement that followed at the end of July 1941 had yet to lead to the genuine rapprochement hoped for. To be sure, diplomatic relations had been restored and the promised amnesty at least partially carried out. But the Polish Army on which Sikorski was pinning his greatest hopes was experiencing mounting food and equipment problems; and its failure to go into action on the Russian front was jeopardizing the all too modest improvement in political relations between the two governments. The prime minister's December 1941 visit to Moscow had seemed to smooth over most of the military difficulties. Although Stalin had initially pressed for a settlement of the outstanding boundary issue, he later relented, saying they could discuss the matter later once Poland's army had gone into battle and professing to want to see a large and strong Poland in the future. But on his return to London, Sikorski learned that the Russian dictator had turned around and demanded from the British immediate recognition of the Soviet Union's 1941 frontiers. The British, embarrassed at their inability to relieve the Russian front and fearful lest Stalin conclude a separate peace, were inclined to give in. The Polish-Soviet boundary was to be excluded from the proposed Anglo-Soviet treaty. But the Poles understandably felt that recognition of the Soviet annexation of the three Baltic States, together with the two Rumanian areas of Bessarabia and Bukovina, would prejudice in advance the status of their own eastern provinces and possibly even undermine their program for Central Europe. Indeed, after a brief interlude of more or less benevolent neutrality, the Soviets had begun to voice their displeasure at the prospect of a Polish-Czech federation which otherwise had been making substantial, if uneven progress.

At the same time, the fact that the United States was now a belligerent

---

[78] Mitkiewicz, *Z gen. Sikorskim*, pp. 216-17; this is his phrasing rather than a quote from the memorandum.

had not improved the outlook for gaining support there. On the contrary, American policy on territorial questions had hardened into a set of abstract principles, whose strictures against territorial aggrandizement and reen-thronement of self-determination-by-plebiscite were diametrically opposed to the concept of "real guarantees" on which the Sikorski government's policy was based. And while the British were leaning toward making an exception in the case of Soviet "security requirements," they were stead-fast in refusing to discuss the similar requirements of the Poles.

The effect of these countervailing pressures, which all came to bear in the first months of 1942, was to put the Polish exile leader in the paradoxical position of having to rely in the short run on a policy he knew to be a serious obstacle to his long-range strategy—i.e., the Atlantic Charter. On the one hand, the need to reach as soon as possible an overall political accommodation with the Soviet Union made it imperative to push ahead with his postwar program and, in particular, to gain approval for an ad-equate territorial settlement on Poland's northern and western flanks. To acquiesce in the former, which by now he understood would involve concessions in the east, without a firm commitment on the latter would leave Poland in a geographical limbo and bound by a principle that did not promise her an adequate settlement in the future. On the other hand, if he was to stave off the pending Anglo-Soviet treaty to gain the time he felt he needed, he had to invoke in the short run the very Atlantic Charter principles for "self-determination" and against "territorial aggrandize-ment" that posed such a threat to his long-term hopes.

In the end, he chose the latter course. Hence the defensive tone of most accounts of his Washington talks. Hence also the fact that even the sanitized version of his territorial aspirations was in all probability never presented.[79]

Finally, and before passing on to the third and final trip, we should take note of several developments in Sikorski's conception of the composition

---

[79] The only memorandum prepared for this trip that I have been able to locate in the archives is one drafted by the Ministry of Finance with the participation of the Foreign Ministry, and is clearly not the one referred to by either the *Observer* correspondent or Mitkiewicz—although it is closer in scope and tone to the latter's account. In Polish and twenty-one pages long, this memo says nothing about boundaries or security per se, but focuses instead on the urgency of remedying the economic underdevelopment of the countries of East-Central Europe as the only means of permanently ending their vulnerability to German domination. The memo is accompanied by a draft of a covering letter to the U.S. secretary of state with instructions, dated March 13, 1942, from the Foreign Ministry in London to the embassy in Washington to prepare a translation in advance of Sikorski's arrival, and to send back to London three copies of the final text "following its submission to the Department of State." Ciechanowski Deposit, Box 67[84], folio: "Gen. W. Sikorski w USA (III-IV/1942), II," HIWRP. However, no translation of this memo was found, and there is no evidence whatever that it was submitted to the Americans.

and internal structure of a Central European federation, all of which appear to reflect the influence of the "West-Slavonic" group as well as the pressure of events. In the north, as part of his developing strategy of compromise with the Soviets, Polish proposals spoke now in terms of including only Lithuania of the three Baltic States.[80] In the south, he seemed uncertain whether Yugoslavia should be part of a single federation with the northern tier of states, or should be the core of a "Southern European Federation" with which the northern tier would be united by alliance.[81] In any event Sikorski now seemed to be making a distinction, in the manner of the *Bulletin* program, between a special Polish-Czechoslovak relationship and the broader regional organization, in terms not only of timing but more particularly of the degree of economic unity anticipated.[82] Moreover, whatever residue of Polish chauvinism had marked earlier statements on the federation—the notion of Poland's "special mission" or leadership role bestowed by virtue of past grandeur—no such overtones were evident in the draft Constitutional Act presented by the Poles to the joint Polish-Czechoslovak Coordinating committee in the fall of 1941. On the contrary, while proposing gradual integration rather than mere coordination of policies, it nevertheless included elaborate checks and balances to protect the small nations from domination by the larger (Poland being the most populous state in Central Europe).[83]

December 1942. This brings us back, finally, to our starting point—the memorandum on Poland's western boundaries that General Sikorski brought with him on his third trip to Washington.[84] By now it should be apparent

---

[80] Emphasis on the importance of Lithuania, as distinct from Latvia or Estonia, to Poland's security was also apparent in the talks Raczyński and Sikorski had in Washington. See *Documents*, 1:310-12; *FRUS, 1942*, 3:112-13; and Kukiel, *Generał Sikorski*, p. 196. Ciechanowski (*Defeat in Victory*, pp. 93-103) does not make this distinction.

[81] Mitkiewicz (*Z gen. Sikorskim*, p. 221) admits that the confusion could be his. Earlier, in a July 1941 meeting with Eden, Sikorski related that he had discussed with the Yugoslav prime minister and foreign minister "the possibilities of creating federal blocs of countries in Central Europe which would provide mutual support for each other. One of such blocs would have Poland as its core and the other would be a Balkan bloc." *Documents*, 1:114. (In January 1942, Yugoslavia and Greece had signed a preliminary agreement to form a Balkan Federation.)

[82] Mitkiewicz, *Z gen. Sikorskim*, pp. 216-17 and 221-22.

[83] For a discussion of the Polish draft, see Wandycz, *Czechoslovak-Polish Confederation*, pp. 61-65.

[84] See pp. 3-4 above. That this time the memorandum was actually submitted to the Americans is indicated by the handwritten notes, summarizing its key points, located among the records of the Department of State in the National Archives in Washington. Although undated and unsigned, the notes are clipped to a December 7th memo (also related to Sikorski's visit) from Under Secretary Welles to Ray Atherton, then acting chief of the Division of

that the new element in his policy was not the substance of the memorandum, which was merely the logical outgrowth of the strategy developed over the preceding three years, but the forthrightness of his approach to the Americans. One need not look far for the reasons behind this change. Where at the time of his first trip Sikorski had been hopeful about the prospects for his program and, at the time of the second, somewhat defensive, by December 1942 his situation was fast becoming desperate. It was this desperation, rather than any change in Washington's policy of deferring consideration of territorial and other postwar issues, that accounts for the boldness of Sikorski's presentation.

The most serious blow to his program had been the final evacuation of the Polish Army from the Soviet Union the previous summer. The withdrawal had come about against his wishes and under circumstances that gave the Soviets ample excuse to prohibit further recruitment and to shut down the aid program for Polish civilian deportees. Not surprisingly, the deterioration of Polish-Soviet relations had led to a suspension of Polish-Czech negotiations toward the planned federation, which had always been dependent on at least the tacit approval of Moscow. Moreover, while the British-Soviet negotiations of the previous spring had not led, as the Poles feared, to recognition of the Russians' 1939-40 conquests, the continued failure of the western Allies to open a second front in Europe gave the Soviet Union a psychological advantage in renewing its boundary demands. In these circumstances, Sikorski felt that the only hope of salvaging his carefully balanced strategy was to negotiate all outstanding differences directly with Stalin; yet he also knew he would have little chance of reaching an acceptable agreement without the staunch support of the British and Americans, and especially without a reasonable assurance that an arrangement arrived at with Stalin would be respected at a future peace conference. So it is hardly surprising that, as Polish-Soviet relations continued to deteriorate during the summer and fall of 1942, Sikorski decided to do what he had abstained from doing in March—to journey yet again to Washington, this time to lay his whole program before the Americans in a last desperate effort to solicit their support before undertaking talks with the Russians.[85]

European Affairs [U.S. Department of State Decimal File, 1940-1944: 860C.014/12-842, NA]; it was Atherton to whom the several memoranda submitted by the Polish prime minister at this time were transmitted for analysis and comment. See also the Polish records of Sikorski's meetings with Welles on December 4, 1942 and January 4, 1943, where reference is made to the memoranda; Ciechanowski Deposit, Box 67[84], folio: "Raporty podczas pobytu Premiera Generała Sikorskiego w USA (1.XII.1942-10.I.1943)," HIWRP.

[85] See, e.g., Mitkiewicz, *Z gen. Sikorskim*, pp. 295 and 302-304; Raczyński, *W sojuszniczym Londynie*, p. 161; and *Documents* 1:457-58. Sikorski originally wanted to make the trip in October, but was put off by Washington until after the congressional elections; see *FRUS, 1942*, 3:189-90.

The brief memorandum reproduced at the beginning of Chapter I was not the only one submitted to Under Secretary of State Sumner Welles in that first week of December. It was in fact a summary of three much longer memoranda, each one elaborating on one of the three paragraphs of the shorter document: 1) "The German Problem with Special Relation to Poland," a twenty-one-page defense of Poland's territorial claims in the west and north; 2) "Measures to be Applied to Germany Immediately after Cessation of Hostilities," corresponding to paragraph 2 and discussing the truce and occupation conditions to be imposed on Germany; and 3) "The Problem of Central and South-Eastern Europe," corresponding to paragraph 3 and elaborating on the proposed federation.[86] (In addition, the general submitted at least three other memoranda during the course of his stay: one concerning Poland's eastern boundary which had, like the above three, been prepared in advance of the trip but was submitted only several weeks after the others; and two others, on internal French politics and postwar reconstruction, which were apparently solicited by President Roosevelt during their first meeting on December 2nd.)[87]

At this point there would seem to be little need for a lengthy analysis

[86] The English translations of all four memoranda are located in the Ciechanowski Deposit, Box 93[84], folio: "General Sikorski's visit in Washington, Dec. 1942 to Jan. 10, 1943," HIWRP. Of the longer memoranda, at least the first and third were also submitted to the British Foreign Office, on December 1st and 17th respectively; C12169 and C12841/464/55, FO 371/31091, PRO. The longer memoranda were all drawn up in advance, with first drafts originating in the Ministry for Peace Conference Preparations, most likely by the beginning of November 1942. (The old Bureau of Political, Economic and Legal Studies had been upgraded into a separate ministry the previous July.) Polish versions of the second and third memos, on truce conditions and the federation, are located in the Ciechanowski Deposit, Box 33, folio: "Ministerstwo Prac Kongresowych," HIWRP; both were delivered to Welles on December 7th, and were apparently also distributed in late November to Polish diplomatic missions together with several other position papers; see the Foreign Ministry circular of November 27, 1942, Polish Government Collection, Box 507, folio: "Prace przygotowawcze do konferencji pokojowej," HIWRP. By contrast, the first memo ("The German Problem . . ."), which was submitted to Welles on December 4th and then resubmitted with slight revisions on the 31st, was not so distributed. An early Polish draft, marked "secret!" and entitled simply "Aide Mémoire," is located in the Polish Government Collection, Box 976, folio: "Western Boundaries of Poland, 1942," HIWRP. It seems likely that the brief summary memo was drawn up after Sikorski's arrival in Washington, possibly in response to a request from the American side. Ironically, except for the handwritten notes on this summary (see note 84) and the slightly revised draft of the longer boundary memo submitted on December 31st [State Decimal File: 740.0011 European War 1939/26860-1/2, NA], none of these documents has turned up in the State Department Archives; but this is only one of several anomalies in the documentation of this visit.

[87] The memorandum on the eastern boundary is discussed on p. 134 below. Concerning the origin of the other two, see "Note of a conference with President Roosevelt, December 2, 1942," A.XII.23/4: "Trzecia podróż amerykańska," folio 1, no. 5, GSHI. For a rather snide and confused accounting of the materials submitted by Sikorski, see Pobóg-Malinowski, *Najnowsza historia*, 3:245, n. 72, and 247, n. 78.

of these documents; the premises and basic outlines of Sikorski's program had remained constant at least since the November 1940 memo to Bevin. Rather I shall limit myself to highlighting those points over which there has been the most controversy, as well as the striking similarity of Sikorski's vision for Central Europe at its moment of greatest articulation to the program put forth two years earlier by the *West-Slavonic Bulletin.*

Perhaps the issue that has evoked the greatest amount of confusion and controversy is whether, in presenting an Oder-Lusatian Neisse demarcation line, Sikorski intended it as a future Polish-German boundary or merely as the westernmost limit of Polish or Polish-Czech occupation. While it is true that paragraph 2 of the summary "Western Boundaries" memo presents it as a line of occupation—"in connection [with the problem of occupation] the range of our (federated Poland's) interests includes: (a) the zone up to the Oder and Lusatian Neisse with bridgeheads on the left bank . . ."—paragraph 1 would seem to justify the outright incorporation of these areas on grounds of economic necessity and strategic security, and in words that recall the admonitions of the 1940 Bevin memo concerning the need to "weaken the objective bases of German power":

> I. Our approach to the problem of the western boundaries is dictated by the necessity of: . . .
> —control over the mouth of the Oder, which possesses paramount importance for the federation as the artery directly linking our common center of Silesian industry with the sea; . . .
> —the creation of conditions for our effective and rapid intervention against Germany should it attempt to remilitarize. In this regard, Western Pomerania based on the lower Oder and, secondly, the northwestern part of the Sudetes with an outlet toward Leipzig are of paramount importance for the federation.

The memorandum on "Measures to be Applied to Germany Immediately after Cessation of Hostilities" repeated the Oder-Lusatian Neisse formula, and in a context that suggested it was meant to be the future boundary line. After describing the principles that should govern the occupation of central Germany, it continued:

> Apart from the . . . [area of] general occupation, *"strict occupation" is foreseen for territories of Germany in her frontier zones. This term is used to define territories the incorporation of which into other States is foreseen*, or . . . the occupation of which is indispensable from the military viewpoint to exact by force the strict execution of imposed conditions.
> II. Such strict occupation includes the following areas:
> a. *in the East: a line following the left bank of the river Görlitzer*

*[Lusatian] Neisse and the left bank of the Oder, including the nec-
essary bridgeheads; the estuary of the Oder, including Stettin, the
islands of this estuary and the Isle of Rügen.* The occupying power
should be Poland and in the southern area bordering Czechoslovakia—
Poland and Czechoslovakia; . . .

b. in the North: at least the German islands on the North and Baltic
Seas, as well as the [Kiel Canal] and its bordering zones. The occupying powers in the areas of the North Sea and the [Kiel Canal]
should be Great Britain and America; in the area of the Baltic islands
Great Britain and Poland.

Reinforcing the proviso that the zones of "strict occupation" might be
subject to incorporation into neighboring states, paragraph 15 of the same
memo proposed that Germany be obliged "to admit into the area of general
occupation . . . all persons of German extraction, expelled by Allied
Authorities."

On the other hand, the longer memorandum on "The German Problem
with Special Relation to Poland," where one would expect to find a clarification of the issue, is itself somewhat ambiguous. The key passage reads:

Poland's line of national security in relation to Germany is that of
the Oder. This line may be compared with that of the Rhine as a line
of national security for Belgium and France. Like the Rhine in the
West, so in the East the river Oder with its tributaries (flowing from
the Czech frontier), and with the gulf of Stettin, form a vital strategic
axis. The Prussian offensive bases directed against Poland, namely:
East Prussia, the Silesian salient and Prussian Pomerania, are all
situated to the east of this line.[88]

The memorandum then dealt in detail with the problems of East Prussia
(with Danzig), Prussian (or Western) Pomerania, and Silesia (including
the Oppeln district *and* Lower Silesia) from the historical, strategic, and,
to a lesser extent, ethnic points of view. It also analyzed the issue of
security along the Baltic, as well as the possible expulsion of the German
population from territories to be incorporated into Poland. In the end,

[88] This quotation is from the final English draft delivered December 31st; see note 86.
Other versions varied slightly, using the phrase "line of natural [not national] security" and
omitting the reference to the Rhine. This passage was quoted or paraphrased in at least four
different sources between 1945 and 1952: J. M. Winiewicz, *The Polish-German Frontier*,
p. 28; Seyda, *Pół wieku walki*, p. 21; Lipski, Raczyński, and Stroński, *Trzy podróże*, p. 17;
and Aleksander Bregman, "Linia Odry i Nysy, to nie 'wymysł Stalina,' " p. 2. In addition,
excerpts from the Bregman article, including the passage in question, were reprinted in
Gotthold Rhode and Wolfgang Wagner, eds., *Quellen zur Entstehung der Oder-Neisse-Linie*
(Stuttgart: Brentano, 1956), pp. 15-17; and later translated into English in *The Genesis of
the Oder-Neisse Line: Sources and Documents*, ed. Rhode and Wagner, pp. 14-16.

however, the memorandum did not specify a boundary line. Bowing to American sensitivities, it stated:

> The question of Poland's western frontier has not been fully discussed in this memorandum. It will suffice to state at the present juncture that that frontier should be straightened and shortened through indispensable displacement westwards, with a view to giving Poland well earned security.[89]

These ambiguities have generally been interpreted as evidence that Sikorski introduced the Oder-Neisse at this point not as a boundary line, but only as the proposed limit of "strict occupation." Yet, the reverse case can just as easily be made and, indeed, is the more plausible one. That is, given his domestic political difficulties as well as the extreme diplomatic risks involved in raising territorial issues at this stage with the Americans, the very ambiguities in his presentation tend to support the conclusion that he was in fact proposing an Oder-Neisse *boundary*. The most convincing evidence for this conclusion comes from what few insights we have into debates within the exile government during the final weeks of preparations for the prime minister's trip.

One indication of the contradictory pressures weighing on him, especially over his western boundary program, is a pair of memoranda addressed to him by senior advisers on the eve of his departure, warning of the negative reaction his proposals were likely to evoke in Washington. The first, from Ambassador Ciechanowski, came in response to several cables from Sikorski, in which the latter had stated unequivocally his intention to present his ideas on the western boundary.[90] Ciechanowski's advice was equally blunt: "It would not be advisable for the present to raise [the question of our western boundaries] as a problem . . . [requiring] a definitive

---

[89] In his first conversation with Roosevelt on December 2nd (the only one for which there is a detailed record), Sikorski's references to the western boundary were deliberately vague and guarded. When asked for his views on this question, he answered: "They [Poland's western boundaries] should be straightened, and East Prussia and Danzig should belong to Poland." After a brief exchange on East Prussia, he added: "I have brought with me a government memorandum concerning Poland's western boundaries. I will submit this memorandum to Mr. Sumner Welles. I do not ask for a definitive answer in these matters. I know that they are touchy for you at this moment, Mr. President. I ask only for serious consideration of our arguments and [that you] undertake discussion on these subjects with us at the appropriate time." A.XII.23/42, folio 1, no. 5, GSHI. Concerning Sikorski's reluctance to present his views in the form of territorial demands, see also Lipski, Raczyński, and Stroński, *Trzy podróże*, p. 17. See also pp. 298ff. below.

[90] See Sikorski's cables of October 30 and November 12, 1942 [PRM 69/129 and 69/134, GSHI] in which he informed Ciechanowski that "our western boundaries" would be one of the key items on his agenda in Washington. "I am particularly intent," he added, "on advancing our proposals concerning the west, as well as the problem of federation in East-Central Europe."

answer from the President or Government of the United States.'' Not only would such a move ''meet with a refusal even to discuss it'' but could ''have a negative influence on the atmosphere now so favorable'' to Sikorski. Should he insist on raising territorial issues at all, Ciechanowski advised doing so only in the form of an appeal for recognition of territorial integrity of those states that had been victims of aggression (i.e., the *status quo ante*), and warned even against broaching the question of East Prussia for fear of jeopardizing the status of the eastern *kresy*.[91] The second piece of advice came from Foreign Minister Raczyński who, while concurring with Ciechanowski as to the certainty of an adverse reaction, argued that ''this does not release the Polish Government from the necessity of submitting our demands to the American Government already now, and of giving them time to accustom themselves to them.''[92]

At the same time another argument was in process in London, this one over the final text of the longer version of the boundary memorandum (''The German Problem . . .''), between the Prime Minister's Office and the Ministry for Peace Conference Preparations headed by Dr. Marian Seyda. From an exchange of letters that occurred between the 6th and 13th of November, it becomes clear that Seyda was pushing forcefully for a clearer distinction in the memorandum between territories to be subject to incorporation and those subject only to occupation and, for reasons similar to those cited by Ciechanowski, specifically warned Sikorski against succumbing to strategic arguments in favor of demanding incorporation of the entire area up to the Oder and Lusatian Neisse.[93] Although in some points of detail Sikorski seems to have gone along with Seyda's recommendations, on the major issue of strategy he did not, any more than he heeded Ciechanowski's warning. The final draft delivered to Under Secretary Welles does not clarify the distinction between occupation and incorporation; indeed, in places it seems to be deliberately obscured. Moreover, in a number of important passages where Seyda had recommended a narrower construction—''Upper Silesia'' rather than ''Silesia'' or ''German Silesia,''removal of a reference to ''Western Pomerania,'' or the inadvisability of raising the issue of population transfers—the final version retained the more expansive wording, with the clear implication that these areas were among the ''objective bases of German power'' that posed an intolerable threat to the security of Poland and Czechoslovakia.[94]

[91] ''Wnioski dotyczące rozmów oficjalnych Pana Premiera w Waszyngtonie: Załącznik do raportu Nr. 3/SZ-tjn z 28.XI.42''; PRM 71/17, GSHI.

[92] See Raczyński's memo of November 23rd; Polish Government Collection, Box 69, folio: ''Wizyta Pana Premiera w Waszyngtonie,'' HIWRP.

[93] PRM 91/58, GSHI.

[94] For instance, concerning Silesia, the memo stated *inter alia*: ''German Silesia (the Oppeln district of Upper Silesia and Lower Silesia) is an extremely important base for offensive

In light of all this, there would seem to be little room for doubt that, in presenting the Oder-Neisse formula to the Americans at this time, Sikorski was making the case for a future Polish-Germany boundary and not merely a line of "strict occupation." Nor does the fact that he did not couch his proposals in terms of categorical "demands" detract either from this conclusion or from the boldness and clarity of his conception. It is inconceivable that he would have unnecessarily exposed himself to the disapproval of the U.S. president and State Department by casually or inadvertently using formulations that implied more extensive territorial acquisitions than he desired or intended. To conclude otherwise, as do both Polish and German writers,[95] is to suggest that he had suddenly cast aside the basic premise of his foreign policy—i.e., the concept of "real guarantees." For every occupation, no matter how "strict," has to end sometime; thus he would have to have been willing to countenance Poland's eventual loss of control over areas he thought vital to her physical existence.

A second point of interest is the striking similarity of Sikorski's program, as presented here at its moment of greatest articulation, to the program outlined two years earlier by the *West-Slavonic Bulletin*. For instance, he went beyond a simple Oder-Neisse line to ask, as had the *Bulletin* before him, for bridgeheads on the left banks of both rivers, footholds in Lusatia

---

military operations. It represents a wedge driven in to considerable depth between Poland and Czechoslovakia. The salient thus formed runs from the north-west to the south-east, being 185 miles long and on an average 75 miles wide. . . . From a military point of view only a considerable shortening and narrowing of the Silesian salient can ensure the necessary territorial coherence of Poland and Czechoslovakia and their mutual security in the event of war." Another example is the passage on Western Pomerania, which follows directly on a brief paragraph beginning: "Finally, there is the question of Poland's western frontiers." "The Polish sea ports . . . are adjacent to the Western Pomeranian salient which threatens Poland's access to the sea from the west. It is imperative that Germany should be prevented from using Western Pomerania for military concentrations and as an offensive base for attacking the lower Vistula and the Polish ports from the west. Western Pomerania together with the bay of Stettin is of vital strategic importance for Poland. It forms a defensive terrain vis-à-vis Germany. This is why the lower Oder was defined in the introductory remarks of the present Memorandum as forming the natural line of security of Poland and the Central European Federation." Quotations taken from the copy submitted December 31st; see note 86 above.

[95] See, e.g., Kowalski, *ZSRR a granica*, pp. 55-58, and *Walka dyplomatyczna*, pp. 286-87; also Wolfgang Wagner, *The Genesis of the Oder-Neisse Line: A Study in the Diplomatic Negotiations During World War II*, pp. 14-16. Kowalski's handling of this matter is especially questionable. In the earlier work he cited both the definition of Poland's "natural line of security" and the passage concerning the area of "strict occupation," concluding that Sikorski desired only strict occupation of the territories east of the Oder and Lusatian Neisse. However, he must have realized that his argument was unduly tortured; for in the later and much longer book, he took the easier route of citing only the passage on strict occupation.

("the northwestern . . . Sudetes with an outlet toward Leipzig") and Western Pomerania (i.e., including an area west of the lower Oder along the Baltic), as well as a share in the control of key Baltic islands and exits to the North Sea. With respect also to the internal structure of the projected Central European organization, the general's thinking had evolved rather far in the direction of accepting the two distinct but allied federations proposed by the West-Slavonic group. As Under Secretary Welles summarized his views from their December 4th meeting:

> General Sikorski . . . thought there should be two blocs in Eastern Europe, a Balkan bloc, to be created by Yugoslavia and Greece in which Bulgaria and Albania should be included. It was his conception that the northern bloc, of which Poland and Czechoslovakia should be the nucleus, should likewise be joined by Hungary and by what remained of Rumania at the end of the war. . . . [He] went on to say that he believed that there should be some working arrangement in the nature perhaps of an economic link, and one which perhaps would likewise involve joint management of communication facilities between the northern and southern federations.[96]

There were other parallels as well. Of particular interest is what appears to be a briefing paper on the federation proposal for one of Sikorski's meetings with Welles. From this paper it is clear that, far from viewing a Central European organization as a potential vehicle for recapturing Poland's "great power" status, he foresaw that his nation would have to accept limits on its sovereignty and freedom of action as the price of security and economic prosperity. In words reminiscent of the *Bulletin*'s admonition that Poles, Czechs, and Slovaks would be able to achieve their "common ambitions" only insofar as they could "manage already now to restrain their particularist ambitions,"[97] the brief stated:

---

[96] *FRUS, 1942*, 3:201. This conception is reflected also in the memorandum on "The Problem of Central and South-Eastern Europe" (see note 86). For the most part this memorandum reiterates themes articulated as far back as the Bevin memorandum in November 1940, or even earlier: e.g., the insistence on regional federations in which members are linked by common political interests and natural economic ties as opposed to broader and more diffuse unions; the emphasis on self-reliance as essential to the security of the region and to European equilibrium; the economic complementarity and development potential of the nations of Central and South-Eastern Europe. One discrepancy between the Welles account and the memorandum itself is worth mentioning here; this concerns the projected composition of the Central European component. Where in the memorandum both Lithuania and Rumania are included without qualification, Welles omits Lithuania and refers only to "what remains of Rumania." (In the summary memo, Lithuania is included in parentheses, while Rumania is omitted altogether.) For a comment on the significance of these discrepancies, see Chapter VI, note 38, below.

[97] See notes 8 and 9 in this chapter.

It is clear that states like Poland, Lithuania or Yugoslavia, *which are territorially small and which are not self-sufficient economically,* . . . [should] *at the cost of mutual concessions and the exclusion of egotistical and hypocritical policies* . . . approach the realization of the common ideal of defense of their rights and freedom in reliance on [their] common economic and human wealth.

. . . in approaching the problem of the boundaries of the federation, there can be *no territorial questions on the petty scale of the interests of one or another state, of the difficulties of reconciling population questions or feelings [?—text unclear] of historical traditionalism.* The problem of boundaries must find its solution from the viewpoint of giving the entire bloc of federated states powerful bases for development and the defense of its existence.[98]

It is true, of course, that many of the documents related to this trip reflected a more defensive tone toward the Soviet Union, and a more determined rejection of Soviet involvement in Central European affairs. In addition to the reference in the summary memorandum to "any other forces which might again bring Europe to a state of chaos," the longer memo on the federation stated categorically that, in "depriving the Germans of the possibility of conquering Central and South-Eastern Europe, . . . it does not follow at all that the 'leadership' in that part of Europe should be left to Russia." On the contrary,

> The nations of Central and South-Eastern Europe have their national and cultural individualities, as fully developed as those of the nations of Western Europe. The ideals for which the Allies are fighting the present war would be violated if these nations did not recover full independence. There can be no independence under the "leadership" of Russia—a power which pursues a policy aiming at the introduction of the communist system in the neighboring countries, with the purpose of incorporating them into the Soviet Union. . . .
>
> The justified desire of the nations of Central and South-Eastern Europe to set themselves free from Soviet rule would provide Germany with opportunities for intrigue. . . . Consequently, Russian "leadership" . . . would be a source of weakness for Russia and an encouragement to aggression for Germany.

[98] "Notatka w sprawie federacji (dla N[aczelnego] W[odza])," December 12, 1942; A.XII.23/42, folio 1, no. 23, GSHI [original text in Polish; emphasis added]. The brief also betrayed the same sense of urgency over timing as had the *Bulletin*—that is, the need for the federation to be organized immediately after the war, in order that decisions not be taken by default as after World War I; and the certainty that extensive outside investment would be essential to the reconstruction process.

On the other hand, "the central 'bloc' would not have any aggressive designs against Russia. On the contrary, it would serve her as a natural shield against any possible recurrence of German aggression."[99]

Yet this defensiveness should not necessarily be interpreted as signaling that Sikorski had abandoned his policy of reconciliation with Russia, or that he was determined by some unspecified means to prevent the USSR from assuming the role of a great power in the postwar world. Quite the opposite. What is evident from his talks at the White House and State Department during this December 1942 visit is that he still viewed as essential a long-term alliance with Moscow and, indeed, that he hoped to go to Moscow again in the near future to negotiate such an alliance.[100] What he was seeking from the Americans was not support for supposed anti-Soviet machinations, but assistance—especially in the form of a public endorsement of a Central European federation—in avoiding a settlement that would be merely a facade for Soviet domination of Poland's (and Central Europe's) political and economic life.[101] For, as we shall see in more detail below, Stalin had by now made it unmistakably clear that he would oppose as "anti-Soviet" every move that might allow the Central European states to increase their leverage vis-à-vis their larger neighbors.

One disadvantage of having to deal almost entirely with statements, and excerpts of statements, of a programmatic nature is that our knowledge of

[99] "The Problem of Central and South-Eastern Europe"; see note 86 above.

[100] See, e.g., the memorandum on Polish-Soviet relations, personally dictated by Sikorski in preparation for this trip; Ciechanowski Deposit, Box 93[84], folio: "Basic data prepared for Sikorski's visit," HIWRP. It is not clear in what form, if any, this memo was presented to the Americans; see additional comment on p. 134 and note 37 below.

[101] Probably the best indication of the kind of support Sikorski sought from the United States at this time is his draft of a letter he wished to receive from President Roosevelt. On the boundary issue, he asked first that the president affirm Poland's territorial integrity "as consistent with the principles of the Atlantic Charter"; in the west, he did not ask for endorsement of specific territorial gains but only that Roosevelt "not exclude the possibility that the necessity will arise to widen the basis of Poland's security in the West in relation to Germany and thus to strengthen her economic independence." Concerning the federation, however, the draft continued: "I [Roosevelt] have noted with satisfaction your constructive initiative towards the establishment of a Confederation of Poland with Czechoslovakia as a first step in the direction of a European policy of international cooperation, . . . I am looking forward to its further satisfactory development, considering that the establishment of durable peace and security in Central Eastern Europe largely depends on its successful completion." Then on Polish-Soviet relations: "In my opinion, the Polish-Soviet Agreement of July 30th, 1941, and the Stalin-Sikorski Declaration of December 4th, 1941, constitute a most satisfactory basis for Polish-Russian collaboration. It is my hope that this basis will be duly enlarged and strengthened in view of the fact that a Polish-Soviet alliance, based upon the mutual loyalty and mutual respect of the sovereign rights of these two neighboring nations, must be regarded as one of the best guarantees of European peace." *FRUS, 1942*, 3:202-203.

the state of the prime minister's thinking at this juncture remains perforce superficial. Given the limited availability of supporting materials—preliminary working papers, accounts of discussions within his inner circle,[102] or records of the critical meetings with Roosevelt and Welles at which he was informed of the American reaction to his memoranda[103]—it would be easy to conclude that Sikorski was naively optimistic concerning the prospects for his proposals and perhaps oblivious to the enormous difficulties of implementing them. As we shall see later, however, he was often deeply pessimistic about the prospects for his program already months before this third and last visit to Washington, and even warned Roosevelt that Europe would require a massive infusion of economic aid after the war if it were not to succumb to "anarchy and communism"[104]—this nearly five years before the Marshall Plan was announced.

[102] Unfortunately Mitkiewicz, whose accounts are usually the most detailed, spent the second half of 1942 on temporary duty with the Army in Scotland. He was recalled in January 1943 to be the Polish representative to the Combined Allied Staff in Washington and, in this capacity, reviewed the record of Sikorski's trip. His account contains several nuggets from the most important session with Roosevelt, but of course nothing from the discussions preceding the trip. See *Z gen. Sikorskim*, pp. 314-20.

[103] Sikorski may have met with Welles on or about December 12th, and definitely had a meeting with him on the 21st; no record of either meeting has turned up in either Polish or American archives. See Chapter X, note 136, below.

[104] According to Pobóg-Malinowski (*Najnowsza historia*, 3:245, n. 72), this suggestion was included in a "fundamental letter on the matter of the postwar economy" that Sikorski left with Roosevelt.

VI · *The Eastern Boundary: Encounter with Necessity*

INTIMATELY related to Sikorski's vision of Poland's future geographical and political orientation, and most particularly of her relations with the Soviet Union, was his position on the boundary that would divide the two states. Yet this comprises a separate and fourth aspect of his program in the sense that substantial territorial concessions in the east were in all probability not part of his original conception of a rapprochement with Moscow, or at the very least a step he hoped he could avoid. Rather, it seems likely that he came to accept the need for such concessions only gradually and reluctantly in order to salvage the rest of his program.

It is unquestionably the most difficult aspect of his program to pin down and not only because it was the most sensitive issue in Polish wartime politics—a fact dictating that the prime minister's statements even to his own government be cautious and veiled. It is elusive also because, with one exception, sources who were close to Sikorski or who had reason to be aware of his approach to the eastern boundary question have preferred either to remain silent or to allude to it in only the most cursory fashion.[1] Nonetheless, by piecing together the numerous hints and innuendoes (Sikorski's as well as others') with the few more solid bits of evidence (especially from British Foreign Office documents), one arrives at the inescapable conclusion that the real question is not *whether* Sikorski recognized the necessity of compromise on Poland's boundary with the Soviet Union, but *when* he came to this realization, and by how much and under what circumstances he was willing to compromise.

There can be little doubt that Sikorski basically shared the view of most Poles to the effect that the boundary established by the 1921 Riga Treaty had represented a fair compromise at the time, that their prewar eastern provinces comprised an important part of historic Poland, and that the resources of these territories were of far greater value to Poland than they could ever be to the Soviet Union. From an economic point of view, they contained relatively few natural resources, and none that the Soviet Union did not possess in abundance. However, they were Poland's only source of oil, natural gas, and potash, much of her timber and her richest agri-

---

[1] Leon Mitkiewicz's *Z gen. Sikorskim* is the one exception.

cultural soils. In addition, these provinces were more sparsely populated than the rest of the country and, given an aggressive land reform and development program, could have absorbed some of the excess population from the overcrowded central provinces. From a strategic standpoint, the river Bug, along which both the Curzon and Molotov-Ribbentrop lines ran,[2] provided less of a barrier than the Pripet Marshes further east; moreover, the shifting of Poland's boundary to the Curzon line would reduce by more than 50 percent (to approximately 100 miles) the distance from her capital at Warsaw to the frontier, while Moscow lay more than 500 miles to the east. In these circumstances, it is scarcely surprising that the Poles, Sikorski included, tended to see Moscow's territorial claims as motivated less by Soviet security needs than by a desire to deprive Poland and other Central European states of economic resources and natural defenses essential to their independence.[3]

On the other hand, the Poles were well aware even before June 1941 of the Soviets' determination to keep the territories occupied in 1939. As we have already seen, the conditions under which the latter were allegedly willing to reestablish contact with the Poles, as conveyed to the Government-in-Exile first in November 1939 and again in June 1940,[4] included

[2] Both lines are shown on Map 6. What came to be known as the Curzon line was first proposed by the Commission on Polish Affairs at the Paris Peace Conference in April 1919, as ''a 'minimum' eastern frontier within which the Polish Government should be authorised to organise a permanent administration.'' It was at this point that differences among the delegations produced two variants—lines ''A'' and ''B''—for the Eastern Galician sector. Although not included in the final Versailles Treaty, it was again recommended in a Declaration of the Supreme Allied Council on December 8, 1919. It acquired the name Curzon line in July 1920, when Lord Curzon proposed it as a demarcation line between the Polish and Soviet armies after the tide of battle had turned against the Poles. At that time the Bolsheviks rejected the line as too unfavorable to the Poles (although they probably had in mind a Soviet Poland as they continued to press their drive on Warsaw). Despite the fact that, from the outset, the ostensible purpose of the line was to protect Poland's interests by defining the *minimum* territory to be assigned her in the east, presumably without prejudicing a future frontier settlement, the British (in contrast to the French) always opposed Poland's expansion east of this line, and favored line ''A'' in Eastern Galicia, leaving Lwów outside of Poland. See the Foreign Research and Press Service's paper on the ''History of Poland's Eastern Frontier,'' dated August 22, 1942; C9098/1534/55, FO 371/31104, PRO.

[3] For a Polish presentation of these arguments, see *Documents*, 1:312-17 and 469-72. The argument that it was possession of these Polish territories that gave the Soviets the margin in time and distance needed to stave off defeat in the initial German onslaught—an argument on which Moscow relied heavily in pressing its claims on the Allies—is simply not tenable in light of the military history of that campaign. German armies were closing in on Minsk within days of the opening shots; and their failure to proceed toward Moscow after the capture of Smolensk in the late summer of 1941 was apparently due to decisions and disagreements within the German high command rather than to the ability of the Red Army to stop the advance at this point. See Albert Seaton, *The Russo-German War 1941-45*, pp. 116-32.

[4] See pp. 49-50 and note 9 above.

The Polish-Soviet Frontier

STATUTE MILES
0 25 50 75 100

KILOMETERS
25 50 75 100

- – – – International boundaries to September 1, 1939
- ·············· Curzon Line, with
  A B Extensions into Eastern Galicia
- –··–··– Demarcation line established by the Nazi-Soviet Non-Aggression
  Pact, August 23, 1939 (Molotov-Ribbentrop Line)
- –·–·–· Polish-Soviet boundary since 1945

N

LITHUANIA

BALTIC SEA

Kaliningrad
(Königsberg)

Gdańsk
(Danzig)

EAST
PRUSSIA

Wilno
(Vilnius)

•Minsk

Niemen River

Białystok•

Vistula River

Warsaw•

Bug River

Brześć
(Brest)

•Pinsk

U S S R

POLAND

•Lublin

San River

Kraków•

A
Lwów•
(Lvov)
B

CZECHOSLOVAKIA

HUNGARY

ROMANIA

G.W.WARD

18° 19° 20° 21° 22° 23° 26°

55° 55°
54° 54°
53° 53°
52° 52°
51° 51°
50° 50°
49° 49°
48° 48°

Map 6

acceptance of both territorial concessions and the concept of an "ethno-graphical" Poland. Moreover, the Poles were painfully aware of the at-titude of the British who, far from being willing to support Poland's interests in the east, had from the opening days of the war made no secret of their readiness to accept the Molotov-Ribbentrop line as a return to the Curzon line they had proposed (under very different circumstances) at the time of the Polish-Soviet war of 1919-20.[5]

What is notable about Sikorski's response to this situation is surely not his public defense of Poland's territorial integrity within her pre-September 1939 boundaries, a position from which he would not deviate until two months before his death. After all, any other posture would have been political suicide. More intriguing and unquestionably far more indicative of his personal inclinations were the numerous hints—mostly in confidential communications to the British, and occasionally the Americans, but some-times also in internal Polish documents—that he was prepared to be flexible on this touchy question provided Poland's fundamental needs and interests were taken into account. While several of these feelers have already been alluded to, it is useful to review them here to see whether or not they fit a coherent pattern.

The first intimation of this flexibility came at the end of his first official visit to London in mid-November 1939 (and thus barely two and one-half months after the beginning of the war!). According to a report from the Foreign Office's Political Intelligence Department, Sikorski acknowledged "that it will not be possible to have any hard and fast ideas about Poland's future until the end of the war." In addition, the report continued:

> Although [Sikorski] will not admit officially any difference between the two invaders of Poland, he does realize perfectly well that the reconstruction of Poland in her pre-war frontiers is very problematic. If it proves impossible to recover from Russia what has been lost, he aims at finding compensation elsewhere which would at the same time increase Poland's security.[6]

The following June, as we have seen, he hinted very strongly both to the British and indirectly also to the Soviets that he would not insist on specific recognition of the Riga Treaty as a precondition for resuming contacts with the USSR. As he told then Foreign Secretary Halifax, the Polish Govern-

[5] British policy on Poland's eastern boundary is discussed in Chapter VIII below; see especially pp. 151-59.

[6] Letter from Rex Leeper, Political Intelligence Department, to William Strang, Assistant Under Secretary, November 25, 1939, relaying Sikorski's views as reported by Stefan Litauer, London correspondent of the Polish Telegraph Agency; C19288/27/55, FO 371/23131, PRO; excerpted in *The Great Powers and the Polish Question*, ed. Polonsky, pp. 75-76.

ment "did not wish to place any obstacle in the way of an improvement of relations between the Western Powers and the Soviet Union by continuing their predecessors' policy of provocation towards the latter country." Nor was he opposed to direct Polish contacts with Moscow "on condition that the question of the eastern frontier of Poland were freely discussed and the persecution of Poles in Soviet-occupied Poland ceased."[7] Again, in his November 1940 memorandum to Labour Minister Bevin, the eastern boundary question is passed over in silence—an omission whose significance was not missed by at least one Foreign Office observer.[8]

Internal documents from this early period also hint occasionally at a degree of flexibility to which Sikorski could never have admitted publicly. For instance, in his instructions to Ambassador Ciechanowski in January 1941, he wrote:

> At the present moment it is premature to reveal our war aims, and our tactics in this regard will depend on the course of events. For this reason, it is also essential to stand officially and on the surface on . . . the status quo from 1939. This does not of course prejudice our actual position concerning war aims.[9]

In a second and rather curious instruction to Ciechanowski, this one in preparation for his meetings with Under Secretary of State Welles and President Roosevelt in April 1941, he wrote that his government must "in principle" insist that Poland emerge from the war at least with "those same boundaries with which she consciously took up battle against . . . Nazi totalitarianism." However, in the interests of "differentiating Germany from Russia" and of promoting a resolution of Poland's difficulties with the latter, he would "for the moment" ask only that the United States exert pressure on Russia "not to cross the present demarcation line [between Poland and the Soviet Union] at the time of Germany's collapse."[10]

The evidence is hardly sufficient to demonstrate that the general was prepared at this early stage to concede the loss of even part of Poland's

[7] Halifax's report of a conversation with Sikorski, June 19, 1940; C7880/7177/55, FO 371/24482, PRO. For a discussion of this incident, see pp. 48-55 above.

[8] The memorandum to Bevin is summarized on pp. 86-92 above, and 133 below.

[9] PRM 40a/2, GSHI. This is the same letter in which Sikorski attacked Poland's prewar foreign policy and stated that he had not condemned it openly only "for reasons of national interest." See Chapter V, note 59, above.

[10] PRM 40b/2, GSHI. There is no record of his actually having made this curious request. This was, of course, still two months before Hitler's attack on the Soviet Union. More to the point, however, it was also not long after the Polish foreign minister had vigorously protested British suggestions of a similar de facto recognition of Soviet territorial conquests from 1939-40. See p. 86 above.

prewar east.[11] It does suggest, however, that he was acutely conscious of the fact that Poland's recovery of these territories—if, indeed, she had any chance of recovering them—would depend on a genuine reconciliation with the Soviet Union, and that the Poles were in no position to make the one a prerequisite for the other.

This same approach on Sikorski's part is even more evident in the negotiations leading up to the Polish-Soviet Agreement of July 30, 1941. As generally presented, these negotiations began with the Polish prime minister insisting on Soviet recognition of the validity of the boundary established in 1921 by the Riga Treaty and ended with his reluctant acceptance, under heavy British pressure, of a formula that merely declared invalid the German-Soviet treaties of 1939 without settling the boundary issue. Close examination of both Polish and British records of the negotiations, however, offers quite a different picture. Specifically, the record indicates that it was Sikorski himself, without British urging and in full recognition that a future settlement might well entail concessions, who agreed to leave the boundary issue in abeyance—and that his efforts were aimed more at forestalling a public Soviet declaration that the prewar border would not be restored than at wringing from them formal recognition of that border. The record also shows that his handling of this question throughout the negotiations was determined by the need to steer a narrow and difficult course between the requirements of Poland's international position and the demands of his domestic constituency, from which pressure for a more aggressive and public defense of Poland's claims against the USSR had been mounting in the early months of 1941.[12]

During the preliminary meeting on July 4th, at which British Foreign Secretary Eden relayed to him Moscow's conditions for a reconciliation (including the future establishment of a Polish state within "ethnographical" boundaries), Sikorski asked only that "the Soviet Union acknowledge

[11] Nonetheless Kukiel, describing Sikorski's views in mid-1940, wrote: ". . . He did not reject the possibility of boundary changes—with the thought of compensation in East Prussia, Gdańsk and Silesia—but only after a victorious war and with an enlargement, not a reduction of Poland"; *Generał Sikorski*, p. 144. The source cited by Kukiel is Mitkiewicz, *Z gen. Sikorskim*, pp. 64-65; however, Mitkiewicz made no mention here of boundary changes. The Kukiel reference is especially curious since he never again states directly that Sikorski was willing to compromise on the eastern boundary.

[12] British Foreign Office archives document that, by the beginning of 1941, Sikorski's government was coming under serious criticism at home for "not doing enough for the Poles in Soviet-occupied Poland . . . [and] generally neglecting Polish claims *vis-à-vis* the U.S.S.R." In fact, such "neglect" was due to a BBC ban on descriptions of the conditions in Soviet-occupied Poland; nonetheless, the result was pressure on Sikorski to defend Poland's prewar eastern boundary. See C932 and C1175/151/55, FO 371/26718, PRO.

as null the German-Soviet agreements of August and September 1939."[13] The following day, at the first negotiating session with Soviet Ambassador Maisky, Sikorski broached the issue by stating that "the Soviet Government should explicitly revert to the situation as covered by the Treaty of Riga [which] would follow automatically from a Soviet renunciation of the two treaties signed with Germany in . . . 1939." But it appears this was an opening gambit, possibly as much for Polish as for Russian consumption. For when Maisky stated that Moscow "could not explicitly recognize" the 1939 frontier but that "the question might be left open," Sikorski readily assented, adding only that "he could not . . . agree that the Soviet Government should declare that the frontiers of 1939 would *not* be restored."[14] Moreover, while pleading that boundary concessions now could jeopardize Polish-Soviet cooperation, he hinted that he did not rule out changes in the future:

> General Sikorski said that a necessary condition of collaboration between Poland and Russia was a return to normal relations. The Polish people had accepted war with Germany in 1939 on the then existing basis of the Polish State. He was therefore unable *now* to discuss frontier changes. . . . Moreover, were he to recognize even implicitly a surrender of Poland to the USSR, it would be difficult, if not impossible, to create enthusiasm among the Polish soldiers, who are at present in Soviet gaols, concentration camps or deported under distressing conditions.[15]

Just why Sikorski reinjected the issue of the Riga boundary into the later course of the negotiations is not clear. One possibility is that he felt compelled to do so in order to substantiate his government's claim to represent all Polish citizens deported or imprisoned in the Soviet Union since 1939.[16] An equally likely possibility is that the mounting crisis within the Government-in-Exile over the prospect of an agreement excluding explicit recognition of the prewar boundary forced Sikorski to demonstrate that he had made every possible effort to extract such recognition, even while he was attempting to persuade his colleagues that nullification of the

---

[13] *Documents*, 1:114-16. We are discussing here only the territorial aspects of these negotiations; for a more general treatment, see pp. 56-65 above.

[14] Ibid., pp. 117-18 [emphasis in the original]. Eden confirms this in *The Reckoning* (pp. 314-15); see also Mitkiewicz, *Z gen. Sikorskim*, p. 167.

[15] *Documents*, 1:117-18 [emphasis added].

[16] See the protocol of the July 11th session, in ibid., pp. 130-31. The issue of Polish prisoners and deportees proved to be the most intractable and was the last to be settled; see especially Kukiel, *Generał Sikorski*, pp. 171-74; and *The Cadogan Diaries*, ed. Dilks, p. 391.

1939 partition and postponement of a final boundary settlement was the most they could hope for.[17]

On the question of whether Sikorski viewed the postponement of a settlement as affording the Poles a chance to recover their prewar eastern provinces in the future, or merely as a first step toward inevitable compromise, the evidence is suggestive if not entirely conclusive. On the one hand, his public posture remained unchanged. In his broadcast to Poland on July 31st, the day after the agreement was signed, he proclaimed: "The present agreement . . . does not permit even of the suggestion that the 1939 frontiers of the Polish State could ever be in question. It does not allow of any idea that Poland has resigned anything."[18] On the other hand, on July 3rd, two days before the negotiations began, he told Bevin and a high-ranking Foreign Office official that "the Polish Government, without surrendering their claim to the pre-war frontiers, admitted that these frontiers might be a matter for discussion."[19] In the same vein, Mitkiewicz confided to his diary while the negotiations were still in progress:

> If I understand him well, General Sikorski has great hopes that through negotiations and with the help of the Western Allies he will in time succeed in bringing Russia to a more conciliatory position and in checking her tendency to take over the whole of our eastern provinces, and above all Lwów.[20]

Even the American ambassador to the Government-in-Exile, Anthony Drexel Biddle, recognized that the Poles' ardent defense of their prewar eastern boundary might well represent less an inflexible negotiating position than a response to the need, common to exile governments, to "build up a record of having left no stone unturned in defending the interests of their respective countries." "I am aware," he wrote:

> that during the final phase of negotiations which led up to the conclusion of the Polish-Russian Agreement, the Polish Government gained the distinct impression that the Russian Government's ideas on a future

[17] For accounts of this crisis, see especially Mitkiewicz, *Z gen. Sikorskim*, pp. 152-61; and Ambassador Dormer's report to Eden of July 22nd, in C8306/3226/55, FO 371/26756, PRO. Kot (*Listy z Rosji*, p. 14) contends that Sikorski feared another coup attempt. Concerning the possibility that he exaggerated the pressure being exerted on him by the British, see p. 63 above.

[18] *Documents*, 1:144.

[19] C7458/3226/55, FO 371/26755, PRO. In his minute to the report, William Strang of the Foreign Office, who had also attended this meeting, referred even more explicitly to Sikorski's "statement that the Polish Government would be ready to reach a compromise with the Soviet Government about the Polish eastern frontier, and that it was in the west (at the expense of Germany) rather than in the east that Polish aspirations lay."

[20] Mitkiewicz, *Z gen. Sikorskim*, p. 157 [entry for July 22, 1941].

settlement of Polish-Russian frontiers envisaged the retention of certain territories of Eastern Poland, on the grounds that the populations thereof were predominantly Russian [sic].

The Polish Government . . . intend[s], in event of an Allied victory, to insist vigorously upon the re-establishment of Polish-Russian frontiers as defined by the Treaty of Riga.

I am aware, however, that . . . it is not unmindful of Moscow's no less determined point of view in the matter, and of consequent difficulties to be overcome, if ever a settlement satisfactory to Poland's standpoint is to be effected.

Moreover, the Polish Government's concern over Moscow's attitude is not without consideration for its own post-war political ambitions. Hence the acquisition of East Prussia is envisaged not only as the answer to Poland's longstanding "dream," but also as compensation to the people for whatever loss Poland might incur in a settlement of her Eastern Frontiers.[21]

Six months later, the situation had changed in subtle but unmistakable ways. If in mid-1941 Sikorski could still nurture hopes for recovery of all of Poland's prewar east, by early 1942 he knew such hopes to be utterly illusory. During the prime minister's December 1941 trip to Moscow, Stalin had made plain his intention to "solve" the Ukrainian problem once and for all. "Don't worry, we won't harm you," he had added, implying that he would ask only for modest boundary corrections.[22] As we have seen, however, Sikorski learned immediately on his return to London that the Russians had made far more extensive demands of Foreign Secretary Eden, who had followed him to Moscow. The British government was being asked to extend immediate recognition to the western frontiers of the Soviet Union as they existed prior to the German invasion—that is, including the Baltic States and the Rumanian territories of Bukovina and Bessarabia, but excluding the Polish-Soviet boundary which Stalin told Eden he wished to settle directly with the Poles on the basis of the Curzon line.[23]

[21] *FRUS, 1941*, 1:375-77. Biddle mentions only East Prussia here, but other comments in this same letter indicate that he was aware of the Poles' desire for a more general "straightening out of the age-old Polish-German tangle on the Baltic."

[22] This is the exchange in which Stalin is reported to have said he only wanted to change the border "a little bit" [*chut'-chut'* in Russian]. This comment is not included in the Polish "Note" of the conversation in *Documents*, 1:245; but it is recounted by Sikorski in a later meeting with Eden (ibid., p. 365). See also Rozek, *Allied Wartime Diplomacy*, p. 94; and Kukiel, *Generał Sikorski*, p. 188.

[23] The detailed British record of the Eden-Stalin talks [W.P.(42)8, CAB 66/20, PRO] indicates that Stalin did initially demand immediate recognition of a Polish-Soviet boundary along the Curzon line, "with perhaps some slight variations one way or the other," but

It is only at this point, in January 1942, that we begin to find evidence of the kind of compromise Sikorski envisioned. The most detailed evidence comes from the diary entries of his intelligence chief, Leon Mitkiewicz, which indicate that possible compromise solutions to the eastern boundary stalemate were the subject of continuous discussion between the time of Sikorski's return from Moscow and his second departure for Washington in mid-March. The first entry of substance, from January 9th, describes a long briefing session at which the prime minister declared that he had resisted Stalin's efforts to discuss the boundary issue. "But," continued Mitkiewicz:

> from the General's tone, from his reticences and vague hints, I con-clude rather that such a conversation with Stalin did take place and that its result was unfavorable. This followed from the General's additional comments, from which it was evident that he has accus-tomed himself to the thought that we will have to cede something to Russia in the east. For example, about Wilno and about the whole Wilno region, the General spoke in a manner which indicated that it would be necessary to cede this area to the Lithuanians [in exchange] for [their] joining a Central European Federation together with the Poles. About Lwów, too, the General said—rather it was possible to surmise and feel—that he is thinking of defending Eastern Galicia with Lwów and the oil basin, at the possible cost of concessions in the rest of our East.
>
> In a sentence in which the General called the Polish Republic with numerous minorities a weak spot, he intimated that he is rather inclined to base a postwar understanding with Soviet Russia on the basis of rebuilding Poland as an ethnically pure state, a national state. Waxing enthusiastic, Gen. Sikorski also spoke of the fantasies of Poland's pseudo-great power status in the pre-1939 concept, all the while abus-ing [former Foreign Minister] Beck something awful. Jumping from topic to topic, he told us of his directive to the Ministry of Foreign Affairs, in which he has ordered that we insist on retaining Lithuania in our sphere of influence, [expressing] on the other hand *désinté-ressement* in the affairs of Latvia and Estonia.[24]

---

retreated in the face of Eden's protests. See also Eden, *The Reckoning*, pp. 335-45; and Churchill, *The Grand Alliance*, pp. 629-30. Later, however, during the course of the Anglo-Soviet negotiations in the spring of 1942, the Soviets tried to reinsert the Polish question into the discussions; for further discussion, see pp. 253-54 and 296 below.

[24] Mitkiewicz, *Z gen. Sikorskim*, pp. 198-99 [emphasis added]. In this passage Mitkiewicz faithfully reflects the tone of Sikorski's secret report to the Council of Ministers on January 12th, particularly his remarks on prewar Polish policy. These portions of the report were not included in the excerpts published in *Documents*, 1:264-66; for the full text, see C795/19/55, FO 371/31077, PRO. See also note 29 below.

Several weeks later, in his diary entry for January 28th, Mitkiewicz referred to Stalin's intention to solve his Ukrainian problem and speculated on the possibility of a population exchange in Eastern Galicia:

> . . . Stalin has purportedly proposed to Eden and to Sikorski that the Ukrainian problem be left in Russian hands, in order once and for all to remove this focal point of frictions and misunderstandings which exists in the form of two Ukraines: western—our Eastern Galicia—and eastern—lying along the Dnieper. According to Stalin each of them is a Ukrainian "Piedmont" and causes both States, Poland and Russia, many troubles and headaches—which a third side, Germany, eagerly exploits. Unfortunately, in large measure this corresponds to the truth. The Russian proposal is based on the fact that, because the majority of the Ukrainian population is found in the Ukraine along the Dnieper, then Eastern Galicia should be attached to the Soviet Union, to the Ukrainian Republic.

However, in view of the "unconditionally Polish character of Lwów itself" and of other concentrations of Poles in Eastern Galicia, Mitkiewicz suggested that a compromise might be possible whereby the Lwów area would be left to Poland and the Polish and Ukrainian populations exchanged.[25]

In early March, relating a discussion of Sikorski's federation program preparatory to his upcoming Washington visit, Mitkiewicz described a possible course for the future Polish-Soviet frontier:

> Most interesting and important for me was the indication by the General on a large map of Europe . . . of the future eastern boundaries of this Federation, that is of Poland and Lithuania. I watched very carefully, literally in suspense, as the General moved his hand along the map. And so: the former Lithuanian boundary to Dynaburg

---

[25] Mitkiewicz, *Z gen. Sikorskim*, pp. 204-205; see also p. 231 [entry for March 19th], where Mitkiewicz reported a discussion on whether to mention the possibility of such an exchange in a note to the British. In the first passage, he attributes the suggestion of a possible population exchange, as part of a compromise that would leave Lwów to Poland, to Acting Foreign Minister Raczyński. In the course of our conversations and correspondence between 1979 and 1981, however, Count Raczyński stated several times that he did not recall any such discussions and that, in any event, they would have been based on speculation rather than on any specific knowledge of Soviet proposals or intentions. The second passage concerns a discussion that occurred several weeks after Raczyński had left for Washington; here Mitkiewicz mentions Retinger and Józef Lipski as the other participants and notes that, in the end, "General Sikorski decided not to raise this question for the time being, [in part] because . . . the disclosure of this concept by us at the present time would cast the entire onus of undeserved blame [for concessions in the east] on the General." Concerning the extraordinary sensitivity surrounding the eastern boundary question within the exile government, including the apparent lack of candid discussion even among Sikorski's closest colleagues and advisors, see Chapter X, note 47, below.

(Dźwińsk)—lake Narocz—the Nalibocka forest—Baranowicze—Pińsk—the river Styr—the Zgniła Lipa river—the Dniestr river. For Poland, I thought to myself, this would mean the loss of almost all of Polesie, eastern Wołyń [Volhynia] and Podole . . .[26]

Nearly a year later, in a January 1943 entry discussing the memoranda presented by Sikorski during his third trip to the United States, Mitkiewicz wrote that a "special addendum" to the "fundamental" memorandum concerning the postwar organization of Central Europe "emphasized that the Polish Government recognizes that the Ukrainian problem belongs to Soviet Russia."[27]

Clearly it is risky to accept without question the word of a single source on an issue of such import, especially when that source seems to contradict nearly everything else written on this issue for more than thirty years. Yet a number of other bits and pieces of evidence (including some from Sikorski's own conversations and speeches), while not so explicit and detailed, do tend to corroborate Mitkiewicz's testimony. The first of these is the official Polish record of a conversation between General Sikorski and Marshal Stalin at the Kremlin banquet on December 4, 1941, during which the question of amnesty for Polish citizens of non-Polish nationality arose:

> Stalin: What do you need Byelorussians, Ukrainians and Jews for? It is the Poles you need, they are the best soldiers.
> Gen. S.: I do not have individuals in mind, they can be exchanged for the Poles who are Soviet citizens. I am, however, unable to accept, even in principle, any suggestion that the Polish state frontiers could be considered fluid. All Polish citizens within the frontiers of Poland as they existed prior to the war did not cease to be our citizens. One must not create "faits accomplis" by force. . . .
> [Here they discuss the Ukrainians and the issue of Lwów.]
> Gen. S.: It is not the Ukrainians who matter to me, *but the territory in which the Polish element is dominant*, and which you have weakened by deporting 2,000,000 Poles into Russia.[28]

---

[26] Mitkiewicz, *Z gen. Sikorskim*, p. 221. It is interesting to note that this line is quite similar to the boundary proposed by Piłsudski toward the end of 1918; see Wandycz, *Soviet-Polish Relations*, p. 99.

[27] Mitkiewicz, *Z gen. Sikorskim*, p. 315. Between June 1942 and January 1943, Mitkiewicz was on temporary assignment with the Polish Army in Scotland and, therefore, not in touch with day-to-day events within the exile government; he read the memoranda and other papers from Sikorski's trip in connection with his next assignment as the Polish representative to the Combined Allied Staff in Washington.

[28] *Documents*, 1:244-45 [emphasis added].

The second piece of corroborating evidence comes from Sikorski's secret report on his trip to the Soviet Union, delivered to the Polish Council of Ministers on January 12, 1942:

> In the East we know only those frontiers within which Poland entered the war, the frontiers established by way of compromise with Russia. It would be a great mistake to allow any official discussion on this subject, and to accept any suggestion that our frontiers are in a state of fluidity. *The situation is not yet ripe for any such discussion.* Stalin proposed to me a conversation of this nature. He told me of Soviet good will in this direction, and of the assistance which Russia was ready to give us in our disputes with the Ukrainians in the matter of the Polish city of Lwów. He told me of the need to bargain with Russia. He mentioned Poland's mission in the West, and the prospects of her expansion at Germany's cost. I declined these proposals, politely but firmly. Stalin acquiesced, announcing that he would return to the subject at a moment more favorable for us, that is to say, when the Polish Army will begin to fight on the Western [Soviet] front.

This was the same speech in which he expressed the hope that Poland would expand to the west, saying "it is history that pushes us in this direction, providing us with a unique occasion for putting right old wrongs and mistakes." Although these "mistakes" were not further defined, one can only assume from the context that he was referring to past mistakes of the Poles in pushing too far to the east at the cost of their position in the west.[29]

Even U.S. Ambassador Biddle's analysis of the situation corroborates Mitkiewicz's account. In a report to Washington dated February 2, 1942, he wrote that, while Sikorski had expressed confidence "that the question of the frontier was one which could eventually be settled directly between the Poles and the Russians," "I have the impression that he is not optimistic as to the outcome in light of Poland's claims; that he is sufficiently a realist not to count upon a settlement of the question on the basis of the 1939 frontier." Biddle then predicted that the prime minister would be prepared

---

[29] Ibid., pp. 264-65 [emphasis added]; see also p. 104 above. The unpublished portions of this speech make no additional reference to the eastern boundary, but do contain blunt criticism of Poland's prewar policy toward the Soviet Union, as well as the statement that "Polish 'raison d'état' imposes an understanding with one of our great neighbors." C795/19/55, FO 371/31077, PRO. So sensitive was this document that the letter from the Foreign Office to Ambassador Dormer requesting a translation of the text included the following warning: "It is absolutely essential that no one, and particularly no Poles, should know that General Sikorski has shown this document to the Secretary of State. . . . The Secretary of State has undertaken that only one copy of the translation will be made and that it will be kept in the Foreign Office so I am afraid we must ask you not to keep any trace of this document at the Embassy and of course not to allow anybody to know that you are aware of its existence."

to make concessions in the east if he were assured of his political and
territorial program (although he apparently had only limited knowledge of
those desiderata):

> At the back of his head, I believe, he has linked the question of
> possible "adjustments" of the pre-war frontier, with his postwar
> aspirations: annexation of East Prussia, and some form of close eco-
> nomic, political and military tie-up with Lithuania. In other words,
> provided he were assured of realizing these aspirations, he would be
> apt to concede the frontier adjustments.

But Biddle was also aware of the constraints imposed on Sikorski's pursuit
of this strategy by his domestic critics:

> It is not likely, however, that he would air such views to his
> associates as a whole. For with possibly one or two exceptions, their
> desire for a settlement of the Polish-Russian frontier on the basis of
> *status quo ante* is fundamental. Moreover, circles which, importantly
> due to this very question, had opposed Sikorski's signing the Agree-
> ment with Russia, would be quick to seize on any such views, and
> to exploit them against him as well as against his Russian policy.[30]

Still another indication that Sikorski was actively seeking to bargain
with Moscow is the fact that, at this point (early 1942), he did drop his
proposal for the inclusion of all three Baltic States in a future federation,
emphasizing instead the importance to Poland only of Lithuania. Likewise
he began playing down Polish objections to the Soviet annexation of Bessarabia, while continuing to stress the strategic value of Bukovina to Central
European defenses. These shifts were reflected in a number of communications with both London and Washington concerning the pending Anglo-
Soviet treaty.[31] Moreover, as those negotiations proceeded and as it began
to look more and more likely that the final treaty would include the dreaded
territorial clause, the Poles moved still closer to tacit acceptance of concessions. Without retracting their objections to British recognition of Soviet
rights in Lithuania and Bukovina, they began pleading quietly with the
Foreign Office for a formal guarantee, written into the treaty, "that Poland
should receive . . . some counterweight in the West for the prejudice which

---

[30] *FRUS, 1942*, 3:102.

[31] See Chapter V, note 80, above; also "Extract from a conversation between General
Sikorski and Mr. Churchill . . . ," March 11, 1942, and "Memorandum from the Polish
Embassy in London to the Foreign Office concerning Soviet territorial claims," March 27,
1942, in *Documents*, 1:295-99 and 314-17. This shift in Polish policy is also reflected in a
number of British documents from this period; see especially C3438/19/55, FO 371/31081,
and C3999/19/55, FO 371/31082, PRO.

would be done to her interests in the East. It would make it easier for the Polish Government to acquiesce in the treaty . . ."[32]

The significance of these numerous hints and subtle policy shifts was not lost on the British. At the time of Sikorski's lengthy memorandum to Bevin in November 1940, at least one Foreign Office observer perceived that the omission from the memo of any mention of the Riga line reflected Polish (or at least Sikorski's) recognition "that they cannot regain the Ukrainian and White Russian territories."[33] Early in 1942, following the general's return from Moscow, another British official remarked on the duality of the exile government's posture on the eastern boundary—that is, official rigidity combined with unofficial intimations of flexibility:

> The official attitude of the Polish Government regarding the eastern frontiers of Poland is that they cannot now consider or discuss any changes from the position as it existed at the outbreak of the war in August 1939. There is, however, some reason to suppose that, provided they received compensation elsewhere, *e.g.*, in East Prussia, Danzig and Upper Silesia, the Polish Government might be ready at the Peace Conference to consider reduced frontiers in the east. In no circumstances, however, do they appear prepared to contemplate the abandonment of Vilna [Wilno] or Lwów, which have been closely associated with the Polish State for many centuries.

He also suggested that an exchange of the Polish and Ukrainian populations should be considered as one element of a viable solution to this problem, but noted that overall the "attitude of Polish public opinion is . . . likely to be more intransigent than that of the Polish Government."[34]

[32] The plea for a guarantee of compensation was apparently not made in any of the written representations to the Foreign Office, but was recorded in Foreign Office minutes of conversations. The subject was first broached by Sikorski himself in a meeting with Eden, probably on April 15th; it was repeated the following day by Kulski to Strang, and raised again in early May by both Kulski and Raczyński. The only area specifically mentioned was East Prussia, but the Poles appear to have been more anxious to establish the principle of their right to compensation at the expense of the enemy. C4072 and C4077/19/55, FO 371/31082, and C4789/19/55, FO 371/31083, PRO.

[33] E. L. Woodward's comments in C14/14/62, FO 371/26419, PRO; see also Frank Roberts's comments in the same file entry.

[34] F. K. Roberts, "The Eastern Frontier of Poland," March 16, 1942; C3056/19/55, FO 371/31079, PRO. Roberts suggested here that, apart from the pressure of public opinion, official inflexibility on this question might be related to a desire to protect Polish citizens from the eastern provinces. See also the British record of the conversation between Sikorski and Eden on January 22, 1943, in which the latter noted that the Polish position on the eastern boundary, as expressed in the December 23, 1942, memo to the U.S. Department of State, "represent[ed] a more rigid attitude on the part of the Polish Government than that which had been developed to me [Eden] in confidence by General Sikorski in the past." C910/258/55, FO 371/34563, PRO.

One final piece of evidence comes from an entry in Raczyński's diary made during Sikorski's third trip to the United States in December 1942:

> The attempt at improving our relations with Russia is causing a political sensation in Polish circles. From America the general has inspired a number of articles in the press about his intended trip to Moscow. He is at the same time appearing publicly as the champion of our territorial integrity, and negotiating confidentially on this subject with the State Department and President Roosevelt. His policy is, in my opinion, both skillful and bold—let us hope it succeeds.[35]

As is often the case with Raczyński's references to boundary matters, the passage is more tantalizing than informative. Nonetheless it is difficult to imagine that, at this late date, he viewed an inflexible stand on Poland's 1939 eastern boundary either as "skillful and bold" or as an effective means of "improving relations with Russia." Thus it is not unreasonable to suppose that the confidential negotiations of which he speaks had some purpose other than merely extracting American recognition of Poland's territorial integrity. We do know, for instance, that Sikorski submitted the memorandum defending Poland's prewar eastern border several weeks later than those on her western boundaries and the Central European federation, and only after he had been given to understand that he would not get the support he sought on either proposal.[36] Indeed, there is also circumstantial evidence that, prior to submitting the government-prepared memo on the eastern boundary, he presented Welles with a personal statement on Polish-Soviet relations, the latter far more conciliatory in tone and stressing above all the "necessity of seeking an understanding with Russia."[37]

---

[35] Raczyński, *W sojuszniczym Londynie*, p. 159.

[36] The "Memorandum on the Polish-Russian Frontier" was delivered to Under Secretary Welles on December 23, 1942, and is reprinted in both *Documents*, 1:469-72, and *FRUS, 1942*, 3:208-212. We have already seen that the other memoranda were submitted early in December, between the 4th and 7th, and the evidence suggests that Sikorski began getting feedback from the Americans by the 12th at the latest. See Chapter V, especially note 86, above; also Raczyński, *W sojuszniczym Londynie*, p. 157; and *FRUS, 1942*, 3:199-202 and 204-208. The American response is related in Chapter X below, especially pp. 301-311 and note 136.

[37] The Polish record of Sikorski's meeting with Welles on December 4, 1942, includes among the list of items submitted that day "a detailed exposé concerning the matter of the attitude toward Russia and the necessity of seeking an understanding with Russia on the question of Polish-Soviet relations . . ." The brief précis here indicates the statement included also some discussion of the "legal bases of Poland's eastern boundaries" and concluded with a proposal for direct negotiations on outstanding issues between Sikorski and Stalin with the "express support" of the United States and Great Britain. Ciechanowski Deposit, Box 67[84], folio: "Raporty podczas pobytu Premiera Generała Sikorskiego w USA (1.XII.1942-10.I.1943)," HIWRP. No copy of this "exposé" is appended to the record here, but other

What conclusions can one draw from these admittedly scattered and sometimes indirect references? Certainly it is impossible not to conclude that, at least in the period following his return from Moscow and possibly even earlier, General Sikorski seriously contemplated the necessity of making substantial territorial concessions to the Soviet Union. The remaining elements of uncertainty concern the extent to which he would have been willing to compromise and the circumstances under which he would, or could, have done so. With regard to the first, it is quite apparent that he did not—and indeed from the political standpoint could not—recognize as an acceptable basis for negotiation the 1939 Molotov-Ribbentrop partition line, which the Poles understandably viewed as a product of aggression against them. Nor is there any indication that he would have accepted the Curzon line, which with a few digressions was merely a less odious name for essentially the same boundary. If we accept Mitkiewicz's account, however, he had by early March of 1942 conditioned himself to the loss of about half of Poland's eastern provinces and was focusing primarily on salvaging the predominantly Polish centers of Lwów and, through federation with Lithuania, Wilno. Whether, as Poland's diplomatic situation deteriorated during 1942, he modified his view still further we simply do not know.[38] As to the circumstances under which he might have agreed to a compromise, his conditions appear to have been two: first, that a future boundary agreement be the result of genuine give-and-take negotiations and not merely the legitimization of an act of force;[39] and,

papers related to this trip include a lengthy statement on Polish-Soviet relations, in Polish and marked "dictated by Gen. Wł. Sikorski" and "strictly secret"; ibid., Box 93[84], folio: "Basic data prepared for Sikorski's visit," HIWRP. This statement repeats a number of the key passages from the prime minister's secret report of the previous January 12th, particularly his critical references to prewar Polish policy and to the political opposition, the urgency of reaching an understanding with Russia, his inferences about possible boundary changes in the east and west; on the other hand, it does not contain a defense of the Riga boundary.

[38] However, most of the evidence relates to the period (i.e., early 1942) when Sikorski could still believe that Stalin was willing to bargain—at a time, too, when he still foresaw the Polish Army fighting on the Russian front. On the other hand, Sumner Welles's memorandum of his conversation with Sikorski on December 4, 1942, offers by way of omission a hint that the prime minister was considering dropping his objection to Soviet incorporation of Lithuania and Bukovina. (See Chapter V, note 96, above.) Since he had tied his insistence on the inclusion of these two areas in a future Central European structure to Poland's security needs in the east—and, in the case of Lithuania, also to the retention of Wilno within the federation—their omission here may be an indication (very tenuous to be sure) that he was contemplating the need for more far-reaching concessions than he had earlier in the year. See *FRUS, 1942*, 3:201.

[39] Mitkiewicz, reviewing the eastern boundary dispute at about the time of Sikorski's last visit to Washington, wrote: ". . . Here the most far-reaching concession that Gen. Sikorski and his Government could make would be a revision of the eastern boundary and an examination of nationality problems—Ukrainian, Belorussian, and possibly Lithuanian—by

second, that the Poles not be forced to give away their bargaining cards in the east so long as the Allies refused to discuss seriously either Poland's desiderata in the west or, more generally, the requirements of Central European security and independence.

way of amicable bilateral negotiations, barring *faits accomplis* before the time of an agreement." *Z gen. Sikorskim*, p. 303.

VII · Synthesis:
The Precarious Balance

WE HAVE already examined in some detail the interdependence of Sikorski's proposal for a Central European federation and his concept of Poland's future western boundary, with each reinforcing the need and, at the same time, providing justification for the other. It should be obvious by now that much the same kind of reciprocal relationship existed between these two aspects of his program, on the one hand, and his desire for a reconciliation with the Soviet Union, on the other. For instance, the proposed federation reinforced the need for good Polish-Soviet relations, because the reluctance of the Czechs to do anything that might antagonize the Kremlin made the success of any such association with Poland ultimately dependent on Soviet good will—most specifically on a settlement of Poland's boundary dispute with the Soviet Union. (In fact, this was an issue on which the Czechs had consistently refused to support Polish claims since 1918.) Evidence of this dependence is the fact that, while the Polish and Czech exile governments declared their intention to form a postwar union months before Soviet entry into the Grand Alliance, and thus at a time when Poland and the Soviet Union were theoretically still at war with one another, their federation began to assume concrete shape (albeit briefly) only after Polish-Soviet relations were restored in mid-1941. As we shall see in Chapter XI, its subsequent fortunes closely paralleled the later decline and collapse of those relations.[1] At the same time—the apparent paradox

---

[1] Strumph-Wojtkiewicz (*Gwiazda Władysława Sikorskiego*, p. 236) has pointed out this connection between improved Polish-Soviet relations and the Polish-Czech Agreement of January 1942: "It is obvious that this agreement between the Polish and Czech governments could occur only at a moment when relations between Poland and the Soviet Union were being smoothed over. Czechoslovakia, traditionally friendly toward Russia, could enter into close association with Poland only when the Czechs had received assurance that such an association would in no way be directed against Russia. The conclusion of the confederation— or rather the announcement of it—immediately after Sikorski's return from Moscow was an expression of Czech confidence in the policy of General Sikorski, in its correctness and sincerity." Written in 1946, this is one of the very few assessments of the federation (if not the only one) emerging from postwar Poland to acknowledge that it was not anti-Soviet in intent. See also Kukiel, *Generał Sikorski*, p. 181. As we shall see in Chapter XI, the period between the Polish-Soviet Agreement of July 1941 and the declaration of confederation in January 1942 proved to be the high point of Polish-Czech relations, which deteriorated quickly along with the illusion of Soviet benevolence.

notwithstanding—the federation seemed to provide an acceptable vehicle for reducing Poland's (and Czechoslovakia's) vulnerability to Soviet domination and, to that extent, made the prospect of an understanding with Moscow less threatening to the Poles.

The relationship between the question of Poland's boundary in the west and a settlement, particularly a territorial settlement, with Russia was somewhat more complex. Certainly it was not in Sikorski's mind (nor for that matter in Stalin's) a simple matter of compensation. For him, Poland's claim to the lands east of the Oder and Lusatian Neisse were fully justified by her economic and strategic needs; in this sense, the eastern and western boundary questions were unrelated. Nonetheless, in a political sense they were inextricably related. On the one hand, a promise of substantial gains in the west would have greatly facilitated an understanding with Moscow by making it easier for the Poles to accept concessions in the east; on the other, the growing certainty that such concessions would be necessary made gains in the west all the more imperative. Moreover, although Sikorski could not have accepted a situation in which the Soviet Union was the only guarantor of a Polish-German boundary on the Oder and Neisse, the attainment and maintenance of such a boundary without Soviet support was inconceivable, since it would have returned Poland to the "two-enemy" stance against which he had so consistently argued.

THE POINT that has most often been missed in appraisals of the Sikorski period, whether friendly or hostile, is the essentially revolutionary character of his program viewed as a whole. One reason is that, of the varied cast of individuals, governments, political parties, or other institutions with some stake—whether moral, political or territorial—in the outcome of the "Polish Question" at the end of World War II, almost all have found it convenient to play down, distort, or simply ignore the innovative and (in my view) fundamental aspects of the general's strategy. Instead, attention is almost invariably focused on the negative side of his policy, on the defensive tactics forced upon him by the circumstances of Polish exile politics and Grand Alliance diplomacy. Even those few sources that do treat one or another of the positive aspects of his program do so disparately, apparently without perceiving that the whole was greater than the sum of its parts.[2]

A second and equally important reason is that we tend to view the Sikorski period through the lenses of the later wartime and postwar years

[2] Mitkiewicz's diary again seems to be the exception to the rule, in that he recognized both the interrelationships among the various aspects of Sikorski's program and the radical consequences of the whole. The impact of the various vested interests on the treatment of Sikorski's policy in the literature is explored in the Bibliographical Essay.

when, at least in the Central European context, the term "revolutionary" has become the self-proclaimed monopoly of Marxism-Leninism. In the black-or-white climate of the Cold War, only those who sided with the revolution imported from the East have merited the designation of "revolutionary" or "progressive," while all others have at best been relegated to the ranks of defenders of the *status quo ante*. Of course, Sikorski was in no sense a Marxist-Leninist. But then dictionary definitions impart no such exclusive right to the word "revolution." Webster's *Third International*, for instance, defines it in part as: ". . . a sudden, radical, or complete change [as a revolution in thought], a basic reorientation and reorganization. . . ." It is in this generic sense, especially of "a basic reorientation and reorganization," that one can view Sikorski's program as revolutionary in at least three important respects: first, in the transformation of Poland's internal socio-economic structure implicit in a westward territorial shift; second, in the reorientation of her external economic and political relationships resulting both from the territorial shift and from the proposed Central European federation; and, third, in the federation idea itself, which offered a new model for international organization and which, in an all-European context, promised a fundamental alteration of the balance of power. It has been stated earlier, but the point bears repeating here, that none of the elements of Sikorski's program was original to him: the idea of pushing Poland westward toward the Oder and Neisse had numerous advocates before and during the war, at home and in exile; likewise, the notion of federation in various guises had been a familiar part of the Polish and Central European intellectual scene throughout the interwar period. If the general's program can properly be called "revolutionary," it is because he was the first to synthesize these elements into a coherent policy which, if successfully implemented, would have had a profound impact on Poland's internal structure and external geopolitical orientation.

The implications for Poland's socioeconomic structure of a westward territorial shift were enormous. The provinces she stood to lose in the east were overwhelmingly agricultural, with relatively little natural industrial potential; agricultural production was largely unmechchanized and inefficient. In addition, the eastern *kresy* were the last holdout of Poland's feudal past, with a landholding structure dominated by large, often huge estates on the one hand and an impoverished peasantry on the other; land reform here during the interwar period had been halfhearted at best, and the Depression had wiped out the few beneficial effects it had produced. By contrast, the territories that Sikorski proposed Poland gain in the west were more generously endowed with natural resources than all of interwar Poland, with sections of Oppeln and Lower Silesia already heavily industrialized; in the agricultural sector, their acquisition would provide the

Poles with the opportunity to create almost from scratch a stable and independent peasant class similar to that which had existed in the prewar western provinces of Poznania and Pomerania. Between the increased industrial capacity and the added farmlands, Poland would be able to eliminate her surplus rural population—estimated as high as eight million, or nearly 25 percent of the total population—which had so burdened her economic progress. Thus in a single stroke she would emerge with a vastly improved natural resource base, a more favorable balance between agriculture and industry, and a healthier agrarian structure. The domestic political consequences of these changes would also be profound, shifting power away from the vestiges of the landed gentry, whose economic base was largely in the east, in favor of a larger working class and more affluent peasantry.[3]

No less revolutionary would be the combined effects of the territorial shift and the establishment of a Central European federation on Poland's international orientation. As we saw earlier, her prewar configuration was disastrous from virtually every standpoint—whether political, economic, or strategic. Rather than afford her a definitive political orientation, her boundaries were a source of dissatisfaction and discord on all sides, a barrier to normal relations not only with Germany and Russia, but with Czechoslovakia and Lithuania as well. Rather than reinforce natural economic relationships, they served to cut her off from essential sources of support for her economic independence leaving her vulnerable to outside domination. Rather than provide even a minimum of security, they left her most vital centers exposed to German might from three directions, while the military burden imposed by her political isolation and strategic exposure only further undermined her economic viability. In these circumstances, the protection provided by alliances with the West could be little more than illusion.

By contrast, implementation of Sikorski's territorial and federation proposals would yield a new and clearer definition of Poland's external relationships. Strategically, she would still stand face to face with Germany, but now along a single shortened frontier well removed from her main industrial and political centers; and now she would no longer stand alone but as part of a united Central European front in alliance with Russia (assuming a settlement of the Polish-Soviet frontier acceptable to both sides) as well as with the West. More important, however, her primary

---

[3] While Sikorski's ideas for a postwar domestic economic program are beyond the scope of the present study, it is worth noting in passing that he was actively concerned with the question of land reform and the creation of a stable and independent peasantry from an early stage in the war. See, e.g., the British record of his meeting with Bevin and Strang on July 3, 1941 in C7458/3226/55, FO 371/26755, PRO.

political and economic alignment would no longer be along an east-west axis, as the weak point between Germany and Russia. Rather, the establishment of a federation together with the elongation of the Polish-Czech frontier through their respective industrial centers would give Poland a predominantly southward orientation; at the same time, the Oder with its port at Stettin, and to a lesser extent the Vistula with Danzig, would serve as gateways to the world not only for Polish Silesia but for Czech Moravia as well—and potentially, through a series of projected canals, for the rest of Central Europe. As important as the physical reorientation would be the psychological effects of a westward territorial shift. On the one hand, withdrawal from the remaining ethnically non-Polish lands in the east would put an end once and for all to unrealistic dreams of recreating the old Polish-Lithuanian Commonwealth with its implicit message of Poland's cultural and political superiority. On the other hand, her reconstruction within boundaries more consistent with her ethnic strength and economic interests, with a real and vital role to play as an equal partner in a Central European venture, would give the Poles a more realistic sense of their national identity, of their rightful "place in Europe," thereby making the "great power" posturings of the interwar period unnecessary as well as inappropriate.

Finally, the very concept of federation held potentially revolutionary consequences not only for Poland and the other prospective participants, but for the postwar balance on the entire European continent. For its members, the federation would mark an important step beyond the nation-state as the basic unit of political and economic organization, requiring a voluntary sacrifice of the theoretical sovereignty of each in exchange for more of its substance for all. In a broader European context, the federal concept provided a model for continental organization based on a rejection of self-determination as an absolute goal in favor of concerted action by a community of nations whose history and geography gave them common needs and interests, thereby striking a balance between the unworkable universalism of the League of Nations and the more traditional domination of the weak by the strong. If such a solution sounds too far removed from the prewar and postwar realities of Central Europe to have ever been more than a fleeting pipe dream, we should recall the skepticism with which later proposals for West European union were first met. One might go so far as to say that the ideas that postwar statesmen began applying to Western Europe only in the late 1940s, General Sikorski was promoting in already well-developed form for Central Europe in 1941 and 1942.

SINCE Sikorski has often been accused, by critics both to his left and right politically, of relying too heavily on the West at the expense either of the

Soviet Union or of Poland's presumed "great power" potential,[4] it is worth asking at this point just what he did want of his Anglo-American allies and what role he foresaw for them, as well as for the Soviet Union, in the Central Europe of the future. There can be no question that his political preferences lay with the West; he made no secret of his desire not to see communism or satellite status imposed on Poland. Nor can there be any question, as he himself repeated many times, that he wanted firm alliances with the West in the future. But it would be a mistake to read into his preferences a desire to isolate the Soviet Union—either by erecting a new *cordon sanitaire*, as communist writers are so quick to charge, or by turning Washington and London against Moscow. On the contrary, it was essential to the success of the general's program—as it would be later to the program of the Polish Communists—that the Grand Alliance continue into the postwar period. Only thus could the Poles be assured that Germany would be subject to a stringent and uniform occupation policy and not become the focal point of East-West rivalry, ultimately at the expense of Poland and her smaller neighbors.

If Sikorski believed it essential to gain Western support for his proposals, it was because he understood that the circumstances that had allowed Poland at least partially and momentarily to determine her own fate following World War I (specifically the collapse of both Germany and Russia) would not be repeated; that the major decisions affecting the postwar territorial and political structure of Europe would be made by the Great Powers; and that whatever influence Poland might exert on decisions affecting her own future would have to be within the framework of rules established by them. To seek a separate settlement with the Soviet Union—assuming that such was attainable—not only without Anglo-American participation but in the face of their refusal to discuss the postwar settlement during wartime, would have laid the Poles open to the risk that the West might support future German claims and, in turn, to a new round of competition for Germany's allegiance. In other words, the very antithesis of the uniform severe occupation policy he favored. What the Polish leader wanted from both East and West was recognition for his basic premise: that the nations lying between Germany and Russia, by virtue of their history and geography, formed a distinct community whose political independence, economic vitality, and capacity for self-defense would serve not only the interests of its own members, but in equal measure the cause of European security—including, through its ability to check German expansionism, the security of the Soviet Union. Beyond this, he sought Great Power

---

[4] See, e.g., Giertych, *Pół wieku polskiej polityki*, chap. 13; Pobóg-Malinowski, *Najnowsza historia*, 3:chaps. 23-25, *passim*; Kowalski, *ZSRR a granica*, pp. 37 and 58; also his *Walka dyplomatyczna*, pp. 203, 289-90, and 333.

support for the detailed proposals that would transform his premise into reality. The major difference in his approach to Moscow and to the Western capitals was that he anticipated (with ample reason) stiffer resistance to his program from the Soviets and, as a counterweight, sought some persuasive arm-twisting by the British and the Americans.

In light of all this, it is clearly unfair to suggest that Sikorski would have settled for a Poland at odds with her two largest neighbors and dependent on the West for her security. Although a strong advocate of Franco-Polish ties in the interwar period, the failure of both Britain and France to come to Poland's aid in 1939, followed by the swift collapse of the latter less than a year later, had delivered the *coup de grâce* to whatever remained of his faith in the efficacy of alliances with the West as the mainstay of his nation's security.[5] Indeed, it was precisely to avoid a repetition of the whole post-Versailles experience that he developed his strategy of "real guarantees"; if Poland and the other nations of Central Europe were to cease being pawns in someone else's chess game, they must henceforth rely in the first instance on their combined internal strengths. By the same token, it is unfair to describe Sikorski's policy—and especially the federation as the heart of that policy—as "anti-Soviet," or as scarcely distinguishable from those of Piłsudski and Beck. In particular, the suggestion that he sought to use the federation as a vehicle to induce the other Central European states to gang up on the Soviet Union—as Soviet and some Polish sources contend—is a distortion bordering on demagoguery. If anything, creation of a federation such as Sikorski proposed could have turned Poland away from her old preoccupation with the Jagiellonian east, toward her new center of gravity in the southwest and toward her expanded horizons both to the south and north. The real message of his program was Central Europe for the Central Europeans; and one can ascribe to it anti-Soviet motives only if one concedes to the Russians some inherent right to dominate the affairs of that beleaguered region. It is, finally, the most unkind cut of all to suggest that the general's major failing was his inability to break with Poland's past policies and prejudices—with her "great-power" pretensions and her anti-Russian animus. For it would turn out that the real tragedy of Sikorski's tenure was that he was a man ahead

[5] As Mitkiewicz noted in his diary on July 4, 1940 (*Z gen. Sikorskim*, pp. 74-75): ". . . Gen. Sikorski is aware of the fact that staking everything, our existence as a Nation and State, solely on the one British card constitutes a serious danger; for, even in the event of victory by Great Britain in the war with Germany, we ourselves will still have to take care of settling postwar relations with Soviet Russia. Mainly from these considerations, disregarding the fact that Gen. Sikorski clearly sees that two fronts—east and west—with the unconditional participation of America are necessary for the defeat of Germany, he is for an understanding with Soviet Russia already now, during this war."

of his time: ahead of the majority of his countrymen in his ability to recognize the limits and opportunities of Poland's situation, and ahead of her allies as well in his willingness to think in terms of new patterns of international organization.

THE IRONY of Sikorski's program is that its greatest strength was also its greatest weakness. While every element reinforced the others so that progress in any one area tended to promote all, they were so closely interwoven that if one of those elements was removed the whole structure began to come unstuck: take away the prospect of sizable territorial gains in the west and the already difficult problem of compromise in the east becomes insurmountable; reverse progress toward a Polish-Soviet understanding and prospects for a federation with the Czechs vanish; remove the federation and the possibility for a stable structure in Central Europe also disappears; finally, break up the Grand Alliance—especially the prospect of a concerted policy toward Germany—and the heart of Europe becomes a theater for Great Power competition threatening Poland's gains in the west. And so the vicious circle closes. Where Part II has been the story of the development, or the coming together of Sikorski's program, it is to the coming apart of that program that we now turn.

Part Three

Agony and Aftermath

VIII · *Setting for Disaster*

THE OBSTACLES that General Sikorski faced in attempting to realize his program fell into two categories: one external and almost wholly beyond the influence of the Poles; the other internal and, if presumably within the control of the Poles as a nation, certainly beyond the control of one man, even as prime minister of the Government-in-Exile. The first category consisted of the currents and cross-currents within the Grand Alliance, not only over the "Polish Question" itself, but more generally over the premises of a postwar European settlement, and even over wartime relations among the Big Three. While the Poles might reasonably have hoped to exert some influence in the first area, they could do so only insofar as their urgings were not at odds with Allied policies and did not pose a threat to wartime unity. The second category consisted of political and institutional restraints on Sikorski's ability to direct Polish policy, including in particular: deep and bitter divisions among the Poles not only over the best means of attaining their goals, but at times over the goals themselves; the constraints inherent in an exile status as a result of isolation from one's native constituency and a reduced ability to control dissident elements either at home or in the host country; and the political and constitutional compromises attending the establishment of the Govenment-in-Exile.

UNCERTAIN ALLIES

In their treatment of the diplomacy of the Second World War, historians have tended to place greatest emphasis on the events more or less from the middle of 1943 on. There is nothing surprising in this. The period after mid-1943, with its intense diplomatic activity and the Big Three conferences at Teheran, Yalta, and Potsdam, was unquestionably more dramatic than the early war years. Moreover, the focal point of historical research has been less the Allied victory in the war against Germany than the origins of the Cold War that followed. And here the decisions that most directly and immediately shaped the postwar world were made during the later period.

To a certain extent, the "Polish Question" followed the general pattern, at least in the sense that Poland's postwar territorial and political status was decided in the two-year period between Sikorski's death in July 1943 and the Potsdam Conference in July-August 1945. However, if one is seeking to understand not the origin of the Poland that emerged from World War II, but the reasons for the demise of the Poland that perished in the war, then a preoccupation with the later war years at the expense of the earlier Sikorski period leads to gross distortions. These distortions relate to the policy of the Government-in-Exile itself, which after Sikorski became essentially reactive and negative; but more importantly, they relate to the attitudes of the Great Powers toward the Polish Question. If, on the one hand, one concentrates on the events after Teheran, Poland emerges as a test case in which East and West probed each other's intentions in Central Europe and over which the Grand Alliance began to come apart. On the other hand, if one examines more carefully the pre-Teheran period, the issue of Poland's territorial and political future appears as a stepchild to the cause of Allied unity. As damaging to Polish interests as Moscow's ambitions was what came to be known as the "policy of postponement": the reluctance on the part of the Americans, and to a considerable extent also the British, to discuss problems of a postwar settlement, especially territorial problems, during wartime. Sikorski was to learn soon enough that this attempt to divorce the political aspects of war from the military— or, in the case of the British, to let the political follow from the military— veiled views of a postwar order wholly incompatible with his own concept of "real guarantees." He would also learn that under the guise of "postponement" the Western powers, far from playing the role of active champions of Poland's (or Central Europe's) independence, had proven only too ready to mortgage her meager bargaining points for their own advantage or to their own visions of a postwar world in which the Central Europeans themselves would have little voice.

Great Britain. As allies, Poland and Britain were an unlikely match from the start. Despite the British guarantee to Poland in April of 1939 and the Anglo-Polish treaty that followed in August,[1] the alliance remained mostly on paper for nearly a year. It was to France, her traditional ally, that Poland first turned in the wake of defeat; it was there, first in Paris and then Angers, that she organized a government and army in exile. With the fall of France in June of 1940, the Poles found themselves wholly dependent on the British, formal allies to be sure, but ones with whom they had never had close ties and who were little acquainted with Polish affairs. The fact that the Poles were able to capitalize on their meager assets to become for

---

[1] The British guarantee to Poland against German aggression was first issued verbally by Prime Minister Chamberlain in the House of Commons on March 31st, but was formalized in a written agreement only on April 6th; this was followed by a Treaty of Mutual Assistance on August 25th, two days after the signing of the Nazi-Soviet pact. For details see, e.g., Cienciala, *Poland and the Western Powers*, pp. 223-37.

a time Britain's only fighting ally in Europe, and to lay the foundation for future wartime collaboration, was largely to Sikorski's personal credit.[2]

But his success in solidifying a military alliance with the British was not the same as winning them over to his conceptions of Poland's future. Traditionally, Britain's balance-of-power policy had left scant room for long-term commitments to "buffer" states. Indeed, during the First World War, at least until the Bolshevik Revolution in 1917, London actually opposed the resurrection of an independent Polish state, acceding instead to the tsarist government's insistence that the Polish question be treated as an internal Russian affair. The British approach was spelled out most clearly in a November 1916 memorandum by Foreign Secretary Balfour who, while recognizing the need for "some kind of home rule for Poland" as well as the desirability "of diminishing the area from which the Central Powers can draw the men and money required for a policy of aggression," continued:

> . . . Looking at the Polish question from a purely British point of view, . . . I should not like to see the old Kingdom of Poland restored. I should fear that the new Poland will suffer from the diseases through which the old Poland perished; that it would be a theatre of perpetual intrigues between Germany and Russia; and that its existence, so far from promoting the cause of European peace, would be a perpetual occasion of European strife. Moreover, even if such Poland were capable of playing the part of an efficient buffer State (which I doubt) I am not sure that a buffer State between Germany and Russia would be any advantage to Western Europe. If Germany were relieved of all fear of pressure from Russia, and were at liberty to turn her whole strength towards developing her Western ambitions, France and Britain might be the sufferers; and I am not by any means confident that cutting off Russia from her Western neighbours might not divert her interests towards the Far East to an extent which British statesmen could not view without some misgivings. . . .

The solution that, in Balfour's view, "would best suit our interests" was the reconstitution of "a Poland endowed with a large measure of autonomy, while remaining an integral part of the Russian Empire—the new State or province to include not only all Russian Poland but also Austria's and (part at least) of Prussia's share in the plunder of the ancient Kingdom."[3] Although later, during the Peace Conference at Versailles, the British came

---

[2] Raczyński, *W sojuszniczym Londynie*, pp. 201-203.

[3] Quoted in Komarnicki, *Rebirth of the Polish Republic*, pp. 61-62. It should be noted, to his credit, that Balfour foresaw that population transfers might be necessary to give Poland strategically viable boundaries.

around to the idea of a fully independent Poland, it was Lloyd George's protests that led to plebiscites in Upper Silesia and East Prussia and to autonomous status for Danzig, rather than the outright cession of these areas to Poland. For now "balance of power" dictated that Germany not be so weakened as to be incapable of offsetting a Bolshevik Russia.[4] At the same time, the British protested Poland's expansion east of the Curzon line and generally took an unsympathetic view of Polish policy throughout the interwar period. They were especially outraged by the Poles' seizure of Teschen Silesia during the Sudeten crisis in September of 1938.[5]

The fact that after such an inauspicious beginning Britain should have been willing to go to war over Hitler's attack on Poland becomes intelligible only when one realizes that it was less to defend Poland's independence than because, by 1939, even the Chamberlain government had finally awakened to the true magnitude of the danger posed by Nazi Germany. As the émigré Polish historian Edward Rozek later wrote, not without a tinge of bitterness:

> The British decision was motivated not by any specific sympathy for Poland, but by the final realization that a struggle for a redivision of Europe was on, that the traditional balance of power was just about to be upset, and that the struggle for the integrity of the British Isles had to be fought outside the British Isles. The British were certain that the "romantic" Poles would fight and, by so doing, would at least weaken the impact of the German war machine on the West. Thus Poland's resistance would buy a certain amount of the time needed by the Western Powers to arm themselves and temporarily divert from the West the full force of the German Armies.[6]

[4] Ibid., pp. 318-54; and Lundgreen-Nielsen, *The Polish Problem*, pp. 69-70.

[5] Writing later on the Teschen affair, Churchill said of the Poles: "The heroic characteristics of the Polish race must not blind us to their record of folly and ingratitude which over centuries has led them through measureless suffering. We see them, in 1919, a people restored by the victory of the Western Allies after long generations of partition and servitude to be an independent Republic and one of the main Powers in Europe. Now, in 1938, over a question so minor as Teschen, they sundered themselves from all those friends in France, Britain, and the United States who had lifted them once again to a national, coherent life, and whom they were soon to need so sorely. . . . It is a mystery and tragedy of European history that a people capable of every heroic virtue, gifted, valiant, charming, as individuals, should repeatedly show such inveterate faults in almost every aspect of their governmental life. Glorious in revolt and ruin; squalid and shameful in triumph. The bravest of the brave, too often led by the vilest of the vile! . . ." Winston S. Churchill, *The Gathering Storm*, p. 323. In light of Britain's role in the Munich Agreement, which preceded and precipitated Poland's seizure of Teschen, this statement can only be viewed as excessive and hypocritical.

[6] *Allied Wartime Diplomacy*, p. 26. The popular notion that the British "went to war for Poland" was fostered largely by Churchill's later and repeated reminders to the Poles and others as evidence of Britain's good faith. At the time, however, the Chamberlain government

London's tendency to see the future organization of Europe in terms of spheres of influence, and thus to concede to the Soviets virtually without question postwar possession of the territories acquired by virtue of the Molotov-Ribbentrop pact, was already apparent in the first weeks of the war. On October 1, 1939, in a broadcast that contained his now famous "riddle wrapped in a mystery inside an enigma" remark, Winston Churchill saw Russian national interest as the "key" to Soviet behavior:

> Russia has pursued a cold policy of self-interest. We could have wished that the Russian armies should be standing on their present line as the friends and allies of Poland instead of as invaders. But that the Russian armies should stand on this line was clearly necessary for the safety of Russia against the Nazi menace . . .[7]

Later that month Lord Halifax, then British foreign secretary, told the House of Commons that Britain's guarantee to Poland applied only to German aggression and suggested that London was inclined to view Soviet occupation of territories up to the Molotov-Ribbentrop partition line as a return to the Curzon line recommended in 1919-20.[8] A year later, and still months before Moscow was forced into the war, Halifax informed the Poles that his government was prepared to acknowledge de facto Soviet control over all of the territories occupied in 1939-40 as the price for an Anglo-Soviet rapprochement, assuring them at the same time that their interests were not in jeopardy as ultimate sovereignty over the territories in question would not be affected.[9]

Moreover, this willingness to concede Poland's east was not offset by

---

apparently went so far as to attempt to induce Roosevelt to pressure the Poles into making whatever concessions were necessary to stave off war. As Adolf Berle, assistant secretary of state, noted acidly in his diary on August 24, 1939: "I am not quite clear how you would word a strong message to Poland. It would have to begin: 'In view of the fact that your suicide is required, kindly oblige by' etc." *Navigating the Rapids 1918-1971: From the Papers of Adolf A. Berle,* ed. Beatrice Bishop Berle and Travis Beal Jacobs, p. 243; and Robert Dallek, *Franklin D. Roosevelt and American Foreign Policy, 1932-1945,* p. 197. Several months after the war began, Halifax was still wondering if Hitler's demands "hadn't after all been acceptable." See Chapter V, note 36, above.

[7] Churchill, then First Lord of the Admiralty, made the same point even more bluntly in a September 25th paper for the War Cabinet; see *The Gathering Storm,* pp. 448-49.

[8] Kukiel, *Generał Sikorski,* pp. 98-99; for the text of the Anglo-Polish Agreement of Mutual Assistance, see *Documents,* 1:550-52; and Władysław W. Kulski, "The Anglo-Polish Agreement of Aug. 25, 1939," pp. 23-38. In addition, the Poles had to contend with their old nemesis Lloyd George who, in several newspaper articles in September 1939, applauded Soviet annexation of the eastern provinces as an act liberating "Russian peoples" (sic) from Polish oppression. For Ambassador Raczyński's account and rejoinders, see *W sojuszniczym Londynie,* pp. 49-50 and 414-18.

[9] PRM 20/36, GSHI; and *Documents,* 1:98-101. See also Chapter IV, note 14, above.

a similarly indulgent approach to the question of compensation at Germany's expense. Sikorski's first tentative hints concerning East Prussia evoked a decidedly negative response. As one foreign service officer wrote in the internal minutes: "I am sorry to see that General Sikorski is toying with the East Prussian ambition which always struck me as rather silly when advanced by the wilder Polish imperialists before the war." Added Assistant Under Secretary Strang, "the Poles are incurably romantic in their ideas."[10] Nor were these isolated views. A collection of parliamentary views on the postwar settlement published in mid-1940 confirmed the widespread tendency to deny the legitimacy of Polish claims to the eastern *kresy*, but at the same time to discount the idea of compensation; less comprehending still were the views of several contributors who suggested that Poland be required to return part of the "Corridor" and/or Upper Silesia to Germany for any concessions in East Prussia.[11]

But the aspect of British policy most inimical to Sikorski's hopes was ironically their approach to the postwar organization of Europe. For, while they were among the first to encourage the federation idea, and would continue to pay it lip service, in other ways their behavior betrayed an implicit rejection of the underlying premise of the Polish leader's program—to wit, that by joining forces the smaller nations lying between Germany and Russia could play a positive and independent role in maintaining European equilibrium, and that they need not be left to the domination of one or the other of their great neighbors. Disturbing signs on this score were in evidence well before Hitler's armies turned east in June 1941, but it was that event more than anything else that brought London's more traditional balance-of-power outlook to the surface again. Less than six weeks later, by way of editorial comment on the Polish-Soviet Agreement of July 30th, the London *Times* stated:

> The Treaty of Vienna of 1815 was realistic and free of abstract principles so characteristic of the Versailles Treaty. . . . Some leadership in Eastern Europe in the future must replace the chaos of the last twenty years. This leadership may be provided either by Germany or Russia. Therefore, the interests of Great Britain and also of the United

[10] C19288/27/55, FO 371/23131, PRO; the first signature is not legible.

[11] See, e.g., the comments on Sikorski's November 1940 memorandum, C14/14/62, FO 371/26419; and *After the War*, ed. Teeling. An internal Polish analysis of the Teeling book saw the basic problem as one of ignorance about their country and not one of openly anti-Polish views. "The book demonstrates the need for counteraction in the form of familiarizing English society with the problems of Poland's postwar reconstruction. . . Anglo-Polish ties at an emotional level are steadily improving, but this friendship has still not taken root within certain rather influential English circles, in addition to which it is not based on a real knowledge of Polish affairs." "Anglicy o sprawie odbudowy Polski," PRM 20/13, GSHI.

States demand that the German influences will not overshadow the Russian interests in Eastern Europe. . . .[12]

Moreover, there is reason to believe that, as early as that summer of 1941, the British made a "half promise" to the Russians not to oppose a Soviet sphere of influence over the nations on her western flank. In a memorandum dated September 15, 1941, U.S. Assistant Secretary of State Adolf Berle reported the following exchange with one Ralph Stevenson, principal private secretary of the Foreign Office:

> I asked how their thinking was running as to the reorganization of Eastern Europe. Specifically, I asked *whether they had entered into any real commitments with the Russians*, in view of the very extensive commitments which the Russians had asked of the British during the abortive negotiations of 1939 . . . [and] *whether, speaking realistically, the proposed arrangement of a reconstituted Poland, Czechoslovakia and Yugoslavia, under some kind of federated system but in close relations with Russia did not really mean—to the Russians, at least—that they were to dominate that entire area.*
>
> Stevenson said that, speaking frankly, the British Government *had given a half promise to that effect.* At all events, they had permitted the Russians to believe that the British would be favorable.[13]

As to the reasoning behind this "half promise," Berle hinted at a degree of complacency concerning the future Soviet role in Europe:

> Stevenson said that they [the British] *considered that they were merely dealing with the old imperialist Russia.* He implied, and possibly said directly, that he thought conditions at the close of the war would be such that the British half promise in regard to this area might not be brought to fruition; that conditions would be such as to make it virtually impossible to carry out the kind of thing that the Russians had in mind and from which the British had at least not dissented.[14]

---

[12] "Peace and Power," London *Times*, August 1, 1941; quoted in Rozek, *Allied Wartime Diplomacy*, p. 63.

[13] *FRUS, 1941*, 1:188 [emphasis added].

[14] Ibid. [emphasis added]. Churchill later made several statements in a similar vein to Sikorski. On the first occasion, in January 1942, the latter had warned that Stalin was "a staunch Communist . . . [who] would tend to introduce communism in Europe from Norway to Greece"—to which Churchill replied "that Great Britain was not afraid of communism. Should Europe accept communism, Great Britain would not oppose it, . . ." *Documents*, 1:275. In another conversation in March of that year, during which the Briton attempted to convince the Pole of the urgency of the proposed Anglo-Soviet treaty, Churchill declared: "Should Russia come to an agreement with the Reich, all would be lost. It must not happen." Then he added: "If Russia was victorious she would decide on her frontier without consulting

Why Churchill should have been so loath to bargain with Stalin at this stage in the war—why he extended Britain's aid, implicitly recognized a Soviet sphere of influence in East Central Europe and within a few months proposed to accede to their territorial demands, with no quid pro quo either real or implied—is a question that merits more attention than it is generally given. Though understandably relieved to have Russia in the fighting, he was surely aware that Stalin needed him more than he needed Stalin and that he could extract conditions for Britain's assistance. Indeed, even his ambassador in Moscow, the mercurial Mr. Cripps, claimed to have recommended that he do precisely that.[15]

The argument that America was pressuring Churchill to postpone consideration of postwar issues is insufficient. Churchill himself was inclined to put off postwar planning, though more for pragmatic reasons than out of principle.[16] But that did not stop him from signaling both Washington and Moscow early the next spring of his willingness to recognize the Soviet Union's 1941 border in the west.[17] A second argument was that the Soviet position was too precarious—that, as Churchill put it later, "we could not force our new and sorely threatened ally" to concede what she had possessed at the time she was attacked. This was the argument used in July 1941 as the reason for not supporting Poland's prewar eastern boundary; it was used again in the spring of 1942 in a slightly different form—the fear of a separate Russo-German peace—in an attempt to persuade the

---

Great Britain; should she lose the war, the agreement would lose all its importance." *Documents*, 1:298-99.

[15] Eden noted in November 1941: ". . . Winston is impressed with the strength of our hand in dealing with Stalin. His need of us greater than our need of him, I must not go to Moscow except the red carpet is out, etc. There is much force in all this." *The Reckoning*, p. 326. In January 1942, Ambassador Cripps told Sikorski "that as long ago as July 1941 he had urged the importance of establishing and putting into practice general principles concerning the frontiers of post-war Europe. At that time Russia was so dependent on Britain's assistance that she would have accepted all proposed conditions. . . ." *Documents*, 1:269. That Cripps should have been disposed to adopt even the mildly tough-minded stance reported here strains the observer's credulity. If such advice was in fact given, it likely coincided with Cripps's brief "get tough with Moscow" phase, a temporary transformation brought on by the chilly reception accorded him by the Soviets. See Hanak, "Sir Stafford Cripps," pp. 67-69. Certainly by the time of this meeting with Sikorski, he had reverted to his more familiar posture of favoring unconditional concessions to Moscow as the price for Soviet cooperation. See, e.g., Eden's reference to Cripps in his report on "Policy Towards Russia," below.

[16] Concerning British policy on the eve of his December 1941 trip to Moscow, Eden wrote: "There was, however, also the Prime Minister's reluctance to consider post-war problems at all. This was natural enough in one who had to bear the principal burden of the conduct of the war, but it was a position which would become increasingly hard to hold with allies, American [sic] as well as Russian, who wanted to do just this." *The Reckoning*, p. 326.

[17] Churchill, *The Hinge of Fate*, pp. 327-28.

Poles and the Americans to agree to Britain's recognition of Soviet frontier demands.[18]

Yet, neither this line of reasoning nor the argument suggested in Berle's report—to the effect that the Soviet Union, whether out of weakness or disinclination, no longer posed a threat of world revolution—was pursued with any consistency. Rather, both are directly contradicted by a January 1942 memorandum in which Eden advocated immediate recognition of Soviet border demands. Writing just a month after his return from Moscow, and for War Cabinet circulation only, the foreign secretary seems to have been impressed less by Russia's current weakness than by her potential strength, and by the urgency of acceding now to Stalin's demands in the interest of future cooperation. "On the assumption that Germany is defeated," he warned,

> . . . and that France remains, for a long time at least, a weak Power, there will be no counterweight to Russia in Europe. But it may yet be necessary to maintain cooperation with Russia (a) because she might otherwise be tempted to collaborate with Germany in view of the historical tendency to, and economic urge for, these two Powers to work together; (b) in order to recreate in our own interest the balance of power in Europe against the possibility of a revived Germany, which balance has been destroyed by the collapse of France; (c) in order that, militarily speaking, Germany should be encircled. . . .
>   . . . If the defeat of the German armies is brought about chiefly by the action of the Soviet forces . . . , Russia's position on the European continent will be unassailable. Russian prestige will be so great that the establishment of Communist Governments in the majority of European countries will be greatly facilitated, and the Soviet Government will naturally be tempted to work for this. . . . But this possible development is in itself a reason for establishing close relations with the Soviet Union now while their policy is still in a fluid state, in order to exercise as much influence as possible on the moulding of their future course of action. . . .[19]

Although he admitted that the end of the war could find the Soviets in a less favorable position, Eden argued nonetheless that "common prudence

[18] Ibid.; and Churchill, *The Grand Alliance*, pp. 390-93. See also *Documents*, 1:298-99; and Mitkiewicz, *Z gen. Sikorskim*, pp. 223 and 228.

[19] "Policy Towards Russia," January 28, 1942, W.P. (42)48; filed under N563/5/38, FO 371/32875, PRO. See also Eden, *The Reckoning*, pp. 370-71. It is useful to compare the detailed, almost solicitous, attention accorded Stalin's proposals in the upper echelons of the Foreign Office with the condescending dismissal given Sikorski's November 1940 memorandum—"this tiresome paper," as Strang had called it. See Chapter V, note 50, above.

requires that we should lay our plans on the assumption that if we want Russia's collaboration after the war we shall have to be prepared to make such a policy advantageous to her.'' Remarking, moreover, that Stalin's demand for recognition of the Soviet Union's 1941 frontiers was "super-ficially . . . very reasonable when we recall how much M. Stalin might have asked for . . . ,''[20] Eden acknowledged that there was no assurance that this demand would not be followed by others. Turning to Moscow's motives, he confessed that it was "not altogether easy to decide what real object M. Stalin has in view in insisting upon this particular demand at this juncture,'' since Britain's "acquiescence or refusal'' was unlikely to affect Russia's postwar frontiers "one way or the other.'' "Probably,'' he continued:

> M. Stalin's demand is intended as an acid test to find out how far His Majesty's Government are prepared to make unpalatable conces-sions in order to obtain the post-war co-operation of the Soviet Union: in other words, to see what value we attach to that co-operation and *what sacrifice of principle we are prepared to make in order to achieve it*. [emphasis added]

Having identified the key issue, Eden argued for making the sacrifice, since:

> If this is really M. Stalin's object, he is not likely to be prepared to accept any smaller or alternative concession in its place. Sir S. Cripps, whom I have consulted since his return from Russia, holds that this is a case of all or nothing, and that our refusal to satisfy M. Stalin will be the end of any prospect of fruitful co-operation with the Soviet Government in our mutual interests, and that Soviet policy will revert to the pursuit of purely selfish aims, with incalculable consequences for the post-war period.

[20] Here Eden listed: "control of the Dardanelles; spheres of influence in the Balkans; a one-sided imposition on Poland of the Russo-Polish frontier [which was in fact what Stalin intended]; access to the Persian Gulf; access to the Atlantic involving cession of Norwegian and Finnish territory.'' As to the "reasonableness'' of Stalin's demands, Eden declared in the following paragraph: "Looked at purely from the strategic point of view it may well be in the British interest that Russia should be established once again on the Baltic, so as to be able better to dispute with Germany the naval command of that sea . . .'' On the matter of the Polish-Soviet border, while it is true that Eden resisted Stalin's importunings for immediate recognition of the Curzon line, he did so more on procedural than substantive grounds; for the British minutes of the Moscow negotiations, see W.P.(42)8, CAB 66/20, PRO. The foreign secretary revealed his true feelings a few weeks later: "Why does Kot pretend that we are opposed to Curzon line? I have certainly never said so. Are we committed against it by any previous undertaking? What is dept. view of Curzon line *on merits?*'' C347/19/55, FO 371/31077, PRO [emphasis in the original].

Why Eden chose to regard one-sided concessions at the expense of third parties, themselves for the most part victims of aggression, as *un*selfish aims was not made clear. He was aware of the desirability of requiring a "suitable *quid pro quo*"—since Stalin "would, in his oriental mind, interpret such an omission as a sign of weakness"—but in view of what was to be conceded (and at whose expense), his suggestions in this regard can be described only as naive or disingenuous.[21]

The Foreign Office files contain no lack of contrary advice. Particularly in the month following Eden's memorandum, cables and internal minutes reveal widespread concern among senior officials over their failure to follow a consistent and carefully thought-out strategy in relations with Moscow. As one put it:

> . . . I have felt more than a suspicion that our tactics, in so far as they have been consistent at all, have been wrong, and have not only failed to achieve the results we want in specific cases, but (which is obviously of great importance) have given the Russians a completely wrong impression of ourselves.

It was generally conceded that "the rather hysterical magnification of their successes" in the press as well as the tendency to "offer them assistance that they have not asked for" were counterproductive. While it was problematical whether granting their every demand, either for military supplies or political concessions, would allay Soviet suspicions in the longer term— the presumption underlying Eden's approach—it was viewed as almost certain that such tactics would evoke contempt for the West as "soft and decadent" and would not make them any less difficult to deal with now, since "they would have one incentive the less for meeting [our requests]."[22]

---

[21] Eden's two main suggestions here were (1) that Britain, in order to bolster her own security, be allowed to establish bases and other military arrangements in northwestern Europe; and (2) that the Soviet Union be required to subscribe (again) to the provision of the Atlantic Charter against "territorial aggrandizement." The first was merely a repetition of a suggestion made by Stalin during the Moscow talks (see location of record in previous note); the second was meaningless, as Eden had already noted earlier in the memo that there was little in Stalin's demands that could "be reconciled with the principles" of the Charter. It was here that Eden also made his one reference to regional federations, stating that the Soviets should be asked to "formally express their approval of the principle of confederation as applied to the weaker countries of Europe, especially in the Balkans, and as regards Poland and Czechoslovakia."

[22] N927 and N1023/5/38, FO 371/32876, PRO. See especially minutes by Christopher Warner, head of the Northern Department which oversaw relations with the Soviet Union, and William Strang, both in the first entry, and the cables from Baggallay, with the British Embassy in Kuibyshev, in both entries. Warner, who had initiated the discussion and urged formulation of "an agreed doctrine (as to how to deal with the Russians)," later wrote: "It

At the same time, and despite a liberal peppering of the internal memoranda with caustic and patronizing comments about the Poles, there was no lack within the Foreign Office of sympathetic and knowledgeable voices on Polish affairs: those who understood the pressure on exile governments like Poland's to begin developing their postwar programs and to seek Great Power support, who recognized that there was "no particular sanctity" attached to the Curzon line, and who valued General Sikorski's loyalty and candor vis-à-vis His Majesty's Government. While none supported a return to anything approximating the prewar frontier, several of those closest to the Polish situation were sensitive to the complexities of the history and the ethnic-cultural makeup of the eastern provinces, as well as to the patent injustice of seeking cooperation with one ally at the expense of vital interests of a second. In addition, the Foreign Office's research arm, the Foreign Research and Press Service, while not devoid of the pro-Russian bias feared by the Poles back in 1939-40, had by early 1942 begun producing a series of balanced and well-researched background papers on various aspects of the Polish problem. Although these early drafts contained few if any policy recommendations, several pointed toward conclusions favorable to Sikorski's program.[23]

---

was later decided not to proceed with this." The disagreement did not end here, however. During the course of the Anglo-Soviet negotiations in the spring of 1942, Cadogan noted in his diary: "It's curious that A.[Eden], of all people, should have hopes of 'appeasement' ! ! Much better say to the Russians 'We can't discuss post-war frontiers: we want to work with you, now and later: let's have a mutual guarantee. Frontiers can easily be agreed on later. If you like, we will try to get U.S. collaboration—so far as their Constitution allows them to go. If not, we offer you all *we* have. But don't ask us *now*, at the cost of all our principles, to agree to a situation which *we* can't influence! ' I believe, still, it would be better not to crawl to the Russians over the dead bodies of *all* our principles." *The Cadogan Diaries*, ed. Dilks, p. 449 [emphasis in the original]. Still, it is interesting to note the extent to which Eden's tendency to look benignly on the possible expansion of *Soviet* influence in East-Central Europe in 1942 mirrored Cadogan's own view of *German* expansion in that same region in 1937. See Chapter II, note 26, above.

[23] Within the Foreign Office itself, the most notable were Frank Roberts of the Central Department (and head of the department from 1943-45) and Frank Savery, consul-general in the British Embassy in Warsaw before September 1939, counselor of the embassy to the exile government, and likely Britain's foremost expert on nationality relations in Poland. See, e.g., Roberts's memorandum on "The Eastern Frontier of Poland" of March 16, 1942 (C3056/19/55, FO 371/31079, PRO), and his comments on the same question in C9098/1534/55, FO 371/31104, PRO; and Savery's January 1940 memorandum on the federation and eastern boundary questions, "The Problems of the Reconstruction of Poland" (C1762/116/55, FO 371/24470, PRO). See also E. L. Woodward's lengthy comments on Sikorski's November 1940 memorandum to Bevin, in C14/14/62, FO 371/26419, PRO; and the comments on the full text of Sikorski's secret speech to his Council of Ministers on January 12, 1942, in C795/19/55, FO 371/31077, PRO. For the origin of the F.R.P.S., its relationship to the Foreign Office, and early Polish fears concerning its orientation, see pp. 82-84 and 87 above. The early F.R.P.S. drafts, the first on "The Teschen Question" dating from October 29, 1941, are to be found in file FO 371/31104, PRO. See also note 41 below.

In the end, it was the approach advocated by Eden and Cripps that predominated, particularly in the first critical year of the Grand Alliance. Later, when it began to look as if the Red Army would reach Central Europe and Germany ahead of the West, Churchill would argue vigorously for a Balkan invasion as a way of limiting Soviet influence. But later still, during his October 1944 meeting with Stalin, when it had already become clear that the Soviets could take more or less what they wanted, he would cavalierly offer to divvy up the countries of South-Eastern Europe according to percentages of Western and Soviet influence. With the benefit of hindsight, one might be inclined to call this flexible stance on the part of the British realistic and farsighted. But one might also question whether by failing to bargain—to exact a quid pro quo for their aid and support in the early years of the war—they did not in fact invite the Soviets to press their maximum demands, and to interpret British support of Poland (and others) as largely rhetorical.[24]

The United States. In contrast to the British, the American attitude toward Poland was little burdened by the past. Indeed, despite profound differences of history and geography, Polish-American relations had been notable mainly for the role played by a leader of each nation in the birth or rebirth of the other, with generally positive effects on their mutual sympathies.[25] In addition, American policy was unencumbered, at least in principle, by a balance-of-power approach to European politics. To be sure, Poland's seeming tilt toward Germany after 1934, and particularly her seizure of Teschen from Czechoslovakia in 1938, had rather tarnished her image as valiant underdog which was so much a part of her appeal to Americans. But her decision to resist the Germans had rekindled sympathy in the United States, whose verbal defenses of the right of all nations to liberty in turn raised enormous expectations among the Poles.

Nonetheless, the cast of mind that pervaded Washington's thinking on postwar problems was in the end as inimical to Sikorski's aspirations as

[24] For a recent account of the circumstances surrounding the Churchill-Stalin "percentages deal," see Albert Resis, "The Churchill-Stalin Secret 'Percentages' Agreement on the Balkans, Moscow, October 1944," pp. 368-87. Concerning Churchill's overall policy toward the Soviet Union, one British historian has offered the following summary appraisal: "One interpretation which the evidence will not, however, bear is of an implacable hostility on the part of Churchill or the British Government to Russian ambitions, and of a persistent and far-sighted desire, thwarted only by American blindness, to keep Russia at bay further to the East. In short, Churchill's view of Russian policy, though more realistic than the President's, was a fluctuating rather than a settled one." David Dilks on Churchill, in Robert Dallek, Alexander Dallin, and David Dilks, "Allied Leadership in the Second World War," p. 25.

[25] For a history of Polish-American relations from the late eighteenth century to the present, see Piotr S. Wandycz, *The United States and Poland*.

was London's or even Moscow's. No single adjective is sufficiently elastic to capture the essence of that cast of mind. Rather, it appears at first blush to have been a random and unintelligible mix of contradictory precepts— of the Wilsonian with the anti-Wilsonian, of utopianism with *Realpolitik*— all held with an abstract simplicity that gave little quarter to the complexities of the real world. On closer examination, the inconsistencies seem the result less of naiveté than of a variety of contradictory pressures in both the international and domestic political environments, most importantly President Roosevelt's preoccupation with the isolationist mood of Congress and the American public. Yet, however understandable in the context of American politics, such considerations could provide small comfort to the Poles.

The dominant feature of Washington's approach to postwar planning was the "policy of postponement," which was in itself not a single decision but a response to several not always compatible influences.[26] Initially, in the more than two years between the outbreak of the war and the time the United States became a belligerent, Roosevelt's desire to postpone consideration of postwar problems—and especially his adamant refusal to make commitments of a territorial nature or to countenance similar commitments by others—grew in part out of his attachment to the principle of self-determination and in part out of Wilson's unhappy experience at Versailles. As Harry Hopkins warned Eden in the summer of 1941, the United States "would come into the war and did not want to find after the event that [the British] had all kinds of engagements of which they [the Americans] had never been told." Likewise, the signing of the Atlantic Charter in August of that year was motivated more by a desire to forestall secret commitments, and "to dramatize and clarify for American and world opinion the vital principles at stake in the war," than to set practical ground rules for a postwar settlement.[27]

Later, after the United States had entered the war, the policy of postponement was reaffirmed in response now to more practical considerations: a desire not to let differences over postwar aims disrupt the unity of the Alliance in the prosecution of the war and the need to repress, at least until after the 1944 elections, the domestic repercussions of these differ-

---

[26] The most extensive discussion of the pros and cons of the policy of postponement, of the theories behind it as well as the problems it raised in practice, is in Sumner Welles, *Seven Decisions that Shaped History*, pp. 123-45. According to Welles, he himself was opposed to the decision as was Eleanor Roosevelt, who suggested as early as 1939 that an official international body be set up to plan for the future peace.

[27] Dallek, *Roosevelt and American Foreign Policy*, p. 281. See also John Lewis Gaddis, *The United States and the Origins of the Cold War, 1941-1947*, pp. 12-13; and Eden, *The Reckoning*, p. 316.

ences among America's ethnic minorities.[28] In addition, it reflected FDR's personal style, "his old aversion to making decisions and commitments before he had to,"[29] and his optimistic belief that the Soviet Union was moving in a democratic direction.[30] As late as August 1943, when his first ambassador to Moscow, William Bullitt, sought to warn him that "war is an attempt to achieve political objectives by fighting . . . and political objectives must be kept in mind in planning operations," the president replied: "I just have a hunch that Stalin is not that kind of man. Harry [Hopkins] says he's not and that he doesn't want anything but security for his country, and I think that if I give him everything I possibly can and ask nothing from him in return, *noblesse oblige*, he won't try to annex anything and will work with me for a world of democracy and peace." To this Bullitt retorted that Stalin was "a Caucasian bandit whose only thought when he got something for nothing was that the other fellow was an ass." FDR responded: "It's my responsibility and not yours; and I'm going to play my hunch."[31]

Whether Roosevelt was truly as naive and idealistic as this anecdote portrays him is questionable. More likely, practical considerations (though different from those guiding Churchill and Eden) dictated his attitude toward the Soviet Union. Charles Bohlen has discussed the separation of military and political considerations in terms of FDR's distrust of the professional foreign policy establishment and differences in priorities. Noting that the State Department's Soviet specialists "shared the view that the Soviet Union, even though now an ally, had to be closely watched because its ultimate aims clashed with those of the United States," he continued:

> Roosevelt and his chief assistant, Harry Hopkins, were concerned mostly with the present. That meant that they focused on military

[28] Welles, *Seven Decisions*, pp. 127-30 and 133-35. John L. Snell (*Wartime Origins of the East-West Dilemma Over Germany*, pp. 14-15) has also attributed the policy of postponement to the "great differences of opinion [which] developed between policy-making personalities and their technical experts" in each of the three Allied capitals. In Washington, these differences appear to have become important only after the middle of 1943, and may have been less a cause than a result of postponement and the consequent lack of coordination between researchers and policy-makers.

[29] James MacGregor Burns, *Roosevelt: The Soldier of Freedom*, p. 359.

[30] Concerning the influence on American policy of unrealistic expectations of changes in the Soviet political system, see Gaddis, *United States and the Origins of the Cold War*, pp. 32-42; Charles E. Bohlen, *Witness to History, 1929-1969*, pp. 121-26; and Robert Dallek on Roosevelt, in Dallek, Dallin, and Dilks, "Allied Leadership in the Second World War," pp. 6-8.

[31] William C. Bullitt, "How We Won the War and Lost the Peace," *Life*, August 30, 1948, p. 94; quoted in Gaddis, *United States and the Origins of the Cold War*, pp. 63-64.

decisions, because the immediate problem was turning back the Nazis. Eager to prove to the Soviets that the United States was a true ally, the White House thought the State Department's worry about political problems smacked of foot-dragging.[32]

Historian Robert Dallek goes even further to suggest deliberate manipulation of the issues on Roosevelt's part. Arguing that the "portrait of him as utterly naive or unrealistic about the Russians . . . has been much overdrawn" and that the president harbored few illusions over whether Russia "would eventually become a peace-loving, popular government . . . which would not interfere with the integrity of its neighbors," Dallek claims that FDR accepted the extension of Soviet power into East-Central Europe as an inevitable consequence of victory over Germany and in the interest of enlisting future Soviet cooperation. To the extent that he idealized the new Soviet ally, thereby contributing to illusions and false expectations on the part of the American public, it was, ironically, because of his overriding concern to generate public support for the war effort:

> Convinced that only a stark contrast between freedom and totalitarianism would provide the emotional wherewithal for Americans to fight, Roosevelt wished to identify the Russians, regardless of Soviet realities, with Anglo-American ideals as fully as he could. The effort to depict the Soviet Union as reformed, or reforming on the issue of religious freedom was chiefly an expression of this concern.[33]

Whatever the short-run advantages of "postponement" for the Allied war effort—and it is not at all clear that there were many—the long-term consequences for the peace were disastrous and irreversible. First, in avoiding one pitfall of the post-World War I situation (that is, secret wartime commitments), the Americans fell into another: they again failed to use the political and military leverage they possessed when they entered the war at least to promote the kind of postwar settlement they sought. As Sumner Welles later wrote:

> It must be ruefully admitted also that many of our discussions of postwar territorial and political problems with the Soviet Union were undertaken in a singularly haphazard fashion and without full consideration or preparation. The United States had two clear-cut alternatives in January, 1942. One was to create the official international

---

[32] Bohlen, *Witness to History*, p. 121.

[33] Dallek, *Roosevelt and American Foreign Policy*, esp. pp. 297-98, 211, and 533. For instance, as early as September 1941 in an effort to garner Catholic support for American aid to the Soviet Union, Roosevelt was pointing to Article 124 of the Soviet constitution as evidence of freedom of conscience in the Soviet system.

planning commission that Mrs. Roosevelt had suggested, in the hope that the major allies would at that crucial moment in the war be able to work out political and territorial solutions that would be found acceptable at the end of the war. The other alternative was to refuse resolutely to discuss any political or territorial question until a peace conference assembled.

Each course had its advantages and its disadvantages. By sticking neither to one course nor the other we fell, as so often happens in such cases, between two stools. The immense influence that we possessed immediately after Pearl Harbor was not exercised. When we did attempt to negotiate political settlements, our influence was no longer decisive.[34]

Second, the decision not to *commit* themselves on postwar issues became in practice a decision not to *discuss* those issues except in the vaguest generalities, which in turn had a dampening effect on American research and planning for the postwar period. For instance, the official State Department history of the postwar planning effort describes that effort, as of the spring of 1941, as "handicapped and barely in motion." In February of 1942, an Advisory Committee on Post-War Foreign Policy was set up within the Department and organized into several research subcommittees, but coordination between these committees and policy-makers appears to have been haphazard. With specific reference to territorial issues, the author notes: "The views of the Territorial Subcommittee, *while never formally presented as a whole to superior authority*, reached the Secretary of State and the President *selectively* and in several ways." Only in mid-1943, in response to the changing political and military situation, did the Advisory Committee shift from research to decision-making.[35] Thus the policy of postponement served as an excuse to perpetuate, at least at upper levels of the Roosevelt administration, an attachment to excessively rigid and abstract formulas—to "a few favorite panaceas" as Sumner Welles later wrote—which hard thinking on specific problems might have shown to be both inequitable and unattainable.[36]

---

[34] *Seven Decisions*, pp. 138-39. For a similar criticism of United States behavior on entering World War I, see James P. Warburg, *The United States in a Changing World: An Historical Analysis of American Foreign Policy* , pp. 247-50.

[35] Harley Notter, *Postwar Foreign Policy Preparation, 1939-1945*, pp. 45, 78-95, 123, and 163-64 [emphasis added]. Bohlen (*Witness to History*, pp. 126-27) confirms that it was only in mid-1943, after the Soviet victories at Stalingrad and Kursk and the surrender of Italy, that the State Department "thought it was time to discuss with Moscow the shape of the postwar world."

[36] Welles, *Seven Decisions*, p. 136; and Burns, *Roosevelt: Soldier of Freedom*, pp. 359-60.

Particularly unrealistic were FDR's views on territorial questions and international organization. On the one hand, he was inclined to carry the principle of self-determination to its illogical extreme, to view plebiscites as a "universal remedy" for territorial disputes regardless of the economic or strategic consequences for the states involved.[37] Even without waiting for the results of future plebiscites, the president had a ready set of pre-conceptions about the shape of postwar Europe: Serbia should be separated from Croatia and Slovenia; a new state of "Wallonia" might be created by joining the Walloon parts of Belgium with Luxembourg, Alsace-Lorraine and part of northern France. Describing one such discussion, Eden commented:

> Though I enjoyed these conversations, the exercise of the President's charm and the play of his lively mind, they were also perplexing. Roosevelt was familiar with the history and geography of Europe. Perhaps his hobby of stamp-collecting had helped him to this knowledge, but the academic yet sweeping opinions which he built upon it were alarming in their cheerful fecklessness. He seemed to see himself disposing of the fate of many lands, allied no less than enemy. He did all this with so much grace that it was not easy to dissent. Yet it was too like a conjuror, skilfully juggling with balls of dynamite, whose nature he failed to understand.[38]

On the other hand, what Roosevelt gave with one hand, he proposed to take away with the other. His disillusionment with the League of Nations during the 1930s made him wary of international organizations of the universalistic variety; instead, he favored a kind of "peace by dictation" with the Big Four (including China) as the "sheriffs" or "policemen" of the world.[39] Such a system assumed not merely continued cooperation

[37] Welles, *Seven Decisions*, p. 136; and Gaddis, *The United States and the Origins of the Cold War*, pp. 11-12.

[38] Eden, *The Reckoning*, pp. 432-33. George Kennan has been less generous in his assessment of Roosevelt's foreign policy acumen: "The truth is . . . that Franklin Roosevelt, for all his charm and for all his skill as a political leader, was, when it came to foreign policy, a very superficial man, ignorant, dilettantish, with a severely limited intellectual horizon. . . . Either [his] schemes were cynically designed to appeal to a series of opinionated and unenlightened domestic lobbies, without serious regard to their external effect, or they bore witness to a very poor understanding of international affairs on the part of their author. Roosevelt knew nothing about Russia, and very little about Europe. This in itself would not have been so bad. What was worse was that he did not seek or value the advice of those who did know something about these places and could have told him something about them." Kennan's comment in Dallek, Dallin, and Dilks, "Allied Leadership in the Second World War," p. 31.

[39] Gaddis, *United States and the Origins of the Cold War*, pp. 24-25; and Burns, *Roosevelt: Soldier of Freedom*, pp. 358-59.

among the Great Powers after the war but also an identity of purpose, if it were not to degenerate into an old-style sphere of influence arrangement. In this sense, it was either hopelessly utopian or disdainful of the legitimate concern of the smaller nations, whose right to self-determination Roosevelt so staunchly defended, that their interests not be sacrificed to those of the Great Powers. For instance, as the president explained his program to Soviet Foreign Minister Molotov during the latter's visit to Washington in May and June 1942:

> . . . The first step was general disarmament. But the four major nations would maintain sufficient armed forces to impose peace, . . . If any nation menaced the peace, it could be blockaded and then if still recalcitrant, bombed. . . . He thought that all other nations save the Big Four should be disarmed (Germany, Japan, France, Spain, Belgium, Netherlands, Scandanavia, Turkey, Rumania, Hungary, Poland, Czechoslovakia, etc.).
>
> Mr. Molotov remarked that this might be a bitter blow to the prestige of Poland and Turkey. . . . He also inquired about the reestablishment of France as a Great Power. The President replied that might perhaps be possible within 10 or 20 years. He added that other nations might eventually be accepted progressively at various times among the guarantors of peace whenever the original guarantors were satisfied of their reliability. This might be peace by dictation, but he hoped that the peoples of the previous aggressor nations might eventually come to see that they have infinitely more to gain from permanent peace than from periodically recurrent wars.
>
> Mr. Molotov observed warmly that the President's ideas for the preservation of mutual peace would be sympathetically viewed by the Soviet government and people. . . .[40]

One can only speculate as to the conclusion Mr. Molotov drew concerning Washington's commitment to a genuinely independent Poland.

It would eventually prove impossible to maintain the posture of postponement. When it did, the Americans abandoned the policy reluctantly and piecemeal. The inevitable result was a double standard whereby they deferred to British or Soviet pressures when the need for military cooperation seemed to warrant political concessions, while elsewhere continuing to insist on "no commitments."

One final dimension of the policy of postponement merits comment at this point: to wit, the ripple effect that it had on communication between British and American postwar planners and policy-makers. In light of the

[40] *FRUS, 1942*, 3:568-69.

tendency for Washington to regard Poland largely as a British concern, as well as the undisputed fact that the British were infinitely better informed on Polish affairs and Central European affairs in general, a rational procedure would have been for the Foreign Office to share its expertise (and that of the Foreign Research and Press Service) with the State Department. However, so anxious was London not to offend American sensibilities by even seeming to raise forbidden topics that, of a dozen or so papers on Poland produced by the F.R.P.S. in 1942, it appears that only two were deemed sufficiently innocuous to be forwarded to Washington. And even those two—a twelve-page paper on "Poland's Economic Problems" and a seven-page paper on "The Industry of Polish Upper Silesia," dated April 14 and June 19, 1942, respectively—were forwarded only months later, in February 1943. Later, especially after mid-1943, Foreign Office research papers were more or less routinely cleared for transmittal to the State Department. But in that most crucial year for Sikorski, in 1942, when he was urgently seeking Washington's understanding for his program, the Americans were deprived of the results of Britain's superior research effort.[41] From what little we know of the State Department's thinking on postwar problems at this stage, access to the British papers might have gone far to dispel misconceptions on such vital issues for Poland as the "Corridor," Upper Silesia, and East Prussia, as well as the ever-present eastern boundary question.[42] As it was, to the extent that the Americans

[41] See note 23 above. The 1942 F.R.P.S. papers are all located in PRO file FO 371/31104; see especially document C7842/1534/55 in that file for a discussion of criteria for forwarding papers to the State Department. Among papers not forwarded were those on "Polish-Soviet Relations," the "History of Poland's Eastern Frontier," plus separate papers on the Ukrainian and Belorussian problems, Danzig, and the Teschen dispute. These were almost entirely historical in nature, containing few if any policy recommendations. The 1943 papers, largely comprised of revised and expanded versions of the earlier drafts and by then being collated into a *Polish Handbook*, are located in files FO 371/34595 to 34599, PRO. One indication of the sensitivity of these matters is the fact that only in late July 1943 did the Foreign Office decide to send its own embassies in Washington and Moscow some basic "background" documents on the Polish-Soviet boundary question in order to prepare them for discussions with the U.S. and Soviet governments that would arise "sooner or later." C8533/258/55, FO 371/34584, PRO.

[42] American and British views on both the Polish-Soviet and Polish-German boundary questions are discussed in more detail in Chapters X and XI. At this point, it is worth mentioning only three papers on Upper Silesia delivered to the Foreign Office by a U.S. Embassy official in August and September 1943, but dated January 1943. (The authors and originating agency were not identified, but the papers were treated as reflecting State Department opinion.) By comparison with the F.R.P.S./F.O.R.D. analyses (by now it had become the Foreign Office Research Department), the American papers were weak and superficial, especially on the Polish side, and seemed to imply (mistakenly in the view of a knowledgeable British reviewer) "that a united Upper Silesia would be more than Poland could profitably exploit." See C9925, C10852, and C10853/231/55, FO 371/34561, PRO,

were familiar with London's approach to these matters, it was with the Eden/Cripps viewpoint, no doubt magnified by the distinctly anti-Polish bias of Britain's ambassador to the United States, Lord Halifax.

The Soviet Union.   By virtue of history and proximity the Soviet Union, alone of the Big Three, had both a vital interest in the future political and territorial status of Poland and an intimate knowledge of that country. These two elements—interest and knowledge—gave the Russians a distinct advantage over the British and Americans in their three-cornered maneuvering over the "Polish Question." Yet despite this, and despite the certainty with which both apologists and detractors have asserted the benevolence or duplicity of Soviet intentions toward Poland during World War II, Moscow's policy appears to have been as complex and ambivalent as that of the West. Moreover, this observation applies as much to the period of the Nazi-Soviet Non-Aggression Pact as to the years of the Grand Alliance.

One obvious reason for uncertainty is the unavailability of documents and memoirs relating to the Kremlin's policy-making processes, such as exist for British and American policy and without which the historian is often thrown back onto inference and conjecture. But a more important reason is simply that Soviet policy toward Poland was less a function of relations between the two states—either of Moscow's ambitions vis-à-vis Warsaw or of Warsaw's attitude toward Moscow—than a reflection of a broader range of anxieties and expectations on Stalin's part, which were constantly shifting in response to the course of the war and which were related to the "Polish Question" per se largely by virtue of Poland's position across the North European plain between Germany and Russia: Where and when would Hitler strike next? Would Britain and France really declare war in Poland's defense? Once that nation's fate was sealed, would they then make peace with Hitler or, what would be just as bad, succumb quickly to his armies, in either event leaving Russia face to face—alone—with Germany? Should Hitler turn east before defeating or neutralizing the West, would the latter be able to come to Russia's aid and, in view of her prior "neutrality," under what conditions? Even if Russia were eventually to emerge on the side of the victors, could the Soviet system or Stalin himself survive the initial and inevitable reverses? In particular, how would the non-Russian nationalities along the Soviet Union's vital western rim react first to German occupation and later to the return of Soviet rule? Finally, what of Allied intentions in postwar Europe? How would the

---

especially the comments in the first document by A. J. Brown and Mr. Holliday, British consul in Katowice before the war; and Chapter X, note 138, below.

Western Powers receive Moscow's very substantial ambitions for territorial expansion and political influence in Europe? With respect to Germany, would they favor a harsh peace—a course that would offer, on the one hand, the prospect of reparations adequate to repair the devastation of war but, on the other, the opportunity to revive the Rapallo relationship by exploiting German national frustrations? Or would the West seek to rebuild Germany's industrial capacity as a counterweight to a victorious, if weakened, Soviet Union?[43]

Suspicious of ally and enemy alike, acutely aware of the Soviet Union's vulnerability, Stalin's policy was constant only in its striving to retain maximum flexibility—in conceding only the minimum conditions necessary at any given moment to avoid war or, once forced into war, to survive it with the Soviet system and his personal position intact—at the same time keeping open alternative options for the future, including the option of reneging on or reinterpreting earlier commitments when more favorable circumstances allowed. Likewise what Stalin might propose, indeed demand, at a moment of acute danger became less desirable, even unthinkable, once the danger had passed. Stalin's attitude toward the presence of Allied military personnel in the Soviet Union and toward the opening of a second front in Europe are good examples of this latter phenomenon. During the critical autumn months of 1941, he suggested that Britain "could without risk" send twenty-five to thirty divisions to Archangel or, through Iran, to Russia's southern front (!); again, at the height of the Stalingrad campaign, he briefly welcomed Churchill's proposal to send twenty Anglo-American air force squadrons to help defend the Caucasus. Yet later, after the military tide had turned in Russia's favor, he would resist any Allied military presence, whether in the form of observers, a base for shuttle-bombing, or sufficient personnel to assist with the convoys the Soviets wanted so badly.[44] Similarly, where in the early stages of the war Stalin pleaded for a second front anywhere in Europe, even the Bal-

---

[43] For several interpretations of Stalin's anxieties and expectations before and during the war, see: Vojtech Mastny, *Russia's Road to the Cold War: Diplomacy, Warfare, and the Politics of Communism, 1941-1945*, pp. xvii-xix, and chaps. 1-3; Ulam, *Expansion and Coexistence*, especially pp. 270-86, 295-300, and 314-15; and Robert C. Tucker, "The Emergence of Stalin's Foreign Policy," pp. 563-89. Regardless of whether one concludes that Stalin's preference all along had been a pact with Hitler or that he was forced into it by dithering on the part of Britain and France, most would agree that the gamble was fraught with both peril and opportunity. As to the range of Stalin's ambitions even in the earliest stage of the war, the "astounding list of . . . desiderata" presented by Molotov during his November 1940 visit to Berlin is revealing; Mastny, *Russia's Road to the Cold War*, p. 31.

[44] See Ulam, *Expansion and Coexistence*, pp. 319-20; *Correspondence between the Chairman of the Council of Ministers of the U.S.S.R. and the Presidents of the U.S.A. and the Prime Ministers of Great Britain during the Great Patriotic War of 1941-1945*, 1:24 and 74 [cited hereafter as *Correspondence*, 1 and 2]; also Winston S. Churchill, *Closing the Ring*, pp. 264-74.

kans, by the fall of 1943 he would oppose any Allied military operation in what he considered a Russian preserve. Moreover, at about this time, one vice commissar of foreign affairs expressed the view that: "Things are going so well on our front that it might even be better *not* to have the Second Front till next spring. . . . Better to . . . get the Red Army *right up* to Germany, and *then* start the Second Front."[45]

This ambivalence, this concern with maximizing future options and minimizing short-term risks, was present at every turn of Polish-Soviet relations during the period in question. Even (or perhaps most significantly) at those points where Soviet actions seemed most categorical, as in August-September 1939 and again in July 1941, Stalin always hedged his bets in preparation for the time when necessity would compel him—or opportunity allow him—to change his course. In 1939, for instance, while joining Nazi Germany in the destruction of Poland, he never closed the door completely to the revival of some form of Polish state. It is true that the "rump state" originally provided for in the first Nazi-Soviet agreement of August 23rd was dropped in the rearrangement of the following month, and that most of the ethnically Polish districts initially assigned to the Soviet "sphere of interest" were turned over to Germany.[46] Yet within a month, in apparent anticipation of the need to prepare for their acceptance into the Western alliance as well as to gain the use of what remained of Poland's armed forces, the Soviets were quietly trying to organize Polish units for the Red Army, at the same time letting it be known through confidential channels that they would support the creation of a "politically friendly" Poland within "ethnographical" frontiers. And this at a time when Molotov was publicly boasting about the demise of "this ugly offspring of the Versailles Treaty."[47]

[45] Alexander Werth, *Russia at War, 1941-1945*, p. 747 [emphasis in the original]. See also *Correspondence*, 1:20-21; and Eden, *The Reckoning*, pp. 318-19 and 484.

[46] Ulam suggests that Stalin might have wanted this slice of ethnic Poland in the event, unlikely to be sure, of a successful Anglo-French attack on Germany, in which case "Stalin could have had his Lublin Polish government then and there, instead of in 1944." In the wake of Germany's swift victory over Poland and the West's inactivity, however, the idea of a rump state looked more "like a trap" which Hitler might use to convince Britain and France to conclude a peace, again leaving Germany with a free hand in the east. *Expansion and Coexistence*, pp. 276-78 and 282-84. For corroboration from the German point of view, see Martin Broszat, *Nationalsozialistische Polenpolitik, 1939-1945*, pp. 12-17.

[47] See p. 50, especially note 9, above. It is interesting to speculate whether this attempt (unsuccessful as it turned out) to exploit Polish military manpower was a precipitating factor in the Katyń massacre of Polish officers the following spring. Other evidence suggests that the Germans learned of this "stockpiling" of some 15,000 officers and induced the Soviets, at a time when Moscow was extremely nervous about Hitler's intentions, to execute the Poles. See J. K. Zawodny, *Death in the Forest: The Story of the Katyn Forest Massacre*, pp. 127-28; Ulam, *Expansion and Coexistence*, pp. 343-44; and Mastny, *Russia's Road to the Cold War*, p. 28.

Not quite two years later, in July 1941, the tables were turned: finding themselves now under the ultimate pressure of imminent military collapse, the Soviets as we have already seen quietly discarded many of their previous stipulations. Rather than insist on some kind of puppet regime or proceed with the formation of a Polish "national committee," they agreed to recognize the legitimacy of the Government-in-Exile, pledging to leave the future form of Poland's internal government to the Poles themselves. The reference to "ethnographical" frontiers was dropped and the German-Soviet treaties of 1939 were declared to have "lost their validity." Instead of Polish units within or subordinate to the Red Army, Moscow now agreed to the formation of a sovereign Polish Army under the command of the exile government. Perhaps the most unusual concession of all was allowing the Poles to set up a network of outposts to aid their civilian deportees.

Yet these concessions were extracted only after the most tedious and difficult negotiations, clouded by reservations and innuendoes that proved to be a foretaste of later Soviet policy toward Poland. From the outset it was clear that the first obstacle to be overcome was Moscow's extreme reluctance to deal with the exile government at all. During a preliminary meeting with Soviet Ambassador Maisky on June 24th, Eden referred to Sikorski's broadcast of the previous day as "moderate and reasonable . . . in light of past history" and asked whether the Soviet government could not "make a start with the release of some of these prisoners soon." As the foreign secretary recorded the encounter, Maisky was "not responsive to my appeal," replying that:

> if I insisted, he would, of course, transmit my suggestion to his Government, but he much hoped that I would not press him to do this just now. The Soviet Government regarded the Polish Government as a reactionary government which was fundamentally hostile to Russia . . . [and which] had made it plain that they were at war with Russia. How could the Soviet Government be expected to release the prisoners of a country with whom they were still at war?

To Eden's rejoinder that it was "not surprising" that the Poles regarded "the Russian attack on them last year when they were being invaded by Germany [as] a cruel deed," and that the Polish soldiers would provide "invaluable fighting material" against the common enemy, Maisky persisted in his view that "the matter should be allowed to drop."[48] Although

---

[48] C7016/3226/55, FO 371/26755, PRO. At two subsequent meetings on July 4th (the day before the opening of formal negotiations), the Soviet envoy appeared only slightly less hostile, this time ensnaring himself in his own diplomatic trap. At the first session, he demanded on the one hand the establishment of a Polish "national committee" in Moscow, and on the other that Sikorski be willing to sign a treaty "to form a common front against

eventually induced to recognize Sikorski's government and to accept at least in principle the idea of a reconstituted Polish state, the Soviets were careful never to renounce fully what they had gained from Germany—indeed, threatening once to break off negotiations and revert to the preferred format of a "national committee" rather than do so.[49] Not only would Stalin renew his territorial demands at the first occasion; in the final analysis, it would turn out that each concession contained a time bomb, some condition or alternative basis that would allow the Soviets to reinterpret their obligations once their military situation improved.

Meanwhile, even as the negotiations were in progress, Polish intelligence began receiving information suggesting that Moscow harbored serious reservations concerning Poland's political resurrection. In particular, "curious instructions" intended for the British Communist Party were being sent from Moscow to the Soviet Embassy in London, which reportedly said: "Don't concern yourselves with minutiae like boundaries, etc.—in the present situation the Soviet Union needs a new tactic, a new popular front for the struggle against Germany and assurance of Soviet primacy in this operation. In the press avoid the designation 'Polish State' and use only 'Poland'; don't use 'Polish citizens' but merely 'Poles.' "[50] A second set of instructions, this one to the London branch of the party, was rather more candid about long-term Soviet goals. Describing "revolutionary conditions" in Poland as unpromising and the Polish proletariat as being wholly under the influence of the opportunistic and reactionary Polish Socialist Party, these instructions concluded:

German aggression." When he inquired during the second meeting as to Sikorski's willingness to do the latter, Eden replied that it would seem appropriate "to clear up first the question of national committees," and that Maisky could hardly ask for a treaty of nonaggression with a government that the Soviet government did not recognize. C7421 and C7423/3226/55, FO 371/26755, PRO.

[49] See Eden's account of his meeting with Maisky on July 18, 1941; C8028/3226/55, FO 371/26756, PRO. Even during the negotiating sessions, Maisky hinted broadly that his government looked upon the agreement to be signed as an interim expedient involving no irrevocable commitments concerning its future policy toward Poland: "The important thing seemed to be to reach an agreement now. If they dwelt on general political matters and questions regarding frontiers, they would not get this agreement now. *His statement of the Soviet Government's point of view did not mean that this point of view was to be embodied in a document to be agreed here and now by the Polish Government.* The Soviet Government were ready to leave discussion and agreement on this point for the present." *Documents*, 1:130 [emphasis added].

[50] Mitkiewicz, *Z gen. Sikorskim*, p. 156 [entry for July 22, 1941]. Soviet ambivalence over the future of Poland was also apparent in their efforts to groom a number of Polish officers, then POWs, to lead Polish units in the Red Army. During the winter and spring of 1940-41, as part of their indoctrination, the selected prisoners were asked to write essays or give lectures on a variety of political topics, including: "Red Poland—the Seventeenth Republic of the Soviet Union." Zawodny, *Death in the Forest*, pp. 150-52.

In these circumstances it is against the interests of the international proletariat to rebuild Poland either in her "non-ethnographical" frontiers or within any frontiers which might satisfy the national ambitions of the Polish working masses since this would only enable her, by her influence on the Balkan and Baltic countries, to revert to her old role of a barrier to the revolution of Central Europe. Therefore the Communist press must put a check to all Polish ambitions and propagate the idea of a strictly ethnographical Poland, as weak economically as possible. At the same time the Communist press must promote the ideas of the People's Front among the Poles.

Of particular interest was the following sentence which suggested that any support Moscow might express for the idea of a Central European federation was for strictly manipulative purposes: "The programme of a Polish-Czech federation must be taken advantage of to propagate among the Poles a feeling of political weakness and lack of economic self-sufficiency."[51] Small wonder in this light that the Poles so adamantly rejected the idea of an "ethnographical" Poland, or that they remained skeptical of Stalin's pledges to support a strong and independent Poland in the future.

Adding to the opaqueness of Moscow's approach, especially as seen from London and Washington, was the fact that Stalin's policy and tactics toward Poland during the Second World War were reminiscent in several key respects of tsarist policy and tactics during the First World War. Like Stalin, Tsar Nicholas II before him also coveted Eastern Galicia and the northern part of East Prussia, and for essentially the same reasons: in the one instance to gain control of the largest remaining body of Ukrainians outside Russia's borders, in this way depriving her adversaries of a "Piedmont" from which to exploit Ukrainian nationalism against her; and in the second case to acquire the ice-free ports of Memel and Königsberg. With respect to Poland's political and territorial status, tsarist war aims as presented to the Allies in September 1914 foresaw an essentially ethnographical Poland (comprised of Congress Poland enlarged by Poznań and Southern Silesia from Germany and Western Galicia from Austria) restored

---

[51] C8803/3226/55, FO 371/26758, PRO. The quoted passage is from a summary of the instructions by British Ambassador Dormer; the information was received from the Polish Ministry of Foreign Affairs, but its content and tone were verified by Dormer as fully consistent with a variety of other Soviet sources. In this report he also noted that: "The present Polish Government in London is ignored in these instructions. General Sikorski's name is quoted along with those of Marshal Śmigły-Rydz, Beck and Witos as one of the leaders of capitalist and fascist tendencies of the Polish bourgeoisie." Earlier Dormer reported a Maisky interview with some British Communists, during which he "assured them that there was no need for them to fear that Stalin intended to change his policy toward Poland and that the prospective agreement was merely tactics." C8202/3226/55, FO 371/26756, PRO.

within the framework of the Russian Empire—a proposal not very different in substance from Stalin's first offers to the Sikorski government.[52] Finally, both tsar and Soviet dictator sought to convince their respective allies that the "Polish Question" was primarily Russia's problem.[53] In view of the distinction then widely presumed to exist between "Soviet" and "Russian" policies—i.e., between policies determined by ideological considerations and those determined by Russian national interests—it was probably to be expected that Stalin's Western allies would interpret these similarities as evidence that the leopard had changed his spots, that the erstwhile promoter of world revolution had become a Russian nationalist par excellence. What they failed to realize was that, once the first priority of Soviet policy came to be the preservation of the Socialist Fatherland, any distinction between ideological and national interests in an area deemed vital to the security of the Soviet state became meaningless—a rule of thumb that was doubly true in a period of extreme danger. Therefore, any parallels that existed between Stalin's policy toward Poland in 1939 or 1941 and tsarist policy in 1914 were noteworthy not as evidence of the former's reconversion but as specific examples of Poland's enduring misfortune: that her place in Moscow's calculations has been determined in large measure by her hapless geography, which has made her an unwilling accessory to the requirements of Russia's security—whether internal or external, defensive or offensive, tsarist or Soviet.[54]

What tentative conclusions can one draw concerning the likely effects of these several factors on Polish-Soviet relations in the years 1939 to 1943? Two come immediately to mind. The first is that it is impossible, indeed pointless, to try to identify with any certainty fixed Soviet goals

[52] The tsarist government may even have toyed with an Oder line in the opening months of World War I. In the early autumn of 1914, a "Map of the Future Europe" was placed on sale for twenty kopeks in Moscow bookstores, showing *inter alia* a Russian-controlled Poland extended to the line of the Oder; see Kazimierz Rosen-Zawadzki, " 'Karta Buduszczej Jewropy,' " pp. 141-44 + map.

[53] Concerning Russian war aims in 1914, see Komarnicki, *Rebirth of the Polish Republic*, pp. 38-39 and 42. Ulam describes the Ukrainian problem as "one of the main keys to [Soviet] foreign policy"; *Expansion and Coexistence*, pp. 325-27 and 299-300.

[54] Had Western leaders been more attentive to the continuities in Soviet policy, they would have realized that the Polish Communist Party occupied an analogous role in Comintern history. That is, it served primarily as an instrument to promote Moscow's claims to eastern Poland and the interests of a *German* revolution, at the expense of its credibility within Poland. Lenin's views at the time of the Polish-Soviet war of 1919-20 are instructive: While Poland as established by the Treaty of Versailles served as "a buffer . . . to fence off Germany from a contact with Soviet Communism," a Soviet victory in Poland would bring not only security but would "open the road to Germany," "destroying the Versailles Peace on which the entire present system of international relations is based." Wandycz, *Soviet-Polish Relations*, p. 214.

with respect either to Poland's political status or to her future territorial configuration. What Stalin would later demand both from Poland and for her would depend largely on the developing political and military balance as the end of the war approached. The most one can do for the early years is to identify areas of relative rigidity (such as the Ukrainian problem) or flexibility (such as the question of Poland's western boundary) where Stalin's attitude would be shaped by his political prospects in Germany as well as in Poland. The second conclusion is that, in a period in which the rulers of the Soviet Union saw the very existence of their state and system threatened, there was little the Poles themselves could do to improve their bargaining position vis-à-vis their neighbor to the east. Moreover, what was true in 1939 would continue to be true after 1941. This is not said by way of defending the policy of Poland's prewar government, which had an undeniably inflated view of its own merits and influence. It is simply that their behavior was largely irrelevant to their ultimate fate. They could—and indeed did—worsen their position by giving Moscow added incentive and justification for joining in the destruction of their state. But, even had they wanted to, there was by 1939 virtually nothing the Poles could have done to materially improve their own prospects because they could not offer what the Soviets needed most: reprieve from war. The fact that after June 22, 1941, the Poles and Russians were fighting on the same side would do nothing to change the inherent imbalance between Poland's assets and Moscow's ambitions and anxieties. Soviet policy would continue to be shaped less by what the Poles did or did not do than by the pressures exerted and opportunities afforded by the broader political and military situation.

FROM the viewpoint of an exile leader like General Sikorski, whose success or failure would depend in large measure on Allied receptivity to innovative approaches to the solution of Central Europe's perennial traumas, the outlook was inauspicious indeed. For what marked the policies of all three Great Powers with respect to the "Polish Question" was their adherence to old prescriptions: Roosevelt with his rigid fixation on self-determination combined with a curious reluctance to use American military superiority to promote political goals; Churchill with his overriding preoccupation with Empire and, therefore, with European "balance"; Stalin with his determination to solve his Ukrainian problem, his striving for a free hand in the nations along Russia's western flank, and his use of the separate peace ploy. It was almost like a replay of Entente-tsarist relations in World War I. As Titus Komarnicki has written about the fate of Poland at the hands of the earlier alliance:

It was really a very strange and uneasy relationship, by the way, not very different from that which occurred later, in the course of the Second World War. Whichever might have been the situation of Russia, whether strong, or rather supposed to be strong, or weak, in either case the Western Allies were obliged, or felt obliged, to keep in with Russia. *Watching all these moves one cannot help thinking that the Western Powers behaved towards Russia as if they did not possess any bargaining assets or were unwilling to use them.*

All these factors explain to some extent the attitude of the Western Powers toward the Polish question in the first stage of the war. Until the outbreak of the Revolution in Russia in 1917 the Western Powers had followed events, but they had not exercised any influence on Russian policy in relation to the Polish cause, in spite of the fact that their passivity could entail far-reaching consequences for the outcome of war in Eastern Europe and therefore for the outcome of the war in general.[55]

DOMESTIC CRITICS

The Polish Government-in-Exile was indeed a "Government of National Unity" in the sense that it brought together within a single structure most of the warring elements of the prewar political landscape in Poland, with the exception only of the most outrageous factions of the Nationalist and pro-Sanacja Right and the Communists and left-wing Socialists at the other end of the spectrum. But to call it a government of national unity in the sense that it pursued in time of grave crisis a bipartisan (or multipartisan) policy for the sake of some shared view of Poland's higher national interest is patently absurd. Although from a constitutional standpoint General Sikorski's emergence as prime minister, as well as supreme commander of the Polish Army in exile, had all the trappings of a legal transfer of power, politically speaking it was tantamount to a *coup d'état*. In effect, Sikorski parlayed his personal political capital in the West, particularly in France, together with the disrepute into which the pre-September government had fallen, into a position of formal leadership in both the political and military spheres.[56]

[55] Komarnicki, *Rebirth of the Polish Republic*, pp. 35-36 [emphasis added].

[56] Probably the best account of the maneuvering and intrigue surrounding the formation of the Government-in-Exile and particularly Sikorski's selection for both posts (it was the double appointment that especially surprised and galled his opposition) is Micewski, *Z geografii politycznej*, pp. 306-12. See also Pragier, *Czas przeszły dokonany*, pp. 562-80; Popiel, *Generał Sikorski w mojej pamięci*, pp. 90-102; Raczyński, *W sojuszniczym Londynie*, pp. 51-56; Terlecki, *Generał ostatniej legendy*, pp. 84-98; and Kot, *Listy z Rosji*, pp. 532-

However, his hold on the seat of power was at best insecure. Those whom he had outmaneuvered—primarily supporters and officials of the old regime—remained unreconciled from the start. Moreover, their numbers in exile were large and they dominated the key military, diplomatic, and intelligence bureaucracies. Sikorski, on the other hand, possessed little in the way of an organized political base, his main assets being his lack of complicity in the September debacle (indeed, he had warned long before 1939 that Poland's army was hopelessly obsolete), his excellent and long-standing connections with the French military establishment, and his close personal and political relationship with Poland's best known cultural and political figure, Ignacy Paderewski.[57] To be sure, by virtue of his stature as an outspoken opponent of the Piłsudski and post-Piłsudski regimes, Sikorski could count on the support of the center and center-left of Polish politics—most importantly the Peasant and Labor Parties—and to a lesser degree on individual leaders from the democratic wings of the Nationalist and Socialist Parties. But these groups were sparsely represented in the exile population at large, and not at all in the military and governmental establishments.[58] In addition, under the existing constitution—the so-called "April Constitution" of 1935—the potential authority of the prime minister together with his Council of Ministers to set governmental policy was severely circumscribed by the extensive independent powers conferred on the president, now the moderate Piłsudskiite Władysław Raczkiewicz. Raczkiewicz, himself no admirer of Sikorski,[59] favored General Kazimierz

---

33. Two rather tendentious accounts, both decidedly more hostile to Sikorski, are Pobóg-Malinowski, *Najnowsza historia*, 3:68-90; and *Diplomat in Paris 1936-1939: Papers and Memoirs of Juliusz Łukasiewicz, Ambassador of Poland*, ed. Wacław Jędrzejewicz, pp. 341-73. One non-Polish source that takes note of the patchwork character of the exile government is Sharp, *Poland: White Eagle*, pp. 155-56.

[57] Concerning Sikorski's relationship with Paderewski and with the French, see Kukiel, *Generał Sikorski*, pp. 75-77 and 92; and Chapter III above. Even so bitter an opponent as Ambassador Łukasiewicz had to admit in late September that "only if General Sikorski were entrusted with the command of our army in France" could they overcome the "outrage and bitterness" among the Poles over the fact that their president and commander-in-chief had abandoned the country "before the fight was over." *Diplomat in Paris*, pp. 357-58.

[58] Raczyński, *W sojuszniczym Londynie*, pp. 69-70; and Kot, *Listy z Rosji*, p. 10.

[59] During the interwar period Raczkiewicz served several times as minister of internal affairs, both before and after May 1926, as president of the Senate between 1930 and 1935, and as provincial governor in several regions of the country. Perhaps indicative of his political orientation is the fact that he retained as his chief political advisor Stanisław Łepkowski, director of the Chancellery for President Mościcki. For Łepkowski's negative opinion of Sikorski, see Ambassador Kennard's notes of a meeting on July 19, 1940; C7639/252/55, FO 371/24474, PRO. Not surprisingly, Raczkiewicz was not Sikorski's choice either. In fact the general sought to have the former's appointment rescinded in favor of Paderewski, who had been one of the original candidates but had been thought initially to be too ill to take the post. See Raczyński, *W sojuszniczym Londynie*, pp. 54-56.

Sosnkowski (a Piłsudski protégé, hero of the September campaign, and also the favorite candidate of the prewar regime for the presidency in exile) as supreme commander,[60] and August Zaleski (also a Piłsudskiite, a prewar foreign minister and likewise a candidate for the presidency) as prime minister. He accepted Sikorski reluctantly and only after several party leaders refused to serve in a government led by Zaleski.[61]

Sikorski was, then, in no position to flaunt his tactical victory. Since his first concern had to be to establish the continuity of the Polish state and therefore the legitimacy of his government, in the eyes of Poles as well as the Allies, he sought to resolve both the constitutional and political crises by way of a trade-off: in exchange for the president's pledge to act only in "close agreement" with the Council of Ministers—i.e., not to use his extraordinary presidential powers[62]—the prime minister acquiesced in the participation in his government of several of the more moderate members of the Sanacja camp. The inclusion in key positions of Sikorski's two principal rivals—Sosnkowski as the designated successor to the president and ex officio member of the cabinet, Zaleski as foreign minister—gives some indication of the delicacy of the political balance. (Both later resigned in protest over the July 1941 agreement with Russia.)

By and large throughout his tenure Sikorski was able to carry the Council of Ministers on critical issues—although, with the exception of his closest political associates from prewar days, their support was often grudging

[60] Sosnkowski, though slightly younger than Sikorski, was senior to him in military rank. Both had collaborated closely with Piłsudski in the formation of the Polish Legions during World War I but had parted ways after the war, Sosnkowski remaining close to the marshal both before and after 1926. Following Piłsudski's death, however, Sosnkowski also found himself sidelined as a potential rival to Śmigły-Rydz, and was recalled to active duty only during the September crisis.

[61] See especially Micewski, *Z geografii politycznej*, p. 308; and Kot, *Listy z Rosji*, p. 533 and note. Zaleski, an economist by training with a degree from the University of London, joined Poland's nascent diplomatic corps in 1918; in June 1926, just a month after Piłsudski's coup, Zaleski was appointed foreign minister, a post he retained until November 1932. Although he was apparently eased out by his ambitious successor, Colonel Beck, he remained in the good graces of the post-Piłsudski regime, served as chairman of the Bank of Commerce in Warsaw, and had been mentioned as a possible successor to President Mościcki.

[62] This was the so-called "Paris Agreement" first enunciated on October 1, 1939; it was necessitated by the belief of Sikorski and his supporters that the legal continuity of the state could be maintained only on the basis of the 1935 constitution, despite the fact that they themselves felt it had been adopted illegally. Unfortunately the agreement was oral and became the subject of conflicting interpretations, especially over the question of whether the government was also bound to act "in close agreement" with the president. See Pobóg-Malinowski, *Najnowsza historia*, 3:153-54, n. 5, and 162-63, n. 21; Micewski, *Z geografii politycznej*, pp. 308-309; and Popiel, *Generał Sikorski w mojej pamięci*, p. 98. It was, for instance, this agreement that helped both to precipitate and to abort Raczkiewicz's dismissal of Sikorski in July 1940.

and less than total.[63] Rather less manageable was the National Council. Set up in lieu of an elected parliament, its function was to give representation apart from the government or cabinet to all political parties. However, because of the manner of its selection and despite its strictly advisory role, it progressively became a sounding board for the more conservative elements, particularly from the Nationalist and Socialist Parties.[64] But by far the greatest threat to the prime minister's ability to govern, by virtue both of numbers and opportunities to sabotage established policy, were the military officer corps and the civilian and diplomatic bureaucracies. Staffed almost wholly by holdovers from prewar days, their relative importance was magnified by the exigencies of exile. As Mitkiewicz observed in his diary on July 4, 1940:

> The composition of our Government, called the Government of National Unity, only seemingly gives predominance to the parties representing the mass of the Polish people, that is to the Peasant Party and to the Socialists. In our émigré reality, without the support of the home country and the opinion of the peasant and working masses, the opposition has great weight. The political opposition is made up for the most part of officials and numerous [military] officers, people outside the parties. It is easy merely on the basis of conversations and uttered opinions of General Sikorski to determine where the action against him, and against the direction of Polish policy which he represents, originates. Professor Stanisław Kot, although he often exaggerates in detecting everywhere and at every step "sanatorzy" and the "Sanacja," is quite right in [contending] that the group which formerly ruled Poland has not in the least given up and has not recognized its errors, but on the contrary considers itself even as the only [group] presently called to assume the leadership of Poland's governments.[65]

[63] The prime minister's staunchest supporters within his cabinet were consistently those who had been associated with him in the Front Morges in the late 1930s. Concerning the Front, see Polonsky, *Politics in Independent Poland*, pp. 418 and 504; Micewski, *Z geografii politycznej*, pp. 257-59 and 305; and Kukiel, *Generał Sikorski*, pp. 76-77. See also Chapter III, note 12, above, and note 115 below.

[64] The Council (Rada Narodowa) was established by presidential decree in December 1939; its members were in theory appointed by the president on the nomination of the prime minister. However, it became accepted practice that when a higher ranking leader arrived in exile he displaced a lower ranking member of that party. The Council was actually dissolved in the wake of the crisis over the Polish-Soviet Agreement and was reconvened, with a new membership, only in early 1942. See Kowalski, *Walka dyplomatyczna*, p. 127; Pobóg-Malinowski, *Najnowsza historia*, 3:87-88 and 193-94; Raczyński, *W sojuszniczym Londynie*, p. 126; Kukiel, *Generał Sikorski*, pp. 106-107; and C1755/807/55, FO 371/31094, PRO.

[65] Mitkiewicz, *Z gen. Sikorskim*, pp. 75-76. The moderate Socialist, Pragier, though

Several critics have suggested that Sikorski committed a strategic blunder of the first order in not seizing the opportunity in September or October 1939, when the prewar regime was most severely compromised and when, because of French support, his own position was strongest, to rid himself of these restraints and obstacles: to revert to the previous 1921 constitution, which had established a parliamentary democracy with only limited presidential powers; to eliminate prewar elements from the government; and above all to purge the civilian and military bureaucracies of pro-Sanacja officers.[66] Once France fell, so this argument goes, the occasion was lost. His own errors (chiefly his undue confidence in France and the resulting loss of much of the Polish Army in the West) left him open to criticism, some of it justified but much of it not. Also, Poland's September 1939 defeat no longer appeared so shameful in the wake of the precipitous collapse of France nine months later. Meanwhile, the transfer of the government from Angers to London, where Sikorski was at first less well known than some of his opponents—and where, apart from a handful of specialists in the scholarly and diplomatic communities, little of Polish affairs was known at all—emboldened the opposition to take the offensive against him. It was, in fact, this coincidence of events that led to the abortive coup in July 1940, although the triggering incident was the general's unauthorized feeler to Moscow.[67]

Certainly these critics are right in asserting that the constant bickering and recurrent crises within the government reinforced Sikorski's dependence on Allied backing, at the same time reducing the options open to him in the conduct and substance of his policies. Nonetheless one must question

scarcely a supporter of Sikorski, confirms the point: "At first the official apparatus was not numerous. It was created by those people who reached France the earliest, and thus by those who had the means: cars, money, influence. Virtually all had occupied official positions at home, sometimes important ones. There was no lack among them of highly qualified people. Almost all, in one way or another connected with the former governments, now threw themselves more or less ostentatiously to the side of the 'counter-Sanacja.' As I wrote about them later: 'I would rather deal with non-opportunistic Piłsudskiites than with opportunistic anti-Piłsudskiites.' " *Czas przeszły dokonany*, pp. 574-75. Concerning opposition to Sikorski within the military officer corps, see the minute by Frank Roberts, dated July 30, 1940; C7639/252/55, FO 371/24474, PRO.

[66] Ksawery Pruszyński, "Dzieje emigracji londyńskiej," *Wybór pism publicystycznych*, 2:438-44; Micewski, *Z geografii politycznej*, pp. 306-16; Popiel, *Generał Sikorski w mojej pamięci*, p. 99; and Jerzy Klimkowski, *Katastrofa w Gibraltarze: Kulisy śmierci generała Sikorskiego*, pp. 18-22. Characteristically, all are sympathetic critics; his detractors do not fault him for not making these moves because they considered him the interloper.

[67] See pp. 53-56 above and note 112 below. Even some who do not criticize him for not purging the governmental and military apparatus see June 1940 as the real turning point in the struggle between Sikorski and the opposition. See Kot, *Listy z Rosji*, p. 533; and Kukiel, *Generał Sikorski*, pp. 127-31.

whether, in the weeks and months following September 1939, he really had any alternative to compromise. For a government in Poland's situation, there was no escaping a relationship of dependence on the Allies. Moreover, believing as he did that Poland must earn her place in the alliance and that recognition as a full-fledged ally was a necessary precondition (although by no means a guarantee) of her rightful voice in Allied peace councils, Sikorski was anxious that the government and army be operational as soon as possible.[68] Even had he had the time to train new military officers, diplomats, or civil servants, the pool from which he could draw was limited to those who had managed to make their way to France, and later England.[69] Besides, given the narrowness of his political base in exile and the impossibility of appealing to the mass-based parties at home, Sikorski could justifiably fear that any attempt to solidify his position by excluding the opposition would have provoked the latter to organize a competing government, and would almost certainly have damaged relations with the British and French. Avoiding such contingencies was, and throughout his tenure would continue to be, one of his primary concerns.[70]

[68] Responding to criticism of the initial composition of the exile government, Pragier wrote a few months later: "In the dramatic circumstances in which the government was created, a rapid decision was essential. Thus all the deficiencies resulting from the composition of General Sikorski's government had to be deferred to a future reconstruction, but could not be an obstacle to the creation of the government." From the discussion preceding this, it is clear that the Poles in Paris regarded continued international recognition of the legal continuity of the Polish state as the question of prime importance, and that this recognition was being threatened by the transparent efforts of remnants of the *ancien régime*, now interned in Rumania, to hang onto power at least indirectly. *Czas przeszły dokonany*, pp. 567-68 and 580. In addition, and especially in the months before the fall of France demonstrated Germany's truly formidable power, Sikorski faced serious difficulties in organizing his army in France, in part as a result of Allied doubts over Poland's value as an ally, and in part as a residual effect on their distrust of former Foreign Minister Beck. See, e.g., Popiel, *Generał Sikorski w mojej pamięci*, pp. 105-107; and Terlecki, *Generał ostatniej legendy*, pp. 95-96. Indicative of his problems was the British reaction to Sikorski's request, during his November 1939 visit to London, for Polish representation on the Inter-Allied Military Coordinating Committee. After shuffling the request about for several months, it was decided to let the matter drop "unless and until the Poles . . . enquire what has been decided." After all, commented one official, "nobody wants a Pole, and he would cost money." C18714/27/55, FO 371/23131, PRO.

[69] Popiel has charged that Śmigły-Rydz and part of the officer corps in Rumania deliberately tried to sabotage the exile government and army in France by holding the bulk of military officers in the internment camps, particularly young officers fit for active service. At least initially, Popiel claims, the effort was very successful and prevented Sikorski from making contact with the people he wanted, while others of little or no use (for reasons of age or lack of experience) were allowed to leave. *Generał Sikorski w mojej pamięci*, pp. 110-12.

[70] Pruszyński, "Rzecz działa się we Francji," *Wybór pism*, 2:440; Kot, *Listy z Rosji*, p. 532; and Kukiel, *Generał Sikorski*, p. 97. Particularly during the first half of 1940, the Foreign Office commented repeatedly on the "unfortunate zeal" shown by Sikorski and

One other probable element in his decision not to force the issue was his apparent optimism that he could convince the skeptics and critics, or at least a significant number of them, of the urgency and rationality of his policies—that the shock of the September debacle had impressed on them the need for fundamental changes in Poland's domestic and foreign policies.[71] No doubt, also, he reasoned that any government returning to Poland would have to have at least the tacit support of the more moderate wings of the Sanacja and the National Democracy. It was characteristic that he tried, especially in the early years, to involve his rivals in the development of his postwar programs and to force them to cooperate with other members of the government.[72] This effort was not without a few individual successes—most notably Ambassadors Raczyński and Lipski and Dr. Marian Seyda[73]—but by and large it was to be one of his bitterest disappointments.

THE GULF between Sikorski and his supporters on the one hand and the pro-Sanacja/Nationalist opposition on the other ran through virtually every

---

some of his supporters for vengeance against former government personalities, and warned him that it would be harmful to the Polish cause to get rid of those most knowledgeable about the West, and especially Britain—a clear reference to Zaleski. FO 371/24474, PRO (*passim*).

[71] Pruszyński ("Rzecz dziaa się we Francji," 2:440 and 443) and Popiel (*Generał Sikorski w mojej pamięci*, p. 99) both make this point, but also suggest that he underestimated his opponents. Sikorski's hopes in this regard were not wholly unfounded, however. For instance, neither Zaleski nor Sosnkowski was a man of extreme views, and both had had their own difficulties with the post-Pisudski leadership. (See notes 60 and 61 above.) In addition, one authoritative source (Pragier, *Czas przeszły dokonany*, p. 567) recalls that Zaleski was incensed by the behavior of Mościcki and his supporters.

[72] For instance, he named both Sosnkowski and Zaleski to the Polish half of the Polish-Czech Coordinating Committee (the former as chairman), with relatively good results; see Raczyński, *W sojuszniczym Londynie*, pp. 113-15. He also put Sosnkowski in charge of the military Underground in Poland—a position that required him to cooperate with then Minister of Internal Affairs Kot—this time with near disastrous results. See Mitkiewicz, *Z gen. Sikorskim*, pp. 103-104 and 176; Kot, *Listy z Rosji*, pp. 544-46; and C2405/151/55, FO 371/26718, PRO.

[73] Both Raczyński and Lipski, as high-ranking members of the diplomatic corps, were for that reason alone regarded at first with some suspicion by Sikorski, in addition to which Raczyński initially disapproved of the Polish-Soviet Agreement of July 1941. Yet both quickly won his trust and came to be among his closest advisors, Raczyński as acting foreign minister following Zaleski's resignation, Lipski particularly as an advisor on the German problem and on territorial questions. Seyda, then minister of justice, resigned from the government together with Zaleski and Sosnkowski in protest against the Polish-Soviet Agreement; but he returned six months later (and even earlier to his other post as head of the postwar planning office) and went on to work closely with Sikorski, if not in full agreement on all issues. Concerning Seyda's return, see Ambassador's Dormer's report to the Foreign Office of January 21, 1942, in C807/807/55, FO 371/31094, PRO; his continuing differences with Sikorski, especially over boundary questions, are discussed below, pp. 263 and 269-70.

basic issue of Poland's politics, from her international orientation to her political and socio-economic structure. This is not to suggest that the opposition was monolithic. On the contrary, the most important elements—the Sanacja and National Democracy—had themselves been at odds for much of the interwar period, and each camp was characterized by gradations of temperance and illusion.[74] Nonetheless, two common denominators set these groups apart from Sikorski and others of the center-left and made the differences between them irreconcilable. They were, first, an exaggerated image of what Poland had been and could again become, and second, according to some, a paralyzing fear of social and economic revolution in Poland—not merely of a Bolshevik revolution but of any substantial change in the direction of political and economic democracy. These two motivating impulses warped their perception of every ingredient of Poland's international environment—of her geography, of her relative strength vis-à-vis her neighbor to the east, of her moral standing both in Central Europe and in the West, and of her importance to and therefore leverage with her Anglo-American allies. Where Sikorski viewed geography as a constant which must set limits to a nation's aspirations, his opponents saw it as an obstacle to be defied. This attitude was implicit in the "two enemy" concept which had dominated Polish foreign policy in the interwar period, and which at least in some quarters emerged almost unscathed from the experience of renewed partition. Characteristic is the following comment made by a Socialist member of the National Council to some English hosts:

> Suppose someone says to us: You are in a difficult position, so join up with the Soviet Union. My answer would be very short: After you, my friend! But geography protects you, and geography is against us.

[74] Relations between the Nationalist and Sanacja camps in interwar Poland were extremely complicated and cannot be discussed in any detail here. In practice, since the Bolshevik revolution had removed their basic disagreement over policy toward Russia, many Nationalists supported the "post-May" regimes. The picture is further complicated by the rampant factionalism that characterized Polish politics, producing groups that defy simple classification on a traditional right-left spectrum. One important example is the Polish Socialist Party (PPS), whose right wing had remained loyal to Piłsudski and in exile was more or less associated with the Sanacja and opposed to Sikorski, while its moderate center, having been opposed to the prewar regimes, to a certain extent supported the prime minister. (The left-wing Socialists played no part in the London exile picture and were later associated with the "Moscow" Poles.) Nationalist topography is even more confusing; here, moderate supporters of Sikorski's government were limited to a handful of mostly older leaders from Poland's prewar western provinces. An excellent survey of the interwar political landscape in Poland is Micewski's *Z geografii politycznej*, which analyzes groupings according to their geopolitical orientation as well as by more traditional criteria. See also Polonsky, *Politics in Independent Poland*; Terej, *Rzeczywistość i polityka*; and Wynot, *Polish Politics in Transition*.

Very well, then we will do battle against the German aggressors, against Fascism, and against geography.[75]

Where Sikorski accepted the fact that Poland was at best a medium-sized power and, in relation to her great neighbors to the east and west, even a small one who must seek strength in partnership with other small nations, adherents of the Sanacja imagined her to be a "great power." As Juliusz Łukasiewicz, Poland's ambassador to France and later one of the most vociferous critics of Sikorski's person and policies, wrote in 1939 (after Munich and the Teschen affair!):

> Poland is a great power, constituting the cornerstone of the present structure of Central and Eastern Europe. . . . Thanks to a far-sighted, rational and virile foreign policy, thanks to her constantly growing internal strength and to an army which represents her worthily, Poland is emerging from the storm, which has hovered over the West, as a great power. . . . The history of our nation in the course of the past quarter century is an unending series of victories. . . . Our victories have been splendid and will endure forever. . . . The Teschen victory is a new stage in the historical march of the Poland of Piłsudski. . . . [76]

Raczyński has suggested that this "great power" fetish was the result of a belief on the part of Piłsudski, and to a greater extent his successors, that one of their most "urgent" tasks was "to cure the Poles of their alleged humility and submissiveness toward foreigners, resulting from an uncritical awe of the cultural and material superiority of the outside world. Hence," Raczyński continued:

> the slogan of Poland as a Great Power. In the Marshal's time this tactic could without difficulty be explained and justified by political calculations; after his death, however, it degenerated into cant which threatened the continued existence of the Polish state.[77]

[75] Quoted in Tadeusz Katelbach, *Rok złych wróżb (1943)*, p. 77. The alleged speaker was Adam Ciołkosz and following the quotation, Katelbach commented: "Bravo Ciołkosz! What good fortune that, in addition to the 'demons' like Kot and PPS comrades on the order of Grosfeld, Szczyrek, Stańczyk or Beloński, we have in London Socialists of the Ciołkosz variety, who are faithful to the traditions of independence of that party. Unfortunately there are too few of them here."

[76] Łukasiewicz, *Polska jest mocarstwem*, pp. 59-63; also quoted in Kot, *Listy z Rosji*, p. 531. For Łukasiewicz's unflattering appraisal of Sikorski (as well as Raczyński's equally unflattering appraisal of Łukasiewicz), see Raczyński, *W sojuszniczym Londynie*, p. 75.

[77] Raczyński, *W sojuszniczym Londynie*, pp. 200-201.

Both of these attitudes—the defiance of geography and the illusion of Poland as a great power—reflected a fundamental contempt for Russia, the more so for a Soviet Russia, and a belief that history was about to repeat itself: that in a war with Germany the Russians would either be defeated or badly weakened, leading in any event to the disintegration of the Soviet empire and possibly even to the overthrow of the communist system.[78] Such views were not, of course, unique to the Polish opposition. Four days before Hitler launched "Barbarossa," Sikorski told British Ambassador Cripps that the Red Army "will not be able to stand the impact" of the German onslaught (although he was quick to recognize his mistake on this point). Cripps shared his initial pessimism, as did many others, including top U.S. military advisors.[79] As we have seen, Stalin himself was apparently haunted by similar fears. Where Sikorski's views departed most sharply from those of his opposition was over the consequences for Poland of a German victory and, therefore, over the question of what posture the Poles should adopt toward a Russo-German war.

Here views within the opposition also varied widely. Closest to Sikorski were those who professed to believe in the necessity of an agreement with Moscow, but only on Poland's terms. For instance, as Mitkiewicz recorded in mid-July 1941, while the negotiations were in progress:

> The opposition group around General Sosnkowski and Foreign Minister Zaleski as well as President Raczkiewicz's entourage, including the President himself, represent the view that an understanding with Russia is *in principle* necessary *in our present conditions*; but there

[78] Kot (*Listy z Rosji*, pp. 10-11) charged that the Sanacja deluded itself and its followers with the example of the First World War: "The outcome of that war, the orientation of the Legions, the war of 1920, the faith in the prophetic genius of Piłsudski, the inebriation with great-power phrases repeated through the years, and the habit of slighting the strengths of others—all this completely obscured for the Piłsudskiites an appraisal of the world political situation. Dazed by the September disaster, for which they had prepared neither themselves nor the nation, they did not understand the attitude of other nations toward us."

[79] See the "Note" of Sikorski's conversation with Cripps, June 18, 1941, in *Documents*, 1:103-108. Mitkiewicz noted with considerable disapproval that the "mood" at this time in the Polish General Staff was one "of anticipation—I do not wish to say of joyous [anticipation] . . .'"; *Z gen. Sikorskim*, pp. 151-52. See also Eden, *The Reckoning*, p. 314; Werth, *Russia at War*, p. 279; and Dallek, *Roosevelt and American Foreign Policy*, p. 278. Sikorski appears to have been one of the first to change his appraisal. During a luncheon meeting with Bevin and Strang on July 3rd, less than two weeks after the German attack, he remarked that the Germans had not had the "sweeping successes" they might have expected, and that the Soviet Army now "was quite a different thing" from the army that had marched into Poland in 1939 "with no heart in its task." According to the British record of the meeting, in C7458/3226/55, FO 371/26755, PRO.

is no need to press the issue, we should wait until Russia herself offers us favorable terms: boundaries according to the Treaty of Riga.[80]

Noting, however, the "prevalence of utterly woolly-headed views" on this subject, Mitkiewicz was of the opinion that the delaying tactics stemmed "from hopes that several weeks hence the situation will be such that our understanding with *Soviet* Russia will be completely superfluous."[81] In a similar vein, Sir Cecil Dormer, Britain's newly appointed ambassador to the Government-in-Exile, reported back to the Foreign Office on the prevailing mood within official Polish circles:

> One would have expected that General Sikorski's broadcast, issued on the morrow of the German attack on Russia, declaring Poland's readiness to reach an understanding with Moscow, would have met with a more favourable response from Poles in London than it seems to have done. M. Tarnowski, Secretary-General of the Ministry for Foreign Affairs, for instance, when I asked him a day or two later whether there had been any reply from the Russian side, was almost indignant at the suggestion that the reply could be of any interest. The Russians, he anticipated, would soon be driven out of Poland, and as far as they were concerned the question of Poland's frontiers would be no longer worth discussing with them. . . .[82]

To Sikorski such hopes were sheer folly since, in his view, a post-Bolshevik regime would be more likely either to work out a compromise with Hitler or to collapse precipitously into anarchy, in either event giving even greater advantage to the Germans.[83]

Certainly the minimum program of all the groups opposing the Polish-Soviet Agreement—as, indeed, of some who supported Sikorski's decision to sign—was a return to the pre-September 1939 boundary in the east.

---

[80] Mitkiewicz, *Z gen. Sikorskim*, p. 153 [emphasis added].

[81] Ibid. [emphasis in the original]. Even Raczyński shared this view at the time and went so far as to prepare a memorandum to this effect for Sikorski and Zaleski. However, he was also critical of the dominant Polish attitude toward Russia—"When it comes to the Russian problem [our authoritative circles] are ruled by emotional reactions and are therefore always in error"—and within a few months changed his mind about the agreement. *W sojuszniczym Londynie*, pp. 118-25; also Kukiel, *Generał Sikorski*, pp. 179-80.

[82] C8306/3226/55, FO 371/26756, PRO. Dormer also reported that he had not detected any significant change in the Polish attitude after the opening of negotiations, adding that "most of the Poles whom I have seen seem to regard the question of the frontiers as of greater importance than that of the Polish prisoners."

[83] See the record of Sikorski's September 19, 1941, meeting with Averell Harriman in *Documents*, 1:169; also Kot, *Listy z Rosji*, p. 87, n. 2.

Beyond that, their territorial appetites grew in direct proportion to their disdain for Russian might, with maximum demands reaching even beyond the easternmost limits of the Jagiellonian empire in the seventeenth century. Ambassador Kot has described a map that circulated in the Polish Army in the Middle East, showing "the mirage of an enormous Poland" which would arise from "the ruins of the Russian empire" and would reach "from the Oder to the Donets, with Kharkov included."[84] While this map may have been an NKVD provocation, Mitkiewicz too wrote incredulously of those "who in all seriousness conjure up plans whereby the Polish State . . . would take possession of territories in the east up to the Dnieper and Dvina [rivers], recreating in its totality the former Polish Commonwealth of the Jagiellonians—and, in addition, under the scepter and crown of the Duke of Kent or the Slav, King Peter of Yugoslavia."[85]

What was the relative influence of such fantasies? To what extent were those who nurtured them willing to collaborate with the Germans, or to countenance German domination over Poland in order to realize them? Mitkiewicz was of the view that the link between "anti-Russian" and "pro-German" was an inescapable one since "there cannot be any other solution to this problem," and that the whole nexus was related to domestic political and economic cleavages, with the view of Germany as "the lesser evil" widespread among "our aristocratic and landowning circles."[86] In all probability Mitkiewicz's views, especially concerning the influence of the "aristocracy," were both exaggerated and out-of-date. No class in Poland escaped Nazi brutality, and all participated in the resistance. Likewise, mirages of vast territorial expansion, if not entirely the handiwork of the NKVD, could only have been the product of a lunatic fringe.

Still, Mitkiewicz does call our attention to one striking detail which can be confirmed by other, more neutral sources: on both occasions when the prospect of an agreement with Russia arose—that is, in June/July 1940

---

[84] Kot (*Listy z Rosji*, pp. 72 and 428) charges that the map originated in the Propaganda section of the Eastern Command in late 1942, as part of an anti-Sikorski campaign in cooperation with London and New York opposition groups, and that Stalin later displayed it to Churchill as an example of Polish imperialism. The map, which is reproduced on the last two pages of Kot's book, is entitled "To będzie Polska—Matka Wolnych Narodów" (This will be Poland—Mother of Free Nations) and shows the eastern boundary of a future Polish state running to the east of the Baltic States, then southeastward to end near the eastern tip of the Sea of Azov, just short of Rostov on the Don. (In the southwest, it included the two former Rumanian territories of Bukovina and Bessarabia seized by the Soviets in 1940!) Similar maps apparently circulated in the Underground in Poland. See Strumph-Wojtkiewicz (*Siła złego*, pp. 80-83) concerning the prevalence of such views both in the army and in London; see also pp. 261-66 below.

[85] Mitkiewicz, *Z gen. Sikorskim*, p. 165.

[86] Ibid., pp. 157-58. It is not just Sikorski's defenders who emphasize the extent of his opposition; see, e.g., Katelbach, *Rok złych wróżb*, pp. 35-36.

and again in July 1941—proposals for or rumors of a pending settlement with Germany spread through the exile community. On the first occasion he reported "ever more frequent and shrill calls for a settlement of relations with Germany" on the basis of the "eleven points [Hitler] offered last year." "Adherents to this conception," he continued, "were well represented in the military and the Ministry of Foreign Affairs and were "counting . . . on taking advantage of a [future] German campaign against Russia, which supposedly will afford a settlement of Poland's postwar boundaries."[87] A year later, in the midst of the Sikorski-Maisky negotiations, he wrote of "rumors from [Poland]" that the Germans have promised "a change in the regime in Poland and proposals for territorial changes in the east in exchange for Silesia and Pomerania—if Poland participates in the war against Russia." The proposals had reportedly been rejected but had "unfortunately been picked up to a certain extent in Polish London."[88]

One might be inclined to write off Mitkiewicz's allegations to the overactive imagination of a diligent intelligence chief were it not for the corroborating evidence. For instance, a July 1940 entry in the Foreign Office files remarked on the widespread belief that, "if they had to make a choice . . . , the Poles would be more likely to work with the Germans than with the Russians, since collaboration with the Russians implied the

---

[87] Mitkiewicz, *Z gen. Sikorskim,* p. 74; see also *Documents*, 1:118 and 125. Mitkiewicz also says that Sikorski was aware of these views and where they originated, and that he was bitterly opposed to them: "[Sikorski] considers it impermissible to bind the future of the Polish Nation under any pretext to Germany." The "eleven points" is an apparent, though inaccurate, reference to the conditions offered by Hitler to Foreign Minister Beck in January 1939. Hopes of reverting to this point were entirely illusory; after April 1939 Hitler was no longer interested in Polish collaboration on the basis offered in January and had begun to prepare for a military attack on Poland. See, e.g., Martin Broszat, *Zweihundert Jahre deutsche Polenpolitik*, pp. 198-205; and Gerhard L. Weinberg, *The Foreign Policy of Hitler's Germany: Starting World War II, 1937-1939*, pp. 496-505, 538-39, and 560. In an earlier study (*Nationalsozialistische Polenpolitik*, p. 17), Broszat writes that in October 1939 the German Embassy in Geneva reported back to Berlin on the formation of a Polish exile circle in Switzerland which, in opposition to the Sikorski group in France, favored an understanding with Germany aimed at the establishment of a new Polish state. According to Broszat, however, Ribbentrop ordered that contact with this group be broken off. See also Wagner, *The Genesis of the Oder-Neisse Line*, pp. 1-2.

[88] Mitkiewicz, *Z gen. Sikorskim*, p. 153. Mitkiewicz describes Sikorski here as being in an "unprecedentedly difficult position. . . . One senses clearly an almost universal opposition to an understanding with Russia . . . General Sikorski is virtually isolated . . ." Some weeks later, in mid-September, Mitkiewicz reported to Sikorski on the existence within the Foreign Ministry of a group which, "in view of the fact that Soviet Russia was losing the war" and of the inactivity on the part of the Western Allies, was advocating the formation of a government in Poland "to create a *modus vivendi* with Germany." Ibid., p. 180. Strumph-Wojtkiewicz (*Gwiazda Władysława Sikorskiego*, pp. 172-73) also speaks of a pro-German mood in some exile circles.

acceptance of a lower cultural and material standard of existence, the negation of their strong Catholic faith and the acceptance of Communism with all that that implies."[89] In July 1941, Foreign Minister Zaleski himself lent credence to the rumors by his provocative statement, during the first negotiating session with Maisky, to the effect that the Germans were trying to form a puppet government in Warsaw and were promising the Poles "a most considerable extension of their eastern boundaries."[90] Even Sikorski's statements provide indirect confirmation of the persistence of pro-German sympathies by his constant iteration of the theme that: "One of the most dreaded solutions for us would be a negotiated peace with Germany. For Poland it would be a calamity as great as a lost war . . ."[91]

A more moderate position, the one undoubtedly espoused by the great majority of dissidents both inside and outside the government, held that Poland at least for the time being should remain neutral in a Russo-German war. On the very day of Hitler's attack, the Council of Ministers resolved that the government saw no "possibility in present circumstances of committing itself to cooperation with Russia" but that, "with the further development of the situation, the time might come for taking a more precise stand."[92] In a similar vein, Adam Pragier, a prominent Socialist member of the National Council, suggested as one basis for future policy that "Poland will refrain from actions detrimental to Russia's war effort."[93] In advocating neutrality, or at least inaction, some apparently believed or hoped that Germany would soon defeat the Soviet Union, others that the

[89] Comment by Frank Roberts, July 15, 1940; C7880/7177/55, FO 371/24482, PRO.

[90] *Documents*, 1:118. Possibly as a result of this statement, Zaleski found himself largely excluded from subsequent negotiations leading up to the Polish-Soviet Agreement of July 30th.

[91] From Sikorski's report to the Council of Ministers on his trip to Russia, January 12, 1942; *Documents*, 1:266. The full text of this secret speech (C795/19/55, FO 371/31077, PRO) contains other allusions to such views, to "ill-will and out-of-date views of Russia," and to "the London milieu" as "the most unhealthy and weakest part of our emigration." See also his June 23 and July 31, 1941, broadcasts to Poland; *Documents*, 1:110 and 145.

[92] This vague promise of a later change in attitude apparently reflected the view of several key ministers—especially Zaleski and Sosnkowski—that cooperation with Moscow was possible only after the Soviets unequivocally recognized the pre-September 1939 boundary; see Pobóg-Malinowski, *Najnowsza historia*, 3:173-74 and n. 39.

[93] Other points of Pragier's program, which with minor changes was adopted by the exile leadership of the Socialist Party, included demands that "the USSR renounce its annexation of Polish territories" and "transfer [?] the occupied territories . . . to the Polish Government," as well as a declaration that Poland would make "no territorial claims against the USSR and is not interested in the internal structure of the USSR." It is not clear whether the author saw these points as leading to some sort of agreement with Moscow; on the one hand, he called for a British "guarantee" to Poland, on the other, for the Polish Government to hold talks only with Britain. *Czas przeszły dokonany*, pp. 630-32; see also Kukiel, *Generał Sikorski*, p. 178.

two giants would bleed each other to the point of exhaustion. In either event final victory would fall to the West, which would then reinstall its Polish allies within boundaries at least as generous in the east as those of 1939 and with additional protection against Germany in the north and west.[94] Yet even this scenario—though less reckless in its disdain for realities than dreams of vast territorial expansion to the east—took little account of Anglo-American attitudes toward a Nazi-Soviet conflict or of the improbability that a defeated or weakened Russia would long remain defeated or weakened in the wake of an Allied victory over Germany.[95] Also implicit in this outlook was an exaggerated view of Poland's importance to the alliance and, conversely, of the Allies' moral and political obligations to her. Adherents of the Sanacja in particular, being unable to accept that their prewar policy had in any way been wrong, believed that "someone must correct the wrongs done to us." As Ambassador Kot has put it in his rather abrasive style:

> [T]hey limited their tactical sagacity to the instructions: enter into no compromises, point out again and again for the Allies the paragraphs of their obligations and pound [your] fist on the table, agree to nothing and . . . wait. That by waiting the strength of Polish demands would grow, this of course they could not prove. They were incapable of understanding the fact that time would be against us.[96]

Moreover, many felt that Poland "had already made her contribution in the September campaign, that the Allies had not come to her aid and thus were now in her debt, and that we must reserve our forces for the future"— or, at the very least, "every effort should be made conditional on guar-

---

[94] Mitkiewicz, *Z gen. Sikorskim*, pp. 165-66; also Kot, *Listy z Rosji*, pp. 10-13. Ambassador Dormer reported to Eden just a month after Germany's attack that "the news was greeted [at the Polish Embassy] with unconcealed relief at the prospect not only that Poland's two great enemies would now begin killing each other, but also that once the Russians were driven out of Poland there would be only one enemy left to deal with. In that respect the problem for the Poles, it was felt, had become greatly simplified, because no doubt remained that an Allied victory against Germany would entail the restoration of Polish territory in its entirety, whereas if a part of the country were in Russian occupation at the end of the war there would be no such certainty." C8306/3226/55, FO 371/26756, PRO.

[95] It is worth noting that after the war some émigrés transferred their hopes for regaining their prewar political and territorial position from either a German defeat of Russia, or a purely Western defeat of Germany, to a Western defeat of Russia in World War III, which they believed imminent. See, for instance, Giertych, *Pół wieku polskiej polityki*, chap. 20.

[96] Kot, *Listy z Rosji*, p. 11. Writing later in defense of his June 1941 proposal (see note 93 above), Pragier claimed: "In these conditions [our] only chance for salvation was an unyielding policy, without concern for the sensitivities of the Allies." Quoted in Kukiel, *Generał Sikorski*, p. 179.

antees.''[97] As late as February 1943, after the Russian victory at Stalingrad (!), one exponent of this view could write:

> The Soviets' progress and their mushrooming position in the Allied camp are making us increasingly uneasy. The "News Chronicle" is demanding an explanation of Polish-Soviet relations. What a magnificent occasion to explain the Polish side without any evasiveness, starting with a protest resignation of the cabinet and a complete change in the list of ministers. What an effect such a resignation would have in Great Britain, in the States, in the threatened Baltic countries, in Turkey whose favor they are currying so! *The Allies are still dependent on the Poles. They count sedulously on our every soldier. All are essential to them. Simply by relying on favorable world opinion, we could pin the Soviets to the wall.* The Germans, forced by events, speak and write more and more often about the Polish question. This too is grist for our mill.[98]

As one seasoned observer of Poland's international relations is alleged to have remarked, the behavior of his countrymen too often tended "to evoke the impression that we . . . consider ouselves the navel of the world, or at least of Europe."[99]

CONSIDERING the magnitude of the differences dividing the Polish community, it was probably inevitable that they would have serious repercussions on the operations of the Government-in-Exile. Formed at a time when the only course open to the Poles was unanimously to protest the joint Nazi-Soviet dismemberment of their country, the government could maintain a facade of unity only so long as no alternatives for a positive policy existed. Not surprisingly, then, Hitler's attack on the Soviet Union, by offering such an alternative—if only between a policy of slow and painful compromise and one of heroic defiance of reality—also breached that facade,[100] exposing all the political and institutional anomalies of an exile situation. It was one thing to agree with the principle that Poland should seek "real guarantees" of her security, especially at a time when the country lay mute witness to the failure of legal guarantees. But it was quite

---

[97] Kukiel, *Generał Sikorski*, p. 97.

[98] Katelbach, *Rok złych wróżb*, pp. 42-43 [emphasis added].

[99] Mitkiewicz, *Z gen. Sikorskim*, p. 324; the remark is attributed to Józef Lipski, Poland's prewar ambassador to Berlin and during the war an advisor to Sikorski.

[100] Pobóg-Malinowski (*Najnowsza historia*, 3:187) pinpoints the resignations of Ministers Sosnkowski, Zaleski, and Seyda in protest against the Polish-Soviet Agreement as signaling "the breakdown of the last bases of the fiction of a 'government of national unity.' "

another to agree on what real guarantees the Poles should seek, from whom, and at what price.

With no recourse to the normal channels by which a people ratify the policies of a government or eject it from office, the prime minister's hand was both strengthened and weakened. On the one hand, to the extent that he could outmaneuver his adversaries (as he did in July 1940 and again in July 1941), while maintaining good personal relations with Allied leaders, he could at least in the short term pursue his chosen policy at the diplomatic level, even in the face of bitter opposition. He could, within limits, control the composition of the Council of Ministers; that is, he probably would not have been able to get rid of Zaleski and Sosnkowski had they not resigned, but he could retain others whose removal was sought by the opposition.[101] He could even manage to have the National Council disbanded temporarily when some of its members were too outspoken in their criticism of the Polish-Soviet Agreement.[102] Since much of the work of an exile government involves diplomacy and intelligence, he could and often did circumvent a hostile bureaucracy, keeping counsel with a close circle of handpicked advisors. He could even bypass a reluctant minister at critical moments, as he did with then Foreign Minister Zaleski during the July 1941 negotiations.[103] Moreover, he could do all this in the conviction that he was right, that his opponents had failed and thereby lost their mandate, and that, as Paderewski wrote to him in October of 1939, he now represented the will of the Polish nation. Indeed, this letter from Poland's elder statesman may provide an important clue to Sikorski's attitude toward his domestic critics. Warning the newly appointed prime minister "not to let people stand between him and the nation," Paderewski continued:

> . . . The entire responsibility for the future of the Nation rests on you, General. . . . In my eyes and in the eyes of the whole Nation, you are the Leader of the Nation. We want and acknowledge you as such. You should not waste time in lengthy discussions and debates. A military order from the Leader should cut them short. This is not the time for sharing responsibility with anyone else. It is necessary to take it all on yourself, even though it is beyond human strength . . .[104]

[101] Ibid., pp. 193-94.

[102] Ibid.

[103] See note 90 above. Even Mitkiewicz is critical of Sikorski for excluding Zaleski from the negotiations (although he exaggerates the extent of the exclusion); *Z gen. Sikorskim*, pp. 150-52, 159-60, and 167.

[104] Quoted in Kukiel, *Generał Sikorski*, p. 92.

This was a style of leadership that might have been successful so long as Sikorski could show progress. In the absence of progress—or worse, in the face of impending failure, for whatever reason—such tactics were bound to further aggravate relations with his critics. For, if they lacked the institutional means to get rid of him, he also lacked the institutional means to remove or control them. Nor did he have a means of demonstrating that his policy did in fact represent the will of the nation. Moreover, while he might promote his ideas in relative secrecy at the diplomatic level, their implementation, especially of his plans for reconciliation and military collaboration with the Soviet Union, would require the active cooperation of the government, the military, intelligence and diplomatic services and, perhaps most critical of all, the Underground in Poland. As we shall see, the opportunities for mischief were legion. The National Council could embarrass the prime minister in the midst of delicate negotiations by publicly adopting a rigid stand on some key issue. A Foreign Ministry clerk could aggravate a crisis by leaking some confidential communiqué. Dissident military officers could undermine morale in the ranks by lobbying against official policy. A general in the Underground could jeopardize relations with Moscow by refusing to cooperate with Soviet intelligence. Physical separation combined with the precarious political balance within the Government-in-Exile tended to make such breaches of discipline immune to the sanctions usually available to a government.

Further exacerbating the situation was a tendency for differences of a political and philosophical nature to be translated into personal attacks on the character of the prime minister. A difference of opinion, even over a point of fact, became a moral failing or outright heresy. Unable to believe that Sikorski's pursuit of an understanding with Russia represented an honest attempt to protect Poland's national interests within the constraints of her geographical situation, they had to seek a more sinister motivation. For some he was "a Freemason and agent of international Jewry."[105] Others saw him as the dupe of British machinations, the witting or unwitting promoter of Soviet designs, or "the victim of his own ambitions and impulsiveness."[106] Unwilling to accept the limits of Poland's leverage

[105] This was a holdover from the interwar period when Dmowski's Endeks suspected the Front Morges of which Sikorski was a founding member, of "Masonic and Jewish" leanings because of its Francophile and liberal democratic character. See Polonsky, *Politics in Independent Poland*, p. 418; also Terlecki, *Generał ostatniej legendy*, pp. 76-77. According to Strumph-Wojtkiewicz (*Siła złego*, p. 82), who was with the Polish Army in the Soviet Union, this view was popular among Nationalist officers, to whom he attributes "a tendency toward intrigue, slander and an utterly fanatical bitterness."

[106] Pobóg-Malinowski, *Najnowsza historia*, 3:152-57 and 178-81; for Kukiel's comments on the "malicious" criticism of Sikorski in connection with the signing of the Polish-Soviet Agreement, see *Generał Sikorski*, p. 174.

within the alliance, they were inclined to blame the persistence of Rus-sophile tendencies in London and Washington on Sikorski's failure to formulate a ''clear'' (read rigid) policy toward Russia.[107] They interpreted his willingness to compromise, to adjust Polish demands to the conditions and interests of the Central European region as a whole, as a sign of character weaknesses, especially of his vanity and alleged susceptibility to the flatteries of foreign leaders—or, even worse, as evidence of a dis-regard for the ''Polish cause.''[108] This approach to Sikorski's policy had its illogical aspects, since even his most bitter opponents had to admit that Piłsudski had admired Sikorski's talents. Early in 1943, when the anti-Sikorski clamor had reached fever pitch, one of them conceded:

> . . . He is, after all, an intelligent and gifted man. In Lisbon Miedziński told me that Piłsudski valued highly his quality of mind. In the first years after the Polish-Russian war, he [Piłsudski] entertained the idea of basing his governments on two people: Sosnkowski would be supreme commander, Sikorski the permanent prime minister. But Sikorski has always lacked character. It is the same even today. Thus he deludes himself that somehow he can maneuver his way through everything—that is, maneuver his way through personally, losing along the way almost imperceptibly matters of capital importance for Poland. . . .[109]

The question of what influence personal factors had on the definition and conduct of his policy is a difficult and ambiguous one. By all accounts he was indeed a vain and ambitious man, but these qualities would scarcely set him apart from the genre of politician or general. Nor is there any evidence that the prime minister's personality quirks influenced the *substance* of his policies—that, for instance, in seeking to build a Polish army in the Soviet Union, or in pushing the cause of Central European federation, he was motivated by ''personal ambition'' rather than by his perception of Poland's long-term national interests. On the contrary, Raczyński, who is perhaps the most temperate and balanced of all sources in this regard,

---

[107] Pobóg-Malinowski, *Najnowsza historia*, 3:136-40.

[108] Ibid., pp. 245-48 and notes.

[109] Katelbach, *Rok złych wróżb*, p. 49. Sikorski, incidentally, was not the only one whose motives or character were so impugned. Apparently anyone who dared to suggest either that the Russians would not collapse as expected or, later, that the Red Army would reach Poland and Germany before the armies of the West risked being considered pro-Soviet as well as wrong in his appraisal of the military situation. The occasional Pan-Slavist or journalist who openly advocated territorial or political concessions to the Soviet Union was viewed with extreme suspicion, even as a traitor. See, e.g., Mitkiewicz, *Z gen. Sikorskim*, pp. 172-74 and 219; Strumph-Wojtkiewicz, *Gwiazda Władysława Sikorskiego*, p. 183; and Pobóg-Ma-linowski, *Najnowsza historia*, 3:234-35, n. 49.

saw his character weaknesses as a facade that provided a convenient target for his critics but also tended to obscure his real talents and qualities:

. . . General Sikorski had so many foibles and *Schönheitsfehler* that I believe he was one of those people whose true worth is not fully appreciated. His suspiciousness, his desire not only for power but also for its external symbols, and above all his great vanity made it difficult if not impossible for anyone to idealize him as an historical hero. I will say even more: these errors and shortcomings screened him from the eyes of his contemporaries, not allowing a just evaluation of his abilities and contributions. They readily ascribed his decisions to ambition or tactics, and not to a rational patriotism. The quality which distinguished him and raised him above his contemporaries . . . and which is indispensable to a statesman was a *sense of reality*. A seemingly ordinary thing, but in actuality rare, especially in our society. It is comprised above all of two attributes: a capacity for correct reasoning and in addition a kind of instinct, sixth sense, or what the French call second sight. This is the attribute which supplements the information sometimes lacking, which causes one to reject rumor and illusion and without wavering to recognize the genuine fact. . . . These criteria distinguish the politician from the political storyteller, like the precious stone from glass. This is a rare quality, especially in Poland where such stories bloom profusely and, even worse, easily conquer the opinion of society, its emotions and reactions.

. . . Yes, he was inclined to humor foreigners. Beyond that, he did not pass up an occasion to exploit their prestige to ease his own situation with his native firebrands, or merely critics. He was reproached for this method unjustly. [His critics] have consciously forgotten the fact that this skillful politician and fervent patriot never for a moment ceased to plead the cause of his homeland, to interpret it and to make it intelligible.[110]

---

[110] Raczyński, *W sojuszniczym Londynie*, pp. 199-201 [emphasis in the original]; this appraisal of General Sikorski was written August 2, 1943, just a month after his death. Mitkiewicz (*Z gen. Sikorskim*, p. 114) also spoke of the duality of Sikorski's character: "Two features of the General's character seem to me more sharply delineated: a great belief in himself and strong ambition, combined with a sense of historical responsibility"; see pp. 296-301 for a more personal and detailed appraisal of his personality and habits. See also Morawski, *Wspólna droga*, pp. 165-71. Contrary to numerous reports that in personal relations Sikorski was stiff, aloof, and humorless, others have written (or told me personally) that among intimates he was relaxed, informal, with a lively sense of humor; see, e.g., Włodzimierz Onacewicz, "Komentarze do książki Leona Mitkiewicza 'Z Generałem Sikorskim na obczyźnie,' " pp. 160-61.

Equally important is the question of how Sikorski's character affected his relations with the Allies, whether his personal "foibles" in any way detracted from his effectiveness as a spokesman for Poland's interests. As the quote from Raczyński suggests and as the available record confirms, the answer is that for the most part they did not—indeed that, even as his compatriots criticized him as vacillating and indecisive, both the British and the Americans came to value his judgment and forthrightness, and that the British at least gradually developed a healthy appreciation of the difficult circumstances within which he had to operate. While it is true that early references to Sikorski in the Foreign Office records are not entirely flattering and that the British were inclined at first to favor Za-leski,[111] they would soon have reason to revise their opinions. Following the fracas within the Polish government in July 1940, some in the Foreign Office had come to recognize that "it is much more important that the Polish Government should continue to be led by well-known persons who command a following in Poland and have shown some energy and deter-mination than that it should consist of pleasant gentlemen with English connexions, but little force of character or following among the Poles at home." Again: "General Sikorski has won, as we thought he would. There is, in fact, no alternative to him, and we shall just have to bear with his idiosyncrasies. . . . the Poles cannot easily do without him."[112] By

---

[111] In connection with his first visit to London in November 1939, a biographical sketch of Sikorski circulated among British officials stated: "In the early years of Polish independence he made an excellent impression on foreign observers as one of the most capable, energetic and straightforward men in the country, but his long residence in Paris has not improved him; not only has he lost contact with Poland, but the flattery which the French have lavished on him seems to have turned his head." A similar sketch of Zaleski referred to his British education and described his policy as foreign minister between 1926 and 1932 as "broad-minded and pacific" and in economic matters lacking "the narrow nationalistic attitude of most of his cabinet colleagues"; although "notoriously indolent," he was "simple" in manner and "exceedingly pleasant to deal with." C18579/27/55, FO 371/23131 and C16049/16049/55, FO 371/23159, PRO. Both sketches were based on an earlier dispatch from Ambassador Kennard who, as British envoy to the prewar regime, may have reflected some of its biases; see C10430/10430/55, FO 371/23153, PRO.

[112] Comments by Frank Roberts and William Strang, respectively; in C7639/252/55, FO 371/24474, PRO. Roberts's comment was part of a report of a meeting with the Polish-born historian, Lewis B. Namier, who had worked as a Polish expert in the Foreign Office's Political Intelligence Department at the end of World War I. Though describing himself as a close friend of Zaleski, Namier's "main point," as recorded by Roberts, "was that it was essential not to lose those Poles who were really doing the work of organising the Polish cause abroad and whose position is therefore strong with the people in Poland. Dr. Namier referred in particular to General Sikorski and Professor Kot, the latter of whom represented the great mass of the Polish peasantry. Dr. Namier was afraid that M. Zaleski being naturally lazy, although entirely honest, was allowing himself to be used by intriguers, many of whom had been connected with the old colonels' regime, to down General Sikorski." Among the

the middle of 1941, British views had come full circle. As Cadogan (not one to suffer fools gladly or in any other way) remarked during the course of the Polish-Soviet negotiations: "The best hope seems to be Gen. Sikorski who, so far as I am able to judge, is a bigger man than most Poles, and able to rise above domestic squabbles."[113] Likewise, Sumner Welles later wrote that he found Sikorski "one of the most stalwart and attractive statesmen of the war years . . ."[114]

What is apparent, however, is that the atmosphere of political dissension and personal rancor within the exile community *did* have a marked effect on the prime minister's *modus operandi*, if not on the substance of his policy. Unable to restrain his opposition, perhaps buoyed at least initially by his optimism and self-confidence, he tended to keep policy deliberations within a narrow circle of handpicked aides and advisors,[115] meanwhile

main "intriguers" Namier mentioned Jan Ciechanowski, then still secretary-general of the Ministry of Foreign Affairs and soon to become Poland's ambassador in Washington, and President Raczkiewicz's *chef de cabinet*, the Mr. Łepkowski mentioned in note 59 above. In Namier's view, "these people, and even the President himself and M. Zaleski, cut very little ice now in Poland and it would therefore be fatal if they were to win the day." Meanwhile, in his contribution to this discussion, Ambassador Kennard was still dwelling on Sikorski's "colossal" vanity and attempting to bolster the positions of Zaleski and Raczkiewicz. (Kennard was replaced as ambassador to the exile government in May 1941 by Sir Cecil Dormer, who was distinctly better disposed toward Sikorski.)

[113] C8306/3226/55, FO 371/26756, PRO. See also the minute by Frank Roberts in this same entry; and *The Cadogan Diaries*, ed. Dilks, p. 391. These comments did not put an end to British criticism of Sikorski, but henceforth such criticism was tempered by a keener appreciation within the Foreign Office of the difficulties of his situation.

[114] Welles, *Seven Decisions*, pp. 130-31.

[115] The most important of his advisors were: Józef Retinger, a personal advisor to the prime minister without official designation; General Tadeusz Klimecki, chief of the General Staff, and Colonel Andrzej Marecki, also on the General Staff (both died in the plane crash with Sikorski); three political associates from the prewar period, Professor Stanisław Kot, minister of internal affairs and later ambassador to Moscow, Stanisław Stroński, minister of information, and Karol Popiel, a minister and member of the Political Committee of the Council of Ministers; two prewar military colleagues, Generals Józef Haller and Marian Kukiel; and, finally, two members of the professional diplomatic corps, Count Edward Raczyński, ambassador to London and later acting foreign minister, and Józef Lipski, former ambassador to Berlin. These men were often at odds with each other personally and politically, and did not necessarily agree with all aspects of Sikorski's policy; several, such as Kot and Stroński, were abrasive and controversial personalities. But none of the others has excited as much controversy and malicious speculation as Retinger. Disliked especially by the Endeks for his allegedly Jewish origins, suspected by others as a British or even Soviet agent, he has most often been accused of being a malign influence on Sikorski's policy by steering it in directions convenient to the British but contrary to Poland's interests. In truth, Retinger was none of these things. Rather, as a friend and advisor to Sikorski since the early 1920s, they appear to have seen eye to eye on many issues and in particular on the question of federation, of which Retinger was a fervent advocate. To the extent that he was involved in Polish politics, his ties were with the PPS and the trade union movement, but his real interests were inter-

telling the Council of Ministers and National Council only what he wanted them to know—or what he had to tell them to gain their approval for a decision he had already reached in private counsel. This is not to say that his decisions were necessarily arbitrary or that he could dictate the moves of the government. Quite the contrary, Mitkiewicz in particular stresses that Sikorski was at pains to find compromise solutions wherever possible.[116] But he was not averse to stretching (or concealing) the truth, to using foreign pressures to persuade his domestic audience and vice versa, or to pursuing in private ideas which he or his government rejected in public. Thus in July 1941, it seems quite clear that he exaggerated the level of Allied pressure on him in order to extract approval from a wavering Council of Ministers for what he believed to be the best Polish-Soviet agreement attainable.[117] Later, he would try to reverse the process, using the domestic pressures on him as an argument against British concessions to Moscow.[118] Likewise, both as a negotiating strategy and as a means of avoiding a domestic confrontation, he would consistently affirm the inviolability of Poland's 1939 eastern boundary—even when, as is now abundantly clear, he knew concessions to be unavoidable. He would conceal, as much and for as long as possible, the true extent of the deterioration of relations with Moscow; he would also conceal his inability to garner Western support for his federation and western boundary concepts. In line with official Allied policy, he would publicly state that the time was not yet ripe for detailed postwar planning, all the while pressing behind the scenes for commitments along these lines.

---

national. Well-connected in British Labour circles both through marriage and by political conviction, he was indispensable to Sikorski in the early years of the war, when the prime minister was still unsure whom else he could trust. It was Retinger who arranged his most confidential meetings with British leaders—including his dramatic first meeting with Churchill in June 1940, as well as his several meetings with Bevin; again Retinger seems to have been the only other Pole who knew that Sikorski had given a copy of his secret report on his trip to Russia to the Foreign Office. Retinger appears to have played a less important role after the middle of 1942, possibly because of his support for the evacuation of the Polish Army from the Soviet Union. Much of the suspicion and mystery surrounding his role was likely due to his radical pro-labor leanings and to his adventurous approach to life, for which at one time or another he found himself *persona non grata* in Germany, France, Britain, and the United States (where for a time the State Department viewed him as a "Mexican agent" and "a most undesirable and suspicious character"). Of the many references and documents on Retinger, one of the most interesting is a highly favorable report from U.S. Ambassador Biddle sent to the State Department in June 1942; State decimal file: FW860C.00/903, NA. See also *Joseph Retinger*, ed. Pomian.

[116] Mitkiewicz, *Z gen. Sikorskim*, pp 299-300.

[117] See Chapter IV, note 44, above.

[118] See, e.g., the report of his meeting with Churchill, March 11, 1942, in *Documents*, 1:298.

It was inevitable that the two sides of Sikorski's behavior would come into conflict with each other; likewise it is inconceivable that he was unaware of the contradictions. One can only suppose that he pursued these tactics as a means of preserving a semblance of national unity, and of defusing his critics, in the hope that the next turn of events would be in Poland's favor and until he could muster the necessary diplomatic support for his program. Yet the overall effect was bound to be confusion at home and abroad as to the real policy of the exile government and, in the absence of a favorable turn of events, increasing dissension and embitterment. Less than six months after the signing of the Polish-Soviet Agreement, Raczyński, with his usual flair for understatement, described the atmosphere among the London Poles as "paradoxical and insincere":

The critics of the Government have looked everywhere for arguments to show that the Polish-Soviet Agreement was bad and useless since it has not been carried out. Hence the conclusion that General Sikorski is the spoiler and that his opponents were right. This practice has led to the purely negative stance that *the worse* [*our relations with Russia*], the better. The Government, on the other hand, pushed into a false position by its critics, has been inclined in defense of its policy to embellish reality. These political skirmishes and intrigues have obscured our view of the real state of affairs . . .[119]

[119] Raczyński, *W sojuszniczym Londynie*, p. 125 [emphasis added]. In a similar vein, Mitkiewicz noted that the agreement was widely viewed as "the fifth partition of Poland." *Z gen. Sikorskim*, p. 161. See also Frank Savery's very interesting memorandum to the Foreign Office, dated January 11, 1942, on the attitude of the Poles toward the Polish-Soviet Agreement; C496/19/55, FO 371/31077, PRO. While Savery believed that "most" Poles in Britain were "now prepared to accept the agreement as inevitable in the circumstances and as having been beneficial to many Poles in the U.S.S.R.," he noted that there had "not, so far as I can judge [been a change] in their feelings towards Russia and the Russians." He also confirmed the generally poisonous atmosphere within the exile community. Interesting also are his comments that "the overwhelming mass of the Poles in the U.S.S.R." and under German occupation approved of Sikorski's action in signing the agreement.

IX · *Retreat from Rapprochement*

OUR RETROSPECTIVE VIEW, distorted as it often is by the prism of later events, does not generally recognize the Polish Army-in-Exile as a failure, even a qualified one. Freshest in our minds are the memories of the Katyń discovery, which made a mockery of the idea of Polish-Soviet military cooperation, and the unquestioned gallantry of the Poles on the western front, which seemed to justify fully their evacuation from the Soviet Union. What we may forget is that Katyń was not the reason for the evacuation. While it is true that the search for the missing officers cast a deepening pall over Polish-Soviet relations during the year that elapsed between the initial organization of the army and its final departure (August 1941 to August 1942), the discovery of the mass graves in the Katyń forest came a full eight months after the evacuation, in April 1943. More important, we tend to forget that Sikorski conceived of the army primarily as a *political* rather than merely a military instrument (indeed, it was his only tangible political asset); that a Polish force fighting on the Russian front and crossing into Poland together with the Red Army was a key element in his strategy of reconciliation with the Soviet Union; and that the general fought its final evacuation to the very end, pleading not only with Moscow but with the Western Allies as well as with his Polish colleagues. It is from the political standpoint that this first Polish Army in the Soviet Union must be judged a failure.[1] Thus, the army's importance lies in the fact that it was the first aspect of Sikorski's strategy to fail, and that its withdrawal from the Soviet Union occurred for reasons and under circumstances that jeopardized the rest of his policy.

FORMATION OF THE POLISH ARMY IN RUSSIA

With respect to military relations, the Polish-Soviet Agreement signed by Sikorski on July 30, 1941, provided only that the Soviet government would consent to the formation on Soviet territory of a Polish Army under a commander appointed by the Polish government but operationally subordinate to the Supreme Command of the USSR; all other details "as to command, organization and employment of this force" were left to a

---

[1] A second unit, the so-called Kościuszko Division, which did participate in the liberation of Poland was organized later under the auspices of the Communists.

subsequent agreement.[2] This subsequent Military Agreement and several supplementary protocols were negotiated and signed in Moscow during the following month, the signatories for the Polish side being Generals Zygmunt Bohusz-Szyszko, head of the military mission sent from London, and Władysław Anders, fresh from Moscow's Lubianka prison and the newly appointed commander of the Polish Army in the Soviet Union.[3] We shall be concerned here only with those provisions that later became the subject of dispute: the size of the army, how it would be supplied and armed, its disposition and timetable for battle-readiness, and eligibility (that is, whether all Polish citizens or only ethnic Poles would be allowed to join).

Like the political agreement before it, the formal Military Agreement of August 14th was primarily a statement of principles. The army "will be organized in the shortest possible time," but "units will be moved to the front only after they are fully ready for action . . . [and] will operate in groups not smaller than divisions." The "number and strength" of the Polish units "will depend on manpower, equipment and supplies available." Arms, supplies, and transport "will be provided as far as possible" by the Soviet government, otherwise by the Poles themselves through Lend-Lease. Enrollment would be open to "Polish citizens on the territory of the USSR by conscription and voluntary enlistment."

Only at the subsequent meetings did the negotiators get down to figures and dates. According to the first supplementary protocol, dated August 16th, Anders suggested on the basis of the Soviet estimate of the numbers of Polish effectives available (approximately 20,000 plus "a certain number of Polish citizens in Siberia and in the Urals")[4] that he could form two light infantry divisions plus a reserve unit. The head of the Soviet delegation, General Panfilov,[5] allowed that "we think it more appropriate to

[2] *Documents*, 1:141.

[3] For the texts of the principal Military Agreement of August 14, 1941, and two supplementary protocols, dated August 16th and 19th, see ibid., pp. 147-53. The Polish text of the Agreement appears in Kot, *Listy z Rosji*, pp. 449-51.

[4] This figure of 20,000 is the same as used by Soviet Ambassador Maisky during the July negotiations. At that time, Sikorski challenged the figure by citing Soviet statistics claiming approximately 190,000 soldiers in POW camps, including more than 9,000 officers. Maisky later reported that there were now only 20,000 being held as prisoners-of-war, that the rest had been released and "were now dispersed throughout Russia"—he did not add, largely in labor camps. Another possible reason for the discrepancy is that the Soviets were very likely talking in terms of Polish "nationals" while Sikorski always spoke in terms of Polish "citizens." See *Documents*, 1:114-17, 128 and 158-59; also *FRUS, 1941*, 1:242-43.

[5] General A. P. Panfilov, a deputy chief of staff in the Red Army, remained on as the chief liaison officer attached to the Polish Command. His NKVD counterpart was Major (later General) of State Security Georgi S. Zhukov (not the same as the Red Army general of the same name).

create at first one division," but agreed to consider the Polish request. The Poles indicated they had been promised uniforms from Britain and the United States and therefore requested Soviet assistance only in arming the divisions; they also asked that "Poles serving in the Red Army be returned." At a second meeting on August 19th, Panfilov announced Soviet agreement to the formation of two divisions plus a reserve regiment (numbering 25,000 to 30,000 in all) and set a "date of readiness for action" of October 1, 1941. The Soviets also agreed to arm the two divisions and "wishing to placate the Polish Command," to allow Poles in the Red Army to transfer to the new Polish force. There is no indication that the Soviet negotiators made any attempt in these discussions to distinguish between ethnic Poles and Polish citizens of other nationalities; with the exception of the reference to "Poles" in the Red Army, the term "Polish citizens" appears throughout.

Immediately upon receipt of the final text of the Military Agreement in London, General Sikorski protested the provision that Polish units "will operate in groups not smaller than divisions" (10,000 to 12,000 men) as unacceptably vague. With the disastrous experience of the Polish Army in the 1940 French campaign in mind, he instructed Bohusz-Szyszko to renegotiate that article to "guarantee that the Polish Forces in the USSR would be used for operational purposes as a whole under Polish Command."[6] The matter was apparently settled without difficulty, as the latter reported back several weeks later that Panfilov had given him verbal assurances that the Polish interpretation would be respected. Or so it seemed at the time. This issue would return to haunt Polish-Soviet military relations and would eventually be the basis of Soviet charges of Polish bad faith.[7] In addition, it is reasonable to ask whether the Polish military mission did not make a mistake in not disputing either the Soviet estimate of 20,000

[6] See Sikorski's instruction of August 23rd, in *Documents*, 1:156; he wrote that the final text differed in this and other "essential" respects from an earlier draft sent to London. In a subsequent letter of instruction to General Anders (ibid., p. 163), Sikorski elaborated on the reasons for his insistence on this point: "I attach the greatest importance to our troops being used for military operations as a whole, obviously under your command. This is indispensable both from the point of view of our prestige, and of operational considerations which do not allow any breaking up of the Polish troops which would lead to sheer waste of their effort. I am absolutely unrelenting on this point since the French campaign, when, owing to jealousy, meanness and envy our divisions were scattered during the training period, and it could not be remedied in June 1940. I think that the Soviet Command will appreciate this principle, and the advantages of its being put into effect. I advise you, however, to be both firm and vigilant in this question of paramount importance for the Polish Army."

[7] The Soviets were apparently chary of giving written assurances on this point; in response to another Polish inquiry in mid-September, they stated that they saw "no reason for re-examining the existing" agreement and that Polish fears concerning the interpretation of this provision were "groundless." See ibid., pp. 165-67; also Kot, *Listy z Rosji*, pp. 38-40.

POWs or the target date of October 1st (a mere six weeks away!).[8] But, at this point anyway, there seemed little reason to fear that the two-division figure would become a barrier instead of an opening. After all, didn't the agreement specifically state that the number and strength of Polish Army units would be limited only by the men and arms available? Likewise, the Poles could not then know that the physical condition of the recruits and the supply problems that would arise in the intervening weeks would make an October 1st target date unthinkable. Indeed, reports reaching the exile government in London during the first weeks of renewed relations stressed the degree of Soviet cooperation rather than the problems being encountered. On September 5th, just after his arrival in Moscow, Ambassador Kot wrote that recruits were arriving in such numbers that Anders was anticipating an eventual army of 100,000; all who presented themselves as Polish citizens were being admitted without respect to nationality.[9] Dr. Retinger, who had preceded Kot to Moscow as interim chargé, made a similar report to U.S. Ambassador Biddle on his return to London.[10]

Within a few days, however, the Soviets informed the Poles that, due to heavy losses on the battlefield and destruction of industrial capacity, they would be unable to arm more than one Polish division.[11] Whether this was Moscow's only reason there is no way of knowing for sure. It is possible that Stalin hoped to use the Polish Army as leverage in extracting additional Western arms aid during the upcoming Beaverbrook-Harriman mission (the Allied Military Conference held in Moscow at the end of September 1941). It is equally probable that he wanted to limit the exile government's military effort, and therefore also its political influence. Supporting the first supposition was Sikorski's remark to Harriman on September 19th that the Soviets were insisting that the Poles "should exert

---

[8] It is not clear whether the supplementary protocols were communicated to London. Sikorski's letters do not pick up on these points although, as we have seen, he had earlier protested the 20,000 figure and was intent that the Poles not go to the front until the entire army was battle-ready. Kot later complained that he was not kept fully informed of the state of military relations with the Soviets, despite Sikorski's explicit instructions. See *Listy z Rosji*, pp. 42-45; and *Rozmowy z Kremlem*, p. 122, n. 30. Anders later wrote that the October 1st deadline was "sheer fantasy, but I knew it was a waste of time to make any objection." Lt. General W. Anders, *An Army in Exile: The Story of the Second Polish Corps*, p. 54.

[9] Kot, *Listy z Rosji*, pp. 81-83.

[10] See Biddle's report of September 17th, in *FRUS, 1941*, 1:252-53. Both Biddle's reports from London and Steinhardt's from Moscow, between mid-August and mid-September, reflect the steady upward revision in Polish estimates of the potential size of their army from 40,000 to 100,000; ibid., pp. 249-53. By the end of October the Poles had raised their estimate to 150,000; see *Documents*, 1:187 and 207; also Mitkiewicz, *Z gen. Sikorskim*, p. 190. Later events would demonstrate that this was not an exaggerated figure.

[11] See Kot's letter of September 10th, *Listy z Rosji*, p. 91; and Eden's report of his meeting with Sikorski and Retinger on the 15th, in C10394/3226/55, FO 371/26760, PRO.

pressure on the Western Allies to obtain arms and equipment of which they (the Soviets) were short.''[12] (As it turned out of course, Stalin didn't need Polish leverage; indeed, he learned that they didn't have much to exert.) On the other hand, and especially in view of the Kremlin's initial aversion to the idea of an independent Polish military force, the second alternative cannot be overlooked even though the evidence is largely circumstantial at this point. For instance, it was in response to Sikorski's appeal (through Bohusz-Szyszko) that the Polish Army form a single operational unit, an appeal stressing political as well as military factors, that the Soviet government reduced its arms pledge to only one division and first indicated its resistance to the formation of further divisions. The Polish request was submitted at the end of August, the Soviet reply delivered orally on September 10th. Moreover, it was in precisely this time period that Polish estimates of the size army they could form were escalating sharply.[13] Two weeks later, Kot wrote to Retinger: "Things are not progressing too easily. After great promises, nothing. It seems that they have become alarmed at the rampant growth of the army.''[14] Subsequent events would confirm Kot's impression.

In the meantime, the Poles had already applied to the British and Americans for arms to equip their divisions over and above the first two. Now Sikorski appealed directly to Harriman, who was in London en route to the Moscow Conference: Would he "take full account of the necessity of supplying arms to the Polish Army in the USSR, and . . . support that request before his Government,'' and would he "support the request for the participation of the Polish Ambassador and General Anders at the Moscow conference whenever Polish problems or interests require it''?[15] Harriman in turn appealed directly to Roosevelt and Hopkins for instructions. FDR's response supported the Polish position in every respect but one: there would be no Polish participation in the conference, since the proposal and acceptance had been for an Anglo-American mission. However, the note continued: "We feel that it would be preferable to deal with the needs of the Polish forces in Moscow direct with the Poles while you are in the Soviet Union for two reasons:

[12] *Documents*, 1:169. Even before the military agreements, in which the Soviets agreed to arm the two Polish divisions, had been signed, they had begun hinting to the British Military Mission that they would not be able to do so; see General MacFarlane's cables of August 8th and 10th, in C8949/3226/55, FO 371/26758, PRO.

[13] *Documents*, 1:165-67.

[14] *Listy z Rosji*, p. 106.

[15] *Documents*, 1:169-70. Sikorski told Harriman that the Soviets had indicated they would not object to Polish participation in the conference and had advised him, semiofficially, that they "would concede to the Poles priority in obtaining supplies of arms from the West.''

1. We have already decided that Poland is to receive the benefit of Lend-Lease appropriations. Such a decision has not yet been made with regard to Russia. It would therefore be difficult to furnish through Lend-Lease arms and equipment to the Poles through Russia.

2. It is believed that it would be in conformity with our policy of *maintaining so far as possible Polish prestige and influence* in Eastern Europe for us *to deal direct with the Poles with regard to the supplying of the Polish forces in Russia* since such direct negotiations would be likely to enhance the prestige and stress the individuality of those forces now as well as in the future.

"Of course," the president added, any negotiations with the Poles "should be carried on in cooperation with and [with] the consent of the British and Russians" since both "must share responsibility for the transport and delivery" of supplies to the Poles. However, should either object to Harriman's "carrying on direct negotiations with the Poles," he was to inform Washington, with alternative suggestions for handling the problem. General Sikorski was to be informed of the American position.[16]

Yet despite these assurances, the Moscow Conference dealt a crippling blow to the independence of the Polish Army—ironically as a result of actions not by the Soviets, but by the British and Americans. Harriman, as representative of the still nonbelligerent United States, apparently saw his role as secondary to that of the British chief of mission, Lord Beaverbrook, who, unlike the American, was distinctly unsympathetic to the Polish cause. Not only were the Poles denied participation in the conference,[17] they were not even consulted until after the meetings with the

[16] See Harriman's query and Roosevelt's reply in *FRUS, 1941*, 1:253-55 [emphasis added]. British Ambassador Cripps took a somewhat more cautious approach. As he cabled the Foreign Office on September 12th, he saw "no objection in principle" to Polish participation in the Moscow Conference, but advised that "it would not be wise to try to settle the point with the Soviet Government in advance. . . . If when British and American representatives are here they say they would like one of the meetings to be devoted to Polish supplies and to have the Polish Ambassador present, it would be very difficult for the Soviet representative to refuse." C10250/3226/55, FO 371/26760, PRO.

[17] Even Cripps and American Ambassador Steinhardt were excluded from the meetings, in part because both Beaverbrook and Harriman "felt Stalin would be franker if we didn't take the ambassadors along" and in part because of the former's confessed aversion to teetotalers (Cripps), "particularly Socialist teetotalers who were candidates for sainthood." According to Harriman's account, Beaverbrook was pugnacious in style, given to oversimplifying issues "to the point of disregarding other considerations" and, during the mission in question, disposed to promise the Russians everything they asked for. W. Averell Harriman and Elie Abel, *Special Envoy to Churchill and Stalin 1941-1946*, pp. 82-86. Concerning Beaverbrook's unsympathetic attitude toward the Poles, see Strang's report of a conversation with General Ismay who accompanied Beaverbrook to Moscow, in C11104/3226/55, FO 371/26760, PRO.

Russians had adjourned, although they had presented their proposals in advance. Finally, on October 2nd—with the key figures preparing an early departure due to Hitler's "final" offensive on Moscow—U.S. Ambassador Steinhardt, at Kot's insistence, convened a meeting of the British, American, and Polish missions to consider the needs of the Polish Army. The British military representatives argued strongly for a separate supply effort. Harriman presented Washington's view, though in Kot's opinion he did so "timidly." But Beaverbrook held firm: the Allies had already promised so much to the Russians that, even if they could produce enough to give separate aid to the Poles, transport facilities would be inadequate to the task. Instead, arms for the Polish forces must come out of what had been allotted to the Russians, obviously at the latters' discretion.[18]

Nonplused, Kot appealed to Steinhardt to arrange a separate hearing with Harriman before his departure. However, as the ambassador reported back several days later, the grave military situation had forced cancellation of all "secondary" meetings; moreover, Roosevelt's instructions notwithstanding, "Harriman was of the opinion that

> at the outset they [the Allies] must not treat Russia with distrust or burden her with any kind of obligations. If the Russians did not deliver what they should to the Polish Army, then we should make known our claims and Washington would influence their consideration.

Steinhardt assured Kot that the Poles would "not in any way suffer" as a result of this decision; he had briefed Harriman in great detail on their military needs "which, even so, could not be taken care of officially."[19]

[18] See especially Kot, *Listy z Rosji*, pp. 110-12 and 121; also Kukiel, *Generał Sikorski*, p. 183. For general accounts of the conference, without reference to the Polish issue however, see: Sherwood, *Roosevelt and Hopkins*, pp. 384-95; and W. Averell Harriman, *America and Russia in a Changing World: A Half Century of Personal Observation*, pp. 15-23. Ambassador Kot was particularly concerned over Beaverbrook's excessive enthusiasm about the prospects of cooperation with Stalin: "I fear he is not inquiring and does not want to inquire into the hard realities of Russian relations, and that he fancies these people on the model of westerners, also with respect to sincerity and observance of obligations." Sherwood's account tends to support this. Sherwood also suggests by inference a possible explanation at least for Harriman's reluctance to raise the Polish arms question with Stalin in the latter's technique of keeping guests off balance and on the defensive by frequent changes of mood. He notes (p. 395): "Harriman did not realize it at the time but he was to learn on several later occasions that this first experience of a major conference in Moscow set a pattern which was to be followed time and again: extreme cordiality at the start of the conference, changing to disagreeable and even surly hostility at the second meeting—and then harmonious agreement and a jubilantly triumphant banquet with innumerable toasts to Allied cooperation at the finish."

[19] Kot, *Listy z Rosji*, pp. 119-20. In his own report of the conference, Harriman seems to

(In fact, Beaverbrook and Harriman may have held a subsequent meeting with Molotov, at which they were informed that the Soviets were "not in a position" to equip the Polish forces, "but saw no objection" to Britain and the United States doing so[20]—although the Poles were apparently not so informed at the time.)

Sikorski made no attempt to conceal his extreme displeasure at the outcome of the conference. In a courteous but strongly worded note to Churchill, he recalled prior "friendly assurances" from Lord Beaverbrook as well as Washington's instruction to Harriman. He then went on to put the onus for the adverse decision on "the British representative" and to appeal for reconsideration:

> In view of the above it was with profound regret that I learnt of the decision of the British representative to interpret his instructions as restricting the British contribution in material as destined exclusively for the USSR leaving it to the discretion of the Soviet Government to decide whether they can spare [any of the armaments supplied] for the use of the Polish Army . . .
>
> In these circumstances the Conference refrained from making a decision on the question of arms for our troops.
>
> In view of the gravity of the situation which has arisen I am appealing to you to modify the ruling which our British Ally applied in this case. Should it remain unchanged it would place the whole issue at the mercy of the Soviet Government. It would, moreover, seriously jeopardize the adequate armament of the Polish divisions on Soviet territory.[21]

have been of two minds about Soviet sincerity. On the one hand, he wrote of the third and final meeting with Stalin: "I left with the feeling that he had been frank with us and if we came through as had been promised and if personal relations were retained with Stalin, the suspicion that has existed between the Soviet Government and our two governments might well be eradicated." Yet he also saw the risk that the Russians' sincerity might be superficial. Commenting on their response to his advances on the subject of religious freedom—a question to which, for domestic political reasons, Roosevelt attached great importance—he wrote: "In spite of all the comments and assurances I leave with the impression that all the Soviets intend to do is to give lip service and to create certain instances which would give an impression of relaxation without really changing their present practices." Sherwood, *Roosevelt and Hopkins*, pp. 391-92. Nonetheless, Harriman allegedly told one of his fellow delegates that the objective of the mission was to "give and give and give, with no expectation of any return, with no thought of a *quid pro quo*." Quoted in Dallek, *Roosevelt and American Foreign Policy*, p. 295.

[20] See Strang's note of October 13th in C11104/3226/55, FO 371/26760, PRO; and Harriman and Abel, *Special Envoy*, pp. 101-102. It is not entirely clear that this meeting took place after Kot's plea, although most likely it did. Also, while Harriman indicated that the Soviets were still willing to arm one division, Strang's note said nothing on this matter.

[21] *Documents*, 1:174-75.

Whether Churchill answered this letter directly is not clear.[22] What is clear is that both the Poles and Russians eventually received assurances that the British would "do [their] best" to equip the Polish divisions, but only after a month's delay and only if the latter were moved south to the Caucasus to facilitate communications.[23] From the standpoint of Polish-Soviet political relations, however, the damage had already been done. Rather than "maintaining so far as possible Polish prestige and influence" or stressing "the individuality of [the Polish] forces," as Roosevelt's instructions had specified, the British and American negotiators only succeeded in demonstrating all too clearly to Stalin how little real, as opposed to rhetorical, support the Poles had in the West.[24]

Whether or not as a result of their reinforced leverage over the Poles, Moscow now began to exert overtly pressures hitherto applied only indirectly or by inference. General Anders's request, made at the beginning of October, for permission to organize three more divisions and for an

[22] Churchill's account of the Beaverbrook-Harriman mission (*The Grand Alliance*, pp. 465-72) makes no mention of the Polish arms issue. The Foreign Office too, in response to a query from the Prime Minister's Office, professed to be "rather in the dark" as to what "assurances [had] been given to General Sikorski" concerning the equipping of the Polish forces; C11419/3226/55, FO 371/26760, PRO. According to Polish records, however, Beaverbrook had assured Sikorski and Raczyński on the eve of his departure for Moscow that he was fully cognizant of the needs of the Polish Army and would "endeavor to secure preferential treatment" for them; he had also indicated, although without committing himself, that he took a favorable view of Polish participation in the Moscow conference. PRM 39b/14-16, GSHI.

[23] See especially internal Foreign Office discussion and the cable to Cripps of October 21st, in which Eden stated that he had informed Ambassador Maisky of this position; C11419/3226/55, FO 371/26760, PRO. From Moscow, Kot cabled that the British generals on the delegation told him they would try to "get around" Beaverbrook's decision, and Kot thought the army might receive equipment for six divisions. On October 29th, he cabled again: "Can I inform the Soviet Government that England has given official assurance of arming and feeding our troops?" And on November 2nd, he told Deputy Foreign Commissar Vyshinsky that he had that day received "positive assurance in this matter." *Listy z Rosji*, pp. 112, 121 and 143; and *Rozmowy z Kremlem*, p. 102.

[24] See, e.g., Ciechanowski's account of a conversation with Harriman in mid-November, in *Defeat in Victory*, pp. 61-64. During our recent conversations, Count Raczyński several times singled out the Beaverbrook-Harriman mission as the first major blow to Sikorski's strategy, and also as the first great mistake by the British and Americans in their handling of the Russians. Not only, in Raczyński's view, did they undermine the independence of the Polish Army; they also failed to understand Russian psychology and negotiating technique: that is, what they regarded as a gesture of good will and as a starting point for bargaining and compromise Stalin saw as a sign of weakness, of Poland's lack of real influence in London and Washington, and therefore as the occasion to begin posing further demands. Raczyński recalled that, despite promises in private conversation that he would look after Poland's interests, Beaverbrook was basically hostile to the Poles and, rather like Lloyd George, did not take them seriously. However, when Raczyński later complained to Harriman about Beaverbrook's behavior, Harriman replied, "Why put all the blame on him? I was there, too, and was equally responsible."

increase in rations to a total of 70,000, was met first by silence and then, after repeated and insistent inquiries, by a series of objections and road-blocks. In addition to pleading lack of arms and equipment, the Soviets now contended that the several military agreements had foreseen only the two divisions and reserve unit already in existence—implying, despite previous assurances, that it was the Poles who were trying to alter the terms of cooperation. Moreover, they now imposed a new condition, that the Poles themselves be responsible for supplying rations for any additional troops. (There were at this time approximately 44,000 already enrolled.)[25] Then during the last week of October, without waiting to see if the Poles could obtain promises of food as well as arms, Soviet authorities began dispersing 35,000 additional Polish soldiers among the civilian population. Again the reason cited was the inability of the Soviet government to maintain them.[26] Two weeks later, on November 6th, however (and after Ambassador Kot had told Deputy Foreign Commissar Vyshinsky of the British promise to both feed and arm the Polish forces),[27] General Panfilov informed Anders that the total size of the army for 1941 would be limited to the 30,000 figure first set in August.[28] Fearing that such an order if carried out would destroy the future effectiveness of the army,[29] the Poles appealed directly to Stalin. With London and Washington now expressing their interest in the matter and with the Poles threatening to call off Si-

[25] See Kot's conversations with Vyshinsky and Molotov on October 14th and 22nd, respectively, in *Rozmowy z Kremlem*, pp. 84-85 and 96-98; also Kot, *Listy z Rosji* p. 125. (The record of the first conversation is translated in *Documents*, 1:178-82.)

[26] Apparently Kot had a second meeting with Molotov the next day, October 23rd; see *FRUS, 1941*, 1:257.

[27] Kot, *Rozmowy z Kremlem*, pp. 102-103.

[28] *Documents*, 1:197-98. Vyshinsky had tried out the idea on Kot the previous day; see *Rozmowy z Kremlem*, pp. 109-111. As if to reinforce the pressure, additional barracks promised the Poles were not turned over to them; nor did they receive sufficient materials to winterize the two existing (and already overcrowded) camps. *Documents*, 1:201-202.

[29] The Polish argument was not unreasonable. Recruits were arriving in such poor physical condition that considerable time for rehabilitation had to be allowed even before training could begin. The Poles feared that, if these men were dispersed among the civilian population or sent to work in conditions little better than those they had survived for two years, their physical condition would deteriorate even further. Moreover, the Polish command was not asking that the unarmed men remain idle. During their reconditioning period and until arms arrived, they would be used as labor battalions—in particular, to construct winter quarters for the Polish camps. See Kot, *Rozmowy z Kremlem*, pp. 97 and 122; *Documents*, 1:201-202 and 208; and Anders, *An Army in Exile*, pp. 62-64 and 94-96. Two of the most detailed reports of the desperate circumstances of Polish POWs and deportees in the Soviet Union were based on interviews with some of the first evacuees in the spring of 1942, but filtered through to the Foreign Office only in January of 1943; see C1917/258/55, FO 371/34564, PRO [originally marked closed until the year 2019].

korski's visit to Moscow,[30] Stalin, in a long and frank interview with Ambassador Kot on November 14th, agreed provisionally to arm the second Polish division as originally promised and to allow the Poles to form as many divisions as their manpower and additional arms from abroad would allow. These decisions were to be finalized during Sikorski's visit which was now rescheduled (it had been postponed several times) for early December.[31]

Despite Stalin's assurances, other problems that would weigh heavily on the potential success of the army had already begun to surface. Following the optimism of the first weeks, evidence quickly accumulated that the amnesty was not being carried out in accordance with the July 30th Agreement and the subsequent Soviet decree of August 12th. Refugees and recruits reaching the army camps told of many others, often the strongest and most able, who were not being released from labor camps. Many thousands of so-called political prisoners remained in prison; additional thousands—hundreds of thousands in fact—were unaccounted for. In response to Polish protests, the Soviet government now let it be known indirectly that, in its interpretation, the renunciation of its 1939 treaties with Germany contained in the Polish-Soviet Agreement was in no way equivalent to recognition of the inhabitants of Poland's prewar eastern territories as "Polish citizens." During an October 14th meeting, Vyshinsky presented Kot with figures showing that, of a total 388,000 taken prisoner or deported to "special settlements" and "places of compulsory residence" by the Soviet government, all but 42,000 had been released by October 1, 1941. When Kot disputed the figures—conservative Polish estimates of the number deported were on the order of 1.5 million—Vyshinsky admitted that these figures did not include "former Polish citizens" who had acquired Soviet citizenship by a decree of October 1, 1939.[32]

There were similar discrepancies in the execution of the Military Agreement of August 14th. Poles who had been conscripted into the Red Army, the great majority into labor battalions, were not being transferred to the Polish Army as agreed. In early November, the embassy protested to the

---

[30] See *Documents*, 1:187-89 and 191-94; Ciechanowski, *Defeat in Victory*, pp. 59-61; and Kot, *Rozmowy z Kremlem*, p. 115.

[31] The record of the Stalin-Kot meeting appears in Kot, *Rozmowy z Kremlem*, pp. 118-29. See also Kot, *Listy z Rosji*, pp. 169-79; and *Documents*, 1:205-13.

[32] Perhaps as a subtle word of warning Vyshinsky added: "I should like to stress that the Polish-Soviet Treaty was signed by us more from motives of sentiment than of reason. It is also difficult to say that it has any advantages for us, rather the contrary." See Kot's note to Vyshinsky of October 13th, and the record of their conversation on the 14th, in *Documents*, 1:175-82; a more complete version of the latter appears in Kot, *Rozmowy z Kremlem*, pp. 182-89.

Soviet government that contrary to the agreement and implementing protocols, which included no nationality restrictions, the war commissar for Kazakhstan had issued orders that only Polish citizens of Polish nationality were to be given permits to travel to Polish Army centers, while those of Ukrainian, Belorussian, or Jewish origin who met age and fitness requirements were to be enrolled in the Red Army. This time (in a note delivered the day of General Sikorski's arrival in the Soviet Union) the Foreign Commissariat made explicit what Vyshinsky had only implied a month earlier. By virtue of Soviet citizenship laws, "all citizens of the Western districts of the Ukrainian and White-Russian S.S. Republics" (i.e., Poland's prewar eastern provinces) present in those districts between November 1st and 2nd, 1939, had "acquired Soviet citizenship." Moreover, the note continued:

> The readiness of the Soviet Government to recognize as Polish citizens persons of Polish nationality inhabiting the above-mentioned districts till the 1-2 November, 1939, shows the good will and readiness to compromise of the Soviet Government, but can in no case serve as a basis for the analogous recognition as Polish citizens, of persons of other nationalities, in particular, Ukrainian, White-Russian and Jewish; . . .[33]

Most painful of all for the Poles was the unexplained disappearance of more than 7,500 of their officers. Of the 9,500 known to have been taken prisoner, only 2,000 had been found by early October; the missing included not only career officers, but also several thousand reservists—mostly professional men, doctors, lawyers, professors, etc.[34] Although at this early stage the Poles could not have known the true fate of these men, their continued absence could not but impair the morale and training of the army, while the evasiveness of Soviet replies to inquiries as to their whereabouts was a source of increasing strain on Polish-Soviet relations.[35]

[33] See Kot's letter to Raczyński of November 8th, in *Listy z Rosji*, pp. 153-55; also *Documents*, 1:200-201 and 227-28.

[34] The story of the missing officers and the uncovering of the mass graves at Katyń has been told in detail elsewhere; see especially Zawodny, *Death in the Forest*. The final tally of missing officers was 8,300 to 8,400, constituting 45 percent of Poland's land army officer corps at that time; the rest of the 15,000 missing were noncommissioned officers, military police, and civilians mostly involved in law enforcement.

[35] Kot wrote later (*Listy z Rosji*, pp. 60-62) that the Poles suspected from the beginning that the officers had been murdered by the NKVD. However, other sources indicate that, for the first months at least, they took seriously the rumors that the missing men had been sent to the far north, possibly to Novaya Zemlya or Franz Joseph Land; other rumors told of drownings in the Yenisei or White Sea. Since only about one-third of the missing men were accounted for by the discovery of the Katyń graves, some of these rumors may have been true. In addition to the two secret reports cited in note 29 above, see: Kot, *Rozmowy z*

From Moscow's point of view as well, the Polish Army seems to have been something of a disappointment. Evidence suggests that the Soviets, always unenthusiastic about the formation of an independent Polish force, had harbored exaggerated hopes that the rank and file, and particularly the traditionally anti-Polish minority elements, would be amenable to communist influence. When these expectations proved unfounded and when they realized that the army would be both large and highly nationalistic—that is, that it would be the significant political instrument Sikorski wanted—they apparently grew disenchanted.[36] Moreover, they could scarcely have been unaware of what Raczyński described as the "paradoxical and insincere" attitude among the Poles and the widespread belief, in some quarters even the hope, that the Soviet Union would collapse under the German onslaught.[37]

Kremlem, p. 79, n. 21; Anders, *An Army in Exile*, pp. 76-77; Mitkiewicz, *Z gen. Sikorskim*, pp. 196 and 305-306; Pobóg-Malinowski, *Najnowsza historia*, 3:203-204; and Kukiel, *Generał Sikorski*, pp. 183-84. See also the letter to U.S. Ambassador Biddle of May 29, 1942, in *Documents*, 1:355-56. The most detailed contemporary account of the futile search for the missing officers, and of the overwhelming evidence of Soviet responsibility for their deaths, is the secret report dated May 24, 1943, to Eden from then ambassador to the Government-in-Exile, Owen O'Malley; C6160/258/55, FO 371/34577, PRO.

[36] Kot wrote to Raczyński in early November 1941 that he thought the Soviets had released disproportionately large numbers of Poland's minority groups and allowed them to enroll in the army in order to influence its orientation and weaken its Polish character. The Poles apparently proved reasonably diligent in preventing segregation and discord among the various elements and in weeding out the few undesirables (e.g., pro-German Ukrainians). See *Listy z Rosji*, pp. 153-55 and 161-65; also Anders, *An Army in Exile*, pp. 65 and 77; Rozek, *Allied Wartime Diplomacy*, pp. 69-70. In April of 1943, the new British ambassador to the exile government, Owen O'Malley, more than confirmed Kot's earlier report. Referring to the tendency of ethnic minorities to join the Polish Army, he wrote: "Whatever had been the attitude of these persons, whether Jews or Ukrainians or White Russians, in the first months of the Soviet occupation of Eastern Poland, there is no doubt that, when the opportunity was offered of obtaining recognition as non-Soviet citizens, most of them hastened to avail themselves of it with the further intention of getting out of the U.S.S.R. if they possibly could. During the first few months, i.e., until December 1941, the Soviet Government did, in fact, release many thousands of Polish citizens, irrespective of their race. In November, however, of that year, the Soviet military authorities began to conscript for the Red Army Polish citizens of Jewish, and even of Polish, race." C4850/258/55, FO 371/34571, PRO. For a 1942 Polish report of attempts to spread anti-Polish and anti-British propaganda among army recruits, see C6014/19/55, FO 371/31083, PRO, including the comments by Roberts and Warner.

[37] See note 119, Chapter VIII, above. Mitkiewicz, in his diary entry for October 31, 1941, described the view of the Polish command in Russia as follows: "All of them, as a unanimous chorus, . . . report that the military defeat of Russia is a certain and already accomplished fact. General Anders especially emphasizes this in preemptory fashion. . . . The one exception was Ambassador Kot who in his assessment of the situation in Russia, although he leaned toward the above views, added that despite the incredibly difficult military situation . . . Soviet Russia can continue to fight." *Z gen. Sikorskim*, p. 186.

IT WAS against the background of these developments that the idea of evacuating the Polish forces took shape and that General Sikorski undertook his trip to the Soviet Union. Here the picture becomes rather complicated, as the idea of moving the army was the result not of a single proposal but of several, emanating from different quarters, at different times, and motivated by different considerations. Sikorski himself had used the idea of evacuation as a negotiating tool in the very first session with Ambassador Maisky in July, his purpose at that point being to demonstrate the Poles' determination to fight and to gain Soviet agreement to the largest possible army in the Soviet Union.[38] Later he retained the option of evacuation in the event of a Soviet collapse or "should the difficulties arising in connection with the formation of the Polish forces in the USSR turn out to be insuperable."[39] In addition, he foresaw at a very early stage the desirability of evacuating all air force and naval personnel, as well as enough land-based forces to fill out the Polish Corps in Scotland and the brigade already fighting in North Africa. (Evacuation of the former was provided for in the military agreement;[40] the latter he initially expected to come not from the divisions being organized in Russia but directly from POW and labor camps, preferably in the north.) In any event, the numbers involved were small, especially compared to Polish estimates of the potential size of the army.[41] Nor can there be any doubt that, for both political and military reasons, Sikorski wanted the main body of the army to remain in the Soviet Union to fight on the eastern front and to participate from that direction in the liberation of Poland. This was consistent with his belief, already noted, that the collapse of the Soviet regime would not be in Poland's interest.

On the other hand, the general had no intention of allowing his largest

[38] During the July 5th session, the following exchange took place: "Monsieur Maisky inquired what exactly General Sikorski had in mind in regard to Polish prisoners of war in the Soviet Union.

"General Sikorski replied that these men, who according to official statistics, published recently, number 191,000 men and some 9,000 officers, . . . should be formed into an independent, sovereign Polish Army in the Soviet Union. If the Soviet Government did not desire the presence of such an army, it might perhaps be possible to transport it elsewhere to continue the fight against Germany." *Documents*, 1:117.

[39] From Sikorski's letter of instruction to Ambassador Kot, August 28, 1941; ibid., p. 159.

[40] Ibid., p. 147.

[41] Initially he wanted to withdraw 10,000 from Russia—8,000 to Great Britain and 2,000 to Egypt. See his letter to Churchill of September 17th, in ibid., p. 168; also Kot, *Listy z Rosji*, pp. 118 and 122. Later, as the Poles encountered increasing difficulties organizing their army in the Soviet Union, he raised the desired number to 15 to 20,000, and finally to 25,000. See further discussion below; also C12829 and C12982/3226/55, FO 371/26762, PRO.

concentration of troops—this "valuable . . . instrument of the Polish State"—to be swallowed up in the massive Russian front as so much cannon fodder. In his letter of instruction to General Anders, dated September 1, 1941, Sikorski wrote that in developing their strategy the Poles must reckon with the probability that the war would be long. Thus, "although our struggle against the Germans . . . is by no means a token one," "we cannot risk [our forces'] annihilation" either by sending them into battle before "they have attained full combat readiness" or by letting them be used on the main Russian front, "as they would be diluted there, broken up and playing a secondary role." He requested that Anders "do everything possible" to have the Polish Army assigned to a single, strategically important target—he thought the defense of the Caucasian oil fields the "most appropriate"—where it would be in operational contact with the British as well as the Soviet armies. (After all, even at this early date it was assumed that the former would have to arm all but two Polish divisions.) Similarly, he took a cautious approach to the question of Underground strategy, later to be the subject of acrimonious charges of noncooperation by the Soviets. "I do not share the view," he wrote to Anders, "that this organization should be completely inactive during the war. . . . the home country must continue to play an active part in the struggle." However, as "enough Polish blood has been shed already," the nation should not be exposed unnecessarily to enemy reprisals. "We must preserve forces as big as possible for the time of the outbreak of an armed rising, and this moment is still far ahead."[42]

This letter to Anders together with a similar one to Kot[43] provide perhaps the clearest statements available, in Sikorski's own words, of his approach to reconciliation with the Soviet Union. Both belie later charges of naïveté with respect to Soviet intentions. In particular, his instructions for the use of Poland's armed forces defined the limits of his understanding of military cooperation with Moscow. Just as he did not envision political cooperation as extending to "the transplanting of communist ideas on our soil" or Poland's disappearance "in the Pan-Slav melting-pot,"[44] so he was insistent that Polish-Soviet military cooperation not be construed in such a way that Poland's all too meagre reserves be expended for immediate Soviet military benefit at the expense of her own long-term political interests. "One has to agree to many tactical moves in international politics, but it is not permissible to agree to anything that might harm the Polish cause."

It was only in late September and October, in the wake of the rapid German advance and mounting supply problems, that the idea first of

[42] *Documents*, 1:162-65.
[43] Ibid., pp. 158-61.
[44] See p. 39 above.

moving the army south and then of evacuating most or all of it—whether temporarily for equipping and training or permanently for use elsewhere— began to emerge. The initiative, although only to change the army's location within the Soviet Union, appears to have come from the Polish side on the eve of the Beaverbrook-Harriman mission, but after the Soviets had informed the exile government that they would be unable to arm the second Polish division as promised. On Sepember 26th, Sikorski cabled General Ismay with the British military mission in Moscow proposing that, ''in view of latest developments on the Eastern front and particularly . . . in the Southern sector,'' the Polish forces be moved to the Caucasus where they could be armed by the British and participate in the defense of the oil fields. ''Being most anxious to avoid occasioning any suspicion,'' he asked British assistance in gaining Soviet agreement to this plan.[45] Barely a week later, on October 2nd, the Chiefs of Staff Committee of the British War Cabinet supported the move on grounds that, with the Russians able to arm ''only one of the six Polish Divisions,'' the volume of supplies and arms necessary for the rest would overburden the northern route via Archangel, especially ''under winter conditions, quite apart from German operations.''[46] There followed a lengthy period of haggling within the Foreign Office as to whether the Poles or the British should bear the onus of broaching the subject with Moscow. Finally, on October 13th, it fell to Foreign Secretary Eden to suggest somewhat tentatively to Ambassador Maisky that the Polish forces ''be moved to somewhere nearer the Persian front, perhaps to the Caucasus.''[47]

Yet less than two weeks later, it was a decidedly more provocative proposal that Churchill outlined for Sikorski. According to the British record of their October 24th luncheon, the prime minister ''instructed'' his guest ''upon the line which he should take if he made his journey to Russia'':

> General Sikorski should make the following proposition to the Soviet Government. First, the Soviet Government would move their

---

[45] *Documents*, 1:170-71; and C10960/3226/55, FO 371/26760, PRO. Mitkiewicz writes that he made this proposal to Sikorski, suggesting either the Caucasus or Western Siberia; he said the idea could be attributed to the need for access to British supplies, but his primary concern was with the deteriorating military situation. *Z gen. Sikorskim*, p. 181.

[46] C11104/3226/55, FO 371/26760, PRO.

[47] Eden made a point of referring to the recently concluded Beaverbrook-Harriman talks in Moscow, during which, he informed Maisky: ''It seemed that M. Molotov had made it plain that, while the Soviet Government was not in a position to equip the Polish forces, they had no objection to our doing so.'' C11514/3226/55, FO 371/26760, PRO. For the discussions leading up to Eden's request, see C11419/3226/55, FO 371/26760, PRO, and documents cited in the preceding two notes.

forces from Persia to the Caucasus, thus freeing the lines of communication through Persia for supplies to Russia instead of cluttering
them up with supplies for a Russian army of occupation. . . . Secondly,
the Soviet Government would send three or four divisions of Polish
troops down to the Caucasus (or to Persia) where they would be
equipped by the British Government in order to take part in the defence
of the Caucasus in the spring. Thirdly, if the Soviet Government
would accept the first two conditions, General Sikorski would undertake to do everything he could to persuade H[is] M[ajesty's]
G[overnment] to send divisions to defend the Caucasus by the side
of the Polish and Russian troops.[48]

In addition, it was made "clear that this proposal must be made on General
Sikorski's own responsibility and without committing H.M.G. in any way."
Why Churchill should have chosen this moment to introduce the idea of
evacuating the Polish troops, even temporarily, as an alternative to their
transfer to a more accessible location within the Soviet Union, is not
explained. But it seems likely that, apart from a sorely taxed military
supply system, concern for the welfare of the troops was a major consideration. By this time the Soviets were already moving to curtail the size
of the army; and only the day before Ambassador Cripps had cabled a
warning of impending "chaos and tragedy" among the Poles in Russia,
who would "die in numbers" of starvation and typhus unless "drastic"
action, possibly a "large-scale evacuation," were taken immediately.[49]

Nonetheless, there was ample reason to expect that Moscow would
receive Churchill's proposal with something less than good humor. Having
suggested only recently that the British "could safely land 25-30 divisions"
at Archangel or on Russia's southern front,[50] Stalin was unlikely to be
impressed by the argument that they could supply a relative handful of
Polish troops only if the latter were transferred to Iran, and only on condition that the Soviets withdraw their five divisions from that country. Yet
what choice did Sikorski have but to go along with Churchill's "instructions"? His soldiers, unarmed and in ill-health, faced the oncoming Russian

---

[48] C11837/3226/55, FO 371/26760, PRO. According to the Polish record of this meeting
(*Documents*, 1:182-84), the British side regarded a transfer to Persia as "most appropriate,"
and only "should the Russians oppose this move," would the troops "be concentrated on
the northern shores of the Caspian Sea, . . . to where the British would send the necessary
supplies." Sikorski apparently took exception to the idea of sending British troops to the
Caucasus, commenting (according to the British record) that "the Russians were so uncertain
of their own position in the Caucasus, . . . they would not welcome British troops on that
front."

[49] C11893/3226/55, FO 371/26760, PRO.

[50] See p. 168 above.

winter in overcrowded summer camps and with inadequate food supplies. Moreover, it is important to note that the proposal, both as discussed at this meeting and as communicated later to Stalin, spoke at most of a *temporary* evacuation pending the army's combat readiness.[51] Nowhere was it suggested that, apart from reinforcements needed to fill out existing Polish units in Scotland and North Africa,[52] the army would be used on any but the Russian front.

Within a few weeks, however, thinking within both British and Polish military circles began taking a very different turn. That military events—specifically, a collapse of the Russian front—might necessitate a longer-term or even permanent evacuation of the Poles had, of course, always been a possibility.[53] Now the desirability of such a withdrawal under any circumstances seemed to be gaining favor. By mid-to-late November, the War Office had concluded not only that evacuation for purposes of training and equipping was essential, but that Iran was no longer a suitable location. "Owing to direct conflict of maintenance requirements with existing transportation commitments on the Persian Gulf route, and to the need for period of some months for physical recuperation and re-organisation [of the Poles] into fighting formations, concentration area must be somewhere other than Persia or Iraq." India was now mentioned as the preferred destination. And, while the Foreign Office still seemed to assume the return of the bulk of the troops to the Russian front, it is less clear that this is what the military planners had in mind.[54] Indeed, Mitkiewicz writes that

[51] To assuage anticipated Soviet suspicions, Sikorski appealed to President Roosevelt to assist in gaining Moscow's acceptance of the temporary transfer. (Ciechanowski, *Defeat in Victory*, pp. 59-61; and *Documents*, 1:187-89.) At the same time, he instructed Kot to approach the Soviet government directly. Kot, who at this point was trying to gain resumption of recruitment (his meeting with Stalin was not for another two weeks), interpreted his instructions loosely and asked only that the Polish Army be concentrated "at a point easily accessible for British supplies." (*Documents*, 1:185-86 and 190.) Nor did he mention Iran during his November 14th meeting with Stalin. As a result, the American message, which actually came from Harriman (*FRUS, 1941*, 1:258), may have had the opposite effect from what Sikorski hoped, arousing rather than allaying Stalin's suspicions. (See the exchange of cables between Raczyński and Kot, in *Listy z Rosji*, pp. 190-91.)

[52] The same instructions to Kot (see preceding note) raised the number of recruits Sikorski wanted evacuated to Scotland and North Africa to 15-20,000. This request Kot did submit to Molotov, who replied that there would be "no obstacles." *Documents*, 1:185, 190, and 199.

[53] See, e.g., the report of the same Chiefs of Staff Committee meeting that supported the transfer of the Polish troops to the Caucasus (note 46 above): "If things were to go badly wrong in Russia, it would be desirable that the Poles should be able to get out" since these divisions "might be of inestimable value to us as a means of reinforcing our army in the Middle East without the cost of shipping." See also the October 25th letter from General Pownall in the War Office to Cadogan; C11881/3226/55, FO 371/26760, PRO.

[54] C12829 and C12982/3226/55, FO 371/26762, PRO. The several cables and accompa-

by now the British staff had worked out an evacuation plan that foresaw that "the surplus left after the formation of General Anders's infantry division" (presumably the one still being armed by the Russians) would leave "for Palestine via Persia, and later for Egypt . . . and Great Britain." "It should be underscored here," he continued:

> that the plan for withdrawing the Polish Army from Russia to the Near East has found a very favorable, one could say enthusiastic, reception and very considerable support in the British Government and Staff. The English after all would acquire at least one well-trained military corps for free as it were, and that in a region which is very important to them: the Near East: oil.[55]

Among the Poles, those who were less than enthusiastic about the policy of cooperation with the Soviet Union or who anticipated imminent Soviet collapse (they were often one and the same) took an even stronger stance. They favored evacuation of the entire Polish Army, including the division being armed by the Soviets, as well as the largest possible number of Polish civilians. As Mitkiewicz described their point of view on the eve of the Sikorski-Stalin talks:

> . . . According to this conception, the formation of a Polish Army of great strength should take place in the Near East in anticipation of its use in a Western Allied offensive in southern Europe, in Italy or the Balkans. Politically and strategically, the conception of opponents of General Sikorski's Russian conception is based on the assumption, accepted in advance, that in the final stage of the war the Western Allies will strike against Germany simultaneously from Europe's West and South, through France and through the Balkans. *In addition, adherents of this conception make no allowance for Soviet Russia's participation in the final assault on Germany; in their opinion, Soviet Russia will be defeated by Germany, or will be incapable of mounting such an effort.*

nying minutes in these files reveal wide differences of opinion as to whether Stalin, or even Sikorski, should be apprised of this change in plans. Sikorski was in the Middle East at this time, inspecting the Polish Brigade there and waiting for the final go-ahead for his trip to Moscow, and did not take part in these discussions. In fact, it is not clear whether Sikorski was ever informed of the proposed change of location, although both the War Office and the head of the British Military Mission in Moscow, General MacFarlane, advised that he be so informed—the latter adding also, "I do not recommend being anything but quite frank with Stalin." (Unfortunately, our knowledge of the War Office's handling of Polish military matters is limited almost exclusively to documents preserved in the Foreign Office files. The War Office's own records on the Polish Army—WO 193/39, PRO—is marked "weeded 1/5/46" and contains little of interest.)

[55] Mitkiewicz, *Z gen. Sikorskim*, pp. 189-91 [entry for December 1, 1941].

Again, other calculations by opponents of General Sikorski's "Russian" conception look to an end of the war with Germany much earlier on the western than on the eastern front. . . .

On this basis, "the majority" of the officer corps as well as, among others, President Raczkiewicz, expected—"credulously" in Mitkiewicz's opinion—Western armies to reach Poland "much earlier" than the Red Army.[56]

FROM the psychological standpoint, then, the setting could not have been worse when Stalin and Sikorski met at the Kremlin on December 3rd. Whether or not Stalin was aware of these more far-reaching evacuation proposals (not to mention the assessments that inspired them), the Poles by now knew that he had taken umbrage at the suggestion of a temporary withdrawal.[57] Possibly as a not so subtle indication of displeasure, the Soviet note denying Polish citizenship to the non-Polish minorities of the occupied eastern territories was delivered on the day of the prime minister's arrival.[58] Equally relevant to the mood of the meeting was the fact that Hitler's armies were hammering at the gates of Moscow. We now know that by the 3rd, German offensive strength was spent. But the Soviet leaders could not yet be sure of this, while the opening of their counteroffensive was still several days off.[59]

Sikorski presented the temporary withdrawal plan much as it had been discussed with Churchill in October—that is, mentioning only Iran as the intended concentration area.[60] Stressing the symbolic as well as military

[56] Ibid. [emphasis added]. Mitkiewicz emphasized here the contrast between this view and Sikorski's determination to leave the largest possible army on the eastern front. By this time it is evident that, despite earlier doubts shared by many in the West, Sikorski was convinced that the Soviet Union would not be defeated. Very likely he was encouraged in this opinion by Retinger's optimistic report on his return from Moscow. See ibid., p. 182; also Ambassador Dormer's report of December 2nd, C13467/3226/55, FO 371/26762, PRO.

[57] See note 51 above. To the extent that these ideas were topical in Anders's army Stalin must have known, as the headquarters and camps were crawling with NKVD men. Likewise, it is unlikely that echos of the mood in the Polish exile community did not reach Soviet Ambassador Maisky's ears.

[58] See note 33 above. Other warning signs that greeted Sikorski on his arrival were the sudden arrests of two prominent Polish Jewish Socialists, Henryk Ehrlich and Wiktor Alter (later executed on trumped-up charges of spying for the Germans), and the announcement in *Izvestiia* of the first meeting of the Communist-dominated Union of Polish Patriots. For Sikorski's reaction to the latter event, see Kot, *Listy z Rosji*, pp. 64-65; and Rozek, *Allied Wartime Diplomacy*, p. 95. For an account of the Ehrlich-Alter case, see Rozek, *Allied Wartime Diplomacy*, pp. 98-103.

[59] Werth, *Russia at War*, pp. 257-63; and Seaton, *The Russo-German War*, p. 224.

[60] See note 54 above; Sikorski also appears to have avoided raising the issue of the Soviet divisions in Iran. The official Polish record of this meeting appears in *Documents*, 1:227-

importance of the army to Poland—"we have here the only reserve of our youths"—he expressed his fear that, in view of "the present difficulties in feeding, equipping and training," his soldiers were "doomed to slow extinction." "Therefore," he continued:

> I propose that the entire army and all the people eligible for military service be moved, for instance, to Persia where the climate as well as the promised American and British help would allow these people to recover within a short time and form a strong army which would return here to the front and take over the section assigned to them. This has been settled with Churchill. On my part I am ready to declare that these forces will return to the Russian front, and that they might even be strengthened by several British divisions.

He now asked that he be allowed to send 25,000 recruits as reinforcements to Polish units in Scotland and Egypt, but stated that if the need arose these units too could be transferred "here to the East." He thought the Poles "should form about seven divisions with the rest."

Stalin exploded: "I am a person of experience and of age. I know that if you go to Persia you will never return here. I see that England has much to do and needs Polish soldiers." Now the tone of the conversation grew increasingly acrimonious on both sides. Stalin charged again and again that the Poles did not want to fight, at least not in Russia, and intimated that Sikorski, wittingly or unwittingly, was the tool of British machinations: "If the Poles do not want to fight then let them go. We cannot hold back the Poles. If they want to they may go away. . . . I know that where an army is formed, there it remains. . . . I see that the English are in need of good armed forces. . . . When you go to Iran then perhaps you will have to fight in Turkey against the Germans . . . , then against Japan. So as the English will order. Perhaps in Singapore." He seemed particularly offended by references to the poor health of the recruits and the lack of proper conditions for training the army:

> That means that we are savages, and that we cannot improve anything. It amounts to this, that a Russian can only oppress a Pole, but is unable to do anything good for him. However, we can do without you. We can give back all of them. We will manage ourselves. We will conquer Poland and then we will give her back to you. But what will people say to this? They will ridicule us all over the world that we are not able to achieve anything here.

43; Rozek, *Allied Wartime Diplomacy*, pp. 82-94; Kot, *Listy z Rosji*, pp. 191-208, and *Rozmowy z Kremlem*, pp. 153-71. See also the account in Kukiel, *Generał Sikorski*, pp. 186-87.

Sikorski, denying Stalin's charges in equally heated tones, stated that his hand was being forced by conditions beyond the control of the Poles and demanded to be shown "another solution": "If we had been allowed to organize ourselves, we would be fighting already. But, so much time was wasted here for which we are not to blame. . . . I do not want people to perish in vain. I am not presenting an ultimatum, but . . . I cannot look at [the situation] and remain silent. . . . I am still waiting for a new formula and I am ready to accept every just solution. . . . I ask for concrete counterpropositions. I categorically confirm once again that we want to fight for Poland and at your side. . . . The patriotism of the Poles does not have to be proven. I confirm that I still have no clear counterproposition."

At this point, having apparently concluded that Sikorski was sincere, Stalin made his counteroffer:

> Stalin: If you insist—one corps, two to three divisions may leave. However, if you so desire, I shall assign place and means necessary for the forming of seven divisions. I see, however, that the English need Polish soldiers. I, of course, have received Harriman's and Churchill's request to evacuate the Polish Army.
>
> Gen. S[ikorski]: The English are not so badly off that the Polish Army formed here should decide their fate. . . . It was I who demanded that Churchill request the evacuation of our armed forces.[61] I will, however, prove my good will; I am ready to leave the army in Russia, if you assign an adequate region for its concentration and if you assure to it equipment and supplies and proper quarters, and so establish adequate conditions for its training.

With this the tension began to dissipate—indeed, Stalin now readily admitted the truth of the Poles' complaints about their conditions—and the two quickly reached an agreement: the Poles could withdraw the desired 25,000 men for their Scottish and North African units; the rest would remain in the Soviet Union where they would be organized into an army of seven divisions. Stalin agreed to designate a locale in the warmer climate of Central Asia, where the Poles would have easier access to British supply

---

[61] This is almost certainly not true. As we saw earlier (note 48 above), the records of the Churchill-Sikorski meeting on October 24th show that it was Churchill who proposed the evacuation to Iran, but insisted that Sikorski take sole responsibility. This is supported by a cable from the U.S. chargé in the Soviet Union, Thurston, of December 8th, which reads in part: "I judge that Sikorski did as he apparently had been requested to do in London, endeavor to obtain Stalin's consent to the transfer of Poles of military age to India [sic] and other places in the Near East for equipment and training but that he quickly gave way before Stalin's insistence that the Poles should remain within Soviet jurisdiction." *FRUS, 1941*, 1:267.

lines and where the Polish civilian population would be allowed to concentrate. He also agreed to provide rations equivalent to those for Soviet troops. As a further show of good will, Sikorski proposed to transfer several Polish air force units from England to complement the army, and promised to press in the West for speedier arms deliveries to Russia. Although a target date for the army's combat readiness appears not to have been set at this meeting, Sikorski stated shortly after his departure that he expected his troops to be reconditioned and trained by June 1942, at which time he foresaw "that a great German offensive will be launched on the Eastern European Front."[62]

To all appearances this agreement constituted a victory for Sikorski's strategy of reconciliation between Poland and the Soviet Union. Yet he was clearly chastened by the harshness of some of his exchanges with Stalin, and by a new appreciation of the extraordinarily difficult circumstances of Poland's position between Moscow and the West. On the one hand, Stalin had made clear to him in several ways that he would tie the future settlement of political and territorial questions to the strict observance of the military obligations undertaken here. His angry remark during the main negotiating session—"we can do without you. . . . We will conquer Poland and then we will give her back to you"—was not his only warning. "We should settle our common frontiers between ourselves," he had told Sikorski at a Kremlin banquet, "*as soon as the Polish Army enters into action.* . . . Don't worry, we will not harm you."[63] Following the meetings in Moscow, the Polish leader told British Ambassador Cripps that "by yielding with regard to the retention of the Polish forces within the Soviet Union" he felt he "had assured Stalin's full acceptance of the principle that a Polish State should be reconstituted."[64] Moreover, as he reported to American Ambassador Biddle on his return to London, Stalin had attached a firm condition to the withdrawal of troops for Polish units in Scotland and the Near East: "25,000, but no more." As Biddle relayed the conversation to Washington: "If Sikorski wanted more he could take them only from the 40,000 then already organized—moreover, he, Stalin,

[62] As reported to the Department of State in Washington by Ambassador Ciechanowski; ibid., p. 269. Many details of the new agreement for Polish-Soviet military cooperation were left to be worked out by a joint staff meeting discussed below.

[63] *Documents*, 1:245 [emphasis added]. See also Sikorski's January 12, 1942 report to his Council of Ministers, in ibid., pp. 264-65; and Kot, *Listy z Rosji*, pp. 211-12.

[64] As reported by the American chargé, Thurston, in *FRUS, 1941*, 1:195-96 and 267. This report was occasioned by the immediate objections of British military authorities to the decision to leave the bulk of the army in the Soviet Union and their request that Sikorski seek modifications of the Agreement; see further discussion below.

would see to it that no more Poles were allowed to join the Polish forces in Russia.''[65]

On the other hand (even supposing he could keep his domestic dissidents in line), Sikorski's ability to keep his side of the bargain was utterly, and for reasons beyond his control, dependent on the political farsightedness as well as the military capacity of Britain and the United States. What little flexibility he had possessed—or thought he had possessed—was gone. The option of evacuating the Polish forces ''should the difficulties . . . turn out to be insuperable'' was no longer viable, if he was not to risk undermining a cornerstone of his postwar program. It was his first encounter with a lesson he would have occasion to reflect on many times over the next year and a half: for Poland there was no such thing as loyalty to the ''Alliance'' as a whole. The demands and pressures exerted by one side were bound to come into conflict with those exerted by the other; he was at the mercy of either and had growing reason to fear that he was being used by at least one and possibly both.

THE POLITICS OF EVACUATION

The initial results of Sikorski's visit were modestly encouraging. At a follow-up meeting of the Polish and Soviet staffs, the size of the Polish Army to remain in the Soviet Union, although not to approach the 150,000 figure that Sikorski anticipated might be raised, was set at 96,000 (six divisions plus reserves), far higher than previous limits. The Soviets again promised to arm a second division and to provide certain other essential equipment. They also agreed to a loan sufficient to maintain the army for six months—that is, long enough by Polish calculations to bring it to combat readiness. The Poles would be responsible for obtaining the balance of needed arms and equipment from the British and Americans. Finally, new locations for the Polish camps were designated in Central Asia, with head-quarters to be situated at Yangi-Yul near Tashkent.[66] (This would turn out to be a fatal move, immensely complicating supply problems, and exposing the army and civilians alike to uncontrollable epidemics of typhoid, typhus, dysentery, and even malaria. But at the time it seemed a welcome relief from the ravages of winter along the Central Volga.)

In addition, the Soviets apparently agreed (again) to release for service in the Polish Army those Poles conscripted into Red Army labor battalions.[67] Indeed, the Polish Embassy was able to determine that large num-

---

[65] *FRUS, 1942,* 3:101.

[66] These decisions were reported to London by Ambassador Kot in his letter of January 5, 1942; *Listy z Rosji*, pp. 245-46.

[67] See Sikorski's letter to Churchill of December 17, 1941; *Documents*, 1:254.

bers of Poles were now being released from camps and restricted settlements, especially in the far north, and that they were being directed south
in more orderly fashion and in rather better conditions than had obtained
during the the the first wave of releases. Certainly many acute problems remained, in particular the dire material and medical situation of the civilian
population, the still missing officers, and the Soviets' continued refusal to
recognize members of non-Polish minorities as Polish citizens or as eligible
for enlistment in the army. Still, a month after the Sikorski-Stalin talks,
Kot could report to London that "there has been a visible improvement
in the attitude of the Soviet Government toward the Polish population,"
and that "only during December did the Soviet authorities begin to deal
realistically with our requests, which they had put off since September."
Attributing the change not only to political calculations on Stalin's part,
but to "the personal impression" made by Sikorski, the ambassador also
reported that the Soviets now seemed more willing to assist the Polish
Embassy in its efforts to reach and care for Polish civilians and that he
had been able to obtain a substantial loan for this purpose, something that
had earlier been refused.[68]

Yet, despite this apparent progress toward the reconciliation he hoped
for, Sikorski's position began to deteriorate in other respects almost from
the moment he concluded his Moscow visit. One reason was the rising
tide of criticism back in London. Dissidents in the exile community had
taken advantage of the prime minister's absence to mount an intense propaganda campaign against him, including the publication of a clandestine
newsletter *Walka (The Struggle)*. Rumors to the effect that Sikorski had
made secret territorial concessions, that he was "selling Poland out to the
Soviets," spread among Poles on both sides of the Atlantic.[69] In particular,
the decision to leave the bulk of the army in the Soviet Union met with
widespread dissatisfaction both in the officer corps and among the rank
and file, whose "underlying attitude" toward Russia and the Russo-German conflict had undergone little if any change since July.[70] Even the

---

[68] Kot, *Listy z Rosji*, pp. 242-45 and 251-53.

[69] Mitkiewicz, *Z gen. Sikorskim*, p. 198; and Kukiel, *Generał Sikorski*, pp. 200-201.
Mitkiewicz's suspicions that, in view of strict paper rationing, such opposition publications
could not have appeared without the collusion or at least knowledge of "certain British
institutions" were apparently misplaced. The "delicate" legal and political problems posed
by the question of censorship (and not only of the Polish opposition press) were a recurring
subject of discussion within the Foreign Office; see especially C4658/19/55, FO 371/31083,
PRO.

[70] See Ambassador Biddle's cable to Washington of February 2, 1942; *FRUS, 1942*, 3:102-
104. Citing a recent conversation with the editor of an army newspaper, he reported: "As
for their attitude towards the Russian-German conflict, he [the editor] characterized the
thoughts in the back-of-the-mind of the average Polish officer and soldier, by citing a Polish

prime minister's efforts to impress on Washington—as he had promised Stalin he would do—the need for stepped-up arms deliveries to the Soviets and for a second European front in 1942 met with ridicule and suggestions that he sounded like the Soviet ambassador.[71]

But a more immediate source of Sikorski's new difficulties lay elsewhere, in a combination of changes in the overall military situation and a new and, for Poland, dangerous turn in Anglo-Soviet relations. On the morning of December 6th, the Soviet armies, having held the line before Moscow, began their winter counteroffensive; on the following day, the Japanese attacked Pearl Harbor. While American belligerency was something Sikorski had long desired, the short-term effect of the war effort in the Pacific was inevitably to drain resources intended for the European theater, including at least indirectly Poland's unarmed divisions.[72] Meanwhile, both events strengthened Stalin's diplomatic hand—up to the time of Pearl Harbor, he had feared a Japanese attack on his own Far East—just as British Foreign Secretary Eden arrived in Moscow for his mid-December visit.

The substance of the Eden-Stalin talks will be discussed in some detail in the next chapter. Suffice it to say at this point that, while the foreign secretary successfully resisted Stalin's pressure to sign an agreement legitimizing Moscow's territorial gains from 1939-40, he did not, as Polish Foreign Minister Raczyński lamented several weeks later, "refuse to hear out far-reaching Soviet demands embracing the Baltic States and our eastern

legend about a battle between two rats: they fought until all that was left were two tails." Kukiel (*Generał Sikorski*, pp. 200-201) contends that the dissidents, especially what he calls a "Young Turk" movement in the military, did not limit themselves to verbal attacks, but undertook a kind of "psychological warfare" against Sikorski aimed either at frightening the prime minister into abandoning his policy or at overthrowing his government. This campaign even included what Kukiel calls a staged attempt on Sikorski's life during his flight to the United States in March 1942. (For less sanguine accounts of this incident, see Mitkiewicz, *Z gen. Sikorskim*, pp. 234-38 and 251-53; and Klimkowski, *Katastrofa w Gibraltarze*, pp. 24-32.)

[71] Pobóg-Malinowski (*Najnowsza historia*, 3:219-20 and n. 12), citing news reports of Sikorski's public statements on this subject during his March 1942 visit to the United States, calls him "a loyal trumpet" (*wierna tuba*) for "Stalin's demands and pretensions." This reaction was reflected in a report from the British Embassy in Washington to the Foreign Office, which stated *inter alia* that: "Although General Sikorski in his private conversations may have said things to which the Russians might take exception, it is interesting to note that in his public pronouncements he was regarded, at any rate by the Polish Americans, as being a good deal too pro-Russian." C5328/19/55, FO 371/31083, PRO.

[72] Indeed, from this point on direct U.S. arms aid to the Polish Army in Russia was never again a serious factor. During his trip to Washington in March 1942, Sikorski was told that America's war production was not yet sufficient both to supply its own armies and to satisfy the needs of all its allies. Mitkiewicz, *Z gen. Sikorskim*, pp. 246-47.

provinces."[73] Nor, on his return, did Eden or other British officials (especially Cripps) conceal their belief that acceptance of Soviet demands, including a Polish-Soviet boundary approximating the Curzon line, was inevitable. For Sikorski, the blow was all the more bitter coming so hard on the heels of his own apparent agreement with Stalin by which the Soviet dictator had indicated that his territorial demands would be modest and that, in any event, he would not press the issue until the Polish Army had gone to the front. Yet here he was a mere two weeks later trying to foreclose the issue with the British behind the backs of the Poles. It was now more critical than ever that Sikorski get his army combat-ready and on the battlefield as quickly as possible, if only to salvage what he could of his independent bargaining position. But here too he was to encounter unrelenting and, in the end, insurmountable difficulties.

At the outset, British military representatives in Moscow opposed the decision to leave the army in the Soviet Union, ostensibly for logistical reasons—although there were again hints that they had not anticipated that any of the Polish troops, once trained and armed, would be returned to the Russian front. As the American chargé, Thurston, reported to Washington on December 8th:

I have been informed by members of the British Embassy that the agreement entered into by Sikorski during his recent visit to Moscow is unsatisfactory to the British Government inasmuch as, if put into operation, it would place too great a burden upon the transport and other services involved in equipping and maintaining the Polish forces on Soviet territory *while at the same time depriving the British of the use of some fifteen or more thousand Polish troops in the Near Eastern field*.

As a result of British pressure, Thurston presumed, Sikorski might seek to have the agreement modified.[74] In fact, he did nothing of the kind but, instead, with Cripps's support, prevailed on the British military to accept

---

[73] Raczyński, *W sojuszniczym Londynie*, pp. 128-29

[74] *FRUS, 1941*, 1:267 [emphasis added]. Since the Sikorski-Stalin agreement called for the evacuation to the Near East and Britain of 25,000 troops, we are left to suppose that the "15,000 or more" referred to the remainder of the 40,000-odd then enrolled in the Polish Army. Concerning possible pressure on Sikorski to alter the agreement, see General MacFarlane's cable to the War Office of December 6th, in which he wrote: "This [the agreement] completely changes the situation. . . . I consider it imperative that Sikorski be left in no doubt as to the implications of this new plan, at any rate before he returns to Moscow to see Stalin on 12/12. Please therefore inform me urgently extent to which we can arm and equip Poles in this new area and estimate of time required." C13728/3226/55, FO 371/26763, PRO.

his agreement with Stalin.[75] His rationale was most clearly stated in a direct appeal to Churchill. "If I had insisted on evacuation of the Polish Army as at present formed," he wrote from Teheran on December 17th:

> I am certain I should never have been able to recruit any more Poles— nor should I have obtained any advantages for the Polish civilians now in Russia. Stalin's way of putting it was that "the world would laugh at him if the Polish Army had to leave Russia!"
>
> It was quite clear to me that Stalin suspected an Anglo-American intrigue at the back of the suggestion. . . .

After outlining the main points of the agreement, Sikorski continued:

> I think it worth remarking that such a Polish Force on Soviet territory may very well play an important role politically and militarily when the war is over, on behalf of Poland and the Allied cause.
>
> In view of the above facts and as it is hoped that the new Polish divisions will be formed very shortly I beg you to consider the problem of their armament and equipment. Full provision for 4 divisions has already been promised by the War Office, I trust additional arms will be made available for 2 or 3 more divisions. . . . I ask you to take personal interest in this matter as it is the most urgent and important question at the present time.[76]

Although no formal reply to this letter was ever sent,[77] in fact Churchill had already intervened personally in support of Sikorski's position.[78] By

[75] See Thurston's subsequent cable, dated December 9; *FRUS, 1941*, 1:195 and 267, n. 33. This apparently occurred even before MacFarlane received the War Office's reply, dated December 10: "Consider policy agreed by General Sikorski and M. Stalin . . . must be accepted. . . . Must emphasise however that all tonnage for Poles will necessarily be at direct expense of supplies for Russia, and Sikorski will doubtless make this clear to Stalin." C13728/3226/55, FO 371/26763, PRO.

[76] *Documents*, 1:254-55. Sikorski even suggested that the Polish force might "be regarded as an adequate substitute [for the sending of British divisions to Russia]—especially as by far the largest part of their armaments will have come from Great Britain." His reference to the promise of "full provision for 4 divisions" suggests that he had been informed of the War Office's December 10th cable prior to his departure from the Soviet Union.

[77] At the time the letter was delivered, Churchill was in Washington conferring with Roosevelt about the changed military situation in the wake of Pearl Harbor. A reply was discussed within the Foreign Office but in the end not sent. C491/19/55, FO 371/31077, and Frank Roberts's minute in C1861/19/55, FO 371/31078, PRO.

[78] On seeing the December 10th cable to MacFarlane (note 75 above), Churchill fired off an angry note to General Ismay at the War Office: "This most foolish remark"—asking that Sikorski make clear to Stalin that supplies for the Poles would be at the expense of deliveries to the Russians—"must be immediately cancelled. We want to get the Poles armed as soon as possible. Why then should we tell the Russians that it will only be at their expense? Let me know who drafted this. He evidently does not understand the general situation." A

mid-December, the War Office had prepared a tentative supply schedule that foresaw an initial arms shipment in late December or early January, major supplies by March or April, and the balance of weapons on a "war scale" once the divisions were fully trained.[79]

The evidence is overwhelming that despite earlier reservations the British viewed this commitment as a binding one, one which they would do their utmost to honor, and that the Foreign Office in particular was now acutely sensitive to the political as well as military importance of maintaining Polish troops on the Russian front. But the evidence is equally overwhelming that, in that terrible winter of 1941-42, the task was simply beyond Britain's resources and sorely overtaxed transport capacity—that, as one sympathetic Foreign Office official put it, "General Sikorski is asking us to do what was previously considered impossible,"[80] and that promised supplies for the Poles inescapably fell victim to the urgent demands created by Rommel's North African campaign and the expanded war in the Pacific. Twice between late January and the first week of February, shipments of training arms had to be diverted to other destinations.[81] Then in early March, following a month-long review, the War Office determined that, "although we have every intention of fulfilling our commitments to arm the four Polish divisions in Russia, the rate of provision of full equipment may be much slower than we originally expected . . ." General MacFarlane, chief of the British Military Mission in Moscow, thereupon informed the Soviets and Poles, according to the latters' account, that the first shipment would now "probably arrive end-April-beginning-May," and even then "installments [would] consist of single categories of arms and not of complete arms for the units."[82] A few days later, on March

---

correction was sent to Moscow the following day, December 11th. C13728/3226/55, FO 371/26763, PRO.

[79] A copy of this proposed schedule is appended to C1861/19/55, FO 371/31078, PRO.

[80] See Frank Roberts's second minute, dated January 16, 1942, in C491/19/55, FO 371/31077, PRO.

[81] War Office cables informing the British command in the Middle East of the diversions are dated January 24th and February 7th, the latter adding "replacement being considered urgently." C840/19/55, FO 371/31077, PRO.

[82] Letter from Archibald Nye to Alexander Cadogan, March 3, 1942, C2371/19/55, FO 371/31078, PRO; and *Documents*, 1:594, n. 185. Concerning the review process, see especially C1220 and C1861/19/55, FO 371/31078, PRO. These papers reveal some natural but quite distinct differences between the viewpoints of the War and Foreign Offices. While the former stressed strategic and logistical considerations, tended to see arms deliveries primarily as leverage to speed up evacuation of the 25,000—and perhaps showed a declining interest in the military value of the Poles in the Soviet Union as the Russian front recovered somewhat and the military situation elsewhere deteriorated—the Foreign Office focused more clearly on the political ramifications, especially on what one of those involved called "the devastating consequences of this decision [to delay arms shipments] for the Polish Government" (Roger Makins in the last document cited). In the end, however, the War Office

9th, Stalin informed Anders by telegram that, in view of the fact that the Polish troops "are not engaged in fighting," it would be necessary as of March 20th to reduce the army's rations "at least to 30,000." (By early March the army numbered approximately 66,000 men, with 1,000 to 1,500 arriving daily.)[83]

Just what prompted Stalin to take this action at this particular time is not certain. It is possible, of course, that his sole reason was the one he gave Anders: the lack of progress toward combat readiness of the Polish troops, combined with an unexpectedly severe food shortage as a result of the outbreak of war in the Pacific and the curtailment of American grain shipments. However, the timing of the move, as well as the sequence of events both before and after, make it more likely that political motives were uppermost in Stalin's mind and that the delay in arms deliveries merely provided the occasion rather than the cause for the cut in rations. Even the most cursory review of dispatches, whether British or Polish, between Moscow/Kuibyshev and London in the early months of 1942 reveals a transparent and infuriating succession of obstacles to the expeditious implementation of the Sikorski-Stalin agreement. Moreover, these delaying tactics began weeks before the diversion of the first shipment of British arms and tend to belie Stalin's preoccupation with food supplies:

—On January 1st, for example, the Soviets informed Anders that the evacuation of the 25,000 troops agreed to by Stalin would not begin until recruitment of the 96,000-man army to stay in the Soviet Union had been completed; and recruitment would begin only after existing units had been transferred to Uzbekistan. With the transfer due to begin on January 15th, mid-February was viewed as the earliest possible start-up date for the evacuation—although MacFarlane was already anticipating, correctly as it turned out, a longer delay. In the meantime, of course, the 25,000 had to be fed.[84]

---

confirmed its continuing commitment to arm the Poles in unequivocal language, its March 3rd cable to MacFarlane reading in part: "Decision now taken NOT (repeat NOT) withdraw from commitment provide arms and equipment for Polish forces Uzbekistan. Substantial initial installment together with ammunition already released will be shipped earliest possible." C2563/19/55, FO 371/31079, PRO.

[83] *Documents*, 1:294-95; see also Anders, *Army in Exile*, pp. 98-99, and Kukiel, *Generał Sikorski*, p. 202. Initial notification came three days earlier from one General Khrulov, who advised Anders that rations would be cut to 26,000. The situation was especially critical because the soldiers were already going short to help maintain the thousands of Polish civilians who had gathered around the camps. MacFarlane also used the figure of 26,000 in his cable of March 9th; on the 16th, he gave the size of the army as 70-80,000 with 1,500 arriving daily. C2643 and C2907/19/55, FO 371/31079, PRO.

[84] C425/19/55, FO 371/31077, PRO; concerning further delays in transferring the army, see C1113/19/55, FO 371/31077 (cable of February 3rd) and C2609/19/55, FO 371/31079, PRO.

—Despite the signing of a financial agreement in January, as of mid-February the Polish military command was still without operating funds.[85] Soviet authorities were also reneging, or at least stalling, on other aspects of the December agreement—such as the release of Poles conscripted into labor battalions of the Red Army, delivery of the thrice-promised arms for the second division, and the agreement not to press Anders to send individual units to the front.[86]

—Although presumably interested in facilitating delivery of British arms and equipment to the Poles, the Soviets delayed for a full five months—from September 1941 into February 1942—the attachment of a British liaison officer to Anders's headquarters.[87]

—Plans for evacuating the 25,000 were further complicated at the end of January when the Soviets first insisted that arrangements now be made through the Soviet ambassador in Teheran (who was hardly likely to have independent decision-making powers), and then changed the proposed point of transfer after the British had made all of the necessary preparations at the original site.[88]

—In the meantime, General Wolikowski, the military attaché at the Polish Embassy in Kuibyshev who was promised transportation to Moscow on January 31st to draw up an evacuation plan, was informed a week later that no air transport was available and he would have to travel by train; he finally arrived on February 20th.[89]

Unquestionably these delaying tactics, however maddening and counterproductive in purely military terms, can be understood partly as a product of Moscow's inveterate suspiciousness and partly as an attempt to retain some leverage over both the British and the Poles—that is, to ensure that the former would in fact deliver the promised arms, and that the latter

---

[85] C1113/19/55, FO 371/31077, PRO (cable of February 15th) and Kot, *Listy z Rosji*, p. 275.

[86] Kot, *Listy z Rosji*, p. 262; *Documents*, 1:304-309; and C2338/19/55, FO 371/31078, PRO.

[87] C10286/3226/55, FO 371/26760, and C1320/19/55, FO 371/31078, PRO.

[88] C1220 and C1444/19/55, FO 371/31078, PRO. The tone of the second message indicates that MacFarlane's patience was wearing a bit thin. Noting that the British had been prepared since mid-January to receive 2,000 Polish troops per week via the original route and that the change could mean a delay of weeks, he reported that his protests had been unavailing and that his Soviet counterpart, General Panfilov, had adopted an "uncompromising attitude." "The Russians are very clearly out to procrastinate as much as possible and they hold the Poles."

[89] C1535 and C1960/19/55, FO 371/31078, PRO. By now totally exasperated with the constant delays, MacFarlane despaired that he could "bring no more pressure to bear this end" and suggested that both the Poles and British consider diplomatic action in London and Kuibyshev.

would eventually field a sizable force on the Russian front.[90] But another possibility is that Stalin, for reasons related more to his ongoing negotiations with the British and to his long-term political goals than to the immediate military situation, had by now lost interest in keeping a Polish Army—at least *this* Polish Army—in the Soviet Union. Certainly the Poles had proved of negligible value in drawing additional military aid from the West,[91] while from the political standpoint they remained overwhelmingly anti-Soviet. Nor had they shown any signs of abandoning the search for the missing officers; on the contrary, it was now clear that the exile government was intent on pressing the search during the coming spring and summer.[92] Moreover, in the three months since Sikorski's Moscow visit, the Soviets had shown increasing pique at his efforts both to forestall an Anglo-Soviet treaty legitimizing their territorial gains from 1939-40 and to promote his own program for a Central European federation.[93]

In this light it is not unreasonable to suppose that Stalin now saw the army, the one tangible result of Polish-Soviet cooperation, as a liability that imposed obligations he no longer wished to honor. Might it not be better to let the troublesome Poles go, providing of course it could be done without the onus falling on Moscow? Indeed, since the British seemed so eager to use them in the Middle East, such an arrangement might even help smooth the way for an Anglo-Soviet treaty along the lines Stalin

---

[90] The interplay of these two issues provides a good illustration of the way in which Polish interests could be effectively sidetracked by the larger Anglo-Soviet relationship. Although fully aware from the outset that Moscow would likely use the promised partial evacuation as leverage to ensure delivery of British arms (e.g., C1024/19/55, FO 371/31077, PRO), the British were inhibited from intervening effectively on behalf of the Polish Army by their sensitivity to Soviet suspiciousness and by a desire on the part of senior Foreign Office officials not to arouse "renewed Soviet suspicions of our motives." See especially C1220 and C1602/19/55, FO 371/31078, PRO.

[91] Commenting on the ration cut, Mr. Baggallay of the British Embassy in Kuibyshev cabled that, while the food shortage was real, it was not the Soviets' only motive; it was "quite likely" in addition that "disappointment at our inability to arm the Polish [forces] straightaway may have led them to decide that the Polish forces will not be ready to fight in time to make their maintenance meanwhile worth while." C2838/19/55, FO 371/31079, PRO. General Wolikowski also was of the opinion that, even taking into account the food shortage, "the reduction of food rations for Polish troops . . . was either a pressure aiming at the speeding up of the delivery of arms by England or a kind of political pressure." *Documents*, 1:594, n. 185.

[92] C1370 and C1786/19/55, FO 371/31078, PRO; and Kot, *Listy z Rosji*, pp. 283-84. By May 1942, there were growing signs that the British might become actively involved in pressing the search; see especially the minute by Roger Makins, in C5226/19/55, FO 371/31083, PRO.

[93] As one Foreign Office official responsible for relations with the Soviet Union remarked in January, "If the Poles pick a quarrel with the Soviets over the status of Lithuania, they will much increase difficulties over such practical matters as the present." C1024/19/55, FO 371/31077, PRO. See also Kot, *Listy z Rosji*, pp. 287-89; and *FRUS, 1942*, 3:133-34.

wanted.[94] In any event, the threatened cut-off of rations triggered the final chain of events that led some five months later to the complete evacuation of the Polish Army from the Soviet Union and thereby to the collapse of one cornerstone of General Sikorski's strategy. It was a chain of events in which the interests of the Soviets and of those Poles who opposed the general's policy of reconciliation with Moscow, and allegedly of the British as well, all seemed to coincide.

IN RESPONSE to Stalin's telegram, Anders went immediately to Moscow where on March 18th the two reached agreement in a deceptively cordial atmosphere.[95] Full rations would be continued to the end of the month. Thereafter the Poles would be allowed to keep three divisions plus a reserve regiment, for a total of 44,000 instead of the 26,000 to 30,000 first specified. The rest would be evacuated to Iran. It was true, Stalin admitted, that the Soviets had not made good on all of their promises: arms for a second division would be provided "immediately"; Poles in Red Army labor battalions would be transferred to the Polish Army. In addition, Anders asked for and got Stalin's verbal assent to a continuation of recruitment. Indeed, all the concessions seemed to come from the Soviet side. As Anders wrote later, he was "surprised . . . that Stalin had so readily agreed to my suggestions." Either he did not suspect, or did not care to admit he suspected, that Stalin's motive might be to abrogate the December agreement with Sikorski.[96]

[94] Kot was apparently aware that the Soviets were at least preparing for such a contingency. In early March 1942, he warned both Anders and Sikorski that they were gathering all manner of charges and complaints against the Polish military in order, he surmised, "at a given moment to create some sort of incident." *Listy z Rosji*, pp. 279-81. MacFarlane too referred euphemistically to Moscow's "inconsistency": "When talking to Wolikowski two days ago Panfilov said that the Polish evacuation question could be settled between the Poles and the Russians without our interfering. When talking to me last night he proposed that he and I should settle the whole question without being bothered by the Poles." C2170/19/55, FO 371/31078, PRO. It has been suggested that the British did in fact carry on direct negotiations with the Soviets for the evacuation of some of the Polish troops, without the participation or knowledge of the Polish government (*Documents*, 1:595, n. 198). From the detailed coverage of this issue in the Foreign Office papers, however, this allegation appears to be ill-founded. While it is true that the War Office and the Middle Eastern command were eager to secure the release of the promised 25,000, particularly for use in the North African campaign, there is no evidence of independent British initiatives in this regard. Indeed, the Foreign Office was extremely reluctant to intervene even when asked to do so by the exile government. See FO 371/31077 and 31078 *passim*, especially C1220 and C1602/19/55 in the latter file, PRO; also note 90 above.

[95] The Polish record of this meeting is translated in *Documents*, 1:301-310; Anders and a staff aide were the only Polish representatives present. Kot (*Listy z Rosji*, pp. 290-91) has questioned the veracity of at least part of the record.

[96] Anders, *Army in Exile*, pp. 99-100; in general, Anders's account of this meeting is very sketchy and omits many of the most sensitive issues.

Yet both men were playing a double game. For his part, Stalin apparently never had any intention of keeping these promises. The long-awaited arms did not come this time either; in fact, scarcely more than a week after the Anders-Stalin meeting, Panfilov informed a flabbergasted MacFarlane that any Soviet arms made available to the Poles were merely for training purposes and would have to be returned and replaced by British and American arms as the latter became available.[97] As for continuing recruitment or releasing Poles from the Red Army, the flow of men into the Polish forces was cut off completely in early April with prospective recruits being directed *to* rather than from the labor battalions.[98] And once again, Moscow's handling of the actual evacuation suggests that Stalin was more intent on creating chaos among the Poles and headaches for the British than on carrying out the terms of the new agreement.[99]

Anders, on the other hand, failed to keep either Ambassador Kot or the exile government fully informed of his activities. It would appear that he set up his meeting with Stalin without prior clearance from London and, in agreeing to the reduction in the size of the army in the Soviet Union, blatantly overstepped at least the spirit of Sikorski's orders that he not negotiate with Stalin on any "fundamental problems."[100] He again exceeded his authority in appealing directly to the British War Office for assistance in arranging the "evacuation of 40,000 men by April 1st" before obtaining the approval of his commander-in-chief.[101] In Anders's defense,

[97] C3419/19/55, FO 371/31081, PRO. This was on March 27th. Only four days earlier, Ambassador Maisky had confirmed to Eden the Soviet commitment to arm two divisions, asking that Britain arm the third to remain in Russia; he also hinted that the Soviets would welcome the evacuees—whose number he put at 26,000 only—back on the Russian front once trained and armed, despite the earlier agreement that this number could go to the Middle East and Great Britain. C3112/19/55, FO 371/31080, PRO. The internal minutes attached to both documents indicate that the British felt they must honor the commitment to arm the one division (in addition to those that were to be evacuated), but not the other two.

[98] *Documents*, 1:596, n. 198.

[99] This time Moscow procrastinated until the last minute over the appointment of a Soviet liaison officer to help coordinate the operation, and then rushed the evacuation of more than 30,000 people within the space of a few days over a route prepared to handle a maximum of 4,000 per week. One cable to the War Office spoke of the "extremely serious" condition in which the evacuees were arriving. See, e.g., C3171/19/55, FO 371/31080; C3419, C3498, C3611, and C3612/19/55, FO 371/31081; and C3799/19/55, FO 371/31082, PRO.

[100] Kot, *Listy z Rosji*, pp. 282 and 304-305. Although Anders was authorized to discuss matters relating to the army and planned evacuation with Stalin, the reduction in the size of the army to remain and the consequent increase in the number to be evacuated were issues of far-reaching political importance because of the weight attached to them during the Sikorski-Stalin talks the previous December.

[101] C3010/19/55, FO 371/31079, PRO. In a dispatch dated March 19th, the day after Anders's meeting with Stalin, the Foreign Office cabled its Moscow representatives: "We are assuming that General Anders' message correctly represents Soviet intentions . . . Polish

it can be argued that he was only acting out of concern for the welfare of his troops and the accompanying civilian population, who faced dispersal and possible starvation with a cut-off in rations. The evidence suggests however that, motivated at least in part by his own pessimistic view of Soviet prospects in the coming summer campaign, he was by now determined to pursue a strategy fundamentally at odds with Sikorski's policy—that he was more concerned with a total withdrawal of the existing army than with additional recruitment or with maintaining the Polish position in Russia. For, shortly after his meeting with Stalin, Anders's staff agreed to the dismantling of the entire Polish recruitment organization throughout the Soviet Union—a move which meant that any further recruitment (to which Stalin had allegedly agreed) would be wholly at the discretion of Soviet authorities.[102] Moreover, it is almost certain that, while en route to London for consultations several weeks later, Anders himself raised the possibility of a total evacuation with British military authorities in the Middle East.[103]

It was precisely in this time period—that is, between Anders's meeting with Stalin on March 18th and his arrival in London on April 21st—that two issues emerged in the dispatches which together were to be the subject of much confusion and, in all probability, manipulation. The first was the idea of a "second echelon" of Polish troops to be evacuated; the second, the actual number of Polish effectives available for evacuation, either from the existing divisions or as a result of continued recruitment. This "second echelon" idea was also the source of later allegations that the British, out of their own very real need for military manpower but nonetheless in disregard for Polish interests, had conspired with Anders and/or Stalin, and without Sikorski's knowledge, in arranging the final and total evac-

---

Government's approval is being sought and, unless you have reason to doubt the accuracy of General Anders' statement, authority will be given to put these plans into operation as soon as possible.''

[102] Pobóg-Malinowski, *Najnowsza historia*, 3:229; quite likely the Soviets demanded this concession as the price of their cooperation in the first evacuation.

[103] Nearly a week before the Anders-Stalin meeting, Baggallay cabled from Kuibyshev: "Colonel Hulls [the British liaison officer finally allowed to join the Anders command] derived the definite impression that unless real satisfaction is forthcoming at the interview, General Anders will aim at getting the whole Polish Forces out of this country.'' C2838/19/55, FO 371/31079, PRO. See note 110 below; also Strumph-Wojtkiewicz, *Siła złego*, p. 89, and Klimkowski, *Katastrofa w Gibraltarze*, p. 36. The former, then a press officer with the army, contends that Anders was already privately advocating total evacuation before his trip to London. If so, it is most unlikely that Stalin was not apprised of this view; as Kot wrote a few months later, the NKVD is "splendidly informed about what goes on in the army . . .'' *Listy z Rosji*, p. 338, also 45. Anders himself does not admit that he discussed further evacuations during his stopover, but does say he urged this view on Churchill on his arrival in London. *Army in Exile*, pp. 103-104.

uation of the Polish Army from the Soviet Union.[104] At first glance, some circumstantial evidence would seem to support these allegations. Certainly it is true, as we shall see shortly, that the first references to the possibility of a "second echelon" evacuation came from various British representatives in Russia—from Ambassador Clark-Kerr in Kuibyshev, General MacFarlane in Moscow, and Colonel Hulls, the British liaison officer who had finally been allowed to join Anders's headquarters. It is also true that the British commander in the Middle East was eager to have the maximum possible number of Polish soldiers at his disposal, and that the messages passed between London, Moscow/Kuibyshev, and the Middle East often used inflated figures of the number of Poles to be evacuated. However, careful examination of the voluminous cable traffic as well as other documentary evidence strongly suggests that the British, and in particular the War and Foreign Offices, far from pursuing a deliberate policy of undermining the Polish position in Russia, were as much the victims of misinformation (or disinformation as the case may be) as was Sikorski—although the possibility cannot be excluded that some British officers (e.g., Hulls) may have helped engineer the final evacuation.

The most serious points of confusion concerned (1) how many Poles would be available for evacuation, (2) where they could come from, and (3) how soon they could be evacuated. On March 20th, two days after Anders's meeting with Stalin, Ambassador Clark-Kerr cabled the Foreign Office:

> You will see from Moscow telegrams [a reference to MacFarlane] that Stalin has agreed to provide 44,000 rations from April 1st and to the evacuation of all Polish troops recruited now or hereafter in excess of 44,000. This apparently means that anything from 20 to 40,000 men can leave at once and more later.[105]

[104] See Klimkowski, *Katastrofa w Gibraltarze*, pp. 34-39; Kot, *Listy z Rosji*, pp. 42-53 and 68-71; and Kukiel, *Generał Sikorski*, pp. 203-206. These versions differ mainly over whether the primary instigator was the British War Office, Stalin, or Anders. Klimkowski, the most tendentious of the three, sees the British as the main villains, while Kot fingers Stalin, although both see Anders as an all too willing conspirator. Kukiel takes the more neutral view that the interests of all three parties coincided.

[105] C3033/19/55, FO 371/31079, PRO. The rest of this cable suggests the sense of urgency that prevailed among the Poles in Russia: "Polish Embassy are extremely anxious that these men should leave Soviet territory at the earliest possible moment and by any means possible. They fear with good reason that if delays occur new forms of obstruction may appear from the Soviet side." Mentioning "the difficulty entailed by the existence of typhus," Clark-Kerr continued, "but so far as Poles themselves are concerned elaborate organisation is unnecessary. For instance they are so accustomed to going short that for any reasonable period they can well manage on half rations: they would much rather do this than be held up while full scale rations are assembled all along the line."

Three days later, MacFarlane sent the following message to the War Office:

> 1. Soviet Govt. has agreed with Anders that recruiting for Polish forces should continue. Eventual strength Polish forces may reach neighborhood of 150,000 but Anders cannot yet give firm figure.
> 2. Possible final total 150,000 less 44,000 to be held in U.S.S.R. leaving maximum number possible evacuated as approximately 100,000. It will however be some time before this figure can be attained . . .[106]

It is not clear from either of these messages whether the source was the Soviets or Anders reporting on his meeting with Stalin, although MacFarlane's cable seems to imply it was Anders. The message from Colonel Hulls on March 28th, however, was more explicit. Arriving in Teheran just as the first evacuation was getting under way and claiming that his information came from Soviet authorities in Krasnovodsk, the transfer point on the Russian side, Hulls reported that:

> . . . Second echelon expected to commence after interval of some weeks while Poles are being collected from various labour centres etc. all over Russia. Strength anticipated to be 50,000. . . .[107]

What all of these messages implied—Hulls's more directly than the others—was that the Soviets had confirmed their commitment, presumably made to Anders on March 18th, to permit a continuation of recruitment and evacuation. Moreover, while these and other dispatches used quite disparate estimates as to the number of Poles to be evacuated, they all agreed in the assumption that the 44,000 for whom rations would be continued were *not* to be among the evacuees.[108] (In fact, there is evidence of continued War Office planning for the arming of one of the divisions remaining in Central Asia at least to mid-June.)[109] It was only on April 20th, in the wake of Anders's stopover in Cairo, that the possibility was first raised of the "eventual evacuation [of] 44,000 more from Polish divisions now in USSR," which according to the British commander in the Middle East might raise the maximum number of evacuees to 120,000. Even then the British seemed

[106] C3166/19/55, FO 371/31080, PRO.

[107] C3847/19/55, FO 371/31082, PRO; and *Documents*, 1:318.

[108] See, e.g., C3013/19/55, FO 371/31079, and C4902/19/55, FO 371/31083, PRO.

[109] The War Office informed Cadogan on April 28th that "a consignment of arms and equipment intended as a training scale for one division is already at sea on its way to Uzbekistan," although it added that "military considerations . . . make it essential that the completion to war establishments of the Poles in the Middle East should take precedence over the completion of one division in Uzbekistan, . . ." C4502/19/55, FO 371/31082, PRO. By June 15th, however, arrangements had been made to send the remaining arms; C6057/19/55, FO 371/31083, PRO.

quite surprised, indeed skeptical, and concerned primarily with ensuring that the second stage be carried out in less chaotic conditions than the first. That even the military authorities were less interested in pressing for the maximum evacuation than in simply determining the dimensions of the problem they were going to have to cope with is indicated by the following passages of the same dispatch:

1. Lack of any definite information second contingent Poles ex USSR causing much concern. Best information at present incl from Polish H.Q. is (A) Numbers. Say 50,000 incl 5,000 families but figure may vary from 30,000 to 70,000. (B) Date of arrival. No information whatever. (C) Start. Tentative suggestion of end May.
. . .

3. Consider we cannot wait longer before making provision. Services are therefore being instructed to order on basis 120,000 in 6 months time.

4. Cable earliest any information you can obtain.[110]

The Soviets may have made one subtle attempt to throw cold water on these inflated estimates. On March 23rd, Ambassador Maisky told Eden that a *total* of "about 26,000" Poles would be available for evacuation—the 70,000 so far enrolled less the 44,000 to remain in the Soviet Union.[111] Had it been taken seriously, Maisky's statement should have served as a warning that there would be no continuation of recruitment and no "second echelon" evacuation. But faced with an avalanche of contrary reports—not to mention the fact that the first evacuation exceeded Maisky's figure—the Foreign Office concluded that the ambassador's information was "not up to date."[112]

In the meantime, Sikorski had little choice but to consent to the initial evacuation if he did not want a substantial portion of his troops to face slow starvation. Still, he hoped to salvage the situation by having this interpreted as the partial evacuation agreed upon with Stalin in December. In no way did he see it as the first stage of the army's total withdrawal from the Soviet Union; on the contrary, in several communications submitted through the Polish Embassy in Kuibyshev, he sought to impress on Stalin his sincerity in wishing to carry out the terms of the July and

---

[110] C4262/19/55, FO 371/31082, PRO. Hancock of the Foreign Office's Northern Department commented: "The evacuation of the 44,000 seems unlikely." On April 23rd, the War Office replied to Cairo: "We have no information additional to that already given you by Hulls. . . . Agree you adopt figure of 120,000 for planning."

[111] C3112/19/55, FO 371/31080, PRO; see also note 97 above.

[112] C3112/19/55, FO 371/31080, and C3437/19/55; FO 371/31081, PRO. For the resulting confusion, see, e.g., C4902 and C4970/19/55, FO 371/31083, PRO.

December agreements.[113] Sikorski's only mention at this time of a possible "second echelon" was in his April 1st cable to Churchill from Washington in which he reckoned that, in view of the 35,000 evacuated so far, "another 10-15 thousand may be expected."[114] This was consistent with his expectation that the 44,000 would remain in the Soviet Union—and that Stalin would allow recruitment of the full 96,000 agreed to in December. What he could not know at this point, of course, was the extent of the concessions that his commander in Russia had made concerning the potential size of the Polish Army, or that the latter was already maneuvering behind the scenes to liquidate even that position.[115]

The issue came to a head with Anders's arrival in London, where a General Staff strategy conference during the last week of April quickly deteriorated into what can only be described as a donnybrook.[116] The focal point of the conference was a discussion of the probable course of the Russo-German war and therefore of the importance of retaining a strong Polish force in the Soviet Union. Sikorski's view at this time was based on a combined Polish-Czech intelligence estimate for 1942—an estimate that in retrospect appears to have been remarkably accurate: No longer strong enough to strike along the whole Russian front, the Germans would probably concentrate their summer offensive in the southern sector, toward Stalingrad and the Caucasus; while the Soviets still suffered from severe shortages of food and war materiel, they were in a better position to withstand the German onslaught than they had been in 1941. Sikorski was also convinced, despite his own urgings, that there would be no second front during 1942 and therefore that the Allies, Poland included, must do everything possible to aid the Russian war effort.[117]

In direct opposition to this appraisal, Anders predicted a swift defeat

[113] See Sikorski's cables to Kot and Anders of March 14th, 22nd, and 26th-27th, in Kot, *Listy z Rosji*, pp. 282-96.

[114] C3643/19/55, FO 371/31082, PRO; and *Documents*, 1:319-20.

[115] Pobóg-Malinowski (*Najnowsza historia*, 3:230) implies that Sikorski did not have prior knowledge of the first evacuation. This is not true, although because of his absence from London he may not have been apprised of the exact timing. What neither Sikorski nor the Polish General Staff in London expected—and what gave them their first inkling that Anders was "sabotaging" Sikorski's policy—was the sudden appearance in the Middle East of 2,000-odd officers, who were already in short supply in Russia. See Mitkiewicz, *Z gen. Sikorskim*, pp. 254 and 261-62.

[116] Mitkiewicz's account of this conference and the surrounding events is by far the most detailed; *Z gen. Sikorskim*, pp. 264-85. Kukiel, also a participant, in no way disputes Mitkiewicz in his much briefer account; *Generał Sikorski*, pp. 203-204 and 252, n. 25. Anders's own version unfortunately is entirely self-serving and at critical points misleading, especially where he says he brought Sikorski around to his point of view; *Army in Exile*, pp. 104-107.

[117] Mitkiewicz, *Z gen. Sikorskim*, pp. 271 and 275.

for the Soviets in the coming summer campaign and argued vociferously for the concentration of all Polish land forces in the Middle East, whence the shortest route to Poland.[118] Only now did he inform his commander-in-chief of the full extent of his concessions to Stalin. When Sikorski protested that the decision to limit the army in Russia to 44,000 was contrary to his own December agreement with Stalin, Anders retorted that the earlier agreement was no longer valid and that his (i.e., Anders's) March 18th agreement was now the controlling factor. Moreover, Anders appears to have seriously misrepresented that agreement—no doubt in an effort to bolster his own argument that the whole army should be withdrawn—by claiming that Stalin had "conditioned the opening of further recruitment and evacuation from Soviet Russia on the *transfer of a majority of the Polish Army from Russia* to the Middle East, since this will ease the Russians' food problem."[119] When Sikorski cabled Kot for confirmation, the Soviets not only denied this assertion but now claimed that Stalin had not even discussed with Anders the possibility of continuing recruitment or of transferring Poles from Red Army labor battalions to Polish units.[120]

At the end of the conference and with the backing of his cabinet, Sikorski ordered Anders back to his command in the Soviet Union with instructions that, with only a few changes of emphasis to reflect changing circumstances, substantially reaffirmed the position he had held since the army was first established nearly nine months earlier: there was no way of knowing now whether, as the end of the war approached, the shortest route to Poland would be from Russia, the Middle East, or Great Britain; thus it was impermissible to risk annihilation of the Polish forces by concentrating them in any one theater. Polish strength would now be divided more or less equally among the three locations, with Anders to remain with the army corps in Russia "for the time being consisting of three divisions." (At this point, Sikorski still hoped the 44,000-man limit might again be raised.) Transfer of these remaining divisions to the Middle East "would be possible only in the event of the collapse of Russia" which, he warned, was not in Poland's or the general Allied interest. To do so earlier would be to forego their largest pool of potential recruits, as well

[118] Ibid., pp. 275-79; Anders expounded this view with sufficient indiscretion during his stay in London that Churchill admonished Sikorski to silence him. See also Kot, *Listy z Rosji*, pp. 68 and 373. Anders himself does not mention his prediction of Soviet defeat.

[119] Mitkiewicz, *Z gen. Sikorskim*, pp. 278-79 [emphasis added]. Mitkiewicz was scathing in his criticism of Anders's inconsistencies and lack of logic. Later he concluded that Anders had no political strategy, but only wanted "to abandon the Soviets as quickly as possible and at any cost" (p. 290).

[120] Ibid., pp. 284-85 and 291; and *Documents*, 1:351-52. This was confirmed in British dispatches; see, e.g., C4970, C5192, and C5226/19/55, FO 371/31083, PRO.

as to deprive the civilian refugee population of its only source of support. "I have full understanding," he concluded:

> of the feelings of the soldiers in Russia under your command, General, especially after the last evacuation. I appeal, nevertheless, to their patriotism and to their trained will, which has so well stood the test. They should remain in absolute discipline in a post so important for Poland.

This determination on Sikorski's part to maintain the Polish military presence in the Soviet Union persisted throughout May and June in repeated messages to Anders, supported by repeated government resolutions.[121]

Precisely what happened between mid-May, when Anders left for Russia with these instructions, and June 30th, when Stalin offered Churchill three Polish divisions—"well trained, but not yet fully armed"—is far from clear. Nonetheless, out of the maze of conflicting information (not to mention gaps in information at critical points), one can hazard several conclusions with varying degrees of certainty. The first is that, whatever role Anders did or did not play in initiating the partial March evacuation or in concealing from his government the real nature of his deal with Stalin, his complicity in engineering the second and final stage is incontrovertible. The evidence is overwhelming that immediately on his arrival back in the Soviet Union he began maneuvering, with the readily provided assistance of NKVD General Zhukov, to circumvent Sikorski's orders to keep the army in Russia. Indeed, Anders later admitted that he undertook unauthorized negotiations with the NKVD, in the end appealing directly to Stalin—and that these negotiations were aimed not at arranging a second evacuation through a reopening of recruitment, as the Polish prime minister had directed, but at the evacuation of the existing divisions.[122] Second, although several Polish sources implicate the British in these machinations,[123] it is reasonably certain that they, like Sikorski, continued to operate

[121] See Sikorski's letter of instruction, dated May 1, 1942, in *Documents*, 1:344-48. Even after receiving Stalin's refusal to renew recruitment, Sikorski continued to hope that Polish insistence on maintaining the three existing divisions in the Soviet Union would in time break Moscow's resistance; ibid., pp. 597-98, n. 213. See also his telegram of June 12th, in which he warned Anders that NKVD General Zhukov was playing a "dangerous" game, very likely aimed not only at the departure of the army for Teheran but "rather [at] the decomposition and the ruin of the reputation of our army in the USSR." Ibid., pp. 369-70.

[122] Anders, *Army in Exile*, p. 109; and Kot, *Listy z Rosji*, p. 46. Commenting on Stalin's desire to be rid of the Poles, Kot asserted that: "From the time of the March evacuation, the enterprising and numerous officers of the NKVD who were attached to the Polish Army mounted a propaganda campaign among the officers, pushing them toward the idea of leaving Russia and giving them to understand that Stalin would agree to this."

[123] See note 104 above.

on the assumption that Anders was negotiating on the basis of his government's instructions and that the long-awaited "second echelon" evacuation would begin only on the basis of renewed recruitment.[124] In particular, Churchill's suggestion to Molotov, during the Soviet foreign minister's visit to London in early June, that additional Polish troops be transferred to the Middle East was almost certainly not a reference to the existing army; nor was it made without Sikorski's knowledge, but as a result of his urgent appeal for British assistance in the matters of reopening recruitment and locating the still missing Polish officers.[125] If the British let Sikorski down at this point, it was not by deliberately undermining his policy in collusion with Anders and Stalin but—much as had happened earlier in the year—by failing to intervene strenuously in ways that might have helped him maintain the Polish position in the Soviet Union and, in so doing, playing into the hands of those unlikely collaborators. A good illustration is the following War Office cable of June 19th to MacFarlane:

> Relations with Russia have recently improved. . . . Essential avoid compromising this opportunity of discussing whole question of Northern front.
>
> Consequently do not wish at present to press for evacuation if doing so will endanger this cordial atmosphere.
>
> You should leave all negotiations to Anders, in accordance with previous policy, and reply Panfilov by stating W.O. [War Office] regard this as purely Polish-Russian matter. . . .[126]

Still other aspects of these critical weeks remain obscure. Why, for instance, did Stalin wait nearly a month to respond to Churchill's "suggestion"—not, of course, by reopening recruitment but by offering the British the three existing divisions? Is it possible that he still hoped to use these three divisions on the Russian front, though they remained largely

---

[124] It would appear that the British showed excessive confidence in Anders; see especially C4437/19/55, FO 371/31082, and C5226/19/55, FO 371/31083, PRO. There is no way of knowing, of course, whether Hulls or British officers in the Middle East were privy to his real intentions. Concerning London's view of the likely course of the evacuation, see the last two documents cited in note 112 above.

[125] Concerning Sikorski's appeal, see C5889/19/55, FO 371/31083, PRO. Stalin's offer, as relayed through Molotov and Clark-Kerr, recalled only "that the Prime Minister [had said] in London that if there were in Russia any Polish soldiers over and above the needs of the Soviet Government, His Majesty's Government would be glad to take them over and to equip them for use in the Middle East." Molotov himself then mentioned the three existing divisions. C6553/19/55, FO 371/31084, PRO. See also *Documents*, 1:376-77; Raczyński, *W sojuszniczym Londynie*, p. 141; Kukiel, *Generał Sikorski*, p. 206; and Kot, *Listy z Rosji*, p. 49.

[126] C6263/19/55, FO 371/31084, PRO; see also C5008 and C5226/19/55, FO 371/31083, PRO.

unarmed? The evidence is inconclusive but intriguing.[127] It is also possible that he was waiting for a formal request for evacuation from Anders in order that the responsibility for breaking the July 1941 Polish-Soviet Agreement would fall on the Poles. It is probably no accident that the two written documents authorizing the final evacuation—a cable to Anders of July 8th and the evacuation agreement of July 31, 1942—make no mention of Churchill's earlier query, referring only to the Soviet government's decision to accede to "the request of the commander of the Polish Army in the USSR, General Anders . . ."[128]

A second point worth pondering is whether a connection existed—at least in Stalin's mind—between the disposition of the Polish troops and the abortive Anglo-American promise of a second front in 1942. In his letter to Stalin of July 18th, in which he accepted the proffered divisions, Churchill wrote in part: "If we do not get the Poles we should have to fill their places by drawing on preparations now going forward on a vast scale for [the] Anglo-American mass invasion of the Continent."[129] Whether his original query to Molotov was presented in these terms we do not know.[130] If so, it is quite likely that the Soviets thought they had extracted an important and face-saving concession in return for giving up the Poles, in which case they were understandably miffed when they came up empty-handed—neither with British recognition of their 1941 western boundaries (largely through Sikorski's efforts), nor with the much sought after second front. Even if the two issues were wholly unrelated, they were juxtaposed in a way that left an unfortunate impression. For it was in the same letter in which he accepted Stalin's offer of the three Polish divisions, which he now said he could arm "fully" in Palestine, that Churchill broke the news

[127] In response to Sikorski's mid-May inquiry concerning the reopening of recruitment, Stalin ever so vaguely hinted that, if the three existing divisions went to the front, further recruitment might be possible. See *Documents*, 1:351-52 and 355; also Sikorski's warning to his cabinet on May 19th, that talk of evacuation of the remaining divisions was hindering the resumption of recruitment (ibid., p. 598, n. 213). On June 16th, MacFarlane cabled from Moscow that Panfilov was now insisting that there would be no further evacuation *and* that British evacuation facilities at Pahlevi should be closed down; C6136/19/55, FO 371/31084, PRO.

[128] The first document is reprinted in Anders, *Army in Exile*, p. 112; the second in Kot, *Listy z Rosji*, pp. 514-20.

[129] *Correspondence*, 1:55. Concerning the Anglo-American promise of a second front in 1942, see Herbert Feis, *Churchill, Roosevelt, Stalin: The War They Waged and the Peace They Sought*, pp. 64-72.

[130] The phrasing of Stalin's offer suggests that it may have been: ". . . the Soviet Government have been watching with some concern developments in the military situation in Egypt. . . . While the Soviet Government are loathe to weaken their own front . . . , they are ready to place them at the disposal of His Majesty's Government in order to fill the gaps caused by recent severe fighting." C6553/19/55, FO 371/31084, PRO; see note 125 above.

not only that there would be no second front in 1942 but that, due to heavy losses, the North Sea supply convoys to Murmansk would be suspended indefinitely.[131] Worse still, this occurred at a point when the German offensive that was to culminate in the battle of Stalingrad was already in full swing. In effect, at the very time when Sikorski had anticipated the appearance on the Russian front of six or seven Polish divisions, as a symbol both of Polish independence and of a new spirit of Polish-Soviet cooperation, he found his army instead closely identified in Stalin's mind with the failure of the Western Allies to deliver on promises of military aid and relief.

On the other hand, however understandable his suspicions,[132] it is hard to avoid the conclusion that Stalin himself was more to blame for the departure of the Polish Army than either the Poles or the British: that for political reasons, and even at the cost of short-term military advantage,[133] he sought from the outset to limit the size and effectiveness of the army by confronting the Poles with an unending stream of obstacles; and that later, when his bargaining position vis-à-vis the Government-in-Exile had improved, he conspired in the army's withdrawal from the Soviet Union in circumstances which freed him of the obligations undertaken a year earlier with respect to that government. One need only compare the experience of this army with that of the second Polish force formed the following year under communist aegis. In the latter instance, the Soviets relaxed their hitherto rigidly enforced nationality policy, so that anyone from the former eastern provinces of Poland (now the Western Ukraine and Western Belorussia) who "felt" Polish could join the so-called Koś-

---

[131] *Correspondence*, 1:52-55. Churchill reproduced this letter in his memoirs, but did not discuss further the circumstances surrounding the evacuation of the Poles; *Hinge of Fate*, pp. 269-70.

[132] One of the more elusive interpretive problems in this whole story is the extent to which Stalin's persistent demands for a second front and massive military aid reflected unrealistic expectations, the failure of which to materialize nurtured his already deep-seated distrust of the West, and especially of Britain. (See, e.g., Ulam, *Expansion and Coexistence*, pp. 316-20.) Alternatively, to what extent did he know some of his demands were unrealistic but make them in a calculated move to keep the West on the defensive politically and thereby bolster his own bargaining position? In this particular instance, there is good reason to believe that, despite the undeniably critical situation on the eastern front and despite genuine disappointment over the delay in a second front, Stalin was fully aware the Allies had made no firm promise of a second European front in 1942 (Feis, *Churchill, Roosevelt, Stalin*, pp. 71-72) and that, in his elaborate public buildup of the Allied "promise," future political advantage was never far from Stalin's mind.

[133] It is worth recalling that, even at the most desperate stage of the battle of Moscow in the fall of 1941 (at a time when Stalin was asking for twenty-five to thirty British divisions), the Soviets still insisted on keeping five of their own divisions (presumably armed) in Iran—also for political reasons.

ciuszko Division. In addition, Poles previously conscripted into the Red Army were now allowed to transfer to the new Polish unit, something Stalin had consistently refused to do for Sikorski. Moreover, even with a trained officer corps and the massive armaments now readily supplied, the Poles were given six months (from April to October 1943) to bring their division to combat readiness, rather than the incredible six-week limit first imposed on Anders's army.[134]

Even now Sikorski tried to salvage what he could of his strategy. Citing the "unanimous view of the Polish Government that the Polish Army formed in Russia should remain there so as to take part in the fighting on the Eastern front"—as well as "the duty of the Polish Government to assist their citizens in Soviet Russia"—he appealed to the British to make their acceptance of Stalin's offer conditional on Moscow's agreement to a resumption of recruitment "until such time as the complete mobilization of all available men has been effected," the evacuation of auxiliary units of women and boy scouts as well as families of the soldiers, and preparations for the evacuation of an additional 50,000 Polish children. He also asked for "the collaboration of His Majesty's Government in the further search for Polish officers missing in Russia. . . . The matter is urgent as it is only in the short summer months that access is possible to the northern regions where these officers have presumably been removed."[135]

In the end, of course, Sikorski had little choice but to acquiesce in the decision to evacuate the last three divisions. As Kot later summed up the general's position:

> What alternative did the Polish Government have? If Stalin offered the British the assistance of the Polish divisions—of precisely those [divisions] for which the British had not yet managed to send arms to the USSR—and if the British were insisting on the participation of those divisions in the defense of the Near East—and these were the very British on whose intervention depended the amelioration of the situation of the Polish Army in the USSR—Sikorski could not in defiance of one side and the other maintain in Russia an army whose leader, in his haste to flee from Russia, had himself initiated the joint

[134] Werth, *Russia at War*, pp. 653-61. As early as May 1942, there were rumors of a secret "Soviet" Polish Army being formed in the Urals, as well as reports of a concerted anti-Polish and anti-British propaganda campaign among the rank and file of the official Polish Army. See C6014/19/55, FO 371/31083, and C2482/258/55, FO 371/34565, PRO.

[135] See Sikorski's letter to Churchill of July 2nd, and the Polish Government memorandum of the 3rd. C6533 and C6746/19/55, FO 371/31084, PRO; the latter is also in *Documents*, 1:377-78. Sikorski's letter had the effect of delaying outright acceptance of Stalin's offer. For the Soviet rejection of his conditions, especially those regarding a resumption of recruitment and the missing Polish officers, see C6829/19/55, FO 371/31084, PRO.

Soviet-British pressure and had pulled the rug from under his Commander-in-Chief.[136]

From a human standpoint, Sikorski could take some comfort from the fact that the army's evacuation meant the rescue from detention, deprivation, and possible starvation of more than 100,000 Poles. But it also marked the beginning of the end for his strategy of rapprochement. The repercussions of the army's departure were much as he had predicted the previous December. Almost overnight Soviet authorities closed down the entire civilian relief network, while political relations deteriorated steadily, as we shall see, reaching the breaking point even before the grim discovery at Katyń.

[136] Kot, *Listy z Rosji*, p. 49. Yet even Kot is said to have exclaimed following discovery of the graves at Katyń: "Fortune in misfortune that our army is no longer there!" Quoted in Kukiel, *Generał Sikorski*, p. 205.

X · *Boundary Politics:*
East versus West

THE READER will undoubtedly recall a point that was stressed on several occasions in Part II: that Sikorski's vision of Poland's postwar western boundary evolved quite independently of his ideas concerning the eastern boundary. Whereas in the west his primary consideration was securing the strategic and economic prerequisites for Poland's security and independence in federation with Czechoslovakia, his gradual acceptance of concessions in the east was a product of necessity, stemming from his conviction that reconciliation with Russia was more important to his country's future security than retention of the Riga line. To the extent that he saw territorial gains on the one side as compensation for losses on the other, this was decidedly a secondary consideration.

Yet it was inevitable that at the practical political level the two would be linked, and therefore that Sikorski too would have to bargain in these terms: that he would try to use concessions in the east to win commitments of "real guarantees" in the west; and that, in the absence of such commitments, he would hold fast to a public stance of defending Poland's territorial integrity within her 1939 frontiers. Not only was this good diplomatic strategy; it was essential from the standpoint of internal Polish politics, where the only hope—and that even a faint one—of gaining acceptance for a territorial compromise in the east was a firm promise of substantial gains in the west. Moreover, if Poland were not to be held hostage later to East-West competition for Germany's allegiance, it was also essential that any such arrangement be part of an overall Allied peace plan, including a common approach to the postwar treatment of Germany. Thus, in tracing the fate of Sikorski's territorial program, the critical question becomes not merely how one or another aspect of that program was received in this or that capital, but whether or not he was ever confronted with a definitive quid pro quo which, at the very least, he could reasonably expect would be acceptable to all three Great Powers.

DID STALIN REALLY OFFER AN ODER LINE?

One of the key arguments used by those inclined to discredit Sikorski's sincerity in seeking a rapprochement with the Soviet Union is the allegation that he was in fact offered just such a quid pro quo by none other than Stalin, but that he turned it down in favor of maintaining a rigid stand on the Riga line. The most elaborate and far-reaching version of this theory has appeared in the writings of the Polish historian, Włodzimierz Kowalski. In brief, it is Kowalski's contention that during their December 1941 talks Stalin offered Sikorski a western boundary on the Oder River, that his offer stood for more than a year, until January of 1943, and, therefore, that it "strengthened Sikorski's position in negotiations with London and Washington and gave him greater freedom of maneuver." Rather than "take advantage of this possibility," however, Kowalski argues that the Polish exile leader "went in the exact opposite direction after the Moscow visit, . . . concentrat[ing] on the recovery of Poland's prewar boundaries in the east . . . in accordance with the policy traditions of the pre-September governments."[1]

A former official of the Polish Foreign Ministry, W. W. Kulski, argued along similar lines in a 1947 article in *Foreign Affairs*, "The Lost Opportunity for Russian-Polish Friendship."[2] Though less specific in his assertions, especially about Stalin's views on Poland's future boundary in the west, Kulski wrote that in 1942, following Sikorski's Moscow visit, Soviet representatives (presumably in London) told the Poles that they "would support any degree of compensation" at Germany's expense in exchange for a territorial settlement in the east. Moreover—something that for obvious reasons Kowalski does not mention—Kulski claimed that the Soviets were willing, at least at that time, to settle for a compromise between the Riga and Curzon lines, very likely including an exchange of populations that would leave Lwów to the Poles. Stalin's motive, he reasoned, was a fear of Ukrainian separatist tendencies rather than a quest for additional territory. "But," he continued, "General Sikorski did not dare take on himself the responsibility for renouncing the Riga frontier and challenging the opposition of a large section of Polish opinion. . . . [He] perhaps missed a great opportunity."[3]

---

[1] Kowalski, *Walka dyplomatyczna*, pp. 225-32; the quoted passage is repeated verbatim from his earlier book, *ZSRR a granica*, pp. 33-37. More or less similar interpretations of Sikorski's territorial policy appear in Orzechowski, *Odra-Nysa-Bałtyk*, and Stanisław Zabiełło, *O rząd i granice: Walka dyplomatyczna o sprawę Polski w II wojnie światowej.* Kowalski contends that Stalin "withdrew" his offer of a boundary understanding only in January 1943, following Sikorski's last trip to Washington and after the "earlier breaking of the Polish-Soviet agreements by the émigré government." As evidence for this assertion, he cites only the Soviet note of January 16, 1943, withdrawing recognition of the Polish citizenship of ethnic Poles from the former eastern provinces. See *ZSRR a granica*, p. 69.

[2] Pp. 667-84.

[3] Ibid., pp. 676-79; Kulski cited no sources for these and other assertions but, during the period in question, he held the rank of counselor in the Polish Embassy in London. His statement here, however, is all the more curious in that, while he probably was not apprised

The single most important source for the argument that Stalin proposed a clear-cut territorial quid pro quo to the Poles at this early date—indeed, the sole source for the claim that he offered Sikorski a boundary on the Oder—is the general himself, a fact that offhand would seem to lend credibility to Kowalski's thesis. Specifically, the source in question is the official Polish record of a conversation between the Polish and British prime ministers on January 31, 1942, during which the former reported on his Moscow meetings. The record reads in part:

> . . . Stalin . . . was a man who, having spent a few years in Poland, was convinced that Poland's existence was essential for Russia as a rampart against Germany. He declared to General Sikorski that Poland must arise larger and stronger than before, that *East Prussia must belong to Poland, that the Polish Western boundaries must be based on the river Oder*. Stalin's tendency to push Poland to the West was obvious.[4]

On careful analysis, however, other materials relating both to the Moscow visit and to the events immediately following fail to substantiate either Sikorski's statement to Churchill or Kowalski's argument based on that statement. On the contrary, they raise serious questions not only as to whether Stalin proposed a territorial shift in such specific terms as implied above but, more importantly, as to how confidently the general could rely on Stalin's "offer," however vague or specific, in pursuing his own territorial strategy.

The obvious place to begin looking for corroborating evidence is in the official records of the Sikorski-Stalin talks. As we saw in the previous chapter, the Polish protocol indicates that virtually the entire formal negotiating session of December 3rd was devoted to problems connected with the Polish Army and civilian deportees in Russia.[5] The minutes of this session appear to be inordinately detailed; yet there is not a syllable in them about Poland's boundaries, east or west (although Sikorski's later

---

of the full extent of Sikorski's territorial program, he was one of two Foreign Ministry officials (the other was Raczyński) who, during the Anglo-Soviet negotiations in the spring of 1942, unsuccessfully presented Sikorski's pleas for recognition of the principle of territorial compensation as a means of making more palatable Britain's expected acceptance of Soviet territorial claims. For Kulski's role here, see C4072/19/55, FO 371/31082, and C4789/19/55, FO 371/31083, PRO; see also Chapter VI, note 32, above.

[4] *Documents*, 1:274 [emphasis added]. Kowalski quotes this passage in such a way that the underscored part appears to be a direct quote from Stalin instead of Sikorski's report of what Stalin said; see *Walka dyplomatyczna*, p. 225, and *ZSRR a granica*, pp. 33-34.

[5] See pp. 218-22 above. Soviet sources say little about the talks, making no mention at all of boundary matters. See *Istoriia Pol'shi*, 3:566-67; and *Istoriia Velikoi Otechestvennoi Voiny Sovetskogo Soiuza, 1941-1945*, 2:201-203. For further comment on Soviet sources, see the Bibliographical Essay.

statement to Churchill implied that it was during this session that Stalin suggested the Oder and showed an "obvious . . . tendency to push Poland to the West").

The Polish version of the banquet exchanges the following day, however, is more interesting.[6] Here, indeed, Stalin is reported as having delivered "a long and important speech, very friendly to Poland. He emphasized that Poland should be big and strong, stronger than ever before." And he is quoted as saying: " 'We have fought each other continually [in the past]. It is about time to finish this brawl.' " But there is not a shred of evidence here that he offered to support Polish acquisition of any specific territory—even East Prussia or the Oppeln district, to say nothing of the lands up to the Oder. Indeed, it seems unlikely that he would have left a serious proposal of this nature to a ceremonial occasion. On the question of the eastern frontier, on the other hand, it does appear that Stalin indicated a willingness to bargain, especially over Lwów:

> Stalin: We shall not quarrel because of frontiers.
> Gen. S[ikorski]: Have you not said yourself that Lwów is a Polish town?
> Stalin: Yes, but you will have a dispute about it, not with us but with the Ukrainians. . . . Jointly with you we shall destroy them in [the] future. We shall finish with them once and for all.

It was at this point that Stalin suggested: "We should settle our common frontiers between ourselves. . . . Don't worry, we will not harm you"—adding, according to some accounts, we want only a "tiny bit" (*chut'-chut'*).[7] But again there is no indication that he in any way related this to the question of Poland's western boundary.

This impression of Stalin's comments as being friendly, even hinting at the possibility of expansion to the west, yet deliberately nonspecific, is confirmed in another firsthand account of the banquet by the veteran Polish journalist, Ksawery Pruszyński, who attended in his capacity as embassy press officer.[8] His account includes the following description of Stalin's lengthy toast to Sikorski:

---

[6] The official Polish record of the banquet conversation appears in *Documents*, 1:244-46.

[7] Sikorski repeated the Russian phrase some months later to Eden; ibid., p. 365. See also Rozek, *Allied Wartime Diplomacy*, p. 94; Kukiel, *General Sikorski*, p. 188; and Mikołajczyk, *The Pattern of Soviet Domination*, pp. 24-25.

[8] Pruszyński has described the event in his book, published under the partially anglicized name, Xavier Pruszyński, *Russian Year: The Notebook of an Amateur Diplomat*, pp. 104-23. He writes that, during the pre-dinner conversations, Stalin showed little interest in Kot's query about the postwar disposition of the Lusatian Serbs (a small group located just west of the Lusatian Neisse), but did refer to East Prussia in an historical context. Pruszyński was called away and did not hear the conclusion of the discussion, but he indicates that Sikorski was elsewhere at the time.

The climax of the evening was, of course, Stalin's speech. . . . Stalin is a peculiar speaker with a method of his own. He asked questions and proceeded to answer them, he used picturesque examples and anecdotes. He talked like a teacher, who partly instructs his class and partly hints at certain conclusions. He dealt with the relations between Poland and Russia. There were—he said—many quarrels, conflicts and mutual claims. There was a time when the Poles held Moscow; then the Russians took Warsaw.

Stalin then related an incident from which, years before, he had learned firsthand the intensity of Polish resentment of Russia. Pruszyński's account continues:

"I understood," Stalin concluded his toast, "Lenin's lesson of knowledge of other nations' susceptibilities and of respect for them. That is why I drink this toast to General Sikorski and his party, our guests, to their prosperity, to the honour of the famous Polish army and the liberation of Poland from enemy hands. Poland will rise after this war greater than ever."

Pruszyński himself was an early advocate of Poland's westward shift and in all likelihood would have made careful note of more specific comments had they been made.[9]

A letter from Sikorski to Churchill, written from Teheran on December 17, 1941, and reporting on the just-concluded Moscow talks, provides a second basis for comparison—and several more illuminating discrepancies.[10] The bulk of the letter was devoted to the two topics that dominated the talks: the plight of the Polish civilian population and the formation of a Polish Army in Russia. Political issues were treated only briefly and in the most general terms. On the vital matter of Polish-Soviet relations, Sikorski merely conveyed his "impression that Stalin himself and the Soviet peoples in general are sincere in desiring the Polish-Soviet rapprochement," noting that the joint declaration issued at the conclusion of the talks "declares equality of status as between Poland and the Soviet Union." On Soviet attitudes toward the future of Germany, he reported:

Apart from condemning Germany—Hitler's Germany—Stalin told me he was strongly in favor of permanently reducing the power of Germany whatever its form of political Government and he added he put no trust even in so-called German Communists. . . .

[9] Pruszyński's first article advocating a return to the Oder and Neisse appeared only a few months later, in April 1942, in London. See Mitkiewicz, *Z gen. Sikorskim*, pp. 262-63; also pp. 267-68 below.

[10] *Documents*, 1:254-57.

Then, citing the reactions of other diplomats in Russia, he expressed "a reasonable assurance that for the time being Stalin has abandoned the idea of universal communism and the international policy of the Comintern." Sikorski concluded the letter with a restatement of the importance of Poland's military role in the Allied effort and a plea that Poland be added to the Supreme War Council.

Taken as a whole, this letter appears to be a fairly accurate reflection of the tone and substance of the Sikorski-Stalin talks (though it does gloss over several sticky points). However, it is strikingly at odds on at least two counts with Sikorski's verbal report to Churchill on January 31st. First, nowhere in this letter is there any mention of boundaries—either of Soviet territorial demands in the east or of the Polish-German frontier in the west, much less of an offer by Stalin to extend Poland westward to the Oder. Second, at the later meeting with Churchill, Sikorski explicitly contradicted his earlier assessment of Soviet policy. Where in the December 17th letter he concluded that Stalin had "for the time being . . . abandoned the idea of universal communism and the international policy of the Comintern," a bare six weeks later he told Churchill that he was "convinced that Stalin, as a staunch Communist and first disciple of Lenin, would tend to introduce communism in Europe from Norway to Greece."[11]

Still another basis for comparison (one almost completely ignored by Kowalski) is Sikorski's report to his Council of Ministers on his return from Moscow.[12] This report is the more interesting because it fell on January 12th, midway between his letter to Churchill and their meeting on January 31st. Because of its confidential nature, moreover, it is probably the most accurate reflection we have in the prime minister's own words of the status of Poland's boundary crisis at this critical juncture. (Although, as we shall see, he was not entirely candid even with his cabinet.) The relevant portion of the report opens with a cautiously optimistic assessment of the change wrought in Polish-Soviet relations by Hitler's attack on Russia: "The Russo-German war, so much desired by Poland, did not put us in a difficult international position. . . . It was quite clear to us that in joining the camp of fighting democracies Russia was bound to review her

[11] Ibid., p. 275.

[12] Ibid., pp. 264-66. Of this entire report, Kowalski quotes, actually misquotes, only a single phrase toward the end where Sikorski said that the "Polish-Russian frontier must remain . . . a frontier of Western and Christian civilization." Kowalski uses this to substantiate his argument that Sikorski rejected out of hand the notion of shifting Poland to the west, and ignores the overwhelming bulk of the report implying just such a shift. (Actually Sikorski was speaking here of his opposition to Pan-Slavist tendencies, not in defense of a specific border.) See *ZSRR a granica*, p. 37, and *Walka dyplomatyczna*, p. 232; the source is not identified in the latter.

previous attitude toward Poland." Turning then to the boundary question, he spoke first of prospects in the west:

> We do not know what kind of Poland will emerge from this war. It will depend on the precise balance of forces in the ultimate stage of the war. We hope that it will be to our advantage, and that the Polish State will expand its western frontiers. It is history that pushes us in this direction, providing us with a unique occasion for putting right old wrongs and mistakes and enabling us to reinforce our strategic position in the West, to stem the perennial German drive to the East and to force it back. We shall have to do our utmost in this period in order to lay a firm foundation for a strong Poland, a Poland that will be able to face Germany, by regaining old Slav territories, with wide access to the sea, and secure from the military point of view.

Three aspects of this passage are worth noting: First, although Sikorski did not name the Oder as a possible frontier and although he did not further define his phrase "old Slav territories," it is amply clear from the context that he was thinking in terms of territorial gains going substantially beyond the old "plebiscite areas" which alone would only partially solve the problems of Poland's military security and access to the sea. Second, he made absolutely no attempt to attribute this idea to Stalin; rather he spoke in terms of Poland's historic rights and strategic requirements. Third, it is significant that he referred to "a unique occasion" for correcting not only "old wrongs," by which he undoubtedly meant German encroachments upon Poland, but also "mistakes"—a term that would seem to imply criticism of Poland's eastward orientation and past neglect of her western flank. This interpretation is strengthened by the next passage of the report, in which he cautiously advanced the possibility of a compromise on the eastern boundary:

> In the East we know only those frontiers within which Poland entered the war, the frontiers established by way of compromise with Russia. It would be a great mistake to allow any *official* discussion on this subject, and to accept any suggestion that our frontiers are in a state of fluidity. The situation is *not yet ripe* for any such discussion. [Emphasis added.]

Only here did Sikorski refer to Stalin's willingness to bargain over boundaries, and in general terms that more closely reflect accounts of the banquet scene than his later statement to Churchill:

> Stalin proposed to me a conversation of this nature. He told me of Soviet good will in this direction, and of the assistance which Russia

was ready to give us in our disputes with the Ukrainians in the matter of the Polish city of Lwów. He told me of the need to bargain with Russia. He mentioned Poland's mission in the West, and the prospects of her expansion at Germany's cost. I declined these proposals, politely but firmly. Stalin acquiesced, announcing that he would return to the subject at a moment more favorable for us, that is to say, when the Polish Army will begin to fight on the Western front. . . .[13]

One final point of comparison is the Foreign Office record of Sikorski's January 19th meeting with Eden, at which the general recounted his talks with Stalin. Although here he reported that Stalin did mention East Prussia, in other respects this version tends to confirm both his confidential report to his government and accounts of the banquet:

General Sikorski told the Secretary of State that the question of the post-war Polish-Soviet frontiers had not been discussed with Stalin during their official conversations. On a private occasion, however, Stalin had suggested that the Soviet and Polish Governments *might reach an understanding on this subject in advance of the peace settlement without reference to H[is] M[ajesty's] Government.* Stalin said that he was in favour of a strong Poland; that *he would not be difficult about the eastern frontier, and that he thought that East Prussia should be Polish.* He contemplated that Lwów should again become part of Poland and suggested that the trouble there would be the Ukrainians. . . .

General Sikorski said that his answer to Stalin's approach had been that he could not discuss these territorial matters at present, and that he must continue to collaborate with H.M. Government, who had been entirely loyal to the Polish Government. In any event, it was rather early to talk about East Prussia since the Soviet Government were not yet in a position to deliver it to Poland.

[13] The reference to the "Western front" here obviously means the Soviets' western front; in the full Foreign Office text, it is translated as "eastern front." (This latter version contains no passages on boundary questions not included in the excerpts in *Documents*; see C795/19/55, FO 371/31077, PRO.) Sikorski was not entirely candid here concerning the eastern boundary. For, in the next breath he declared: "On the strength of authoritative information I know that the question [of Poland's boundaries] was not discussed with Mr. Eden during his stay in Moscow." In fact, by this time Sikorski knew all too well that the exact opposite was true, and that Stalin had told Eden he wanted a future Polish-Soviet boundary based on the Curzon line. His purpose in denying that Poland's boundaries had been a subject of discussion during the Eden-Stalin talks was apparently more to soften the blow that he knew was coming than simply to mislead his cabinet. For he added: "[The question] will, nevertheless, be reopened in a few weeks' time during Molotov's stay in London, and we must be duly prepared for this contingency."

> Stalin's response to this had been to suggest that these matters *might be reopened when the General returned again to the Soviet Union, say in about six months' time. By that time the Polish army would no doubt be reconstituted and in action.*[14]

The reference to East Prussia here is interesting, but raises more questions than it answers. Most importantly, if Stalin had in fact made a firm offer of East Prussia, why did Sikorski report it only to Eden and not, even in confidence, to his own Council of Ministers? By this time, of course, he knew very well that East Prussia's possible cession to Poland had been discussed during Eden's visit to Moscow (although probably not that Stalin had demanded the northern part of the province). He may well have been trying to probe the British reaction to this idea, just as he was obviously at pains to impress on the foreign secretary his own loyalty to Anglo-American strictures against discussion of a postwar territorial settlement.[15]

Accounts of the Eden-Stalin talks only partially dispel the confusion. For, while the Soviet dictator did mention both East Prussia and the Oder to his British guest, his reference to the latter was distinctly more casual and was not included in the territorial provisions to which Eden was being asked to agree. According to the detailed minutes of their first meeting on December 16th,[16] Stalin proposed that a secret protocol spelling out postwar territorial changes be appended to the Anglo-Soviet treaty. First among the suggested changes was that:

> The boundary of Poland should be extended at the expense of Germany so as to get rid of the Corridor by the transfer of East Prussia to Poland. The portion of Germany containing Tilsit and to the north of the Niemen River should be added to the Lithuanian Republic of the U.S.S.R.

[14] C794/19/55, FO 371/31077, PRO [emphasis added].

[15] In response Eden confirmed that Stalin had said "that he thought East Prussia should go to Poland," and "that he himself was inclined to agree, but that he could not of course speak for H.M. Government." Ibid. Sikorski's desire to hold the British and Americans to *their* policy of postponing territorial questions is especially evident in his report to the Council of Ministers: "I declined [Stalin's] proposal politely, stressing the loyal attitude of our British Ally and emphasizing the value of allied solidarity for all of us, including Russia. This line was maintained during my stay in Russia, and His Majesty's Ambassador and the United States' Chargé d'Affaires in Moscow were duly informed of it. Great Britain and the United States must now maintain this solidarity." Then he added: "In spite of intense German propaganda on that matter, I do not believe that Mr. Eden would sacrifice Poland and recognize Russia's exclusive role in Eastern Europe. . . ." *Documents*, 1:265.

[16] "Mr. Eden's Visit to Moscow, Memorandum by the Secretary of State for Foreign Affairs," W.P. (42)8, CAB 66/20, PRO; detailed minutes of the negotiating sessions, as well as texts of various draft agreements are appended to Eden's summary report, dated January 5, 1942.

Only later, in the course of discussing East Prussia and the Soviet demand for the area around Tilsit, did the subject of the Oder come up, and in a manner suggesting that Stalin had *not* discussed specifics with Sikorski:

> Mr. Eden: Did you say anything about this to the Poles?
> Mr. Stalin: No, but you can tell them it will be necessary. Up as far as the river Oder could be given to Poland and then the rest left for a Berlin state.[17]

Moreover, Stalin's intentions with respect to the Polish-Soviet boundary were, as Eden later described them, "starkly definite."[18] Whatever he had allowed Sikorski to conclude less than two weeks earlier concerning the possibility of a compromise settlement, the record here makes it unmistakably clear that he was seeking immediate British recognition of the Curzon line. And, as with his views on East Prussia, this was among his formal proposals for the secret protocol:

> As to the frontiers of the Soviet Union we should like to see the frontier in Finland and the Baltic Provinces restored to its position in 1941, immediately before the outbreak of war. So far as the frontier with Poland is concerned the Curzon Line should form the basis for this with perhaps some slight variation one way or the other.
> The Roumanian frontier should be so formed as to include Bessarabia and Northern Bukovina in the Soviet Union.[19]

Nor did the fact that Stalin later agreed not to insist on including the Polish sector of the Soviet Union's western boundary in the proposed treaty imply any retreat from this position. "The Polish frontier remains an open question," he said the following day, "and I do not insist upon settling that now. . . . I hope that we shall be able to come to an agreement between the three of us [the Soviet Union, Poland, and Britain]. Generally speaking our idea is to keep to the Curzon Line with certain modifications." This was the position that was reported back to the Poles by Ambassador Cripps.[20]

[17] Eden did not respond directly to the Oder suggestion but did indicate his reservations about "cutting up Germany," noting "you may cause an irredentist movement to unite the country again, rather like the *Anschluss*."

[18] Eden, *The Reckoning*, p. 335.

[19] See note 16 above.

[20] Early in January, just before his final departure for London, Cripps told Kot that "Russia is figuring on the Curzon line, [but] for this is ready to grant Poland the most far-reaching [gains] from a dismembered Germany." Kot, *Listy z Rosji*, p. 241. Later that month he met with Sikorski directly. According to the Polish note of the meeting, Cripps "thought that Russia would present rather far-reaching demands" in the east. "In unofficial [sic] Russian circles the 'Curzon line' had even been mentioned." In the west, however, "Russia was

Writing about these meetings later, Eden did not distinguish between those demands to which the British government was being asked to subscribe and more casual offhand comments such as Stalin's mention of the Oder.[21] At the time, however, he appears to have taken little note of the Oder reference; for, in his initial report to Churchill, he wrote only that Stalin had "proposed that East Prussia should be transferred to Poland," with no mention of any suggested changes in Poland's western boundary.[22] This more limited version is also the one reflected in the American diplomatic papers.[23]

WHAT conclusions can we draw from these various reports surrounding Stalin's alleged offer of an Oder boundary to Sikorski? Perhaps the one thing that can be said with complete confidence is that it is possible to speak only in terms of probabilities rather than certainties. The first such probability—one that applies to Sikorski's as well as to Eden's visit—is that Stalin was both probing the intentions of the other side and hinting at the shape and dimensions of his own preferences, but all without committing himself to any specific settlement. (This is, of course, the same posture he was to adopt nearly two years later at Teheran.)[24] In addition, the weight of evidence suggests that Stalin was willing to be considerably more candid and expansive in his probings and hints with the British foreign secretary than with the Polish prime minister. Eden himself apparently came away with the impression that Stalin was unwilling to make any direct promise to the Poles, even of East Prussia. As late as March 1943, he told President Roosevelt, "the Russians agree privately with this [that Poland should have East Prussia] but are not willing to tell this to the Poles because they want to use it as a bargaining instrument at the Peace Table."[25] Thus, while we cannot discount entirely the possibility that Stalin men-

---

willing to extend Poland's frontiers at the expense of Germany, and above all to annex East Prussia to Poland." "Sir Stafford thought," the note continues, "that Stalin genuinely believed in the necessity of a strong Poland to serve as a rampart against Germany. But he would like the expansion of Poland to be effected at the expense of Germany only." *Documents*, 1:271.

[21] Eden, *The Reckoning*, pp. 335-38.

[22] Churchill, *The Grand Alliance*, pp. 628-29. A few months later, when the Foreign Office turned to detailed consideration of Stalin's territorial proposals, his reference to the Oder was passed over in total silence; see N2182/5/38, FO 371/32880, PRO.

[23] The American ambassador to Britain, John Winant, was allowed to review Eden's cables from Moscow and his summary report to the War Cabinet—but apparently not the detailed minutes (see note 16 above). See Winant's report to Hull and Roosevelt of January 19, 1942, in *FRUS, 1942*, 3:494-503 (especially 499-500).

[24] See especially Bohlen, *Witness to History*, p. 143; and Churchill, *Closing the Ring*, pp. 361-62 and 394-97.

[25] Sherwood, *Roosevelt and Hopkins*, p. 710.

tioned the Oder at some point during his conversations with Sikorski, there is no reasonable basis for concluding that the one actually offered the other an Oder boundary or, for that matter, that *any* specific territorial deal was posed.

In a more positive vein, what does seem likely is that Sikorski understood Stalin's probings and gestures of cordiality as an invitation to bargain—as an indication that Stalin was amenable not only to compensation in the west for Poland, but also to a compromise settlement in the east (more or less along the lines Kulski suggested). Moreover, despite his refusal to dicker over boundaries then and there and despite his later disclaimer to his cabinet ("the situation is not yet ripe for any such discussion"), it is apparent that he returned to London determined to accept Stalin's invitation. This was after all an important opening for his strategy, the first indication on the part of any Great Power of a willingness to see Poland expanded to the west and, by the same token, to see Germany permanently weakened.[26]

Furthermore, we know from evidence already detailed in Chapter VI that, immediately on his return from Moscow, Sikorski began to discuss with his closest aides the probable adjustments that would have to be made in Poland's eastern posture. It was at this point, for instance, that he dropped his plan to include all three Baltic States in the proposed federation and began speaking instead only of Lithuania. It was then also that he reportedly sketched for several aides the approximate course of the boundary he thought Poland would have to accept in the east—one that foresaw the loss of nearly half the area in question to the Soviets as well as the cession of Wilno to Lithuania, while salvaging Lwów through a disentanglement of the Polish and Ukrainian populations. We know, too, that during this same period he returned to the development of his own western boundary and federation programs in preparation for his second trip to the United States. In other words, contrary to Kowalski's contention—that Sikorski rejected Stalin's "offer" but instead "went in the exact opposite direction after the Moscow visit, . . . concentrat[ing] on the recovery of Poland's prewar boundaries in the east . . . in accordance with the policy traditions of the pre-September governments"[27]—the circumstantial evidence points

[26] Strumph-Wojtkiewicz (*Siła złego*, p. 178) claims that Sikorski later told him he had made a mistake in not settling the boundary question in Moscow. Whatever the truth of this contention, we do know that Sikorski had planned to return to Moscow by December 12th for another meeting with Stalin, following his inspection tour of the Polish Army camps, at which he presumably wanted to discuss still unresolved issues. But illness delayed his schedule, and he decided it might be awkward to be in Moscow just as Foreign Secretary Eden was arriving for his talks with Stalin. Kot, *Listy z Rosji*, pp. 208-209; and C13728/3226/55, FO 371/26763, PRO.

[27] See note 1 above.

strongly to the conclusion that he was preparing in all seriousness both to seek a genuine compromise with Moscow on the eastern boundary and to take advantage of the opening that Stalin's apparent flexibility gave him in his dealings with the West.

What Sikorski undoubtedly was not prepared for were the results of Eden's talks in Moscow—and not only because Stalin had demanded a treaty recognizing the Soviet Union's western borders as of June 22, 1941. Equally disturbing was the apparent inclination first of Eden and Cripps, and later of Churchill himself, to view the Soviet claims as reasonable and to see Allied recognition of them as essential to "full cooperation in the war effort."[28] The fact that Stalin had stated he would not insist on including the boundary with Poland in the proposed treaty could be of scant comfort to the Poles. Not only would recognition of other Soviet conquests in Finland, the Baltic States, and Rumania set a dangerous precedent; it would leave the Polish east as an exposed enclave in Soviet territory and foreclose completely the possibility of settling the Wilno question through Lithuania's inclusion in a federation.

In addition, Cripps's statements concerning Soviet insistence on a boundary approximating the Curzon line—and his warning that the Poles should seek immediate American support for their claim to Lwów and Wilno "because Russia will press for a quick settlement"[29]—seemed to negate the understanding Sikorski thought he had reached with Stalin. Whether because of the improved military situation on the Moscow front or because his British guests, despite disclaimers, had betrayed their disposition to accept Soviet demands—or whether Stalin's apparent cordiality toward Sikorski had simply been an act—clearly the latter could no longer assume that the Soviet dictator was willing to strike a genuine compromise on the eastern boundary,[30] or that he would wait as promised for the Polish Army to reach the front before forcing a decision. Moreover, if Stalin could reverse himself almost overnight on these matters, then how much stock could the Poles place in his vague, if sweeping, references to Poland arising "big and strong, stronger than ever before" at Germany's expense? (One

[28] *FRUS, 1942*, 3:491-92. Kot cabled London on January 6th that Cripps, "despite all his criticism of Russia," did not think England "could resist Russia's demand." *Listy z Rosji*, p. 255.

[29] Kot, *Listy z Rosji*, p. 241 [cable of January 3, 1942]. A few days later, Kot cabled that Cripps considered Wilno a "hopeless" cause (p. 255).

[30] Sikorski's worst fears were confirmed in early January when the Soviets circulated a note to all diplomatic missions in Moscow, the ostensible purpose of which was to inform them of the German atrocities being committed in occupied areas, but which was also used as a vehicle to announce the Soviet claim to Lwów as a Ukrainian city. Ambassador Kot protested and in response was informed that the Foreign Commissariat deemed such protests unacceptable. *Documents*, 1:259-61 and 266-67.

failing of Kulski's contention that the Poles could have attained a compromise boundary in the east, leaving Lwów to Poland, is that he totally disregarded the pall cast by the Eden-Stalin talks on Sikorski's own Kremlin discussions. Kowalski, of course, does not—presumably cannot—even mention that the Soviets ever intimated they might accept such a compromise.)[31]

This reading of events is corroborated by contemporary accounts of a change in Sikorski's mood just after his arrival back in London on January 6th. (The general had left the Soviet Union on December 15th, following an inspection tour of the Polish camps, and had spent the next several weeks in the Middle East, in part for a rest as well as to inspect the Polish brigade already in operation there. As a result, he was unaware of the outcome of Eden's Moscow trip until his own return to London.) As Raczyński confided to his diary on January 11th:[32] "The General returned in a good and optimistic mood. Yet, from the very moment of his departure from Moscow, our horizon has darkened considerably." The Soviet "tone" toward the Polish embassy was "sharpening," with "almost daily" manifestations of their claim to Poland's eastern territories—developments that Raczyński attributed to the altered military situation (both the outbreak of war in the Pacific and the counteroffensive on the Russian front) as well as to Eden's Moscow sojourn. "In such an atmosphere," he continued:

> it is difficult to indulge one's optimism. I have devised a defensive tactic and am preparing to leave soon for the United States to draw that government into the action. Gen. Sikorski agrees with this plan and has asked me to prepare for his possible visit to the States.

[31] One other point that Kulski fails to mention is that Stalin never offered a compromise on Lwów to the Polish Communists, although he presumably had an interest in boosting their national image at home. Some indication of how sensitive the Lwów issue remains even today is a discussion in another book by Kowalski of negotiations between the Soviet government and the Polish Committee of National Liberation (the so-called "Lublin Committee") during July 1944, to fix the Polish-Soviet boundary. Kowalski writes that, on the basis of Soviet promises to consider corrections of the Curzon line in Poland's favor, the Polish representatives "sought to gain the most favorable shifts." However, he then discusses Polish demands for changes only along the East Prussian and Belorussian sectors of the boundary, without a word about Lwów. See Włodzimierz T. Kowalski, *Polityka zagraniczna RP, 1944-1947*, pp. 3-4 and 360-61, n. 7. The story widely circulated in Poland at the time was that Edward Osóbka-Morawski, then chairman of the Lublin Committee, had in fact raised the Lwów question and had been roundly rebuffed by Stalin. Later, during the January 1957 election campaign, Osóbka-Morawski, who was now trying for a political comeback, again raised the issue in a public campaign speech in Lublin, after which he was stricken overnight from the list of candidates. (This information comes from a conversation with Roman Szporluk, a resident of the Lublin area until 1958 and now Professor of History at the University of Michigan.)

[32] Raczyński, *W sojuszniczym Londynie*, pp. 128-29.

Similarly, as Mitkiewicz described the airport arrival: "General Sikorski looks marvelous—he is in a splendid humor, cracks jokes in abundance while greeting everyone."[33] Yet, two days later, following a briefing by Sikorski, he wrote:

> At the end of the conference, Gen. Sikorski repeated several times that news of the results of Stalin's talks with Eden should not be received with fear, for these are not definitive talks. The General added that, in March of this year, he will go to Washington for talks with President Roosevelt. *Our contest with Soviet Russia is at an extremely dangerous turn. If we do not bring about now—right away, immediately—the recognition of our boundaries by Great Britain and by the United States, then we will be plundered by Stalin.*[34]

This interpretation would also go far to explain the curious discrepancies already noted between Sikorski's rather sanguine assessment of Soviet policy in his December 17th letter to Churchill and the much more apprehensive tone of his remarks during their January 31st meeting. And this brings us back to our starting point; for it casts a rather different light on his statement to Churchill, during this same meeting, that Stalin had offered him a western boundary on the Oder. Was this really an accurate report of what Stalin had said to *him*? Or was it perhaps an embellishment of Stalin's less specific remarks, based on what he knew to have transpired with Eden?[35] Or—an even more intriguing possibility—was Sikorski taking

---

[33] Mitkiewicz, *Z gen. Sikorskim*, p. 194 [entry for January 7, 1942]. Later in this same entry (pp. 196-97), Mitkiewicz reported that he was receiving "unfavorable" news from "other sources"—from Moscow (presumably Kot) and from the Polish military attaché in Washington: "Soviet Russia is posing a categorical demand to receive all the Baltic states . . . , Bessarabia and Bukovina; and, as for the boundary with Poland, Stalin is calling for final talks in Moscow with Gen. Sikorski and for an understanding concluded between them. . . . I have the impression that the struggle with Soviet Russia over the former eastern border, and at least over Lwów and Wilno, has begun."

[34] Ibid., p. 199 [entry for January 9, 1942; emphasis added]. The reference here to the need for Western recognition of Poland's boundaries should not be interpreted as indicating a rigid stand on the 1939 eastern boundary, but more likely as a diplomatic maneuver; for it was in this same entry that Mitkiewicz wrote, "it is evident that [Sikorski] has accustomed himself to the thought that we will have to cede something to Russia in the east. . . . that he is thinking of defending Eastern Galicia with Lwów and the oil basin, at the possible cost of concessions in the rest of our East." See p. 128 above.

[35] When or through whom Sikorski might have learned of Stalin's reference to the Oder is not readily apparent from the record. Cripps's reports to Kot and Sikorski (see note 20 above) were suggestive but not specific, and it is most unlikely that Eden made any reference to it during his meeting with the general on January 19th (notes 14 and 15 above). In fact, during a weekend in Scotland shortly after Eden's return from Moscow, when Raczyński tried to sound him out concerning *British* views on Poland's future boundary in the west, Eden was evasive and the question of Stalin's views was not mentioned at all. (From personal

advantage of an occasion to probe Churchill's reaction to his own boundary concepts and to the very notion of a quid pro quo territorial exchange? There is probably some truth to both suppositions. (And, as we shall see later, he got a negative response.)

One final footnote to this rather complicated story: nowhere have I been able to find any evidence that the subject of an Oder line was raised again in Allied councils until the time of the Teheran Conference nearly two years later. It was, of course, raised by Sikorski in his December 1942 memoranda to the American and British governments and, in response to those memoranda, does begin to appear in *internal* Foreign Office papers early in 1943. But it is a virtual certainty that it did not come up for discussion among the Big Three during this time. As for Moscow's position, whatever Stalin meant by his casual reference to the Oder during his December 1941 talks with Eden, the reference was not repeated until Teheran. During his May/June 1942 visit to London, Foreign Minister Molotov told Eden only that Poland "ought to acquire East Prussia and perhaps a part of Upper Silesia," while the following March Ambassador Maisky apparently mentioned only East Prussia.[36] It is significant as well that even these limited positions were conveyed to the British and not to the Poles, although Molotov met with Sikorski on June 10th, shortly before returning to Moscow.[37]

---

correspondence with Raczyński, 1981.) On the other hand, the Polish notes of Sikorski's meeting with Ministers Bevin and Dalton on January 28th, just three days before his meeting with Churchill, do contain a passing mention of the Oder. According to the final draft of these notes, "General Sikorski declared that it would be megalomania to demand the cession to Poland of German lands up to the Oder . . . ." However, the original notes state only that he concurred with the opinion of his two British hosts to this effect. PRM 68/3, GSHI. In any event, it would appear that by this time, at least, he had learned of Stalin's reference to the Oder.

[36] The Molotov and Maisky statements, respectively, are reported in C5814/19/55, FO 371/31083, and N1605/499/38, FO 371/36991, PRO; both repeat Moscow's insistence on the Curzon line in the east. Polish documents contain a slightly different version of the first statement (as relayed by Eden to Sikorski) according to which Molotov "repeated Stalin's opinion that after the war Poland should be strong and should receive East Prussia and former Polish territories, lately in German possession, which were indispensable to Poland in the West." *Documents*, 1:365. On the basis of this "less precise" wording, the Polish historian Kowalski has argued that this actually represented an "enrichment" of Stalin's earlier offer of an Oder line because it added a "new element—the recovery of historical boundaries." *ZSRR a granica*, pp. 46-47. The most one can say for this explanation is that it requires a generous rendering of Molotov's remarks (as relayed by Eden) to conclude that by "lately in German possession" he was referring to lands lost by Poland before the fifteenth century, and not to pre-World War II Polish territories that had been reincorporated into the Reich. (This argument was not repeated in Kowalski's later study, *Walka dyplomatyczna*.)

[37] See Raczyński, *W sojuszniczym Londynie*, pp. 142-43; and pp. 296-97 below.

THE DOMESTIC CONNECTION

Even under more favorable circumstances—that is, even if the situation had not been aggravated by the threat of an Anglo-Soviet treaty legitimizing the Soviet Union's 1941 western boundary—two serious obstacles stood in the way of any attempt to take advantage of Stalin's supposed offer to Sikorski, however vague or specific, to grant Poland compensation in the west in exchange for a compromise settlement in the east. One—the steadfast refusal of the Western Allies, as symbolized by the Atlantic Charter, to consider such proposals during wartime—is the subject of the third section of this chapter. The other, and the subject of this section, was the domestic resistance—not only among Sikorski's opponents, but among many of his supporters as well—to concessions on the eastern boundary.

As mentioned earlier, the Oder-Neisse concept experienced a revival in popularity with the outbreak of World War II. Where in the interwar period westward expansion was strictly an Endek-sponsored idea with little real currency even in that movement, during the war it was espoused by groups of widely divergent political persuasions. Not all favored shifting the border as far west as the Oder and Lusatian Neisse, although this variant seems to have been especially prevalent in the Underground press. Some sought an Oder-Eastern Neisse line (i.e., including the Oppeln district but not most of Lower Silesia); still others, a straightening of the boundary to a line running through central Pomerania and Silesia. But there was almost no group that did not favor some correction of the Polish-German frontier, with minimum demands approximating those presented by the Polish National Committee to the Versailles Peace Conference in 1919: all of Upper Silesia (that is, the addition of the Oppeln district to prewar Polish Upper Silesia), Danzig, and at least the southern part of East Prussia, with the rest of the province removed from German control.

Had the issue been merely one of whether or how far Poland should expand to the west, it would hardly have been the source of great controversy that it became. Where the rending differences arose was in the connection between the eastern and western boundary questions and in the conflicting images of Poland's potential place in the European scheme. As it became clearer to all but the most out-of-touch that any meaningful gains in the west, if they were to be had at all, could be had only at the price of concessions in the east, all the emotionalism attached to the latter issue was transferred to the former. Adding to the confusion was the fact that many of those who advocated an Oder-Neisse line in the west were in reality no closer to Sikorski's overall conception of Poland's proper international posture—indeed, often more estranged—than those who favored only minimal boundary corrections. Farthest from the prime minister in spirit were those who combined a demand for the Oder and Neisse in the west with illusions of resurrecting in some form the old Polish-Lithuanian Commonwealth in the east. At the other extreme, some of those closest to Sikorski in their appreciation of the limits of Poland's power—including some key supporters in his cabinet—pulled back from urging a bolder program in the west for fear of jeopardizing their claim to the prewar boundary in the east.

Some examples may be useful to illustrate the wide range of positions. As might be expected, the earliest advocates of westward expansion in the Underground were to be found among the Nationalists. However, their early focus on a return to a "western orientation" and the "Piast idea" quickly yielded to renewed interest in the east with the outbreak of the Russo-German war, which they welcomed not as an opportunity for reconciliation with the Soviet Union, but because it would "bring disintegration and death to one side and the other." From the ensuing political vacuum would arise a "Greater Poland" stretching from the Oder and Lusatian Neisse in the west to the Smolensk Gate and the Dnieper in the east (although they retreated to the Riga line once a Soviet victory seemed inevitable). In accordance with the Nationalist tradition, this was to be a unitary state rather than a federation; indeed, they had no interest in federation with Czechoslovakia, viewed the Ukraine and Belorussia as a "no-man's land," and saw incorporation into Poland as the "only solution" to the problem of Lithuania and Wilno.[38] An offshoot of the National Party, publishing under the name *Rampart* (*Szaniec*), was somewhat more consistent in its western orientation. Favoring an Oder-Neisse boundary with an additional "defensive line" even further to the west, the group's basic thesis was that Poland arose in the west and there she must return; the "myth of the east" must not blind Poles to their destiny in the west. On the other hand, despite their relative realism toward Russia (they basically accepted the Riga line and did not foresee a breakup of the Soviet Union), the "Rampart" group adopted a neutral stance toward the war and did not exclude eastward expansion at some future time. In sum: "Toward the Saale [!] we must strive, toward the Dnieper maybe."[39]

By contrast, the two factions of the National Party in exile exhibited relative moderation. The more influential group, under National Council member Tadeusz Bielecki, spelled out its position only at the end of 1942:

---

[38] See Orzechowski, *Odra-Nysa-Bałtyk*, pp. 14-23; and Terej, *Rzeczywistość i polityka*, pp. 206-207 and 243-47. This was by no means the most extreme point of view found on the Nationalist right; see, e.g., the description of a Polish-dominated Slav Empire put forward by the group associated with Falangist Bolesław Piasecki, in Terej, *Rzeczywistość i polityka*, pp. 157-58, n. 110.

[39] Orzechowski, *Odra-Nysa-Bałtyk*, pp. 72-75.

Plebiscites were no longer an acceptable means of determining boundaries. For strategic reasons, Poland's boundary in the west must be based on the island of Rügen, the Oder and Lusatian Neisse rivers with further safeguards on the Baltic, the long-term occupation of areas to the west of this line, and the permanent disabling of Germany as a military power; in addition, the German population must be expelled from the incorporated areas. Despite the obvious similarities to Sikorski's territorial program in the west, Bielecki was a vociferous critic of the exile government for its territorial "minimalism" and its promotion of a Central European federation and Polish-Soviet reconciliation. While he warned his more exuberant colleagues that eastward expansion to the Dnieper had "weakened Poland internally" in the past, he also rejected any suggestion that the gains he desired in the west would necessitate concessions to the Soviet Union. A strong Poland was possible only with an increase in total territory, not a curtailment. And such a Poland was attainable only by "conducting policy in the truly grand style" of Dmowski.[40]

By far the most cautious and realistic branch of the Nationalist movement was the handful of mostly older moderates clustered around Marian Seyda, himself a former professor, newspaper publisher, member of the Polish National Committee in Paris during World War I, and minister in the exile government. They were also the only Endeks who openly supported and participated in the Sikorski government (for which they were denied recognition as official representatives of the National Party by the Underground leadership). Where Bielecki appealed to Dmowski's "grand style," Seyda appealed to his mentor's "realism," on which ground he urged that Poland restrict her demands in the west to the 1919 formula (of which he was a coauthor) together with a general "shortening and straightening" of the boundary with Germany. He considered an Oder-Neisse line wholly unrealistic, especially as these territories were "already completely germanized"; such a demand could only subject Poland to a "charge of imperialism" and "undercut the defense of the eastern boundary." On the other hand, he rejected a "two-enemy" stance and favored the "maintenance of as good relations as possible with Russia"—but only on the condition that the latter recognize the integrity of the Riga boundary. (Seyda, of course, was one of three ministers to resign from the Government-in-Exile in July 1941 in protest against Sikorski's signing of the Polish-Soviet Agreement, although unlike the other two he returned to the government six months later.)[41]

[40] Ibid., pp. 24-25; Tadeusz Bielecki, "Zagadnienie główne."

[41] Orzechowski, *Odra-Nysa-Bałtyk*, pp. 25-27. Other moderate Endeks who participated in the Sikorski government were Stanisław Stroński and Wacław Komarnicki; Stroński had left the party in 1938, while Komarnicki, like Seyda, was disowned upon entering the exile

Overall the Peasant and Labor Parties, both participants in the exile government, were far closer to Sikorski in their appreciation of Poland's relative international position and the need for a rapprochement with Moscow, and in their support for his federation program. Yet the general pattern of division between Underground and exile branches held true for these parties as well—with the former espousing more far-reaching positions, and in more uncompromising terms, than their counterparts in London. On the one hand, the conspiratorial wings of both parties viewed an Oder-Neisse boundary as essential to Poland's security in the west, but clung steadfastly to the Riga line as her minimum demand in the east. (Apparently, however, only occasional and isolated voices flirted with the hope of further eastward expansion or the collapse and disintegration of the Soviet Union.) On the other hand, their colleagues in exile were somewhat more cautious, adopting a position quite similar to Seyda's and for much the same reasons.[42]

The Socialist Party and the Sanacja exhibited a similar pattern of Underground/exile division, but with this important difference: in neither of these movements, generally speaking, did the subject of Poland's western boundary evoke the same degree of interest as in the other parties. The focal point of the Socialists in the Underground—who operated under the name *Wolność, Równość, Niepodległość* (WRN), or "Freedom, Equality, Independence"—was their plan for a "European Union of Free Peoples," a kind of United States of Europe composed of units whose political-administrative boundaries would approximate ethnic lines (although they also gave some weight to economic, strategic, and moral arguments). On this basis Poland should receive East Prussia with Danzig, the rest of Upper Silesia (Oppeln) and an additional slice of Pomerania in the northwest; Lusatia should become an autonomous state associated with Czechoslovakia. On the other hand, while eschewing "great power" slogans or schemes for eastward expansion, the WRN also opposed the "Soviet" program of "shifting Poland from east to west," proposing instead a reorganization of the Soviet Union into national states, or at least the separation from it of an independent Belorussia and Ukraine. By contrast, the Socialists in exile (who with few exceptions remained in opposition

government in early 1942. Confidence in Komarnicki's loyalty may have been misplaced, however; see Chapter XI, note 65, below. For a good discussion of the differences between Seyda and Bielecki, see Terej, *Rzeczywistość i polityka*, pp. 200-205.

[42] Orzechowski, *Odra-Nysa-Bałtyk*, pp. 28-34. Peasant Party participants in Sikorski's cabinet were Professor Stanisław Kot, later ambassador to the Soviet Union, and Stanisław Mikołajczyk, Sikorski's eventual successor as prime minister of the Government-in-Exile. Karol Popiel and General Józef Haller belonged to the Labor Party, successor to the earlier Christian Democratic Party.

to Sikorski's government)[43] displayed little interest in federations, whether continental or regional in scope. Adhering more closely to the later Piłsudski tradition, they stressed Poland's "position of separateness and independent role . . . in the east of Europe." Their territorial demands in the west were only vaguely formulated and seem to have approximated the 1919 demands, although later in the war they also asked for a zone of occupation between the new boundary and the Oder-Neisse line. In the east, they stood resolutely for a return to the Riga line, with the proviso that predominantly Belorussian and Ukrainian districts would be allowed internal autonomy. On the other hand, their concept of Polish-Soviet reconciliation appears to have been limited to the notion that neither side would put forward territorial demands against the other.[44]

Most unrelenting in its affirmation of the Jagiellonian conception was the Sanacja, although neither the Underground nor exile wing appears to have seriously advanced the vast claims in the east characteristic of some Nationalist programs. Their primary focus instead was on the retention of the Riga line as a minimum condition enabling Poland to assume "a preeminent role . . . in the new natural political arrangement," which variously took the form of a Central European federation under Poland's "primacy" or a more literal recreation of the old Jagiellonian Commonwealth—for which, of course, an indispensable condition was the disintegration of the Soviet Union and the creation of an independent Belorussia and Ukraine. This does not mean they disclaimed interest in the west. On the contrary, in the conspiratorial wing in particular demands ranged from a general straightening of the border with Germany to the Oder-Neisse, but always in the context of guaranteeing Poland the power "commensurate with our historic role." Exile spokesmen of the Sanacja, however, put forward only the most minimal claims, and these only on condition that the status quo in the east was maintained.[45]

THE IRONY of Sikorski's dilemma can scarcely be overstated. On the one hand, the great majority of those who advocated an Oder-Neisse boundary in the west rejected out of hand any suggestion that the price of such substantial gains on one side might be losses on the other—indeed, the

---

[43] The Socialist contingent in the government consisted of Herman Lieberman (who died in October 1941) and Jan Stańczyk. The following comments refer to the dominant Pragier-Ciołkosz wing of the exile branch.

[44] See Orzechowski, *Odra-Nysa-Bałtyk*, pp. 34-37; Pragier, *Czas przeszły dokonany*, pp. 630-32; Kukiel, *Generał Sikorski*, pp. 178-79; and Raczyński, *W sojuszniczym Londynie*, p. 133.

[45] Orzechowski, *Odra-Nysa-Bałtyk*, pp. 79-83. A few Sanacja adherents in the West disclaimed all interest in German territory, attributing such claims to the Communists; even East Prussia should be an international mandate.

most adamant among them entertained what can only be described as outrageous claims in the east as well.[46] On the other hand, more realistic voices both inside and outside the government, who foresaw (or feared) that the Oder-Neisse or even more limited gains could be had only at the price of concessions to Russia, opted with varying degrees of rigidity to curtail demands in the west in order not to jeopardize claims to Poland's prewar eastern boundary. In the meantime, the prime minister, himself more and more convinced that a reinstatement of the Riga line was unattainable and that he must move boldly and quickly to gain Allied support for adequate compensation and security in the west, was being pushed by external events in a direction acceptable to neither.

In this atmosphere, it was perhaps to be expected that every mention of the Oder-Neisse or intimation of compromise in the east would send shock waves through the exile community. Karol Popiel wrote later that he had not shared the general enthusiasm at the time over Sikorski's refusal to discuss the boundary question with Stalin, that it might have been better to probe Stalin's intentions then and there in order to be better prepared to put forward "a compromise that would salvage our most vital interests." But in the next breath he admits that he "did not have the courage to voice his doubts openly," since with one "possible" exception no one among his closest acquaintances "shared my fears and expectations."[47] As if to demonstrate Popiel's point, shortly after Sikorski returned from Moscow a rumor began circulating through the army in Scotland purporting to relate the terms of a secret agreement with Moscow, including: "corrections"

[46] One former member of the Underground, himself very much involved both during and after the war with the question of the western boundary, told me during a recent visit to Poland that the prevalence of extremist views within the Underground was virtually inevitable, that the isolated and conspiratorial environment bred a detachment from reality and a posture of intransigence. More than thirty years later, he still felt that Sikorski faced an impossible task in attempting to persuade political leaders at home of the necessity of compromise in the east. Concerning the western boundary, he confirmed that it was a subject of active discussion in some quarters from the earliest days of the war, but stressed that views were rather more fluid than recent historians would have one believe. While the Oder line was the point of departure for most, beyond that there was a plurality of views, with most attention given initially to the Kłodzka (Eastern) rather than the Lusatian Neisse. By and large, communication between London and the Underground on the boundary question was minimal; he had not been aware, for instance, of the activities of the *West-Slavonic Bulletin* and learned only much later of Sikorski's December 1942 memoranda.

[47] Popiel, *Generał Sikorski w mojej pamięci*, p. 159. Popiel's account of the aftermath of the Sikorski-Stalin talks, while it contains several factual errors, is interesting as evidence of how closely the prime minister held his cards on these sensitive issues. Even more revealing of how little such matters were discussed within Sikorski's inner circle is the fact that Raczyński, who (as he told me in 1981) also felt that it had been a mistake on the general's part not to probe Stalin's intentions further, did not know at the time that Popiel shared his view.

of unspecified dimensions in the eastern boundary, a Russian promise "to push the Germans back to the Oder-Neisse line," and the cession of the Wilno area to Lithuania which would remain "under joint Soviet and Polish control." Surmising that the episode was a provocation instigated most likely by radical Nationalists, Mitkiewicz nonetheless lamented that it had had "an extremely dispiriting effect on the officer corps and among the rank and file."[48]

Several months later, Ksawery Pruszyński published a short article urging that Poland return politically and geographically to the Piast conception— "that the moment had arrived for Poland, with Russia's help, to take the historic breakthrough decision of turning her face expressly toward the West, against Germanism." While he specifically mentioned the Oder and Lusatian Neisse as the desirable boundary in the west, he apparently only implied the extent of concessions in the east. Still Mitkiewicz reported that the article had "evoked a veritable storm in all of London, Polish and non-Polish." "One needs," he added, "to approach this kind of question with great caution and with an understanding of all the imponderables."[49]

Pruszyński, who was one of the few intrepid enough to broach the subject openly, then proceeded to write a second and longer article, entitled "In the Presence of Russia," which appeared in London on October 4, 1942. Referring to one of the founders of the Union of Polish Patriots in Moscow, he wrote:

> Wanda Wasilewska spoke of "the Poland of Bolesław Wry-Mouth." If this is not merely a slogan, it means just one thing: a Poland which reaches barely to the Bug and San in the east, but is pushed to Szczecin and embraces Wrocław in the west. Before our eyes, the eyes of the Poles from England, on red banners of revolution flew, as if as an inducement or provocation, precisely this proposal: "Cancel out five hundred years of history, surrender the east, but take the Baltic, return to the Oder, recover the lands for which Długosz prayed in the last words of his *History of Poland*."

It was as if the writer were appealing to Sikorski to take up the challenge; yet he also recognized the enormity of the task:

[48] Mitkiewicz, *Z gen. Sikorskim*, pp. 211-12 [entry for February 6, 1942]. Commenting on the incident, Mitkiewicz expressed his dismay that even "the above-cited version of a boundary agreement with Soviet Russia evokes the desired [i.e., negative] effects among groups in our army opposed to General Sikorski." For independent reports of continued opposition to Sikorski's policy of reconciliation with the Soviet Union, especially in the army, see Ambassador Biddle's report of February 2, 1942, in *FRUS, 1942*, 3:102-104; and Counselor Savery's report to the Foreign Office of January 11, 1942, in C496/19/55, FO 371/31077, PRO.

[49] Mitkiewicz, *Z gen. Sikorskim*, pp. 262-63 [entry for April 10, 1942].

But to respond in this matter one must be more than an ambassador, more than a prime minister. What is needed is a Bolesław the Brave, a Peter the Great, a Kemal Pasha. Someone who can take on his shoulders the decision for a whole nation, and for whole centuries. . . . No wonder it is difficult [to find] shoulders strong enough to bear the burden of a decision so enormous and so terrible. . . .[50]

Whether or not in reaction to Pruszyński's article, just three days later, on October 7th, the Council of Ministers passed a resolution that amounted to a rejection of his challenge. "It is detrimental in the highest degree," resolved the Council, "to advance fantastic territorial demands, reaching for example to the Lusatian Neisse or the Bober (Bobrawa) and embracing the whole of Lower Silesia with its fanatically anti-Polish population." Not only would the expulsion of such a large German population be "unfeasible," the possibility of their "re-Slavization" was an illusion. Moreover, "the advancement of such boundless territorial demands discredits the Poles in the eyes of Anglo-Saxon opinion as a people of unrestrained greed, which does irreparable harm to our real territorial aspirations . . . [and], in the present state of affairs, could foster thoughts of depriving Poland of part of the eastern territories in exchange for acquisitions in the west." Instead the Council put forward the more limited and deliberately vague formula of "the incorporation of Danzig, East Prussia and Opole Silesia, as well as a general westward shift of the boundary with Germany and a guarantee of freedom of the Baltic."[51]

Whether Sikorski tried on this occasion to get cabinet approval for a more precise and far-reaching definition of Poland's territorial designs in the west is not clear. But there is at least a hint that he did—and that he failed.[52] Perhaps the best indication of his isolation on this issue is the fact

[50] "Wobec Rosji," *Wiadomości Polskie* (London). The article was reprinted in full in Pruszyński, *Wybór pism*, 2:306-16; substantial excerpts also appear in *The Genesis of the Oder-Neisse Line: Sources and Documents*, ed. Rhode and Wagner, pp. 27-29. Although the quote from Wasilewska suggests that the Polish Communists already had a well-developed program for Poland's western boundary, this was not the case; they began articulating such a program, and hesitantly at that, only in 1943. For further comment, see Chapter XI, note 105, below.

[51] Polish Government Collection, Box 507, folio: "Prace przygotowawcze do konferencji pokojowej," HIWRP. By way of explaining the vagueness of this formulation, the resolution warned against a "premature definition of the western boundary line," as it might lead to asking "either for too much or for too little" and "either course would be a mistake." Kowalski (*ZSRR a granica*, pp. 51-53) mentions a supplementary document which argued for the incorporation of a strip of Lower Silesia along the right bank of the Oder and adjoining the prewar Polish-German boundary. I found no such supplement; the resolution itself, however, does refer to the desirability of pointing out the basically Polish or Slavic character of the lands between the prewar boundary and the Oder.

[52] In his letter of November 6, 1942, in which he pleaded with Sikorski not to succumb

that even the member of his cabinet most responsible for defining Poland's postwar goals, and therefore for the first drafts of the December 1942 memoranda to Roosevelt, was in disagreement with the prime minister on the key point. This was, of course, Marian Seyda, who after his return to the government in January 1942 was the minister in charge of preparations for the peace conference[53] and whose general position has been described above. In Sepember 1942, when the memoranda were presumably in preparation, Seyda set forth his own views in a privately circulated thirty-five page essay entitled *Poland and Germany and the Post-War Reconstruction of Europe*, which he described as an attempt "to assemble into a whole the results of [many months'] considerations" of "the problems of post-war reconstruction of Europe with special reference to Polish-German relations."[54] In its general line of argumentation Seyda's essay was very close to what we know of the Sikorski memoranda, as well as to the program of the *West-Slavonic Bulletin*—so close to the latter in fact that it provides graphic evidence of a link between the *Bulletin* group and the Sikorski government.[55] Areas of similarity included: an emphasis on economic and strategic, as opposed to ethnic, criteria in determining Poland's postwar boundary with Germany; the relationship between Poland's western border and future cooperation with Czechoslovakia; the essential integrity of Central and South-Eastern Europe and the right of this region to organize itself free from outside domination, including the "leadership" of Russia; a rejection of the universalistic approach to European security characteristic of the Versailles settlement; and a demand for harsh treatment of Germany, including long-term occupation, territorial curtailment in both

to pressure from some of his military advisors to ask for incorporation of lands up to the Oder-Lusatian Neisse instead of merely a zone of occupation (see Chapter V, note 93, above), Seyda added this curious footnote: "Later it will be said, General, that you yourself recognized that it is necessary to secure this (with the expulsion of 9 million Germans!), but you and the government did not prevail on this [issue] but *lost*." PRM 91/58, GSHI [emphasis in the original]. Seyda's reference to "and the government" is odd since the Polish verbs are in the singular form; moreover, it was "the government" that Sikorski was presumably trying to win over.

[53] This was the Ministerstwo Prac Kongresowych. Though established only in July 1942, it was preceded by a Bureau of Political, Economic and Legal Studies (Biuro Studiów Politycznych, Ekonomicznych i Prawnych), which Seyda also headed except for a brief period in late 1941 following his resignation from the cabinet, when the bureau was attached to the Ministry of Foreign Affairs. See Raczyński, *W sojuszniczym Londynie*, p. 125; Kowalski, *Walka dyplomatyczna*, p. 272; and Chapter VIII, note 73, above.

[54] A Polish version, "O nowy porządek rzeczy," was distributed to all government ministers; Ciechanowski Deposit, Box 33, folio: "Ministerstwo Prac Kongresowych," HIWRP. The English version was reissued as a pamphlet in January 1943, as a vehicle offering "foreigners . . . a concise presentation of our general aspirations." See Seyda's letter to Sikorski of November 11, 1942; PRM 91/55, GSHI.

[55] See especially Tadeusz Sulimirski, "Geopolityka ziem polskich," *Biuletyn Zachodnio-Słowiański*, no. 4/5 (August 1941), pp. 5-12; see also pp. 77-79 above.

east and west, and expulsion of the German population from areas incorporated into other countries.

The one issue on which Seyda's essay did not agree with Sikorski's memos was in its formulation of Poland's boundary demands in the west. Where the latter specifically asked for an Oder and Lusatian Neisse line with additional safeguards on the left banks of these rivers, the former used a more limited formula similar to that in the October 7th Council of Ministers resolution: East Prussia with Danzig, Opole Silesia, plus "a further shortening of the Polish-German frontier . . . by straightening it as far as possible and by moving it westward in accordance with the interests of Poland's security and especially the security of her ports."[56] After the war Seyda explained that the Poles did not formulate "precisely" their claim to "the maximum boundary on the Oder and Lusatian Neisse . . . in the first years of the war" because "such a pushy approach would have done serious harm to Polish proposals" in Britain and the United States, where opinion "was not fully prepared" for this demand. But he admitted obliquely that the eastern boundary question also played a role—that apart from "tactical" considerations "the view [favoring] presentation of the Polish issue as a whole, including the eastern territories, restrained us."[57] Yet we know for a fact that Sikorski did present Poland's case for an Oder-Neisse boundary—very likely overstepping once again the mandate from his cabinet—and that he handed this and the other memoranda on the postwar European settlement to the Americans weeks before submitting the one defending the Riga boundary in the east. We also know that he substantially reworked Seyda's drafts, apparently much to the latter's chagrin, paying special attention to the western boundary question.[58]

Small wonder in this atmosphere that the prime minister chose to pursue his territorial program through a combination of private probing and public circumspection: that, by his repeated defense of the integrity of Poland's 1939 boundary, he concealed not only from the public but from members of his own government the true extent of the threat to the eastern provinces;[59] likewise, that his public statements only hinted at the extent of his territorial desiderata in the west and that, even in official communications,

---

[56] However, Seyda did ask for strict occupation of additional territories up to the Oder and Lusatian Neisse. He also implied that Poland might claim other territories in Lower Silesia and elsewhere where there were "aggregations of Polish population" whose "Germanization is of a recent date." *Poland and Germany*, pp. 6-7 and 11-12.

[57] Seyda, *Pół wieku walki*, pp. 11-12; he does not admit here his differences with Sikorski on this question.

[58] Lipski, Raczyński, and Stroński, *Trzy podróże*, p. 17; and Kukiel, *Generał Sikorski*, p. 211.

[59] See, e.g., Pobóg-Malinowski, *Najnowsza historia*, 3:212-14; and Mitkiewicz, *Z gen. Sikorskim*, pp. 264-66.

he restricted himself to the minimum demands accepted by virtually all factions.[60] Yet it was inevitable that Sikorski's isolation on this issue, together with the general mood of intransigence in the exile community, would affect not only his tactics but the substance of his policy, setting limits beyond which he dared not go. "It seems to me," Mitkiewicz concluded early in 1942, "that the maximum concession to which [any] politicians, even [those] most disposed to compromise could agree, would be a slight correction in the boundary such that Lwów would remain forever with Poland, while Wilno could be returned to Lithuania as the price for her joining the federation."[61] Moreover, it was inconceivable that from a practical political standpoint Sikorski could have agreed even to these concessions—that is, that he could have garnered sufficient support for them to remain in office—if they were not accompanied by very firm assurances, if not outright guarantees, of corresponding gains in the west.

Likewise it was inevitable that, in avoiding open confrontation on this issue, he ran the very serious risk of compounding the confusion at home and abroad over what his policy really was, possibly even of undermining the credibility of his diplomatic efforts. The National Council, for instance, succeeded in embarrassing him during both his March and December 1942 visits to the United States. On the first occasion, it passed a resolution that, while rejecting Lithuania's "unjustified pretensions" to the city of Wilno, nonetheless wished her "the swiftest possible return to the road of progress of its Christian western culture, in cooperation with the nations of central Europe, after it . . . had recovered complete independence." Published during Sikorski's absence, the resolution could not have been more skillfully designed both to further irritate the Russians, who were already annoyed at his trip, and at the same time to weaken the prime minister's negotiating hand with the Lithuanians.[62] On the second occasion, the Council issued another statement, this one asking for a shortening and straightening of the boundary in the west but also reaffirming its stand on

[60] See, e.g., his letters to General Anders of May 1, 1942, and to the Underground commander, General Grot-Rowecki, of November 28, 1942, both in *Documents*, 1:346 and 457; also excerpts from his press conference in Chicago, December 18, 1942, in *War and Peace Aims*, ed. Holborn, 1:482-83.

[61] Mitkiewicz, *Z gen. Sikorskim*, p. 212.

[62] *FRUS, 1942*, 3:135. This is Ambassador Biddle's paraphrase of the resolution in a report to Washington. Biddle felt that this among other developments might have contributed to Stalin's apparent desire to force the Polish Army out of the Soviet Union. The "other developments" included two transparently anti-Soviet statements also made during Sikorski's absence: an article by Professor Stanisław Grabski, president of the National Council, on "The Historical Idea of the Nation"; and a broadcast by Minister of Information Stroński on the anniversary of the signing of the Treaty of Riga. For the Soviet reaction and Foreign Office comment, see C3330/19/55, FO 371/31080 and C3415/19/55, FO 371/31081, PRO.

the Riga line in the east.[63] This occurred on December 2nd, just one day after Sikorski's arrival in Washington for his third visit and at a time when he was preparing to discuss with the Americans for the first time his definitive proposals for Poland's postwar western boundary. On his return to London in early January 1943, he told the cabinet that the National Council's resolution had made "a bad impression" and had "aroused suspicions" of Polish "imperialism." He admonished his ministers "to limit themselves to the business of their own departments" and warned them that "the confidentiality of sensitive matters must be observed with strictest discipline."[64] Yet, in the absence of a public clarification of his own position, he was at a loss to counter effectively the influence of those who, whether in an official or unofficial capacity, were very vocally expressing theirs.[65]

THE ATLANTIC CHARTER: A DOUBLE STANDARD

Sikorski's position as 1942 opened was an unenviable one. Had he been confronted only with Stalin's seemingly friendly (but in fact illusory) intimations of a compromise with compensation, he could have responded positively. Indeed, although such a settlement would have involved a painful and, from a domestic political standpoint, risky decision on the eastern boundary, in other respects it was not incompatible with his own hopes for territorial gains at Germany's expense. However, with the sudden

[63] For the text of this resolution, see *The Genesis of the Oder-Neisse Line: Sources and Documents*, ed. Rhode and Wagner, p. 13.

[64] See Sikorski's confidential report to the Council of Ministers, January 21, 1943; Dz. Cz. N.W./I/1943, GSHI; also Pobóg-Malinowski, *Najnowsza historia*, 3:250, n. 85. The jab at the ministers to mind their own business may have been aimed at Seyda, the apparent instigator of the December 2nd resolution (see Orzechowski, *Odra-Nysa-Bałtyk*, p. 62). Seyda had then added insult to injury by holding a press conference on December 23rd, at which he repeated his firm stand on the Riga boundary ("after all, we gave up then 30,000 square kilometers") and declared that talk of "incorporating [the lands] up to the Lusatian Neisse is deception, for Poland cannot digest all this." Quoted in Witold Leitgeber, *W kwaterze prasowej: Dziennik z lat wojny 1939-1945*, p. 207.

[65] In addition to the National Council's actions, there were other unofficial groups who issued their own statements on the boundary question and, in at least one instance, made a direct appeal to the White House. Pobóg-Malinowski, *Najnowsza historia*, 3:250-51 and n. 86. One slightly comical attempt at free-lance diplomacy was Bielecki's suggestion on April 1st, while Sikorski was still in the United States, that inasmuch as he "no longer had any obligations" vis-à-vis Sikorski (an apparent reference to his exclusion from the reconstituted National Council) he should pay a personal call on Churchill or Eden. Reporting this incident back to the Foreign Office, Savery in the British Embassy commented ruefully on the lack of contact that Bielecki and many other Poles had outside their own exile circles and their consequent lack of realism. C3482/807/55, FO 371/31094, PRO; see also C1089/807/55 in the same file for other comments on Bielecki and on the Nationalists' repudiation of Seyda and Komarnicki for joining the government.

Kremlin pressure for immediate recognition of all Soviet territorial conquests, he found himself in a cruel dilemma. Should he press ahead faster to gain Allied support for his own program of federation and westward expansion? Or should he concentrate his efforts on forestalling the proposed Anglo-Soviet treaty? If he took the first course, he would have to challenge head-on that shibboleth of Anglo-American policy, the Atlantic Charter; and should his challenge be unsuccessful, he risked coming up empty-handed in both east and west. If he took the second course, he would have the Charter as a shield; but, in using it, he would undercut arguments that would later be crucial to his own program, at the same time possibly destroying the already shaky foundations of his rapprochement with Stalin.

In the end, he failed to make a clear-cut decision—or perhaps he chose not to. But in trying to play both sides, he was forced by the sheer pressure of events to give precedence to the latter course. It was a fateful, even a fatal decision. For it meant that his policy took on an increasingly negative cast—that, at least in the public mind, his positive and genuinely creative strategy for the future became hopelessly entangled with his tactical defense of the past. Never would he be able to regain the initiative he lost here. Yet, as we review Sikorski's diplomatic efforts during the year 1942, we should ask ourselves whether in fact he had an alternative, or whether the inconsistencies in his behavior were not forced upon him by the conflicting requirements of loyalty to the two sides of the Grand Alliance.

The Atlantic Charter and the "Polish Question."　　One irony of Sikorski's dilemma was that a primary obstacle to the realization of his territorial program came in the form of a declaration of principles—the Atlantic Charter—whose ostensible purpose was to assure the victims of Hitler's aggression a restoration of their independence, security, and well-being. What made it such an insuperable obstacle was the fact that, as historian Herbert Feis observed: "It was hailed not solely as a moral code by which nations ought to try to live but as a definite guide for settling the numberless questions that the war would bring forward."[66] From the Polish point of view, the Charter posed three fundamental problems: two related to its substance (the postponement of political and territorial decisions to the postwar period and the reaffirmation of self-determination as the cardinal principle in arriving at these decisions), and the third related to the uneven manner in which it was applied.

Of the two substantive issues, only self-determination was explicitly invoked in the Charter's text. Most ominous to the Polish ear was the wording of point 2:

---

[66] For accounts of how the Charter was conceived and drawn up, see Feis, *Churchill, Roosevelt, Stalin*, pp. 20-23; Dallek, *Roosevelt and American Foreign Policy*, pp. 281-84; and Churchill, *The Grand Alliance*, pp. 433-45.

Second, they [the president of the United States and the prime
minister of the United Kingdom] desire to see no territorial changes
that do not accord with the freely expressed wishes of the peoples
concerned.

For behind the simple language and noble sentiment lurked the specter of
Versailles—of a reimposition, in the form of plebiscites, of the narrow
ethnic criteria that had deprived Poland of economically viable and strategically defensible boundaries between 1919 and 1939. More alarming
still in light of the brutality of the German occupation was the justifiable
fear on the part of the Poles that strict application of this clause of Atlantic
policy might foreclose not only the acquisition of the additional German
territories they hoped for, but even the recovery of those prewar Polish
districts which had been reincorporated into the Reich in 1939 and from
which ethnic Poles had been forcibly expelled.

During the month preceding the September 1941 Inter-Allied meeting
at which more than a dozen governments announced their formal adherence
to the principles of the Anglo-American declaration, the Polish government
lobbied strenuously, though unsuccessfully, for some reassurance, whether
public or private, that the Charter "should not be applied with regard to
enemy countries in a way excluding adaptations imposed by the needs of
European security and by economic necessities" and that "the future
frontiers of Poland should not in any case embrace a territory less important
than that which Poland possessed before the German aggression." As
Foreign Minister Raczyński presented his case to U.S. Ambassador Biddle
and to the Foreign Office, the exile government felt that "the abstract
character of the policy of justice, as set forth [in the Declaration], would
render its practice inadequate to meet actual conditions on the continent."
For example, he continued:

> mass deportation which had taken place in certain sections of Poland,
> rendered the principle of self-determination set forth in point 2 of the
> Declaration, difficult, to say the least. . . . Moreover the Declaration
> made no reference to compensation for losses inflicted by the in-
> vader—no reference to righting the wrongs already done.
>
> The Polish nation, . . . which had consistently rejected . . . all
> German suggestions of collaboration with the Nazi regime, and which
> was the first nation to oppose the military power of Germany at a
> tremendous cost in masses of victims, in the cultural achievements
> of many generations, and in material worth, had the undoubted right
> to expect reparations of the wrongs inflicted on it. . . .

In addition, Raczyński expressed the fear that point 8, concerning disarmament of the aggressors and the creation of a "system of general se-

curity,'' would reinforce the Charter's bias against strategic considerations in the drawing of postwar boundaries. "Disarmament," he protested,

> could hardly . . . remain as the sole guarantee. Experience of the past 20 years was there to prove it. It would be necessary to find other additional guarantees, such as limiting the war potential of nations which had shown an inclination to provoke wars—also strengthening of the defensive position of nations which were the victims of the first or second war. Insofar as Poland was concerned, Poland earnestly hoped for greater security in light of strategic considerations. In the Polish mind, this called for straightening out of the age-old Polish-German tangle on the Baltic: for securing Poland's position on the sea, and for doing away with the East Prussian enclave, which had for so long afforded Germany a strangle grip on Poland.[67]

Although the reaction within the Foreign Office at least was not entirely unsympathetic, in the end no reassurances were given, and the Poles, having informed both London and Washington of the full extent of their reservations, had to settle for a somewhat sanitized public statement of their own.[68]

[67] Biddle's report of September 12th, *FRUS, 1941*, 1:374-75; and Raczyński's letter to Eden of August 25th, C10382/14/62, FO 371/26424, PRO. The Polish appeal was not made solely on the merits of their case, but also in the hope of strengthening Sikorski's hand vis-à-vis his domestic opposition. As Strang reported on September 5th, Raczyński "pleaded very hard . . . [saying] in effect that the Polish Government found themselves between the Scylla of the Atlantic Declaration and the Charybdis of the Soviet-Polish Treaty [of July 30, 1941] taken with the Secretary of State's announcement in the House of Commons that the exchange of notes at the time of the conclusion of the [treaty] did not involve any guarantee of frontiers by His Majesty's Government. The consequence was that General Sikorski's position had been very considerably weakened, and that a severe strain had been placed upon the loyalty and will to resist of the Poles in Poland. His Majesty's Government must not under-rate the effect of the Atlantic Declaration upon the home Poles, particularly in the form in which it would be presented by German propaganda." Raczyński "urged," Strang continued, that the Polish government be given "some form of reassurance, either public or confidential even in general terms, and if necessary without special reference to the Atlantic Declaration." C9994/5996/55, FO 371/26775, PRO.

[68] After much discussion, the British considered informing the Poles privately that they did not regard the Charter as "standing in the way of the equitable settlement" of Poland's future boundaries. But largely as a result of Eden's objections and doubts as to whether such private assurances would meet with Washington's approval, this was not done. In addition to the Foreign Office entries cited in note 67, see C9671/5996/55, FO 371/26775, PRO. For Raczyński's statement to the Inter-Allied meeting on September 24, 1941, see *War and Peace Aims*, ed. Holborn, 1:461-62. The key passages are almost identical to those recorded in Biddle's report above, but with the omission of references to specific territories and the phrase concerning "limiting the war potential" of aggressor nations; in addition, the British had insisted on removal of the word "reparations."

The policy of postponement, though not explicit in the text, was no less important a component of the Atlantic Charter than self-determination. Indeed, one of Roosevelt's primary motivations in seeking a joint declaration of this sort had been to ensure that the Americans would not be confronted at the peace table, as Wilson had been in 1919, with a spate of secret commitments. Such commitments, he felt, had contributed to public disillusionment with the Versailles settlement and, by their violation of self-determination, had sown the seeds of the present war. Moreover, nations under occupation or fighting for their survival were in no position to take advantage of the rights granted them under the Charter. "The important thing now," Roosevelt declared during one of his fireside chats, "is to get on with the war—and to win it." In the interim, he was impatient with those who demanded to know "what are you going to do about such and such a five-square kilometer area in the world."[69]

But where the post-World War I experience had instilled in the American president a dread of secret treaties and premature decisions, it had instilled in the Poles an equal dread of the vacuum left by failure to resolve in advance fundamental political and territorial issues—a situation that they felt had prejudiced later decisions to their disadvantage. We have already noted the eagerness of the exile government, even in the first weeks of its existence, to begin "already now to coordinate war aims and the structure of Europe with our allies" and "to mold [their] opinion" toward a peace "which would assure Poland . . . the foundations of security."[70] Now that Stalin was pressing for an immediate decision on the eastern boundary, it was only natural that the Poles should seek simultaneous discussions of an overall settlement. Even Sumner Welles, who had the unpleasant duty of informing Sikorski on several occasions that Washington could in no way commit itself on any of the Polish proposals, later acknowledged the legitimacy of the prime minister's concern and sense of urgency:

> Yet it was, of course, inconceivable that some of our smaller allies who had territorial or political problems, should not *try during the war* to get by direct negotiation *a settlement that would be confirmed after the victory*. If any demonstration of this had been needed, it was soon afforded, first, by the several visits to Washington of General Sikorski, the Prime Minister of the Polish Government-in-Exile, and, later, by the visits of President Beneš of Czechoslovakia.
>
> Sikorski I found one of the most stalwart and attractive statesmen

---

[69] Gaddis, *The United States and the Origins of the Cold War*, pp. 12-13. The American position was forcefully restated by Secretary of State Hull in a message to Eden on the eve of the latter's departure for Moscow; see *FRUS, 1941*, 1:194; also Welles, *Seven Decisions*, pp. 126-27.

[70] See Chapter V, note 35, above.

of the war years, and I conferred with him at great length during his weeks in Washington. He recognized, of course, as he told me repeatedly, that no final commitments on the future status of Poland or the future extension of Polish territory could be made by any Polish Government-in-Exile, but must await the freely expressed decision of the Polish people themselves. Nevertheless, he felt he would be criminally short-sighted *not to try during the war* to reach an agreement with the Soviet Union and with Czechoslovakia on political and territorial issues, *so that the entire problem could be successfully clarified before any peace conference was held.*[71]

One reason these two aspects of the Atlantic Charter—self-determination and postponement—proved so unsettling to the Poles was that, in their early exchanges with London and Washington, refusals to discuss postwar problems had been phrased in more pragmatic terms: the British had said it was "too early," while the Americans were concerned with maintaining the neutral stance dictated by their nonbelligerent status. But nowhere did either indicate that consideration of outstanding issues would be relegated to the postwar period or that their approach to these issues would be based on precepts so at odds with the concept of "real guarantees" central to the thinking of the Sikorski government. On the contrary, in the first years of the war the Poles had good reason to hope that British opinion, at least, would be receptive to their strategic and economic arguments.[72]

[71] Welles, *Seven Decisions*, pp. 130-31 [emphasis added]. Welles wrote here that he himself opposed the decision to postpone consideration of postwar problems, favoring instead a plan originally proposed by *Mrs*. Roosevelt to set up a representative body that would "begin without delay to study the future structure of the world, . . . and . . . be prepared at the end of the war to present for the final approval of the peace conference a series of settlements and of postwar policies already agreed upon in principle." The idea was discussed, with mixed reception, in the State Department, but was "summarily turned down" at the "highest level." Ibid., pp. 125-26 and 132-33.

[72] As noted earlier (p. 85 above), the British were early enthusiasts of the federation concept. In addition, occasional well-placed Britons came out publicly in favor of substantial corrections of the Polish-German boundary—including at least one suggestion by a member of Parliament that Poland's enduring well-being would require the recovery of Danzig and the Oder together with the "industrial region of Silesia in its entirety." From the essay by Alan Graham, M.P., in *After the War*, ed. Teeling; quoted in Bregman, "Linia Odry i Nysy," and Bloński, *Wracamy nad Odrę*, pp. 115-16. Perhaps most encouraging to the Poles was a lengthy memorandum on "The Problem of the Reconstruction of Poland" by Frank Savery, counselor of the British Embassy to the Polish Government-in-Exile, which argued *inter alia* for federation with a greater Lithuania (expanded to include the Wilno area), Polish retention of Lwów, plus the acquisition by Poland of East Prussia and additional parts of Silesia (with the expulsion of the German population). Dated January 27, 1940, the memo was regarded as highly confidential by the Foreign Office; but it must have been leaked to the Poles, as a copy of the bulk of the memo also appears in their files. See C1762/116/55,

As serious as these reservations concerning the substance of the Atlantic Charter was the failure on the part of the Western Powers to apply it evenhandedly. If the principles of the Charter were to be respected by some, they had to be respected by all. One could not in fairness insist on strict observance of ethnic criteria in one instance, but accept strategic criteria somewhere else; nor could one tell some that solutions to their problems must await the final peace, while making advance commitments to others. Above all, it would be unfair in the extreme to tell a nation that its boundary on one side must be established at the end of the war on the basis of "self-determination" (or possibly with due consideration for the economic well-being of its hostile neighbor), but that it would have to accept now the curtailment of its other flank in the name of someone else's security—*and* in order to insure this third party's cooperation in establishing a "just" peace. Never, of course, was this corruption of principle so crudely articulated. Yet, in essence, this was the squeeze in which Sikorski found himself during the critical year of 1942.

ONE ASPECT of the problem facing the Poles predated the signing of the Charter. This was the predisposition on the part of both the British and the Americans, despite their formal policy of not recognizing territorial changes brought about by war, to write off Poland's prewar holdings east of the Curzon line as never legitimately Polish—a view that reflected the West's none too profound knowledge of Central and East European history or geography. As we have seen, the British in particular, having disapproved from the outset Poland's eastward expansion after World War I, made no effort even in the first weeks of the Second World War to disguise their acceptance of the Molotov-Ribbentrop partition line as a return to the boundary they had favored twenty years earlier.[73] Later, at the time of the signing of the Polish-Soviet Agreement, Eden made it clear that the accompanying Foreign Office statement reiterating Britain's nonrecognition

---

FO 371/24470, PRO; and Polish Government Collection, Box 976, folio: "Ukrainian Question, 1942," HIWRP. What the Poles may well not have known was that, as indicated in the accompanying minutes, Savery's memorandum evoked a largely negative reaction concerning not only the future status of Wilno and Lwów and the prospects for a federation with Lithuania, but also possible changes in the Polish-German boundary (viewed by one as "fundamentally just") and population transfers. On rare occasions even American sources broached postwar issues in the early war years. See, e.g., "A Federation for Eastern Europe," pp. 117-21, in which an anonymous "Group of U.S. Military Experts" acknowledged that "on strictly military grounds it would be desirable to push [Poland's] boundary westward to the Oder River." Although the authors rejected such a move as too drastic, the mere mention of such a possibility may have encouraged the Poles to believe their views could find a positive reception.

[73] See pp. 151 and 155-56 above, esp. notes 7, 8, and 20.

of the "territorial changes which have been effected in Poland since August 1939" in no way "involved any guarantee of frontiers by His Majesty's Government."[74] The official British approach to this question was perhaps best summed up in the foreign secretary's March 1943 remark to President Roosevelt, that "he thought that Russia would demand very little territory of Poland, possibly up to the 'Curzon Line.' " Loss of that half of her prewar territory to the east of this line "would not affect Poland unduly from an economic point of view."[75]

This was by no means the unanimous view of the Foreign Office. On the contrary, among those closest to the Polish situation, several were inclined to acknowledge the validity of Poland's claim to Lwów and Wilno, as well as the more practical political considerations behind the exile government's juridical stand on the Riga boundary—including the need to reserve not only their future negotiating position but their right to represent and protect Polish citizens from the disputed territories.[76] Even among those less inclined to concede the merits of the Polish position, there was some recognition of Britain's "special obligations" toward the Sikorski government. As Roger Makins, then head of the Foreign Office's Central Department, wrote in the midst of a rather "intemperate" exchange early in 1942:

> It is of course our policy not to make any territorial commitments anywhere in Central or Eastern Europe. With reference to M. Dew's minute it must be remembered that Poland was our first belligerent ally, and that we have many special obligations toward her both of a moral and political kind. Unlike Soviet Russia which did her utmost to injure our interests in the first two years of the war, Poland has sacrificed everything and her policy has been simple and direct. The Polish population, under the severest strain, has not produced a single Quisling, and the Polish Govt. has shown unusual courage in making a treaty with Russia.
>
> Polish faults are obvious; little political sense and exaggerated ambitions. But to compare them to the Bourbons is just as great an exaggeration as anything the Poles are capable of.[77]

[74] *Documents*, 1:142-44.

[75] Sherwood, *Roosevelt and Hopkins*, p. 709.

[76] In addition to the Savery memorandum mentioned in note 72 above, see Frank Roberts's memo, marked "most secret," on "The Eastern Frontier of Poland" (C3056/19/55, FO 371/31079, PRO), as well as Roberts's earlier comments, dated January 29, 1942, in C1071/19/55, FO 371/31077, PRO.

[77] C2188/464/55, FO 371/31091, PRO. Makins's reference here was to a previous comment by Mr. Dew of the Northern Department that: "It would be an act of mercy if the Poles could be induced without further delay to bring their ambitions from the vaulting to the

In addition, there was considerable discussion at this time as to whether Britain was not obliged under the terms of the Anglo-Polish Mutual Assistance Agreement of August 1939, in particular the Secret Protocol thereto, to recognize Poland's special interest in an independent Lithuania. It was eventually determined that no such obligation existed, or rather that it could be invoked only in the event that Lithuanian independence was threatened by Germany.[78] On the other hand, the internal Foreign Office analysis of the territorial demands that Stalin had presented to Eden in December 1941 concluded that Moscow's insistence on the inclusion of northern East Prussia in a Lithuanian Republic of the U.S.S.R.:

> implies . . . the use of Tilsit as a bridgehead into Polish territory, . . . [and] would revive Polish suspicions about the strategic encirclement of Poland by the U.S.S.R. H.M. Government might take the line that as the disposal of the area in question affected the future frontier of Poland, which was reserved for further discussion, we could not commit ourselves at this stage.[79]

Only much later, beginning in the spring of 1943, would there develop a more general consensus that Poland's future boundaries should not be decided in piecemeal fashion and that her bargaining position in the east should not be compromised until the question of compensation could also be settled.[80] In the meantime, such considerations appear to have carried little weight with either Eden or Churchill.[81]

The American approach to the question of Poland's prewar eastern boundary, though more inscrutable and legalistic than the British, was in the end scarcely more helpful to the Poles. From the very beginning of

---

skipping level. If they cannot . . . , they will, I fear, suffer the same fate as the Bourbons whom they appear so closely to resemble.'' Strang attempted to paper over the differences between the departments by suggesting they didn't really exist and advising against "intemperate minutes.'' Yet, elsewhere both Dew and Strang had termed "ridiculous'' (Dew) or "unwise'' (Strang) Polish attempts to invoke the Atlantic Charter in support of their opposition to Soviet annexations of 1939-40—a view that Roberts definitely did not share. See C1071/19/55, FO 371/31077, PRO.

[78] For the texts of the Agreement and Protocol, as well as the Polish interpretation of their legal significance, see *Documents*, 1:550-53; and Kulski, "The Anglo-Polish Agreement.'' Detailed British comments are found in C1071/19/55, FO 371/31077 and C3056/19/55, FO 371/31079, PRO.

[79] N2182/5/38, FO 371/32880, PRO; dated April 21, 1942.

[80] See pp. 343-46 below.

[81] See discussion of Eden's position on pp. 155-59 above, especially notes 19 to 21. Eden was particularly irritated over even the appearance of an obligation with respect to Lithuania: "Foolish of us,'' he noted in the margin. And later: "Yes, the secret protocol is a most unwelcome embarrassment. We shall have to bear it in mind when we come to reconsider the Russian demand. A. E. Feb. 17.'' C1071/19/55, FO 371/31077, PRO.

the war, even while maintaining a posture of "nonrecognition," Washington chose to treat Soviet occupation of Poland's eastern half as somehow less an act of war than Germany's occupation of her western half.[82] A good example of the potential for misunderstanding in this neither-nor stance was the brouhaha that erupted during the July 1941 Polish-Soviet negotiations, when State Department officials repeated to Polish Ambassador Ciechanowski on several occasions "that the United States Government continued to adhere to its policy of refusing to recognize the acquisition of territory obtained by aggression." On the basis of Ciechanowski's reports to this effect, as well as the ambassador's own interpolation that Washington looked with disfavor on the agreement as drafted, President Raczkiewicz ordered Sikorski to delay the signing of the agreement until the arrival of an anticipated American "guarantee" which, it was thought, would go further in defending Polish claims than the declaration offered by the British. Sikorski, having determined for himself that Ciechanowski's impression of American disapproval was inaccurate, went ahead and signed the agreement[83]—an act that Raczkiewicz promptly disavowed and that brought on the prime minister harsh criticism for passing up an opportunity to gain open American recognition of Poland's territorial integrity within her 1939 boundaries.

Papers now available show, however, that no such opportunity ever existed. According to a State Department cable drafted on August 5th (but never sent), the much touted American "guarantee" would have amounted to nothing more than a suggestion to the British government that the Polish government be allowed to issue a statement to the effect that, in signing the agreement with the Soviets, it had "not in any way admitted any change in its pre-war territorial boundaries or the existence of any basis for the discussion of such changes." Moreover, it is apparent from the cable that, in reaffirming its posture of nonrecognition, the Department

[82] Secretary of State Hull wrote of this decision: "Although Russia's invasion of Poland could be considered an act of war, the President and I decided not to include Russia in our application of the Neutrality Act. We did not wish to place her on the same belligerent footing as Germany, since to do so might thrust her further into Hitler's arms. . . . On September 21 . . . information . . . came from an official Chinese source in Moscow . . . to the effect that the Soviet invasion . . . was solely to secure the frontier and protect the Russian [sic] minorities in eastern Poland." Hull, *Memoirs*, 1: p. 685.

[83] See exchange of cables between Eden and Halifax, July 29-30, 1941; C8498 and C8567/3226/55, FO 371/26756, PRO, and *The Great Powers and the Polish Question*, ed. Polonsky, p. 84; also the exchange of cables between Sikorski and Ciechanowski, August 5-6, 1941, PRM 40a/10, GSHI. In his response, Ciechanowski referred to Anglo-American differences that were not reflected in official policy and, in particular, to a more skeptical approach to the Soviet Union on Washington's part. This proved to be no more than a brief interlude in American policy, and had already passed at the time of Ciechanowski's cable. See, e.g., Dallek, *Roosevelt and American Foreign Policy*, pp. 278-80.

was concerned more with keeping U.S. policy on a "moral plane" than with the merits of Poland's claims to her eastern boundary and that the American government was "adhering to its policy of taking upon itself no obligations with regard to what the boundaries of continental Europe are to be following the conclusion of the present war . . ."[84] Indeed, other sources indicate that high American officials shared the bias of their British counterparts in favor of the Curzon line—that, as Sumner Welles later expressed it, "the 'Curzon Line' had long been regarded in the West as a legitimate boundary between Poland and Russia, for ethnic as well as strategic reasons."[85]

It is worth noting here that the conclusions reached by the Territorial and Political Subcommittees of the State Department's Advisory Committee on Post-War Foreign Policy, which worked on the Polish-Soviet boundary issue during late 1942 and early 1943, differed markedly from such blanket dismissals of Poland's claims in the east and were in several respects similar to dissident British views as well as to Sikorski's own position. Recognizing the validity of Poland's ethnic claims to the more populous urban areas, especially to Wilno and Lwów—recognizing as well the impossibility of drawing a boundary that would not leave significant numbers of Poles or Ukrainians on the wrong side—the subcommittees favored a compromise between the Riga and Curzon lines, one that at a minimum would leave the better part of Eastern Galicia to the Poles. In addition to ethnic considerations, the committees advanced both economic and strategic arguments for Poland's retention of this area. In particular, Eastern Galicia's oil and other mineral resources were seen as vastly more important to the Polish economy than the Soviet. Likewise, the committees recognized that possession of the Carpathian line and the rail links to Rumania would be critical to the creation of a regional federation—and, conversely, that one Soviet motive for claiming all of Eastern Galicia would be a "desire to play an active role in Central Europe." Finally, with an eye to achieving a genuine compromise settlement, the Territorial Subcommittee recommended "that the Riga Line be regarded as the eastern boundary of Poland as a starting-point for negotiations"—a position that

[84] *FRUS, 1941*, 1:245-48 and notes. See also Pobóg-Malinowski, *Najnowsza historia*, 3:181 and n. 50, and 188-92; Rozek, *Allied Wartime Diplomacy*, pp. 61-63; Jędrzejewicz, *Polonia amerykańska w polityce polskiej*, pp. 51-52; and Ciechanowski, *Defeat in Victory*, pp. 28-41.

[85] Welles, *Seven Decisions*, p. 142. See also Warburg, *The United States in a Changing World*, p. 361. Referring to the discussion of the Curzon line at Teheran and the possibility of an exchange of populations, Warburg writes: "This seemed to settle the question without doing violence to the Atlantic Charter pledges, since Russia was demanding only the return of territory which all agreed had never rightfully belonged to Poland. The [Soviet] claim to Koenigsberg, however, was a wholly different matter. . . ."

would presumably imply interim recognition of the integrity of the prewar frontier. None of the relevant papers was available to American policymakers at the time of Sikorski's 1942 visits—the first factual presentation is dated January 12, 1943, and the final recommendations, May 19, 1943—but this probably made little difference, as the committees' conclusions appear to have had negligible influence on later U.S. policy.[86]

This is not the place to discuss in detail the relative merits of Poland's claim to her prewar eastern provinces. What should not be overlooked, however, is the erosive effect that the policy of "nonrecognition," combined with Western inclinations to accept the Curzon line, had on the exile government's potential bargaining strength at the negotiating table. First, if nonrecognition was to carry any practical weight, it had to be accompanied by de jure recognition of the *status quo ante*, at least until such time as an alternative settlement could be reached. This was especially true in the case of territorial changes brought about not by an adversary such as Germany, whose conquests were repudiated by all, but by an adversary-turned-ally (or, as many Poles chose to refer to the Soviet Union, "the ally of our allies") who would also come to the peace table as victor rather than vanquished. It is understandable that the British and the Americans preferred the tidier policy of recognizing nothing to the risks of taking sides between allies. Yet failure to recognize the integrity of what had existed before implied de facto recognition of the change and, in so implying, deprived the Poles (and others) of what meager bargaining influence they possessed. This erosive effect applied to their ability to defend not only their territorial claims but other vital interests as well, most painfully the rights of erstwhile citizens now reclassed at Moscow's will as subjects of the Soviet Union.

In addition, the disposition of the Western Powers to look on the Curzon line as the easternmost limit of Poland's legitimate territorial claims could not but affect their view of what constituted proper compensation for her losses. If the lands to the east of this line were never rightfully Polish,

---

[86] Notter, *Postwar Foreign Policy Preparation*, pp. 492-512. At Teheran Roosevelt sat out the discussion of Poland's future boundaries, without taking exception to the tentative agreement between Churchill and Stalin on the Curzon line as the Polish-Soviet frontier, with Lwów going to the Soviet Union—Churchill: "I was not going to break my heart . . . about Lvov"—although the Americans would later try to convince the Poles that the president had defended their interests in Eastern Galicia. At Yalta Roosevelt made only the most feeble attempt to save Lwów for Poland, although this recommendation was included in the State Department's briefing paper on the Polish problem. See Churchill, *Closing the Ring*, pp. 395-97 and 403; Bohlen, *Witness to History*, pp. 151-52; Stettinius, *Roosevelt and the Russians*, pp. 86-87 and 151-52; and *FRUS: Malta and Yalta*, pp. 202-206 and 230-34. See also Sharp, *Poland: White Eagle*, pp. 300-301; and Rozek, *Allied Wartime Diplomacy*, pp. 338-39.

then the fact that they constituted nearly half of the prewar state was of little consequence; if, as Eden averred, their loss "would not affect Poland unduly from an economic point of view," then reparation for the economic loss was incidental to the determination of her future boundary in the west. As Roosevelt remarked to Eden during their March 1943 discussion:

> . . . after all, the big powers would have to decide what Poland should have and . . . he, the President, did not intend to go to the Peace Conference and bargain with Poland or the other small states; as far as Poland is concerned, the important thing is to set it up in a way that will help maintain the peace of the world.[87]

In the final analysis, however, what the Great Powers viewed as contributing to the peace of the world had little in common with the prerequisites of Central European prosperity, security, and independence so central to Sikorski's program.

The Anglo-Soviet treaty and Sikorski's second American visit. Prime Minister Churchill's initial reaction to the Soviet demand for immediate recognition of their 1941 western frontier was abruptly negative, for reasons of principle as well as timing. "Stalin's demand about Finland, Baltic States, and Rumania," he cabled the War Cabinet, "are directly contrary to the first, second, and third articles of the Atlantic Charter, to which Stalin has subscribed." And to Eden in Moscow: "We are bound to United States not to enter into secret and special pacts. . . . Even to raise [these proposals] informally with President Roosevelt at this time would, in my opinion, be inexpedient."[88] Later, in a second cable to Eden, he expanded on his views:

> We have never recognized the 1941 frontiers of Russia except *de facto*. They were acquired by acts of aggression in shameful collusion with Hitler. The transfer of the peoples of the Baltic States to Soviet Russia against their will would be contrary to all the principles for which we are fighting this war and would dishonour our cause. This also applies to Bessarabia and to Northern Bukhovina, and in a lesser degree to Finland, . . .

"Strategical security," he added, might be "invoked at certain points on the frontiers of Bukhovina or Bessarabia," in which case "the population would have to be offered evacuation and compensation." However,

[87] Sherwood, *Roosevelt and Hopkins*, p. 710.

[88] Churchill, *The Grand Alliance*, pp. 630-31; one reason for Churchill's very keen concern over Roosevelt's reaction was that he received Eden's first message en route to see the American president for the first time since the attack on Pearl Harbor.

In all other cases transference of territory must be regulated after the war is over by freely and fairly conducted plebiscites, very differently from what is suggested. In any case there can be no question of settling frontiers until the Peace Conference.[89]

It is not immediately clear from Churchill's account whether he omitted mention here of Soviet demands vis-à-vis Poland because Stalin was not insisting on the inclusion of this sector of the boundary in the proposed treaty or because he, Churchill, did not find these demands objectionable. In light of earlier British views on the Curzon and Molotov-Ribbentrop lines, one is led to suspect the latter. Indeed, as the prime minister himself admitted, it was Stalin's claim to the Baltic States that aroused his special ire.[90]

In any event, Churchill's views on the general question of territorial changes appear to have been unchanged when he met with General Sikorski on January 31, 1942. The reader will recall that this was the interview at which the general told Churchill: "[Stalin declared] that East Prussia must belong to Poland, that the Polish Western boundaries must be based on the river Oder." He also mentioned the Soviet dictator's apparent flexibility on the disposition of Lwów in the east adding: "Stalin would like to open the discussion on the Polish-Russian frontier at the time when the Polish Army in the USSR was already at the front." In the total context of the moment, it now seems likely that Sikorski's purpose in raising this issue was not simply to report what Stalin had said (if in fact he had said it at all) but to sound out, without revealing his own hand, the British leader's reaction to a package territorial deal with Stalin, involving concessions to Russia in the east with compensation in the west based on Poland's economic and security needs, rather than on narrow ethnic criteria. If this hypothesis is correct, then the general's probe produced a negative reaction—although in so responding Churchill also seemed to be saying, contrary to the impression left by Cripps, that the British would refuse to consider Soviet claims as well. According to the official Polish record of the meeting, the prime minister, "referring to the authority of an agreed opinion between Great Britain and the United States," assured Sikorski "that the principles of self-determination, proclaimed in the Atlantic Charter, would be the basis of just and peaceful plebiscite voting by which the population of a territory would decide on the incorporation of their land into a given State." He foresaw only two possible exceptions: first, in areas of mixed populations, where "a method of resettlement might be adopted"; and second, in the case of Prussia, which he distinguished from

[89] Ibid., p. 695.
[90] Ibid., p. 629-30 and 694-95.

southern Germany and Austria and toward which "measures would be adopted to break her power." Here Churchill implied he favored partition but gave no indication of his views on a possible reduction of Prussian territory, or even on the disposition of East Prussia. On the contrary, he insisted that "as long as victory has not been achieved, the problem of the future State boundaries in Europe would be in no way discussed."[91]

This was on January 31st. Yet scarcely more than a month later, Churchill reversed his stand on Soviet claims. "The increasing gravity of the war," he cabled to President Roosevelt on March 7th, "has led me to feel that the principles of the Atlantic Charter ought not to be construed so as to deny Russia the frontiers she occupied when Germany attacked her. This was," he now said, "the basis on which Russia acceded to the Charter, . . ."[92] Two factors appear to have influenced Churchill's change of heart. The first was the one mentioned in the cable—i.e., Britain's deteriorating military position and the declining likelihood that she could make good her promises of military aid, much less open the second European front the Soviets were calling for. "Everything portends," he continued to FDR, "an immense renewal of the German invasion of Russia in the spring, and there is very little we can do to help the only country that is heavily engaged with the German armies." Implied here but left unsaid was the fear that, without a substitute for the second front in the form of the territorial concessions demanded, the Soviets might be inclined to seek a separate peace with Germany. This was the argument with which the British initially tried to extract Polish acquiescence to the proposed treaty.[93]

It seems likely, however, that a second factor was more important. This was the conviction on the part of three key advisors to Churchill—Eden, who reportedly returned from Moscow "personally impressed with the reasonableness of the Russian demand," Cripps, who after eighteen trying months as Britain's ambassador to the Soviet Union was impressed by the

[91] *Documents*, 1:274-76.

[92] Churchill, *The Hinge of Fate*, pp. 326-28. Two days later, on March 9th, Churchill cabled Stalin, informing him: "I have sent a message to President Roosevelt urging him to approve our signing the agreement with you about the frontiers of Russia at the end of the war." The decision to negotiate on the basis of Stalin's demands was apparently taken at least a month earlier; see Eden's instructions to Ambassador Halifax in Washington, beginning February 10th, in W.P. (42)96, filed also in N1093/5/38, FO 371/32876, PRO.

[93] Sikorski had several rather tense interviews with Eden and Churchill on this subject in early March—Mitkiewicz called them "dramatic"—during which Churchill warned that, if the Soviets signed a separate peace, "we will all go down together" and implied that the territorial provisions of the proposed treaty were of little practical importance: "If Russia was victorious she would decide on her frontiers without consulting Great Britain; should she lose the war, the agreement would lose all its importance." See *Documents*, 1:295-99 and 595, n. 189; Mitkiewicz, *Z gen. Sikorskim*, pp. 223 and 228; also note 95 below.

fragility of Anglo-Soviet relations, and Lord Halifax, who had been foreign secretary at the time of the abortive Anglo-French negotiations with the Soviets in the summer of 1939—that acceptance of Stalin's territorial claims was a prerequisite to future Anglo-Soviet cooperation.[94] As Eden cabled Ambassador Halifax in Washington on March 30th:

> As you are aware from my [earlier] telegrams . . . real reason for importance we attach to conclusion of treaty is not so much that we fear separate peace but that, at this critical stage of war, we are convinced that we must leave nothing undone to establish a basis for real co-operation and confidence with Stalin. We cannot allow Polish interest in Lithuania and Polish suspicions of Soviet motives to stand in the way of this all-important object. I trust that you will press this home with President.[95]

American Ambassador to London, John Winant, later confirmed this line of reasoning. Churchill and Eden felt, he reported, that Stalin was making the territorial issue "the basis of trust in Britain as a friendly ally." "They believe that if mutual confidence could be established it would mean a great deal in the prosecution of the war and in building the future peace." However, he added, "they do not believe that failure to meet Stalin's wishes would lead to a Russian-German arrangement."[96]

Although at this stage (March 1942) there was still no question of including the Polish-Soviet boundary in the proposed treaty, British recognition of Soviet conquests in the Baltic States and Rumania threatened to undercut Sikorski's position from several standpoints. In the north, Lithuania's absorption into the Soviet Union would automatically foreclose the possibility of including that country in a Central European federation. This in turn would eliminate the one solution to the Wilno problem that he could hope might be acceptable to his Polish constituency—that is,

[94] *FRUS, 1942*, 3:492, 509, and 513-14; and *Documents*, 1:339. Concerning Eden's views, see also pp. 155-59 above.

[95] C3353/19/55, FO 371/31081, PRO. A day or so earlier, Eden had described the treaty as "a political substitute for material military assistance . . . [which] under present conditions, Great Britian is unable to give . . . in the sense of a second front, or even in the sense of any considerable supply of materiel." Despite Eden's views to the contrary, Halifax inferred that such a state of affairs might lead the Soviets to seek a separate peace. As Under Secretary Welles reported their conversation on the evening of March 30th, the British ambassador "implied that, were the war situation to continue to go badly for Great Britain and Stalin were then either to negotiate a separate peace with Hitler or to demonstrate marked hostility to Great Britain, Mr. Churchill's Government would probably fall and, in that event, Sir Stafford Cripps would replace him, with the probability that under such a government a frankly Communist, pro-Moscow policy would be pursued." *FRUS, 1942*, 3:536-38. See also Mastny, *Russia's Road to the Cold War*, pp. 41-45.

[96] *FRUS, 1942*, 3:552.

cession of the city and its environs to Lithuania within the framework of a federation. In the south, Soviet possession of northern Bukovina would drive a wedge between Poland and Rumania, leaving Moscow in possession of key communication lines as well as a strategic bridgehead on the western side of the Carpathians. Perhaps most important of all, Sikorski could rightly fear that blanket acceptance of Soviet demands, with no reciprocal concessions on their part and with no reference to an overall territorial settlement in Central and Eastern Europe, would prejudice in advance his own chances for arriving at an acceptable compromise settlement of the Polish-Soviet boundary that would at the same time recognize Poland's right to substantial compensation in the west.[97] In fact, he protested the separation of the Polish issue from the general territorial settlement in Central and Eastern Europe, proposing instead that the British delay their treaty with the Soviets at least until the summer, when a general agreement to which Poland and the United States would also be signatories could be reached.[98] No doubt uppermost in his mind at this point was his expectation that, by the summer of 1942, the Polish Army would be ready for service on the Russian front, thereby putting the Poles in a better bargaining position. (This was still several weeks before the Russians sharply reduced the army's rations and forced the first stage of evacuation.)

His efforts to dissuade the British unavailing, Sikorski had little choice but to alter his own plans accordingly. First to be affected was the agenda for his forthcoming visit to the United States, already scheduled for the end of March. Preparations for the trip—in fact all his activities between his return from the Soviet Union in early January and the first of March[99]—

[97] See especially notes of Sikorski's meeting with Churchill and other British leaders on March 11th, in *Documents*, 1:295-99; and Raczyński's note to Eden of April 21st, ibid., pp. 332-35. In the latter, the Polish foreign minister spoke of "the importance which [the Polish government] attach[ed] to the maintenance of the independence of Lithuania and the retention of Bukovina within the area of Central Europe, to which it properly belongs for both historical and geographical reasons," and warned that "the principle of the Atlantic Charter cannot be reconciled with sacrificing weaker nations and states to the interests of a powerful neighbour." He also implied that conclusion of the treaty along the lines demanded by Moscow would not provide the desired security against a separate peace, since "the projected agreement [would] in no way commit the Soviet Government in relation to Germany, considering that the expansion of Soviet possessions is to be effected not at the expense of Germany but at that of third parties." Thus "being able to prove that . . . they have not in any way prejudiced Germany's interests, the Soviet Government would retain a valuable trump card in relation to any, even the present German Government, a fact which would become apparent to all the interested parties as soon as the agreement has become public."

[98] Ibid., p. 595, n. 189; and Mitkiewicz, *Z gen. Sikorskim*, p. 223 [entry for March 9, 1942].

[99] In addition to the memorandum prepared for this visit and the efforts within his inner circle to work out a compromise position on the eastern boundary (see pp. 102-104 and 128-33 above), Sikorski devoted much of his time during these weeks to trying to accelerate plans for a Central European federation. See, e.g., *FRUS, 1942*, 3:108-110 and 120-22.

suggest that the general's original purpose in going to Washington at this time was not merely to enlist the aid of the Americans in his efforts to prevent British concessions to Moscow, but in the first instance to gain American support for his postwar program as a basis for a second round of talks with Stalin. As Mitkiewicz noted in his diary on March 1st, during the period when the memorandum for this second trip was being drafted:

> General Sikorski and some of his political advisors are inclined to undertake talks directly with Soviet Russia. Prior to this, however, the General would like to obtain Anglo-American support in the form of a kind of *guarantee that the decisions taken in these talks will be respected in a future peace treaty. . . .*[100]

And again a week later, in connection with Sikorski's suggestion that negotiations with the Soviets be postponed until the summer: "The General is counting unbelievably on gaining President Roosevelt's support for his political desiderata in Central and Eastern Europe."[101]

Yet in the end, the substance of his talks with Roosevelt and Under Secretary Welles was almost wholly negative, devoted to arguing the case against the pending Anglo-Soviet treaty, with no attempt to present in coherent fashion his own positive program for the postwar reorganization of Central Europe. Moreover, it is virtually certain that the memorandum prepared prior to Sikorski's departure from London, detailing his federation concept and at least by inference his view of essential territorial gains for Poland in the west, was never presented to the Americans. Both Polish Embassy and State Department records show that the Poles did indeed present several other memoranda: two submitted by Foreign Minister Raczyński in advance of Sikorski's arrival, one on the status of Polish-Soviet relations since the signing of the July 1941 agreement, the other on Poland's vital interest in the independence of the Baltic States and, in particular, of Lithuania; a copy of a March 27th memo to the British Foreign Office detailing Polish objections to the territorial provisions of the proposed treaty; two concerning the treatment of Polish citizens under German occupation; and a sixth, delivered after Sikorski's departure from Washington, reiterating the Polish government's insistence on its right to participate in all discussions concerning Poland's boundaries and the future status of Lithuania and Bukovina. But there is no reference to a memorandum on Poland's postwar goals. As for the talks themselves, prior to Sikorski's arrival the subject of East Prussia and Upper Silesia came up briefly and quite inadvertently during Raczyński's meeting with Roosevelt on February 25th, but with no attempt on the foreign minister's part to press Polish

---

[100] Mitkiewicz, *Z gen. Sikorskim*, p. 218 [entry for March 1, 1942; emphasis added].
[101] Ibid., p. 223.

claims.[102] The subject of boundary corrections vis-à-vis Germany came up again, during Sikorski's March 25th meeting with Welles, but only in connection with the general's Moscow trip the previous December. And this time, in relating Stalin's offer of a private deal, he mentioned only East Prussia without repeating his earlier statement to Churchill about the Oder line. Most surprising of all, he appears to have raised the federation idea only once, in this same session with Welles, but did not pursue the subject, possibly because Welles did not encourage discussion.[103]

Sikorski's failure to present his postwar program during this second Washington stay cannot be attributed solely or even primarily to deference to the American policy of postponement, although this was undoubtedly an added factor. For Welles told his Polish guests that, while the American government would make no commitments on postwar issues during the war, it would "be glad to receive the views of [other nations] . . . in order that it may give full consideration to these problems and be in a position to determine its own views . . . when the time comes for these questions to be finally settled."[104] We are left to conclude that Sikorski did not take advantage of this opening because he did not want to dilute the force of his case against the British position, which was based on a strict application of the Atlantic Charter, by interjecting into the discussion his own objections to the Charter's provisions.[105]

[102] It was the president who raised the matter, remarking "spontaneously" that East Prussia as a stronghold of "pro-Hitler Junkers" should be separated from Germany and placed under "trusteeship"—a solution that he also saw as applicable to the Sudetenlands. Roosevelt then mentioned "Oberschlesien," which he declared a "predominantly German" region. When Raczyński protested, Roosevelt dropped the subject, "obviously desiring not to go beyond general observations. He merely noted once more that the whole subject will require thorough consideration. Decisions can be made only after the war. For the present, the less said about it the better it will be for this matter from several points of view." The record of this conversation appears only in the Polish archives; see note immediately following for location.

[103] For records of Raczyński's talks, see Ciechanowski Deposit, Box 67[84], folio: "Amb. E. Raczyński w Waszyngtonie (II-III/1942)," HIWRP; and *FRUS, 1942*, 3:106-108 and 111-16. Accounts of Sikorski's meetings and presentations are in *FRUS, 1942*, 3:123-33 and 139, n. 79; and *Documents*, 1:310-12. Ambassador Ciechanowski's final report of the trip, as well as numerous cables related to the preparations and results of the visit are in Polish Government Collection, Box 424, folio: "Stosunki Polsko-Amerykańskie: Podróż Ministra Spraw Zagr[anicznych] i Premiera, 1941-1942r," HIWRP. For other accounts of the trip, see Lipski, Raczyński, and Stroński, *Trzy podróże*, pp. 9-15; Raczyński, *W sojuszniczym Londynie*, pp. 134-38; and Ciechanowski, *Defeat in Victory*, pp. 93-102.

[104] *FRUS, 1942*, 3:130; also Raczyński, *W sojuszniczym Londynie*, p. 138n.

[105] The conclusion that Sikorski's posture during this second American visit was determined mainly by his desire to invoke the Atlantic Charter and postponement as the most effective means of opposing the Anglo-Soviet treaty is supported by a related decision not to include in the memorandum to the Foreign Office mention of the Poles' willingness to accept a compromise settlement in Eastern Galicia accompanied by an exchange of populations. See Mitkiewicz, *Z gen. Sikorskim*, p. 231 [entry for March 19, 1942]. Later, of course, during

There is some evidence to suggest that he was not entirely comfortable with the negative posture he felt compelled to assume during this trip, and here we get a brief glimpse into the nuances of policy that divided the prime minister even from some of his closest collaborators. For instance, Raczyński has suggested, a bit too critically I think, that Sikorski was encouraged to make the trip only after his own (i.e., the foreign minister's) advance work had proved successful. "Prior to this," Raczyński continued, "he did not seem to appreciate fully the danger that would have resulted from the agreement between London and Moscow. Or, if he even perceived it, he hesitated to assume the risk of a diplomatic defeat in Washington. This risk turned out to be nonexistent, . . ."[106] It is likely, however, that Sikorski hesitated for reasons other than fear of a diplomatic defeat. After all, even Churchill told him that his opposition to the British position on Russian border demands would get a sympathetic hearing in Washington; moreover, the record of talks between Sikorski and various British leaders amply demonstrates that he was acutely aware of the danger not only to Poland's interests, but to his own political position as well.[107] It is far more likely that whatever reluctance Sikorski showed was due to two quite different considerations: first, his uneasiness over the prospect of seeking even temporary refuge in a principle which he feared could not in the long run protect Poland's interests in the east and which was incompatible with her aspirations in the west; and second, his fear that too aggressive a lobbying effort against Soviet demands would irreparably damage his already very fragile reconciliation with Moscow.[108] From this vantage point the risks involved in his trip, far from being "nonexistent," were very great indeed.

This reading of Sikorski's mood corresponds to several entries in Mitkiewicz's diary from this period that call attention to the growing tension the general felt among the demands being made of him by three different sides: by the Soviets, who were pressing for an immediate settlement, involving in all probability far-reaching political and territorial concessions;

April and May when it appeared almost certain that a treaty incorporating Stalin's territorial demands would be signed after all, the Poles did request explicit recognition of their right to compensation. See especially Chapter VI, notes 25 and 32, above.

[106] Raczyński, *W sojuszniczym Londynie*, p. 137.

[107] At one point, Sikorski told Churchill that, having assumed sole responsibility for a reconciliation with Russia the previous July, he could not accept the consequences of the far-reaching concessions proposed by the British and warned that he would no longer be able to stop publication of a "Red Book" exposing the unbelievably brutal treatment of Poles in the Soviet Union. See *Documents*, 1:298-99.

[108] No doubt Sikorski's very vocal support of Soviet demands for a second front and stepped-up military aid during this visit (a posture that led him to be compared with Litvinov) was an attempt to offset Soviet annoyance with his opposition to the treaty with Britain. See Chapter IX, note 71, above.

by the Western Allies, who were insisting on the one hand that the Poles compose their relations with Russia, but on the other that they remain loyal to the Atlantic Charter; and by his Polish constituency, which was demanding above all a resolute stand on the Riga boundary. Writing on March 19th, Mitkiewicz described Sikorski's position as "exceptionally difficult." Posing the question "to go or not to go to the States?" he continued:

> Involuntarily the thought comes to mind that it might be better and more advantageous if the General went straight to Moscow, to Stalin, and there, without third parties, settled all issues, posing the question: "to be or not to be?"
>
> General Sikorski, however, cannot do this. Disregarding the not small resistance of his opposition, our ties with the West are too strong in exile for any one person to be able to decide on such a step; rather, someone from the Country might be able to assume the risk of such a change—a 180-degree shift of Poland's entire policy in the matter of the eastern boundaries.
>
> It seems, then, that we will go to Washington, to Roosevelt . . .[109]

Four days later, already in Washington, Mitkiewicz recounted several long walks with Sikorski during which the latter reportedly was in a very bad humor:

> I sense that the closer we come to fundamental discussions, which will perhaps decide the fate of the Polish Republic after this war, the more General Sikorski betrays enormous anxiety and agitation, . . .
> During this walk, the General expressed highly pessimistic views as to the future structure of relations between Soviet Russia and the Western powers; he saw the Polish question in an especially black light. At one point, he blurted out with genuine bitterness: "If even here, in America, they will do nothing to help me, then nothing will remain for me but to move with the Staff, and perhaps also the Government of Poland, to Moscow, and to go the whole way [*pójść na całego*] with Stalin."

Reflecting later on these talks Mitkiewicz continued,

> . . . I conclude from numerous of the General's statements that he sees clearly a total aversion on the part of the Western powers to interfering in the matter of our boundaries in the east and to the Polish question in general—an aversion similar to the position taken by the

---

[109] Mitkiewicz, *Z gen. Sikorskim*, p. 230.

whole West in 1920. I see also that the General is struggling hard with himself over *the ultimate decision concerning our future policy: whether to go with Soviet Russia, or to remain faithful to the Western powers. At the same time, [he] does not see the possibility of . . . [a third alternative]*. He takes very seriously the opposition voices among the émigrés and in the Country. Responsibility for the fate of the Polish Republic weighs as a monstrous burden on the General . . .

"It is precisely from this," Mitkiewicz concluded, "that all his vacillations flow."[110]

JUDGED solely in terms of their immediate goal of enlisting American diplomacy in the struggle to prevent British recognition of Soviet territorial demands, this trip has to be ranked as a success for the Poles. Without question the opinions they found among many American officials were quite similar to their own on such matters as Stalin's postwar ambitions, his motives in posing territorial demands at this stage of the war, as well as the probable consequences of conceding those demands. A State Department memorandum prepared for Secretary of State Hull and President Roosevelt in early February 1942 ascribed Stalin's "insistence upon obtaining at least certain territorial commitments at this time" to his desire:

1. to break down the principle thus far observed by the American and British Governments not to make any territorial commitments prior to the peace conference;
2. to make use of the recognition of his territorial claims as evidence of the justification of the Soviet Union in invading Poland and the Baltic States and in making war on Finland in 1939 and 1940;
3. to have promises now with regard to Soviet frontiers which might be useful to him later at the Peace Conference in case the war should end with a weakened Soviet Union not in occupation of the territories which he has demanded.

"At no time" since Hitler's attack on the Soviet Union, continued the memorandum, had the Department "been in doubt that

Stalin's references to the desirability of entering into negotiations for a political agreement with Great Britain were in fact part of a maneuver the purpose of which was to place the British Government in such a position that it would be embarrassing for it to reject Soviet demands that it recognize certain Soviet territorial claims and that it promise to agree to certain territorial adjustments on the European continent

[110] Ibid., pp. 239-41 [entry for March 23, 1942; emphasis added].

and to other arrangements which would make the Soviet Union the dominating power of Eastern Europe if not of the whole continent.

Moreover, the Americans warned, abandonment of the principle of postponement, while weakening Allied unity, "would result in only a temporary improvement" in Anglo-Soviet relations:

> If the British Government, with the tacit or expressed approval of this Government, should abandon the principle of no territorial commitments prior to the Peace Conference, it would be placed in a difficult position to resist additional Soviet demands relating to frontiers, territory, or to spheres of influence which would almost certainly follow whenever the Soviet Government would find itself in a favorable bargaining position. There is no doubt that the Soviet Government has tremendous ambitions with regard to Europe and that at some time or other the United States and Great Britain will be forced to state that they cannot agree, at least in advance, to all of its demands. It would seem that it is preferable to take a firm attitude now, rather than to retreat and to be compelled to take a firm attitude later when our position has been weakened by the abandonment of the general principles referred to above.[111]

As welcome as these views may have been, from a broader perspective the Poles must have come away from Washington profoundly unsettled over prospects for future American support of their own postwar program. Raczyński noted in his diary on his return that, in all his official meetings, he had encountered a determination to "defend the principles of the Atlantic Charter" and a "unanimous" rejection of " 'security' considerations as grounds for Soviet territorial claims." Yet in the very next sentence he had to admit that "these same arguments can be turned against us when our territorial claims are up for discussion."[112] Moreover, it was clear that behind the smokescreen of Charter principles the Americans lacked a coherent policy and, for the most part, took an overly simplistic view of postwar problems. On the one hand, Roosevelt and Welles told Sikorski and Raczyński on separate occasions that, with the disarmament of Germany at the end of the war, the security of the Soviet Union would no longer be threatened and therefore she would no longer have any grounds for pressing her territorial demands. On the other hand, Assistant Secretary of State Adolf Berle expounded a view more compatible with the British

---

[111] *FRUS, 1942*, 3:504-512. For the detailed record of Anglo-American exchanges on the subject of the Anglo-Soviet treaty, see ibid., pp. 490-561; also Hull, *Memoirs*, 2:1165-74.

[112] Raczyński, *W sojuszniczym Londynie*, p. 137; this passage is omitted from the English edition.

balance-of-power outlook than with the Atlantic Charter. Russia would emerge from the war as a great power, he told Raczyński and Ciechanowski, and it was "inevitable that the interests and demands of such an organism [would] receive special consideration." It was also "inconceivable that the unlimited sovereignty of small states . . . could stand in the way of the inevitable and natural political and economic expansion of a great power." Using the example of the American hemisphere, Berle thought it would be possible to "secure the free development of the smaller states [on Russia's periphery] while simultaneously taking into account [her defensive] requirements."[113]

Most damaging of all in light of Sikorski's current dilemma was the rigid American stand on the postponement to the postwar period of "all questions involving definitive boundaries and territorial readjustments." As Welles told the Poles in no uncertain terms, the United States would make no commitments itself during wartime, and would brook no such arrangements arrived at by others.[114] From the general's point of view, this was a clear warning that even should he be able to reach an acceptable settlement with Stalin, he could have no assurance that such a settlement would be respected at the peace conference; indeed, he could reasonably expect it to be denounced.

Sikorski's trip to the United States did not end the struggle over the Anglo-Soviet treaty. The wrangling went on for another two months, coming to an end only on May 26th with the signing of a twenty-year alliance omitting all references to frontiers.[115] But for the Poles it was a Pyrrhic victory, won at great political cost. For, while the British had shown their willingness to entertain Soviet demands at the expense of third (and mostly Allied) countries, they had proven quite unwilling to commit themselves to the principle of compensation at Germany's expense, on grounds of the negative results of "any announcement about the handing over of East Prussia to Poland from the point of view of its effects on

[113] Lipski, Raczyński, and Stroński, *Trzy podróże*, p. 13; see also note 100 above, and Ciechanowski, *Defeat in Victory*, pp. 93-94. Berle's memo of this conversation is less specific; *FRUS, 1942*, 3:111-12.

[114] *FRUS, 1942*, 3:130. It is worth recalling that, while Sikorski did not present his territorial program during this visit, the State Department was not unapprised of the Poles' desire for some boundary corrections with Germany, both for strategic and economic reasons and as compensation for lands they might lose in the east. See Biddle's letters of September 1941 and February 1942; *FRUS, 1941*, 1:375-77, and *FRUS, 1942*, 3:102.

[115] See especially Churchill, *The Hinge of Fate*, pp. 332-36; and Eden, *The Reckoning*, pp. 370-72 and 375-82. *The Cadogan Diaries* (ed. Dilks, pp. 449-55) indicate that by this time Eden was "longing to get out of his promise about frontiers. . . . But it's a bit late for that now!"

German policy and propaganda.''[116] Moreover, although it was American influence, together with ill-advised promises of a second front in 1942, that proved decisive in dissuading both the British and Russians,[117] it was the Poles who provided an easy mark for Moscow's irritation.[118]

Evidence of Soviet pique was ample. As we have already seen in some detail, the maneuvers that eventually led to the total evacuation of the Polish Army from the Soviet Union began in earnest on the eve of Sikorski's departure for Washington; by the time of the treaty's signing, recruitment had been halted and the Soviets had declared that there was no possibility of its being reopened. Equally ominous was Molotov's last minute attempt to reinsert in the text recognition of the 1941 frontier with Poland.[119] Since Stalin had previously stated that he wanted to settle this frontier directly with the Poles, was this perhaps a signal that he no longer wished to traffic with the exile government? Molotov had also taken advantage of his London stay to step up pressure on the Czechs to abandon their federation plans with the Poles, and by mid-year the talks were in a state of unofficial suspension.[120]

In an effort to reopen channels of communication, Sikorski asked Eden to arrange a meeting with Molotov before the latter's return to Moscow.

[116] See especially C4789/19/55, FO 371/31083, and N2182/5/38, FO 371/32880, PRO. As one Foreign Office official commented on the Polish request for explicit recognition of the principle of compensation (see note 105, this chapter, and Chapter VI, note 32, above): ''The question whether we can give any guarantee to Poland about East Prussia has already been considered and turned down. It may be that in our own minds we have already allocated East Prussia to Poland, but to allow this to be known, either directly or indirectly, at the present time, would be the greatest mistake. It would not only oblige us to give other territorial assurances in Europe, but it would completely wreck our propaganda policy to Germany . . .''

[117] As indicated in Chapter IX above (pp. 241-42), what finally persuaded the Russians to drop their territorial demands for the moment was not the moral force of the American arguments against recognition of territorial changes during war, but a desire not to antagonize the United States at a time when it had begun to hint at the possibility of a second front in 1942, See Dallek, *Roosevelt and American Foreign Policy*, pp. 342-47; Feis, *Churchill, Roosevelt, Stalin*, pp. 62-64; and *FRUS, 1942*, 3:558-61.

[118] Raczyński noted in his diary on July 10th: ''Despite public pronouncements of a good reception in Moscow, the Anglo-Soviet treaty has left an ample store of ill-humor there. This treaty is only a makeshift [version] of what they wanted. To a certain extent they probably ascribe their defeat to Polish diplomacy.'' *W sojuszniczym Londynie*, p. 141. At the time, Eden was effusive in giving Sikorski ''100%'' of the credit for averting a treaty containing territorial concessions, although he does not mention the Polish role in his memoirs; *Documents*, 1:364-65.

[119] Churchill, *The Hinge of Fate*, p. 332; Eden, *The Reckoning*, pp. 380-81; and Feis, *Churchill, Roosevelt, Stalin*, p. 61.

[120] Wandycz, *Czechoslovak-Polish Confederation*, pp. 79-82; also Raczyński, *W sojuszniczym Londynie*, p. 154; and pp. 327-28 below.

As Raczyński has described the meeting (a luncheon on June 10th), it was a stiff, unproductive affair which dragged on for three hours in "atrocious French" (a reference to Soviet Ambassador Bogomolov's interpreting). The Poles talked about the need for "friendship," the Russians about "understanding." Sikorski's suggestion that he pay a second visit to Russia "was met with casual politeness, making it clear that the offer was accepted only *ad referendum*"; the parties adjourned "having achieved nothing positive."[121] Within the month the decision to evacuate the remainder of the army had been reached, and the Soviets had begun to close down the Polish civilian relief organization, arresting scores of embassy delegates throughout the Soviet Union.

Thus not quite a year after the signing of the Polish-Soviet Agreement of July 1941, and scarcely more than six months after his apparently successful talks with Stalin, Sikorski's policy was stalled and his basic dilemma unchanged. Toward the end of June, Mitkiewicz confided to his diary:

> . . . The General reflected at length on the difficulties we are having in our relations with Soviet Russia, and in this connection with the Western Allies, and especially with the British. The British, said the General, would like us to be absolutely and utterly faithful to them as present and future allies, but at the same time they would like us, by ourselves, to find some sort of adjustment of our affairs with Russia. Whereas Russia and Stalin . . . tell us explicitly that we have only one course: to accept their conditions and to subordinate ourselves politically—now and in the future. The one clearly contradicts the other. . . .
>
> General Sikorski mentioned the great difficulties he is encountering in the internal sphere—i.e., our opposition. He claims that it is impossible to convince our people that we have no choice as to the direction of our foreign policy. The entire opposition . . . would like the Polish government to stand inflexibly on the pre-September [1939] position in the matter of our eastern boundaries and, in general, in relation to Soviet Russia, paying no heed to the Western Allies.

The core of his dilemma was evident in the further course he outlined to Mitkiewicz. He hoped, he said, to go to Moscow again either at the end of 1942 or early in 1943, to try to reach "a final settlement of our affairs with Soviet Russia." On the other hand, he indicated that he had little choice, for the time being at least, but to accept the strictures of Atlantic

---

[121] Raczyński, *W sojuszniczym Londynie*, pp. 142-43; and Eden, *The Reckoning*, p. 383. For Sikorski's request that Eden arrange the meeting, see the record of the Eden-Sikorski meeting, June 8th; C5814/19/55, FO 371/31083, PRO.

policy and "to continue his policy of total unity with the Allies, avoiding all matters which could because of the Polish question breach Allied unity, in particular with Russia."[122] It was a paralyzing situation and one that he could not long tolerate.

Sikorski's last American visit, December 1942. So it is not surprising that, as Polish-Soviet relations continued to deteriorate during the summer and early fall of 1942, General Sikorski decided to do what he had failed to do in March—to journey yet again to Washington and to lay his whole program before the Americans in a last desperate effort to solicit their support before seeking another round of talks with Stalin. Originally projected for October, this third and final American visit spanned six weeks, from December 1st through January 10th of the new year.[123] In contrast with his earlier trips, there can be no doubt that on this occasion Sikorski did submit the prepared memoranda. Nor can there be any doubt that, instead of merely presenting general principles for a postwar settlement in Central Europe and despite warnings of an adverse reception, these memoranda set forth Poland's war aims in great detail, most importantly in the areas of Poland's western boundary, the regional organization of Central Europe and its relationship to the Great Powers, and the postwar treatment of Germany.

Since these proposals have already been discussed at considerable length,[124] there is no need to repeat them here. Before turning to the substance of the American response, however, there are several questions concerning Sikorski's expectations from this trip that bear examination. First, in view of the fact that his second trip earlier in the year had been instrumental in souring Polish-Soviet relations, was he now justified in believing that Stalin would be willing to receive him after this one? With the benefits of hindsight, the answer is probably no. But at the time the prospects, though

[122] Mitkiewicz, *Z gen. Sikorskim*, p. 295 [entry for June 21, 1942]. In an earlier entry, Mitkiewicz reported that Sikorski "has ordered us all to be calm and composed—it is impermissible for us to break from Allied ranks. Indeed, where would we go?" He then quoted the general's words, "spoken with genuine bitterness: 'English policy in relation to Poland is insincere, just like Soviet [policy]; we are in a very difficult position and are thrown back more and more on ourselves.'" Ibid., p. 284.

[123] The Americans asked Sikorski to postpone his visit until after the November congressional elections; the trip was probably further delayed by problems related to the evacuation of the army and the termination of the civilian relief effort in the Soviet Union. In addition to his conferences in Washington, the general made several speaking trips to other cities and spent a week in Mexico to arrange asylum for the Polish children he hoped to evacuate from Russia. See *FRUS, 1942*, 3:189-90; Kukiel, *Generał Sikorski*, pp. 212-13; and Lipski, Raczyński, and Stroński, *Trzy Podróże*, p. 15. For a detailed account of his activities during this six-week period, see the Dz.Cz.N.W./XII.1942 and I.1943, GSHI.

[124] See pp. 107-118 above.

bleak, did not appear entirely hopeless. True, his efforts to elicit an invitation from Molotov in June had gone unanswered; true also, the Soviets had consistently refused to discuss a renewal of military recruitment and had proven exceedingly stubborn in the matters of the arrested Polish delegates and requests to evacuate Polish children. On the other hand, strenuous American intervention had resulted in the eventual release of most of the delegates;[125] likewise, in the wake of a temporary lull in press polemics on both sides, Sikorski's conciliatory letter of introduction for Poland's new ambassador to the Soviet Union, Tadeusz Romer, had produced a brief but also conciliatory reply from Stalin.[126] However, it is likely that the general was animated less by optimism over the prospects for a renewed rapprochement than by sheer necessity born of the realization that "[Russia's] position is constantly strengthening."[127] Moreover, even if he thought he could reach an acceptable settlement with Stalin without the staunch diplomatic backing of the Western Allies (at this point a most unlikely eventuality), he could scarcely have been expected to do so at the risk of forfeiting the West's support at a future peace conference.

The other area of ambiguity concerns the nature and form of the assistance Sikorski hoped to receive from the Americans. On the one hand,

[125] *FRUS, 1942*, 3:196; and p. 11 of Ambassador O'Malley's review of Soviet policy toward Poland of April 29, 1943, in C4850/258/55, FO 371/34571, PRO. See also the notes of Sikorski's meeting with Averell Harriman, September 21, 1942, in PRM 71/14, GSHI; and his meeting with Wendell Willkie, who had personally made the appeal to Stalin in Roosevelt's name, on January 9, 1943, in Dz.Cz.N.W./I.1943, GSHI. That the release of the Polish delegates was little more than a short-lived tactical maneuver on Moscow's part is indicated by the Aide-Mémoire delivered to Raczyński by Bogomolov on October 31, 1942, accusing them of "many instances of intelligence activities, detrimental to the interests of the Soviet Union"; translated in State Decimal File: 740.0011 European War 1939/26685, NA.

[126] See Sikorski's letter of October 26, 1942, in *Documents*, 1:441-42; Stalin's reply, received December 3rd in Washington, appears in *FRUS, 1942*, 3:199. Concerning the accompanying lull in hostile press commentary, see C10219/19/55, FO 371/31088, PRO.

[127] See especially Sikorski's letter of November 28, 1942, to Underground commander, General Grot-Rowecki, in *Documents*, 1:457-58; also Raczyński, *W sojuszniczym Londynie*, p. 161. Although some describe him as optimistic at this point about future Polish-Soviet relations (e.g., Kukiel, *General Sikorski*, p. 208), Mitkiewicz saw his East versus West dilemma as reaching a climax: "I presume also that Gen. Sikorski's role becomes more difficult with every moment. Political events are forcing [him] to make decisions on which will depend the building of a new edifice for the Polish State. Whether to stay with the concept arrived at back in 1939 and continued to the present, or to opt for fundamental change? Or perhaps to seek compromises on all sides and wait until the end of the war for a decision, as we are advised in London and Washington.

"As it appears to me, Gen. Sikorski has thrashed about like a wounded lion in a net, seeking a way out of this situation, but ultimately he accepted the advice of the Western Allies. Although Klimecki told me not long ago that, following the visit to Washington, the General will be leaving again for Moscow." *Z gen. Sikorskim*, p. 304.

every aspect of his handling of the western boundary issue suggests that he neither asked for nor expected an immediate or public commitment on his proposals. On first informing Roosevelt that he would submit a memorandum on this subject, he said: "I do not ask for a definitive answer on these matters. I know that they are touchy for you at this moment, Mr. President. I ask only for serious consideration of our arguments and [that you] undertake discussion on this subject at the appropriate time."[128] Similarly, in the Polish draft of the letter he hoped to receive from Roosevelt, he did not ask for an endorsement of specific territorial gains in the west, but only that the president "not exclude the possibility that the necessity will arise to widen the basis of Poland's security in the West in relation to Germany and thus to strengthen her economic independence."[129]

On the other hand, the sequence in which Sikorski submitted the various memoranda also rules out the possibility that he was merely seeking support for an inflexible stand on the Riga boundary in the east. It has been stated before, but will bear repeating, that the three detailed memoranda on the German problem with relation to Poland, a Central European federation, and the postwar occupation of Germany—together with the summary "western boundaries" memo—were handed to Under Secretary Welles within a few days of the general's arrival, between December 4th and 7th. As will become clear shortly, they were sent first to the European Division of the State Department for study and comment. The weight of the evidence suggests that he began receiving preliminary feedback on his proposals within a few days, perhaps as early as December 9th, and that he was officially apprised of the American reaction either on the 12th or on the 21st, following his return from a week-long speaking tour outside of Washington. However, it was only on December 23rd that he submitted the fourth major memorandum defending Poland's prewar boundary in the east. Finally, although the draft letter did ask for an affirmation of Poland's integrity as of August 31, 1939, it added the phrase "consistent with the principles of the Atlantic Charter"—a formula that did not foreclose acceptance of changes in the future.

Unfortunately, deciding what Sikorski did not expect is somewhat easier than determining with any certainty what he was seeking. It is possible to interpret his draft letter as a plea for evenhanded application of the Atlantic Charter, and therefore for American support for a postponement of a decision on Poland's eastern boundary. Or it may simply have reflected his deference to the American position. Certainly he could not have be-

[128] "Notatka z konferencji z Prezydentem Roosveltem odbytej w dniu 2-go grudnia 1942r," A.XII.23/42, folio 1, no. 5, GSHI. Part of this note appears (in sometimes faulty translation) in *Documents*, 2:688-91.

[129] *FRUS, 1942*, 3:202-203; see also Chapter V, note 101, above.

lieved at this late date that postponement would satisfy Stalin—or, for that matter, that the Poles themselves could risk postponing a decision at a time when they were beginning to contemplate the probability of a Soviet liberation of Poland.[130] My own conclusion, based admittedly on circumstantial evidence, is that Sikorski hoped that by laying bare the totality of his predicament—the full extent of Poland's difficulties with the Soviet Union and the pressure he was under to reach an immediate settlement there—he could obtain Washington's support in three specific areas: first, recognition of the principle of Poland's territorial integrity within her prewar boundaries as a counterweight to Stalin's ever more insistent demand for the Curzon line, thereby measurably increasing his chances of obtaining a compromise in the east; second, tacit approval of his boundary proposals in the west, or at least of the principle of compensation based on Poland's economic and strategic needs, giving him reasonable assurance that whatever promise of compensation he could get from Stalin would not be rejected later by the Western Allies;[131] and third, public expression of American support for "a Confederation of Poland with Czechoslovakia as a first step in the direction of a European policy of international cooperation."[132] Only Washington's response in the first two areas will be discussed here; U.S. views on the federation idea are related in Chapter XI.

DURING their first meeting on December 2nd, President Roosevelt made several remarks concerning Poland's boundaries with Germany and the postwar treatment of Germany in general that must have been at least

---

[130] In his letter to General Rowecki (*Documents*, 1:457-58; see note 124 above), Sikorski implied that, with or without American support, he thought it imperative to seek a rapid improvement in Polish-Soviet relations: "I hope to be able to convince Roosevelt of the necessity of keeping a joint and strong line of action with respect to Russia, should the latter try to infringe upon Polish territorial sovereignty. However, I have to reckon also with such developments which might lead to the Red Army entering the frontiers of the Republic, in pursuit of the enemy. . . ." He went on to describe the prospect of armed struggle between the Underground army and Soviet troops as "sheer madness" and to order Rowecki to prepare to bring the army into the open and to stress its "positive attitude toward Soviet Russia."

[131] In this same letter to Rowecki (see preceding note), Sikorski wrote: "*Maybe* the Polish Government, with British and American support, will eventually induce the Soviet Government to recognize our rights in the East with a simultaneous support for our claims in the West, which include East Prussia, Danzig, and such a rectification of our frontier as may be necessary for the security of our ports on the Baltic; Opole Silesia should return to Poland. *I envisage a direct approach to Soviet Russia* by us in relation to these questions." [emphasis added]

[132] See Sikorski's draft letter, *FRUS, 1942*, 3:202-203.

mildly encouraging to his Polish guest. It was, for instance, Roosevelt who first raised the boundary issue:

> Roosevelt: And now, General, what are your thoughts on Poland's western boundaries?
> Sikorski: They should be straightened, and East Prussia and Danzig should belong to Poland.
> Roosevelt: And what will become of the German population of this province?
> Sikorski: They will flee to Germany. And for the rest, I think we will apply to the Germans the same methods of transfer which they applied to the conquered nations.

Here they discuss briefly the ethnic structure of the population, after which the president declared: "Yes, East Prussia should be yours, but this is a very difficult problem." Turning then to the problem of Germany itself, he continued:

> We have no intention of concluding this war with any kind of armistice or treaty. Germany must surrender unconditionally. We must then dismember her and subject her to the harshest possible quarantine, if need be for thirty years. We must eradicate Hitlerism completely, for only on its ruins can we build peace.[133]

This apparent willingness to see East Prussia incorporated into a postwar Poland was repeated to Sikorski two days later during a meeting with Sumner Welles, although the under secretary now indicated that Washington would *not* approve forcible expulsion of the German population.[134]

However, whatever optimism these remarks may have engendered over prospects of a favorable reception for his other territorial aspirations proved unfounded. A December 9th memorandum, prepared for Welles by the State Department's Division of European Affairs in response to the Sikorski memos, began with a reaffirmation of the Department's attachment to collective security, listing as one of "a number of considerations which must be kept constantly in mind":

> a. The degree to which a proposed territorial settlement will further or obstruct the creation in postwar Europe of a general system of collective security rather than the acquisition at the expense of others by one state or another of strategically important frontiers or areas which it considers necessary for its national security against its neighbors.

[133] See note 128 above.
[134] *FRUS, 1942*, 3:200; see also note 138 below.

The memo went on to temper this view somewhat, first with respect to East Prussia and Poland's access to the sea:

> Poland must . . . have free and unthreatened access to the sea. The annexation of East Prussia to Poland would appear to be a reasonable means of achieving such access to the sea while at the same time removing a constant threat to Poland's security.

Then, in an apparent reference to the Silesian and Pomeranian wedges, it continued:

> There is some force to the argument that Poland's western frontier should be so established that Germany should not have an enclave into the vitals of Poland and also that the greatest security for Poland's access to the sea be assured. It is worth keeping in mind, however, that there is no natural frontier between Poland and Germany.

Having made these rather hopeful observations, the memo concluded with the following assessment of Sikorski's proposals:

> It is very important to observe that in the aggregate the proposals presented by General Sikorski set forth a point of view greatly at variance with the basic principles we have adopted as the real general war aims included in such documents as the Atlantic Charter and the Declaration by United Nations. An examination of the several documents now presented shows that they cover reparations, war guilt, frontier pretensions, occupation, military booty, land and sea bases, et cetera, all in the spirit of extreme nationalism, with only a mild suggestion of Poland's own plans for international collaboration [?], . . . The proposals in effect lay down Poland's maximum nationalistic demands. It is suggested that some indication be given to General Sikorski that we view them in that light.[135]

There is no way of knowing in how great detail these views were communicated to Sikorski, since records of the subsequent meeting or

[135] Ibid., pp. 204-208. This memorandum was addressed to the secretary of state, but as Hull was in poor health at the time it was Under Secretary Welles who conducted all the substantive talks with Sikorski. Kowalski's handling of this memo and the western boundary question in general deserves passing mention here. By ignoring the discrepancy in dates, he treats this final paragraph as a response to Sikorski's memo on the *eastern* boundaries, and to his alleged "great power" aspirations and anti-Soviet machinations. He then goes on to describe the American response on the *western* boundaries as "considerably more favorable," while ignoring every shred of evidence to the contrary. See *Walka dyplomatyczna*, pp. 285-301, and, to a lesser extent, *ZSRR a granica*, pp. 63-67.

meetings with Welles are not available.[136] It would be particularly interesting to know whether he was informed of the European Division's opinion "that Germany should not have an enclave into the vitals of Poland"—a formulation that could be interpreted as support for the incorporation into Poland of Upper Silesia in the southwest as well as an additional slice of Eastern Pomerania in the northwest. This was the position eventually adopted by the United States at Yalta,[137] and one that would have approximated the Poles' minimum demands. On the other hand, this was not the conclusion implied by a U.S. paper on Upper Silesia submitted to the Foreign Office in 1943, which suggested instead that "a united Upper Silesia would be more than Poland could profitably exploit." Nor is there any evidence that the State Department's planners had yet begun to consider changes in the Pomeranian sector.[138]

[136] Sikorski may have met with Welles on December 12th, three days after this analysis was prepared, and unquestionably met with him on the 21st. No record of either meeting appears in either the Polish or American archives. The official journal of the general's activities (*Dziennik Czynności Naczelnego Wodza*) mentions only the meeting on the 21st, but without even the usual abstract of topics covered, not to mention a more detailed record of the session. However, other sources indicate the possibility of an earlier meeting, most likely on the 12th. For instance, Welles's account of the December 4th meeting mentions a second the following week, after the Department had had a chance to study the Polish memoranda. *FRUS, 1942*, 3:202. In addition, a program of Sikorski's visit from the embassy files indicates such a meeting on December 12th, from 9:30 to 11:00; but again there is no record of the substance of the talks. Ciechanowski Deposit, Box 93[84], folio: "General W. Sikorski's visit in Washington, December 1942 to January 10th, 1943," no. 22, HIWRP. The absence of these records is perhaps more understandable on the Polish than on the American side, in that Sikorski made the official records of his meetings during this, and apparently other, trips available to his cabinet, and obviously did not want to be embarrassed by a detailed exposition of an American rejection of proposals that his cabinet had not authorized him to make in the first place. In this connection, there are also very substantial discrepancies between Welles's version of the December 4th conversation and the Polish notes written up by Ambassador Ciechanowski—discrepancies that on balance cast doubt on the reliability of the latter. Most striking is the predominance given to the eastern boundary in the Polish version, while the Welles account gives distinctly more attention to a discussion of East Prussia and the western boundary not mentioned in the former. In fact, Ciechanowski's notes indicate that Sikorski rejected out of hand the idea of compensation. What makes this version additionally suspect is the fact that it was written up only on December 21st, after Sikorski had met again with Welles and presumably been given the American rejection of his federation and western boundary proposals. In this light, it is quite possible that what purports to be a record of the December 4th meeting actually represents a composite *and partial* record of several meetings, from which the most sensitive parts have been omitted. Ciechanowski Deposit, Box 67[84], folio: "Raporty podczas pobytu Premiera Generała Sikorskiego w U.S.A. (1.XII.1942—10.I.1943)," HIWRP.

[137] *FRUS: Malta and Yalta*, pp. 230-33.

[138] C9925/231/55, FO 371/34561, PRO; and Chapter VIII, note 42, above. The quoted comment is from a critical appraisal of the U.S. paper by Mr. Holliday, British consul in Katowice (capital of Polish Upper Silesia) before the war. Contesting the view of the American

There is nothing in the credible Polish sources to indicate that General Sikorski was given any inkling of the more favorable interpretation, or any real hope that, beyond East Prussia, the Americans had seriously considered the question of territorial gains for Poland in the west. (Indeed, the State Department memorandum specifically recommended against any "weakening" of the American position of "not negotiat[ing] on questions of European frontiers at this stage of the war.") Raczyński's diary contains the following entry for December 13th: "From the telegrams that have reached us, it appears that the federation concept has met with a very favorable reception, but there is no sympathy for our territorial claims."[139] Mitkiewicz, on reviewing documents from the trip, wrote that "only the inclusion of the former Free City of Danzig presented no doubts" and that

---

author that the resources of prewar Polish Upper Silesia were more than enough to meet the country's needs, Holliday concluded: "Pre-war figures would, on the contrary, show that compared to Western European countries Poland would still be under-equipped industrially relative to area and population even if she disposed of the combined resources of a united Upper Silesia." There were other signs as well that, regardless of the mildly positive aspects of the December 9th memorandum, the trend of thinking within the State Department was deeply inimical even to Sikorski's minimum program. For instance, a November 1943 comparison by the Department's Division of Political Studies [formerly the Advisory Committee on Post-War Foreign Policy (p. 163 above)] of British and American views on the Polish-German boundary noted U.S. objections to the Poles' basic demands in East Prussia, Upper Silesia, and Eastern Pomerania: For instance, while the Political Subcommittee "tended to favor" incorporation of East Prussia and Danzig into Poland, though *without* forced evacuation of the German population, the Territorial Subcommittee "favored retention of East Prussia by Germany" on grounds that "the solidly German character of the population, the difficulties of transfer, and the certainty of lasting irredentism if the province were to be taken from Germany, were considerations which outweighed those of strategy." In the southwest, the British recommendation that all of German Upper Silesia be transferred to Poland would have given that country "more than twice as much territory as the solution preferred by the Territorial Subcommittee." As for the Pomeranian sector, this analysis admitted that the Division of Political Studies had made "no studies . . . concerning possible modification of the Polish-German frontier between Upper Silesia and the Baltic Sea"—that the subcommittees had "not considered the possibility of revising it in favor of Poland" because there was "no ethnic or economic basis for such revision." State Decimal File: 860C.0144/10-1243, NA. See also Chapter XI, notes 89 and 107, below.

[139] Raczyński, *W sojuszniczym Londynie*, p. 157. It is not clear whether this passage reflects Sikorski's cable of December 9th or some later (unavailable) report. On the 9th, Sikorski cabled back to London that the federation idea had met with a much more favorable response than had been foreseen. On the other hand, "[the question of] our boundaries has not yet matured in opinion here, but the American Government has undertaken confidential discussions on this subject with me." At the same time, he requested that the memoranda on the federation and Poland's western boundary be submitted to the Foreign Office. Dz.Cz.N.W./XII.1942, GSHI. At this point, of course, the Americans had *not* yet undertaken confidential discussions on boundary questions, and even Sikorski's optimism on the American response to the federation idea turned out to be premature.

even East Prussia was viewed as posing "a difficult problem."[140] Kukiel, who also had access to the records, wrote: "Our plans for incorporating the whole area up to the Oder and Lusatian Neisse in an East-Central European 'Federation' were not treated realistically. . . . Sikorski's 'minimum' demands for Opole Silesia and a broadening of access to the sea were taken under advisement; but [the Americans] fretted over whether East Prussia wasn't sufficient compensation for the lands taken from Poland by the Soviets."[141] Sikorski himself reported to his cabinet after his return to London that, while Roosevelt "understands the need to incorporate [East Prussia and] Danzig," Polish proposals concerning "the necessity of straightening the western boundary, in particular in Silesia, arouse reservations."[142]

In fact, during one of his conferences with the president, it was even suggested that Poland should return part of the "Corridor" to Germany (!) in exchange for receiving East Prussia.[143] Although this exchange too is omitted from the record of his talks with Roosevelt, it was an obvious reference to a plan for partitioning Germany that Welles had been nursing along for at least a year and that reached full flower in his 1944 book *The Time for Decision*.[144] Welles believed that the conjunction of two factors—unification under Prussian control and the cult of militarism—were responsible for the German menace, and that "partition will do more than anything else to break the hold which German militarism has on the German people." In order that such partition not lead to economic or political chaos or to a renewed effort at unification, he specified as a basic premise of his plan that each of his three proposed German states be capable of "ensur[ing] the eventual prosperity of the German people." Turning to the problem

---

[140] Mitkiewicz, *Z gen. Sikorskim*, p. 316. Earlier, as news of the visit filtered back to London, he wrote: "Gen. Sikorski's trip to America seems to have been completely unsuccessful. The news of this trip, edited by the inseparable Dr. Retinger, sounds disastrous. . . ." (p. 306).

[141] Kukiel, *Generał Sikorski*, pp. 215-16.

[142] "Sprawozdanie Prezesa Rady Ministrów z podróży do U.S.A.," January 21, 1943, Dz.Cz.N.W./I.1943, GSHI; and Pobóg-Malinowski, *Najnowsza historia*, 3:247, n. 78. It was at this point in his report that Sikorski chastised his colleagues for the December 2nd National Council resolution defending the Riga boundary (see note 64 above), stating that it had created "a bad impression, not only arousing suspicions of [Polish] imperialism, but also giving ammunition to the Polish opposition . . ." Both this report and the record of his farewell visit with Roosevelt on January 5th indicate that Sikorski had some difficulty persuading the president that Danzig as well as East Prussia were essential to Poland. For the latter record, see Ciechanowski Deposit, Box 67[84], folio: "raporty pobytu . . . ," HIWRP.

[143] Mitkiewicz, *Z gen. Sikorskim*, p. 316; and Kukiel, *Generał Sikorski*, p. 215.

[144] Chap. IX: "The German Menace Can Be Ended," pp. 336-61. For an early reference to Welles's ideas on postwar Germany, see the memo of his conversation with Lord Halifax on February 18, 1942, in *FRUS, 1942*, 3:520.

of the boundary between Poland and a future northeastern German state (provisionally composed of Prussia, Mecklenburg, and Saxony), he continued:

> The only solution . . . is to give Poland the province of East Prussia, *at the same time readjusting the frontier between Western Prussia and the old Polish Corridor so as to give the new German state*, of which Western Prussia will form a part, *an area of the old Corridor*. [emphasis added]

Welles did add that the final border through the Corridor should be based on prevailing ethnographic and economic conditions; population transfers "from one sovereignty to another" would be voluntary, with "full and equitable compensation" for property left behind.

These were all commendable democratic principles. But it is quite clear that the focus of Welles's concern was German economic prosperity and that he had not long pondered the practicality or morality of asking Poland to compensate Germany or to suffer permanent disadvantage as a result of acts of war against her. He seems to have been wholly unaware, for instance, that the ratio of population to cultivated land was more than 60 percent greater in prewar Poland than in prewar Germany,[145] or that the Poles had been forcibly expelled from the territories reincorporated into the Reich in 1939. Moreover, the map accompanying Welles's plan indicates that the area subject to possible return to Germany included not only the Corridor but also the western part of Poznania, prewar Poland's most modern agricultural province, up to a line running south to the boundary with Lower Silesia at a point somewhat north and west of Breslau.[146]

Without access to the record, we are left to imagine Sikorski's reaction on being exposed to even a preliminary version of this plan. On his return to London, he reported: "I succeeded . . . in completely unburdening Roosevelt's views of the notion foisted upon him of giving back (Polish) Pomerania for East Prussia."[147] But the fact that it was suggested to him at all is indicative of the backhanded, almost casual way in which the

[145] Polonsky, *Politics in Independent Poland*, p. 12.

[146] Welles, *The Time for Decision*, map inserted opposite p. 342 (reproduced as Map 7). It should be noted that Welles assumed here that Poland's eastern boundary would be based on the Curzon line (p. 354).

[147] See Sikorski's report cited in note 142 above. Contrary to Kukiel's statement that this was a State Department plan (*Generał Sikorski*, p. 215), the Department never favored partition. However, in this instance, Welles had the ear of the president who for personal reasons was susceptible to Welles's arguments, as he would later be to Morgenthau's. For discussion of the differences between Roosevelt and the State Department on this issue, see Gaddis, *The United States and the Origins of the Cold War*, pp. 97-100 and 119-20; also Notter, *Postwar Foreign Policy Preparation*, pp. 554-60.

Map 7

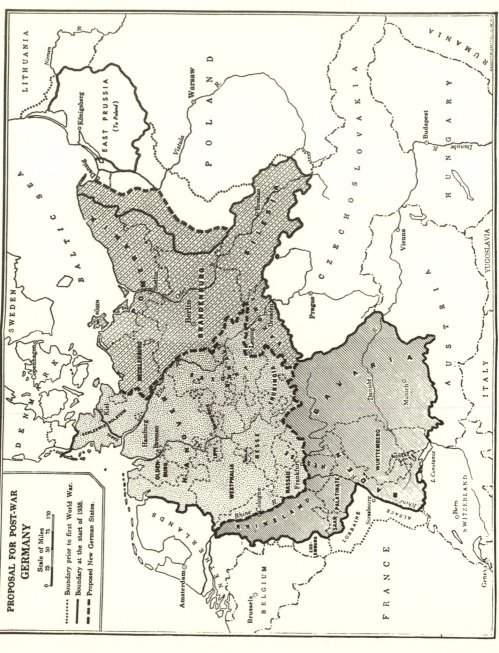

PROPOSAL FOR POST-WAR
GERMANY

Scale of Miles
0   25   50   75   100

.... Boundary prior to first World War.
———— Boundary at the start of 1938.
- - - - Proposed New German States.

SOURCE: Sumner Welles, *The Time for Decision* (New York: Harper & Brothers, 1944). Courtesy of Benjamin

Americans approached the problems of the small Central European nations lodged between Germany and Russia. (Ironically, it was Welles himself who later wrote, without however recalling his own earlier plan: "[The Curzon line] constituted a frontier which many of the more realistic Poles would have accepted, however reluctantly, if it had been combined with concessions to Poland in the form of a part in East Prussia and a part of Germany's eastern agricultural provinces.")[148]

Sikorski was, if anything, even less successful in impressing the Americans with the seriousness of Poland's difficulties with the Russians. During their first conference on December 2nd, he gave the president a confidential briefing on the true state of Polish-Soviet relations, after which the following exchange took place:

> Roosevelt: But Stalin is a realist with whom one can come to an understanding.
>
> Sikorski: Stalin is a realist, but his realism is extremely egoistic. We have canceled out past wrongs suffered from Russia. We have done this in the name of higher goals, but above all for the sake of international solidarity. We are adhering to your policy, Mr. President. Russia depends on the material aid of the United States today, and so will she tomorrow. We must take advantage of this fact to clarify the situation. . . .
>
> Roosevelt: . . . It seems to me, however, that your difficulties with Russia are not substantial. Stalin is demanding Petsamo—the neutralization of Karelia—Latvia and Estonia, and Bessarabia in the west. This does not affect Poland either directly or indirectly; thus there is ground for an understanding. I appreciate the far-sightedness and magnanimity of your policy, General. You must continue it.

Sikorski responded that he intended to do so—"my policy is bold and will remain so in the future"—and that he was ready to go to Moscow again, "but only on the condition that I have your and Churchill's support." And here he asked Roosevelt for a letter of support for his policies to use in his negotiations with Stalin. The president replied that he would be happy to give him such a letter so long as it was in keeping with the Atlantic Charter, and asked Sikorski to submit his draft to Welles.[149]

---

[148] Welles, *Seven Decisions*, p. 142. There is no question that he was referring here to Sikorski, who was the only Polish prime minister he dealt with; see also his direct reference to Sikorski, pp. 130-31.

[149] See note 128 above. Most of Sikorski's briefing on Polish-Soviet relations has been excised from the transcript. The letter referred to here is the "draft letter" already mentioned. The *Documents* translation says this was to be a letter to Stalin, but the original Polish text states clearly that it was to be addressed to Sikorski, as is the Polish draft printed in *FRUS, 1942*, 3:202-203.

On reading the Polish draft, however, the under secretary found reason to object to every major point. Apart from the assurances of a private nature that had been given to Sikorski, he said, the United States could neither make any commitments relative to Poland's future boundaries, nor could it recognize her integrity within her 1939 boundaries.[150] In fact, it is quite apparent that by this time the operations side of the State Department, Welles, and possibly the president himself, had already concluded that the Curzon line provided an equitable settlement of Poland's boundary in the east (although it should be recalled that this was not the position then being developed by the Department's postwar planners).[151] Whether Sikorski was told this in so many words is not made clear, but according to Mitkiewicz, Welles did inform him "most explicitly" that: "The Government of the United States would regard as most appropriate a direct understanding between the Polish Government and the Soviet Government on all disputed matters." Then, having told the general he could expect no commitments on Poland's future boundaries with Germany, he asked: "Doesn't the Government of Poland consider it possible to make certain concessions, even the smallest, in favor of Soviet Russia relative to the boundary established by the Riga Treaty?"[152]

Moreover, Sikorski's effort to convince the Americans that Stalin's territorial demands were only a harbinger of his intention to extend Soviet domination over all of Central and South-Eastern Europe fell on deaf ears, despite the fact that the State Department had made the same point earlier in the year. At one point, the president told his guest that, while Russia's

[150] See Welles's reports of his meetings with Sikorski on December 4th and January 4th, in *FRUS, 1942*, 3:199-202; and *FRUS, 1943*, 3:314-18. The Polish account of the January 4th meeting corresponds quite closely to Welles's; Ciechanowski Deposit, Box 67[84], folio: "Raporty pobytu," HIWRP.

[151] See the reference to the Curzon line as being "in accordance with ethnic considerations" in the Department's December 9th memo; *FRUS, 1942*, 3:206. Certainly Welles was of this view, as was Roosevelt by the following March when Eden came to Washington; see *The Reckoning*, p. 432. Likewise, Beneš wrote that Roosevelt told him in June of 1943: "He expects the final solution will be the Curzon line somewhat modified in Poland's favor and the incorporation of East Prussia in Poland. He considers this a just and right compensation which the Poles could and should accept." *Memoirs of Dr. Eduard Beneš: From Munich to New War and New Victory*, trans. Godfrey Lias, p. 195. For a departmental view more favorable to the Poles, see pp. 282-83 and note 86 above.

[152] *Z gen. Sikorskim*, pp. 316-17. According to Mitkiewicz, Sikorski's immediate reaction to this question was not recorded, but in further discussion he maintained a "strictly legal position . . . agree[ing] to an examination only at the peace conference, after the war, of fundamental problems, such as the Ukrainian problem, and that with the participation of interested parties." In general, Mitkiewicz described the American response on Polish-Soviet relations as "highly alarming from our point of view." These passages reflect fairly closely the Polish version of the December 4th meeting; but, as indicated in note 136 above, this may actually be a partial and composite account of two or three sessions with Welles.

position was still "equivocal," she was "destined to evolve in a democratic direction" and it was necessary to draw her into cooperation "on the basis of reciprocity."[153] Later Sikorski tried, without success, to impress upon Welles that "the question of Poland's eastern frontier . . . was in the nature of a precedent" or "test case" of Western resistance to Soviet ambitions:

> [I]f at this stage Stalin were definitely informed that the Government of the United States would not agree to the submerging of eastern and southern Poland in the future Soviet Union, Stalin would accede to that point of view without any material difficulty since intrinsically the territory involved was of no great importance to Stalin. But, . . . if no opposition to such imposition on the part of Stalin were evidenced now, he will take it for granted that neither the United States nor Great Britain are going to lift a finger to prevent the domination at the close of the war of most of eastern and southern Europe by the Soviet Union, and the imperialistic ambitions of the Soviet Union will be greatly accelerated and enhanced as the result of any present failure on the part of the United States to make its views known.[154]

Similarly, Sikorski's desire to insert in the final version of Roosevelt's letter, where it referred to the "re-emergence of a strong and independent Poland," the phrase "capable of effective defense and capable of economic development" brought a rebuff from Welles that the first implied "a program of rearmament which was entirely counter to the objectives of this Government."[155] The under secretary even objected to that portion of Sikorski's draft which mentioned the agreements of July and December 1941 as providing the basis for "a Polish-Soviet alliance, . . . as one of the best guarantees of European peace," on grounds that "the conclusion of military alliances of this character would have no valid basis if an effective international security were to be established."[156]

[153] "Streszczenie rozmowy z Prezydentem Roosevelt'em," PRM 97/2 and Dz. Cz.N.W./I.1943, GSHI. This conversation is mistakenly marked as having taken place on January 3rd, in part because this summary was written up by Sikorski himself only on the 5th; it is almost surely the general's account of his second meeting with the president on December 3rd. See also Pobóg-Malinowski, *Najnowsza historia*, 3:248, n. 80; and Lipski, Raczyński, and Stroński, *Trzy podróże*, p. 22. For the earlier and less sanguine State Department view, see pp. 293-94 above.

[154] See references to Sikorski's January 4th meeting with Welles in note 150 above. Apart from the term "test case" which is from the Polish account, quoted passages are from Welles's version. For a report of similar fears expressed at about this time to the British Foreign Office, see C11601/19/55, FO 371/31088, PRO.

[155] *FRUS, 1943*, 3:320-21; the final version of Roosevelt's letter to Sikorski appears on pp. 319-20.

[156] *FRUS, 1942*, 3:201-202.

THUS as 1942 ended, Sikorski was no closer to the attainment of a satisfactory boundary settlement than he had been at the beginning of the year. Indeed, to the extent that he could no longer hope for a genuine compromise in the east and that he had so far been unable to obtain assurances of adequate compensation in the west, he was that much farther away. Twelve months earlier, two courses of action had been open to him: using the Atlantic Charter as a shield, he could insist on a postponement of all territorial decisions, including consideration of Soviet demands, at least until such time as all three Great Powers were willing to agree on an overall settlement taking into account Poland's basic economic and security requirements; or, accepting the need for an immediate understanding on the eastern boundary, he could challenge the Charter head-on and press for immediate Allied approval of his program in the west.

In a year of intense diplomatic activity, he had tried one and then the other option, both with a singular lack of success. Although he had been able to avert formal concessions to the Soviets, first the British and now the Americans had let him know that, while Poland could expect no definitive consideration or commitments regarding her future boundary with Germany, neither could she expect help from the West in settling her difficulties with Moscow, either in postponing a decision or in salvaging at least part of her prewar east. In other words, while she would be bound by the Charter's restrictions in the west, she could not avail herself of its protection, even temporarily, in the east.

Moreover, the Americans had now told Sikorski in unmistakable terms that, apart from East Prussia with Danzig (on which they would give him only informal and private assurances), they were wholly unsympathetic not only to his specific proposals for the rest of Poland's boundary with Germany, but also to the economic and strategic arguments on which those proposals were based. Indeed, they had shown greater concern for Germany's postwar economic stability than for Poland's. He could not even be sure that, in taking over East Prussia, the Poles would be allowed to rid themselves of a hostile German population. In effect, Washington had told Sikorski that, in place of the "real guarantees" he sought, Poland must do what he had said she could not risk doing again—that is, throw her security "into the melting-pot of [the] general security."[157]

To this point the British, too, had given the Poles no indication of their position on compensation. But even had Foreign Secretary Eden been willing to discuss the matter, his views would have been scarcely more comforting to Sikorski than those he had encountered in Washington. In early March of 1943, on the eve of his departure for exploratory postwar

---

[157] *Documents*, 1:265; see also p. 80 above.

planning talks with Roosevelt, Eden warned the War Cabinet that "a policy of handing large areas of German territory, complete with their populations, to neighbouring states [could not] be made to last." Some boundary rectifications "might be possible and even necessary," he conceded, and he thought that Poland "could probably absorb East Prussia and part of Silesia." But, in general, he saw "a voluntary federation in Germany" as "the best long-term solution."[158] With slight variations in formulation, this remained the basic British position until Teheran, but even these minimal concessions seem to have been communicated to the Poles only in September of 1943.[159]

Both the British and the Americans would shortly begin to alter their views not only with respect to the timing of postwar decisions, but also on some of the substantive points raised by the Poles. Indeed, Foreign Office papers show that such changes, stimulated largely by Sikorski's memoranda, were already underway behind the scenes.[160] But these changes would come too late to help Sikorski, or even his successors. For, in the meantime, Moscow had had ample opportunity to observe just how little tangible support the Poles could muster in the West, with the result that, whatever Stalin had or had not been willing to offer the Poles in December of 1941, the Soviets too were now speaking only in terms of East Prussia and were beginning to hint that they might not be willing to offer even this to the exile Poles.[161]

Toward the end of 1942, Ambassador Romer, Poland's new envoy in Moscow, wrote of the "suffocating dilemma" facing Polish policy:

> on the one hand, "victory is already beginning to dawn"; on the other, "we are still sinking in the twilight of dangers, threats and

[158] Eden, *The Reckoning*, p. 429. Describing his talks with Roosevelt, he mentioned East Prussia "and perhaps some concessions in Silesia" (ibid., p. 432); Sherwood (*Roosevelt and Hopkins*, p. 710) mentions only East Prussia.

[159] See the Polish records of two meetings between Eden and Mikołajczyk on September 9th and October 5th, in *Documents*, 2:49 and 63; also Eden's account of his mid-November meeting with Raczyński, in *The Reckoning*, pp. 488-89. Churchill first spoke of the possibility of compensation to the Poles in an April 15, 1943, meeting with Sikorski, but apparently without mentioning specific territories; Raczyński, *W sojuszniczym Londynie*, p. 170.

[160] Copies of the two long memoranda on "The German Problem with Special Relation to Poland" and "The Problem of Central and South-Eastern Europe" were also submitted to the Foreign Office at the time of Sikorski's trip; see C12169 and C12841/4641/55, FO 371/31091, PRO. Although at the time these memoranda were merely acknowledged without comment, the internal minutes show a surprisingly positive reaction to some of the Polish arguments. The subject of compensation came under detailed discussion within the Foreign Office and British postwar planning agencies starting around the end of January 1943; see discussion pp. 343-46 below.

[161] See Eden's report of his talk with Maisky on March 10, 1943; N1605/499/38, FO 371/36991, PRO; also Sherwood, *Roosevelt and Hopkins*, pp. 713-14.

insinuations.'' ''At practically every step'' . . . , it is necessary to glide over ''difficulties'' at the core of which lies ''in one or another form the matter of our eastern boundaries.'' The final outcome will be determined by ''the relationship of forces at the dawn of victory.'' . . . but ''exceedingly painful for us [at the moment] is the necessity of realizing how little, at bottom, we can throw onto the scale of our most vital matters'' . . .[162]

Romer wrote, of course, with specific reference to Polish-Soviet relations and the eastern boundary, but his message applied with equal force to the state of Poland's relations with Britain and the United States and the issue of her western boundary.

[162] Romer's letter as paraphrased in Pobóg-Malinowski, *Najnowsza historia*, 3:244.

XI · *The Consequences of Failure*

FEDERATION: DISSOLUTION OF A DREAM

OF THE THREE FACETS of Sikorski's postwar strategy—rapprochement with Russia, westward territorial expansion, and Central European federation—it was the last mentioned that, in the early stages of the war at least, seemed to hold out the greatest promise of success. On November 11, 1940, the Polish and Czechoslovak exile governments had issued a joint declaration of their intention "on the conclusion of this war, to enter as independent and sovereign States into a closer political and economic association which would become the basis of a new order in Central Europe and a guarantee of its stability."[1] This was followed in the spring of 1941 by the establishment of a Polish-Czech Coordinating Committee and a number of specialized joint commissions to study the proposals submitted by each side.[2] On January 23, 1942, a second declaration was issued, this one an agreement describing in very general terms the scope of "the future Confederation of Poland and Czechoslovakia."[3] Although from the standpoint of Sikorski's desire for a closely integrated political structure this second agreement was undoubtedly something of a disappointment, it represented visible progress nonetheless. Moreover, early support from Allied quarters seemed genuine, even enthusiastic. Regional cooperation in general, including some form of Central European federation or confederation, was actively promoted in both official and unofficial British circles, while President Roosevelt pronounced it "a great idea" on first being presented with it in April 1941. Yet by mid-1942, less than six months after the signing of the second declaration, the work of the commissions had been suspended, and a year later negotiations were formally broken off.

It is not my intention here to recount in detail the course of the Polish-Czech negotiations, as that has been done adequately elsewhere.[4] Instead,

---

[1] For the text of this declaration, see Wandycz, *Czechoslovak-Polish Confederation*, pp. 128-29.

[2] Ibid., pp. 46-47 and 130; and Raczyński, *W sojuszniczym Londynie*, pp. 106-107 and 114.

[3] For the text, see Wandycz, *Czechoslovak-Polish Confederation*, pp. 133-35.

[4] In addition to the Wandycz study, see the following articles for the Czech and Polish views respectively: Eduard Táborský, "A Polish-Czechoslovak Confederation: A Story of the First Soviet Veto," pp. 379-95; and T. Komarnicki, "Próby stworzenia związku polsko-czeskiego w okresie drugiej wojny światowej."

it will suffice to highlight the causes for the breakdown of the talks: in particular, the parallel course of Polish-Soviet and Polish-Czech relations and the adverse impact of growing Western ambivalence toward, or even opposition to, the federation idea following Russia's entry into the war. In focusing on the external reasons for the federation's collapse, I do not mean to imply that there were no important differences between the Poles and Czechs themselves, or in their respective approaches to their future relationship. Even a cursory survey of the most important of these differences will show, however, that they were neither as great as is sometimes supposed, nor would they necessarily have proved insurmountable had the external environment been more propitious.

The first problem area was, of course, the dispute over Teschen Silesia, which more than any other issue symbolized the ill feeling that had existed between the two states in the interwar period. Here both sides nursed legitimate grievances. Taken by force of Czech arms in 1919, retaken under duress by the Poles during the Munich crisis of 1938, the province had a predominantly Polish population but was vital to the Czech economy.[5] Still, although both Sikorski and Czech President Beneš stood squarely on the integrity of the boundaries within which their respective countries had entered the war (thus both claiming Teschen),[6] even this emotion-charged issue was amenable to solution, the more easily so within the framework of a political and economic union. The two sides agreed at a rather early stage in the negotiations that the Teschen problem should be shelved while work on the basic structure of their relations went forward,[7] a postponement that seemed to presage an eventual compromise. For his part, as a long-time advocate of Polish-Czech cooperation, the general made no secret of the fact that he thought Poland had behaved shamefully in 1938. Although he did not (and could not) say so openly, he undoubtedly hoped that as plans for a federation progressed the question of which side should have Teschen would fade in importance, much as he foresaw that the Wilno issue could be resolved through a federal association with Lithuania. Undoubtedly, too, he hoped that the prospect of territorial gains in the west—

---

[5] See Chapter II above; also Wandycz, *Czechoslovak-Polish Confederation*, chap. I.

[6] The Czechs of course claimed their pre-Munich boundaries, the Poles their pre-September 1939 borders, including the disputed duchy which they had taken over in the meantime. Sikorski and Beneš each claimed his government could not do otherwise without compromising its mandate from the nation. See Sikorski's letter to Beneš of February 10, 1941, and Beneš's reply of February 25, 1941; Polish Government Collection, Box 64, folio: "Zasadnicze akty współpracy polsko-czechosłowackiej," HIWRP.

[7] See, e.g., Beneš's memorandum to Sikorski of November 1, 1940, and the draft of the Polish reply of December 3, 1940, in PRM 19/14 and 19/26, GSHI; and the exchange of letters cited in preceding note. See also Wandycz, *Czechoslovak-Polish Confederation*, p. 40.

in which, according to his plan, Czechoslovakia would share with Poland—would remove the lingering animosities that the Teschen dispute had engendered on both sides of the border.[8] Beneš, as a principal architect of prewar Czech policy, was in a more difficult position and would later revert to an inflexible stance on this question. There seems also to have been an element of personal rivalry in his relationship with Sikorski. But initially he too appears to have supported a compromise solution, whether through arbitration or some form of partition.[9]

By far the most serious problems arose over the very different attitudes of the two governments toward the Soviet Union. In contrast to the Poles, the Czechs had maintained cordial relations with Moscow during the in-

[8] Wandycz, *Czechoslovak-Polish Confederation*, pp. 33-34. It is not clear whether Sikorski was willing to see all of the Teschen district eventually returned to Czechoslovakia or whether he hoped for partition as originally envisioned in 1919; it is most unlikely, however, that he would have insisted on Poland's retention of the whole district. In any event he believed, as he wrote Beneš in October 1941, that the importance of this question should be "inversely proportional to the closeness of the union between the two countries." PRM 38a/10, GSHI. In general, the Poles seemed eager to involve the Czechs as soon as possible in the development of a joint plan for territorial changes in the west; see, e.g., Raczyński's record of his meeting with Beneš on August 23rd, and his memo of September 4, 1940, as well as Sikorski's letter of February 10, 1941, all in the file cited in note 6 above.

[9] See Raczyński's report of his meeting with Beneš on December 2, 1939, in the file cited in note 6 above. Once his hand had been strengthened by Allied recognition of his government and Soviet entry into the war, however, Beneš reverted to a more rigid position. See, e.g., his letter and memorandum to Sikorski of October 6 and 29, 1941, in which he denied having admitted that the Czechs had committed errors with respect to Teschen in 1919; PRM 38a/9 and 38a/11, GSHI. These two items were passed along (by the Czechs) to the British Foreign Office, where they evoked rather unflattering comments about the author. As Roger Makins, head of the Central Department noted: "I am afraid Dr. Beneš's attitude as revealed in the memorandum of October 29th augurs ill for the future of Polish-Czech collaboration. A man who repels the slightest hint of criticism and who claims to have been invariably right is apt to wrong his would-be allies." C151/151/12, FO 371/30827, PRO. Elsewhere Makins wrote: "The full recognition accorded Dr. Beneš (which rather went to his head) combined with the entry of Russia into the war effected a marked change in [his] position." C5534/151/12, in the same file. The question of personal relations between Beneš and Sikorski is an elusive one. The former's references to the latter in his memoirs were generally unflattering, and have often been quoted by those who have wished to portray the general as arrogant and pompous as well as unalterably anti-Soviet. See, e.g., *Memoirs of Dr. Eduard Beneš*, trans. Lias, pp. 147-49. On the other hand, there is more than a hint that Beneš resented Sikorski's prominence among exile leaders (the result in part of the fact that the Poles got their government organized nearly a year ahead of the Czechs and Slovaks), and that he was quick to "tattle" on him—to report to the Foreign Office that Sikorski was about to do this or that, of which the British might not approve. See, e.g., C3226/3226/55, FO 371/26755, PRO. During our recent correspondence, former Ambassador Raczyński agreed that, of the Czechoslovak leaders in London, Beneš was the "least friendly toward the Poles" and that he tended "to belittle Sikorski in the eyes of the British, possibly because he wanted to replace him as leader of the smaller allied governments."

terwar period and had consistently urged the USSR's inclusion in the European diplomatic community. With no history of territorial or other disputes, they were more trusting too of Soviet motives and future intentions, a posture that understandably alarmed many Poles. There is no question but that the latter were also disturbed by Beneš's long-held view on their eastern boundary—to wit, that Poland must accept her ethnic limits in the east as a precondition to a reconciliation with the Soviet Union.[10] For their part, the Czechs were similarly distrustful of Poland's traditional friendship with Hungary and sympathy for the latter's irredentist claims along the Slovakian border. These contrasts in historical experience and geopolitical outlook led to serious tactical differences. For instance, the Poles felt that each side should in principle back the vital territorial interests of the other—i.e., restoration of Poland's eastern boundary on the one hand, and Czechoslovakia's western boundary on the other—but were eventually compelled to accept Beneš's formula of mutual disinterestedness in the other's boundary disputes with third parties.[11] In addition, while Sikorski felt strongly that it would be a mistake to let Moscow intervene in any way in the Central European negotiations and that Western pressure should be brought to bear on the Soviets, the Czech leader firmly believed that all problems could be ironed out in direct dealings with Stalin.[12]

However, the differences between the two men did not extend to the fundamental substantive questions of the role of the proposed federation in the postwar European system, or of its proper relationship to the Soviet Union. Here the one was neither as anti-Soviet, nor the other as pro-Soviet as is often assumed. On the one hand, Sikorski believed as steadfastly as did Beneš that the future Central European organization must be on friendly terms with Moscow, and even that it should maintain an alliance with Russia against a potentially resurgent Germany. As we have seen, he also came to accept the necessity of territorial concessions in the east; in fact,

[10] Wandycz, *Czechoslovak-Polish Confederation*, pp. 2 and 41. Beneš felt compelled on several occasions to deny that he was anti-Polish or unduly pro-Russian, although he had to admit that there was a kind of "Russian mystique" among his countrymen. See Raczyński's reports of their meetings on December 2, 1939 and August 23, 1940, in the file cited in note 6 above; also Beneš's November 1940 memo, PRM 19/14, GSHI.

[11] Beneš's formula was first proposed in his letter of February 25, 1941 (note 6 above), and was finally accepted by Sikorski after several exchanges in October of that year; see PRM 38a/8, 38a/9 and 38a/10, GSHI.

[12] During their December 1939 meeting (note 9 above) Beneš told Raczyński that he was convinced Moscow recognized the value of a Central European "buffer separating Russia from Germany." For a summary of his appraisal of Soviet policy in 1942, see N2625/50/38, FO 371/32918, PRO. Only much later would Beneš recognize his error. In one of his last letters to his former political secretary, Eduard Táborský, he wrote: "My greatest mistake was that I refused to believe to the very last that even Stalin lied to me cynically both in 1935 and later, and that his assurances to me and to Masaryk were an intentional deceit." Quoted in Wandycz, *Czechoslovak-Polish Confederation*, p. 84.

his overriding commitment to the federation was in all probability one of the factors influencing this decision. On the other hand, despite his more sanguine appraisal of Soviet policy, Beneš shared Sikorski's vision of creating a new kind of European balance, as well as his desire to avoid direct Soviet participation in or domination of Central European affairs. Writing for *Foreign Affairs* in early 1942, he foresaw the need for "a permanent and general European equilibrium . . . based both politically and economically upon the balance of forces between a number of large political units. . . . [T]he weakness of small states must not in the future tempt large states to fall upon them." The creation of such a larger unit in Central Europe was, he continued, the only means by which "the smaller states of [this region can] avoid violent social revolution and attempts to establish Communism."[13] Nor was this a view formulated to appeal to a Western audience. From his earliest contacts with the Poles, Beneš stressed that his insistence on cordial relations with Moscow in no way diminished his view that "Russia is an Eastern power," while "we jointly [Czechs and Poles] represent Western culture." On the contrary, he repeatedly voiced fears that the collapse of the Reich might spark a communist revolution in Germany, bringing with it the danger of Soviet troops entering Central Europe, and that every effort must be made to avert this possibility.[14]

A third area of major difference between the Poles and Czechs concerned the internal structure and jurisdictional scope of their proposed union. In a lengthy memorandum to Sikorski of November 1, 1940, Beneš outlined his plan for a loose "confederation *sui generis*"— something more than a "simple alliance" but less than political union: the participants would maintain their separate national governments, parliaments, and armies; they would also retain full sovereignty except in economic matters, where the plan proposed a customs union and common trade policy. The central organs of the confederation would consist of several joint councils, each disposing only of coordinating functions in such areas as foreign and defense policy.[15] By contrast, the Polish plan submitted the following year proposed a highly integrated political union—the Polish word *związek* was

[13] Eduard Beneš, "The Organization of Postwar Europe," pp. 227 and 240.

[14] The reference to Russia as an "Eastern power" was made during a September 1940 meeting with Sikorski; PRM 19/11, GSHI. Beneš's fears of Soviet military intervention in Central Europe were first expressed to Raczyński in December 1939 (note 9 above), and were repeated in his November 1940 memo (note 7 above) and letter of February 25, 1941 (note 6 above). Beneš seems not to have seen any discrepancy between these fears and his expectation that Moscow would welcome a Polish-Czech "buffer" between Russia and Germany.

[15] The original French text of the memorandum appears in PRM 19/14, GSHI; it is discussed in detail in both Wandycz, *Czechoslovak-Polish Confederation*, pp. 39-41; and Táborský, "A Polish-Czechoslovak Confederation," pp. 382-85.

used—in which the central authorities (including a Supreme Council, a Council of State Secretaries, and a directly elected Assembly) would have extensive executive and legislative powers. Under the Polish plan, economic integration would depend on the degree of political unity achieved, the ultimate goal being full economic integration.[16]

Practical rather than theoretical considerations appear to have been largely responsible for the different approaches. For their part, the Poles were fearful that one-sided concentration on economic union would leave them at a disadvantage relative to the more industrialized and less devastated economy of the Czechs.[17] On the other hand, the latter, as the most democratic of the Central European nations, were understandably wary of tying themselves too closely to the far less democratic structure of prewar Poland, especially as that country was by far the more populous. In fact, both Beneš and the Slovak leader, Milan Hodža, initially expressed reservations about joining a regional organization in which Poland was the only other member.[18] The Slovaks themselves were the source of additional complications. Frustrated by Czech domination of the prewar political structure, they had unsuccessfully opposed the establishment of the unitary Czechoslovak exile government that Beneš wanted (and got), preferring instead a dual Czecho-Slovak organization to reflect their demand for equal status in the postwar state. They may even have contemplated participation in a regional federation as a separate entity. Because Polish-Slovak relations had traditionally been more cordial than those between Poles and Czechs, this issue now became an irritant between the two exile governments.[19]

[16] See Wandycz, *Czechoslovak-Polish Confederation*, pp. 61-65; also the draft Polish reply to Beneš, in PRM 19/26, GSHI.

[17] Wandycz, *Czechoslovak-Polish Confederation*, pp. 40-41; and the Polish draft cited in the preceding note.

[18] Beneš's reservations were especially evident in his first meeting with Raczyński in December 1939 (note 9 above), in which he stated that economic and historical ties tended to pull the Czechoslovaks "rather toward the south," but that they would be "ready for a closer association with Poland as well." During their August 1940 meeting (note 8 above), he warned that "serious psychological differences" between the Poles and Czechs could prove to be a source of misunderstandings. See also Raczyński's record of his November 1939 meeting with Hodža; PRM 19/9, GSHI. By the time of his November 1940 memorandum (note 15 above), Beneš appears to have come around fully to the Polish view that Poland and Czechoslovakia must be the core of any Central European regional organization and that the adherence of other countries was a matter for later consideration.

[19] See especially the meeting between Raczyński and Beneš in August 1940 (note 8 above), in which the latter warned that it would be impossible to establish a relationship of trust between the two countries if the Poles attempted to inflame or support "Slovak antagonisms toward the Czechs." See also Hodža's bitter remarks about the Czechs to Raczyński in November 1939 (preceding note); and Wandycz, *Czechoslovak-Polish Confederation*, pp. 34-35.

However, each side showed an acceptable degree of sensitivity to the anxieties of the other. Once the Beneš government had gained Allied recognition, for instance, the Polish government appears to have exercised considerable restraint in avoiding the Slovak issue (although Czech suspicions were not easily allayed).[20] In addition, the federation plan submitted by the Poles contained an elaborate system of checks and balances to prevent larger states (such as Poland) from dominating the less populous ones. Similarly, Beneš's memo declared that the Czechs were prepared "to examine with favor and understanding" all proposals for collaboration, and presented his more limited plan as the basis upon which "all the political and economic machinery for unifying the two countries" might develop in the future.[21] Equally important, a territorial shift along the lines sought by Sikorski would have gone far toward dispelling fears on both sides; for the resulting radical alteration of Poland's socio-economic structure would have made closer political integration less onerous to the Czechs, while making economic union less threatening to the Poles.

CERTAINLY it would be inaccurate to suggest that these contrasts in historical and political outlook—what some called "psychological" differences between the Poles and Czechs—did not pose serious problems, or that any of them was close to solution at the time substantive talks were suspended in mid-1942. But neither were the divisions sufficiently acrimonious in and of themselves to have caused the breakdown.[22] It would be more accurate to say that the talks stalled for want of the favorable international climate so essential to their development. And the reasons for this must be sought elsewhere—specifically in the structure of relations within the Grand Alliance which allowed the Soviets, virtually by default, to become the sole arbiters of Central Europe's future, not in 1944 and

[20] In his memorandum on Polish-Czech relations of September 4, 1940 (included in file cited in note 6 above), Raczyński specifically recommended that Poland agree "not to support the decentralizing aspirations of the Slovaks, inasmuch as a harmonious settlement of relations between the Czechs and Slovaks will contribute to the strengthening . . . of the Polish-Czechoslovak federation." The Poles appear to have abided by this policy for some time; for, it was only much later, after the federation plans had begun to fall apart, that Raczyński began to think about playing "the Slovak card." *W sojuszniczym Londynie*, p. 155.

[21] Wandycz, *Czechoslovak-Polish Confederation*, pp. 62-63; and note 15 above. On October 6, 1941, Beneš wrote Sikorski that "events of recent months" have made possible "a fundamental step forward in our mutual negotiations" which "can now take on a more concrete form." PRM 38a/9, GSHI. (Ironically, this was also the letter in which he began to hedge on Teschen.)

[22] In January 1942, Beneš described the difficulties between the Poles and Czechs as "in any case . . . not great." "The Organization of Postwar Europe," p. 231. See also Wandycz, *Czechoslovak-Polish Confederation*, pp. 79-80.

1945 as a result of military occupation, but in 1941 and 1942 even before the tide of war had turned in their favor.

Two factors were involved here. First, in view of the Czech attitude toward the Soviet Union, it was a foregone conclusion well before June 22, 1941, that a sine qua non of any future association between Poland and Czechoslovakia would be the ability of the former to establish at least correct, if not friendly, relations with Moscow. As Beneš wrote to Sikorski in November 1940, at a time when Poland was still technically at war with her eastern neighbor, "we must not have the Russians against us."[23] So it was to be expected that, once the Soviets were in the war, the Czechs would seek their approval for the federation plan—although perhaps not that they would allow Moscow to dictate the terms of its realization.

It was the second factor, however, that provided the more serious obstacle, at the same time magnifying the impact of the Czech position: namely, the change in the attitude of the Western Powers toward the very idea of a Central European federation, a change more or less coincident with the appearance of the Soviet Union in the Allied camp. The British in particular, having actively promoted the idea in the early days of the war, now seemed willing to consign the entire region to Soviet hegemony (very much as some of them had been eager to consign it to German hegemony before the war).[24] Although Sikorski undoubtedly did not know of the British "half promise" to that effect given already in the summer of 1941,[25] he was alert to the shift in prevailing opinion; for he complained to Churchill in the latter part of August that "the Great Powers are beginning to act as if they recognized only Russia's role in this part of the world."[26]

---

[23] See note 15 above. In his first conversation with Raczyński, in December 1939 (note 9 above), Beneš made it plain that Czechoslovakia would in no way associate itself with aspirations for a " 'northern federation' (Poland, Lithuania, Belorussia, Ukraine)." In October 1940, however, the Czechs said they would not object to the inclusion of Lithuania so long as this did not give the federation an anti-Russian orientation; see the report of Raczyński's meeting with Hubert Ripka, October 14, 1940, in the file cited in note 6 above.

[24] Actually, the British attitude had begun to shift with the first signs of serious Nazi-Soviet tension in late 1940; see pp. 86-87 above. By this time also a number of people in the Foreign Office had begun to ponder the implications for Britain's traditional posture of disengagement from the continent of the Sikorski/Beneš concept of European equilibrium; hence "the advisability of keeping to generalities over war aims . . ." C14/14/62, FO 371/26419, PRO [this entry consists of comments on Sikorski's November 1940 memorandum to Ernest Bevin]. Concerning Britain's earlier readiness to consign the region to the German sphere of influence, see Cadogan's 1937 memo in *The Cadogan Diaries*, ed. Dilks, pp. 14-15 (also Chapter II, note 26, above); and the London *Times* editorial of August 1, 1941, quoted in Rozek, *Allied Wartime Diplomacy*, p. 63; and pp. 152-53 above.

[25] See p. 153 above.

[26] *Documents*, 1:156.

In the ensuing months, the British seem to have made several attempts to retract or hedge their "half promise." Both in December 1941 and the following spring, during the negotiations for an Anglo-Soviet treaty, Eden suggested the insertion of a clause on "safeguarding and strengthening the economic and political independence of all European countries either as unitary or federated states." In December, Stalin is reported to have remarked that "if certain of the countries of Europe wish to federate then the Soviet Union will have no objection to such a course." On the second occasion, Molotov first tried to ignore the British proposal, then to oppose it on grounds that the Soviet government "had certain information to show that some federations might be directed against the Soviet Union." After some pressuring, he reluctantly agreed to the inclusion of an amended clause, adding the words "on the basis of friendly relations towards the U.S.S.R and Great Britain." But the clause disappeared entirely when it was decided to conclude a treaty along different lines. As Eden noted in his diary:

> With the disappearance from the Treaty of any mention of frontiers it would no longer be necessary for us to safeguard the Polish position and to reassure our other Allies in Eastern Europe by the insertion of special stipulations about the confederation of these States and about collaborating in the postwar settlement with the other United Nations.[27]

From this and other episodes, it is hard to escape the impression that, at the policy level at least, the British regarded the cause of Central European federation as a peripheral but hardly urgent one to which they would give verbal support when the occasion arose, but which they would not pursue at the risk of irritation in Moscow—although there is ample evidence of greater support and understanding for the idea at lower levels of the Foreign Office.[28]

One result of London's reticence on this issue was ironically to convince the Poles that their only recourse was to seek support in Washington. Yet American policy was if anything even more damaging to the cause of Central European federation than British. The reasons were several, al-

---

[27] Eden, *The Reckoning*, pp. 378-79. Concerning the prior sequence of events, see: *FRUS, 1942*, 3:496 and 516; D. Allen's minute in C7636/151/12, FO 371/30827, PRO; and a Foreign Office paper summarizing the "Soviet Attitude to Federations in Eastern Europe" in N4906/499/38, FO 371/36992, PRO.

[28] For the ongoing discussion within the Foreign Office as to just what posture the British ought to adopt toward the federation, see especially: C7636/151/12, FO 371/30827; C10670/151/12, FO 371/30828; and N4912/50/38, FO 371/32918, PRO [minutes by Messrs. Roberts, Warner, Strang, Cadogan, and Eden are particularly instructive].

though on this as on other issues the American position defies easy definition. The first was ideological: that is, President Roosevelt's penchant for a universalistic approach, coupled with his attachment to an extreme form of self-determination and, the contradiction notwithstanding, his optimism over the prospects of reaching a satisfactory settlement with Stalin. Far from understanding the need for grouping smaller nations into regional organizations for their own defense and prosperity—and despite his exclamation of approval to Sikorski in 1941—he actually favored the breakup of such existing federal states as Yugoslavia. As Sumner Welles lamented later, in favoring continued fragmentation in Central Europe, Roosevelt "did [not] have much in mind the impoverishment and general misery that had spread over most of the Danube basin after the Treaty of Versailles had dissolved the Austro-Hungarian Empire and the economic federation that the Empire represented."[29]

A second reason was political and administrative: the tardiness of Washington's postwar planning effort. In fact, while most of the study groups were set up in the spring of 1942, the decision to establish a Special Subcommittee on Problems of European Organization was made only a year later, and that subcommittee did not begin to meet until June 1943. Even then, however, the regional federation approach was viewed largely as a "fallback" position which "might have sufficient merit . . . in the event the plan for United States entrance into a universal international organization failed of fruition."[30]

Still a third reason was that, in the absence of a definitive policy on regional organizations, the Americans like the British were inclined to humor the Soviets, to impose no conditions for aid given, and to discourage any move that might displease Moscow. Early in 1942, for instance, when

[29] Welles, *Seven Decisions*, p. 136; and Eden, *The Reckoning*, pp. 432-33. Wandycz (*The United States and Poland*, p. 250) suggests that the president's apparent enthusiasm for the federation idea during Sikorski's 1941 visit was due to the fact that "at this point Roosevelt found it useful to propagandize Poland's cause in order to mobilize American public opinion against Germany," rather than to his approval of the substance of the proposal. However, there were apparently some in the United States who were thinking along lines very close to Sikorski's. See, e.g., the article by an anonymous "Group of U.S. Military Experts," "A Federation for Eastern Europe," pp. 117-21. The federation proposed by the authors envisioned the retention by Poland of her prewar eastern boundary, as well as the inclusion of Lithuania which was viewed as "not essential" to Russia either for defensive purposes or to ensure adequate access to the Baltic. The western boundary of Poland, "and thus of the federation," posed greater difficulties. Although "on strictly military grounds it would be desirable to push this boundary westward to the Oder river," the authors thought this might create an intolerable minority problem. Nonetheless, they proposed that the German salient between Poland and Czechoslovakia be eliminated by including virtually all of *Lower* Silesia within the federation.

[30] Notter, *Postwar Foreign Policy Preparation*, pp. 146-48.

Sikorski was trying to induce the other exile governments in London to take some positive action toward federation, Roosevelt wrote in a memo: "I think Sikorski should be definitely discouraged on this proposition. This is no time to talk about the post-war position of small nations, and it would cause serious trouble with Russia."[31] At this point the American position did not necessarily imply a willingness to concede to the Soviet Union hegemony over Central Europe (although there were already differences on this point).[32] But there seems to have been scant recognition in the upper echelons of the Roosevelt administration, despite cogent (and in retrospect accurate) warnings from some quarters in the State Department, that failure to resist Soviet designs at the outset might well foreclose future prospects.[33]

Perhaps the most astonishing and revealing aspect of both British and American policy on this question, as on territorial matters, was the lack of communication between the two. It was only in October 1942, when the idea of a Central European federation was for all intents and purposes a dead letter, that some in the Foreign Office began to consider whether "the time has not come for us to have a talk with the Americans 'off the record' [!] as to how we see this question of federation in Eastern Europe . . . ." Even then it was decided that raising the matter with Washington might only exacerbate Moscow's suspicions and, since "the present is not a good moment to broach the question with the Russians, there is not much we can do, except perhaps to peg away patiently with the Poles and Czechs as occasion offers."[34]

[31] *FRUS, 1942*, 3:113, n. 34.

[32] One such exception was the view expressed by Assistant Secretary of State Berle to Raczyński and Ciechanowski in February 1942; see Chapter X, note 113, above. A few weeks later, on the other hand, Welles wrote to Ambassador Biddle in London: "Now is not the time to launch movements for post war settlements which might be offensive to the Russians. On the other hand we are not inclined to take the position that in order to keep the Russians in good humor we should agree at this time to all of their various projects for a post war Europe." *FRUS, 1942*, 3:137. Later, however, Welles apparently came around to Berle's view; for, in his 1944 book *Time for Decision* (pp. 332-33), he wrote: "The Soviet government is as legitimately entitled to promote a regional system of Eastern Europe, composed of co-operative and well-disposed independent governments among the countries adjacent to Russia, as the United States has been justified in promoting an inter-American system . . . I can only assume, until evidence to the contrary is presented, that the recent constitutional modification of the Soviet Union, as a result of which a federal system of sixteen nominally autonomous Soviet republics has been established, is the first step in this direction, motivated by the Soviet government's belief that regional arrangements can thus more readily be perfected. . . ."

[33] See, e.g., the Department's February 4, 1942, memorandum to Roosevelt, quoted at length on pp. 293-94 above; also Bohlen, *Witness to History*, pp. 39-41 and 121-25.

[34] See especially N4912/50/38, FO 371/32918; and C10670/151/12, FO 371/30828, PRO.

The net effect of both the British and American positions was to obscure the distinction between a Central European organization that was genuinely hostile to the Soviet Union and posed a threat to that power's legitimate security interests, and one that in the name of its members' security and economic prosperity was designed to reduce their vulnerability to outside domination, whether German or Soviet. As a result, it was left to Moscow to define what was or was not "anti-Soviet" and to decide where and under what conditions any form of supranational association would be tolerated in the vicinity of her frontiers. Indeed, the Soviets did not even have to state their opposition openly, but needed only to show irritation or suspicion to achieve their aim. We need only briefly review the course of the federation plans in the nearly two years between June 1941 and the breakdown of Polish-Czech negotiations to see how adroitly they played their hand.

When the Czechs first approached Moscow on the federation question in August 1941, the reaction seemed almost enthusiastic. Czech Ambassador Fierlinger wired back to Beneš:

> According to your instructions I explained to Vyshinsky for the first time in detail our view of the cooperation with Poland and the establishment of a Polish-Czechoslovak confederation, completely independent, but at the same time being in friendly relations to the Soviet Union. He vividly expressed to me his personal approval, adding that he would inform me of the exact official attitude. He assumed that no objection or difficulties would arise.[35]

Similar assurances were conveyed directly to the Czech president several days later by Ambassador Maisky, and it was under this umbrella of apparent Soviet approval that negotiations went forward to the Polish-Czech Agreement of January 23, 1942.[36] Yet this very same day saw the first overt move by Moscow against the federation in the form of a letter from Ambassador Bogomolov, the Soviet envoy to the several exile governments in London, protesting an interview given by Raczyński to the London *Times*. Bogomolov objected in particular to the emphasis placed by Raczyński on the independence of the proposed Central European association, charging that this would deny the Soviet Union "a positive role in the solution of European problems" and "does not correspond to the spirit of the agreement between the U.S.S.R. and Poland, which finds its expression in the declaration of friendship and mutual assistance." Bo-

---

[35] Táborský, "A Polish-Czechoslovak Confederation," p. 388.

[36] At that time, Maisky repeated to Beneš that "in Moscow there were no objections against the Polish-Czechoslovak agreement." Ibid.

gomolov likewise protested mention of Lithuania as a potential member of the federation.[37]

Other warning signs followed quickly. In early February, Fierlinger reported from Moscow that unnamed "Soviet circles" were now warning the Czechs that their policy of cooperation with the Poles "runs ahead of events and does not take a realistic view of the future," and that they should not give up their independence "in favor of some kind of political union the consequences of which cannot today be assessed."[38] At the same time, Soviet representatives in London began a quiet campaign among the Allied governments obviously aimed at isolating the Poles, who were spearheading efforts to give concrete shape to the federation idea, while Czech politicians were approached with "personal" opinions expressing doubts as to the advisability of a union with the Poles.[39] In Washington, Raczyński was asked by Ambassador Litvinov whether "your government [has] consulted with the Soviet Government on this matter [of the federation]."[40] Perhaps the most candid explanation of Moscow's position in this period was that offered by Bogomolov in early March. In an interview with Kajetan Morawski, a high-ranking official in the Polish Foreign Ministry, he declared that "*there cannot be and must not be any European arrangement, and especially in Eastern Europe, from which Russia would be excluded*." Morawski replied that he "did not see any logical relationship between the idea which we all share, namely that of the necessity for establishing the best possible co-operation between the Allied European States and the Soviet Union, and Russia's demand that those States should not enter into any other commitment without her." But the Soviet ambassador was unmoved.[41]

Then in June Moscow began courting the Czechs openly and in such a way as to inflame their simmering differences with the Poles. On the 9th of that month, Molotov, who was still in London following the signing of the treaty with the British, met with Beneš and reached an understanding that, in the words of a Foreign Office report, "went very far in arriving at a Soviet-Czechoslovak agreement at the expense of the Poles." The "salient points" were that:

---

[37] See Bogomolov's letter and Sikorski's reply in *Documents*, 1:268-69 and 272-74; the original *Times* interview of January 11, 1942, appears in Raczyński, *W sojuszniczym Londynie*, pp. 427-30. It is worth noting that Beneš's article in the January issue of *Foreign Affairs* (note 13 above) made many of the same points without evoking a Soviet protest.

[38] Táborský, "A Polish-Czechoslovak Confederation," p. 388.

[39] Ibid.

[40] Ciechanowski, *Defeat in Victory*, p. 93.

[41] *Documents*, 1:285-86 [emphasis added].

a. M. Molotov recognised the pre-Munich frontiers of Czechoslovakia, which involves the recognition of Teschen as part of Czechoslovakia; this issue had however been reserved for settlement between
the Czechs and the Poles;

b. Dr. Beneš agreed with M. Molotov that Polish-Czechoslovak
confederation would be dependent upon the Poles agreeing to satisfy
Soviet demands generally and their territorial demands in particular.
Dr. Beneš has therefore in effect supported Soviet claims against those
of his own partner, Poland.[42]

By mid-summer the ever tedious Bogomolov had made it plain, in unequivocal if still unofficial terms—he persisted in citing *"les milieux russes"*
rather than the Soviet government—that Polish-Czech collaboration along
the lines projected was unacceptable to Moscow. Furthermore he had
extracted from Beneš, apparently with only minimal effort, a statement to
the effect that while "Czechoslovakia [was] in favour of a Czech-Polish
Confederation . . . she [was] not prepared to pursue the scheme in the
face of direct Soviet opposition."[43]

---

[42] C5813/151/12, FO 371/30827, PRO. According to the Czech record of the meeting,
Molotov stated Moscow's view in the following terms: "We have no differences with Czechoslovakia, but we have such with the Poles. If the Czechoslovaks enter into a confederation
with the Poles, are they not accepting Polish points of view *and by so doing do they not
become our enemies*? We believe that Czechoslovakia does not wish to convey that interpretation." Táborský, "A Polish-Czechoslovak Confederation," p. 389 [emphasis added].
Even before this meeting the head of the Foreign Office's Central Department, Roger Makins,
had remarked with respect to deteriorating Polish-Czech relations: "Although, as we know,
the Poles are intolerably difficult to deal with, I am quite satisfied that the main fault in this
matter lies with the Czechs. . . . I hope that the Secretary of State may be willing to send
for Dr. Beneš and give him a good dressing down. Dr. Beneš is already thinking of suggesting
to the Russians the conclusion of a Czechoslovak-Soviet treaty and is also angling for a visit
to Moscow. I suggest that he ought to be firmly discouraged from these schemes and told
that his first and most important task is to reach a proper understanding with the Poles before
he ventures further afield." Eden responded that he thought "the fault [could] be pretty
evenly divided," and apparently did not follow Makins's suggestions. C5534/151/12, FO
371/30827, PRO. Other entries in this file are replete with examples of growing bad feeling
(and bad manners) between the two exile governments. Apparently not all of the Czech exile
leaders were in agreement with Beneš's policy however. During a conversation in 1981,
Raczyński recalled vividly a meeting with Masaryk and Ripka in mid-1942, during which
Masaryk expressed support for the federation and his dissatisfaction with the slow pace of
progress to date—something that he blamed on Ripka who, although Raczyński remembered
him as the Czech leader most friendly to the Poles, sat by silently. Only later did Raczyński
learn that the real target of Masaryk's criticism had been Beneš.

[43] See C7401, C7636, and especially C9156/151/12, FO 371/30827, PRO. Bogomolov
was by all accounts a dour and inscrutable diplomat, even by Soviet standards. While this
impression might be ascribed in part to what one British diplomat generously called his
"rather uneven French"—"atrocious" was the adjective used by Raczyński (p. 297 above)—

How should one interpret this apparent shift in Soviet policy from a year earlier? One could, of course, accept Moscow's explanation that it was solely a response to Poland's increasingly ''anti-Soviet'' policy—most importantly, her alleged intention of turning a federation into the nucleus of a *cordon sanitaire* isolating the Soviet Union and her refusal to recognize Soviet claims to her prewar eastern territories or to Lithuania. In retrospect at least, it can hardly be denied that Sikorski's adamant stance on Lithuania was a serious error of judgment. Whether he genuinely thought he had more support for Lithuania's participation in a regional organization than was actually the case we cannot say for sure.[44] Certainly he must have believed that the domestic political consequences of abandoning this solution to the Wilno problem would be as unpalatable and damaging to his policy as the external consequences of clinging to his position a while longer. But just as certainly his stubbornness on this issue was a constant irritant in relations with Moscow and lent at least superficial credence to

Beneš had scarcely better results attempting to communicate in Russian. Whether he came by his obtuseness naturally, or whether it was a convenient affectation, Bogomolov would appear to have been ideally suited to the task of conveying Soviet displeasure with the federation idea without officially committing his government for or against anything. Although his motives were transparent—no one could have been fooled by his references to ''*les milieux russes*'' and most seemed to grasp that Moscow's game here was to isolate the Poles—the tactic was effective nonetheless.

[44] The Poles may well have thought they had at least potential support for Lithuania's inclusion from several quarters. The earliest and most important evidence to this effect was a January 1940 memorandum on ''The Problem of the Reconstruction of Poland,'' written by Frank Savery, counselor of the British Embassy to the Polish exile government. The author, long familiar with the problems of Poland's eastern provinces, strongly supported the idea of a Polish-Lithuanian federation. (He also supported Polish retention of Lwów, their claims to East Prussia, and the expulsion of the Germans from any German territories taken over by Poland.) C1762/116/55, FO 371/24470, PRO. Although the Poles were not even supposed to know of the memo's existence, a partial copy appears in the Polish files; Polish Government Collection, Box 976, folio: ''Ukrainian question, 1942,'' HIWRP. Concerning the attitude of the Czechoslovak government and an unofficial American view, see notes 23 and 29 above. During late January and the first half of February 1942, there was lengthy and intense discussion within the Foreign Office concerning the advisability of warning the Poles that Lithuania was a lost cause—indeed that they, the British, were then preparing to recognize the Soviet annexation of all three Baltic states. It was finally decided not to send the letter, already drafted, largely because the incorporation of Wilno into Soviet Lithuania had created an embarrassing problem involving Britain's treaty obligations to Poland. See C1071/19/55, FO 371/31077, PRO. Although Sikorski became aware of the threat to Lithuania during the Anglo-Soviet negotiations that spring, he may have hoped that the dropping of the territorial clauses from the final treaty kept open the option of Lithuania's participation in a federation. It is possible that he was even encouraged in this illusion by Maj. Victor Cazalet, the British liaison officer attached to Sikorski's government who, as late as April 1943, referred to the idea in a memorandum on ''The Polish Eastern Frontier.'' See C3454/258/55, FO 371/34567, PRO.

the suggestion, made by Beneš, that the Soviets were withholding their approval of a Polish-Czech federation as leverage to bring about the desired territorial concessions.[45]

Yet none of this can adequately explain such discrepancies as the fact that the Soviets approved in August 1941 precisely the same concept that they began discrediting less than six months later—that is, of a Central European federation independent of but well-disposed toward Moscow.[46] Nor does it take into account Stalin's tactics toward Sikorski following the latter's December 1941 visit, especially the hardening of his posture on the eastern boundary question and the maneuverings to diminish the importance and ultimately force the evacuation of the Polish Army—all of which seemed to negate the understanding Sikorski thought he had reached while in Moscow. In light of all the events related here and in the preceding chapters, a more plausible explanation of the apparent shift in Soviet policy is that it was just that, only an apparent shift.[47] Just as with the issues of the eastern boundary, the army, and the reclassification of Polish citizens, the initial months of ''approval'' of the federation coincided with the period of greatest Soviet weakness and uncertainty over Western policy.[48] Likewise, the carefully orchestrated campaign against it came in the wake of a significant improvement in the military situation on the Russian front—

---

[45] C9156/151/12, FO 371/30827, PRO. Beneš's hypothesis does not seem to have persuaded the Foreign Office. As Frank Roberts of the Central Department commented, with the concurrence of several others: ''I think it may be a little far-fetched to suppose that the Russians are reserving their approval of the Confederation as a bargaining counter. Their doubts are surely of a more fundamental nature . . .'' And elsewhere: ''The recent deterioration in Soviet-Polish relations has clearly presented the Czechs with an awkward problem. But I think they would be better advised to keep their own counsel and not make it so easy for the Russians to play the Czechs off against the Poles.'' C7401/151/12, FO 371/30827, PRO.

[46] In this connection, the following postwar Soviet assessment of the federation is worth quoting: ''In the fall of 1940, on order of the imperialists, Sikorski's 'government' undertook negotiations with the émigré government of Beneš concerning the creation of a new anti-Soviet bloc of states, to be called an 'East European federation'' [sic! neither Beneš nor Sikorski ever spoke in terms of an *East* European federation], under the domination of the English imperialists. In addition to Poland and Czechoslovakia, the Anglo-American imperialists intended after the war to include in this 'East European federation' also Hungary, Rumania, Yugoslavia and Austria, having consolidated there beforehand reactionary bourgeois regimes. In this way [the imperialists intended] to create a new 'cordon sanitaire' against national liberation movements and against the Soviet state.'' *Istoriia Pol'shi*, 3:548.

[47] Wandycz (*Czechoslovak-Polish Confederation*, p. 82) cites several other hypotheses: that the shift in Soviet policy reflected disappointment over the lack of a second European front; or that there were divergent views in Moscow and that Molotov (!) had been overruled. Wandycz himself, however, concludes that there was no ''sudden'' change in Soviet policy.

[48] Even at this stage, however, Moscow was apparently intent on manipulating any federation—for instance, to engender in the Poles ''a feeling of political weakness and lack of economic self-sufficiency.'' See p. 172 above.

and at a time when Moscow could be increasingly sure that the cause of Central European organization had little genuine support or understanding in the West, or at least that London and Washington were not prepared to promote it in the face of Soviet stonewalling. Moreover, the Soviets could hardly have been unaware of the squeeze Sikorski was in as a result of the conflict between their own pressure for an immediate territorial settlement and the West's uneven adherence to the Atlantic Charter. In this light, it seems likely that the dispute over boundaries and the question of Lithuania's status were less the cause for Soviet opposition to the Polish-Czech negotiations than a convenient excuse. And it was undoubtedly no coincidence that the final veto from Moscow came on the heels of the decision to evacuate the remaining Polish divisions.

During the remainder of the summer of 1942 and throughout the fall, sporadic efforts were made to revive the talks. In an effort to break the stalemate on boundary issues, Sikorski and Raczyński tried to induce Beneš and Masaryk, the Czech foreign minister, to join in a proposal for their mutual frontier with Germany. Sikorski even suggested that the two governments immediately conclude an Act of Confederation, in effect presenting the Great Powers with a *fait accompli*. But Beneš, unwilling to incur the consequences of Soviet displeasure that such an act would surely bring, now abandoned the idea of an independent federation (or confederation) altogether, proposing instead a simple alliance between the two countries—an alternative that also proved unacceptable to Moscow.[49]

Such was the situation when Sikorski left on his third and final trip to the United States. As noted earlier, one of his primary aims on this trip was to elicit from Roosevelt a public declaration of support for an independent regional organization in Central Europe. The relevant paragraph of the Polish draft of the letter to be given by the president to the general read:

> I [i.e. Roosevelt] have noted with satisfaction your constructive initiative towards the establishment of a Confederation of Poland with Czechoslovakia as a first step in the direction of a European policy of international cooperation, and I am pleased to hear that the development of this idea is progressing satisfactorily. I am looking forward to its further satisfactory development, considering that the establishment of durable peace and security in Central Eastern Europe

[49] See, e.g., Wandycz, *Czechoslovak-Polish Confederation*, pp. 82-86; Raczyński, *W sojuszniczym Londynie*, pp. 147-48 and 154-55; and Táborský, "A Polish-Czechoslovak Confederation," pp. 392-93. For the British record of this phase of the negotiations, see file FO 371/30828, PRO, especially document C12165/151/12; concerning Soviet rejection of the alliance proposal, see note 63 below.

largely depends on its successful completion. I have no doubt that the creation of such a close international understanding in that part of Europe will be generally appreciated and approved by all the United Nations.[50]

In retrospect, it is clear that his hopes were wholly unfounded, although Sikorski could not have known this at the time. For one thing, it seems probable that he was not fully apprised of American reservations the previous March.[51] Moreover, in contrast to territorial questions where he was more circumspect in his request for support, the federation concept was not in conflict with the Atlantic Charter and, therefore, he might reasonably have expected that a request for support on this issue would not be offensive to the Americans. Finally, in light of the status of the Polish-Czech negotiations at this point, Sikorski's overture was clearly a last desperate gamble to salvage a cornerstone of his postwar strategy.

Thus Washington's response on this issue must have been one of his bitterest disappointments. On the one hand, the Americans seemed totally unprepared to discuss his federation plans in detail. As Welles recorded his final conversation with Sikorski on January 4th:

General Sikorski then inquired whether he could understand that this Government officially favored a federation or union of eastern European states, including Poland. I replied that as I had endeavored in a previous conversation to make clear, certain officials of this Government were studying very carefully the possibility of the creation of an eastern European union of which Poland could be a member, but that so far as I knew, the matter had not been discussed with the President and I could not therefore give him any indication about such an objective officially favored by this Government.[52]

This was not an entirely truthful statement on Welles's part. The Department was not yet studying these matters "very carefully" and, in fact, would not begin to do so for another six months.[53] Moreover, despite the under secretary's noncommital stance here, less than six *weeks* later, the Foreign Office received a report of a decidedly negative American attitude toward regional organizations in Central and South-Eastern Europe.[54]

[50] *FRUS, 1942,* 3:203.
[51] Ibid., pp. 117-18 and 130.
[52] *FRUS, 1943,* 3:317.
[53] See p. 324 above; also Lipski, Raczyński, and Stroński, *Trzy podróże,* p. 23.
[54] C2595/231/55, FO 371/34560, PRO. On reading the report, one British official was prompted to wonder "whether the State Dept. have not swallowed some of the copious German propaganda" to the effect that such regional organizations would be primarily anti-Soviet in nature.

Nor did Washington seem to understand that external support was essential to further progress even between the Poles and Czechs. For, in its memo of December 9th, the State Department recommended the general be told that:

> . . . not until such time as the powers concerned had tried among themselves to reduce their mutual problems to basic points of agreement and disagreement would it be possible for the United States to discuss these questions, in consultation with other interested powers, with a view to reaching a constructive and final solution of the eastern European problem.[55]

On the other hand, both Roosevelt and Welles made it amply clear that, despite their confidence in Sikorski's desire for a full understanding with Russia, they were unwilling to exert the least pressure on Moscow to soften its opposition to the Polish-Czech negotiations.[56] The paragraph of the final letter from Roosevelt to the general relating to postwar European organization was a masterpiece of obfuscation:

> In an effort to build a solid foundation for a lasting peace in eastern Europe based upon careful considerations of political, ethnic, and economic factors, the United States Government desires to encourage the countries of Eastern Europe to continue to make careful studies of their mutual problems to determine points of agreement and disagreement in order that they may be in a position to present a plan under which lasting relationships would be assured. The United States Government would then be prepared to participate in efforts to reach a constructive and final solution of the Eastern European problem within the framework of a general world settlement.[57]

Small wonder that Sikorski chose to keep the letter secret rather than admit the extent of his failure.[58]

As the deterioration of Polish-Soviet relations gathered momentum in the early months of 1943, Moscow felt emboldened to make more explicit its opposition to federations (and not only of the Polish-Czechoslovak variety) along its western flank. On the eve of Eden's March 1943 visit to Washington, Ambassador Maisky told the foreign secretary "off the

---

[55] *FRUS, 1942*, 3:208.

[56] Ibid., p. 205; and Mitkiewicz, *Z gen. Sikorskim*, pp. 317-18. The same view was repeated by Welles to Ambassador Ciechanowski later in January 1943; see Ciechanowski, *Defeat in Victory*, p. 140.

[57] *FRUS, 1943*, 3:319-20.

[58] See especially Raczyński, *W sojuszniczym Londynie*, p. 161; Mitkiewicz, *Z gen. Sikorskim*, p. 326; and the comment by Frank Roberts in C923/258/55, FO 371/34563, PRO.

record'' that ''his Government was not enthusiastic'' about federations. Under further questioning, he allowed that the Soviet Union ''would probably not be opposed to Balkan federation provided it excluded Roumania, nor to Scandinavian federation if it excluded Finland''—although the ''latter arrangement'' would be ''of little significance and 'vegetarian.' '' As for a Polish-Czech federation, Moscow's attitude would depend on ''what Poland is going to be'' but, in any event, Maisky thought such units could have only economic and not political significance.[59] By May, following the rupture in diplomatic relations between Moscow and the Government-in-Exile, Polish-Czech negotiations were formally suspended.[60]

KATYŃ AND GIBRALTAR

Two events in the spring and early summer of 1943—revelation by Germany of their discovery of mass graves of thousands of Polish officers in the Katyń forest in mid-April, followed in early July by the death of General Sikorski in a plane crash off Gibraltar—have generally been accepted as the major turning points in the destiny of the Polish Government-in-Exile: the first as the precipitating cause of the rupture in Polish-Soviet relations and the occasion for the formation in Moscow of the nucleus of a future communist government; the second as removing from the stage at a critical moment the one exile leader who was thought capable of repairing relations with Moscow. As should now be clear, however, Sikorski's policy lay in ruins well before the first German announcement of their grisly discovery, and to many Poles a break in relations seemed only a matter of time. I certainly do not want to deny the dramatic impact of either Katyń or Gibraltar. But from the perspective of the general's futile two-year search for a solution to the problem of Poland's place in Europe, it is hard to view these two events as much more than an anticlimax, marking the end of an era but not themselves the cause of that end.

The pace of events quickened perceptibly following Sikorski's return from Washington in early January. Whether he intended to pursue his strategy of trying to reconcile the conflicting demands within the Alliance, despite the lack of substantive support from Roosevelt, is not entirely clear,

[59] N1605/499/38, FO 371/36991, PRO; Maisky insisted here that his remarks be ''regarded as strictly 'off the record' '' and that he was ''speaking for himself alone.'' Shades of Bogomolov's ''*les milieux russes*''! (See note 43 above.) By June and July of 1943, outright Soviet rejection of the federation idea was even more explicit, as was their tendency to ascribe it largely to Poland's anti-Soviet machinations. See the Foreign Office's review of the ''Soviet Attitude to Federations in Eastern Europe,'' dated August 10, 1943; N4906/499/38, FO 371/36992, PRO.

[60] On the final breakdown of the talks, see Raczyński, *W sojuszniczym Londynie*, pp. 177-80.

although he apparently remained firm in his resolve to journey again to Moscow.[61] Whatever his plans, however, they were soon cut short by a new crisis, this time in the form of a January 16th note from the Soviet government informing the Poles that it was withdrawing recognition of Polish citizenship from persons of Polish origin resident in the "Western districts of the Ukrainian and White Ruthenian [Belorussian] Soviet Socialist Republics" as of November 1-2, 1939. Recognition of such citizenship had been "by way of exception," the note continued, demonstrating "the good will of the Soviet Government." Until now, only Polish citizens of non-Polish nationality had been reclassed as Soviet citizens; however,

> [as] the Polish Government had adopted a negative attitude to . . . [the position] of the Soviet Government and has refused to take the appropriate steps, putting forward demands contrary to the sovereign rights of the Soviet Union in respect to these territories . . . the question of the possible non-application to such persons of the laws governing citizenship of the Union of Soviet Socialist Republics has ceased to exist.[62]

[61] Sikorski's attempts to disguise his failure to gain American support for his policy—attempts aimed primarily at keeping his Polish opposition at bay and including rumors that Roosevelt's still secret letter contained solid expressions of support—convinced some in the Foreign Office that the general had "exaggerated" expectations of help from that quarter. See, e.g., C910/258/55, FO 371/34563, PRO. That this was not so is indicated by Mitkiewicz's account of a conversation he had early in 1943 with Józef Lipski, a principal advisor to General Sikorski who had accompanied the latter to Washington. Lipski, he wrote, returned convinced that a "consequential declaration by the government of the United States is very unlikely . . . [and that] the most that we can expect . . . would be a postponement of the settlement of the boundary question until the peace conference, . . . [W]e don't know whether Russia, who by every means is insisting that the territorial annexations carried out by her in 1939 and 1940 be sanctioned now, would agree to this. Nonetheless, says Lipski, the United States is presently [our] only point of support . . . , and for this reason we must seek understanding for our causes and assistance there. . . . [A]s for Soviet Russia, Lipski is of the opinion that, at all costs, it is necessary to maintain a calm, cold-blooded and conciliatory position in order, God forbid, that we not find ourselves in total isolation. In Lipski's opinion, it is essential to negotiate our eastern boundaries with Russia." *Z gen. Sikorskim*, pp. 323-24. For a more sanguine but not very consistent appraisal of Sikorski's position on his return from Washington, see Kukiel, *Generał Sikorski*, pp. 216-18.

[62] For the texts of the Soviet note and the Polish reply, see *Documents*, 1:463-76. See also Raczyński, *W sojuszniczym Londynie*, p. 162; and Rozek, *Allied Wartime Diplomacy*, p. 119. The immediate effect of the Soviet action was to cut short the slight progress that had been made toward the end of 1942 in rebuilding the relief programs for Polish deportees in the Soviet Union. See, respectively, Roberts's minute and Raczyński's note in C1089 and C1566/258/55, FO 371/34563, PRO; and pp. 11-12 of Ambassador O'Malley's review of Soviet policy toward Poland since September 1939, dated April 29, 1943, in C4850/258/55, FO 371/34571, PRO.

If the note itself posed a blatantly unacceptable demand—that is, abandonment by the Poles of all of their citizens from the former eastern territories—its timing was no coincidence. Delivered on the eve of the final Soviet victory at Stalingrad, as the war entered a new political as well as military phase, it served notice that Stalin now felt strong enough to solve the "Polish question" on his own terms. In fact, the January 16th note was merely the opening shot in an all-out diplomatic and propaganda barrage against the Government-in-Exile, which the Poles could rightly fear was intended to provoke a break in relations.[63] Even more ominous, this new campaign was accompanied by increased activity on the part of the Communist-dominated Union of Polish Patriots in Moscow, including renewed rumors of the formation of a "Polish Red Army" and the inauguration at the beginning of March of *Wolna Polska (Free Poland)*, a new weekly that took a more critical tone toward the exile government than had earlier publications and for the first time indulged in direct attacks on Sikorski.[64]

In addition, the Soviet note further complicated Sikorski's internal situation, already aggravated by his inability to display to his public some positive results from his Washington talks (especially in the form of concrete guarantees of Poland's territorial integrity). Now publication in the clandestine press of the texts of the Soviet note and Polish reply (both kept

[63] It was just after delivery of this Soviet note that Bogomolov informed Beneš that Moscow "saw no difference between a confederation and an alliance and opposed both." Wandycz, *Czechoslovak-Polish Confederation*, p. 86; see also note 49 above. That Moscow had for some months been laying the basis for a campaign to discredit the exile government is indicated by Bogomolov's remark to U.S. Ambassador Biddle the previous October that Poland "lacked the qualifications of nationhood." As Biddle reported the conversation, Bogomolov "said that he had recently been giving considerable thought to the essential qualifying factors of nationhood. These were not only territory, people, and system, but one which included important heavy industry. The United States, as in the case of Russia, had all these factors, but Poland had no heavy industry, nor any distinctive economic system— yet she posed as a powerful nation. Her authorities now, as before the war, put on the airs of representatives of a great nation. He thought this ridiculous, for Poland lacked the qualifications of nationhood." Biddle did not record his response (if any), but did conclude that Bogomolov "was possibly instructed (a) to 'run down' the Poles, in our minds; and (b) to plant the idea in our minds that Russia would like to do business with us after the war, but . . . [only] on the basis of pre-arranged spheres of political-economic influence." State Decimal File: 860C.00/909, NA.

[64] C2482 and C2703/258/55, FO 371/34565, PRO; Werth, *Russia at War*, pp. 639-40; Raczyński, *W sojuszniczym Londynie*, pp. 164-66; and Ciechanowski, *Defeat in Victory*, pp. 138-42. For texts of additional notes and statements exchanged by the two governments, see *Documents*, 1:482-523. Kukiel (*Generał Sikorski*, p. 223) claims that, by the end of March, the Soviets had prepared a lengthy note justifying a break in relations. At the same time, the Foreign Office was concerned lest the Poles, in their frustration, take some "rash action" such as withdrawing their ambassador or otherwise precipitating a diplomatic rupture; C3385/258/55, FO 371/34566, PRO (especially memos by Roberts and O'Malley).

secret by the government), as well as subsequent exchanges of public statements, brought the opposition to a fever pitch.[65] There were demands for Sikorski's resignation, even for a protest resignation of the entire government. Nationalist leader Bielecki declared that the prime minister bore "full responsibility" for the state of Polish-Soviet relations, presumably because he had not stood up more resolutely to Soviet demands. In the army, where many soldiers recently evacuated to the Middle East had been anticipating the arrival of their families from the Soviet Union, the situation bordered on mutiny. As the usually temperate Raczyński wrote in his diary in early March, ". . . a war is raging on several fronts at once: the Soviets against us and our opposition against General Sikorski's government."[66]

In all probability, it was this building mood of dissension and outrage rather than surprise at the Katyń revelations that was responsible for the Polish reaction to the German broadcast on April 13th. After eighteen months of evasions, contradictions, and rumors, there could after all have been little surprise. What happened next is well known. Three days later, on April 16th, the Polish government issued a statement reviewing its efforts since August 1941 to find the missing officers, and reluctantly concluding that the "abundant and detailed German information" warranted impartial investigation; it had, the statement continued, appealed to the International Red Cross for this purpose. Although the language was moderate, there could be little doubt that the Poles believed the Soviets guilty of the murders. Stalin reacted swiftly. On April 25th, following a frantic but vain effort on Churchill's part to forestall the inevitable, the Soviet Union severed relations with the exile government, accusing it of collaborating with Nazi Germany in a campaign of anti-Soviet "fascist slander."[67]

---

[65] Public silence over the Soviet note of January 16th was broken by the clandestine newsletter *Walka* (see p. 223 above), which put out a particularly venomous issue in February entitled "The Fourth Partition of Poland." Two members of the Polish Army in Scotland were later arrested, but not before the issue had caused a furor among the soldiers and exile community. Counselor Savery of the British Embassy suspected that the source of the leak was Minister of Justice Wacław Komarnicki, an Endek who, according to Savery, had "the reputation of being a *mauvais coucheur* [unsavory bedfellow]" and who had shown earlier indications of sympathy with the Nationalist opposition. See C1728/258/55, FO 371/34563; and C1983, C2054, C2114, and C2115/258/55, FO 371/34564, PRO.

[66] For descriptions of the internal Polish situation from a viewpoint sympathetic to Sikorski, see especially Raczyński, *W sojuszniczym Londynie*, pp. 162-66; and Kukiel, *Generał Sikorski*, pp. 218-20. For the opposition point of view, see Pobóg-Malinowski, *Najnowsza historia*, 3:252-59; and Katelbach, *Rok złych wróżb*, pp. 21-50.

[67] See *Documents*, 1:523-36; also *Correspondence*, 1:120-25. No doubt the most complete record of these two hectic weeks is to be found in the Foreign Office files, FO 371/34568

One lingering question about this sequence of events is just what role Sikorski himself played in it. Certainly the Polish response was not consistent with his long-standing tactic of doing nothing that would give Stalin sufficient cause to break relations. Only a month earlier, he had written to Anders, who among others had demanded the general's resignation and the adoption of a stiffer posture vis-à-vis Moscow, that any action by Poles provoking such a break would be "political suicide" leading to their "complete isolation" within the Allied camp.[68] There is some evidence to suggest that, during both the Katyń crisis and the preceding weeks of mounting tensions, Sikorski played a relatively passive role in directing Polish policy, even that he was depressed and withdrawn. It is well established, for instance, that the Polish statement of April 16th was primarily the work of General Kukiel, the minister of defense, and former Ambassador Kot, now minister of information—both of whom were more rigid in their approach to a Polish-Soviet reconciliation than was the prime minister.[69] Likewise in March, in reference to a crisis produced by an earlier Soviet statement, Raczyński noted: "Perhaps because of criticism and dissension within the government, Sikorski recently took to his bed and took no part in the sessions of the Council of Ministers which discussed our reply to Moscow."[70] One possible explanation for his behavior is that he was simply no longer able or willing to stem the flood tide of anti-Soviet feeling among the Poles—that with all the brutalities they had suffered at Soviet hands now coming into the open, he could not and did not want to bear the onus of enforcing silence, whatever the consequences.[71] In addition, it is evident from several sources that the years of unending toil, frustration, and disappointment had taken their toll on his health and that he was suffering from exhaustion and nervous strain, possibly complicated by a heart problem.[72]

---

to 34570, PRO. As one British official commented after the fact, it seemed "clear" that the Soviets had "seized on [the Polish appeal to the Red Cross] as a not entirely unwelcome pretext." Minute by D. Allen in C4764/258/55, FO 371/34571, PRO.

[68] Pobóg-Malinowski, *Najnowsza historia*, 3:269. See also the report of an article either inspired or written by Sikorski, which warned of the danger that Polish-Soviet friction could play into German hands; "German Temptations and the Polish-Soviet Pact," *Dziennik Polski*, February 17, 1943, reported in C1830/258/55, FO 371/34563, PRO.

[69] Raczyński, *W sojuszniczym Londynie*, pp. 171-72; Feis, *Churchill, Roosevelt, Stalin*, p. 193n; Kukiel, *Generał Sikorski*, pp. 223-31; and Pruszyński, "Katyń i Gibraltar," *Wybór pism*, 2:461-62.

[70] Raczyński, *W sojuszniczym Londynie*, pp. 164-65.

[71] Ibid., pp. 171-72; Mitkiewicz, *Z gen. Sikorskim*, p. 342; and Pruszyński, "Katyńi i Gibraltar," pp. 461-62.

[72] Pruszyński, "Katyń i Gibraltar," pp. 464-65; Mitkiewicz, *Z gen. Sikorskim*, pp. 298-99; Morawski, *Wspólna droga*, p. 170; and David Irving, *Accident: The Death of General Sikorski*, pp. 44-45 and 50. A number of Foreign Office documents from these weeks also

The general's moves during the remaining weeks of his life present an intriguing but incomplete picture. Despite the fatigue that was evident to all who saw him, he seemed to emerge from the Katyń crisis with renewed resolve to seek an accommodation with Moscow. It seemed, too, that his policy now would be bolder than before, less constrained by his domestic opposition, possibly more independent of the Western Allies. On May 1st, he told Averell Harriman that he now realized the Polish statement on Katyń had been a serious error. He would try, he said, to put aside personal feelings and "go as far as he could, consistent with the dignity and views of his colleagues and people," to restore relations, and he asked if the United States would do what it could to help."[73] Three days later, in a broadcast to Poland, he reiterated that "the securing of friendly relations with Soviet Russia has been and continues to be one of the main guiding principles of the Polish Government and of the Polish Nation." He spoke too of "concessions," only obliquely to be sure, but it was the first time that this word had been uttered in an official pronouncement.[74] Then in the latter part of May, amidst rumors of assassination threats and pleas from his friends that he not go, Sikorski left for the Middle East—the purpose of his trip being not only to bolster morale in the army, but above all to reassert his personal control over a rebellious officer corps.[75] It was there in Cairo on July 2nd, just two days before his death, that he gave his last press conference. He spoke now in terms possibly implying a shift toward a policy similar to that of Czech President Beneš. He hoped, he said, to find as soon as possible a means to an understanding with Moscow, based on friendship and alliance between the "West-Slavonic nations and the nations of the Soviet Union." Describing the press conference in his

---

make reference to the general's erratic behavior. For instance, in late January, in a clear reference to Sikorski, Strang wrote: "The Poles are rather rattled these days and inclined to act foolishly." C1125/684/55, FO 371/34602, PRO.

[73] Feis, *Churchill, Roosevelt, Stalin*, p. 193n.

[74] *Documents*, 2:4. Unfortunately, there is an omission in this portion of the text; the available part reads: "[. . .] But there are limits to concessions, which no one in the Polish nation will pass." He then went on to imply that he saw the formation of a puppet communist regime as such a limit. See also Strumph-Wojtkiewicz, *Siła złego*, pp. 135-36.

[75] It was not only the Polish government that was concerned over the unrest among the Polish units in the Middle East. By the end of 1942 the British, both in Baghdad and in London, were expressing alarm over General Anders's penchant for "dangerous talk"—in this case, his expectation (wrong as it turned out) of a German success, or at least a standoff, in the winter campaign in Russia. By early February, the British Middle Eastern Command was equally disturbed over growing unrest in the Polish Army (due especially to the soldiers' anxiety about family members still in the Soviet Union), and was urging that Sikorski "visit here earliest possible." The urgency of the situation is indicated by Churchill's query to Eden: "Foreign Secretary: This is important. Pray advise. W.S.C. 8.2.43" See C258 and C1465/258/55, FO 371/34563, PRO.

diary, already after Sikorski's death, Mitkiewicz added that he had heard "unofficially" that the general had been planning to approach Stalin for direct talks on "the whole gamut of disputed issues."[76]

What did these statements portend? Had he decided that he could no longer straddle the two sides of the Alliance—that, regardless of the strictures of Atlantic policy, he had to strike the best deal he could with Stalin now? Did he still hope to salvage some of Poland's east, or would he have accepted the Curzon line? Did he hope for immediate assurances on Poland's boundary with Germany? From Stalin alone? Did he still intend to insist on a federation entirely independent of the Soviet Union? Or was he now resigned to accepting some degree of political dependence? Unfortunately, the scarcity of hard information concerning the state of Sikorski's thinking during these last weeks reduces any attempt to answer these questions to the level of idle speculation.

But if the extent of the pending shift in Sikorski's policy remains obscure, the motives for it do not. On the one hand, the break in relations with Moscow had in a curious way strengthened his hand vis-à-vis his Polish opposition. In particular, the ambivalent, even negative reaction to the Polish stance on Katyń in Britain and the United States had finally and irrefutably demonstrated to the London Poles what many had hitherto refused to accept—that is, the enormous popularity of Russia in the West and by contrast their own lack of leverage.[77] On the other hand, Sikorski's own hand was being forced by events in Moscow: by the announcement

[76] Mitkiewicz, *Z gen. Sikorskim*, p. 359. (Mitkiewicz had been in Washington since March as the Polish representative to the Combined Allied Staff, and therefore had not had direct contact with Sikorski for some months.)

[77] Ibid., pp. 343-44 and 347; also Pruszyński, "Katyń i Gibraltar," pp. 461-63. British reports from the Middle East during Sikorski's visit there in May and June indicate that he was regaining control of the situation in the army as well; see especially C5992, C6115, and C6730/5889/55, FO 371/34614A, PRO. British ambivalence over Katyń is best seen in the minutes attached to Ambassador O'Malley's May 1943 review of the evidence surrounding the massacre (C6160/258/55, FO 371/34577, PRO). For instance, Cadogan wrote in part: "This is very disturbing. I confess that, in cowardly fashion, I had turned my head away from the scene at Katyń—for fear of what I should find there. There may be evidence, that we do not know of, that may point in another direction. But on the evidence that we have, it is difficult to escape from the presumption of Russian guilt. . . . However, quite clearly for the moment there is nothing to be done. As to what circulation we give to this explosive material, I find it difficult to make up my mind. Of course it would be only honest to circulate it. But as we know (all admit) that the knowledge of this evidence cannot affect our course of action, or policy, is there any advantage in exposing more individuals than necessary to the spiritual conflict that a reading of this dispatch excites." ("Circulation" here refers only to the War Cabinet; this was eventually done.) Earlier Secretary of State Hull had told Ambassador Halifax that "American opinion was not as yet greatly interested" in the Katyń affair or the break in Polish-Soviet relations; Halifax's cable of April 28th, in C4764/258/55, FO 371/34571, PRO.

in early May that the long-rumored "Polish Red Army" (actually only a division named after the eighteenth-century Polish military hero Koś-ciuszko) was being formed under the aegis of the Union of Polish Patriots; and by the stepped-up political activities of the Communists, which clearly foreshadowed the creation of a competing government. It was an eventuality that had worried him ever since the emergence of the Communist-dominated group at the time of his trip to Russia in December of 1941,[78] and one that he was determined to avert at all costs, just as he had avoided the emergence of an official opposition in France in September 1939.[79] Referring to the developments in Moscow, Mitkiewicz wrote: "[T]here was not the least doubt that General Sikorski . . . was ready to do everything, even at the cost of national injuries, . . . to prevent the coming into being of two Polish governments. It was precisely for this purpose that he intended to go to Moscow, to Stalin."[80]

FROM the personal standpoint, as a guide to a better understanding of the man and his policies, it would be interesting to know just how far Sikorski was prepared to bend to salvage his rapprochement with Stalin. But from the standpoint of history it does not really matter. For, on the night of July 4, 1943, en route back to London from his tour of the Polish Army in the Middle East, his plane crashed on takeoff from Gibraltar. All aboard except the pilot were lost.

Although the circumstances of Sikorski's death are not material here (if only because the cause of the crash has never been established), the incident has evoked too much speculation and controversy to be passed over without at least a brief comment. The findings of the British Court of Inquiry, which conducted its investigations hurriedly and without Polish participation, were: first, that there was no sabotage; second, that pilot error was not involved; and third, that the probable cause of the crash was the accidental jamming of the plane's elevator controls, which would have prevented the pilot from continuing his ascent. The only problem with this finding was that there was not the slightest physical evidence that the controls had in fact jammed, or even that they could be jammed. The Poles themselves, stubbornly unconvinced, refused to approve the report of the

[78] See Chapter IX, note 58, and note 74 above. Also Ciechanowski, *Defeat in Victory*, p. 216; and *Documents*, 2:14-17.

[79] See p. 180 above.

[80] Mitkiewicz, *Z gen. Sikorskim*, pp. 359-60. Raczyński's entry for July 10, 1943, the first after news of Sikorski's death, is also suggestive: "We were all preparing for his return, which was to be the signal for a great renewal of our activity on all fronts. I had already had a conversation with Beneš in order to dissuade him from his intention of concluding now a long-term alliance with Moscow without regard for us, [thus] causing a further cooling of our relations." *W sojuszniczym Londynie*, p. 183.

inquiry, which was then issued over their protests. Most were convinced, then and later, that the crash was not an accident.[81]

Evidence of sabotage, however, was strictly circumstantial. First, there was the "accident" during Sikorski's flight to Washington the previous December, in which the engines of his plane failed on takeoff from Montreal. Sumner Welles later told the Polish leader that American investigators were convinced it was an act of sabotage. There were the rumors of assassination plots that were circulating both in London and the Middle East. Then there were the mysterious phone calls to several ministers in the exile government announcing a fatal crash off Gibraltar while Sikorski was en route *to* Cairo—a full six weeks before the real crash occurred. And finally, there were unexplained anomalies in the actions of the pilot, leading some to suspect that he had deliberately caused the crash.[82]

But if sabotage, then by whom? Many Poles blamed Sikorski's opponents among their own countrymen. But this begs the question of how. It was after all a British plane, under strict British control. The most spectacular theory advanced so far is that of German playwright, Rolf Hochhuth, who in his 1967 play *The Soldiers* accused Churchill of murdering Sikorski. Claiming to have seen convincing evidence locked in a Swiss bank vault, Hochhuth attributed Churchill's action to fear that the general's "anti-Soviet" policy would disrupt Allied unity.[83] By now it should be

---

[81] After being told several years before that the Foreign Office file on Sikorski's death had probably been lost or destroyed, I stumbled on it by accident in 1981 while examining records of his Middle Eastern trip (FO 371/34614, with an identifying number, according to which Foreign Office documents are filed, of 5889). Through a clerical anomaly, the cable of July 5th from Gibraltar reporting the crash was originally numbered C7683/*5889*/55 and later renumbered C7683/*7683*/55, indicating the beginning of a new topical file (General Sikorski's death). Instead of assigning a separate file number, file 34614 was divided into sections A and B; however, that division and the second topic number (7683) were not recorded in the all important "Class Lists" through which a researcher locates the proper files. I am inclined to think that the omission was accidental and not a deliberate attempt to hide the file; for, once found, it contained little of historical interest. The only "Green," or secret, document in the file (C9840/7683/55) is the British cover letter to the Polish government, accompanying the findings of the Court of Inquiry on Sikorski's death. The report itself is not there.

[82] For several accounts of the crash and events both before and after, see: Irving, *Accident*; Strumph-Wojtkiewicz, *Siła złego*; and Klimkowski, *Katastrofa w Gibraltarze*. Irving gives a very detailed account of the crash and inquiry; he leaves the reader with little doubt that he believes sabotage cannot be ruled out, but stops short of pointing a finger of blame. (However, Irving also takes a very simplistic, conventional view of Sikorski's policy.) Klimkowski's book is the most tendentious and illogical; he accuses Anders of complicity but assigns primary responsibility to the British who, he claims, wanted to prevent a patching up of relations between Sikorski and Stalin. Strumph-Wojtkiewicz falls somewhere in between; offering a Marxist analysis of British imperial policy, he concludes that they must bear at least moral responsibility but holds the Poles themselves primarily responsible.

[83] For a discussion of the Hochhuth theory, see Martin Esslin, "A Playwright Who Drops Political Blockbusters," pp. 48ff.

obvious that there are serious logical flaws to this theory, not the least of which is that Churchill himself had written to Stalin only in April that Sikorski was "far the most helpful man you or we are likely to find for the purposes of the common cause."[84] One other theory, which I have seen mentioned only in passing, offers more food for thought: that is, to the extent the British were involved in the crash, the key man would have been one Kim Philby, only much later exposed as a long-time Soviet agent, but in July of 1943 the chief of British intelligence in Gibraltar and the man with final responsibility for the security of Sikorski's plane.[85]

AFTER SIKORSKI

Of the many ironies in this story perhaps the bitterest of all is the fact that, just at the time of General Sikorski's death, Western and, in particular, British policy was beginning to move in directions he had been urging in vain for so long—most importantly, toward acceptance of the need to begin discussing *now* the shape of the postwar settlement, and with respect to Poland, to deal with the eastern boundary question in the context of a comprehensive settlement that would afford her adequate compensation in the west. To be sure, this shift was as much if not more the result of the changing military and political balance signaled by the Soviet victory at Stalingrad as of Polish importunings.[86] Nor did it necessarily imply Allied recognition of the premises of Sikorski's policy—that is, the concept of "real guarantees" or the logical consequences thereof for Poland's boundaries and the postwar organization of Central Europe. Still, it seemed to mark an important opening for the Poles, a potential break in the vicious circle of conflicting demands imposed by East and West.

Although Sikorski could not have known it at the time, his December 1942 memorandum on "The German Problem with Special Relation to Poland," which had been submitted to the Foreign Office as well as the State Department,[87] had been referred for analysis and comment to the Military Sub-Committee of Britain's Reconstruction Secretariat. From the correspondence between the two agencies in the early weeks of 1943 it is

[84] *Correspondence*, 1:125.

[85] See the Introduction by John le Carré to *The Philby Conspiracy*, by Bruce Page, David Leitch, and Phillip Knightley, p. 7. The Soviets did not mention Sikorski's death until July 9th. Then *Izvestiia* called his death "tragic" but expressed "regret that his will to consolidate friendship and collaboration between the U.S.S.R. and Poland was able to be broken by circles whose policy had proved ruinous to pre-war Poland." Translated in *Soviet Monitor* (July 9, 1943) and *Soviet War News* (July 12, 1943), in C7990/7683/55, FO 371/34614B, PRO.

[86] See p. 163 and note 35 above; also Eden, *The Reckoning*, p. 425; and Bohlen, *Witness to History*, pp. 126-27.

[87] See Chapter X, note 160, above.

clear that the British fully understood that the Poles had been deliberately vague in defining their territorial desiderata in the west and that, even in the absence of a clearly stated demand for an Oder or Oder-Neisse frontier, they were at least laying the basis for putting forward such a claim in the future. With this understanding, the Military Sub-Committee was asked to study the desirability of shortening and straightening Poland's frontiers with Germany especially from the strategic point of view.[88] The Sub-Committee's recommendations, submitted at the end of June, included cession to Poland of all of East Prussia with Danzig, the Oppeln district, and the Pomeranian salient east of a line that would run approximately due north from the westernmost part of the prewar boundary; expulsion of the German population, estimated at 4.25 million, was deemed "essential." In addition, the report recognized that the Oder line had "the advantage of being the only continuous natural feature that a frontier could follow" and that, "from the purely strategical point of view," inclusion of Lower Silesia in Poland "would be the most satisfactory solution" in the southwest. The authors recommended against pushing the boundary this far west, however, primarily because of the large numbers of Germans who would be displaced and because they questioned Poland's capacity to replace them.[89]

In the meantime, the Foreign Office was discussing the question of compensation in more general terms. Wouldn't it be necessary "when the time comes for Polish-Soviet frontier negotiations . . . to strengthen General Sikorski's hand with his own people by confirming the intention of all the United Nations and not merely of Russia to give Poland adequate territorial compensation in the West"? Wouldn't it be "possible to find a compromise by which Russian security, prestige and minority problems [could] be satisfied, and which, at the same time, [would] be acceptable to the Polish nation" *if* that compromise were "presented to Poland as a whole and not piecemeal"?[90] Citing intense and mounting Soviet pressure for immediate

---

[88] C849/231/55, FO 371/34560, PRO. See especially the letter of January 11, 1943, from Gladwyn Jebb of the Foreign Office to Admiral Bellairs of the Military Sub-Committee, in which the former wrote: "The Polish memorandum, however, contains certain passages which imply that the cession of territory up to the ODER is demanded." See also the letter of February 2nd, summarizing the Foreign Office's interpretation for the Sub-Committee.

[89] M.S.C./54: "The Future Polish-German Frontier," Parts I and II, dated June 28, 1943, and Admiral Bellairs's covering letter of June 30th; C7553/231/55, FO 371/34560, PRO. Essentially the same recommendations were carried over into the final report of what was by now called the Post-Hostilities Planning Sub-Committee; P.H.P. (44)10, May 5, 1944, in C6538/871/55, FO 371/39507, PRO.

[90] C3246/258/55, FO 371/34566 and C3454/258/55, FO 371/34567, PRO. Mention in the first quote of Russian assurances of "adequate territorial compensation" is a reference to a secret radio broadcast in which the Soviets allegedly promised the Poles East Prussia, hardly "adequate" compensation in the Polish view.

acceptance of their boundary claims, the deputy under-secretary, Sir Orme Sargent, proposed that the Polish matter be dealt with at the same time. "Even the exiled Government," he suggested (ironically on April 15th, two days after the Katyń revelations):

> might acquiesce—even though under protest—in the imposition by the three Great Powers of a comprehensive settlement, provided that it stated not only what Poland was to give up in the way of territory but also what she would gain in compensation, and provided that the Poles were not required to sign the document embodying the agreement. For it is surely in the interests of the Poles themselves that this problem of Poland's future frontiers should be resolved before the end of the war, and that the Soviet Government's claims should at any rate be defined and limited now rather than that they should be still unsettled when the fighting stops and may well be followed up by a state of chaos in Eastern Europe.[91]

For the most part such suggestions were based more on the urgency of preserving Allied unity than on sympathy for the Polish case; nor did these discussions, which took place in late March and April, reflect any progress beyond a minimal program of compensation. Indeed, Sargent advanced the outrageous proposition that, while it was "just possible to argue" that Soviet territorial demands would "not constitute a territorial aggrandisement" under the Atlantic Charter, cession of East Prussia and Upper Silesia to Poland could not be so reconciled.[92]

In the end, and despite the critical state of Polish-Soviet relations, it was decided that such a settlement, even in the form of an informal understanding, was out of the question for the time being—that the proposed course was still unacceptable to Washington and should it leak out, as it almost certainly would, would only serve to stiffen German resistance.[93]

---

[91] C4133/258/55, FO 371/34568, PRO.

[92] Ibid. Of key Foreign Office officials under Eden, Sargent appears to have been one of the least sympathetic to the Poles; he was also the under-secretary with purview over the Northern Department (which included relations with the Soviet Union), while William Strang held comparable supervisory authority over the Central Department. Ambassador O'Malley may have helped stimulate some of this discussion about compensation; in his April 1st memo to Eden, he reminded his Foreign Office colleagues that Sikorski and others had earlier indicated in "confidential conversations" a willingness to consider territorial concessions to Russia, "but up to now we have never given the Poles much encouragement to look for compensation . . ." C3641/258/55, FO 371/34567, PRO.

[93] C4133/258/55, FO 371/34568, PRO. Roberts's minute of April 18th is instructive. Suggesting that the question was not yet of "real immediate practical importance, since the Russians are still far from the 1939 Polish frontier," he concluded: "To sum up, I cannot help feeling that we have not yet reached a stage in the war when we can jeopardise our immediate war requirements for post-war considerations. The action now proposed would,

In the process, however, the principle of compensation and the need for a comprehensive approach seem to have won general acceptance. In fact, when the Military Sub-Committee's recommendations were presented several months later, they were welcomed as "useful" and as "providing a solid basis for discussing substantial cessions of German territory to Poland . . . in compensation for" losses in the east; and it was again stated that the two questions be considered simultaneously.[94] At the same time, while the Foreign Office had long regarded the Curzon line as an acceptable basis for negotiations in the east, there was now active discussion of how best to go about salvaging Lwów for the Poles.[95]

Developments at the policy level proceeded rather more slowly, a fact due in part (but only in part) to Roosevelt's continued reluctance to consider territorial issues in detail. The first mention of compensation between the British and Americans, during Eden's March 1943 talks in Washington, was predictably stingy: the Curzon line in the east in exchange for East Prussia with Danzig and, according to Eden, "perhaps some concessions in Silesia."[96] More surprising is the fact that the foreign secretary's position remained essentially unchanged the following October as he prepared for the foreign ministers' conference in Moscow, although by now he seemed more firmly committed to the cession of the rest of Upper Silesia as well as to the need for population transfers.[97] It was this limited view of compensation, rather than the more generous recommendations of the Military

---

I fear, harm the United Nations war effort, in which must be included the resistance of the occupied populations and especially of the Poles, more even than the existing tension between the Poles and the Russians. I submit that we should concentrate upon bringing this home to the Russians and so endeavor once again to plaster over the cracks in the facade of Allied unity." See also minutes in the two entries cited in note 90 above.

[94] See especially D. Allen's minute in C7553/231/55, FO 371/34560, PRO. Not all were in full agreement with the recommendations however. Lord Hood, for example, questioned the exclusion of Lower Silesia, suggesting that the Poles might well have the capacity to repopulate it. More seriously, he continued: "The alignment of the western frontier is considered from the defensive angle only. This seems to be historically and temperamentally unsound. What the *gascons de l'Europe* [braggarts of Europe] need is an 'offensive' frontier: a frontier from which they will constantly threaten Prussia and can launch a lightning offensive against Berlin. In this way they would make a real contribution to the security of Europe." Others took a less generous view, questioning, e. g., the MSC's recommendation concerning Eastern Pomerania; see C9308 and C11491/231/55, FO 371/34561, PRO.

[95] N4447/499/38, FO 371/36991, and N6004/499/38, FO 371/36992, PRO.

[96] Although Eden discussed territorial questions in a general way with Roosevelt during his March 1943 visit, he clearly came away with the impression that the president was not yet ready to commit himself to specific settlements. See especially Eden's marginal comments on Sargent's April 15th memorandum; C4133/258/55, FO 371/34568, PRO.

[97] See Eden's memorandum for the War Cabinet on the "Western Frontier of the U.S.S.R.," dated October 5, 1943; W.P. (43) 438, copy filed in N6004/499/38, FO 371/36992, PRO.

Sub-Committee's report, that was communicated to the Poles when Eden finally decided to broach the issue with them in September.[98]

Yet in November, at Teheran, Churchill—who had visibly bridled at the mention of the Oder the previous March[99]—seized on Stalin's casual reference to such a line with undisguised enthusiasm. He "liked the picture" of a Poland between the Curzon line and the Oder, he said. And after some haggling, in which the Russians extracted a promise of Lwów and Königsberg for themselves while tentatively agreeing that Oppeln might go to the Poles, Churchill said he would recommend the formula to them.[100] There followed one of the better-remembered scenes of Allied wartime diplomacy, one repeated in fact on several occasions: on the one hand, of the British prime minister, in his eloquent and inimitable style, forcefully pressuring the Poles not merely to accept the Teheran formula, but "to accept it enthusiastically as well, . . . because I consider it as just," and warning that if they refused he would wash his hands of them; on the other hand, of the Poles—"mulish" and "silly" Cadogan called them—stubbornly protesting the partition of Poland without their participation and refusing out of hand to accept either the Curzon or Oder line.[101] Later Churchill berated them in the most brutal terms, telling them that, had they not been so unreasonable following Teheran, Stalin would have been willing to see the exile government return to an independent Poland whose new and more favorable boundaries would be guaranteed by the Great Powers. They therefore had only themselves to blame for the existence of the Lublin Committee, that "frightful nuisance" as he called it.[102]

Did the Poles, as Churchill asserted, miss a genuine opportunity here, or were these urgings and posturings on his part the product of so much wishful thinking? By now, it is true, the Government-in-Exile was in weaker, less decisive hands than it had been under Sikorski. The new

[98] See p. 313 and note 159 above; and C10409/231/55, FO 371/34561, PRO.

[99] In the midst of a public flap over a *Times* editorial on March 10, 1943, in which the Oder was referred to as Russia's (!) line of security in Europe, Churchill fired off a one-line memo to the Foreign Office: "Please show also the line of the Oder referred to so foolishly by the *Times*." (The "also" refers to his earlier request for information about the Curzon line which the *Times* editorial had likewise supported.) C3102/258/55, FO 371/34566, PRO.

[100] Churchill, *Closing the Ring*, pp. 361-62, 394-97, and 403; Sherwood, *Roosevelt and Hopkins*, pp. 782 and 797; and Bohlen, *Witness to History*, pp. 143-44 and 150-52.

[101] See the Polish records of three meetings with Churchill on January 20, February 6 and 16, 1944, in *Documents*, 2:144-49, 165-71, and 180-87; also Rozek, *Allied Wartime Diplomacy*, pp. 194-97; *The Cadogan Diaries*, pp. 592-607; and Mikołajczyk, *The Pattern of Soviet Domination*, pp. 52-60.

[102] Mikołajczyk, *The Pattern of Soviet Domination*, pp. 108-111; and *Documents*, 2:416-24.

prime minister, Stanisław Mikołajczyk, did not have his predecessor's stature either at home or abroad; nor did he share entirely the latter's breadth of outlook.[103] But one may reasonably question whether the shift in Western policy did not come too late to have helped even Sikorski had he lived—whether, having failed so utterly to show tangible support for Poland's independence and integrity during the early stages of the war when the Soviets were weak, London and Washington could reasonably have expected to exert much leverage over Stalin now that the tide of war had turned in his favor. On the contrary, all the evidence we have seen indicates that, as early as the middle of 1942, he had exploited Western indifference to maneuver the exile government into a position that would allow him to free himself of his obligations to it at a moment of his choosing. That moment happened to come with the Katyń discovery in April 1943, but it would have come soon thereafter in any event. No doubt Stalin would have been willing to use Sikorski as he later used Mikołajczyk, or as he used Beneš in Czechoslovakia; but that he would have been willing to resume relations with the London Poles under any circumstances is unlikely in the extreme.[104]

Even Churchill's own account of the Teheran proceedings does not support his contention that Stalin was willing to offer an Oder boundary to the exile government—or, indeed, that he actually committed himself to an Oder boundary at all. He would not do that, nor would he openly mention the Western Neisse extension of the Oder line, until he could be certain that Soviet armies would be in control and that the future Polish government would be one of his choosing.[105] As Khrushchev in his memoirs has so ingenuously revealed Soviet motives:

[103] In the midst of the post-Teheran crisis for the exile government, Raczyński lamented in his diary: "I regret more and more the loss of General Sikorski . . ." *W sojuszniczym Londynie*, p. 217. Even President Raczkiewicz complained that "since his death we live in isolation." Onacewicz, "Komentarze do książki Mitkiewicza," p. 162.

[104] See, e.g., Werth, *Russia at War*, pp. 640-41. A few days after he called the Poles "mulish" and "silly," even Cadogan had to admit: "I am beginning to share Polish suspicions that Soviet intentions are wholly dishonorable." *The Cadogan Diaries*, ed. Dilks, p. 597.

[105] Stalin first committed himself to seek an Oder-Western Neisse boundary for Poland in a secret agreement of July 27, 1944, with the newly formed Polish Committee of National Liberation (the "Lublin Committee"). (A second agreement of the preceding day regulating relations between Polish civilian authorities and the Soviet High Command in Poland was published immediately.) Several vague references to this secret agreement were made in Poland just after the war, but the text appears not to have been published until 1967. Whether it has ever been made public by the Soviets is not clear. See Kowalski, *Polityka zagraniczna RP, 1944-1947*, pp. 4-5; and *Stosunki polsko-radzieckie w latach 1917-1945: Dokumenty i materiały*, ed. Euzebiusz Basiński, pp. 399-401. Stalin first mentioned the Western Neisse publicly only in December 1944, during talks with General de Gaulle. See *FRUS: Conferences at Malta and Yalta*, pp. 219-21. Another barometer of Soviet caution on this score was the

The Oder-Neisse Line was advantageous for both Poland and the Soviet Union. We knew that sooner or later Poland would be a socialist country and our ally. Many of us felt, myself included, that someday Poland would be part of one great country or socialist commonwealth of nations. Therefore we were glad to have the Polish-German border moved as far west as possible.[106]

By inverse logic, Western enthusiasm for the Oder line turned out to be short-lived. Once it became clear that Poland's postwar government would be dominated by Moscow rather than the London Poles, the British beat a hasty retreat toward what had now become the State Department's position. (Although Roosevelt had not protested the discussion of the Oder line at Teheran, the Americans never, then or later, favored giving Poland more than East Prussia with Danzig, Upper Silesia, plus the Pomeranian salient—i.e., more or less the same line recommended by the British Military Sub-Committee in June 1943.)[107] Now, following Churchill's talks with Stalin in October 1944, talks that saw the final unsuccessful effort to bring about a reconciliation between Moscow and the exile government, Eden told the Poles that it would be "sheer madness" for them to claim German lands as far as the Oder.[108] On the eve of the Yalta Conference, he wrote to Churchill that "we should keep the position fluid as regards the Oder line frontier, . . . since we need not make the same concessions to the Lublin Poles which we were prepared to make to M. Mikołajczyk in order to obtain a solution of the Polish problem."[109] Churchill, apparently so eager at Teheran for Stalin's agreement to broad compensation

---

tardiness of the Polish Communists in spelling out their program for the western boundary. Having first mentioned the Oder in April 1943, they later retreated to vague and open-ended formulas in their programmatic statements, openly espousing an Oder-Lusatian Neisse line only in November 1944. See, e.g., Kowalski, *ZSRR a granica*, pp. 75-76; and Norbert Kołomejczyk, "Sprawa Ziem Zachodnich w programie i działalności Polskiej Partii Robotniczej," in *Polska Partia Robotnicza na Pomorzu Zachodnim: Studia i materiały*, ed. Bogdan Dopierała, pp. 20-21.

[106] *Khrushchev Remembers: The Last Testament*, trans. and ed. Strobe Talbott, p. 158. Khrushchev here confirms that the Polish Communists (Bierut included!) did ask that Lwów be returned to Poland (pp. 163-65); see Chapter X, note 31, above.

[107] This was the American position by the time of the Yalta Conference. See *FRUS: Conferences at Malta and Yalta*, pp. 232-33 and 510. As indicated in Chapter X, note 138, above, however, as late as the fall of 1943 (approximately the time of Teheran) the State Department's postwar planners foresaw only minimal corrections in Poland's boundary with Germany.

[108] *Documents*, 2:459; for a full discussion of the Polish government's inability to obtain firm Western commitments on the western boundary, see: "Nieznane exposé: Przemówienie Prezesa Rady Ministrów Tomasza Arciszewskiego na posiedzeniu Rady Narodowej w Londynie w dniu 15.I.1945r.," ed. Adam Ciołkosz, pp. 9-25.

[109] *FRUS: Conferences at Malta and Yalta*, p. 509.

for Poland in the west, now uttered his memorable warning about what a "great pity" it would be "to stuff the Polish goose so full of German food that it died of indigestion."[110]

THIS being a study of Sikorski's efforts to promote an Oder-Neisse boundary for Poland—and, more particularly, of the failure of those efforts—I do not propose to venture further into later events that eventually led to the establishment of that line as the boundary between Poland and Germany, the more so as these events have been recounted in detail on many occasions. My intention here is simply to point out that for the Polish Government-in-Exile the critical year was not 1944 or even 1943, but 1942; that in retrospect at least it was Sikorski's failure and not Mikołajczyk's that marked the end of hopes for a genuinely independent and democratic Poland. This is not to say that what transpired after Sikorski was not important. On the contrary, it was these later events that directly shaped Poland's place in postwar Europe. But the collapse of the general's program, even more than his death, was a watershed in Polish wartime politics, after which the Poles could no longer hope to offset the overwhelming preponderance of the Soviet Union, or to lessen their vulnerability to a new Russo-German settlement at their expense.

Whether Sikorski's program ever had a chance for success, assuming he had found early understanding for his proposals in London and Washington, is one of those unanswered and unanswerable questions. If so, then the political structure of postwar Europe would have been profoundly different from that which in fact emerged. But the fact remains that he did not succeed. One consequence of his failure was that his successors were faced with a choice essentially between accepting or rejecting a settlement that would inevitably leave Poland a dependency of the Soviet Union. A second consequence was that the Communists were in the end the only ones who could have obtained the boundary settlement as finally effected, not as they insist because they were the only ones with the foresight to seek it, but because an Oder-Western Neisse (or even Eastern Neisse) line was never a realistic possibility for the London Poles. The Communists would learn soon enough that adherence to the faith of their Soviet mentors could not protect them from the misfortune of Poland's geography. But that is part of another and still unfinished story.

---

[110] It is by no means clear from the context that Churchill was merely registering his objection here to the Western Neisse line, as opposed to the Oder-Eastern Neisse variant implied in the Teheran formula. See ibid., pp. 717 and 720; and Winston S. Churchill, *Triumph and Tragedy*, p. 374.

Epilogue · Sikorski: Realist or Visionary?

IN THE PRECEDING CHAPTERS, we have examined Sikorski's program and the Allied response to it largely from the Polish perspective. What remains is, first, to review the balance sheet on the general himself and, second, to set the Allied response to Sikorski's efforts in the broader perspective of Great Power responsibility to the lesser nations over whose fate they preside.

IN RETROSPECT it is all too easy to criticize Sikorski. Clearly he was excessively optimistic about the possibilities of achieving a genuine reconciliation with the Soviet Union, one that would lead to a compromise settlement of the eastern boundary question and, within a framework of cooperation and even military alliance, would respect the separate community of interests shared by Poland with her Central European neighbors. Possibly his most serious miscalculation here was his stubborn resistance to the Soviet incorporation of Lithuania, a position that made him an easy target for accusations of anti-Soviet bias and of plotting to revive a *cordon sanitaire*. Similarly he placed too much faith in the West, in the possibility of finding there either understanding for Poland's difficulties with Moscow or support for his federation idea and territorial aspirations in the west. One could fault him also for indecisiveness at critical moments—for not taking advantage of Stalin's apparent offer of a compromise settlement in December 1941, or for adopting a defensive and negative posture in the face of the Anglo-Soviet negotiations rather than pursuing more forcefully his own positive ideas at an earlier date. Finally, one could criticize him for a lack of leadership and candor in dealing with his Polish constituencies both at home and in exile, for concealing from them the gravity of Poland's plight and for not trying harder to bring them around to a more realistic point of view, especially on prospects for regaining the eastern provinces. There can be little question but that his attempts to maintain the facade of national unity, by putting him in a position of having to espouse in public positions that he knew to be hopeless, led to confusion over his policy and very likely damaged the credibility of his protestations of sincerity toward the Soviet Union.

If I have chosen not to dwell on these failings, it is not because I do not see them as possible errors of perception or judgment, but because I see them largely as a result rather than a cause of his dilemma and because I do not think that a different course of action on his part would have produced a more favorable outcome. Take first Sikorski's attitude toward the Soviet Union. The fact that those skeptical of his policy of rapprochement turned out to be correct, at least in their assessment of Soviet intentions, does not mean that their prescriptions for Polish policy would have brought greater success. Those who favored a stiffer posture toward Moscow were often the same ones who criticized the general for being too dependent on London and Washington. Their demand for a policy of greater self-reliance was based on the futile hope that history would repeat itself and that the war would end with the collapse, or permanent weakening, of both Germany and Russia. They simply refused to comprehend the realities of Poland's exile status, or the narrowness of her political and moral support. Nor do they appear to have understood that, while Sikorski's policy sought to retain some initiative and leverage for the Poles, their insistence on Soviet recognition of the Riga boundary as a condition for renewing relations would have rendered them wholly dependent on Britain and the United States, both of whom were unwilling under any circumstances to support Poland's claims against Russia. In all likelihood such a course would only have caused the West to discard the exile government sooner than it did—in 1941 or 1942 rather than in late 1944. In the end, it was not so much differing perceptions of Moscow's intentions that separated Sikorski from his opponents[1]—indeed, the general's views on this subject would have done justice to Machiavelli compared to the woolly-headed naiveté that flourished at high levels in London and Washington. Where they differed was in their respective appraisals of Poland's relative bargaining strength, and here it was Sikorski whose vision was clearer.

On the other hand, some, like Kulski and Pruszyński,[2] have argued that had he followed Beneš's example, resigning himself to Western indifference and seeking a settlement of all outstanding issues directly with Stalin, he might have avoided the communization of Poland and possibly even have saved the federation in some form. Frankly the Czech analogy has always struck me as inappropriate—although in Kulski's and Pruszyński's defense it should be pointed out that both wrote before the Communist coup of February 1948, which forced even Beneš to change his mind. For one thing, Czechoslovakia's geographic position, while hardly secure, was not as exposed as Poland's. Czechoslovakia did not stand across the main invasion route into Russia; nor were Russia and Germany accustomed to

[1] See especially Morawski, *Wspólna droga*, p. 166.
[2] Kulski, "The Lost Opportunity for Russian Polish Friendship," and Pruszyński, "Katyń i Gibraltar."

settling their accounts at her expense. Second, the Czechs did not share the Poles' long history of rivalry and conflict with the Russians. Beneš therefore did not face the necessity of overcoming centuries of hostility in pursuing a policy of cooperation with Moscow. Perhaps the most important difference, however, was the fact that the Czechs were seeking no territorial gains but only a return to the *status quo ante*, which the Soviets did not (yet) challenge and which the Western powers were bound to recognize to expiate their guilt over Munich. Sikorski, on the other hand, was being pressed to concede almost half of Poland's prewar territory. Even if he could have gotten a promise of like compensation from Stalin—as we have seen a highly questionable proposition—there was no guarantee that the Soviet Union would be in a position to carry out that promise at the end of the war or that, if the West protested, Stalin, always more sensitive to the German issue than the Polish, would not find it to his advantage to renege.

As for the questions of Sikorski's leadership and candor, had he stated his case bluntly and openly, either to the Polish nation or to the world at large, history would undoubtedly have treated him more kindly. But it is hard to see how this would have served his or Poland's immediate needs. On the contrary, at least until the shock of Katyń (and especially the shock of the Western reaction to Katyń), a frank discussion of the state of Polish-Soviet relations would almost certainly have produced open revolt in the exile community and Underground. On the other hand, had he publicly revealed the full extent of his territorial proposals in the west, he had every reason to expect he would be promptly rebuffed by London and Washington. In either event, it is likely that his government would have fallen or, if he had managed to outwit his opponents again, that a rival government would have emerged, leading to still further confusion and to a further deterioration of Poland's standing in the Alliance.[3] The real tragedy of Sikorski's position was not a lack of leadership on his part, but a lack of any workable solution toward which to lead his beleaguered nation. In this atmosphere of frustration and uncertainty, dissident elements could exert an influence far greater than their numbers might have warranted, their actions lending credibility to Stalin's worst suspicions about the Poles and, on the Polish side, poisoning whatever spirit of cooperation existed.

There is another category of criticisms that I have insofar as possible avoided discussing—namely, the real or imagined influence of the flaws in Sikorski's character on his performance in office. I have done so in the belief that these alleged defects of character were irrelevant. To be sure,

---

[3] This was a possibility that was well recognized in the Foreign Office; see, e.g., C3385/258/55, FO 371/34566 and C3641/258/55, FO 371/34567, PRO.

there were in effect two Sikorskis: on the one hand there was the public leader, rather stiff and aloof, suspicious of others and jealous of his prerogatives, attempting to preserve a semblance of national unity and to defuse his critics by assuring the Poles of what they most wanted to believe—that Poland was and would continue to be a great nation, that her eastern boundary had not been jeopardized, and that the Western Powers understood and supported her need for security and independence. On the other hand, there was the private Sikorski, tormented by his responsibilities, at times deeply pessimistic about the Allied commitment to a truly independent Poland, struggling with increasingly unpleasant alternatives that he knew to be unacceptable to many of his countrymen—at first believing, later only hoping, that at the next turn events would begin to break in Poland's favor. The most damaging criticism, if it were true, would be that the negative aspects of his character, his vanity and ambitions, in some way interfered with his relations with the Allied leaders on whom the success of his policy depended. However, there is considerable evidence to indicate that this simply was not true—that, on the contrary, even as they rejected his proposals, he won their genuine respect and admiration. There is no reason to doubt the sincerity of the complimentary views expressed within the State Department,[4] or Welles's opinion, written after the war, that he "found [Sikorski] one of the most stalwart and attractive statesmen of the war years, . . ."[5] Nor is there reason to doubt the truth of Raczyński's remark that the British regarded Sikorski as the greatest of the European statesmen driven into exile by the war, and that they could not comprehend why the Poles did not look upon him as a hero equal to Piłsudski.[6] The few sour notes that one encounters in Western sources reflect either early opinions, before Western leaders had come to appreciate Sikorski's qualities, or adverse reactions to one or another of his attempts to mollify his domestic opposition, or to some action of which the West disapproved (usually because it might displease Stalin).[7] Moreover, one likely explanation for some of the charges—for instance, of his alleged aloofness and arbitrariness, and his extreme suspiciousness—is that these qualities were the result of, or at the very least were aggravated by, the venomous atmosphere within the exile community. By and large, however, I feel that the character issue has been blown up out of proportion by his critics—that, unable to accept Poland's impotence within the Al-

[4] *FRUS, 1942*, 3:110, 120-22, and 206.

[5] See p. 196 above.

[6] Raczyński, *W sojuszniczym Londynie*, pp. 201-202; see also *The Cadogan Diaries*, ed. Dilks, p. 540.

[7] *The Cadogan Diaries*, ed. Dilks, pp. 390-91; Sherwood, *Roosevelt and Hopkins*, p. 710; and *FRUS, 1942*, 3:108-110 and 120-22.

liance, they have sought a scapegoat for difficulties that were beyond his or anyone else's power to surmount.

WAS Sikorski then a realist, or was he a visionary whose ideas, while appealing, never represented a feasible alternative for his nation or its Central European neighbors? The answer to this question depends in part on how realism is defined. If one uses that term in the special Polish sense discussed in Chapter II, of accepting a position of political dependence on Russia as the only available means of national survival in Poland's geographic location, then the answer is, no, he was not a "realist" in this sense; although he was closer to this tradition than to the "idealist" tradition with which he is usually identified.

If, however, one means realism in its broader, more common usage, then I think the answer must be a qualified yes. Certainly he was a realist in his geopolitical concepts, in his understanding of the limits and conditions of Poland's independence. And not only because he recognized the futility of "great power" pretensions or a "two-enemy" posture, but because he also understood that one-sided reliance on Russia (i.e., the "realist" solution in the strictly Polish sense) in the long run offered no greater guarantee of Poland's survival, that as long as Poland remained weak and dependent she would invite mischief from her more powerful neighbors to the east and west. The real significance of Sikorski's program was that it was an attempt—and a carefully thought-out, integrated attempt—to find some middle ground between the "idealist" and "realist" courses, a third alternative that would avoid the self-defeating consequences of either extreme.[8] For him, cooperation among the nations of Central Europe was not an optional luxury or an act of national self-denial, but an essential condition of their collective independence, without which none of these nations could expect to play a positive and creative role in determining its own destiny.

Where Sikorski's realism failed him was in his optimism that he would be able to bring together the disparate interests necessary to implement his ideas (although, as we have seen, public optimism masked growing private despair during the last year and a half of his life). Each facet of his program was so dependent on progress in the others that, as with a chain, the failure of any one link would lead to the collapse of the whole. In the final analysis

[8] A basic thesis of Bromke's study, *Poland's Politics*, is that the essence of Gomułka's policy following his return to power in 1956 was to find just such a third alternative to the "realist" and "idealist" traditions. My argument with Bromke would be that the attempt began with Sikorski in the early years of World War II, not with Gomułka after the war, and that in fact there are some very interesting parallels between the two—although, of course, some fundamental differences as well.

then he was a visionary, not as is so often alleged because he was unable
to break with Poland's past policies and prejudices, but because he was a
man ahead of his time, ahead both of the majority of his own countrymen
and of Poland's major allies in his willingness to think in terms of new
patterns of national life and new forms of international cooperation.

Still, one measure of the underlying realism of Sikorski's vision is the
extent to which subsequent events have vindicated for better or worse some
of his basic ideas, although often through twists of history and circumstance
that he could not have foreseen. On the plus side, the Oder-Neisse line
has become the boundary between Poland and Germany, and Germany
has eventually come to accept not only that boundary but permanent partition as well—in effect, the harsh peace that the West was afraid to impose.
This acceptance did not come quickly or easily (but then Sikorski thought
that the occupation might have to last a full generation). Nor were these
developments the result of a careful consideration of Central Europe's
economic and security requirements, or of the uniform Allied policy Sikorski hoped for. Instead they grew out of the breakdown of the Grand
Alliance and a scramble by each side to solidify its position at the center
of Europe. Ironically, it was this hardening of Cold War divisions that in
all probability was responsible for the durability of the Oder-Neisse line,
by effectively restraining open East-West competition for the allegiance
of a united Germany during the critical years of readjustment.

On the negative side, the lack of Western recognition of this boundary
was for twenty-five years a source of constant insecurity for Poland, reinforcing her dependence on the Soviet Union, but at the same time causing
her acute anxiety (what one might call "Rapallo jitters") with every thaw
in the Cold War. Likewise, she has paid a heavy economic price, in terms
of outright exploitation and distorted development, for her one-sided dependence and for the absence of an effective organization for cooperation
in their own interests among the Central European nations—although it is
worth noting that this idea, which was so central to Sikorski's program,
has been a recurring theme in the postwar period whenever reduced tensions
have raised hopes of loosening bonds with Moscow. It is perhaps a final
unwitting tribute to his realism, and particularly to the validity of his fear
of one-sided dependence on a single power for the security of Poland's
frontiers, that on several occasions during the Polish crisis of 1980/81 the
Soviets sought to increase their leverage over Warsaw by resurrecting the
bogeyman of German "revanchism" and subtly calling into question the
permanence of the Oder-Neisse line.

BUT are there larger lessons to be drawn from Sikorski's failure—lessons
concerning the role that small powers do or should play in alliances with

great powers, or the voice they have or ought to have in determining their own fate? It seems to me that there are and that, especially from the perspective of 1981-82, his failure can tell us a good deal about the underlying causes of Poland's continuing instability.

During the war, as we have seen, the London Poles were variously described as unrealistic, nationalistic, reactionary and, most of all, troublesome. The Poles were also "troublesome" in 1919 at Versailles. Since the end of World War II, they have proved "troublesome" on no less than four occasions—1956, 1970, 1976, and now since August of 1980. Indeed, over the last two hundred years, every ruler of Germany from Frederick the Great through Hitler, like every ruler of Russia from Catherine the Great through Brezhnev, has found the Poles "troublesome." Yet, in those same two hundred years, the basic decisions concerning Poland's fate have almost always been made by someone else, by the Great Powers of the time. The Poles themselves, when given a say at all, have generally been able to make only the smaller decisions, within the established framework or in response to it—decisions that, to be sure, were not always wise, but that have repeatedly been thrown back at them as evidence of their folly and as the cause of their misfortunes.

In truth, of course, the sources of Poland's "troublesomeness" are that she lies astride a coveted and strategically vital piece of real estate and that, while the Polish nation is too small to fend off stronger neighbors, it is also too large and too keenly aware of its separate identity to be absorbed or long subdued. Then, when one Polish leader proposed a program to remedy some of the ill-considered features of the old system, and to give not only Poland but the other small nations of the region more responsibility and control over their own affairs, the Great Powers either ignored or actively opposed him. It could be (and has been) argued that, at such an early and critical stage of the war, the Great Powers could not take the time to study the multitude of individual problems presented by the Poles and other lesser allies—that, whatever the validity of their claims in the abstract, they could not be allowed to threaten the larger interests of Allied unity now and European stability in the future. The answer to this argument is that, in the absence both of an early postwar planning effort and of an evenhanded application of such statements of principle as the Atlantic Charter, the policy-makers of Washington and London were de facto deciding these issues in ways that could not later be reversed, often on the basis of partial and biased data, or even of woeful ignorance. Moreover, the policy of postponement in the end rendered impossible what Roosevelt and Churchill claimed they wanted most—a reconciliation between Stalin and Sikorski.

Had London and Washington adopted a different course, it is entirely possible, even likely, that it would not have brought markedly different results. With the benefits of hindsight, it is clear that, given the power to do so, the Soviets were determined to retain the territories (Polish and other) that they had seized in 1939 and 1940 under the terms of the Nazi-Soviet pact. It is also clear that Stalin viewed a truly independent Poland, of whatever political persuasion, as a barrier to the expansion of Soviet influence in Europe and, equally important, as the linchpin of a stable and prosperous community of nations in Central or East-Central Europe. Without Poland, with her larger population, strategic location, and considerable resources, any such organization would be, to use Ambassador Maisky's word, "vegetarian."

Yet, as Moscow moves again to stifle the Poles' quest for independence, one can question whether Stalin's solution has provided the Soviet Union with its much sought after stability and security. Since 1945, successive crises in Poland and elsewhere in the region have proven both costly and a potential source of instability in the USSR itself. The most recent Polish crisis provides food for thought in East and West alike. Whatever the final outcome—and at this writing, January 1982, it is still unclear whether the martial law imposed a month ago foreshadows a total reversal of the reform process, or whether Poland's "renewal" will be allowed to continue, albeit in truncated form—the crisis will cost an already strained Soviet economy billions (in both dollars and rubles) and has refueled the fires of East-West tension. Moreover, while the "Polish virus" has not yet spread, it is only the most spectacular example of the economic and political malaise that in varying degrees afflicts all of the Soviet Union's European allies—a malaise that will be deepened by the ripple effects of Poland's disintegrating economy. One can only wonder if there are not some in the Kremlin today who, as they survey the multiple burdens imposed by these sullen and stagnating dependencies, silently wish that Sikorski had been more successful.

Bibliographical Essay

The purpose of this essay is not the usual one of surveying the major sources used in this study. Rather, my purpose is to explore the biblio-graphical dimension of a question posed briefly in Chapter I: namely, why has the conventional wisdom concerning the origin of the Oder-Neisse boundary been accepted for so long, while General Sikorski's pursuit of a similar boundary for Poland has remained obscured? It is a question that has puzzled me throughout my research. Even more, why should it fall to me—a non-Pole, who must still struggle with the finer points of the lan-guage—to unravel a story so intimately and quintessentially Polish? I set out, now some years ago, with no intention of writing on this topic as I, too, assumed that it had been adequately researched. In fact, I rather resented the first nagging doubts that crept into my research.

In retrospect, it is hard to recall what it was that finally pricked my curiosity, what caused me to pursue the few apparently aberrant pieces of a puzzle that did not fit the assembled picture. But the impulse is common enough and has been well expressed by Robin Winks in the Introduction to his charming and edifying collection of essays on *The Historian as Detective*—or, in my case, the political scientist masquerading as historian. "Much of the historian's work," wrote Winks,

> . . . may to the outsider seem to consist of deadening routine. Many miles of intellectual shoe leather will be used, . . . and [much] trivia will stand between the researcher and his answer. Yet the routine must be pursued or the clue may be missed; the apparently false trail must be followed in order to be certain that it is false; the mute witnesses must be asked the reasons for their silence, for the piece of evidence that is missing from where one might reasonably expect to find it is, after all, a form of evidence in itself.[1]

There have been many "mute witnesses" to this story, and it is to them that one must look for the origin of the mystery. Let us begin by looking at the range of Polish sources.

Sikorski's successors in the Government-in-Exile, whose policies were based with increasing rigidity on the inviolability of the 1939 frontier in the east, and consequently on the foolhardiness of making "excessive" demands in the west, stood to gain nothing by advertising the fact that the

---

[1] Robin W. Winks, ed., *The Historian as Detective: Essays on Evidence*, p. xvii.

general himself had accepted the need to compromise on the one side or that he favored a boundary approximating the Oder-Neisse on the other. On the contrary, they had a vested interest in invoking the name of Poland's best-known exile leader in defense of their policies. This tendency was reinforced at the end of the war by the refusal of Britain and the United States to recognize the new Polish-German boundary and by fears of Western support for German revisionism. As a result, for the first fifteen years after the war, a virtual wall of silence surrounded Polish policy on the western boundary in émigré literature. One can, for example, read through the three most influential Polish books on the war years—Ciechanowski's *Defeat in Victory*, Mikołajczyk's *The Pattern of Soviet Domination*, and Rozek's *Allied Wartime Diplomacy*—without encountering so much as a whisper of Polish initiatives on this question, much less an admission that it was broached by the Sikorski government as early as November 1939![2]

There were of course scattered exceptions even in the early postwar years, in several small pamphlets and an occasional article. Between 1945 and 1952, no less than four sources referred to the phrase in one of Sikorski's December 1942 memoranda that defined the Oder with its tributaries to the Czech frontier as Poland's natural line of security in the west.[3] But the critical passages consisted at most of a few sentences, which could do little more than hint at the totality of Sikorski's strategy. In any event, these sources did not attract the attention they merited.

The wall of silence did not really begin to crack until the 1960s, and then only gradually with the easing of the Cold War and mounting signs

---

[2] Émigré books of this early period divide more or less along lines of association with or opposition to the Sikorski and Mikołajczyk governments. On the one hand, these three books stress the necessity and sincerity of Sikorski's policy of reconciliation with the Soviet Union, while playing down or ignoring the divisions within the exile community. (Ciechanowski is something of an anomaly in this group, as he was actively opposed to Sikorski in 1940 and tried to delay the signing of the Polish-Soviet Agreement of July 1941.) On the other hand, those who remained outside the government are sharply critical of the general's entire foreign policy, and especially of his Russian policy, and admit in varying degrees the extent of internal dissension. See, e.g.: Pobóg-Malinowski, *Najnowsza historia*, 3; Anders, *An Army in Exile*; Katelbach, *Rok złych wróżb*; Pragier, *Czas przeszły dokonany*; and Giertych, *Pół wieku polskiej polityki*. While this second group of books is useful to an understanding of the political atmosphere in the exile community, by and large they are poor guides to Sikorski's policy. See also Chapter IV, especially notes 37 and 42, above.

[3] The four, in order of publication, were Winiewicz, *The Polish-German Frontier*; Seyda, *Pół wieku walki*; Lipski, Raczyński, and Stroński, *Trzy podróże*; and Bregman, ''Linia Odry i Nysy, to nie 'wymysł Stalina.' '' See also Chapter V, note 88, above. Of these, the Bregman article and Lipski's account of Sikorski's third trip to the United States are the most useful; both have been used (or abused) by a number of writers, who generally have not accepted their conclusion that Sikorski favored an Oder-Neisse boundary.

on all sides of acceptance of (or resignation to) the territorial status quo in Central Europe. Yet even in these more recent books, although they are often extremely useful, one senses a deep reluctance on the part of those closely associated with the exile government to discuss fully and openly either the extent of Sikorski's commitment to westward expansion or the relationship of this aspect of his policy to his overall strategy, and especially to the eastern boundary question. Let us look quickly at the most important sources in this group: The great virtue of Ambassador Raczyński's diary (*W sojuszniczym Londynie*) is the writer's indomitable objectivity; however, he offers only the most obscure hints as to Sikorski's territorial program, east or west. While the fact that a number of important passages concerning the internal political scene and Polish-Czech relations were omitted from the English edition (*In Allied London*) was in all probability due to the expectation that these matters would be of little interest to the English-speaking reader,[4] their omission further distorts the picture for those who cannot read the Polish. The two volumes of documents edited by the General Sikorski Historical Institute (*Documents on Polish-Soviet Relations, 1939-1945*), although weighted heavily in defense of the eastern boundary, contain a number of important passages that are helpful in filling in the total picture. Kajetan Morawski's memoirs (*Wspólna droga*) include only a brief chapter on the Sikorski period which, while short on detail, provides a balanced perspective on the general political situation. On the other hand, General Kukiel's biography (*Generał Sikorski: Żołnierz i mąż stanu Polski walczącej*) contains a wealth of detail but is spotty in its treatment of controversial issues (especially territorial ones) and short on analysis of Sikorski's overall political strategy. Similarly, Karol Popiel's account (*Generał Sikorski w mojej pamięci*) details the divisions within the exile community but skirts the issues underlying those divisions. Leon Mitkiewicz's diary (*Z gen. Sikorskim na obczyźnie*) is exceptional in this group for its candor about the most critical and sensitive issues; especially valuable are the detailed accounts of discussions within Sikorski's inner circle of advisors. Kukiel has suggested that Mitkiewicz is not altogether accurate[5] but, at a number of critical points where the two differ, the external evidence tends to corroborate the latter.

Literature on this period out of postwar Poland has, with the exception of a special category of sources discussed below, followed a similar cycle of denial and cautious reassessment, but with important differences. The Communists on coming to power had several excellent reasons for wanting to gloss over the divisions within the London camp on the boundary issue

---

[4] Compare, for instance, the entries for June 18 and December 28, 1941, and May 17, 1942, in the two editions.

[5] Kukiel, *Generał Sikorski*, p. 121.

and to focus attention instead on the eastern, anti-Soviet orientation of the last exile government. Certainly they could have had little interest in sharing the credit for the policy on which rested their hopes for refurbishing their patriotic image. Indeed, the territorial minimalism of the exile government was their best argument for discrediting their political opponents in the initial "coalition" phase, just as Western nonrecognition of the new boundary later provided a convenient justification for cementing Poland's ties to the Soviet Union as well as a deterrent to domestic upheaval. By the same token, in other areas where the Communists attempted to build on earlier exile policy—as in the abortive postwar plans for Polish-Czechoslovak economic cooperation—they had every reason not to advertise a continuity that could only intensify Soviet suspicions.

As in émigré literature, the reappraisal of the early exile period began only in the 1960s—possibly signaled by Gomułka's statement in a January 1962 speech that the underground Polish Workers' Party had "not excluded the possibility that he [Sikorski] would head the government after the liberation of Poland."[6] Initially, references to the advocacy of an Oder-Neisse boundary in exile circles were made only in passing, as in the following: "The demand for the Oder and Lusatian Neisse, very popular in the press and publications of the London camp until 1942, . . ."[7] Since then several substantial studies, based in part on hitherto untapped archival materials, have appeared that go considerably beyond émigré sources in their coverage of certain aspects of the western boundary question, including the very early efforts at postwar planning by the Sikorski government and the prevalence of the Oder-Neisse idea among groups associated with the London camp and the non-communist Underground. Despite the undeniable value of these sources, however, they still reflect some taboos of communist analysis and should be approached with an eye toward these weaknesses. For one thing, their political obligation to affirm the benevolence of Soviet motives in any and all circumstances automatically reduces their usefulness as sources in all matters related to Polish-Soviet relations. The enormous gap between a Sikorski and a Piłsudski in their attitudes toward Russia becomes a minor difference of degree; the plan to federate the small nations of Central Europe for their own defense and prosperity, a revival of Polish "imperialism." In addition, communist sources are still unwilling to admit the possibility that anything approaching an Oder-Neisse boundary was ever an official war aim of the exile government with the

---

[6] Quoted in Kowalski, *Walka dyplomatyczna*, pp. 336-37.

[7] Marian Orzechowski, "Koncepcja granic zachodnich w programie i działalności Polskiej Partii Robotniczej i lewicy rewolucyjnej na emigracji," pp. 8-46. See also Norbert Kołomejczyk, "Sprawa Ziem Zachodnich w programie i działalności PPR."

result that, the closer the evidence shows Sikorski to articulating such a proposal, the more unreliable these sources tend to become.[8]

Still a third category of Polish sources consists of books and articles by writers who spent the war in exile, usually associated with the exile government in some capacity, but who returned to Poland after the war. Possibly because of their disaffection from exile politics, also because they lacked the ideological biases of the Communists (although clearly there have been restraints on what they too could publish), these writers as a group have been extremely candid in their discussions of the Polish political scene in wartime London. While they add little to our understanding of the boundary question itself, these sources do provide insights into the formation of the Government-in-Exile and the nature of the opposition to Sikorski. Generally sympathetic to the first exile prime minister, they are useful also as a counterweight to the anti-Sikorski bias of much of the émigré literature.[9] Although published in London, Stanisław Kot's two volumes, *Listy z Rosji* and *Rozmowy z Kremlem*, seem to belong more to this category than to the émigré writings of former members of Sikorski's government.[10] And while his treatment of the opposition to the general

[8] See, e.g.: Kowalski, *ZSRR a granica* and *Walka dyplomatyczna*; Orzechowski, *Odra-Nysa-Bałtyk*; and Zabiełło, *O rząd i granice*. In particular, Kowalski's sins of omission and commission are noted in Chapter V, note 95, and Chapter X, notes 1, 4, 12, and 135, above. Several more recent books out of Poland are worthy of note: Eugeniusz Duraczyński's 1977 book, *Kontrowersje i konflikty, 1939-1941*, marks a significant improvement over earlier books in its attention to conflicts within the exile government; indeed they are the focus of the book. Wapiński (*Władysław Sikorski*) also deserves some credit on this score, as well as on his more objective appraisal of Sikorski's policy in the interwar period; however, his treatment of problems surrounding the Polish Army in the Soviet Union borders on the scandalous, and his handling of Sikorski's three trips to the United States is weak and questionable. By far the most sympathetic treatment of Sikorski to emerge from Poland in recent years is the collection of articles published in honor of the 100th anniversary of his birth in May 1881: *Generał Władysław Sikorski, żołnierz i polityk: Materiały na sympozjum poświęcone 100 rocznicy urodzin*. The preface begins with the statement that General Sikorski "remains in the hearts of Poles as the symbol and personification of Poland, which during World War II fought for its independent existence" (p. 5). The articles themselves, however, are thin on detail and on balance demonstrate the paucity of research on Sikorski, especially on the wartime period.

[9] See especially the four articles written in 1945 by Ksawery Pruszyński: "Rzecz działa się we Francji," "Bieg na przelaj," "Irański odmarsz," and "Katyń i Gibraltar," *Wybór pism*, II; and Strumph-Wojtkiewicz, *Gwiazda Władysława Sikorskiego*. Also useful but more tendentious, each in its own way, are: Strumph-Wojtkiewicz, *Siła złego*; and Klimkowski, *Katastrofa w Gibraltarze*. Rather similar to Pruszyński in outlook, although the writer did not spend the war years in exile, is Andrzej Micewski's excellent study of Polish politics in the interwar period, *Z geografii politycznej II Rzeczypospolitej*, especially chap. 5: "Sikorski a opozycja."

[10] See Kot's own comments on émigré writings in *Listy z Rosji*, pp. 5 and 73-74.

seemed excessively abrasive when the first book came out in 1955, later sources have corroborated the general tenor if not all details of his account.

Western sources have been fully as reticent on the subject of Sikorski's territorial aspirations as the Polish, and for reasons that are not difficult to surmise. Eager on the one hand to demonstrate that they had done everything in their power to preserve an independent and democratic Poland, neither the British nor the Americans were likely to advertise the fact that they had rejected his proposal for the same western boundary they later accorded, however grudgingly or provisionally, to a Communist-dominated Poland at Potsdam. On the other hand, as the division of Europe hardened, it was obviously to the advantage of the Western Powers, especially in their relations with Germany, to let the Communists (Polish and Soviet) bear the full onus for the Oder-Lusatian Neisse boundary, while emphasizing that neither they nor the London Poles themselves had wanted to push Poland so far to the west. In any event, one can read through the published diplomatic papers, as well as the voluminous wartime reminiscences of those British or American officials who had reason to be aware of Sikorski's boundary desiderata, without encountering more than the most occasional and vague inference that the subject of corrections in Poland's boundary with Germany—*any* corrections, much less a shifting of the boundary to the Oder and Neisse—was ever *initiated* by the exile government, or even discussed during the Sikorski years. As I noted in Chapter I, it is as if the idea of shifting Poland westward dated from Churchill's matchstick demonstration for Stalin at Teheran in November of 1943.[11]

Such Soviet sources as are available are of even less value in this regard—a judgment confirmed by the fact that Polish Communist writers rely almost exclusively on Polish and Western sources. Still, they are interesting for what they fail to say. Not unexpectedly, the Soviets pay little attention to the Sikorski period, which they assess in terms only slightly less negative than later exile governments; certainly there is no intimation of Stalin's alleged offer of an Oder line to Sikorski in December 1941. More intriguing is their obvious reluctance to acknowledge the extent of their own role in sponsoring an Oder-Neisse boundary in the period beginning with the Teheran Conference.[12]

[11] See p. 9 above. Both Churchill (*The Grand Alliance*) and Eden (*The Reckoning*) record early talk of such changes with Stalin (see section 1 of Chapter X), but not with the Poles. Only Welles (*Seven Decisions That Shaped History*, chap. V) and an occasional entry in the *Foreign Relations of the United States* series give the reader any inkling of Polish initiatives on the western boundary.

[12] See, e.g.: *Istoriia Velikoi Otechestvennoi Voiny Sovetskogo Soiuza, 1941-1945*, 2:184-85 and 201-203; 3:502-509; 4:237-40 and 667; and 6:132-33. See also *Vneshniaia politika Sovetskogo Soiuza v period Otechestvennoi Voiny: Dokumenty i materialy; Istoriia Pol'shi,*

There have been some exceptions to the general disregard of the Sikorski period in Western sources, most notably among German writers who have understandably had a keener interest in the boundary matter than the British or Americans. While they have been more assiduous than others in detailing interest in westward expansion among non-communist Poles, however, they too have generally been eager to emphasize the "moderation" of the exile government and to give Stalin credit for originating the Oder-Neisse line. Even those German writers who were among the first to openly urge acceptance of the boundary showed little interest in delving into the pre-Teheran origins of the idea, although at least one was critical of his countrymen for their fixation on the "communist" rather than the "Polish" aspect of the issue.[13]

One result of this pervasive silence on, or outright distortion of, the Sikorski period is that the conventional wisdom concerning the general's policy has been carried over into secondary sources of all political persuasions. It is not surprising, of course, that this should be true of books published before the major archival collections were opened to researchers. Nor is it particularly surprising that the revisionist historians should want to stress the uniformly anti-Soviet orientation of all of the Polish exile leaders.[14] What is more surprising is that some of these same misconceptions—that Sikorski signed the Polish-Soviet agreement of July 1941 only under heavy British pressure, that he preferred to evacuate the Polish Army

---

vol. 3; Ivan Maisky, *Memoirs of a Soviet Ambassador: The War 1939-43*, trans. Andrew Rothstein; and I. D. Kundiuba, *Sovetsko-pol'skie otnosheniia (1939-1945 gg.)*. The last mentioned virtually ignores the existence of the Government-in-Exile, not to mention the fact that Moscow maintained relations with it for almost two years, or the existence of the first Polish Army in the Soviet Union. A minor curiosity in the Soviet literature is a collection of articles on Polish-Soviet relations published by the Institute of Slavic and Balkan Studies of the Soviet Academy of Sciences (*Sovetsko-pol'skie otnosheniia, 1918-1945: Sbornik statei*, which includes an article on "The Soviet Government's Struggle for the Establishment of the Oder-Lusatian Neisse Boundary" by the Polish historian W. T. Kowalski (see note 1, Chapter X, and note 8 above). Kowalski here embellishes his earlier statement that Stalin offered Sikorski an Oder line, but cites no sources, not even his own Polish books (p. 250).

[13] See, e.g., Heinz Günther Sasse, "The Prelude to the Expulsions and the Oder-Neisse Line from 1939-1945," in *Eastern Germany: A Handbook*, Vol. II: *History*, ed. Göttinger Arbeitskreis, pp. 371-428; Wolfgang Wagner, *The Genesis of the Oder-Neisse Line*; Gotthold Rhode and Wolfgang Wagner, ed., *The Genesis of the Oder-Neisse Line: Sources and Documents*. Some German revisionists also took up the cause of Poland's lost eastern provinces; see *The Polish Eastern Territories and Their Importance to Poland and Europe*, ed. Göttinger Arbeitskreis. Those who urged acceptance of the boundary include: Hansjakob Stehle, *Deutschlands Osten—Polens Westen? Ein Dokumentation*, pp. 17-18. See also Georg Bluhm, *Die Oder-Neisse-Linie in der deutschen Aussenpolitik*; and Hansjakob Stehle, *Nachbar Polen*.

[14] See, e.g., Gabriel Kolko, *The Politics of War: The World and United States Foreign Policy, 1943-1945*; and Gar Alperovitz, *Atomic Diplomacy: Hiroshima and Potsdam, The Use of the Atomic Bomb and the American Confrontation with Soviet Power*.

from the Soviet Union, that he was unrelenting in his opposition to territorial concessions in the east—continue to appear in later books, including some that draw heavily on archival materials.[15] This is not meant as a criticism, as the focus of these books is generally much broader than the question of Polish exile policy under Sikorski, and the authors make no claim to having researched that question anew. However, it is a comment on the indelibility with which certain ideas about the Sikorski period have been imprinted on the collective memory and have thus escaped critical reexamination.

It was, of course, the opening up of various archival collections that has made it possible to reconstruct many missing pieces of the preceding story. In particular, the change in 1972 from a fifty- to a thirty-year rule by the British archives has made available voluminous files. For my purposes, it is the Foreign Office papers that have provided the great bulk of relevant documentation. The Cabinet papers were also useful, while the War Office files proved disappointing (see note 54, Chapter IX, above)—although many of the relevant War Office papers, especially cable traffic, have been preserved in the Foreign Office files. Still, there are some frustrating gaps and anomalies in the latter. For instance, some documents or whole files remain closed under a seventy-five year rule. In addition, the "Green," or secret, documents, which have been added to the files but do not appear in the printed index, have generally had to be renumbered. Thus tracking down cross-referenced documents is often a time-consuming, and occasionally hopeless, paper chase. These problems are more than compensated for, however, by the British institution of "minutes"—the comments or memoranda appended to documents as they wend their way from the desk and department levels on up to the offices of the under secretaries and the foreign secretary himself. Not only are these minutes the source of much factual information, but they give the researcher a sense of the personalities involved, of conflicts both within the Foreign Office and between it and other agencies, as well as invaluable insights into the policy process.

The American archives proved less interesting for my purposes. A search of the Franklin D. Roosevelt Library at Hyde Park revealed almost nothing on the topic in question that was not already in the public domain (e.g., as in the *FRUS* series or Sherwood's *Roosevelt and Hopkins*). Especially disappointing was the absence of any record whatsoever of Sikorski's several meetings with Roosevelt. Of course, a vital missing link here are the papers of Sumner Welles, which have not yet been released to the

[15] E.g., Lynn Etheridge Davis, *The Cold War Begins: Soviet-American Conflict over Eastern Europe*; Geir Lundestad, *The American Non-Policy Towards Eastern Europe, 1943-1947*; Richard C. Lukas, *The Strange Allies: The United States and Poland, 1941-1945*; and Mastny, *Russia's Road to the Cold War*.

Library by his family. The State Department files, located in the National Archives in Washington, were more useful though only marginally so. As with the Foreign Office papers, many documents were declassified in the early 1970s; however, some documents appear to have been deposited in haphazard fashion (hence the high frequency of fractional document numbers). And, again, critical items are missing: e.g., the Polish memoranda from which the barely decipherable handwritten notes mentioned in notes 84 and 86, Chapter V, above, were made, and records of Sikorski's crucial meetings with Welles on December 12 and 21, 1942. In a more general sense, one misses the British habit of appending "minutes" or internal memoranda, which give the raw documents a three-dimensional quality.

By contrast, Polish exile records are vastly more revealing, although still less voluminous and less thoroughly annotated than the Foreign Office files. The two main collections are located at the Polish Institute (formerly the General Sikorski Historical Institute) in London, and at Stanford University's Hoover Institution. The former has been meticulously organized and catalogued by the late Mrs. Regina Oppman, although again key documents seem to be missing or to have been tailored to suit Sikorski's immediate political needs. The collections at Hoover are extensive, but their use presents substantial problems. The archives of the Government-in-Exile, brought from London to Stanford, comprise nearly one thousand manuscript boxes but remain in a rudimentary state of organization and largely uncatalogued. The smaller Ciechanowski Deposit [now listed as "Poland. Ambasada (U.S.)"] was only in the early stages of being inventoried and organized when I used it in mid-1977.

I had also hoped to make use of archival collections in Poland, in particular the Archive of the Ministry of Foreign Affairs [Archiwum Ministerstwa Spraw Zagranicznych, or AMSZ], cited by several sources published in Poland. Having previously gained access to early postwar sources, I anticipated no problems when I applied for access to the wartime materials as an exchange scholar to Poland in the fall of 1976. Although accepted for the exchange, I was informed on my arrival of a law barring foreign scholars from archives dating from September 1, 1939. Polish scholar-acquaintances assured me that the law was applied capriciously, and generally honored in the breach; but I had had the misfortune of arriving just as the Directorate of State Archives was taken over by a former official of the security police. The incident was not without its more amusing moments—as when I caused several archive officials to turn pale at the list of materials to which I had earlier been granted access (really quite innocuous)—but, in the end, I was still denied access to the materials relevant to this study.

Selected Bibliography

ARCHIVAL MATERIALS

AMERICAN

National Archives [NA], Washington, D.C.:
U.S. Department of State Decimal File, 1940-44.
Franklin D. Roosevelt Library [FDRL], Hyde Park, New York:
Harry Hopkins Papers
President's Secretary File [PSF]: Departmental Correspondence, State Department

BRITISH

Public Record Office [PRO], London:
Foreign Office: General Correspondence [FO 371]
War Cabinet Minutes and Conclusions [C.A.B.]

POLISH

General Sikorski Historical Institute [GSHI], later renamed the Polish Institute and General Sikorski Historical Museum, London:
Dziennik Czynności Naczelnego Wodza [Dz.Cz.N.W.]—Journal of activities of the Supreme Commander
Prezes Rady Ministrów [PRM]—Prime Minister's files
Hoover Institution on War, Revolution, and Peace [HIWRP], Stanford University, Stanford, California:
Ciechanowski Deposit (presently in the process of reorganization as "Poland. Ambasada [U.S.]"); box nos. in notes are the original ones; new box nos., when known, are in brackets.
Leon Mitkiewicz Collection
Ignacy Jan Paderewski Collection
Polish Government Collection

PUBLISHED DOCUMENTS

The Beginnings of Communist Rule in Poland: December 1943-June 1945. Edited by Antony Polonsky and Bolesław Drukier. London: Routledge and Kegan Paul, 1980.

Correspondence between the Chairman of the Council of Ministers of the U.S.S.R. and the Presidents of the U.S.A. and the Prime Ministers of Great Britain during the Great Patriotic War of 1941-1945. 2 vols. Moscow: Ministry of Foreign Affairs, 1957.

Documents on Polish-Soviet Relations, 1939-1945. Edited by the General Sikorski Historical Institute. 2 vols. London: Heinemann, 1961-1967.

The Genesis of the Oder-Neisse Line in the Diplomatic Negotiations during World War II: Sources and Documents. Compiled and edited by Gotthold Rhode and Wolfgang Wagner. Stuttgart: Brentano-Verlag, 1959.

The Great Powers and the Polish Question, 1941-1945: A Documentary Study in Cold War Origins. Edited by Antony Polonsky. London: London School of Economics, 1976.

Roosevelt and Churchill: Their Secret Wartime Correspondence. Edited by Francis L. Loewenheim, Harold D. Langley, and Manfred Jonas. New York: Saturday Review Press/E. P. Dutton, 1975.

Stosunki polsko-radzieckie w latach 1917-1945: Dokumenty i materiały. Edited by Euzebiusz Basiński. Warsaw: Książka i Wiedza, 1967.

U.S. Department of State. *Foreign Relations of the United States: Diplomatic Papers*. Washington, D.C., 1955-1963.

1941: Vol. 1 (1958).

1942: Vol. 3 (1961).

1943: Vol. 3 (1963).

The Conferences at Cairo and Teheran, 1943 (1961).

The Conferences at Malta and Yalta, 1945 (1955).

The Conference of Berlin (The Potsdam Conference), 1945 (2 vols., 1960).

Vneshniaia politika Sovetskogo Soiuza v period Otechestvennoi Voiny: Dokumenty i materialy. 3 vols. Moscow: Gospolitizdat, 1946.

War and Peace Aims of the United Nations. Vol. 1: *September 1, 1939-December 31, 1942*. Edited by Louise W. Holborn. Boston: World Peace Foundation, 1943.

Diaries and Memoirs

Anders, Lt.-General W. *An Army in Exile: The Story of the Second Polish Corps*. London: Macmillan, 1949.

[Beneš, E.] *Memoirs of Dr. Eduard Beneš: From Munich to New War and New Victory*. Translated by Godfrey Lias. Boston: Houghton Mifflin, [1954].

[Berle, Adolf A.] *Navigating the Rapids, 1918-1971: From the Papers of Adolf A. Berle*. Edited by Beatrice Bishop Berle and Travis Beal Jacobs. New York: Harcourt Brace Jovanovich, 1973.

Bohlen, Charles E. *Witness to History, 1929-1969*. New York: Norton, 1973.

Byrnes, James F. *Speaking Frankly*. New York: Harper, 1947.

[Cadogan, A.] *The Diaries of Sir Alexander Cadogan, O.M., 1939-1945*. Edited by David Dilks. New York: G. P. Putnams Sons, 1971.

Churchill, Winston S. *The Second World War*. 6 vols. Boston: Houghton Mifflin, 1948-1953: *The Gathering Storm* (1948); *Their Finest Hour* (1949); *The Grand Alliance* (1950); *The Hinge of Fate* (1950); *Closing the Ring* (1951); *Triumph and Tragedy* (1953).

Ciechanowski, Jan. *Defeat in Victory*. Garden City, N.Y.: Doubleday, 1947.

Eden, Anthony. *The Reckoning: The Memoirs of Anthony Eden, Earl of Avon*. Boston: Houghton Mifflin, 1965.

Harriman, W. Averell. *America and Russia in a Changing World: A Half Century of Personal Observation*. Garden City, N.Y.: Doubleday, 1971.

————, and Elie Abel. *Special Envoy to Churchill and Stalin, 1941-1946*. New York: Random House, 1975.

Hull, Cordell. *The Memoirs of Cordell Hull*. 2 vols. New York: Macmillan, 1948.

Katelbach, Tadeusz. *Rok złych wróżb (1943)*. Paris: Instytut Literacki, 1959.

Kennan, George F. *Memoirs: 1925-1950*. Boston: Little, Brown, 1967.

[Khrushchev, N. S.] *Khrushchev Remembers: The Last Testament*. Translated and edited by Strobe Talbott. Boston: Little, Brown, 1974.

Kmiecik, Edward. *Przystanek Berlin*. Warsaw: Książka i Wiedza, 1971.

Kot, Stanisław. *Listy z Rosji do Gen. Sikorskiego*. London: Jutro Polski, 1955.

————. *Rozmowy z Kremlem*. London: Jutro Polski, 1959.

[Lipski, Józef]. *Diplomat in Berlin, 1933-1939: Papers and Memoirs of Józef Lipski, Ambassador of Poland*. Edited by Wacław Jędrzejewicz. New York: Columbia University Press, 1968.

[Łukasiewicz, Juliusz]. *Diplomat in Paris, 1936-1939: Papers and Memoirs of Juliusz Łukasiewicz, Ambassador of Poland*. Edited by Wacław Jędrzejewicz. New York: Columbia University Press, 1970.

Maisky, Ivan. *Memoirs of a Soviet Ambassador: The War 1939-43*. Translated by Andrew Rothstein. New York: Scribner, 1968.

Mikołajczyk, Stanisław. *The Pattern of Soviet Domination*. London: Sampson Low, Marston, 1948.

Miłosz, Czesław. *Native Realm: A Search for Self-Definition*. Translated by Catherine S. Leach. Garden City, N.Y.: Doubleday, 1968.

Mitkiewicz, Leon. *Z gen. Sikorskim na obczyźnie (fragmenty wspomnień)*. Paris: Instytut Literacki, 1968.

Morawski, Kajetan. *Wspólna droga: Wspomnienia*. Paris: Księgarnia Polska, [1963].

Popiel, Karol. *Generał Sikorski w mojej pamięci*. London: Odnowa, 1978.

Pragier, Adam. *Czas przeszły dokonany*. London: B. Świderski, 1966.

Pruszyński, Xavier. *Russian Year: The Notebook of an Amateur Diplomat*. New York: Roy Publishers, 1944.

Raczyński, Count Edward. *In Allied London*. London: Weidenfeld and Nicolson, 1962.

————. *W sojuszniczym Londynie: Dziennik Ambasadora Edwarda Raczyńskiego, 1939-1945*. London: Polish Research Centre, 1960.

[Retinger, J.]. *Joseph Retinger: Memoirs of an Eminence Grise*. Edited by John Pomian. Sussex: Sussex University Press, 1972.

[Sikorski, W.]. "General Sikorski's 1936-9 Diary (extracts)." Translated by Edward Rothert. *Polish Perspectives* (Warsaw) 13 (May 1970): 26-42.

Sokolnicki, Michał. *Dziennik Ankarski, 1939-1943*. London: Gryf, 1965.

Stettinius, Edward R., Jr. *Roosevelt and the Russians: The Yalta Conference*. Edited by Walter Johnson. Garden City, N.Y.: Doubleday, 1949.

SECONDARY SOURCES

After the War: A Symposium of Peace Aims. Edited by William Teeling. London: Sedgwick and Jackson, 1940.

Alperovitz, Gar. *Atomic Diplomacy: Hiroshima and Potsdam, The Use of the Atomic Bomb and the American Confrontation with Soviet Power*. New York: Vintage Books, 1965.

[Arciszewski, Tomasz]. "Nieznane exposé: Przemówienie Prezesa Rady Ministrów Tomasza Arciszewskiego na posiedzeniu Rady Narodowej w Londynie w dniu 15.I.1945 r." Edited by Adam Ciołkosz. *Zeszyty Historyczne* (Paris), no. 1 (1962):9-25.

Backus, Oswald P. III; Halecki, Oscar; and Jakstas, Joseph. "The Problem of Unity in the Polish-Lithuanian State: A Discussion." *Slavic Review* 22 (September 1963):411-55.

Bagiński, Henryk. *Gospodarcze uzasadnienie żądań terytorialnych dorzecza Odry*. London, 1943.

————. *Polski i Bałtyk: Zagadnienie dostępu Polski do morza*. London, 1942.

Beneš, Eduard. "The Organization of Postwar Europe." *Foreign Affairs* 20 (January 1942):226-42.

Bielecki, Tadeusz. "Zagadnienie główne." *Myśl Polska* (London), December 15, 1942.

Biuletyn Zachodnio-Słowiański (Edinburgh). A total of nine issues was published irregularly between September 1940 and June 1942; title changed to *Ruch Zachodnio-Słowiański* for nos. 7 and 8; no. 9, in English, was called "No. 1 English Series."

Błoński, Antoni [Pałucki, Władysław]. *Wracamy nad Odrę: Historyczne, geograficzne i etnograficzne podstawy zachodnich granic Polski*. London: F. Mildner & Sons, 1942.

Bluhm, Georg. *Die Oder-Neisse-Linie in der deutschen Aussenpolitik*. Freiburg: Romback, 1963.

Borowik, Józef. "Nauka polska a Pomorze Szczecińskie." *Jantar: Przegląd Naukowy Zagadnień Pomorskich i Bałtyckich*, 5 (July-September 1947):177-88.

Borsody, Stephen. *The Tragedy of Central Europe: The Nazi and Soviet Conquest of Central Europe*. New York: Collier, 1962. [Originally published as *The Triumph of Tyranny*. New York: Macmillan, 1960.]

Bregman, Aleksander. "Linia Odry i Nysy, to nie 'wymysł Stalina.' " *Dziennik Polski i Dziennik Żołnierza* (London), December 9, 1952, p. 2.

Bromke, Adam. *Poland's Politics: Idealism vs. Realism*. Cambridge: Harvard University Press, 1967.

Broszat, Martin. *Nationalsozialistische Polenpolitik, 1939-1945*. Stuttgart: Deutsche Verlags-Anstalt, 1961.

———. *Zweihundert Jahre deutsche Polenpolitik*. Munich: Ehrenwirth, 1963.

Buell, Raymond Leslie. *Poland: Key to Europe*. 2nd ed. New York: Knopf, 1939.

Burns, James MacGregor. *Roosevelt: The Soldier of Freedom*. New York: Harcourt Brace Jovanovich, 1970.

Ciechanowski, Jan. "Generał ostatniej nadziei (Refleksje i uwagi na marginiesie ostatnio wydanych prac o politycznej i wojskowej działalności gen. Władysława Sikorskiego)." *Zeszyty Historyczne*, no. 51 (1980):172-91.

Cienciala, Anna M. *Poland and the Western Powers, 1938-1939: A Study in the Interdependence of Eastern and Western Europe*. London: Routledge & Kegan Paul, 1968.

Cobban, Alfred. *The Nation State and National Self-Determination*. New York: Thomas Crowell, 1970.

Consulibus [pseudonym]. *Doświadczenia i błędy naszej polityki zagranicznej wobec zadań chwili*. Warsaw: Biuro Społeczne Literackie, 1926.

Dallek, Robert. *Franklin D. Roosevelt and American Foreign Policy, 1932-1945*. New York: Oxford University Press, 1979.

———; Dallin, Alexander; and Dilks, David. "Allied Leadership in the Second World War" (with a comment by George F. Kennan). *Survey* 21 (Winter/Spring 1975):1-36.

Davies, Norman. *White Eagle, Red Star: The Polish-Soviet War, 1919-20*. London: Macdonald, 1972.

Davis, Lynn E. *The Cold War Begins: Soviet-American Conflict over Eastern Europe*. Princeton: Princeton University Press, 1974.

Dulczewski, Zygmunt, and Kwilecki, Andrzej. *Społeczeństwo wielkopolskie w osadnictwie Ziem Zachodnich*. Poznań: Wydawnictwo Poznańskie, 1962.

Duraczyński, Eugeniusz. *Kontrowersje i konflikty, 1939-1941*. Warsaw: Państwowe Wydawnictwo Naukowe, 1977.

Dziewanowski, M. K. *The Communist Party of Poland: An Outline of History*. Cambridge: Harvard University Press, 1959.

———. *Joseph Piłsudski: A European Federalist, 1918-1922*. Stanford: Hoover Institution, 1969.

Esslin, Martin. "A Playwright Who Drops Political Blockbusters." *The New York Times Magazine*, November 19, 1967, pp. 48ff.

Feis, Herbert. *Between War and Peace: The Potsdam Conference*. Princeton: Princeton University Press, 1960.

———. *Churchill, Roosevelt, Stalin: The War They Waged and the Peace They Sought*. Princeton: Princeton University Press, 1957.

Gaddis, John Lewis. *The United States and the Origins of the Cold War, 1941-1947*. New York: Columbia University Press, 1972.

Generał Władysław Sikorski, żołnierz i polityk: Materiały na sympozjum poświęcone 100 rocznicy urodzin. Warsaw: Wojskowy Instytut Historyczny, 1981.

Giertych, Jędrzej. *Pół wieku polskiej polityki: Uwagi o polityce Dmowskiego i polityce polskiej lat 1919-1939 i 1939-1947*. West Germany, 1947.

Gluck, Leopold. *Od ziem postulowanych do ziem odzyskanych*. Warsaw: Pax, 1971.

A Group of U.S. Military Experts. "A Federation for Eastern Europe." *New Europe: Monthly Review of International Affairs* (New York), 1 (April 1941):117-21.

Gruchman, Bohdan; Klafkowski, Alfons; Kolipiński, Juliusz; Piwarski, Kazimierz; Serwański, Edward; Zajchowska, Stanisława; and Ziółkowski, Janusz. *Polskie Ziemie Zachodnie*. Poznań: Instytut Zachodni, 1959.

Halecki, Oscar. *Borderlands of Western Civilization: A History of East Central Europe*. New York: Ronald Press, 1952.

Hanak, H. "Sir Stafford Cripps as British Ambassador in Moscow, May 1940 to June 1941." *The English Historical Journal* 94 (January 1979):48-70.

Hansen, Ernst R. B. *Poland's Westward Trend*. London: Allen and Unwin, 1928.

Haskins, Charles Homer, and Lord, Robert Howard. *Some Problems of the Peace Conference*. Cambridge: Harvard University Press, 1920.

Horak, Stephan. *Poland and Her National Minorities, 1919-1939: A Case Study*. New York: Vantage Press, 1961.

Institut Slavianovedeniia i Balkanistiki, Akademiia Nauk SSSR. *Sovetsko-pol'skie otnosheniia, 1918-1945: Sbornik statei*. Moscow: Nauka, 1974.

Irving, David. *Accident: The Death of General Sikorski*. London: Wm. Kimber, 1967.

Istoriia Pol'shi. Vol. III. Edited by F. T. Zuev, A. Ia.Manusevich, and I. A. Khrenov. Moscow: Academy of Sciences, 1958.

Istoriia Velikoi Otechestvennoi Voiny Sovetskogo Soiuza, 1941-1945. 6 vols. Moscow: Institute of Marxism-Leninism, 1960-65.

Jędrzejewicz, Wacław. *Polonia amerykańska w polityce polskiej: Historia Komitetu Narodowego Amerykanów Polskiego Pochodzenia*. New York: National Committee of Americans of Polish Descent, 1954.

Jordan, Z. *Oder-Neisse Line: A Study of the Political, Economic and European Significance of Poland's Western Frontier*. London: Polish Freedom Movement, 1952.

Kaiser, David E. *Economic Diplomacy and the Origins of the Second World War: Germany, Britain, France, and Eastern Europe, 1930-1939*. Princeton: Princeton University Press, 1981.

Kiełczewska, Maria. *O podstawy geograficzne Polski*. Poznań: Instytut Zachodni, 1946.

Kisielewski, Józef. *Ziemie gromadzi prochy*. Poznań: Księgarnia Św. Wojciecha, [1939].

Klimkowski, Jerzy. *Katastrofa w Gibraltarze: Kulisy śmierci generała Sikorskiego*. Katowice: Śląsk, 1965.

Kolko, Gabriel. *The Politics of War: The World and United States Foreign Policy, 1943-1945*. New York: Random House, 1968.

Kołomejczyk, Norbert. "Sprawa Ziem Zachodnich w programie i działalności Polskiej Partii Robotniczej." In *Polska Partia Robotnicza na Pomorzu Zachodnim: Studia i materiały*, edited by Bogdan Dopierała, pp. 7-50. Poznań: Instytut Zachodnio-Pomorski, 1965.

Komarnicki, Titus. "Próby stworzenia związku polsko-czeskiego w okresie drugiej wojny światowej." *Sprawy Międzynarodowe*, nos. 2/3 (1947) and 1/5 (1948).

Komarnicki, Titus. *Rebirth of the Polish Republic: A Study in the Diplomatic History of Europe, 1914-1920*. London: Heinemann, 1957.

Korboński, Stefan. *Polskie Państwo Podziemne: Przewodnik po Podziemiu z lat 1939-1945*. Paris: Instytut Literacki, 1975.

Korowicz, Marek Stanisław. *W Polsce pod sowieckim jarzmem*. London: Veritas, 1955.

Kowalczyk, Józef. *Za kulisami wydarzeń politycznych z lat 1936-1938 (w świetle raportów posła Czechosłowacji w Warszawie i innych archiwaliów)*. Warsaw: Książka i Wiedza, 1976.

Kowalski, Włodzimierz T. *Polityka zagraniczna RP, 1944-1947*. Warsaw: Instytut Spraw Międzynarodowych, 1971.

————. "Problem niemiecki w polityce ZSRR (1941-1945)." *Przegląd Zachodni* 23 (May-August 1967):95-119.

————. "Problem granicy polsko-niemieckiej przed konferencja w Jałcie (1943-1944)." *Sprawy Międzynarodowe* 15 (May 1962):44-71.

————. *Walka dyplomatyczna o miejsce Polski w Europie (1939-1945)*. 3rd ed. Warsaw: Książka i Wiedza, 1970.

————. *ZSRR a granica na Odrze i Nysie, 1941-1945*. Warsaw: Ministerstwo Obrony Narodowej, 1965.

Kruszewski, Z. Anthony. *The Oder-Neisse Boundary and Poland's Modernization: The Socioeconomic and Political Impact*. New York: Praeger, 1972.

Kukiel, Marian. *Generał Sikorski: Żołnierz i mąż stanu Polski walczącej*. London: Instytut Polski, 1970.

Kulski, Władysław W. *Germany and Poland: From War to Peaceful Relations*. Syracuse: Syracuse University Press, 1976.

————. "The Anglo-Polish Agreement of Aug. 25, 1939: Highlight of My Diplomatic Career." *Polish Review* 21 (1976):23-38.

————. "The Lost Opportunity for Russian-Polish Friendship." *Foreign Affairs* 25 (July 1947):667-84.

Kundiuba, I. D. *Sovetsko-pol'skie otnosheniia (1939-1945 gg.)*. Kiev: Izdatel'stvo Kievskogo Universiteta, 1963.

Leitgeber, Witold. *W kwaterze prasowej: Dziennik z lat wojny 1939-1945*. London: Katolicki Ośrodek Wydawniczy Veritas, 1972.

Lipski, Józef; Raczyński, Edward; and Stroński, Stanisław. *Trzy podróże gen. Sikorskiego do Ameryki*. London: Instytut Historyczny im. Generała Sikorskiego, 1949.

Lukas, Richard C. *The Strange Allies: The United States and Poland, 1941-1945*. Knoxville: University of Tennessee Press, 1978.

Łukasiewicz, Juliusz. *Polska jest mocarstwem*. 2nd ed. Warsaw: Gebethner and Wolff, 1939.

Lundestad, Geir. *The American Non-Policy Towards Eastern Europe, 1943-1947*. Oslo: Universitetsforlaget, 1978.

Lundgreen-Nielsen, Kay. *The Polish Problem at the Paris Peace Conference: A Study of the Policies of the Great Powers and the Poles, 1918-1919*. Translated by Alison Borch-Johansen. Odense, Denmark: Odense University Press, 1979.

Machray, Robert. *The Polish-German Problem*. London: Allen and Unwin, 1941.
————. *The Problem of Upper Silesia*. London, Allen and Unwin, 1945.
Malinowski, Marian. "Kształtowanie się założeń programowych polskiego ruchu komunistycznego w latach 1939-1942." *Z Pola Walki* 4, no. 4 (1961):19-44.
Mastny, Vojtech. *Russia's Road to the Cold War: Diplomacy, Warfare and the Politics of Communism, 1941-1945*. New York: Columbia University Press, 1979.
Męclewski, Edmund. *Powrót Polski nad Odrę, Nysę Łużycką, Bałtyk*. Warsaw: Ministerstwo Obrony Narodowej, 1971.
Micewski, Andrzej. *Z geografii politycznej II Rzeczypospolitej: Szkice*. Cracow: Znak, 1964.
Mitkiewicz, Leon. "Napastliwe komentarze." *Zeszyty Historyczne*, no. 19 (1971):193-207.
Mroczko, Marian. *Związek Obrony Kresów Zachodnich, 1921-1934: Powstanie i działalność*. Gdańsk: Wydawnictwo Morskie, 1977.
Notter, Harley. *Postwar Foreign Policy Preparation, 1939-1945*. Washington, D.C.: Department of State, 1949.
Nowosad, Ryszard. "Największa bitwa pancerna września (Tomaszów Lubelski, 18-20.XI.1939 r.)." *Mowią Wieki: Magazyn Historyczny* (Warsaw) 23 (September 1980):1-5.
Onacewicz, Włodzimierz. "Komentarze do książki Leona Mitkiewicza 'Z Generałem Sikorskim na obczyźnie.' " *Zeszyty Historyczne*, no. 18 (1970):154-83.
Orzechowski, Marian. "Koncepcja granic zachodnich w programie i działalności Polskiej Partii Robotniczej i lewicy rewolucyjnej na emigracji." *Sobótka: Śląski Kwartalnik Historyczny*, no. 2a (1962):8-46.
————. *Odra-Nysa Łużycka-Bałtyk w polskiej myśli politycznej okresu drugiej wojny światowej*. Wrocław: Ossolineum, 1969.
Osmańczyk, Edmund Jan. *Był rok 1945*. 2nd ed. Warsaw: Państwowy Instytut Wydawniczy, 1973.
Page, Bruce; Leitch, David; and Knightley, Phillip. *The Philby Conspiracy*. With an Introduction by John le Carré. Garden City, N.Y.: Doubleday, 1968.
Pałucki, Władysław (Antoni Błoński). *Ziemie Odzyskane: Szkice historyczne*. London: F. Mildner & Sons, 1947.
Pobóg-Malinowski, Władysław. *Najnowsza historia polityczna Polski, 1864-1945*. Vol. 3: *Okres 1939-1945*. London: n.p., 1960.
The Polish Eastern Territories and Their Importance to Poland and Europe. Edited by the Göttinger Arbeitskreis. Göttingen, 1948.
Polonsky, Antony. *Politics in Independent Poland 1921-1939: The Crisis of Constitutional Government*. London: Oxford University Press, 1972.
Popiołck, Kazimierz. "Instytut Śląski." *Myśl Współczesna* (January 1947):125-29.
Pragier, Adam. *Polish Peace Aims*. London: MaxLove Publishing [1944].
Pruszyński, Ksawery. *Wybór pism publicystycznych*. 2 vols. Cracow: Wydawnictwo Literackie, 1966.

Przybylski, Henryk. *Front Morges w okresie II Rzeczypospolitej.* Warsaw: Państwowe Wydawnictwo Naukowe, 1972.

Resis, Albert. "The Churchill-Stalin Secret 'Percentages' Agreement on the Balkans, Moscow, October 1944." *The American Historical Review* 83 (April 1978):368-87.

Romer, Tadeusz. "Moja misja jako Ambasadora R. P. w Związku Sowieckim." *Zeszyty Historyczne,* no. 30 (1974):138-66.

Rosen-Zawadzki, Kazimierz. " 'Karta Buduszczej Jewropy.' " *Studia z Dziejów ZSRR i Europy Środkowej* 8 (1972):141-44 + map.

Royal Institute of International Affairs. *The Problem of Germany* (An Interim Report by a Chatham House Study Group). London: Oxford University Press, 1943.

Rozek, Edward J. *Allied Wartime Diplomacy: A Pattern in Poland.* New York: Wiley, 1958.

Sasse, Heinz Günther. "The Prelude to the Expulsions and the Oder-Neisse Line from 1939-1945." In *Eastern Germany: A Handbook,* Vol. II: *History,* edited by the Göttinger Arbeitskreis, pp. 371-428. Würzburg: Holzner, 1963.

Schechtman, Joseph B. "The Polish-Soviet Exchange of Population." *Journal of Central European Affairs* 9 (October 1949):289-314.

Seaton, Albert. *The Russo-German War 1941-45.* New York: Praeger, 1970.

Seton-Watson, Hugh. *Eastern Europe Between the Wars, 1918-1941.* Cambridge: Cambridge University Press, 1945.

Seyda, Marian. *Poland and Germany and the Post-War Reconstruction of Europe.* London, 1943. First issued for private circulation in September 1942.

———. *Pół wieku walki o granicę polsko-niemiecką.* London: n.p., February 1946.

———. *Territoires polonais sous la domination prussienne.* Paris: Section de Press du Comité National Polonais, 1919.

Sharp, Samuel L. *Poland: White Eagle on a Red Field.* Cambridge: Harvard University Press, 1953.

Sherwood, Robert E. *Roosevelt and Hopkins: An Intimate History.* New York: Harper, 1948.

Siemaszko, Z. S. "Szara eminencja w miniaturze." *Zeszyty Historyczne,* no. 23 (1973):172-85.

Sikorski, General W. *Modern Warfare: Its Character, Its Problems.* London: Hutchinson [1942]. English translation of *Przyszła wojna: Jej możliwości i charakter oraz związane z nim zagadnienia obrony kraju* (Warsaw, 1934).

Snell, John L. *Wartime Origins of the East-West Dilemma Over Germany.* New Orleans: Hauser Press, 1959.

Sosnowski, Kiryl. "Polska wraca na Dolny Śląsk." *Przegląd Zachodni* 3 (April 1947):278-92.

Stehle, Hansjakob. *Deutschlands Osten—Polens Westen? Eine Dokumentation.* Frankfurt: Fischer, 1965.

———. *Nachbar Polen.* Frankfurt: Fischer, 1963.

Stern-Rubarth, Edgar. *Exit Prussia: A Plan for Europe.* London: Duckworth, 1940.

Stevenson, William. *A Man Called Intrepid: The Secret War*. New York: Harcourt Brace Jovanovich, 1976.

Stroński, Stanisław. "O układzie polsko-rosyjskim z 30.7.1941." *Kultura* (Paris), no. 4(42) (April 1951): pp. 100-113.

Strumph-Wojtkiewicz, Stanisław. *Gwiazda Władysława Sikorskiego*. Warsaw: Czytelnik, 1946.

————. *Siła złego*. Warsaw: Książka i Wiedza, 1971.

Sulimirski, Tadeusz. *Poland and Germany: Past and Future*. London and Edinburgh: West-Slavonic Bulletin, 1942.

Táborský, Eduard. "A Polish-Czechoslovak Confederation: A Story of the First Soviet Veto." *Journal of Central European Affairs* 9 (January 1950):379-95.

Terej, Jerzy Janusz. *Rzeczywistość i polityka: Ze studiów nad dziejami najnowszymi Narodowej Demokracji*. Warsaw: Książka i Wiedza, 1971.

Terlecki, Olgierd. *Generał ostatniej legendy: Rzecz o gen. Władysławie Sikorskim*. Chicago: Polonia, 1976.

Terry, Sarah Meiklejohn. "The Oder-Neisse Line Revisited: Sikorski's Program for Poland's Postwar Western Boundary, 1939-42." *East Central Europe* 5, Pt. I (1978):39-68.

Tucker, Robert C. "The Emergence of Stalin's Foreign Policy." *Slavic Review* 36 (December 1977):563-89.

Turlej, Stefan. *Koncepcje ustrojowe obozu londyńskiego*. Warsaw: Książka i Wiedza, 1978.

Ulam, Adam B. *Expansion and Coexistence: The History of Soviet Foreign Policy, 1917-1967*. New York: Praeger, 1968.

Wagner, Wolfgang. *The Genesis of the Oder-Neisse Line: A Study in the Diplomatic Negotiations during World War II*. Stuttgart: Brentano, 1957.

Wandycz, Piotr S. *Czechoslovak-Polish Confederation and the Great Powers, 1940-43*. Slavic and East European Series, Vol. 3. Bloomington, Ind.: Indiana University Publications, 1956.

————. *France and Her Eastern Allies, 1919-1925: French-Czechoslovak-Polish Relations from the Paris Peace Conference to Locarno*. Minneapolis: University of Minnesota Press, 1962.

————. "Pierwsza Republika a Druga Rzeczpospolita: Szkic." *Zeszyty Historyczne*, no. 28 (1974), pp. 3-20.

————. *Soviet-Polish Relations, 1917-1921*. Cambridge: Harvard University Press, 1969.

————. *The United States and Poland*. Cambridge: Harvard University Press, 1980.

Wapiński, Roman. *Władysław Sikorski*. Warsaw: Wiedza Powszechna, 1978.

————. "Koncepcje polityczne Władysława Sikorskiego." In *Twórcy polskiej myśli politycznej: Zbiór studiów*, edited by Jan St. Miś. Wrocław: Ossolenium, 1978.

Warburg, James P. *Germany—Bridge or Battleground*. New York: Harcourt Brace, 1947.

Warburg, James P. *The United States in a Changing World: An Historical Analysis of American Foreign Policy*. New York: G. P. Putnam's Sons, 1954.

Weinberg, Gerhard L. *The Foreign Policy of Hitler's Germany: Starting World War II, 1937-1939*. Chicago: University of Chicago Press, 1980.

Welles, Sumner. *Seven Decisions that Shaped History*. New York: Harper, 1951.

———. *The Time for Decision*. New York: Harper, 1944.

Werth, Alexander. *Russia at War, 1941-1945*. New York: E. P. Dutton, 1964.

Winiewicz, J. M. *The Polish-German Frontier*. 2nd ed. London: Wm. Hodge, 1945.

Winks, Robin W., ed. *The Historian as Detective: Essays on Evidence*. New York: Harper & Row, 1968.

Wiskemann, Elizabeth. *Germany's Eastern Neighbours: Problems Relating to the Oder-Neisse Line and the Czech Frontier Regions*. London: Royal Institute of International Affairs, 1956.

Wojciechowski, Marian. *Stosunki polsko-niemieckie, 1933-1938*. Poznań: Instytut Zachodni, 1965.

Wojciechowski, Zygmunt, ed. *Poland's Place in Europe*. Poznań: Instytut Zachodni, 1947.

Wójcik, Andrzej J. *The Teheran Conference and the Odra-Nisa Boundary*. New York: Arlington Printing Co., 1959.

———. *The War Settlement in Eastern Europe*. New York: Czas Publishing Co., 1964.

Wynot, Edward D., Jr. *Polish Politics in Transition: The Camp of National Unity and the Struggle for Power, 1935-1939*. Athens: University of Georgia Press, 1974.

Yergin, Daniel. *Shattered Peace: The Origins of the Cold War and the National Security State*. Boston: Houghton Mifflin, 1977.

Zabiełło, Stanisław. *O rząd i granice: Walka dyplomatyczna o sprawę Polski w II wojnie światowej*. 3rd ed. Warsaw: Pax, 1970.

———. "Sprawa polska na konferencji w Jałcie." *Z Pola Walki*, 2, no. 2 (1959):30-55.

Zawodny, J. K. *Death in the Forest: The Story of the Katyn Forest Massacre*. Notre Dame: University of Notre Dame Press, 1962.

Zieliński, Henryk. "Poglądy polskich ugrupowań politycznych na sprawę Ziem Zachodnich i granicy polsko-niemieckiej (1914-1919)." In *Problem polsko-niemiecki w Traktacie Wersalskim*, edited by J. Pajewski, pp. 181-216. Poznań: Instytut Zachodni, 1963.

———. "Polska myśl polityczna a sprawa ziem zachodnich (przed rokiem 1914)." *Sobótka: Śląski Kwartalnik Historyczny*, no. 1 (1964):143-61.

Zieliński, Ryszard. *Gibraltarska katastrofa 1943*. Warsaw: Ministerstwo Obrony Narodowej, 1973.

Zweig, Ferdynand. *Poland Between Two Wars: A Critical Study of Social and Economic Change*. London: Secker and Warburg, 1944.

Żuchowski, Stanisław. *Brytyska polityka wobec Polski, 1916-1948*. Brisbane and London: n.p., 1979.

Index

Library of Congress Cataloging in Publication Data

Terry, Sarah Meiklejohn, 1937-
  Poland's place in Europe.

  Bibliography: p.
  Includes index.
  1. Oder-Neisse Line (Germany and Poland). 2. Poland—
History—Occupation, 1939-1945.   3. World War, 1939-
1945—Territorial questions—Poland.   4. Sikorski,
Władysław, 1881-1943. I. Title.
D821.P7T47 1983   940.53′438   82-47617
ISBN 0-691-07643-X   AACR2
ISBN 0-691-10136-1 (pbk.)

Sarah Meiklejohn Terry is Assistant Professor of Political Science at Tufts University and a Fellow of the Russian Research Center of Harvard University. She is the editor of a book on Soviet Policy in Eastern Europe and a contributor to other anthologies and journals on the politics of the Soviet bloc.